PREVENTING EATING DISORDERS

PREVENTING EATING DISORDERS

A Handbook of Interventions and Special Challenges

edited by

Niva Piran
Michael P. Levine
Catherine Steiner-Adair

BRUNNER/MAZEL
Taylor & Francis Group

USA	Publishing Office:	BRUNNER/MAZEL *A member of the Taylor & Francis Group* 325 Chestnut Street Philadelphia, PA 19106 Tel: (215) 625–8900 Fax: (215) 625–2940
	Distribution Center:	BRUNNER/MAZEL *A member of the Taylor & Francis Group* 47 Runway Road, Suite G Levittown, PA 19057 Tel: (215) 269–0400 Fax: (215) 269–0363
UK		BRUNNER/MAZEL *A member of the Taylor & Francis Group* 1 Gunpowder Square London EC4A 3DE Tel: +44 171 583 0490 Fax: +44 171 583 0581

Preventing Eating Disorders: A Handbook of Interventions and Special Challenges

1 2 3 4 5 6 7 8 9 0

Printed by Edwards Brothers, Ann Arbor, MI, 1999
Cover design by Joseph Dieter Visual Communications.

A CIP catalog record for this book is available from the British Library.
♾ The paper in this publication meets the requirements of the ANSI Standard Z39.48–1984 (Permanence of Paper).

Library of Congress Cataloging-in-Publication Data
CIP information available from publishers.

ISBN 087630–968–6

CONTENTS

PART I
ADDRESSING SOCIETAL INSTITUTIONS AND VALUES

PART II
PREVENTION PROGRAMS FOR ELEMENTARY
AND MIDDLE SCHOOLS

CONTRIBUTORS

Andrea Bastiani Archibald
Doctoral Candidate in Developmental Psychology, Center for Children & Families, Teachers College, Columbia University, 525 W. 120th St., Box 39, New York, NY 10027.

Jeanne Brooks-Gunn Ph.D.
Virginia & Leonard Marx Professor in Child Development and Education, Teachers College, Columbia University, 525 W. 120th St., Box 39, New York, NY 10027.

Patricia A. Colton, M.D.
Research Fellow, Department of Psychiatry, University of Toronto and The Toronto Hospital, Ontario CANADA M5G 2C4.

Denis Daneman, M.B., B.Ch., FRCPC
Professor, Department of Endocrinology, University of Toronto, and Endocrinologist-in-Chief, The Hospital for Sick Children, Toronto, CANADA, M5G 2C4.

Monica Dempsey, M.A.
School Psychologist, Department of Counseling & Educational Psychology, State University of New York, 409 Baldy, Buffalo, NY 14260-1000.

Sandra Susan Friedman, BSW, M.A.
Salal Communications, Ltd., 101-1184 Denman Street, #309, Vancouver, BC CANADA V6G 2M9.

Julia A. Graber, Ph.D.
Research Scientist, The Adolescent Study Program & Center for Young Children & Families, Teachers College, Columbia University, 525 W. 120th St., Box 39, New York, NY 10027.

Kathy Hotelling, Ph.D.
Director, Counseling and Student Development Center, Northern Illinois University, DeKalb, IL 60115.

Lori M. Irving, Ph.D.
Assistant Professor, Department of Psychology, Washington State University, 14204 N. E. Salmon Creek Avenue, Vancouver, WA 98686.

Craig L. Johnson, Ph.D.
Director, Eating Disorders Program, Laureate Psychiatric Clinic and Hospital, 6655 S. Yale Avenue, Tulsa, OK 74136.

Debra K. Katzman, M.D.
Associate Professor of Pediatrics, Hospital for Sick Children and University of Toronto, Adolescent Medicine Clinic, 555 University Avenue, Toronto, Ontario CANADA M5G 1X8.

Melanie Katzman, Ph.D.
Senior Lecturer, University of London, Institute of Psychiatry, DeCrespigney Park, London SE5 8AF, ENGLAND, and Assistant Professor, Cornell Medical Center, 10 East 78th Street, Suite 4A, New York, NY 10021, USA.

June Larkin, Ph.D.
Women's Sexual Harassment Caucus, The Ontario Institute for Studies in Education, University of Toronto, 252 Bloor Street West, Toronto, Ontario CANADA M5S 1V6.

Michael P. Levine, Ph.D.
Professor of Psychology, Kenyon College, Gambier, OH, USA 43022-9623.

Mervat Nasser, M.D., MRCPsych
Senior Lecturer/Consultant Psychiatrist, Department of Psychiatry, Leicester University, United Kingdom.

Linda Nelson, Ph.D.
School Psychologist, Department of Counseling & Educational Psychology, State University of New York, 409 Baldy, Buffalo, NY 14260-1000.

Mimi Nichter
Assistant Professor of Public Health, Arizona Prevention Center, University of Arizona, Tucson, AZ 85716.

Marion P. Olmsted, Ph.D., CPsych
Associate Professor, Department of Psychiatry, University of Toronto, and Director, Eating Disorders Ambulatory Care, The Toronto Hospital, Toronto, Ontario CANADA M5G 2C4.

Sheila Parker, Dr.P.H.
Arizona Prevention Center, University of Arizona, Tucson, AZ 85716.

Susan J. Paxton, Ph.D.
Department of Psychology, University of Melbourne, Parkville, Melbourne, Victoria, AUSTRALIA 3052.

LeAdelle Phelps, Ph.D.
Professor & Director, School Psychology Program, Department of Counseling & Educational Psychology, State University of New York, 409 Baldy, Buffalo, NY 14260-1000.

Niva Piran, Ph.D., CPsych
Professor, Department of Adult Education, Community Development &
Counseling Psychology, Ontario Institute for Studies in Education,
University of Toronto, 252 Bloor Street West, Toronto, Ontario CANADA
M5S 1V6.

Pauline S. Powers, M.D.
Professor of Psychiatry and Behavioral Medicine, University of South
Florida, 3515 E. Fletcher Avenue, Tampa, FL 33613.

Carla Rice, M.Ed.,
Doctoral Candidate, Women's Studies, York University, and Coordinator
of the Body Image Project, Women's College Hospital, 790 Bay St., 8th
Floor, Toronto, Ontario CANADA M5G 1N9.

Gary M. Rodin, M.D., FRCPC
Professor, Department of Psychiatry, University of Toronto, and Psychiatrist-
in-Chief, The Toronto Hospital, Toronto, Ontario CANADA M5G 2C4.

Vanessa Russell, B.Ed., M.Ed.
The Toronto Board of Education, 155 College St., Toronto, Ontario
CANADA M5T 1P6.

Jennifer Sapia, MSW
Department of Counseling & Educational Psychology, State University of
New York, 409 Baldy, Buffalo, NY 14260-1000.

Brenda Alpert Sigall, Ph.D.
Clinical Psychologist, Private Practice, and Counseling Center, University
of Maryland, Shoemaker Hall, College Park, MD 20742.

Linda Smolak, Ph.D.
Professor of Psychology, Kenyon College, Gambier, OH 43022-9623.

Catherine Steiner-Adair
Director of Education, Prevention, and Outreach, Harvard Eating
Disorder Center, 356 Boylston Street, Boston, MA 02116.

Charlie Stoddard, B.A.
Eating Disorders Awareness & Prevention, Inc., 603 Stewart Street, Suite
803, Seattle, WA 91801.

Amy Purcell Vorenberg, B.A.
Shady Hill School, 178 Coolidge Hill, Cambridge, MA 02138.

Nancy Vuckovic, Ph.D.
Kaiser Permanente Center for Health Research, Portland, OR 97207.

Roslyn G. Weiner, Ph.D.
Director, Child and Adolescent Eating Disorder Clinic, and Director,
Weight Control Clinic for Children, The Floating Hospital for Children at
the New England Medical Center, 750 Washington Street, Box 213,
Boston, MA 02116.

ACKNOWLEDGMENTS

This book grew out of a special "prevention issue" of *Eating Disorders: The Journal of Treatment and Prevention* (1996, vol. 4, no. 4) edited by Niva and Michael and featuring a lead article by Catherine and Amy Purcell Vorenberg. We gratefully acknowledge the guidance and inspiration of Leigh Cohn, editor of *ED:JTP*, in making both the special issue and this book a reality.

In some respects, however, this book was developed at innumerable conferences and across countless e-mails, telephone calls, restaurant conversations, and other collaborations. Although familiar with each other's work for many years, Niva and Michael began doing prevention work together in 1993 as members of the volunteer board of directors of Eating Disorders Awareness & Prevention, Inc., headquartered in Seattle, Washington. We thank Jennifer Biely (Executive Director), Sarah Roth, Charlie Stoddard, Robin Gray, Holly Huff, and the rest of the EDAP staff for providing the opportunities (e.g., Eating Disorders Awareness Week) that enabled us to become very familiar with the work of many important contributors to the field of primary prevention, including Margo Maine, Kathy Hotelling, Lori Irving, and Brenda Alpert Sigall.

Niva and Catherine first met in Boston during an academic leave Niva took in 1991. This meeting gave us the opportunity to develop a strong mutual appreciation of each other's work and to collaborate in numerous workshops, conferences, and other meetings. Michael and Catherine first met in Boston in 1986. Their paths have continued to cross, primarily at the annual conferences of the National Anorexic Aid Society (now the National Eating Disorders Organization), and now through the Academy for Eating Disorders, the Harvard Eating Disorders Center, EDAP, and the annual conference of the Renfrew Center. We gratefully acknowledge the support for prevention and to us provided over the years by various people connected to these important organizations. We especially want to thank William Davis, Amy Baker Dennis, Barbara Fleming, Judi Goldstein, Laura Hill, Craig Johnson, Paula Levine, and Pat Warner. Over the years their leadership and vision provided the opportunity to clarify and express our ideas about prevention, and to get to know people such as Melanie Katzman, Susan Paxton, Pauline Powers, Linda Smolak, Roslyn Weiner, and Kathy Hotelling.

Linda Smolak continues to be extremely important to Michael's work, as a colleague, a disturbingly helpful critic, a statistical consultant, and a friend. Participation in different conferences (including the first national conference for school-based eating disorders prevention, organized by Catherine) and, especially, work on this volume has given Niva the opportunity to work more closely with Linda. We thank her, not only for her contribution to this volume, but for her continued insistence on the ideal of a rigorous theoretical, empirical, developmental and feminist approach to the prevention of disordered eating. Linda's leadership in bringing a developmental perspective to the field of eating disorders was instrumental in helping us to establish ongoing connections with Julia Graber, Jeanne Brooks-Gunn, Mimi Nichter, and Susan Paxton.

Niva has had the opportunity to work within the context of a network of women and men who conduct academic research and are similarly interested and involved in prevention and other work in the community. The collegial support and collaboration of Meryl Bear, Paul Garfinkel, Karin Jasper, Ann Kerr, June Larkin, Heather Maclean, Leora Pinhas, Brenda Toner, Carla Rice, Deborah Katzman, Gary Rodin, and Lana Stermac has been very important to her. Niva also wishes to thank Mrs. Mavis Staine, Artistic Director of the National Ballet School, for the support of her work and the shared commitment to the well being of students and dancers.

Over the 20 years during which Catherine has worked as a school consultant and clinical psychologist, she has had the opportunity for ongoing collaboration with several inspiring colleagues: Carol Gilligan, Alexander Merrill, Amy Purcell Vorenberg, and Lisa Sjostrom. Each, with his or her unique vision of how education can foster psychological health and social change, has been central to her work. Catherine also wants to acknowledge the support and collaboration of her colleagues at the Harvard Eating Disorders Center who share her commitment to research, outreach, and the prevention of eating disorders: Anne Becker, Deborah Franko, Tricia Guest, David Herzog, and Deborah Warner.

As friends and from afar, the work of Arnold Andersen, Runi Borrenson Gresco, Sandra Friedman, Patricia Fallon, Catherine Shisslak, Ruth Striegel-Moore, Becky Thompson, J. Kevin Thompson, Joel Killen, Susan Willard, and Susan Wooley has inspired our work in the field of prevention.

They also want to thank Sonja Gallagher, Secretary to the Science Division and Women's & Gender Studies at Kenyon College. Without her computer skills, dedication to accuracy, and patient tolerance for last-minute demands and shifting professorial requirements, this book would never have been completed.

Niva writes: I wish to thank Michael and Catherine for the process of collaboration that was the basis for creating this book. Gratitude is extended to Michael for his critical reflections, thoughtful editing, and consistent committment and friendship. Thanks are extended to Catherine for her insightful editing role, and her vital ongoing support and caring friendship. My family and friends have provided the loving context within which my work could grow. I would like to thank my friends, in particular Judith Schapira, for their friendship and support. I also wish to extend a special note of gratitude to Yuval and Talilah Menipaz, Esther and Ehud Menipaz, and Tova and David Menipaz for their love and support. Victor, Josh, Grace, and Mal Garber are thanked similarly. I thank my husband Steven Garber for his love and his strong belief in my work. I thank Laurel Currie for being a member of our family, and I thank my two sons, Adam Garber and Andre Garber, for inspiring my life.

Catherine writes: I want to thank Niva and Michael for inviting me to join them as editors of this volume. I cannot imagine working in this field without either of them. Niva's and Michael's ideas and passion push mine, and their friendship sustain me through the inevitable highs and lows. Thanks also to my partners in private practice—Walter Abrams and Nick Browning.

Thanks to Rebecca Ramsey, John Reusser, and Alan Slobodnick—for the depth of our peer supervision over all those years, and their patience when I had to miss meetings to work on this book. Lisa Pearl has been a career-long friend, partner, and teacher with me in prevention and clinical work. Thanks also to Susan Willard, my "partner" down South, for years of collaborating on clinical and prevention work. And, of course, my love to Fred, for being home and believing in my work, and to Daniel and Lily, who inspire my vision of a happier and healthier world for children.

And, finally, Michael writes: In the spirit of collaboration that we hope infuses this book, I offer my thanks and gratitude to Niva and Catherine, and especially to my wife, Mary Suydam, for her patience, her postmodern sensibilities, her skill with computers, her love, and her collaboration in raising a 12-year-old daughter for whom "voice" is quite clearly not a problem. I also wish to thank the spouses of my collaborators—Steven and Fred—for their support, sense of humor, skill with fax machines, and willingness to be cheerful no matter how many phone messages it takes for me to get it right.

Niva Piran
Michael P. Levine
Catherine Steiner-Adair

INTRODUCTION

This book is situated at the intersection of three complex "fields" (Albee & Gullotta, 1997; Levine, 1998; Piran, 1995, 1997): prevention, eating disorders, and epistemology. The last involves issues and methods related to questions of knowledge production, such as what approaches may we use to arrive at the type of knowledge required to prevent eating disorders effectively. Our central purpose in developing this book is to describe a variety of approaches to the prevention of eating disorders that could be used by professionals from the disciplines of health, mental health, and education, as well as by community members interested in public education and advocacy. Thus, we have brought together approaches that can be applied to social and institutional policies; to the media; to specific target groups such as physicians, parents, peers, athletes, or dancers; to elementary, middle, and high school settings; and to colleges.

The domain of prevention customarily has been seen as comprising three subcomponents (Kessler & Albee, 1975). *Primary prevention* refers to attempts to reduce the occurrence of new cases, that is, the incidence, of a specific disorder. *Secondary prevention* refers to the early identification of individuals at risk and to interventions that aim to arrest the development of a full-blown disorder. *Tertiary prevention* involves the prompt identification and treatment of individuals who have developed the full syndrome. This book concentrates on programs for the primary and secondary prevention of a spectrum of disordered eating patterns running from negative body image and calorie-restrictive dieting through severe anorexia nervosa and bulimia nervosa.

Prevention work has been described as occurring at different levels of existing societal structures (Prilleltensky, 1994; Sullivan, 1984). Prevention programs may occur at the "macro" level, targeting larger societal values, institutions, and policies. Interventions also may focus on the "meso" level of specific societal institutions such as hospitals or schools, and on the "micro" level of families or individuals. This book addresses issues relevant to all three levels of interventions. We believe that effective prevention in the field of eating disorders requires a collaborative endeavor within and across all three levels.

The prevention of eating disorders is a relatively young field that has gained momentum principally during the past 15 years. There are several important reasons for this growing interest. One is the large number of individuals suffering from eating disorders and the severe complications associated with these disorders. In North America, anorexia nervosa occurs in about 5 to 10 out of 1000 young women between the ages of 16 and 25; while bulimia nervosa occurs in about 20 to 50 out of 1000 girls and women in this age range (Crowther, Wolf, & Sherwood, 1992; Hsu, 1996). Moreover, eating difficulties and extreme preoccupation with weight and shape, which do not fulfill the complete diagnostic criteria for anorexia nervosa or bulimia nervosa, occur in much larger numbers in girls and women (Crowther et al., 1992; Shisslak, Crago, & Estes, 1995). Serious medical, psychological, social, and vocational complications have been documented in individuals who meet the clinical criteria and in those who have so-called "subthreshold" or "partial" syndromes (Andersen, 1985; Hill, 1993; Shisslak et al., 1995). Currently, the incidence rates of eating disorders are growing in countries in Eastern Europe, South America, and the Far East (see Chapter 2 in this book). Prevention work is necessary to reduce the incidence of eating disorders, because treatment (attempts to reduce the prevalence) has never been able to eradicate a disorder (Albee, 1981). To compound the problem, treatment resources have been limited in most countries because of insufficient funds, insurance policies, or lack of expertise.

In addition to the wish to alleviate human suffering, prevention may be motivated by the desire to make an impact on a larger social scale, working with and benefiting the community. Because prevention work inherently focuses on the interface between the individual and society, it may expose societal values, mores, and institutions that adversely affect body esteem and self-esteem, such as different forms of violence against women (see Chapters 9 and 12), weightism (see Chapter 6), and racism (Thompson, 1994). The role of sociocultural factors and sociocultural changes in the prevention of eating disorders gives prevention work an added political dimension and raises questions about the likelihood of success of prevention work that does not challenge the social status quo (Albee & Gullotta, 1997; Levine, 1994; Piran, 1995, 1997, Steiner-Adair, 1990).

Despite the growing interest in both prevention and social factors that may account for the documented increase in the incidence of eating disorders in the past four decades, and despite the admirable concern and energy that abound in many people committed to reducing the incidence of disordered eating, primary prevention has proven to be demanding (Levine, 1998; Piran, 1995, 1997) and, at times, controversial (Mann et al., 1997). There are a fair number of curricula and programmatic ideas for primary prevention available (see the resource list provided by Eating Disorders Awareness & Prevention, Inc., at the web site: members.aol.com/edapinc/home.html). However, relatively few have been evaluated systematically, and those that have been researched yield a mosaic of failures (e.g., Killen, 1996; Paxton, 1993) and encouraging successes (e.g., Moreno & Thelen, 1993; Newumark-Sztainer, Butler, & Palti, 1995; Piran, in press). Comprehensive reviews of this literature are available (Franko & Orosan-Weine, 1998; Levine & Piran, 1998; Shisslak, Crago, Estes, & Gray, 1996), and we recommend them to practitioners as a context for thinking about many of the programs described in this book.

As editors, we honor and respect the multitude of approaches to the prevention of eating disorders and the dedication of professionals and community members to the cause. We see the programs described in this book as providing a "snapshot" of current programs or approaches to prevention that seem to show some promise. Moreover, informed by a critical review of published work in the field of prevention, we hope to contribute to future developments in the field through compiling in this book chapters that address, to varying degrees, several principles that we consider important in achieving the goal of prevention (Levine & Piran, 1998; Piran, in 1998-b). These principles include the incorporation of research findings from other domains of prevention and the reliance on knowledge derived from varied life experiences of girls and women or from the study of community, rather than clinical, samples.

The field of primary prevention provides professionals and community members working towards the goal of prevention of eating disorders with a wealth of relevant information (Albee & Gullotta, 1997; Bloom, 1996). A central tenet in primary prevention that has been communicated repeatedly by Albee and his collaborators is that health is enhanced through provision of *general* factors such as economic and social power, coping skills, and positive self-esteem. Programs included in this book tend to incorporate general resilience factors, such as empowerment and coping skills, in addition to trying to eliminate risk factors specific to the development of eating disorders. In agreement with another principle described by the prevention literature, that of intervening at the societal, institutional, and individual levels (Bloom, 1996; Pentz et al., 1996; Prilleltensky, 1994), several programs included in this book either address more than one level of intervention or offer guidelines for interventions at the societal and institutional levels.

Another overall guide for the selection of chapters for this book relates to its stated goal of forming links to the community. Various programs described in the book are based on research gathered in community-based studies, some of them qualitative in nature. These programs therefore address diverse and complex normative developmental processes, rather than the concerns found among clinical samples. It follows that these programs also aim at addressing the whole spectrum of diverse eating symptomatology uncovered in epidemiological studies (Shisslak et al., 1995) rather than addressing one or another diagnosis of clinical eating disorders. Moreover, several chapters reflect rich and long-term experience in working within varied professional, community-based domains and therefore are written in the first person.

The honoring of life experiences in guiding prevention-program development is expressed further through the critical examination of adverse and protective social factors. Piran (1995, 1997) has suggested that community-based prevention studies have paid insufficient attention to social variables such as exposure to physical or sexual harassment, lack of support for the competence of young girls, and other expressions of social prejudice (see also Striegel-Moore, 1994). This book extends these challenges to mainstream prevention approaches, arguing that cultural concepts such as "Westernization" (see Chapter 2), "pressures for thinness" (see Chapter 9), and "self esteem" (see Chapter 10) have been oversimplified and not well understood. Similarly, mechanisms that underlie the influence on the individual of the mass media, peers, and other "sociocultural" influences have not been explored thoroughly until very recently (see Chapters 2 and 8). In short, most prevention programs have not integrated important information about the challenges girls face as they navigate through puberty and adolescence (Levine & Piran, 1998; Smolak & Levine, 1996; see also Chapters 6, 7, 9, and 12). Consequently, prevention programs have tended to be quite disparate from girls' experiences and have tended to concentrate almost exclusively on issues of weight and shape while overlooking or minimizing other experience-based challenges (Piran, 1995, 1997; Striegel-Moore, 1994). The programs included in this book tend to respond to the concerns expressed by youth.

The book also features programs that utilize varied processes of transformation among participants. Foucault (1979) and other critical theorists have emphasized the experiential components of learning about one's social worth and power through the way one's body is treated in the culture. Most prevention programs for eating disorders have emphasized didactic approaches without providing a healthier experiential environment (Piran, 1995). This book presents a variety of programs that emphasize experience-based components such as empowerment, a safe relational environment, and modeling by older women in prevention programs.

Although many barriers exist to successful prevention, important work has emerged in the field during the past 15 years. Knowledge has started to accumulate that can provide some initial guidelines for future work in the field (Levine & Piran, 1998; Piran, 1997). In this book, we aim to bring together a body of work conducted by experienced and dedicated people who are ready to share lessons they have learned from their work. We hope that the projects described in this book intersect with other ongoing projects in the field. We further recognize that this is a field in transition and that the book can provide a snapshot of a growing field of inquiry and activism. We are looking forward to following future developments in the field and hope that the book contributes to the practice of prevention. We also hope that the field will see a growth in outcome research that systematically evaluates the programs and approaches put forward in this book.

This book grew out of our collaboration in editing and contributing to a special issue of *Eating Disorders: The Journal of Treatment & Prevention* (Piran & Levine, 1996). Through ongoing dialogues with colleagues around the world, we have learned to appreciate the creativity, commitment, and evolving expertise of professionals heavily involved in the prevention of eating disorders. We have also learned to appreciate the process of professional growth-in-relation, which highlights the development of knowledge through intense discussions and, at times, controversy. We hope that this book creates new colleagues and that it invites all those interested in the prevention of eating disorders to examine varied approaches to prevention and to use their own creativity to extend the field through application and systemic evaluation.

All three of us all have been immersed in the application of varied approaches to prevention and in outcome evaluation. We feel committed to the well-being of children and other members of the community at large. Rather than viewing eating disorders as a distant difficulty, we view them as reflecting a complex structure of societal prejudices, structures, and values. We recognize that not only may we be affected by the same social structures, but we may recreate them unless we develop a personal and professional awareness about key social issues that relate to the intersection of body and culture (Bordo, 1993; Levine, 1994; Maine, 1991).

We close this introduction with two conclusions that serve equally well as figure and ground to our own professional, personal, and political work in primary prevention. Goldston (1977, p. 18) writes:

> In my opinion, primary prevention is the most misunderstood, undersupported, and neglected aspect of mental health work. Nonetheless, its allure, excitement, and promise tend to reinforce the graphic analogy in which primary prevention is compared to the Okefenokee swamp: If one explores and survives, the area becomes compelling, even addictive (Kessler & Albee, 1975).

To this we append the passage by Margaret Mead that constitutes the postscript to any e-mail that one receives from Dr. Lori Irving (see Chapter 3):

Never doubt that a small group of thoughtful committed citizens can change the world. Indeed, it's the only thing that ever has.

Niva Piran, Michael P. Levine, and Catherine Steiner-Adair

☐ References

Albee, G. W. (1981). Politics, power, prevention, and social change. In J. M. Joffee & G. W. Albee (Eds.), *Prevention through political action and social change* (pp. 3–24). Hanover, NH: University Press of New England.

Albee, G. W., & Gullotta, T. P. (1997). Primary prevntion's evolution. In G. W. Albee & T. P. Gullotta (Eds.), *Primary prevention works* (pp. 3–22). Thousand Oaks, CA: Sage.

Andersen, A. (1985). *Practical comprehensive treatment of anorexia nervosa and bulimia.* Baltimore: Johns Hopkins University.

Bloom, M. (1996). *Primary prevention practices.* Thousand Oaks, CA: Sage.

Bordo, S. (1993). *Unbearable weight: Feminism, Western culture, and the body.* Berkeley: University of California Press.

Crowther, J., Wolf, E. M., & Sherwood, N. E. (1992). Epidemiology of bulimia nervosa. In J. Crowther, D. L. Tennenbaum, S. E. Hobfoll, & M. A. P. Stephens (Eds.), *The etiology of bulimia nervosa: The individual and family context* (pp. 1–26). Washington, DC: Hemisphere/Taylor & Francis.

Foucault, M. (1979). *Discipline and punish: The birth of the prison.* New York: Vintage Books.

Franko, D. L., & Orosan-Weine, P. (1998). The prevention of eating disorders: Empirical, methodological and conceptual considerations. *Clinical Psychology: Science and Practice, 5,* 459–477.

Goldston, S. E. (1977). Defining primary prevention. In G. W. Albee & J. M. Joffee (Eds.), *Primary prevention of psychopathology: Vol I. The issues* (pp. 18–23). Hanover, NH: University Press of New England.

Hill, A. J. (1993). Pre-adolescent dieting: Implications for eating disorders. *International Review of Psychiatry, 5,* 87–100.

Hsu, L. K. G. (1996). Epidemiology of the eating disorders. In J. Yager (Ed.), *The Psychiatric Clinics of North America 19,* 681–700.

Kessler, M., & Albee, G. W. (1975). Primary prevention. *Annual Review of Psychology, 26,* 7–15.

Killen, J. D. (1996). Development and evolution of a school-based eating disorder symptoms prevention program. In L. Smolak, M. P. Levine, & R. Striegel-Moore (Eds.), *The developmental psychopathology of eating disorders: Implications for research, prevention, and treatment* (pp. 313–339). Mahwah, NJ: Lawrence Erlbaum Associates.

Levine, M. P. (1994). Beauty myth and the beast: What men can do and be to help prevent eating disorders. *Eating Disorders: The Journal of Treatment & Prevention, 2,* 101–113.

Levine, M. P. (1998, April). *Yearned optimism: Reason and research in primary prevention.* Plenary presentation at the 8th International Conference on Eating Disorders, New York.

Levine, M. P., & Piran, N. (1998). *Approaches to health promotion in the prevention of eating disorders.* Manuscript submitted for publication.

Maine, M. (1991). *Father hunger: Fathers, daughters & food.* Carlsbad, CA: Gurze Books.

Mann, T., Nolen-Hoeksema, S., Huang, K., Burgard, D., Wright, A., & Hanson, K. (1997). Are two interventions worse than none? Joint primary and secondary prevention of eating disorders in college females. *Health Psychology, 16*(3), 1–11.

Moreno, A. B., & Thelen, A. H. (1993). A preliminary prevention program for eating disorders in a junior high school population. *Journal of Youth and Adolescence, 22,* 109–124.

Neumark-Sztainer, D., Butler, R., & Palti, H. (1995). Eating disturbances among adolescent girls: Evaluation of a school-based primary prevention program. *Journal of Nutrition Education, 27*(1), 24–30.

Paxton, S. J. (1993). A prevention program for disturbed eating and body dissatisfaction in adolescent girls: A 1-year follow-up. *Health Education Research: Theory & Practice, 8,* 43–51.

Pentz, M. A., Dwyer, J., MacKinnon, D. P., Flay, B. R., Hansen, W. B., Wang, E. Y., & Johnson, C. A. (1989). A multicommunity trial for primary prevention of adolescent drug abuse: Effects on drug use prevalence. *Journal of the American Medical Association, 261,* 3259–3266.

Piran, N. (1995). Prevention: Can early lessons lead to a delineation of an alternative model? A critical look at prevention with school children. *Eating Disorders: The Journal of Treatment and Prevention, 3*(1), 28–36.

Piran, N. (1997). Prevention of eating disorders: Directions for future research. *Psychopharmacology Bulletin, 33,* 419–423.

Piran, N. (in press). Eating disorders: A trial of prevention in a high risk school setting. *Journal of Primary Prevention.*

Piran, N. (1998). Prevention of eating disorders: The struggle to chart new territories. *Eating Disorders: The Journal of Treatment and Prevention, 6,* 365–371.

Piran, N., & Levine, M.P. (Eds.). (1996). Special prevention issue. *Eating Disorders: Journal of Treatment & Prevention, 4,* 291–384.

Prilleltensky, I. (1994). *The morals and politics of psychology: Psychological discourse and the status quo.* Albany, NY: SUNY Press.

Shisslak, C. M., Crago, M., & Estes, L. S. (1995). The spectrum of eating disorders. *International Journal of Eating Disorders, 18,* 209–219.

Shisslak, C. M., Crago, M., Estes, L., & Gray, N. (1996). Content and method of developmentally appropriate prevention programs. In L. Smolak, M. P. Levine, & R. Striegel-Moore (Eds.), *The developmental psychopathology of eating disorders: Implications for research, prevention, and treatment* (pp. 341–363). Mahwah, NJ: Lawrence Erlbaum Associates.

Smolak, L., & Levine, M. P. (1996). Adolescent transitions and the development of eating problems. In L. Smolak, M. P. Levine, & R. Striegel-Moore (Eds.), *The developmental psychopathology of eaing disorders: Implications for research, prevention, and treatment* (pp. 207–233). Mahwah, NJ: Lawrence Erlbaum Associates.

Steiner-Adair, C. (1990). The body politic: Normal female development and the development of eating disorders. In C. Gilligan, N. P. Lyons, & T. J. Hammer (Eds.), *Making connections: The relational worlds of adolescent girls at Emma Willard School* (pp. 162–181). Cambridge, MA: Harvard University Press.

Striegel-Moore, R. (1994). A feminist agenda for psychological research on eating disorders. In P. Fallon, M. Katzman, & S. C. Wooley (Eds.), *Feminist perspectives on eating disorders* (pp. 438–454). New York: Guilford.

Sullivan, E. V. (1984). *A critical psychology.* New York: Plenum.

Thompson, B. W. (1994). *A hunger so wide and so deep.* Minneapolis: University of Minnesota Press.

I

ADDRESSING SOCIETAL INSTITUTIONS AND VALUES

One of the central values that pervade this book is that adult members of society should take responsibility and be accountable for changing values and structures that undermine the well-being of youth, especially girls, and of other members of society. For that reason, the first section of the book focuses on prevention work with larger societal institutions and norms, and with more circumscribed purveyors of values, such as parents. In addressing societal prejudices and mores, it is of relevance to recognize that diverse members of one culture may be exposed to varied adverse societal experiences (Bordo, 1993).

The mass media are seen by professionals and community members alike as a major adverse sociocultural influence unifying standards of thinness and appearance and cultural stereotypes of women and members of other social groups. Chapter 1, by Michael P. Levine, Niva Piran, and Charlie Stoddard, reviews the current status of knowledge regarding the mass media and its effects and suggests ways of "using" the media for the goal of prevention. In Chapter 2, Mervat Nasser and Melanie Katzman expand our thinking about the concept of "sociocultural" factors and demonstrate the necessity of incorporating transcultural, historical, and feminist perspectives in the understanding and prevention of eating disorders.

Families are the smallest social institutions. In Chapter 3, Julia A. Graber, Andrea Bastiani Archibald, and Jeanne Brooks-Gunn describe the prevention implications of the ways in which families may either buffer and protect against, or accentuate, adverse societal norms. Individual adult members of society play an important role in transforming institutional and community norms. In Chapter 4, Lori M. Irving describes how she has combined research, teaching, mentoring, and activism to produce an ongoing transformation of institutional and community norms at the college level. Her work demonstrates another important link, namely the deepening ties between academic and community settings.

☐ Reference

Bordo, S. (1993). *Unbearable weight: Feminism, Western culture, and the body.* Berkeley: University of California Press.

Michael P. Levine
Niva Piran
Charlie Stoddard

CHAPTER 1

Mission More Probable: Media Literacy, Activism, and Advocacy as Primary Prevention

A democratic civilization will save itself only if it makes the language of the image into a stimulus for critical reflection—not an invitation for hypnosis.
　　　　—Umberto Eco (quoted by the Media Education Foundation, 1997)

Mass media such as fashion magazines and television programs have long been considered one of the "sociocultural factors" that set the stage for the emergence of negative body image, calorie-restrictive dieting, and eating disorders as significant health problems for millions of women in the United States and around the world. This chapter begins with an extension of previous reviews by Levine and Smolak (1996, 1998; Levine, Smolak, & Hayden, 1994; Smolak & Levine, 1996) that address the possible role of mass media in influencing weight and body shape concerns in girls and women. It then continues with a discussion of theory and research that view the audience for media as active consumers who can critically evaluate and possibly change the messages transmitted. The chapter concludes with a description of two prevention programs that enhance activism among consumers, a discussion of the role of the World Wide Web in prevention, and suggestions for future work in this area.

For their assistance with this project, thanks are extended to Dr. Linda Smolak and Ms. Jennifer Duvernay of Kenyon College; to the entire staff of Eating Disorders Awareness and Prevention, Inc.; to Susan Berel; to Dr. Renee Hobbs and Elizabeth Thoman; and to Drs. Mary Martin, Susan Stormer, Kristen Harrison, and Heidi Posavac.

Based on our previous reviews of the literature on media and disordered eating (e.g., Levine & Smolak, 1996, 1998), as well as our extensive experience at various conferences, we believe that people interested in prevention often fail to appreciate fully the sheer complexity of people's relationships to magazines, television, movies, and the World Wide Web (see also Hobbs, 1997). Consequently, it is important for people interested in the relationships between culture, media, and prevention to study a variety of sources that examine media influences from the perspectives of research-oriented models of multiple sociocultural and personal factors (e.g., Heinberg, 1996; Stice, 1994); the psychology of advertising for women (Kilbourne, 1994); patterns of psychosomatic and affective disorder during the past 125 years (Silverstein & Perlick, 1995); and postmodern discourse on gender, power, and the body (Bordo, 1993). This chapter covers selected segments of this literature.

☐ The Influence of Mass Media on Negative Body Image and Disordered Eating

Content

Over the past 30 years, magazines and television programs have frequently, persistently, and increasingly glorified a tall, willowy, youthful "look" and emphasized strict weight management while vilifying fat as unhealthy, ugly, and immoral. Research by Silverstein and Perlick (1995) shows that, during the periods from 1910 through 1930 and 1950 through 1980, increases in the presence of slender models in women's magazines and slender actresses in films presaged and accompanied increases in disordered eating. In this regard, meta-analyses by Feingold and Mazzella (1996) have shown that over the past 20 to 30 years the tendency for females—and, in particular, adolescent females—to have a more negative body image than males has been increasing.

Over the past 30 to 40 years females also have received an increasing number of contradictory, irreconcilable messages from magazines and television about the importance of being "fit" and "toned" and "in control," while also "feeling free" to "let go" and "consume" various products, including high-calorie food (see, e.g., Guillen & Barr, 1994; Wiseman, Gray, Mosimann, & Ahrens, 1992). During this period, magazines targeted at young adolescent girls became relentless in driving home the message that self-management in the name of slender beauty is more important than intelligence, careers, friendships, social causes, and even health (Guillen & Barr, 1994; Peirce, 1990).

Prevention programs incorporating a critical evaluation of media content must help adolescents to identify, analyze, and ultimately challenge the "thinness schema" so easily extracted from today's mass media (Bordo, 1993; Levine & Smolak, 1998; Smolak & Levine, 1996): Beauty is a woman's principal project in life; slenderness is crucial for success and goodness; image is in fact substance; it is natural and acceptable for a woman to be self-conscious, anxious, and ashamed about her body; "fat" is a transparent sign of personal responsibility for weakness, failure, and helplessness; a "winner" can and should control, transform, and renew herself through the technology of fashion, dieting, and rigorous exercise. This normative perspective is perilously close to the "nervosa" underlying disordered eating (Gordon, 1990). However, because this set of attitudes is so embedded in our cultures, various methods of experiential learning and social activism are needed to destabilize the thinness schema and to re-define "femininity" in terms of a multifaceted self-concept that reflects both personal substance and personal style; multiple interests and multiple compe-tencies; multiple relationships with an emphasis on social consciousness; and the flexibility to be effective, imperfect, and self-accepting (Levine, 1994; Steiner-Adair, 1991; see also Chapters 4, 9, 10).

Audience

Many prepubescent and adolescent girls, as well as young women (and preven-tion specialists), enjoy, use, and "consume" mass media (Arnett, 1995; Harris, 1994). For example, nearly 2,000,000 girls subscribe to *Seventeen* magazine, and the estimated readership (many of whom are girls ages 11–14) exceeds 11,000,000. It is almost impossible to comprehend the size of the audience for a television program like *Friends* or *Ally McBeal*, but it is known that a huge num-ber of prepubescent and adolescent girls watch such adult shows expressly in order to learn about the world and themselves (Levine & Smolak, 1998). Conse-quently, many girls frequently are exposed to, if not immersed in, this thinness schema (Levine et al., 1994; Murray, Touyz, & Beumont, 1996; see also Chapter 11). In terms of motivation, there is a fair amount of evidence that, relative to adolescent boys, adolescent girls are more concerned about attractiveness in re-gard to interpersonal success and self-concept and are more susceptible to per-suasion by advertisements and other media relevant to "appearances" (see review by Martin, Gentry, & Hill, in press). Prevention efforts that critically evaluate mass media must be careful not to disparage mass media in general and the myriad functions they serve in our society (Harris, 1994; Worsnop, 1994).

Influence

Correlational Studies of the Extent of Exposure

Murray et al. (1996) found that, compared with community controls, young women with eating disorders were significantly more likely to report that maga-zines or newspapers influenced their eating habits and how they felt about their bodies, and that they wanted to look like the ideal, slender models shown in the print media and on television.

   The negative impact of mass media on the hearts, minds, and bodies of young girls and women is taken as gospel by most people committed to the prevention of eating disorders. This assumption implies that greater levels of exposure to (and immersion in the symbolic world of) mass media lead to greater "cultiva-tion" (Signorielli & Morgan, 1990) of the thinness schema and perhaps disor-dered eating. However, there are surprisingly few well-conducted studies to support or challenge this simple proposition, and overall the evidence is mixed (Levine & Smolak, 1996; Stice, 1994). For example, a well-known cross-sectional study by Stice, Schupak-Neuberg, Shaw, and Stein (1994) found that a direct relationship between exposure and disordered eating was one of sev-eral paths accounting for the variance in Eating Attitudes Test (EAT) scores among college women. On the other hand, Cusamano and Thompson (1997) found that negative body image and disordered eating in college women were related to awareness and internalization of the slender beauty ideal, but not to the self-reported amount of exposure to slender models in fashion and beauty magazines.

The theoretical and methodological complexities of the issues involved are clearly revealed in two studies of college students by Harrison (1997; Harrison & Cantor, 1997). She examined the relationship between use of *"thinness-depicting and thinness-promoting* (TDP) television shows and magazines" (1997, p. 45; italics in the original), reasons for interest in media, and psychological variables involved in disordered eating. Harrison has found that in general, media consumption variables were significant but very modest predictors of EAT scores, body dissatisfaction, and drive for thinness. Neither overall exposure to television shows nor exposure to television shows with primarily thin characters was related to eating-disorder symptomatology or body dissatisfaction, and attraction to thin media personalities accounts for less than 5% of the variance in EAT scores. Reading "fitness" magazines plus having a stated interest in dieting and fitness did account for 31% of the variance in EAT scores.

Certainly, more research is needed, and the questions of correlation and causality remain a perplexing tangle. Nevertheless, the findings of Cusamano and Thompson (1997) and Harrison (1997; Harrison & Cantor, 1997) strongly suggest that prevention specialists and eating-disorders researchers in general need to focus more attention on the psychological processes involved in motivation for media use and the extraction of messages and themes from media content (Austin & Johnson, 1997; Harris, 1994; Smolak & Levine, 1996; Stice, 1994).

Experimental Presentation of the Slender Ideal

Turner, Hamilton, Jacobs, Angood, and Dwyer (1997) arranged for young, white undergraduate women attending a private New England college to wait 13 minutes prior to completing a set of questionnaires about their body ideal, dieting history, and body image. Half were assigned randomly to wait in a room containing either four fashion magazines or four news magazines. Compared with those experiencing the news condition, the 80% who read a fashion magazine while waiting reported more frustration about their weight, more guilt during and after eating, more fear of getting fat, and more body dissatisfaction. This finding points to the "role of the media in shaping, rather than merely reflecting, societal perceptions of the female body" (Turner et al., 1997, p. 610).

However, a truly surprising conclusion from our literature reviews (Levine & Smolak, 1996, 1998) is the *lack* of strong evidence for the often heard contention that controlled (experimental) exposure to pictures of slender models causes an immediate increase in a woman's negative feelings about her body (see also Henderson-King & Henderson-King, 1997). For example, close inspection of the data from Stice and Shaw (1994, p. 298)—a study commonly cited as supporting the immediate negative effects of exposure to thin models—reveals that, relative to a no-model control condition, brief exposure to "thin-ideal" models produced no significant difference in body dissatisfaction and inconsistent effects on emotional states such as anxiety and guilt.

In general, studies by Waller and Shaw in the United Kingdom (see review by Shaw & Waller, 1995) and by the Posavacs (Posavac, Posavac, & Posavac, 1998; Posavac, Posavac, & Weigel, 1998) in the United States indicate that the immediate negative impact of a series of 20 or so of these images of slender beauty is confined to girls and women who come to the study already feeling self-conscious or badly about their bodies. This person-environment interaction may be more likely to generate or intensify body dissatisfaction if the observer is an adolescent and the standard of comparison is an adult and a fashion model instead of just an attractive woman (Posavac, Posavac, & Posavac, 1998; Posavac, Posavac, & Weigel, 1998; Shaw, 1995). Consistent with these findings, Martin and her colleagues (Martin & Gentry, 1997; Martin et al., in press; Martin & Kennedy, 1993) have shown that girls (but not boys) ages 10 to 25 who have low self-esteem and/or a poor body image are particularly likely to enjoy advertisements with slender, attractive models and particularly susceptible to the influence of attractive models in advertising.

Social Comparison Studies

Martin and Kennedy (1993, 1994) also have shown that, for a majority of girls ages 8 through 18, reading fashion magazines activates a process of "social comparison" with the models in the advertisements and fashion layouts. This often results in feeling badly about one's own appearance, a tendency that, as noted previously, is greater for girls who consider themselves more physically unattractive. The proposition that females who read fashion magazines and compare themselves to the models will report greater body dissatisfaction and higher levels of disordered eating is supported by other studies of elementary-school girls (Taylor et al., 1998), middle-school girls (Levine et al., 1994; Meade & Levine, 1996), and young women in college (Heinberg, Thompson, & Stormer, 1995; Stormer & Thompson, 1996).

Martin and Gentry (1997) randomly assigned fourth-, sixth-, and eighth-grade girls to receive one of four different instructions for reading pseudo-advertisements constructed with pictures of models from very popular magazines for young teenage girls. The different reading instructions were designed to activate different motives for social comparison. Girls in the *self-evaluation* condition were instructed explicitly to compare their own physical attractiveness with that of the model to determine if they are as pretty on dimensions such as hair, eyes, and body. Girls in the *self-improvement* condition were to think about the model's features as inspiration for their own improvement, girls in the two *self-enhancement* conditions either looked for ways in which they were prettier than the model or sought to avoid or discount any explicit comparison.

The results of Martin and Gentry's (1997) study reinforce the importance of motivation and information processing in the effects of the thin ideal but offer only mixed support for a simple theory of social-comparison motives. As predicted, activation of self-evaluation motives resulted in reduced perceptions of one's self as physically attractive (for all grades). But the effects of the other motives are not summarized easily because they varied as a function of measure and grade. Cautiously, these researchers suggest that preventive education should promote self-improvement as a motive or, in some instances, self-enhancement through downward comparison or discounting of the "models" as relevant (Martin & Gentry, 1997). The question of motives for "upward" or even "downward" social comparison to fashion models is clearly an intriguing and important one for people seeking to understand and dilute the negative impact of media on body image and other aspects of disordered eating (Levine & Smolak, 1996, 1998; Meade & Levine, 1996; Martin & Gentry, 1997; Smolak & Levine, 1996).

Summary

It is very difficult to offer a coherent summary of the current state of theory and research in regard to the relationships among media, negative body image, and disordered eating (Berel & Irving, 1998; Levine & Smolak, 1996). The theoretical foundation is either missing or too simple, and the research findings are either surprising or too complex. With this overriding set of problems in mind, there is some evidence that media portrayals of slenderness *both reflect and contribute to* awareness and internalization of the slender ideal, as well as body dissatisfaction, unhealthy weight management, and disordered eating in girls and women who are vulnerable to these influences (Heinberg, 1996; Levine & Smolak, 1996; Stice, 1994). Moreover, vulnerability to media influence needs to be defined in contextual and personal terms (Berel & Irving, 1998; Smolak & Levine, 1996; Stice, 1994). Contextual factors supporting media glorification of slenderness and other features of "nervosa" include teasing and shape-related criticism from family and peers, the modeling of weight and shape concerns by various people, and direct weight-management messages from significant adults such as parents, teachers, coaches, and physicians (Heinberg, 1996; Levine et al., 1994; Smolak & Levine, 1996; Stice, 1994; see also Chapter 5). Personal factors that increase susceptibility to acceptance and consolidation of these messages probably include, for example, low self-esteem (Martin & Kennedy, 1993), social anxiety, a dispositional tendency to compare one's self with others (Stormer & Thompson, 1996), and deficits in body image and interoceptive awareness attributable to the contextual "factor" of physical or sexual abuse (Smolak & Levine, 1996; see also Chapter 12). The interactions and transactions between these contextual and personal factors almost certainly increase the probability that a person would be seeking to evaluate and improve the self in terms of appearance ideals, assimilate the slender ideal and compare herself to it, and be highly motivated by the ensuing dissatisfaction to take potentially unhealthy steps toward weight and shape preoccupation, restrictive dieting, and so forth (Smolak & Levine, 1996; Stice, 1994; see also Chapter 5).

☐ Media Literacy, Activism, and Advocacy

The safest and most practical assumption at the moment is that there is a need to focus concurrently on reducing messages about slenderness emanating from the media *and* from family, school staff, peers, and so forth, while somehow enhancing the desire, skills, self-confidence, and social support necessary to resist those influences (see Chapters 4–6, 9, and 11). We now consider several lines of prevention theory and research that share the fundamental belief that, because people are "active" processors (mediators) of media messages, active engagement in the analysis, protest, production, and use of media can reduce one's susceptibility to unhealthy images and information.

Media Literacy

According to Renee Hobbs (1998), director of the Media Literacy Project at Clark University's Hiatt Center for Urban Education, media "literacy" refers to "the ability to access, analyze, evaluate, and communicate messages in a wide variety of forms (Aufderheide, 1993). It is a term used by a growing number of scholars and educators to refer to the process of critically analyzing *and* learning to create one's own messages in print, audio, video, and multimedia" (p. 16; italics added for emphasis). Many scholar-activists in the media-literacy "movement" see this set of attitudes and abilities as crucial for citizen participation in a democracy suffused with, if not dominated by, mass media such as television, radio, and newspapers (Center for Media Literacy web site at www.medialit.org; Hobbs, 1997, 1998; Thoman, 1998).

Austin and colleagues at Washington State University (see, e.g., Austin & Johnson, 1997) have found that children and adolescents can change their knowledge, beliefs, attitudes, and behaviors toward alcohol and other health concerns when they are guided to consider certain basic questions that facilitate an "understanding of persuasive intent" and a reduction in the "perceived realism" of the media "portrayals." Austin's Message-Interpretation Process model supports the potential of enhancing media literacy skills in children and adolescents towards the goal of preventing poor body image and disordered eating (Berel & Irving, 1998; see also Chapters 4 and 6). As noted, media-literacy education assumes that the students are active, decisive, individual "information processors and consumers," rather than passive victims of an insidious media (Hobbs, 1997; Worsnop, 1994). Explicit and implicit messages to this effect set the stage for healthy, flexible processing, including active resistance and protest, of media messages.

Several studies have been conducted recently in the area of media literacy and disordered eating. Irving, DuPen, and Berel (1998) evaluated a peer-led, "one-shot" media-literacy program for high-school students. Applying Austin's model, a high-school junior (DuPen) guided 24 female sophomores to consider the following questions: Do *real* women look like the models in advertising? Will buying the product being advertised make me look like this model? Does this model look like this because of this product? Does thinness really guarantee happiness and success? More specifically, the program opened with a discussion of the glorification of slenderness in the media, including a presentation of Jean Kilbourne's (1995) half-hour video *Slim Hopes: Advertising and the Obsession with Slimness*. The students were helped to consider ways to "critically evaluate and 'de-construct' media images," how to challenge and change unrealistic standards, and the importance of developing self-esteem in realms other than physical appearance. Post-test–only comparisons indicated that, compared with the control group, participating students reported less internalization of the slender beauty ideal, and they perceived the media images as less realistic. There were no significant differences in body dissatisfaction, anxiety about weight and shape, the desirability of looking like slender models, or positive expectations associated with being slender.

Stormer and Thompson have found that a similar "psychoeducational" program can produce some significant changes in young women attending college.
The half-hour program implemented by Stormer and Thompson (1995) discussed the nature and impact of the slender beauty ideal and then considered
how fashion models and the production staff of magazines use plastic surgery,
airbrushing, computer graphics, and other technology to "construct" the idealized images. The contrast between such unreal, "perfect" images and the average American woman was emphasized. The program ended with a 6-minute
presentation of cognitive techniques for reducing the negative effects of social
comparisons by focusing on the unreality of the images.

Not surprisingly, Stormer and Thompson's (1995) very brief instruction in
"media literacy" had no significant between-group effect on dispositional measures of body image or disordered eating. However, it did produce significant
pre- to post-program reductions in appearance- and weight-related anxiety, and
in idealization of the slenderness embodied by fashion models and actresses.
Stormer, Thompson, and Huff (1998) recently replicated these findings, adding
a new component designed to help women reduce their overestimation of the
degree of slenderness that males consider an attractive, ideal body size.

Posavac, Posavac, and Weigel (1998) found that female college students with
a negative body image who are given a 7-minute "psychoeducational" intervention involving media analysis are less likely to engage in social comparison
and less likely to experience body image disturbances following experimental
exposure to images of slender beauty than students who see the same images
without the prior intervention. Consistent with the work of Stormer and Irving, the most effective "inoculation" developed by Posavac et al. (1998) emphasized the clash between the artificial, constructed nature of the slender,
flawless, "model look" versus biogenetic realities pertaining to both the diversity
of women's actual weights and shapes and to the negative effects of calorie-
restrictive dieting.

Media Activism

Media *activism* refers to efforts to protest—or praise—media products that have
been identified and analyzed as conveying—or contradicting—undesirable, unhealthy messages. Actions taken to change the media and interconnected businesses deepen and extend media literacy to further enhance self-efficacy and
well-being among consumers (Thoman, 1998). In the area of eating disorders,
media activism typically involves protest against advertisements and commercials that promote the thinness schema, such as depictions of the dull, heavy-
lidded, emaciated look known as "heroin chic" (see, e.g., the web site of
About-Face, Inc.: www.about-face.org). Dr. Vivian Meehan of Anorexia Nervosa and Associated Disorders (ANAD; web site: members.aol.com/anad20/
index.html) and Dr. Liza Berzins of Vitality, Inc. (web site: www.tiac.net/
users/VILTY) have led the way in protesting unhealthy advertising and communicating directly to businesses, advertisers, and legislators ways to promote body
positive image and appreciation of diverse body shapes. For example, in September of 1988 ANAD mounted a petition and letter-writing campaign to
protest the Hershey Foods Corporation's decision to advertise a chocolate bar

with the slogan, "You can never be too rich or too thin." The company withdrew the advertisement on October 17, 1988.

Activism also encompasses praise for companies who intentionally or unintentionally advocate—through advertising, company policies, or programming—more flexible, healthier approaches to beauty, femininity, eating, and exercising. An example of a praiseworthy company and advertisement would be the Body Shop's recent campaign (web site: www.the-body-shop.com/fullvoice/index.html). It intentionally "uses" a nude, full-figured, but otherwise Barbie-like doll named Ruby (because her features are Rubenesque) who reclines on a love seat and encourages women to "love your body," proclaiming that "there are 3 billion women who don't look like supermodels and only 8 who do" (Elliott, 1997).

Media Advocacy

Media *advocacy* refers to a set of tactics "for community groups to communicate their own story in their own words. It [combines] community advocacy approaches with the strategic and innovative use of media to better pressure decision makers to change policy" (Wallack, Dorfman, Jernigan, & Themba, 1993, p. xi). Thus, advocacy is another type of educational and liberating activity within the cycle that expands media "literacy" to encompass access, awareness, analysis, action, more access, deeper awareness, and so forth (Hobbs, 1997; Thoman, 1998). One challenge for prevention-oriented organizations such as ANAD and Eating Disorders Awareness & Prevention, Inc. (EDAP) in the new millenium is learning how to collaborate with and "use" mass media to promote a sociocultural perspective instead of the "individual illness" model of eating disorders, to insist on responsibility in advertising and business, and to "market" a variety of messages that present and represent respect for girls and women (Levine & Smolak, 1998).

EDAP's Media Activism/Advocacy Campaign

Structure

As a step toward meeting this challenge, in the summer of 1997 EDAP developed a campaign to combine activism, advocacy, and public education. Along with EDAP staff and board members, volunteer participants ("watchdogs") around the United States (many of whom are professionals involved in the treatment and prevention of eating disorders) monitor various fashion magazines and other media for the presence of images and text that either promote or work against negative body image, unhealthy eating patterns, and the objectification of women. These advertisements are informally rated on 15 bipolar dimensions pertaining to themes such as the idealization of slenderness, the denigration of fat and heavier people, and the promotion of binge eating as a way of coping with negative emotions. These dimensions are based on the EDAP booklet *Constructing Healthy Media Messages for Every Body* (Piran, Levine, & the EDAP staff, 1997).

Stoddard and other EDAP staff ultimately decide which advertisements or commercials to protest or praise. When the intent is protest, a letter to the company is drafted which details EDAP's specific concerns and feelings about the advertisement, strongly requests that the advertisement be discontinued, and expresses EDAP's willingness to help the company to abandon that type of advertising in favor of advertising that clearly supports the health and well-being of girls and women. The letter (but not the advertisement) also is posted on EDAP's web site (members.aol.com/edapinc/home.html) so that any visitor who wishes may read about our outrage and become a signee.

The letter ultimately is signed by EDAP staff, EDAP board members (including Levine and Piran), and all EDAP media watchdogs and anyone else who wish to be signees. If no action is forthcoming in a reasonable time, a second letter is sent reaffirming the sentiments of the first letter and indicating our intention to report the company's inaction or intransigence to both the mass media (e.g., *USA Today*) and a media-business publication (e.g., *Advertising Age*). In the case of advertisements that convey positive images of women unrelated to their appearance, portray a diversity of weights and shapes as beautiful, or acknowledge the nutritional needs of adolescent females, EDAP sends the business a letter of praise accompanied by an offer to work closely with the company to maintain, extend, and publicize positive messages.

Results

This campaign has been successful. As of this writing (January 1999) letters of protest have been sent to the National Dairy Council (have since discontinued the offending advertisement), Jarlsberg Cheese (who discontinued their advertisement after receiving the second, threatening letter), Avia (who discontinued the advertisement, although the company made no response to EDAP other than a "promise" to consult us during future campaigns), Nicole Shoes (who discontinued the advertisements and sent EDAP a formal apology), and Keds (who replied to the second letter with only a claim that their focus groups show that women like the offending advertisement and then did not reply to a third letter). Letters of praise have been sent to Nike, Kellogg, and Champion Sportswear. On July 1, 1998, *USA Today* and *Advertising Age* were sent a press release that lauded those companies who promote healthy messages, encouraged those companies that were responsive to our protests, and chastized Keds for being unwilling to change a pernicious message.

Implications

Many people—ranging from adolescents and college students to veteran therapists associated with eating disorder organizations—are surprised and inspired to learn that an ostensibly monolithic "sociocultural factor" such as mass media can be influenced to a small degree (for now) by organized citizen action (see Wallack et al., 1993). Clearly, media-related initiatives have the potential to expand the cycle of media literacy (Thoman, 1998) in the direction of united political and economic action by various organizations and individuals. Networking with other organizations is crucial for effective media activism and advocacy work. With regard to the latter, EDAP's commitment to activism and its small but meaningful successes have become part of the "story" that this organization shares and advocates in working with various media (magazines, television, video producers) to increase awareness of the problem of eating disorders and the factors that contribute to it.

☐ The GO GIRLS!™ Project

GO GIRLS!™ is an EDAP-sponsored prevention project for high-school students that integrates (to form the aforementioned cycle of media literacy) the domains of media awareness and analysis (Hobbs, 1997; Worsnop, 1994; see also Chapters 6 and 11), media activism, and media advocacy, as well as feminist group work (see Chapters 7 and 9). GO GIRLS!™ is an acronym for "*Giving Our Girls Inspiration and Resources for Lasting Self-esteem!*"

Goals

For the Students

The superordinate goal of the GO GIRLS!™ program is to help adolescent girls learn about *and* challenge the current relationships between the media's construction and portrayal of "ideal" women, the business of marketing, and the resultant negative effects on the self-image, bodies, and spirit of many women (Kilbourne, 1994, 1995). Based on the feminist perspective (see Chapters 7 and 9), EDAP seeks to create an organized but flexible set of media-related activities to give adolescent girls a chance to understand, through experience *and* action, that they have a "voice" as consumers and citizens, and that together they can use their voices and skills to effect social, political, corporate, and personal change.

More specifically, we believe that an action-oriented media-literacy program will help adolescent girls to: (1) develop critical thinking skills, including an enhanced ability to "read" and "decode" media messages about femininity and beauty; (2) challenge the thinness schema and reduce their glorification of slenderness; (3) have a healthier body image; (4) become more self-confident and have a stronger sense of both autonomy and collaboration with peers; (5) improve their communication skills, including oral and written methods for effectively expressing a desire for change directly to businesses; and (6) learn how to "use" the mass media for the social marketing and promotion of healthy messages.

For the Organization

As a nonprofit prevention organization, EDAP hopes to develop an engaging, experiential, action-oriented, curricular prevention program that will be more effective than many of the traditional and minimally effective primary prevention programs available to date (see Chapters 5 and 9). EDAP is also exploring the value of working with adolescents who have a particular interest in marketing, advertising, and business. A fair number of these women and men eventually will be in business and civic positions with the power to help change cultural standards concerning beauty, weight, shape, femininity, and success.

Research Design

Groups

The design was quasi-experimental. Volunteer students in one class at each of four different high schools participated in the GO GIRLS!™ program, while students in one class at each of two other high schools served as the no-program comparison group. It is important to note that all the adolescents were students in DECA, a national program to engage high school students in learning about business, leadership, and marketing. The composite experimental group consisted of 28 girls and 2 boys. The control group consisted of 22 girls and 10 boys who expressed an interest in the program but were told, truthfully, that it was not yet available in their school. The students' ages ranged from 14 through 18. Only the data from the girls are reported here.

Measures

At the end of the first lesson (February 1998) and again at the end of the program (June 1998), each student completed a packet of questionnaires. These were designed to obtain demographic information and to measure whether the program led to reductions (or no change for the experimental group, as compared with increases in the control group) in the following: objectification of one's own body as (measured by the surveillance, body shame, and belief in body control subscales of the Objectified Body Consciousness Scale [McKinley & Hyde, 1996]); internalization of the cultural ideal of slender beauty as (measured by that subscale of the Sociocultural Attitudes Towards Appearance Questionnaire (SATAQ [Heinberg, Thompson, & Stormer, 1995]); weight-related appearance anxiety as measured by (a subscale of the trait version of the Physical Appearance State and Trait Anxiety Scale (PASTAS) [Reed, Thompson, Brannick, & Sacco, 1991]), and concerns about weight, fat, and shape (measured by the Weight Concerns Scale; [Killen, 1996]). We also predicted that the program would increase general self-esteem (as measured by the Self-Esteem Scale; [Rosenberg, 1979]) and autonomy and self-acceptance (as measured by those subscales of the Psychological Well-Being Inventory; [Ryff, 1989]). There were no significant experimental versus control differences on any of the pretest measures.

Each student who participated in the program also completed an anonymous post-test evaluation that encouraged open-ended, personal reflections and asked her to rate such things as how helpful the class was in teaching critical thinking about the media and in increasing her confidence in expressing opinions.

The Facilitators

The program was facilitated by Charlie Stoddard and Nancy Lee in consultation with EDAP's Board of Directors and EDAP's other staff. Stoddard is EDAP's media specialist. She has a background in philosophy, economics, and public relations. Lee has an MBA in Marketing and extensive experience in business and social marketing, health promotion, and education of high school students. She served as a paid consultant to EDAP and the project.

Structure of the Program

There were 16 50-minute "lessons" presented once per week. In addition, all students had structured homework assignments and in conjunction kept a journal of their observations and feelings concerning culture, media, body image, and anything else they wished to express. Journal entries, which were seen periodically by the facilitators but not by other students, sometimes served as starting points for discussion.

The program is described most easily in terms of four-session segments. Given that the program encouraged critical inquiry, creativity, self-expression, and clear communication, in each of the four classrooms the pace of presentation and the exchange of ideas were necessarily different. This unpredictability was intensified by the fact that many students are motivated to learn about media and body image because they have family and friends with eating disorders. This genuine and powerful motive should not be ignored because it fuels interest in prevention through activism and advocacy. However, a deep, general interest in disordered eating also ensures that there are unexpected, interesting, important, and time-consuming discussions of such issues as helping friends with eating disorders and the impact of boys on the weight and shape concerns of girls.

Segment 1: Introduction and Foundation

Participants were informed carefully about EDAP, the general goals of the project, their rights as research participants, and ground rules for meaningful group interactions. Homework assignments, short presentations by the facilitators, and group discussions were combined to address the definition and implications of "positive" and "negative" body image; various determinants of body image, including the mass media; and depictions of girls and women in media such as *Seventeen* and *Vogue* magazines. The EDAP guidelines (Piran et al., 1997), examples of EDAP's letters of protest and praise, and student and facilitator reactions all were used to analyze what determines the potential "negative" or "positive" impact on girls and women of an advertisement or article.

Toward the end of this four-session segment students saw and discussed the video *Behind Closed Doors*, an 8-minute news special that aired January 27, 1997.[1] This is an exposé of tricks—ranging from painfully awkward poses to computer "enhancement"—used to make models such as Cindy Crawford look more slender, more "beautiful," more fashionable, and more "perfect" in clothes that do not fit all that well without the aggressive use of duct tape to hold them in place for that "natural" look. Students at two schools also discussed Cosy Sheridan's (1996) song "The Losing Game," which offers a lyrical and critical perspective on media, the drive for thinness, dieting, and self-rejection.

To facilitate critical inquiry, as opposed to passive acceptance of the facilitators' pronouncements about the importance of media, students were helped to design, administer, and analyze the data from a survey of their peers as to the influence of various sociocultural factors on the body image of girls. One finding turned out to be crucial for later discussions with business and media people: 93% of the respondents wanted to see a greater diversity of weights and body shapes portrayed as beautiful and desirable in advertisements.

> I was totally and most utterly shocked when we watched that short video on models and the way clothing is made to fit them just right. It is definitely true, there is more to what you see. I also was pretty outraged when the video talked about how supermodel's pictures are taken and completely redone. It is just sick that the most beautiful women aren't even enough.
>
> —*B, lesson 5*

Segment 2: Analysis and Activism

Students were assigned to bring in advertisements with which to construct collages representing negative (the "Wall of Shame") and positive messages (the "Rave Wall"). This activity was accompanied by further discussions of the content, structure, intention, implicit and explicit messages, and various effects of the advertisements, including what girls and women would gain from looking like models in the advertisements and what they would lose or sacrifice. Based on the EDAP templates for activism, students drafted, received feedback on, and revised letters of protest and praise.

During the second segment, Lee made a presentation on "social marketing." This helped students conceptualize their specific goals in trying to change the attitudes and behaviors of advertisers and marketers who target adolescent girls. It also helped students develop specific questions to ask a group of professionals involved in modeling, merchandising, and marketing, such as, "How do advertisers determine both their 'target audience' and the images, messages, and models needed to 'capture' that audience?"

This segment concluded with two important events. First, Lee and Stoddard arranged for the students to meet in person and ask those questions of professional business people from two major department stores (Bon Marche and Nordstrom), two different advertising agencies, two different modeling agencies, and a company specializing in computer imaging of fashion layouts. This "fact-finding" event was designed to supplement Lee's efforts to help student learn to "speak the language" of advertisers and marketers and to understand their points of view, such as their motivation for selecting and constructing the images that go into advertising. Second, students began to reflect on and organize what they had learned so that they could begin creating projects to challenge unhealthy depictions of women and to raise their peers' awareness of the connections between media and body image.

Segment 3: Preparation for Activism and Advocacy

This 4-week period was spent refining plans to raise the awareness levels of specific local businesses, local media, and peers. In addition, during week 10 the news team for the local Fox network affiliate filmed one of the GO GIRLS!™ classes in a group discussion and while the students were working on the Wall of Shame. Stoddard and several of the students also were interviewed individually. At another school one of the more involved students completed her own letter to *Seventeen*, requesting that more diverse images of women be used in their fashion layouts. The rest of the class signed the letter, which was mailed April 24. Three of the girls at a third school spoke passionately and eloquently for approximately five minutes each to an audience of well over 200 people who were attending an EDAP-sponsored luncheon designed to raise awareness about and money for the GO GIRLS!™ program.

Segment 4: Activism, Advocacy, and Evaluation

During the final segment, students completed their activism and advocacy projects. Working with a professional editor at a local cable-access channel, two of the girls at one high school created a 6-minute prevention video containing images and music (including the GO GIRLS!™ luncheon slide show and Cosy Sheridan's song), text, and voice-overs. In one of the project's most exciting developments, the students in one class collaborated in making a presentation to the Divisional Vice President of Visual Merchandising at the Bon Marche, requesting that she diversify the body shapes and sizes of the mannequins displayed in this upscale department store, particularly in the "teen" section. During the discussion, one student repeatedly insisted that the store could change, that the store needs to listen to its customers, and that other stores have more diverse mannequins. Another student, combining activism and advocacy by cleverly calling attention to the fact that the *Seattle Times* was following the GO GIRLS!™ project, got the people at Bon Marche to agree to use a larger "form" (headless mannequin) to display some of the clothing being sold in their teen department. By the end of this exhilarating meeting the business people were less defensive and began to brainstorm with the girls about solutions to the problem.

Despite the company's initial suspicions about possible criticism, another class and the facilitators managed to meet with the marketing director and nearly 10 other employees from the Seattle-based Union Bay Sportswear company. The purpose was to *commend* this company for their magazine advertisements depicting teenagers of many different sizes and shapes. The students gave a great presentation about their knowledge and concerns, and they responded very well to the many questions asked about why this is so important and what they in fact would like to see in advertisements. The students acknowledged that they would like to see Union Bay receive positive publicity from their efforts, so that other companies would notice and follow suit. In yet another illustration of Thoman's (1998) cycle of media awareness–analysis–activism–advocacy, this effort was one of the featured sections of a *Seattle Times* story about the GO GIRLS!™ program (Cronin, 1998).

Although the process undoubtedly was educational, not all the students' efforts at activism were successful. Efforts by students at a third school to convince the Vice President of Corporate Display at Nordstrom to diversify the size and shape of mannequins were met with counterarguments and long-term delay. Students at the fourth school conducted videotaped interviews of people on the streets of Seattle to inquire about the "realism" and effects of ways in which women are portrayed in magazine advertisements and in the mannequins in store windows. Students in this class also filmed themselves looking through magazines, discussing the negative impact of specific ads, and using the *Cosmopolitan* "makeover kit" on their own computers to demonstrate how technology can be used to alter images to look real. Another subgroup in this class worked on a narrative (voice-over) concerning what they had learned. Because of combination of unforeseen exigencies plus poor planning and procrastination by the students, however, these efforts were not integrated and the video was never completed. This outcome reminds us that media-literacy training sometimes requires a tricky balance of student initiative and participation and substantial adult guidance.

Portions of each final class in the program were devoted to program evaluation, completion of the post-test measures, reflection on what was learned and done, and the saying of goodbyes, which in two instances included a bouquet of flowers for Stoddard.

Results

As of this writing, we still are sifting through the students' actions, journal entries, numerical and qualitative evaluations of the class, and survey responses, as well as the observations of Stoddard and Lee. A basic analysis of these data suggests that the GO GIRLS!™ program met a fair number of its goals but failed to effect certain desired changes.

Student Actions and Activism

The program definitely was successful in guiding students to *learn through action* about conducting research, analyzing and producing media, and confronting businesses and advertisers. To summarize, all or some of the students conducted surveys about media influence among peers; met with and tried to influence professionals in advertising, marketing, and media; wrote letters of protest to companies and to media; made a presentation at a well-attended luncheon covered by the media; were featured in television and newspaper stories that published the results of their surveys and their activism, created their own video, and conducted several smaller individual research projects.

This "activism effect" and the sense of empowerment it produced are reflected in the girls' open-ended comments at the conclusion of the program. One girl wrote: "I was really impressed with how many out-of-class activities we had. It was such a great experience going to all the different things, especially the Bon [Marche] meeting." Another girl remarked: "We got to plan and make decisions. We were the ones taking the action!" Yet another girl echoed this sense of feeling through doing: "We made plans and followed through with them; everyone contributed and got to do something they really believed in. . . . [There was] hands-on experience to learn from."

Numerical Evaluations

Student ratings on the evaluation form (10 = maximum positive response) indicated that, in general, they were satisfied with the program (Mean = 8.81), they felt the program improved their critical thinking and gave them "tools for reacting to media" (Means = 8.74 and 8.32, respectively). On her evaluation sheet one girl stated, "[This class] made people aware of how advertising and the media influences us, and we got to make a difference." Another girl from a different class agreed: "[One of the] strengths [was] the look at the magazine ads. All the girls were into it. Made us realize about the media."

The program also increased the girls' confidence in expressing opinions (Mean = 8.39). For example, one girl wrote: "If anything, it helped me with public speaking, with speaking my mind. The final presentation with Union Bay was a great experience talking in front of people." Another girl in a different class, referring to the GO GIRLS!™ luncheon, felt similarly: "It was also great that both my parents got to come and see me speak. Now, I have no fear of speaking in front of adults and would like to do it again."

Their reports concerning self-confidence (Mean = 6.87), feeling better about one's body (Mean = 6.81), and learning to work effectively with classmates (Mean = 7.68) suggested that the program was moderately useful in these areas but less so than in other areas. Nevertheless, one girl spoke for several others at several schools when she wrote that she liked "the fact that it helped me realize that all of us are just as 'good' as all the skinny girls. I also realized how fake some of them could be." Another girl at a different school stated that the program helped her "show my family and friends what I am capable of. I learned a lot about myself in terms of how confident and creative I can be. I surprised myself."

Attendance records, compliance with the journal assignment, and facilitator observations strongly suggested that two of the classes were much more involved in the program. Comparison of their ratings across the seven variables (Mean = 8.89; range = 8.11–9.59) with those of the less involved classes (Mean = 6.98; range = 5.60–8.14) clearly indicates that, not surprisingly, the program was more effective in meeting some of its goals for those students who were more engaged with and by the program.

Survey Data

Twenty-four of the 28 girls (86%) in the GO GIRLS!™ program completed both the pretest and post-test surveys, while the comparable figure for the comparison girls was 20 of 22 (91%). The pre-to-post change scores for each of the 10 survey variables were subjected to an independent groups t-test analysis. Collapsing across all four classes in the experimental condition there were no statistically significant differences ($p < .05$) between the experimental and control condition. The experimental group reported a small mean increase in self acceptance and a small mean decrease in weight and shape concerns, whereas the control group changed in the opposite direction to a modest degree (p values < .10, one-tailed). One perplexing finding was that the control group reported a small mean *decrease* in body surveillance, whereas the experimental group reported no change ($p < .10$, two-tailed).

Each of the dependent variables then was reanalyzed as a function of level of engagement, ranging from none (comparison group) to moderate to high. Owing to large within-group variability, there were still no statistically significant differences. However, on 7 of the 10 variables, the two more engaged classes displayed the most positive changes. Moreover, these two classes were the only ones to show, on average, nonsignificant reductions in internalization of the thin standard of beauty, in weight-related anxiety, and in weight and shape concerns.

☐ Conclusions and Future Directions

GO GIRLS!™

The first phase of the GO GIRLS!™ prevention project indicates that high school students in marketing classes are receptive to participating in a media literacy program that educates them in various active ways, including mentorship, about the relationships between business, media, gender, and body image. Moreover, a preliminary analysis of the data suggests that this type of program can help students develop beliefs and skills in some areas thought to reduce vulnerability to disordered eating, namely community activism, critical thinking, media analysis, and communication via assertive speech, all of which can contribute to a sense of individual and collective empowerment (Steiner-Adair, 1991; see also Chapters 9 and 16). According to the open-ended statements of the girls during both the evaluation process and entries in their journals, a very important element of the program is the opportunity to critically evaluate the situation, formulate a plan, make decisions, take action in the community, and in so doing be "seen" and "heard" by business people, the facilitators, and other adults. The need to expand our efforts to think about and measure "empowerment" and its effects is highlighted by an occurrence in the class following the GO GIRLS!™ luncheon. When asked by one of the facilitators if she felt comfortable calling the woman in charge of print ads for Bon Marche, A responded: "I just spoke in front of 230 people; I can do anything!"

There is also some tentative evidence that students who are engaged more deeply by the program develop greater self-confidence and reduced concerns about weight and shape. The latter is an important outcome, as Killen and colleagues have shown that a simple measure of these concerns is predictive of later disordered eating (Killen, 1996).

This type of short-term pre- and post-program design cannot address the question of whether the GO GIRLS!™ program will *prevent* eating disorders. It appears, however, that the program needs to be refined in order to effect significant changes in important psychological variables such as the internalization of the thin beauty ideal (Heinberg et al., 1995), self-objectification of the body (McKinley & Hyde, 1996), and the aforementioned weight and shape concerns (Killen, 1996). One productive direction suggested by other prevention research that emphasizes personal and communal activism (Wallerstein, Sanchez-Merki, & Dow, 1997) is more opportunity for students to reflect upon and discuss the implications of sociocultural factors for *their own*—and not just their "peers" or "women's"—body image, dieting behavior, and weight preoccupation; and *their own* sense of choice, commitment, and control in regard to their own lives (Kobasa & Puccetti, 1983; see also Chapters 9 and 16).

The finding that girls in the control group, on average, slightly reduced their body-surveillance scores, whereas the experimental group remained unchanged over time, warrants further examination. Although this may represent random variation, we cannot ignore the possibility that, in the short-term at least, heightened awareness of media glorification of slenderness and media objectification of women's bodies may somehow adversely affect one's experience of her body.

At the most abstract, yet most practical level, this pilot project points to a need for increased clarity in regard to the theoretical foundations and specific goals of this type of media literacy–through–activism program (Berel & Irving, 1998); the best teaching methods for engaging students in learning about the media (Worsnop, 1994; see also Chapter 6) and about themselves in their world; and effective ways to transform program goals and evaluative concepts into valid measures of short-term change (e.g., in empowerment or in weight and shape concerns) and long-term prevention (i.e., a reduction in the incidence of disordered eating).

The "New Media"

The World Wide Web currently serves as a source of health-related information for many citizens, as well as a potent means of exchanging treatment and prevention information between professionals in many countries. There are (as of July 1998) a number of informative Web sites for general information about eating disorders (e.g., http://something-fishy.com/ed.html; Harvard Eating Disorders Center at www.hedc.org), primary prevention tips (e.g., http://members.aol.com/edapinc/home.html), and media activism and advocacy in regard to body image and disordered eating (e.g., http://members.aol.com/edapwatch/watchdog.html; http://www.about-face.org). There are also many excellent, provocative Web sites pertaining to the intersection between media literacy and child and adolescent development, including *Girl Power!* at www.health.org/gpower; the *Just Think Foundation* at www.justhink.org; the *Center for Media Education* at www.cme.org/cme; and the *Media Education Foundation* at www.igc.org/mef.

In the all too near future, the Web is likely to be an increasingly important resource for engaging students in both the analysis of media and the creation of their own preventive-education "sites." The Web offers many exciting, evolving possibilities, including electronic bulletin boards (Gleason, 1995) and various forms of interactive, health-related psychoeducation (Dede & Fontana, 1995; Winzelberg et al., 1998). In addition, Springer, Winzelberg, Perkins, and Taylor (in press) have found that a college course providing "traditional" education about the nature and multiple determinants of body image produced significant positive changes in body image and eating behavior, even though there was no explicit emphasis whatsoever on personal change as part of the course. If this finding is robust, such a course easily could be adopted to an interactive CD-ROM format and to distance learning over the Web.

Dede and Fontana (1995) described the Multimedia and Thinking Skills Project (MTSP) at George Mason University. The MTSP's emphasis on interactive, multimedia, Web-integrated learning certainly could be applied to the GO GIRLS!™ project. The MTSP is creating "multi-user shared environments" that incorporate independent and collaborative exploration, learning by observation and discussion, experiential learning through data gathering and simulations, hypothesis development and testing, and multimedia productions (e.g., Web sites, interactive CD-ROMs) for communication of what is learned to various audiences (Dede & Fontana, 1995). Multi-user shared environments should not and will not replace certain aspects of interpersonal learning through face-to-face discussion with mentors, peers, and business people (see Chapter 9). However, this type of "virtual" project could provide an engaging supplement to the GO GIRLS!™ focus on individual expression, collaborative learning, learning by doing, usable learning products, and more sophisticated access to and use of mass media.

In considering the exciting possibilities of the worldwide Web, one also should be aware of potential adverse effects of widely disseminated information, especially on a minority of people vulnerable to disordered eating. As uncomfortable as it may be, there is no denying the evidence the mass media might introduce people to calorie-restrictive dieting and abusive exercising or help people learn how to binge eat and purge (e.g., Murray, Touyz, & Beumont, 1990).

A Final Note

We believe that it is now time for people committed to the prevention of eating disorders to pursue three interrelated goals. First, researchers need to follow the lead of Stice (1994) and Martin and Gentry (1997) in conceptualizing and researching the mechanisms by which mass media contribute to disordered eating, rather than simply including media in multidimensional, biopsychosocial models. Second, eating disorders organizations and others committed to primary prevention need to continue to understand and utilize the mass media as a tool for advocating and marketing a sociocultural, prevention perspective (Wallack et al., 1993). Finally, prevention specialists need to continue to explore the value of critical inquiry, activism, and advocacy for the development of prevention organizations and for curricular preventions programs like GO GIRLS!™ In this regard we strongly recommend that eating disorders specialists broaden their thinking about primary prevention to incorporate the writings of theorists and researchers in the fields of media literacy (Hobbs, 1997, 1998), "critical" consumer psychology (Ozanne & Murray, 1995) and liberation education (Wallerstein et al., 1997).

> "The 90's woman isn't a size 2, she's sometimes a 12, 14, or 18, and she's powerful and strong, and those size 2 girls are just skinny . . ."
> —*S, journal entry for lesson 3 of GO GIRLS!™*

☐ References

Arnett, J. J. (1995). Adolescents' use of media for self-socialization. *Journal of Youth and Adolescence, 24,* 519–533.

Austin, E., & Johnson, K. (1997). Immediate and delayed effects of media literacy training on third graders' decision making for alcohol. *Health Communication, 9,* 323–349.

Berel, S., & Irving, L. M. (1998). Media and disturbed eating: An analysis of media influence and implications for prevention. *Journal of Primary Prevention 18,* 415–430.

Bordo, S. (1993). *Unbearable weight: Feminism, Western culture, and the body.* Berkeley: University of California Press.

Cronin, M. E. (1998, June 11). Body type, body hype: Local high-school students challenge marketing of super-thin image. *The Seattle Times,* Section E, 1–2.

Cusamano, D. L., & Thompson, J. K. (1997). Body image and body shape ideals in magazines: Exposure, awareness, and internalization. *Sex Roles, 37,* 701–721.

Dede, C., & Fontana, L. (1995). Transforming health education via new media. In L. M. Harris (Ed.), *Health and the new media: Technologies transforming personal and public health* (pp. 163–183). Mahwah, NJ: Lawrence Erlbaum Associates.

Elliott, S. (1997, August 26). Advertising: The Body Shop's campaign offers reality, not miracles. *New York Times.*

Feingold, A., & Mazzella, R. (1996). Gender differences in body image are increasing. *The General Psychologist, 32,* 90–98.

Gordon, R. A. (1990). *Anorexia and bulimia: Anatomy of a social epidemic.* Cambridge, MA: Basil Blackwell.

Gleason, N. A. (1995). A new approach to disordered eating: Using an electronic bulletin board to control social pressure on body image. *Journal of American College Health, 44,* 78–80.

Guillen, E. O., & Barr, S. I. (1994). Nutrition, dieting, and fitness messages in a magazine for adolescent women, 1970–1990. *Journal of Adolescent Health, 15,* 464–472.

Harris, R. J. (1994). *A cognitive psychology of mass communication* (2nd ed.). Hillsdale, NJ: Lawrence Erlbaum Associates.

Harrison, K. (1997). Does interpersonal attraction to thin media personalities promote eating disorders? *Journal of Broadcasting & Electronic Media, 41,* 478–500.

Harrison, K., & Cantor, J. (1997). The relationship between media consumption and eating disorders. *Journal of Communication, 47,* 40–66.

Heinberg, L. J. (1996). Theories of body image disturbance: Perceptual, developmental, and sociocultural factors. In J. K. Thompson (Ed.), *Body image, eating disorders, and obesity: An integrative guide for assessment and treatment* (pp. 27–47). Washington, DC: American Psychological Association.

Heinberg, L. J., Thompson, J. K., & Stormer, S. (1995). Development and validation of the Sociocultural Attitudes Towards Appearance Questionnaire. *International Journal of Eating Disorders, 17,* 81–89.

Henderson-King, E., & Henderson-King, D. (1997). Media effects on women's body esteem: Social and individual difference factors. *Journal of Applied Social Psychology, 27,* 399–417.

Hobbs, R. (1997). Literacy for the information age. In J. Flood, S. B. Heath, & D. Lapp (Eds.), *Handbook of research on teaching literacy through the communicative and visual arts* (pp. 7–14). New York: Simon & Schuster.

Hobbs, R. (1998, Winter). The seven great debates in the media literacy movement. *Journal of Communication,* 16–32.

Irving, L. M., DuPen, J., & Berel, S. (1998). A media literacy program for high school females. *Eating Disorders: The Journal of Treatment and Prevention, 6*(2), 119–131.

Kilbourne, J. (1994). Still killing us softly: Advertising and the obsession with thinness. In P. Fallon, M. Katzman, & S. C. Wooley (Eds.), *Feminist perspectives on eating disorders* (pp. 395–418). New York: Guilford.

Kilbourne, J. (1995). *Slim hopes: Advertising & the obsession with thinness* [video]. (Available from the Media Education Foundation, 28 Center Street, Northampton, MA 01060; http://www.igc.apc.org/mef/mef.html)

Killen, J. D. (1996). Development and evaluation of a school-based eating disorder symptoms prevention program. In L. Smolak, M. P. Levine, & R. Striegel-Moore (Eds.), *The developmental psychopathology of eating disorders* (pp. 313–339). Mahwah, NJ: Lawrence Erlbaum Associates.

Kobasa, S., & Puccetti, M. C. (1983). Personality and social resources in stress resistance. *Journal of Personality & Social Psychology, 45,* 839–850.

Levine, M. P. (1994). Beauty myth and the beast: What men can do and be to help prevent eating disorders. *Eating Disorders: The Journal of Treatment & Prevention, 2,* 101–113.

Levine, M. P., & Smolak, L. (1996). Media as a context for the development of disordered eating. In L. Smolak, M. P. Levine, & R. Striegel-Moore (Eds.), *The developmental psychopathology of eating disorders* (pp. 235–257). Mahwah, NJ: Lawrence Erlbaum Associates.

Levine, M. P., & Smolak, L. (1998). The mass media and disordered eating: Implications for primary prevention. In W. Vandereycken & G. Van Noordenbos (Eds.), *Prevention of eating disorders.* (pp. 23–56). London: Athlone.

Levine, M. P., Smolak, L., & Hayden, H. (1994). The relation of sociocultural factors to eating attitudes and behaviors among middle school girls. *Journal of Early Adolescence, 14,* 472–491.

Martin, M. C., & Gentry, J. W. (1997). Stuck in the model trap: The effects of beautiful models in ads on female pre-adolescents and adolescents. *The Journal of Advertising, 26*(2), 19–33.

Martin, M. C., Gentry, J. W., & Hill, R. P. (in press). The beauty myth and the persuasiveness of advertisements: A look at adolescent girls and boys. In C. Macklin (Ed.), *Advertising and children*. Newbury Park, CA: Sage.

Martin, M. C., & Kennedy, P. F. (1993). Advertising and social comparison: Consequences for female preadolescents and adolescents. *Psychology & Marketing, 10,* 513–530.

Martin, M. C., & Kennedy, P. F. (1994). Social comparison and the beauty of advertising models: The role of motives for comparison. *Advances in Consumer Research, 21,* 365–371.

McKinley, N. M., & Hyde, J. S. (1996). The Objectified Body Consciousness Scale: Development and validation. *Psychology of Women Quarterly, 20,* 181–215.

Meade, M., & Levine, M. P. (1996, April). *Media cultivation, motives for media use, and disordered eating in middle school girls.* Paper presented at the Seventh International Conference on Eating Disorders, New York.

Media Education Foundation. (1997). *Catalog: Video resources for the 21st century.* (Available from the MEF, 26 Center Street, Northampton, MA 01060; e-mail: mediaed@mediaed.org; web address: http://www.igc.org/mef)

Murray, S. H., Touyz, S. W., & Beumont, P. J. V. (1990). Knowledge about eating disorders in the community. *International Journal of Eating Disorders, 9,* 87–93.

Murray, S. H., Touyz, S. W., & Beumont, P. J. V. (1996). Awareness and perceived influence of body ideals in the media: A comparison of eating disorder patients and the general community. *Eating Disorders: The Journal of Treatment and Prevention, 4,* 33–46.

Ozanne, J. L., & Murray, J. B. (1995). Uniting critical theory and public policy to create the reflexively defiant consumer. *American Behavioral Scientist, 38,* 516–525.

Peirce, K. (1990). A feminist theoretical perspective on the socialization of teenage girls through *Seventeen* magazine. *Sex Roles, 23,* 491–500.

Piran, N., Levine, M. P., & the EDAP staff. (1997). *Constructing healthy media messages for every body.* (Available from Eating Disorders Awareness & Prevention, Inc., 603 Stewart St., Suite 803, Seattle, WA 98101; 206-382-3587)

Posavac, H. D., Posavac, S. S., & Posavac, E. J. (1998). Exposure to media images of female attractiveness and concern with body weight among young women. *Sex Roles, 38,* 187–201.

Posavac, H. D., Posavac, S. S., & Weigel, R. G. (1998). *Reducing the impact of exposure to idealized media images of female attractiveness on women's body image: An investigation of three psychoeducational interventions.* Manuscript submitted for publication.

Reed, D. L., Thompson, J. K., Brannick, M. T., & Sacco, W. P. (1991). Development and validation of the Physical Appearance State and Trait Anxiety Scale (PASTAS). *Journal of Anxiety Disorders, 5,* 323–332.

Rosenberg, M. (1979). *Conceiving the self.* New York: Basic Books.

Ryff, C. D. (1989). Happiness is everything, or is it? Explorations of the meaning of psychological well-being. *Journal of Personality and Social Psychology, 57,* 1069–1081.

Shaw, J. (1995). Effects on fashion magazines on body dissatisfaction and eating psychopathology in adolescent and adult females. *European Eating Disorders Review, 3,* 15–23.

Shaw, J., & Waller, G. (1995). The media's impact on body image: Implications for prevention and treatment. *Eating Disorders: The Journal of Treatment & Prevention, 3,* 115–123.

Sheridan, C. (1996). The losing game. On *One sure thing* [CD]. Evanston, IL: Waterbug Records.

Signorielli, N., & Morgan, M. (Eds.). (1990). *Cultivation analysis: New directions in media effects research.* Newbury Park, CA: Sage.

Silverstein, B., & Perlick, D. (1995). *The cost of competence: Why inequality causes depression, eating disorders, and illness in women.* New York: Oxford University Press.

Smolak, L., & Levine, M. P. (1996). Adolescent transitions and the development of eating problems. In L. Smolak, M. P. Levine, & R. Striegel-Moore (Eds.), *The developmental psychopathology of eating disorders* (pp. 207–233). Mahwah, NJ: Lawrence Erlbaum Associates.

Springer, E. A., Winzelberg, A. J., Perkins, R., & Taylor, C. B. (in press). Effects of a body image curriculum for college students on improved body image. *International Journal of Eating Disorders.*

Steiner-Adair, C. (1991). New maps of development, new models of therapy: The psychology of women and the treatment of eating disorders. In C. Johnson (Ed.), *Psychodynamic treatment of anorexia nervosa and bulimia* (pp. 225–244). New York: Guilford.

Stice, E. (1994). Review of the evidence for a sociocultural model of bulimia nervosa and an exploration of the mechanisms of action. *Clinical Psychology Review, 14,* 633–661.

Stice, E., Schupak-Neuberg, E., Shaw, H. E., & Stein, R. I. (1994). Relation of media exposure to eating disorder symptomatology: An examination of mediating mechanisms. *Journal of Abnormal Psychology, 103,* 836–840.

Stice, E., & Shaw, H. E. (1994). Adverse effects of the media portrayed thin-ideal on women and linkages to bulimic symptomatology. *Journal of Social and Clinical Psychology, 13,* 288–308.

Stormer, S. M., & Thompson, J. K. (1995, November). *The effect of media images and sociocultural beauty ideals on college-age women: A proposed psychoeducational program.* Paper presented at the annual meeting of the Association for the Advancement of Behavior Therapy, Washington, DC.

Stormer, S. M., & Thompson, J. K. (1996). Explanations of body image disturbance: A test of maturational status, negative verbal commentary, social comparison, and sociocultural hypotheses. *International Journal of Eating Disorders, 19,* 193–202.

Stormer, S. M., Thompson, J. K., & Huff, B. (1998, November). *An evaluation of two media-focused psychoeducation programs for body image: Preliminary findings.* Paper presented at the annual meeting of the Association for the Advancement of Behavior Therapy.

Taylor, C. B., Sharpe, T., Shisslak, C., Bryson, S., Estes, L. S., Gray, N., McKnight, K. M., Crago, M., Kraemer, H. C., & Killen, J. D. (1998). Factors associated with weight concerns in adolescent girls. *International Journal of Eating Disorders, 24,* 31–42.

Thoman, E. (1998, June). *What's it all about? A crash course in core principles and key concept.* Workshop presented at the National Media Education Conference ("A Paradigm for Public Health"), Colorado Springs, CO.

Turner, S. L., Hamilton, H., Jacobs, M., Angood, L. M., & Dwyer, D. H. (1997). The influence of fashion magazines on the body image satisfaction of college women: An exploratory analysis. *Adolescence, 32,* 603–610.

Wallack, L., Dorfman L., Jernigan, D. & Themba, M. (1993). *Media advocacy and public health: Power for prevention.* Newbury Park, CA: Sage.

Wallerstein, N., Sanchez-Merki, V., & Dow, L. (1997). Freirian praxis in health education and community organizing: A case study of an adolescent prevention program. In M. Hinkler (Ed.), *Community organizing and community building for health* (pp. 195–211). New Brunswick, NJ: Rutgers University Press.

Winzelberg, A. J., Eldredge, K. L., Wilfley, D., Eppstein, D., Dasmahapatra, R., Dev, P., & Taylor, C. B. (1998). *Effectiveness of an internet-based program for reducing risk factors for eating disorders.* Manuscript submitted for publication.

Wiseman, C. V., Gray, J. J., Mosimann, J. E., & Ahrens, A. H. (1992). Cultural expectations of thinness in women: An update. *International Journal of Eating Disorders, 11,* 85–89.

Worsnop, C. M. (1994). *Screening images: Ideas for media education.* Mississauga, Ontario: Wright Communications.

☐ Note

1. Until recently, the 6-minute "modeling segment" of *Behind Closed Doors* was available for $35.00 from the producer, Eric Schotz of LMNO productions in Sherman Oaks, California. However, this company now states that they are no longer providing the video. We currently are investigating how this video might be obtained from another source. For an update, interested parties should contact Eating Disorders Awareness & Prevention, Inc., 603 Stewart St., Suite 803, Seattle, WA 98101 (206-382-3587).

2

CHAPTER

Mervat Nasser
Melanie Katzman

Eating Disorders: Transcultural Perspectives Inform Prevention

The world is shrinking and the supposed ideal body size is shrinking, so is it time for our prevention efforts to grow larger? Go more global? Is it time to recognize that societal evolutions contribute to changes in symptoms and that we can affect (and possibly prevent) syndromes by tackling their cultural underpinnings?

In this chapter we argue that culture impacts not only the expression of eating disorders but the development of neurosis in general—that changes in society result in altered expressions of distress and variations on its relief (both medically and politically). We begin with a review of "assumed social causes" of eating problems, revealing that over the past century cultural explanations have always been entertained if not fully understood. We then discuss the past three decades in more detail and pose a challenge for the millennium. Specifically, we consider how the 1970s sought to define a syndrome and the 1980s explored Western cultural influences on eating patterns. The contributions and criticisms of feminist approaches highlighted in the 1990s follow, building to a review of cross-cultural literature that heads the subsequent section.

The globalization of eating disorders is our focus in the second section, in which we examine the effects of immigration, acculturation, modernization, and culture change. Our third section then discusses the global forces that affect the development of eating disorders—political, religious, and familial alterations in society that may in fact change the face of neurosis. We close with suggestions for prevention that encompass a global, cross-disciplinary notion of intervention.

☐ Thinness, Self, and Society: Evolution of the Causal Link

The contribution of social forces to the development of eating pathology is commonly believed to be a recent and clever insight, developed only in the past two decades as a way of explaining the reasons behind the apparent rise in the incidence of eating disorders. However, the link between social forces and eating pathology was by no means absent from the original description of the syndrome. Gull (1868) emphasized the unique propensity of women to develop these disorders, particularly if they were at a certain age: "The subjects of this affliction are mostly of the female sex and chiefly between the ages of 16–23 . . . and it will be admitted that young women at the ages named are especially obnoxious to mental perversity."

One explanation given in retrospect for Gull's emphasis on women's vulnerability was the fact that both London and Paris were, at the time he was describing this syndrome, witnessing their first feminist movement. In keeping with this, in 1888 Playfair (cited in Brumberg, 1988) was of the opinion that anorexia nervosa was a form of "neurasthenia" that resulted from the recent entry of women into the academic arena, with too much intellectual work and advanced schooling: "I have seen many instances of anorexia nervosa in young girls which have followed the various studies for some of the higher examinations for women, now so much in vogue." Gull and Playfair may have implied a possible social causation for this new syndrome, but it was Lasègue (1873) who was able to formulate a clear link between his new syndrome, *anorexie hystérique,* and the disintegration of the aristocracy and the growth of the middle class in France following the French revolution. Eating habits emerged among the middle class as a new style, one that set its members apart from the working class. Meal times symbolized the spirit and values of the newly redefined nuclear family in which the child and (later adolescent) took center stage (Brumberg, 1988; Selvini-Pallazzoli, 1985). The class symbolism has remained an important social dimension in eating pathology.

However, the significance of Lasègue's contribution perhaps lies more in his ability to see that social transformation in itself is capable of producing a *new neurotic syndrome*. The breakdown of the old social structure gave way to the spread of bourgeois values and the subsequent susceptibility of women to manipulation by fashion and external imagery. Study of American newspaper accounts in the 1920s identified an epidemic of self-starvation among American college students, coinciding with the flapper look dictated by the fashion of the time (Silverstein & Perlick, 1995). The relationship between fashion and this new syndrome of self starvation was later confirmed by Ryle (1936): "[T]he spread of the slimming fashion, now happily on the wane, and the more emotional lives of the younger generation since the war, might have been expected to provide a general increase in anorexia nervosa." These quotes extracted from the works of 19th-century authors clearly demonstrate that the recognition of societal forces in the area of eating pathology is as old as the syndrome itself. It appears that all of the major dimensions that shape our current thinking in this domain, namely women's vulnerability, women's drive for achievement, the role of fashion, and the susceptibility of neurosis to change its nature upon social change, were there from the start.

The 1970s: The Specific Syndrome

In the first half of this century, anorexia nervosa continued to be seen as an expression of an underlying neurotic disorder and not an entity on its own right. It was believed that the condition was merely a constellation of symptoms stemming from diverse psychopathology (Kay & Leigh, 1954). In the 1960s attempts were made to give the syndrome some independence (King, 1963), but the situation remained unaltered until Russell (1970) described it as a distinct clinical entity with clear-cut diagnostic features such as amenorrhea. This temporarily shifted the causal argument towards organicity, a plausible explanation given the perceived rarity of the condition at that time. Although Bruch (1973) emphasized both the importance of self-determination as a source of the tension in the patient's family and the young female's efforts to establish identity in the face of a pervasive sense of ineffectiveness, fat-focused theories already were taking precedence. Russell (1970) maintained that the anorexic girl's pursuit of thinness was a result of a her "dread of fatness," which he considered to be the fundamental psychopathology underpinning this disorder. Crisp (1967) referred to it as "weight phobia" and later acknowledged its clear association with dieting behavior. His impression was confirmed by several studies conducted at that time that revealed dieting to be highly prevalent. Anorexic behavior began to be seen on a continuum of severity merging with the culturally normative behavior of dieting (Nylander, 1971). This clearly swayed the argument once more in favor of sociocultural determinism and affirmed the position of fat phobia as the primary cultural cause.

The 1980s: The Culture-Specific Syndrome

Considerable support was given to sociocultural theory in the 1980s. This was largely because of advances in epidemiological research that showed significant morbid concern over weight issues in general populations. In community studies nearly 2% to 5% of girls and women were found to have a partial or subclinical form of an eating pathology (e.g., Button & Whitehouse, 1981; Johnson-Sabine, Wood, Patton, Mann, & Wakeling, 1988; King, 1989).

These findings were in keeping with the "spectrum hypothesis" and ran parallel to the suggested steady increase in the rate of occurrence of these disorders. Some studies showed an increase from 80% to 150% over a period of two decades (Jones, Fox, Babigan, & Hutton, 1980). The phenomenon was linked to increased pressures on women by the mass media, fashion, and diet industry to pursue thinness (Brumberg, 1988; Garner & Garfinkel, 1980). Relevant to this was the realization that individuals who had to focus attention on their body weight for their career demands, such as ballerinas, risked developing such disorders (Garner & Garfinkel, 1980; see also Chapter 16). The contribution of environmental factors such as pressure to achieve and competitiveness in maintaining the problem also was noted. One of the most significant contributions of the 1980s, however, was the emergence of "bulimia." The term was introduced by Russell (1979) as a variant of anorexia nervosa, but in the course of time began to be seen as a distinct entity that is probably four times more prevalent than anorexia nervosa. The emergence of bulimia nervosa in the past decade raised the question of the possible change in the nature of anorexia nervosa and more specifically the changing nature of neurosis in general (Russell, 1985). Cultural forces were considered to be behind these changes. The desirability of thinness as promoted by Western culture was seen as capable of exercising a pathoplastic role on neurotic illness, ultimately producing a range of eating psychopathology (Russell, 1985).

Prince (1983) argued that eating pathology fulfills all the criteria required for the syndrome to be regarded as "culture bound." The culture-boundedness of eating pathology stood first on the assumption that societal mandates regarding thinness were rooted in Western cultural values and conflicts. The anorexic disorder was seen to be consistent with Devereux's model of an "ethnic disorder" in which symptoms reflect exaggerations of normal attitudes and behaviors that are pervasive in a particular culture (Gordon, 1990). The notion of the cultural specificity of eating pathology clearly was strengthened at that time by the apparent absence of eating disorders in other cultures.

The 1990s: The Politics of Gender

Towards the end of the 1980s there was a genuine attempt to decode the role of societal pressures in eating psychopathology. In the 1990s the cultural notion of thinness began to be seen as an illusory answer to the dilemma that many women in the Western world face. The thinness ideal appeared to represent a metaphorical synthesis of the old notions of female attractiveness, frailty, and fashionability and the new, modern values of autonomy, achievement, and self-control (see, e.g., Gordon, 1990; Orbach, 1986). The emphasis on beautifying the body and the symbolic significance of thinness reinforced the notion that women had limited access to power beyond corporal power (Thompson, 1994). Feminist analyses emphasized, however, the "gendered nature" of these disorders, possibly at the expense of examining the true interplay between pathology and culture and the other societal systems of oppression, for example, racism. Moreover, this gendered approach to the problem often was restricted to one culture. The living laboratory of other cultures remained untapped, with little or no cross-fertilization taking place between the feminist and the transcultural schools of thought (Katzman & Lee, 1997). The majority of non-Western cultures continued to be seen as struggling with economic difficulties, and therefore possibly not at risk for the disordered eating commonly considered to be a by-product of wealthy and affluent societies.

However, if properly examined, these economic difficulties could provide a window to political structures that influence eating pathology. Women from non-Western societies also were assumed to be entertaining different beauty ideals from the West, with a tendency to associate plumpness with positive attributes of fertility and femininity. These other societies also were considered protected from the turmoil facing women in the West through rigidly enforced traditional familial expectations and clear-cut gender roles. Through these assumptions the cultural-feminist perspective failed to integrate international findings and thus maintained a stereotyped and fixed notion of other cultures, often seeing non-Western societies as primarily static and lacking the potential for change (Nasser, 1997). As a result the feminist approach did not deal with "women and culture" in its wider context, thus overlooking the true implications of culture itself.

☐ The Globalization of Eating Disorders

Nearly a century after anorexia nervosa first was described in Europe, we now have a body of truly cross-cultural research derived from different ethnicities, cultures, and societies. These studies aim to explore the impact of immigration, acculturation, and overall cultural change in the pathogenesis of these disorders.

Minority Status and the Immigrant Dilemma

The experience of women from other ethnicities and cultures has accumulated after the publication of several case reports of anorexia nervosa in the black communities in both the United States and the United Kingdom (see, e.g., Andersen & Hay, 1985; Hsu, 1987; Lacey & Dolan,1988; Jones et al., 1980; Thomas & Szmukler, 1985). These authors observed the psychological problems of girls who struggled with their "racial identity" and the powerful need to fit into a new society, hoping to become "integrated" through rigid dieting and adoption of prevailing social standards of thinness (Lacey & Dolan, 1988). Immigration and acculturation were regarded in a great number of these studies to be behind the immigrant's susceptibility to developing weight concerns. Such studies also were carried out on an array of individuals, including Eastern European immigrants, Asian and Black minorities in the United States and the United Kingdom, along with Soviet Jews and Vietnamese refugees (see, e.g., Davis & Katzman, 1999; Fumham & Alibhai, 1983; Kope & Sack, 1987).

Among the Hispanic, Asian, and Black populations in the United States, a correlation was found between the level of acculturation and morbid concern over weight, such that adherence to the Western culture was speculated to increase individuals' vulnerability to eating pathology (see, e.g., Abrams, Allen, & Gray, 1993; Davis & Katzman, 1998; Smith & Krejci, 1991). Dieting behavior was found to be equal among both black and white females in the United States (Gray, Ford, & Kelly, 1987; but see Chapter 11), and dysfunctional eating patterns with a tendency to develop bulimia also were found to be more prevalent in the African-Caribbean population in Britain than their White counterparts (Reiss, 1996).

Culture Change: The Western Toxin

The cases of eating disorders identified among ethnic minorities in the United States and United Kingdom can be regarded as orphan cases that could have resulted from a process of acculturation, that is, the identification of a small group with the values of the larger group. A similar process of acculturation also can occur through "culture change" subsequent to the identification of a peripheral culture with a more central and dominant one (Hannerz, 1995). A number of cases of eating disorders reported from non-Western cultures also suggest acculturation as a possible explanation for their results. Reports of eating morbidity have appeared in publications from Nigeria, Zimbabwe, Hong Kong, Malaysia, India, Chile, Brazil, and the United Arab Emirates (Abou-Saleh, Younis, & Karim, 1998; Buchan & Gregory, 1984; Famuyiwa, 1988; Khandelwal, Sharan, & Saxena, 1995; Lee, Hsu, & Wing, 1992; Nunes, Bagatini, & Salvador, 1991; Pumarino & Vivanco, 1982).

Some studies have attempted to decode culture change by examining the relation between exposure to Western cultural norms and values and increased vulnerability to eating disorders. Arab female students in London and Cairo universities (Nasser, 1986) and Greek students in Greece and Munich (Fichter, Weyerer, Sourdi, & Sourdi, 1983) were compared on their eating attitudes. Concern with body weight existed in both the Egyptian and the Greek societies, but this concern amounted to actual clinical cases only in the Greeks in Munich and the Arabs in London.

The impression that eating morbidity could be present in the Egyptian society later was confirmed in a study carried out on Egyptian secondary-school girls, in whom the rate of eating morbidity was comparable to what was found in the same age group in the United Kingdom (Nasser, 1994a). The idealized Western cultural norm of thinness was shown to have been assimilated by the Egyptian female students attending the American University in Cairo; their body-shape preference was found to be similar to that of the American population (Ford, Dolan, & Evans, 1990). Lesser exposure to Western ideals of slimness also was offered as a possible explanation for the apparent reduced risk for eating morbidity in the Turkish students in Istanbul compared with the Greek population in Greece and Germany (Fichter, Eiton, Sourdi, Weyerer, & Koptagel-Ilal, 1988). A similar finding was identified in Asian women attending American schools in the United States and in Hong Kong (Davis & Katzman, 1997, 1998) . These studies strongly suggest the immunity of these cultural groups until they have been exposed to or infiltrated by those specific Western ideals that subsequently render them vulnerable to develop this particular psychopathology.

Native Cultures: Immunity, Vulnerability, and Culture Change in Cross-cultural Studies

Other studies followed, most of which were structured around a recurring binary hypothesis aiming to identify if eating pathology did exist in non-Western cultures or not. A number of surveys conducted in Japan suggested that the prevalence of eating disturbance could be higher in Japan than in the West (e.g., Kamata, Nogami, & Momma, 1987; Mukai, Crago, & Shisslak, 1994). Disordered eating and body dissatisfaction also were reported to be on the increase in Hong Kong (Katzman, 1995; Lee & Lee, 1996). Abnormal eating patterns and eating morbidity in Lahore, Pakistan, were comparable to the West and were closely correlated to high levels of Westernization and what was described as the prevailing dieting milieu (Mumford, Whitehouse, & Choudry, 1992). Identification with Western modes of dieting also was demonstrated to be on the increase among Indians (Khandelwal & Saxena, 1990). In Buenos Aires a significant proportion of female students were reported to have disordered eating patterns associated with figure-consciousness and heightened fashion orientation (Bello, 1995). In Israel, where both Arab and Jewish Israeli schoolgirls were examined, the Kibbutz women were found to have the highest risk for eating morbidity followed by the Arab Muslims, who were thought to have strong Western influences in their attitudes, particularly about body image, which could make them easily prone to developing eating disorders (Apter et al., 1994).

Most of these studies by and large were modeled on Western studies, and the majority used Eating Attitudes Test (EAT; Garner & Garfinkel, 1979) scores as a crude index of eating morbidity. However, a number of reports have raised doubts about the validity of the EAT in different cultural settings and its susceptibility to cultural variations and cultural misinterpretation (Boyadjieva & Steinhausen, 1996; King & Bhugra, 1989). Thus it has been argued that these methods could yield spurious information and provide a false sense of knowledge (Katzman & Lee, 1997). Despite those concerns, the EAT was nonetheless helpful in facilitating research and allowing preliminary comparisons across cultures. In addition, the dieting factor of the EAT has been fairly robust across different cultural groups (Mumford, Whitehouse, & Platts, 1991; Mukai et al., 1994; Nasser, 1994b). The ongoing debate concerning the wisdom of using such instruments in transcultural research cannot be disentangled from the overall debate about the nature of these syndromes, particularly the relationship between dieting behavior and the full-blown picture of an eating disorder.

Katzman and Lee (1997) have criticized the thinness-focused orientation of these studies, arguing that the overreliance on the "dread of fatness" as a diagnostic criterion could lead to an underestimation of the true rates of these problems in some societies. Self-starvation in a population that is normally underweight even by Western standards, as is the case in China, Japan, or India, clearly invites different explanations and meanings. Highlighting this issue has pushed research towards a deeper understanding of these problems by focusing attention on the question of whether the morbidity is mere weight pathology or perhaps a reflection of an as yet uncovered meaning for self-starvation.

Not withstanding the argument about the centrality of "weight issues " in these syndromes, the deduction from transcultural studies remained that identification with Western cultural norms gave rise to a new psychopathology. The process of acculturation commonly referred to as *Westernization* was consistently offered as an explanation for the emergence of eating pathology in non-Western societies, although a clear distinction was not made between Westernization and modernization, and few studies actually attempted to measure this culture change (Katzman & Leung, 1996). Westernization even was given as a plausible explanation for the epidemiological differences in eating pathology between "both Europes." Eating disorders that were largely unreported in Eastern Europe before the political changes began to emerge as a problem by the mid-1990s. When the German Democratic Republic, Austria, and Hungary were compared, Hungary was shown to have the highest rates (Rathner et al., 1995). High rates of abnormal eating attitudes also were detected among Polish students (Warczyk-Bisage & Dolan, 1996). It also was said that the increase in the incidence of anorexia nervosa created the need for specialized treatment units in Prague (Faltus, 1986).

However, Westernization could not possibly explain epidemiological differences within the West itself, inter-European differences, or the greater prevalence of eating disorders in the United States than in Europe. The distinct possibility of genuine intracultural differences made European research workers warn against taking American levels of morbidity as representative of middle Europe (e.g., Mangweth, Pope, Hudson, & Biebl, 1996; Raich et al., 1992). There also was evidence of intra-European variations in which rates could be somewhat higher in the United Kingdom than the rest of Europe, and particularly low in Germany.

Also, Westernization would not explain the 100% increase in incidence of anorexia nervosa reported over a 5-year period in Japan or the rural/urban differences in this respect (e.g., Ohzeki et al., 1990; Suematsu, Ishikawa, Kuboki, & Ito, 1985). It also does not tell us why eating morbidity increased by 800% in the Kibbutz over the past 25 years, or why there should be any differences in eating morbidity rates between the north and the south of Italy (Kaffman & Sadeh, 1989; Ruggiero et al., 1998). It is also doubtful that the concept of Westernization is able to address why eating pathology is now emerging among Black South African girls (Le Grange, Telch, & Tibbs, 1998). Westernization also failed to explain why Indian girls were particularly more vulnerable to eating pathology than their less traditional Indian or their Caucasian counterparts (Mumford & Whitehouse, 1988).

The trend in the study of culture and psychopathology has been to divide the world into Western and non-Western cultures. The time has come to challenge this rather simplistic dichotomy (Nasser, 1997). Emphasis on the issue of identification with the West per se clearly reduces the body to a passive template open to manipulations by simple imagery. The use of Westernization as a concept fails to address the true societal forces that shape bodies and genders. The question, "How does the 'outside' get 'inside'?," critically raised in connection to the feminist split between culture and the individual, still needs to be answered.

This begs us to find true meaning behind the adoption of a particular mode of behavior or symptomatology. In discussing the technology of the self, Foucault (1986) speaks of an ensemble of culturally meaningful practices working on the body, which constitute and transform the self and through which the self becomes an attitude or a way of thinking relating to contemporary society. We need, therefore, to attempt to clarify the meaning of body image as it is created in the context of relationships or societal roles. Consequently, Westernization needs to be broken down to its basic elements to see the forces that may lie behind the concept. These forces include urbanization, global markets, the threat to national identity, the experience of discontinuity, and the disappearance of traditional cultural idioms for articulating personal distress.

☐ The Global Forces

Urbanization and the Traditional Family

One of the recent explanations for the emergence of eating pathology is the nuclearization of the family structure in Europe (Selvini-Pallazoli, 1985). With increased urbanization, social mobility, and migration to the cities, the nuclear family is steadily becoming the norm for a great number of societies. However, with increased levels of modernization, the nuclear family itself increasingly will come under threat and may not remain intact. Social mobility brought with it economic growth and higher expectations in the levels of attention and protection given to children. Interestingly, several related variables have been measured in eating disorders research that reflect an association between changes in family structure and the development of eating problems. Maternal protection and control were found to be associated with increased vulnerability of Indian and Japanese girls to morbid eating attitudes (e.g., Lee, 1995), while paternal absence from home for work reasons was correlated with high EAT scores in Japanese society (Takagi, Nishizono-Maher, & Asai, 1991).

In Japan and Europe, city as opposed to rural life has been associated with higher incidence of eating morbidity (Hoek et al., 1995; Ohzeki et al., 1990). Urbanization also was put forward as an explanation for the finding of eating pathology in cities like Cairo and Johannesburg (Nasser, 1997). Cities undergoing transformation were seen to be capable of producing eating psychopathology (Katzman & Lee, 1997), as shown by research in Beijing, Shanghai, and Hong Kong (Lee et al., 1992; Song & Fang, 1990; Zhu, Sheng, Li, Fu, & Zhai, 1994).

As cities urbanized, meal times appeared to shift, and expectations that families eat together slackened. It was once commonplace in many societies to have the main meal in the afternoon, but as city dwellers worked longer uninterrupted hours there was less time for leisurely, healthy lunches, and the heavier meal was relocated to the evening. Such changes in the nature of the food and the shifting of meal times are likely to contribute to increased rates of obesity, with a subsequent increase in weight consciousness and disordered eating patterns in many societies. For example, weight increase, possibly caused by dietary changes and confusion in the living patterns of people after politico-economic changes, was thought to be a considerable risk factor for developing eating disorders in Hungary and the Czech Republic (Szabo & Tury, 1991). In short, increased levels of urbanization in many societies have brought with them the following significant societal changes: breakdown of the traditional family structure; less emphasis and time given to proper healthy meals and shifting of meal times; and increased access to fast, fat, and trendy American food. These factors operate together to place more urbanized individuals at risk for shaping and expressing their urban distress in the form of an eating psychopathology.

Socialist Structure and Gender-Role Confusion

The argument for the immunity of women in "other societies" against developing eating pathology assumed that women's roles in these societies remained by and large static and traditional. In an extensive analysis of "feminism across cultures," Nasser (1997) challenged this assumption and showed that the majority of non-Western women have significantly changed their social position, with increasing numbers being highly educated and working outside the family. Feminist movements similar to those in the West arose in some of these societies and traditional gender roles were questioned and revised. Nasser posited, however, that there are new forces currently reformulating definitions for gender in the wake of the post-socialist era. For example, she argued that the emergence of eating pathology in East Europe after the political changes was closely linked to the decline of communism and the readiness to adopt a free-market economy. The undermining of socialist collectivist structures in former communist Europe, as well as in the Kibbutz, China, and other countries that have experimented with socialist regimes, has been responsible for a surge in consumerism and subsequent major changes in the value systems of these societies. As noted previously, in the course of a quarter of a century eating disorders in the Kibbutz were reported to have increased by 800%. Kaffman and Sadeh (1989) suggested that this was caused by major transformation in the structure of the Kibbutz, which fostered changes in women's perception of themselves, notably a greater emphasis on appearance and physical beauty.

Under socialist policies women were by and large directed and protected in their education, health, employment, and child care. In countries while socialist policies prevailed for a time, women's sense of value appeared to derive from taking part in an overall social philosophy, with no correlation between their senses of inner worth and their external appearances (Nasser, 1997). Women's expectations of themselves seemed to be more reconciled with those of their society. On the other hand, with the liberalization of the economy, greater disparity began to emerge between what women expected of themselves and what they thought society expected of them. In a profit-motivated economy some of the social provisions that were part of the socialist regimes had to go. This caused greater ambivalence about women's positions in the workplace and a subsequent increase in the rate of unemployment among highly qualified women in post-socialist countries. This societal ambivalence about women's roles is likely to cause greater ambivalence among women themselves.

Another dimension to this is the rise of fundamentalist religion in a great number of societies that experimented with socialism. The revivals of Islam in the Middle East and of Catholicism in Poland are examples of the post-socialism ideological transformation that affected these societies. This type of religious reaction may fill the intellectual vacuum created by the death of communism and in some instances may be instrumental in supporting the "new" economic structures that promote home as the right place for women. Increased ambiguity and confusion over gender-role definition now clearly are seen as sequels to the decaying socialist structure and offer a deeper explanation for the increased propensity of women in these societies to morbid eating patterns (Nasser, 1997).

National Boundaries, Information Networks, and Global Media

The whole world now, including areas once considered far outposts of the Western world, is rapidly integrating into a "global superculture." The non-Western world's access to Western media has increased considerably in recent years as satellite channels offering global networks such as the BBC and CNN have virtually covered the globe. How many media-free cultures remain in this age of television, videos, and satellite broadcasts? Information technology now is playing a similar role, with a great many people almost everywhere easily communicating with each other on the Internet (Nasser, 1997). The contribution of the media to eating pathology has been studied mainly in the West, where the media are seen to present images of thinness through role models or through images and text that infer and confer social desirability (see Chapter 1). The impact of television, advertising, and magazine pictures with reference to self- and body valuation of the body and the self tentatively was referred to in some studies of ethnic and non-Western populations. For example, the time the girls in Japan spent watching television was speculated to increase their susceptibility to eating disorders (Mukai et al., 1994).

As noted by Levine et al. (Chapter 1), the role of the mass media in generating eating psychopathology is far from being fully understood, in part because of inadequate knowledge about the mechanisms or pathways that lead from media messages to eating morbidity. In fact, common use of the construct "mass media" is very similar to the use and misuse of the broad concept of Westernization: that is, there is a tendency to deal with it superficially without attempts to truly analyze it. There is a need, therefore, to examine the ways in which deregulation of media and information technologies may deregulate the relationship between the individual and society, with society no longer normally perceived as a country or national entity. The greatest influence of the media may be that they shrink the world, break national boundaries, and threaten national identity. This threat is capable in itself of producing a sense of cultural identity confusion, which may motivate some individuals to try to assert identity through pathological modes of behavior, including disordered eating.

Eating Pathology and Cultures in Transition

Half a century ago, Margret Mead said: "In the history of culture or subculture, periods will be found in which adequate forms for expression of tension will be lacking and the individual will be forced back upon his own body for symbolic expression." From the previous discussion it is clear that we currently live in a culture that is characterized by changes in and a breakdown of older and more familiar structures, be they family, national boundaries, or state-controlled economy.

It has been suggested that eating pathology has an affinity towards cultural transition and a habit of emerging at times when particularly the female role in society is being revised. In keeping with this Di Nicola (1990) considered eating pathology a "reaction to culture change," Nasser (1997) referred to it as a "culture chaos syndrome," and Gordon (1998) called it "symptomatic of cultures at cross roads." The historical periods that witnessed a surge in eating pathology include the late medieval period, the last half of the 19th century, and the late 20th century (Gordon, 1998; Silverstein & Perlick, 1995). The asceticism of the medieval "holy anorexic" was seen as a form of moral rebellion parallel to the striving for purity characteristic of the modern anorexic; the ascetic's quest for perfection, control, and self-denial are all familiar aspects of modern self-starvation. Given the proposition that the Christian vigil against sin was also a vigil against fat (Schwartz, 1986), it is interesting that a clear relationship was found between the revival of fundamentalist Christian belief in the United States and dieting behavior (Gordon, 1990). Dieting is commonly practiced in non-Western countries within the framework of religious fasting (e.g., Khandelwal & Saxena, 1991; Nasser, 1986).

Perhaps it is not mere coincidence that many of the cultures we live in at the moment are characterized by extremes of both eating and religious behaviors. The revivals of religion and of eating morbidity may both be responses to conflicting cultural messages. The new "veiling phenomenon," for instance, is regarded as a considered response on the part of the young, educated, working Moslem woman, acting metaphorically as a form of desexualization or liberation, forcing society to see women as human beings and less as sexual objects (MacLeod, 1991).

Veiling is a form of *rebellion through conformity*—a social analysis similar to that made of the anorexic position (Nasser, 1997). Both extreme positions represent body politics and convey (embody) similar messages. In either East or West, it is perhaps an expression of a "lost voice" in a social world perceived to be oppressive (Katzman & Lee, 1997). It certainly appears that neurotic illness is a byproduct of social problem solving and therefore culturally pathoplastic (Murphy, 1973). Selvini-Pallazoli (1974) considered anorexia nervosa a *social disease*. The reasons, however, why a young woman would choose an extreme religious stance and not extreme food avoidance (self-starvation), or vice-versa, are open to speculation but certainly bound by a set of circumstances, including the prevailing economic and political structures. For instance, a more intense achievement orientation has been linked to rapidly developing economic changes that lead to a widening of the gap between social aspirations and fulfilment. The frustrated need for achievement could generate political or religious forms of extremism as a way of responding to this perceived sense of deprivation and oppression. Food refusal is one form of social morbidity used particularly by women to come to terms with their experience of living in two worlds, be they two generations work and family, or traditional and modern (Katzman & Lee, 1997; Silverstein & Perlick, 1995). Eating psychopathology therefore should be seen as a "form of expressing distress" that needs to considered along with many other forms of extremist behaviors on the spectrum of social morbidity (Gordon, 1990; Nasser, 1997; Silverstein & Perlick, 1995).

☐ Prevention: The Global Intervention

It is clear that the sociocultural genesis and origins of eating disorders have always been present, even if at times they were not made so explicit. A major contribution of feminist thinking has been the initial attempt to integrate the sum of cultural knowledge we possess into the formulation of the true meaning of these disorders. However, most feminists' attention was restricted to Western cultures and Western women, at the expense of other cultures and the other woman. The enthusiasm to deconstruct the individual in the traditional medical sense may have unknowingly created a split between culture and the individual. In the feminist project, cultural discourses are written on the body, with no direct or predictable linkage to the internal processes of the person (Lester, 1997). But the societal determinants of food denial clearly go beyond caricatured cosmetic compliance; the latter is only the socially sanctioned coloring of distress and not the cause (Russell & Treasure, 1989).

For a proper integration of both cultural and gender issues into the eating-disorders equation, the argument should be shifted towards *powerlessness* and not *weight* (Katzman, 1997; Katzman & Lee, 1997). Mental-health professionals working in the field of prevention, despite their acknowledgment of the sociocultural substrate of these problems, were too ready to dismiss strategies to manipulate the sociocultural environment as simply unworkable. This is a predictable product of a theoretical framework that remains firmly focused on weight issues. The common strategies normally employed in this respect have focused mainly on addressing "societal pressures for thinness," either through highlighting the role of the media in disseminating distorted images or helping schools to detect early weight-comparison practices among school girls. Unless more comprehensive and deeper definitions of sociocultural influences are adopted, plans for prevention are deemed to fail (Piran, 1996; see also Chapters 9 and 16).

This conclusion clearly urges those who are truly concerned with primary intervention to look more seriously into other sociocultural aspects that recently have been shown to be likely contributors to the formation of these problems. To move forward with prevention strategies we need to think more broadly and relinquish the current theoretical rituals that esteem weight issues, in favor of a deeper analysis of *transition*. For example, the transition from state-controlled to market economies and the destruction of social networks appear to have had a greater effect on women who were by and large protected in their education, health, employment, and childcare under socialist policies (Nasser, 1997). Under market economies many women no longer feel secure about work or childcare rights and risk a true confusion about their role in society.

Prevention Objective 1: Promoting Social Provisions for Women

Katzman and Lee (1997) suggested *disconnection* as an underlying problem in eating disorders and proposed it, along with transition and oppression, as a new model for thinking about the relationship between culture and eating disorders. Women who undergo economic changes, change countries, or cross gender boundaries are bound to lose the logical reference to the group or the community with which they identify and may use eating as a method of coping with the disconnection endured.

Marketization of economies in many societies and the possible threat to national identities by deregulated media and information technologies are other sources for disconnection and social identity confusion (Nasser, 1997; Rathner et al., 1995). In several critical reviews of existing preventative strategies, Piran has outlined her participatory approach to the prevention of eating disorders based on addressing societal prejudices and other social systems of oppression. She explained the need to explore and stress the role of larger cultural values and norms under which the body of the adolescent woman becomes an arena of conformity to idealized social image and the target for all these prejudicial pressures (Piran, 1995, 1996; see also Chapters 9 and 16). Although identifying and tackling unhealthy societal forces does not guarantee transformation of those social structures, realistically assisting the individual to achieve the desired internal transformation may change the sense of disconnection into a connection between body and voice (Reason, 1994; see also Chapters 9 and 16).

Prevention Objective 2: Individual "Empowerment"

In order to achieve this connection between body and voice, the emphasis should be on *competency rather than pathology* (Peters & Fallon, 1994; Weiss, Katzman, & Wolchik, 1984; see also Chapter 10). The link between power and knowledge production has been explored in a number of preventative strategies. For example, in the participatory model empowering knowledge is constructed through dialogue, self-inquiry, and reflection based on life experiences (Gavent, 1993; Piran, 1995, 1996). However, the question remains as how to generate dialogue and engage individuals who share the same predicament worldwide? Perhaps the answer lies in taking advantages of the existing information technology.

In her participatory model Piran (1995, 1996) explains and promotes knowledge as the product of inquiries made by people who are interested in seeking information about the contribution of societal mechanisms in generating personal distress and the shape this distress takes (see also Chapters 9 and 16). The meaning of symptoms can then be further explored, and new social roles to help the individual to become more effectual also can be forged. The knowledge construction, the questions asked, and the actions taken are determined by the participants. To maximize the efficacy of the participatory model in a global sense, the role of the facilitator perhaps could be taken over by specifically designed computer programs. Other models of prevention also can be employed, again through producing computer programs or other types of mass media geared towards the enhancement of self-esteem, teaching coping skills, and promoting positive cognitions related to negotiations of power and control and to the significance of the individual in relation to the environment.

Several authors in the field of prevention have written about the importance of mentoring and role modeling by women who have managed to "navigate their way" in this challenging and changing world (Levine, 1994; Piran, 1995). Electronic connections may provide a new way of achieving female connectedness, one in which women may be able to help other women whom they would not have been able to access in the past. Linked by computer technology, women may overcome their social and political isolation and gain new insights into formulas for success and survival.

We hope that recognition of these forces and these new mechanisms will stimulate theory and more research devoted to a transnational perspective for the prevention of eating disorders. The aim would not be to focus on particular symptom patterns, but instead to see these symptoms within the context of other mental-health syndromes and also the spectrum of social morbidity (Silverstein & Perlick, 1995; Striegel-Moore & Steiner-Adair, 1998). As the position of individuals, particularly women, is changed and challenged internationally, we sincerely hope that technology and economics will succeed in shifting "the body ideal" from individual cosmetics to cosmic consciousness. Although this remains a dream at the moment, it is clear that prevention in the future will depend on deepening and broadening our understanding of many social forces and on our commitment to social change to bring symptom change.

☐ References

Abou-Saleh, M., Younis, Y., & Karim, L. (1998). Anorexia nervosa in the Arab culture. *International Journal of Eating Disorders, 23,* 207–212.

Abrams, K. K., Allen, L. R., & Gray, J. J. (1993). Disordered eating attitudes and behaviors, psychological adjustment, and ethnic identity: A comparison of black and white female college students. *International Journal of Eating Disorders,* 49–57.

Andersen, A., & Hay, A. (1985). Racial and socioeconomic influences in anorexia nervosa and bulimia. *International Journal of Eating Disorders, 4,* 479–487.

Apter, A., Shah, M., Iancu, I., Abramovitch, H., Weizman, A., & Tanyo, S (1994). Cultural effects on eating attitudes in Israeli sub-populations and hospitalised anorectics. *Genetic Social and General Psychological Monographs, 120,* 83–99.

Bello, M. (1995, September). *Prevalence of eating disorders in a school population in Buenos Aires, Argentina.* Paper presented at the meeting of the European Council on Eating Disorders, Dublin.

Boyadjieva, S., & Steinhausen, H. (1996). The Eating Attitudes Test and the Eating Disorders Inventory in four Bulgarian clinical and non-clinical samples. *International Journal of Eating Disorders, 19,* 93–98

Bruch, H. (1973). *Eating disorders: Obesity, anorexia and the person within.* New York: Basic Books.

Brumberg, J. (1988). *Fasting girls: The emergence of anorexia nervosa as a modern disease.* Cambridge, MA: Harvard University Press.

Buchan T., & Gregory, D. (1984). Anorexia nervosa in a black Zimbabwean. *British Journal of Psychiatry, 145,* 326–330

Button, E. J., & Whitehouse, A. (1981). Subclinical anorexia nervosa. *Psychological Medicine, 11,* 509–516.

Crisp, A. (1967). Anorexia nervosa. *Hospital Medicine, 5,* 713–718.

Davis, C., & Katzman, M. A. (1997). Charting new territory: Body esteem, weight satisfaction, depression and self esteem among Chinese males and females in Hong Kong. *Sex Roles, 36*(7/8), 119–126.

Davis, C., & Katzman, M. A. (1998). Chinese men and women in the USA and Hong Kong: Body and self esteem ratings as a prelude to dieting and exercise. *International Journal of Eating Disorders, 23,* 99–102.

Davis, C., & Katzman, M. A. (1999). Perfection as acculturation. *International Journal of Eating Disorders, 25,* 65–70.

Di Nicola, V. F. (1990). Anorexia: Multiform self-starvation in historical and cultural context. *Transcultural Research Review, 27,* 165–196.

Faetus, F. (1986). Anorexia nervosa in Czechoslovakia. *International Journal of Eating Disorders, 3,* 581–585.

Famuyiwa, O. (1988). Anorexia nervosa in two Nigerians. *Acta Psychiatrica Scandinavia, 78,* 550–554.

Fichter, M., Eiton, M., Sourdi, S., Weyerer, S., & Koptage Ilal, G. (1988). Anorexia nervosa in Greek and Turkish adolescents. *Eureopean Archives of Psychiatry and Neurological Science, 37,* 200–208.

Fichter, M. M., Weyerer, S., Sourdi, L., & Sourdi, Z. (1983). The epidemiology of anorexia nervosa: A comparison of Greek adolescents living in Germany and Greek adolescents living in Greece. In P. L. Darby, P. Garfinkel, D. M. Garner, & D. V. Coscina (Eds.), *Anorexia nervosa: Recent developments in research* (pp. 95–105). New York: Liss.

Ford, K., Dolan, B., & Evans, C. (1990). Cultural factors in the aetiology of eating disorders: Evidence from body shape preference of Arab students. *Journal of Psychosomatic Research, 5,* 501–507.

Foucault, M. (1986). *The care of the self: Vol. 3 The history of sexuality.* New York: Vintage Books.

Furnham, A. C., & Alibhai, N. (1983). Cross cultural differences in the perception of female body shapes. *Psychological Medicine, 13,* 829–837.

Garner, D. M., & Garfinkel, P. E. (1979). The Eating Attitudes Test: An index of the symptoms of anorexia nervosa. *Psychological Medicine, 9,* 273–279.

Garner, D. M., & Garfinkel, P. E. (1980). Sociocultural factors in the development of anorexia nervosa. *Psychological Medicine, 10,* 647–656.

Gavent, J. (1993). The powerful, the powerless and the experts: Knowledge struggles in an information age. In P. Park, M. Bryden-Miller, B. Hall, & T. Jackson (Eds.), *Voices of change* (pp. 21–40). Toronto: OISE Press.

Gordon, R. (1990). *Anorexia and bulimia: Anatomy of a social epidemic.* Cambridge, MA: Basil Blackwell.

Gordon, R. (1998). Concepts of eating disorders: A historical reflection. In H. Hoek, J. Treasure, & M. Katzman (Eds.), *Neurobiology of eating disorders.* London: John Wiley & Sons.

Gray, J., Ford, K., & Kelly, L. (1987). The prevalence of bulimia in a black college population. *International Journal of Eating Disorders, 6,* 733–740.

Gull, W. W. (1868). The address in medicine delivered before the annual meeting of the British Medical Association at Oxford, *Lancet, ii,* 171.

Hannerz, U. (1995). Culture between centre and periphery: Towards a macroanthropology. *Ethnos, 54,* 200–216

Hoek, H., Bartelds, A., Bosveld, J., van der Graaf, Y., Limpens, V., Maiwald, M., & Spaaij, M. (1995). Impact of urbanisation on detection rates of eating disorders. *American Journal of Psychiatry, 152,* 1272–1285.

Hsu, L. K. G. (1987). Are eating disorders becoming more common in Blacks? *International Journal of Eating Disorders, 6,* 113–124.

Johnson-Sabine, E., Wood, K., Patton, G., Mann, A., & Wakeling, A. (1988). Abnormal eating attitudes in London school girls: A prospective epidemiological study: Factors associated with abnormal response on screening questionnaire. *Psychological Medicine, 18,* 615–622.

Jones, D. J., Fox, M. M., Babigan, H. M., & Hutton, H. E. (1980). Epidemiology of anorexia nervosa in Monroe County, New York: 1960–1967. *Psychosomatic Medicine, 42,* 551–558.

Kaffman, M., & Sadeh, T. (1989). Anorexia nervosa in the Kibbutz: Factors influencing the development of monoideistic fixation. *International Journal of Eating Disorders, 8,* 33–53.

Kamata, K., Nogami, Y., & Momma, K. (1987). Binge eating among female students. *Japanese Journal of Psychiatry and Neurology, 41,* 151–152.

Katzman, M. A. (1995). Asia on my mind: Are eating disorders a problem in Hong Kong? *Eating Disorders: The Journal of Treatment and Prevention, 3,* 378–380.

Katzman, M. A. (1997). Getting the difference right: It's power not gender that matters. *European Eating Disorders Review, 5,* 71–74.

Katzman, M. A., & Lee, S. (1997). Beyond body image: The integration of feminist and transcultural theories in the understanding of self starvation. *International Journal of Eating Disorders, 22,* 385–394

Katzman, M., & Leung, F. (1996, April). *When East meets West: Does disordered eating follow?* Paper presented at the Seventh International Conference on Eating Disorders, New York.

Kay, D. W., & Leigh, D. (1954). Natural history, treatment and prognosis of anorexia nervosa based on study of 38 patients. *Journal of Mental Science, 100,* 411–431.

Khandelwal, S. K., & Saxena, S. (1990). Anorexia Nervosa in adolescents of Asian extraction. *British Journal of Psychiatry, 157,* 783–784.

Khandelwal, S. K., Sharan, P., & Saxena, S. (1995). Eating disorders in Indian perspective. *International of Social Psychiatry, 41*(2), 132–146.

King, A. (1963). Primary and secondary anorexia nervosa syndromes. *British Journal Psychiatry, 109,* 470–479.

King, M. B. (1989). Eating disorders in general practice population: Prevalence, characteristics and follow up at 12–18 months. *Psychological Medicine Monographs 14,* (suppl), 134.

King, M. B., & Bhugra, D. (1989). Eating disorders: Lessons from a cross-cultural study. *Psychological Medicine, 19,* 955–958.

Kope, T. M., & Sack, W. H. (1987). Anorexia nervosa in South East Asian refugees: A report on three cases. *Journal of American Academy of Child Adolescent of Psychiatry, 26,* 795–797.

Lacey, H., & Dolan, B. (1988). Bulimia in British Blacks and Asians: A catchment area study. *British Journal of Psychiatry, 152,* 73–79.

Lasègue, C. (1873). De l'anorexie hystérique reprinted in R. M. Kaufman & M. Heinman (Eds.), *Evolution of psychosomatic concepts: Anorexia nervosa, a paradigm* (1964). New York: International University Press.

Lee, S. (1995). Self starvation in context: Towards a culturally sensitive understanding of anorexia nervosa. *Social Science and Medicine, 41,* 25–36.

Lee, S., Hsu, G., & Wing, Y. (1992). Bulimia nervosa in Hong Kong Chinese patients. *British Journal Psychiatry, 161,* 545–551.

Lee, S., & Lee, A. (1996). Disordered eating and its psychosocial correlates among Chinese adolescent females in Hong Kong. *International Journal of Eating Disorders, 20,* 177–183.

Le Grange D., Telch, C., & Tibbs, J. (1998). Eating attitudes and behaviours in 1,435 South African caucasian and non-caucasian college students. *American Journal of Psychiatry, 155,* 250–254.

Lester, R. J. (1997). The (dis)embodied self in anorexia nervosa. *Social Sciences and Medicine, 44,* 479–489.

Levine, M. P. (1994). Beauty myth and the beast: What men can do and be to help prevent eating disorders. *Eating Disorders: The Journal of Treatment and Prevention, 2,* 101–113.

MacLeod, A. (1991). *Accomodating protest: Working women, the new veiling and change in Cairo.* New York: Columbia University Press.

Mangweth, B., Pope, H. G., Hudson J., & Biebl, W. (1996). Bulimia nervosa in Austria and the United States: A controlled cross-cultural study. *International Journal of Eating Disorders, 20,* 263–270

Mukai, T., Crago, M., & Shisslak, C. (1994). Eating attitudes and weight preoccupation among female high school students in Japan. *Journal of Child Psychology and Psychiatry, 33,* 677–688.

Mumford, D. B., & Whitehouse, A. M. (1988). Increased prevalence of bulimia nervosa among Asian school girls. *British Medical Journal, 297,* 718.

Mumford, D. B., Whitehouse, A. M., & Choudry, L. (1992). Survey of eating disorders in English-medium Schools in Lahore, Pakistan. *International Journal of Eating Disorders, 11,* 173–184.

Mumford, D. B., Whitehouse, A. M., & Platts, M. (1991). Socio-cultural correlates of eating disorders among Asian school girls in Bradford. *British Journal of Psychiatry, 158,* 222–228.

Murphy, H. B. M. (1973). History and evolution of syndromes: The striking case of Latah and Amok. In M. Hammer, K. Salzinger, & S. Sutton (Eds.), *Psychopathology: Contributions from the social, behavioural and biological sciences.* New York: John Wiley & Sons.

Nasser, M. (1986). Comparative study of the prevalence of abnormal eating attitudes among Arab female students at both London and Cairo Universities. *Psychological Medicine, 16,* 621–625.

Nasser, M. (1994a). The psychometric properties of the Eating Attitudes Test in a non-western population. *Social Psychiatry & Psychiatric Epidemiology, 29,* 88–94.

Nasser, M. (1994b). Screening for abnormal eating attitudes in a population of Egyptian secondary school girls. *Social Psychiatry & Psychiatric Epidemiology, 29,* 25–30.

Nasser, M. (1997). *Culture and weight consciousness.* London: Routledge.

Nunes, M., Bagatini, L, & Salvador, C. (1991, April). *What to think of anorexia nervosa in Brazil, a country of hunger and undernourishment?* Poster presentation at the International Symposium on Eating Disorders, Paris.

Nylander, I. (1971). The feeling of being fat and dieting and dieting in a school population. *Acta Sociologica Medica Scandinavia, 1,* 17–26.

Ohzeki, T., Hanaki, K., Motozumi, H., Ishitani, N., Matsuda Ohtahara, H., Sunaguchi, M., & Shiraki, K. (1990). Prevalence of obesity, leanness and anorexia nervosa in Japanese boys and girls aged 12–14 years. *Annals of Nutrition and Metabolism, 34,* 208–212.

Orbach, S. (1986). *Hunger strike: The anorectic's struggle as a metaphor for our age.* New York: W. W. Norton.

Peters, L., & Fallon, P. (1994). The journey of recovery. Dimensions of change. In P. Fallon, M. Katzman, & S. C. Wooley (Eds.), *Feminist perspectives on eating disorders* (pp. 339–354). New York: Guilford Press.

Piran, N. (1995). Prevention: Can early lessons lead to a delineation of an alternative model? A critical look at prevention with school children. *Eating Disorders: The Journal of Treatment & Prevention, 3,* 28–36.

Piran, N. (1996). The reduction of preoccupation with body weight and shape in schools: A feminist approach. *Eating Disorders: The Journal of Treatment & Prevention, 4,* 323–333.

Prince, R. (1983). Is anorexia nervosa a culture-bound syndrome? *Transcultural Psychiatry Research and Review, 20,* 299.

Pumarino, H., & Vivanco, N. (1982). Anorexia nervosa: Medical and psychiatric characteristics of 30 patients. *Revista Medica de Chile, 110,* 1081–1092.

Raich, R. M., Resen, J. C., Dens, J., Perez, O., Requena, A., & Green, J. (1992). Eating disorder symptoms among adolescents in the USA and Spain: A comparative study. *International Journal of Eating Disorders, 11,* 63–72.

Rathner, G., Tury, F., Szabo, P., Geyer, M., Rumpold, G., Forgaces, A., Sollner, W., & Plottner, N. (1995). Prevalence of eating disorders and minor psychiatric morbidity in Central Europe before the political changes of 1989: A cross-cultural study. *Psychological Medicine, 25,* 1027–1035.

Reason, P. (1994). Three approaches to participative enquiry. In N. K. Danzin & Y. S. Lincoln (Eds.), *Handbook of qualitative research* (pp. 324–339). London: Sage Publications.

Reiss, D. (1996). Abnormal eating attitudes and behaviours in two ethnic groups from a female British urban population. *Psychological Medicine, 26,* 289–299.

Ruggiero, G. M. , Hanover, W., Mantero, M., Ferrari, N., Papa, R., & Cavagnini, X. (1998). *Body dissatisfaction and acceptance of mass media appearance ideals in northern and southern Italian non clinical girls and in underweight and non underweight eating disorders girls.* Manuscript submitted for publication.

Russell, G. (1970). Anorexia nervosa: Its identity as an illness and its treatment. In J. Harding-Price (Ed.), *Modern psychological medicine* (vol. II, pp. 131–164). London: Butterworth.

Russell, G. (1979). Bulimia nervosa: An ominous variant of anorexia nervosa. *Psychological Medicine, 9,* 429–448.

Russell, G. (1985). The changing nature of anorexia nervosa. *Journal of Psychiatric Research, 19*(2/3), 101–109.

Russell, G., & Treasure, J. (1989). The modern history of anorexia nervosa: An interpretation of why the illness has changed. In L. Shneider, S. J. Copper, & K. A. Halmi (Eds), *The psychopathology of human eating disorders: Preclinical and clinical perspectives* (pp. 13–30). New York: The New York Academy of Science.

Ryle, J. A. (1936). Anorexia nervosa. *Lancet, ii,* 892–894.

Schwartz, H. (1986). *Never satisfied: A cultural history of diets, fantasies and fat.* New York: Macmillan.

Selvini-Pallazoli, M. (1974). *Self starvation: From individual to family therapy in the treatment of anorexia nervosa* (A. Pomerans, Trans.). New York: Jason Aronson.

Selvini-Pallazoli, M. (1985). Anorexia nervosa: A syndrome of the affluent society. *Transcultural Psychiatry Research and Review, 22,* 199–205.

Silverstein, B., & Perlick, D. (1995). *The cost of competence: Why inequality causes depression, eating disorders and illness in women.* New York: Oxford University Press.

Smith, J., & Krejci, J. (1991). Minorities join the majority: Eating disturbance among Hispanics and native American youth. *International Journal of Eating Disorders, 10,* 179–186.

Song, Y. H., & Fang, Y. K. (1990). A clinical report of nine cases of anorexia nervosa. *Chinese Mental Health Journal, 4,* 24.

Striegel-Moore, R., & Steiner-Adair, C. (1998). Primary prevention of eating disorders: further considerations from a feminist perspective. In W. Vandereyecken & G. Noordenbos (Eds.), *The prevention of eating disorders.* London: Athlone.

Suematsu, H., Ishikawa, H., Kuboki, T., & Ito, T. (1985). Statistical studies of anorexia nervosa in Japan: Detailed clinical data on 1,011 patients. *Psychotherapy and Psvchosomatics, 43,* 96–103.

Szabo, P., & Tury, F. (1991). The prevalence of bulimia nervosa in a Hungarian college and secondary school population. *Psychotherapy and Psychosomatics 56,* 43–47.

Takagi, S., Nishizono-Maher, A., & Asai, M. (1991, April). *Study of predisposing factors and initiating factors of eating disorders in Japan.* Paper presented at the International Symposium on Eating Disorders, Paris.

Thomas, J., & Szmukler, G. (1985). Anorexia nervosa in patients of Afro-Caribbean extraction. *British Journal of Psychiatry, 146,* 653–656.

Thompson, B. (1994). Food, bodies and growing up female: Childhood lessons about culture, race and class. In P. Fallon, M. Katzman, & S. C. Wooley (Eds.), *Feminist perspectives on eating disorders* (pp. 355–378). New York: Guilford Press.

Warczyk-Bisage, K., & Dolan, B. (1996). A two-stage epidemiological study of abnormal eating attitudes and their prospective risk factors in Polish school girls. *Psychological Medicine, 26,* 1021–1032.

Weiss, L., Katzman, M. A., & Wolchik, S. (1984). *You can't have your cake and eat it too: A program for controlling bulimia.* Phoenix, AZ: Golden Psych Press.

Zhu, Y.H., Sheng, S. N., Li, B. L., Fu, S. W., & Zhai, S. T. (1994). A clinical and follow up study on anorexia nervosa. *Journal of Clinical and Psychological Medicine, 4,* 206.

3

CHAPTER

Julia A. Graber
Andrea Bastiani Archibald
Jeanne Brooks-Gunn

The Role of Parents in the Emergence, Maintenance, and Prevention of Eating Problems and Disorders

Research on the developmental course of eating problems and disorders has identified the late childhood years and the entry into adolescence as crucial transitions for understanding the early behaviors that may be precursors to more serious eating problems and disorders (Attie & Brooks-Gunn, 1995; Tyrka, Graber, & Brooks-Gunn, in press). For researchers, parents, and practitioners, the potential for the development of unhealthy behaviors at this time has indicated the need for more comprehensive health promotion, nutrition education, and prevention programming targeting eating problems and disorders for girls of this age. Eating disorders are relatively rare for adolescents in comparison with the rates of other disorders such as depression (Lewinsohn, Hops, Roberts, Seeley, & Andrews, 1993). However, subclinical eating problems marked by elevated symptoms and unhealthy eating behaviors and attitudes are prevalent for girls in adolescence (e.g., Fairburn & Beglin, 1990; Story et al., 1991). Subclinical problems include strict dieting, occasional bingeing and purging, excessive exercising, and having a negative/distorted body image.

Literature on correlates and predictors of eating disorders primarily has been clinical in nature and has focused on girls who met diagnostic criteria for anorexia nervosa or bulimia established by the American Psychiatric Association (1994). Developmental research on the other hand, predominantly has examined the symptoms of disorders, ranging from those that are slightly elevated up to those that are more serious, in normal populations (Attie & Brooks-Gunn, 1989, 1995; Graber, Brooks-Gunn, Paikoff, & Warren, 1994; Swarr & Richards,

The authors were supported by grants from the National Institute of Child Health and Development (HD24770, HD32376) during the writing of this paper. They also would like to acknowledge the support of the W. T. Grant Foundation for support of the Adolescent Study Program from which findings are reported, and the National Institute of Child Health and Development Research Network on Child Well-being.

1996). A subset of this work has focused on girls who, although not in treatment for clinical eating disorders, are reporting high levels of eating problems. High levels are determined by scores that are at or above established cut-offs on psychometric measures or interviews designed to identify girls at risk for developing clinical disorders. These eating problems may pose physical and emotional health risks to girls of this age in and of themselves. Although not all girls with eating problems go on to develop disorders, having a prior problem is the best predictor of the subsequent development of an eating disorder (see, e.g., King, 1989; Vollrath, Koch, & Angst, 1992). Hence, many girls potentially would benefit from prevention and early intervention programs addressing eating behaviors in a developmental context.

It has been suggested that parents play a role in the emergence or maintenance of each type or level of eating problem or disorder in some families and may be sources of protection against unhealthy eating practices in other families. This chapter focuses on what is known about the role of parents in the development of eating problems or disorders. Based on the literature to date, we also consider the nature and extent of involvement that may be beneficial for parents to have in prevention or intervention programming for their children.

☐ Linking Health Promotion, Prevention, and Development

Just as multiple levels of eating symptoms have been noted as potential health problems for adolescent girls, programming to offset those problems can be classified into broad levels or types. These span the range through universal prevention, targeted prevention, and intervention; the value of each strategy has been debated (Killen et al., 1993; Offord, Kraemer, Kazdin, Jensen, & Harrington, in press; Smolak & Levine, 1994). The term *prevention*, as we are using it, is in reference to deterring the onset of subclinical eating problems. The term *intervention*, as we use it, refers to treatment for, or tertiary prevention of, clinical eating disorders (e.g., anorexia nervosa and bulimia nervosa). Primary prevention initiatives are generally universal and therefore implemented with all girls, or all girls in particular communities or settings. In contrast, secondary prevention programs are those developed to target a particular group or groups of girls (Offord et al., in press). For example, programs could target girls with higher scores on eating-problem inventories, as they might be considered a group at risk for the development of more serious eating problems or disorders. Similarly, programs could target girls who might be considered at sociodemographic risk for developing eating problems or disorders. That is, one might choose to target White girls or girls in higher socioeconomic groups, as these girls more frequently exhibit eating problems. Prevention and intervention programs also could target groups by specific contexts. Private schools, particularly single-sex, private schools, dance classes, and gymnastic or skating teams frequently have higher concentrations of girls with eating problems (Brooks-Gunn, Burrow, & Warren, 1988). Because adolescent girls experience far more eating problems and express far more weight concerns than do boys, gender generally is not considered a target variable in the area of eating problems or disorders (Rolls, Federoff, & Guthrie, 1991), and most prevention and intervention efforts in this area are conducted with girls.

Another important consideration in the development of prevention and intervention programs is the "unit" of the program being developed. That is, to whom is the program being delivered: girl, parent, parent and daughter, family, school classroom, or so forth? The unit of the program is also the level at which any anticipated change behavior is evaluated. For example, if a drug intervention program targets the family as the unit of the program for evaluation, one would test the program's effectiveness by documenting whether the family as a whole decreased its drug use. Similar to those developed for drug prevention, most eating-disorder prevention programs developed thus far have used girls or school classrooms as the units of the programs (Killen et al., 1993; Neumark-Sztainer, Butler, & Palti, 1995; Smolak, Levine, & Schermer, 1998).

Health promotion and prevention of psychopathology programs require an emphasis on the enhancement of adaptive skills or an emphasis on competency rather than pathology (Compas, 1993; Petersen et al., 1993), so these programs usually target all youth in a classroom or grade or of a particular age. In other words, adolescents can learn and practice skills that they can utilize when confronting the challenges of adolescence. Health promotion encompasses the development of health in multiple domains, including physical health, psychological health, and social health (Millstein, Petersen, & Nightingale, 1993; Perry, 1984). Health-promotion efforts with adolescents primarily have been used in programs targeting smoking, alcohol, and other drug use and sex education. More recently, promoting physical health has been an emphasis of nutrition-education programs that have focused on teaching adolescents and children about nutritional requirements and healthy foods. A review of nutrition-education programs reports that programs targeting specific foods or behaviors achieve success over short-term analysis but often fail to influence a broader range of behaviors or persist in longer-term follow-ups (Contento, Manning, & Shannon, 1992).

An example of an effective prevention program that focuses on many aspects of health promotion while also targeting specific behaviors is the Life-Skills Training (LST) program (e.g., Botvin, Schinke, Epstein, & Diaz, 1994; Botvin, Schinke, Epstein, Diaz, & Botvin, 1995). The LST program is a school-based program for middle-school students that has demonstrated effectiveness in lowering the likelihood of initiation of drug, tobacco, and alcohol use in randomized designs. The program includes both problem-specific material concerning drug abuse and violence prevention and general personal self-management skills and social skills, including decision making, problem solving, goal setting, interpreting and resisting media influences, coping with anxiety and anger, communication skills, and assertiveness training. Thus, not only does LST provide young adolescents with the motivation and skills necessary to resist peer and media pressure to use drugs, it also provides youth with the skills needed to deal with the challenges of life as an adolescent. Given the success of LST and other health-promotion initiatives, the incorporation of similar program elements may prove useful for programs focused on the prevention of eating disorders.

Comprehensive eating-disorder prevention programs only recently have been attempted with children and adolescents, resulting in limited information on which to base any debate over the merits of different types of programs. In addition, few, if any, prevention programs targeting eating attitudes and behaviors have included parents along with their children. In contrast, prevention programs targeting nutrition education (to offset obesity or decrease cardiovascular risk) as well as interventions targeting obesity have effectively employed two-generation approaches (e.g., Fitzgibbon, Stolley, & Kirschenbaum, 1995).

The absence of programs addressing eating problems that incorporate parents is surprising for several reasons; each is presented briefly here but reviewed more thoroughly in the following sections. First, changes in relationships between children and parents, as evidenced by increased conflict and role change, are part of the normative changes of the early adolescent transition (e.g., Paikoff & Brooks-Gunn, 1991; Steinberg, 1990). Thus, families with young adolescents must meet new challenges and resolve more conflicts, so they may be particularly vulnerable to difficulties stemming from poor parent-child interactions. Second, family characteristics commonly have been cited as having a causal role in the development of eating problems and disorders (see Attie & Brooks-Gunn, 1995, for a review). Parents may be exhibiting unhealthy responses to the challenges of adolescence in the form of conflict that is elevated above the normal level or poorly resolved, or lowered cohesion or warmth in the parent-child relationship. Interestingly, no research to date has examined specifically whether or not adolescents with eating problems experience conflicts around particular issues. Not surprisingly however, accounts of families of adolescents with eating disorders often identify conflicts around food consumption, weight, appearance, and control (Garfinkel & Garner, 1980; Minuchin, Rosman, & Baker, 1978). Finally, in the majority of the most recent prevention and targeted intervention work with younger children (regardless of the specific health outcome being addressed), two-generation programs are considered essential for improving child outcome (Fitzgibbon et al., 1995; Smith, 1995).

Normative Adolescent Challenges and the Development of Eating Problems

Our work has emphasized not just parent-child relationships but the multiple dimensions of an older child's or younger adolescent's life that may be important in the development of eating problems or pathology (Attie & Brooks-Gunn, 1989; Graber et al., 1994). The transition into adolescence is important in the development of eating problems because of the developmental changes and challenges normally occurring at that time. Many of these changes have been identified as potential predictors of eating problems and disorders in the clinical literature and of increased symptoms or behaviors such as dieting in the developmental literature (Attie & Brooks-Gunn, 1995; Levine and Smolak, 1992; Tyrka et al., in press).

The physical changes of puberty such as breast development and weight gain have been linked to increased dieting and unhealthy eating practices in young adolescent girls (Attie & Brooks-Gunn, 1989). Girls who mature earlier than their peers gain weight when all other girls still have prepubescent body shapes; thus poorer body image and increased dieting would be expected to be most common for these girls. In fact, we found support for this hypothesis such that girls with persistent serious eating problems in young and mid-adolescence went through puberty earlier than other girls (Graber et al., 1994). What is striking about this finding is that the early maturing girls were reporting serious eating problems several years after their pubertal development was complete. Notably, early maturation also has been linked recently to eating disorders, not just problems (Graber, Lewinsohn, Seeley, & Brooks-Gunn, 1997). Furthermore, the links between pubertal development and dieting or eating problems may vary or be accentuated in certain contexts that require a low weight and thin body shape (e.g., ballet dancers, gymnasts, figure skaters; Brooks-Gunn et al., 1988). In one of our studies of such contexts, what normally would be considered on-time development was a disadvantage to maintaining the preferred body shape for a dancer. Late maturing dancers, in fact, had healthier eating attitudes and behaviors than on-time and early maturing dancers (Brooks-Gunn & Warren, 1985). Given that most girls begin puberty around the age of 9 years, and early maturers begin puberty at even younger ages (Marshall & Tanner, 1969), prevention or early intervention strategies for offsetting unhealthy eating behaviors need to be tested in middle childhood and the early adolescent years. (This strategy recently has been undertaken by Smolak, Levine, and Schermer [1998].)

In addition to navigating the challenges of puberty, young adolescents face new school environments and changing social pressures. Middle and junior high school environments seem to be at odds with the developmental needs of adolescents. Eccles and her colleagues (1993) have shown that middle and junior high school organizational and educational structures actually restrict independence and decision making at exactly the time at which children have acquired more sophisticated cognitive reasoning skills. With the acquisition of cognitive reasoning skills, adolescents are in fact more capable of independent decision making (Keating, 1990) but may not use good judgment in weighing the consequences of behavior (Beyth-Marom & Fischoff, 1997; Brooks-Gunn & Graber, 1994). Prevention programs implemented in the middle-school years have the potential to meet this need for building skills, especially if parents are encouraged in the promotion of these behaviors concurrently.

Peer behaviors and the advent of dating behaviors may be particularly influential on girls' eating behaviors during early adolescence (e.g., Cauffman & Steinberg, 1996; Gralen, Levine, Smolak, & Murnen, 1990). As adolescents have more freedom in how they spend time outside of school, time with friends, closeness to them, and influence of friends increases in early and midadolescence (Berndt, 1996). Interestingly, whereas time with parents may decrease over adolescence, parental influence still is maintained, especially on issues such as career planning and major life decisions (Kandel, 1985). Most importantly, it is not merely that external forces such as the media, friends, or family act upon adolescents, but rather how much importance adolescents place on the negative influence of these external forces. Hence, some girls may be more strongly influenced by media information or peer behaviors than other girls. The influences of peers and parents on behavior are not purely independent; Kandel (1985) has reported that adolescent behavior is most strongly influenced if peers and parents share similar behavioral expectations or beliefs. Similarly, in their investigation of the association of multiple sociocultural factors to eating attitudes and behaviors of early adolescent girls, Levine, Smolak, Moodey, Schuman, and Hessen (1994) found that some middle-school girls lived in what the investigators termed a "subculture" of intense weight and body-shape concern. These girls perceived multiple sociocultural messages from family, peer, and media domains concerning the importance of thinness. Compared with other girls, those who lived in the subculture reported significantly greater drive for thinness and body dissatisfaction, increased weight-management behavior, and disturbed eating (Levine, Smolak, & Hayden, 1994). At this time, it is unclear how adolescent girls balance information from parents and peers about eating attitudes and behavior, although it is likely that these additive effects are particularly salient in not only the development of unhealthy behaviors and attitudes but also protective factors against such development.

Social contact with boys, in particular, has been suggested as a factor in the increase in dieting behaviors and weight consciousness observed in young adolescent girls (Gargiulo, Attie, Brooks-Gunn, & Warren, 1987; Gralen et al., 1990). A recent investigation examining both pubertal timing and dating behaviors reported that early maturing girls who had begun dating had the highest reported incidence of dieting (Cauffman & Steinberg, 1996). Consideration of the interactive influences of social experiences and physical development is essential for understanding the complexities of healthy or unhealthy development during adolescence. Interestingly, such considerations of dating and peer influences have not incorporated parents into the equation of social interactions. It is certainly feasible that girls who look more physically mature and are interacting more intimately with boys than same-age peers also have parents with heightened concerns about these social interactions. Just like the early maturing girls themselves, their parents may feel less prepared to deal with their daughter's transition to dating.

Hence, a range of social and contextual factors has been considered influential on the development of eating problems in girls and as such has been the target of prevention and early intervention. However, interactions and relationships with parents are connected to girls' behavior both directly and indirectly through these other contextual factors. That is, girls' abilities to face multiple new social challenges is likely to be dependent on the nature of their parent-child relationships during early adolescence. Although the transition to and through adolescence is accompanied by an increase in independence for the adolescent, the maintenance of warmth in the parent-adolescent relationship may serve to buffer the adolescent against the development of psychological and behavioral difficulties (Resnick et al., 1997), including unhealthy eating symptoms (Swarr & Richards, 1996). A better understanding of parent-child relationships and how they influence eating attitudes and behaviors is necessary for better intervention with adolescent girls.

☐ Changes in Parent-Child Relationships at Adolescence

Multiple dimensions of parenting have been identified as important for child and adolescent development. These include parenting style, parenting practices, discrepancies between parent and child viewpoints regarding family and peer issues, familial conflict and cohesion, and parental sensitivity to the child's developmental status (e.g., Collins & Russell, 1991; Smetana, 1988). The salience of these dimensions to adjustment, or more specifically eating behaviors, probably changes over time, and the form of parental behavior is altered over developmental periods even if the function remains the same.

Research indicates that parent-child relationships change as children become adolescents (Paikoff & Brooks-Gunn, 1991; Steinberg, 1990). Conflict between parents and adolescents increases as the adolescents begin pubertal development, peaking around the time of mid-puberty (Steinberg, 1990). For most adolescents and parents, conflict dissipates slowly over time as new roles and relationships are negotiated. In fact, adolescents and parents report that conflict is often over parent-imposed rules or requirements such as curfews or chores (Montemayor & Hanson, 1985; Smetana, 1988). Cognitive changes coupled with pubertal changes increase the likelihood that children will begin to question the legitimacy of parental authority in these domains (Smetana, 1988). Although many parents find challenges to their authority irritating and unnerving initially, most work with their adolescents to find compromises.

Conflict and its resolution happen in the context of an existing parent-child relationship. Most parents and adolescents report feeling close to one another and having warm relationships. Although cohesion and closeness have not been examined as frequently as patterns of conflict in development, evidence to date suggests that closeness often is maintained and is not diminished during early adolescence (see Graber & Brooks-Gunn, 1999, and Steinberg, 1990, for reviews.) Such patterns of relationships parallel models of attachment in infancy and early childhood (Graber & Brooks-Gunn, 1999). For example, young children who feel secure attachment relationships with their mothers are able to explore the world around them and refer back to her as a "secure base" providing reassurance or support. Comparably, young adolescents seek out greater independence and become more adept at asserting their own autonomy but still rely on parents for reassurance and support. The ability to balance conflict and its resolution with the maintenance of a stable, warm relationship may be an important discriminator between families who find healthy versus unhealthy responses to the challenges of adolescence.

☐ Family Correlates of Eating Problems and Disorders

Family correlates of eating disorders have been identified in several studies of clinically diagnosed women (see Attie & Brooks-Gunn, 1995, and Wonderlich, 1992, for reviews). Families of adolescents with anorexia nervosa long have been depicted as having enmeshed relationships marked by a lack of boundaries between individuals within the family system and an inability for individuals within the relationships to act and think autonomously (Garfinkel & Garner, 1980; Minuchin et al., 1978). Communication difficulties, involving both high levels of contradiction and low levels of openness and sharing, also have been noted for young adult women with disorders (Humphrey, 1989; Minuchin et al., 1978; Waller, Calam, & Slade, 1988). Lack of nurturance on the parts of both parents has also been implicated in similar studies (Humphrey, 1989). However, Attie and Brooks-Gunn (1995) suggest that there are many inconsistencies in links between family relationship problems and eating disorders not accountable for merely by type of eating disorder. One difficulty with drawing upon information based on comparisons of families with a child experiencing a disorder versus those without has to do with the direction of the effect. That is, it is impossible to differentiate whether poor family relationships were important in causing the disorder or whether the strain of having a child with an eating disorder actually is causing problems in family interactions.

Further studies of normal adolescent girls and their parents may help to determine causal family patterns as well as precursors to disorders and problems that are good targets for early intervention. Research to date has addressed several aspects of parent-child (or -adolescent) relationships as potential causes of eating problems. Our discussion focuses on relational correlates (e.g., conflict or warmth) of eating problems, modeling of behaviors, criticism of appearance or weight, and time spent with parents. Interestingly, these different dimensions of relational correlates of eating problems often lead to differential effects. We also highlight aspects of parent-child relationships that seem to promote healthier attitudes and behaviors.

Relational Correlates of Eating Problems

In work by members of our group on mother-daughter relationships during midadolescence (around age 16), mother and daughter reports of conflict were not associated individually with unhealthy eating behaviors or attitudes (Paikoff, Carlton-Ford, & Brooks-Gunn, 1994). In contrast, mothers' perceptions of cohesion or closeness and warmth in the family environment were associated with an increased likelihood of eating problems by adolescent girls (Attie & Brooks-Gunn, 1989). In addition, there was a discrepancy in how mothers and daughters perceived the cohesion and warmth of their family environment, a discrepancy particularly linked to girls' dieting behavior. Mothers' feelings about family cohesion also were associated with their own and their daughters' body images such that if mothers reported greater cohesion they and their daughters had better feelings about their bodies (Paikoff et al., 1994). We have suggested elsewhere that this set of findings may indicate that these families are not engaging in meaningful interactions (Graber & Brooks-Gunn, 1999). In support of this hypothesis, Swarr and Richards' (1996) examination of closeness with mothers and fathers as well as time spent with each parent found that both factors were associated with healthier eating attitudes for young adolescent girls. Girls who spent less time with their mothers when they were young adolescents (seventh, eighth, or ninth grade) had more disturbed eating 2 years later when they were mid-adolescents.

Given that changes do occur in parent-child relationships with puberty, recent investigations have considered whether these two dimensions of adolescents' lives are interacting to contribute to eating problems. Swarr and Richards (1996) report that spending more time with parents and being normal in the timing of pubertal development resulted in the healthiest eating attitudes. Both earlier pubertal maturation and less closeness with mothers were risks for less healthy behavior patterns. It should be noted that, in this study, eating problems were looked at as a continuous variable, and "less healthy eating attitudes and behavior" were not necessarily indicative of pathological eating patterns. Although quality and amount of time spent with both parents was important for the promotion of healthier attitudes, of particular note is that spending more time with fathers seemed to offset the negative influence of early pubertal development for girls. Although it is possible that fathers play a key role in the development of their daughters' healthy body image and eating, this is an area that has not been given thorough attention in the literature (see Levine, 1994, for an exception). Consideration of both the quality of relationships and actual time spent with each parent may be particularly important for understanding buffers to the development of unhealthy eating behaviors.

Interestingly, recent work has suggested that poor family relationships may be associated less strongly with eating problems than with other disorders or problems that are co-occurring with the eating problem (Graber & Brooks-Gunn, 1998; Herzog, Keller, Sacks, Yeh, & Lavori, 1992). Specifically, eating disorders and problems are frequently comorbid with both depression and depressive problems. In one study of young women in treatment for an eating disorder, only young women who also reported depressive problems had poor family relationships (Wonderlich & Swift, 1990). In our own work, on subclinical eating and depressive problems in adolescent girls, we found that girls with eating and depressive problems had poor family relationships as well as poor peer relationships; these interpersonal-relationship deficits also were present for girls with a depressive problem but not an eating problem (Graber & Brooks-Gunn, 1998). If girls had an eating problem in the absence of a depressive problem, they appeared to be satisfied with their relationships with peers and reported only somewhat more conflict or less warmth than girls with positive adjustment in adolescence. Notably, we also found evidence that eating problems preceded depressive problems for girls who developed both.

Such a pattern might support the idea that the eating problems began to tax the girls' social support systems and produced stress for these girls and their parents, resulting in the development of a subsequent or concurrent depressive problem. As yet, not enough longitudinal research beginning before the development of these problems has been conducted to ascertain whether poor parent-child relationships were the cause or the result of eating problems in adolescent girls. Most likely, the relationships and problems are interacting. As girls enter adolescence some families are having communication or other relational difficulties. The increased challenges to parent-child relationships at adolescence provide an additional stressor to these relationships. If girls with less supportive family relationships do not cope well with pubertal or other changes, they may develop eating problems. In turn, the eating problem may lead to the further breakdown of family relations, resulting in more severe psychopathology for the adolescent girl in the form of a comorbid depressive problem or the development of an actual eating disorder. However, it could also be that more positive family relationships serve to buffer adolescent girls with eating problems from developing co-occuring depressive symptoms. Finally, it could be that families have little to do with the development of co-occurring eating and depressive problems. That is, girls may become more depressed as eating problems becomes central in their lives and they are unable to control or lose weight.

In a preliminary short-term longitudinal study of the relationship between parent-adolescent relations and two symptoms of clinical eating disorders (dieting and body image) in 12- and 13-year-old girls (Archibald, Graber, & Brooks-Gunn, in press), we tested the possibility of bi-directional effects between parental relationships and dieting or body image. Using dieting, body image, and parental relations as continuous variables, path models revealed significant longitudinal effects of parent-adolescent relations on dieting, but not of dieting on parent-adolescent relations over a 1-year period. Similar results were found for parental relations and body image. Considered alone, these results confirm the direction of causality implied in prior studies: problematic family relations lead to increased symptomatology of clinical eating disorders (Archibald et al., submitted). However, in a separate study of predominantly middle and late adolescent girls (ages 12–18 years), we found different results when we examined the possibility of bi-directional effects between parental relationships and eating problems (Archibald, Linver, Graber, & Brooks-Gunn, submitted 1998). Interestingly, results for this age cohort showed significant effects of eating problems on parental relationships, but not of parental relationships on eating problems. These studies support the possibility that problematic family relationships influence the development of eating problems but only in early adolescence. By mid- to late adolescence, when eating problems may be well underway, relationships may be less influential in maintaining the eating problems, and instead eating problems may serve to minimize positive or neutral, or maintain poor, parental relations.

It also should be noted that difficulties in family relations are probably not specific to eating problems and may be more generally associated with psychopathologies and problem behaviors of adolescence (Garmezy & Masten, 1991; Rubin et al., 1992). Low levels of family cohesion and high levels of family conflict also have been associated with depressive symptomatology (e.g., Carlton-Ford, Paikoff, Oakley, & Brooks-Gunn, 1996) and conduct disorders (Eron, Huesmann, & Zelli, 1991).

Monitoring and Modeling of Eating Attitudes and Behaviors

Time spent with parents may be tapping aspects of behavioral monitoring that are also salient to eating behaviors separate from quality-of-relationship factors. One area in which adolescent girls (and boys) assert more personal independence from parental control is in food choice. With greater independence, adolescents are less likely to eat meals with their parents, as they eat more meals with friends or on their own. Unfortunately, the result of this independence is that unhealthy nutritional patterns abound, with increased consumption of junk food and skipping meals (Crawford, 1996). In particular, poor nutrition patterns as evidenced by deficits in calcium (most likely through the reduction in milk consumption) are common for pre-adolescent girls, especially if they already have begun to eat fewer meals with parents (Crawford, 1996). Recently, our research group found differences in food choice and subsequent nutritional patterns in groups of adolescent girls who were engaged in different levels of dieting behavior. In this study, we compared the eating patterns of adolescent girls who engaged in high levels of dieting behavior (upper 35% of sample) with those of girls who engaged in little or no dieting behavior (lower 35% of sample). Dieters were not merely consuming fewer food items in a day but frequently were skipping breakfast completely and drinking diet soft drinks instead of milk (Hoy, Contento, Brooks-Gunn, Graber, & Warren, 1996). Parents may be relinquishing their power to monitor and assist their daughters in making healthy food choices earlier than when adolescents are able to make healthy decisions on their own.

Along with eating with their children or monitoring what their children eat, parents also have their own attitudes about eating and weight, and consequently they model healthy or unhealthy beliefs and practices. However, findings on whether eating problems correspond between mothers and adolescent girls have been inconsistent (e.g., Attie & Brooks-Gunn, 1989, 1995; Byely, Archibald, Graber, & Brooks-Gunn, in press; Pike & Rodin, 1991).

Some studies have found correspondence between mothers' and daughters' eating attitudes and behaviors. For example, Paxton and colleagues (1991) found that girls with eating problems were more likely to report that one or both of their parents were engaged in dieting. Similarly, Levine Smolak, Moodey, Schuman, and Hessen (1994) found that girls with eating problems were more likely to report that their mothers were very concerned about their own weight than were other girls. However, in a short-term longitudinal study recently conducted by our group of dieting behaviors during early adolescence, we did not find that mothers' dieting predicted daughters' dieting (Byely et al., in press). In this study, we separately investigated the influence of family relations, mothers' own dieting and body-image concerns, and social factors (familial and peer) on early-adolescent girls' dieting and body image. Girls' perception of family relations and social factors were associated with their increased dieting and negative body image 1 year later. However, mothers' own dieting and body image failed to be associated with their daughters' dieting or body image (Byely et al., in press). It should be noted, however, that it is unclear if these findings hold true for girls in middle or late adolescence.

In other work by members of our group, *both* daughter's and mother's reproductive status were considered in connection to unhealthy eating behaviors (Paikoff, Brooks-Gunn, & Carlton-Ford, 1991). Women often experience weight gain in the later stages of menopause and with hormone-replacement therapies for menopause (Matthews, 1992), much as adolescent girls experience weight gain with puberty. In fact, in this investigation postmenopausal mothers were significantly heavier and engaged in more dieting behavior than premenopausal mothers. Moreover, the daughters of these postmenopausal women also were most likely to engage in dieting behavior, but only if the girls were early-maturers. Thus, mother-daughter pairs who were most at risk for unhealthy eating practices and attitudes were those who were experiencing reproductive transitions similarly. Mothers' modeling of behaviors were most influential under these circumstances. Comparing findings across studies, the extent to which mothers actively model unhealthy eating attitudes and behaviors has been associated with their own tendencies toward psychopathology, as well as their own stages of development (Paikoff et al., 1991).

It also has been suggested that, beyond modeling of unhealthy feelings about oneself or unhealthy practices, parents may criticize actively their daughters' appearance or eating behaviors. In their cross-sectional study, Pike and Rodin (1991) found both correspondence in disordered eating symptoms between mothers and their adolescent daughters and that mothers of girls with eating problems were more critical of their daughters' weight and physical appearance. Not only did girls with more eating problems perceive their mothers as more critical of their appearances, but their mothers rated them as less attractive and needing to lose more weight than did other mothers, even after controlling for daughters' body mass. Similarly, Levine, et al. (1994) found that weight- and body shape–related teasing and criticism by family members were strong correlates of disturbed patterns of eating in middle-school girls and of the girls' own investment in thinness. In a large study of parents' attitudes about their children's appearance, Striegel-Moore and Kearney-Cooke (1994) found that parents who had recently dieted were more likely to encourage their children (both girls and boys) to diet. They also noted that parents were usually very positive about their children's general appearance (not particular to weight/shape) but were increasingly less positive with older than with younger children. That is, parents of preschoolers were more satisfied with their child's appearance than parents of elementary-school children, who were, in turn, more satisfied than parents of adolescents. At the same time, parents were more likely to rate daughters as fatter than sons were rated, even though the reported height and weight information for same-age children would suggest that boys were actually fatter than girls. Interestingly, parents satisfaction with their own appearances did not seem to influence their satisfaction with their children's appearances. Striegel-Moore and Kearney-Cooke (1994) hypothesize that parents are applying the culturally pervasive thin ideal to the assessment of their daughter's weight.

Although there are links among poor family relationships, normative adolescent challenges, and development of problematic eating attitudes and behaviors, there are several points at which parents and their adolescent daughters can alter the course of this pattern and improve relationships and behavior. The fact that most girls do not develop serious psychopathology during adolescence suggests that even among girls with periods of problems, most manage to avert the path to disorder. Each parent-child correlate of eating attitudes and behavior identified—amount of time spent in and quality of parent-child relationships, parental monitoring and modeling of eating attitudes and behaviors, and parental criticism—potentially could be addressed through prevention and early intervention programming.

Linking Development and Health Promotion in the Prevention of Eating Problems

Although a number of nutrition and health programs have been developed for use with adolescents, few programs have emphasized the important physical, psychological, and social transitions that challenge developing adolescents. Compas (1993) notes that because of development across childhood and adolescence, prevention programs are not effective for all ages but must address the skills and challenges at each period of development. Moreover, very few programs focused on the prevention of eating disorders have been developed and tested. Even fewer of these programs have included parent components (see Smolak, Levine, and Schermer, 1998, as a notable exception), and none have incorporated parents and girls as their unit of focus.

To illustrate how we have conceptualized linking health promotion, nutrition education, and the prevention of eating problems, the following is a brief description of a pilot program developed by our group (Schuman, Contento, Graber, & Brooks-Gunn, 1994). The program was conducted with sixth-grade girls (ages 11–12 years) and divided into three modules of instruction. The first, *Knowing the Issues,* consisted of four sessions providing an overview of the program and covering the topics of cultural norms about weight and attractiveness, and adolescent transitions such as pubertal development. The second module, *How We Eat,* consisted of six sessions covering nutrition, health, eating disorders and behaviors, and exercise. The third module, *Working It Out,* consisted of six sessions addressing the social and psychological correlates of eating and strategies for making personal choices and implementing those choices in the environment. Along the psychosocial dimension, emphasis also was placed on the roles of others in shaping beliefs about oneself and one's behaviors, including the roles of parents, male peers, and girlfriends.

Each module included interactive activities (e.g., watching a videotape of girls talking about puberty and weight change; discussing the feelings and experiences elicited by the video; role playing conflict negotiation) and outside-of-class projects (e.g., finding an example of unhealthy images in the media) along with curricula on nutrition and health-related information (e.g., how much calcium girls need per day and good sources of calcium). Prevention classes were co-led by a teacher at the school paired with a member of our team. In this way, the program was developed to be implemented in schools on an ongoing basis rather than requiring restructuring for incorporation into schools independent of the research project. Pilot work with this program with 60 girls indicated that it was effective in preventing normative increases in dieting behaviors (Schuman et al., 1994). That is, girls in a control school exhibited increases in dieting behavior over the 2-month pre- and post-test period, similar to increases we have seen in other studies with girls this age (Archibald Graber, & Brooks-Gunn., in press), whereas girls in the program maintained low levels of dieting.

Other universal programs have been implemented and tested in larger samples of girls (e.g., Killen et al., 1993; Neumark-Sztainer et al., 1995; Smolak et al., 1998). Such programs have used varying levels of participation and have had limited effectiveness in their evaluations. A most promising evaluation recently was undertaken by Smolak and colleagues (1998). Their school-based program, *Eating Smart, Eating For Me,* was undertaken with fifth-grade boys and girls. Although the focus of the program was on healthy eating, exercise, and body image, developmentally relevant and related issues such as pubertal development also were addressed. Notably, their program included two parental components: informative newsletters to parents and homework assignments to be done with parents. Results of their controlled evaluation indicated that although children's eating and exercise behaviors were not changed as a result of the program, knowledge was improved by the curriculum. Whether or not the specific incorporation of parental components contributed to the program's effectiveness is as yet unknown.

The limited successes in behavioral change for this program and other programs could be attributed to the fact that they focused solely on eating attitudes and behaviors and failed to incorporate more comprehensive elements of health promotion and general personal skills related to the challenges of adolescence. As discussed previously in regard to the LST program (Botvin et al., 1994, 1995), incorporation of such elements has been found to be very effective in the prevention of alcohol and other drug use with middle-school girls and boys.

At a minimum, given the relational correlates of eating problems in adolescence, we would advocate the addition of parental components to these programs. Parental components, such as newsletters and homework assignments, might at least increase parent-adolescent communication around eating attitudes and behaviors and related adolescent challenges. In this vein, we have considered the incorporation of a parent component as a future addition to our own work on the development of an eating-problems prevention program rather than as a first step (Schuman et al., 1994). Ideally, we would advocate for parallel or joint programs so that both adolescents and their parents have the opportunity to build knowledge and skills individually as well as reinforce what each is learning. Increased time spent together also would be an added positive effect of participation in joint programs.

As noted, at the same time that adolescents seek and are granted greater personal responsibility, parents clearly still are influencing their eating-related behaviors and attitudes via the mechanisms we have noted already. In addition, parents themselves frequently report an increase in anxieties and concerns over the demands of parenting adolescents (Brooks-Gunn & Zahaykevich, 1989; Steinberg, 1990). These concerns are in part based on the erroneous popular-press view of adolescence as a period of strife and conflict. Of course, as indicated, adolescent-parent relationships do demonstrate normal increases in conflict that dissipate over time for most families. Also, given increased exposure to violence, alcohol, and sexual messages in the media, parents do have legitimate concerns about the safety and overall well-being of their adolescent children at exactly the time that they need to help their children prepare for adult roles and responsibilities. As such, parents may benefit personally from inclusion in programs that provide accurate information on health behaviors.

Prior research (Perry et al., 1989) on nutrition-education programs has reported significantly more behavioral changes in programs that have involved parents in addition to the target child or adolescent. Even though this effect did not persist in longer follow-ups, the work of Perry and her colleagues demonstrates the feasibility of parent involvement and the possibility for enhanced treatment effects (Contento et al., 1992). As maternal attitudes towards eating, weight, and dieting have demonstrated some associations with adolescent girls' behaviors and attitudes (Pike & Rodin, 1991), mothers' involvement in particular, may prove to be critical for altering girls' behavior.

Research on health promotion with children and adolescents conducted by Perry and her colleagues (1989) has demonstrated that parents are willing to participate in these types of programs, with a majority of families beginning and completing the program. Perry and others (e.g., Nader, Sallis, Patterson, Abramson, & Rupp, 1989) have used a *home-team* program in which students are given assignments to be conducted with parents at home. Hence, rather than expecting parents to spend time away from home and, in fact, spend less time with their adolescents, the parents and adolescents complete tasks together at home. In the later weeks of the program, "fun nights" at school are conducted at which more experiential programs can be conducted (Nader et al., 1989). Experiential components often include role-playing activities that help parents develop conflict resolution and communication skills. These approaches have demonstrated effectiveness in attracting and maintaining parent participation as well as in influencing nutrition and smoking behaviors in both children and young adolescents (Perry et al., 1989). In order to avoid creating anxiety over their grades for the homework assignments and making adolescents responsible for their parents' behavior, such school-based programs specifically have not made class grades dependent upon parental participation. Interestingly, in the evaluation of their programs, Nader and colleagues (1989) have found that those parents who participate in group sessions in addition to completing their home assignments are most likely to maintain their healthy dietary changes.

It is of course important to emphasize that for truly pathological or dysfunctional family environments (as seen with cases of physical or sexual abuse), parent participation in intervention programs could be detrimental to the adolescent. In these cases, the interactive tasks of the program would force the adolescent into situations that could exacerbate existing problems rather than promote healthy interactions. However, prevention programs of the type discussed earlier in this chapter are not designed for the needs of individuals already experiencing a disorder or serious pathology. Such families are better serviced in treatment programs.

☐ Conclusions

In this chapter we argue that parents need to be included as participants in pre-vention programs specifically targeting the development of subclinical eating problems by adolescent girls, as well as more comprehensive health and nutri-tion-education programs. Through parallel or joint programming, adolescents and their parents have the opportunity to spend time together, build skills, and develop knowledge, both individually and cooperatively. We suggest that the following aspects of parental behavior and parent-child relationships potentially could improve via such programs.

First, comparable program components for girls and parents should include providing information on normal development at adolescence. Parents and girls need accurate information about what to expect at puberty in terms of physical changes such as normal weight gain as well as relational changes such as in-creased parent-child conflict. As indicated, many parents and adolescents express concern over how to talk effectively with one another; thus, even for parents who have not had prior difficulties in conflict resolution or communication, adoles-cence may pose new challenges to even the most skillful negotiator. Unique de-velopmental experiences that may place girls at risk for unhealthy development need to be identified for parents, as they may be unaware of risk associated with certain experiences, or whether certain experiences fall within normal develop-ment. Informal discussions reveal that many mothers of girls beginning puberty in the middle childhood years (ages 8 and 9 years) are surprised at how early their daughters' maturation has begun. Even though these mothers are not aware of research studies on pubertal timing, they seem particularly (and appropriately) concerned that their daughters' development may elicit responses from older boys and put them in situations for which the girls are not prepared. Making par-ents aware that their concerns are realistic and that they can influence negative effects of pubertal timing through such simple activities as spending time with their daughters (as demonstrated by Swarr & Richards [1996]) not only alleviates worry but also provides constructive methods for coping with their concerns.

Second, parents and adolescents need better information about healthy nutri-tional practices, and they need to engage in activities that promote healthier eating. Obesity-intervention programs have demonstrated effectiveness in im-proving behavior of both mothers and daughters (Fitzgibbon et al., 1995). In ad-dition, parents need more specific information on the importance of monitoring their young adolescents' eating behaviors. The fact that children and young adolescents increasingly are eating meals without parents suggests that parents may be allowing adolescents to assert too much independence in this area. It also may be that employment and other parenting-related demands disrupt the routine of regular family meals. The fact that adolescents and older children can make their own breakfast or dinner, if need be, may be a relief to busy parents. Strategies for improving the monitoring of children's eating would have to be developed with these constraints in mind.

Finally, parental components need to address how parents feel about them-selves and their own development, how they may transmit their unhealthy concerns to their children, and how they may be influenced by cultural norms. Parents may benefit from activities that help them explore and identify their own behaviors as well as information on the effects that certain behaviors may have on their daughters. Certainly girls in eating-problem prevention programs must address many of the same issues. Hence, feelings about the self and cultural pressures may be two of the most important topics for girls and parents to address individually and together.

These types of components of parent-adolescent programs have been identified for the purposes of prevention programs, under the assumption that most parents and adolescents would find such programs useful. As previously noted, others have argued that prevention programming in the area of eating problems is not appropriate, and that instead intervention programs should only be developed for and targeted at girls who have already begun to experience difficulties (Killen et al., 1993). However, such decisions are based on limited tests of prevention programming, and, in the absence of evaluation of two-generation programs, seem premature. Comprehensive programs should include not only nutrition education and health promotion but also concerns particular to the changing nature of parent-adolescent relationships, as these areas (amount of time spent together, cohesion and warmth, conflict) have been linked to healthier eating attitudes and behaviors (Archibald, Livner et al., in press; Swarr & Richards, 1996). Obesity-reduction programs with low-income and non-White mothers and daughters have demonstrated that nutrition and health programs are relevant to the lives of women of diverse backgrounds and ages (Fitzgibbon et al., 1995). Recent identification of binge-eating disorder and its prevalence in African-American women in their 30s and 40s (Striegel-Moore & Smolak, 1996), the age at which women often have teenage daughters, supports the need for more broadly based prevention programs that move beyond nutrition and include psychological functioning and well-being. Given the age at which eating-problems typically begin, and given the demonstrated links between girls' positive parental relationships and healthier eating attitudes and behavior, the inclusion of parents in eating-problems prevention work is a logical and potentially fruitful area of further development, implementation, and evaluation.

☐ References

American Psychiatric Association. (1994). *Diagnostic and statistical manual of mental disorders* (4th ed). Washington, DC: Author.

Archibald, A. B., Graber, J. A., & Brooks-Gunn, J. (1998). *Parental relations and pubertal development as predictors of dieting and body image in early-adolescent girls: A short term longitudinal study. Journal of Research on Adolescence.*

Archibald, A. B., Linver, M. R., Graber, J. A., & Brooks-Gunn, J. (1998) *One problem feeding another? Reciprocal associations between eating problems and parental relations in adolescent girls.* Manuscript submitted for publication.

Attie, I., & Brooks-Gunn, J. (1989). The development of eating problems in adolescent girls: A longitudinal study. *Developmental Psychology, 25(1),* 70–79.

Attie, I., & Brooks-Gunn, J. (1995). The development of eating regulation across the lifespan. In D. Cicchetti & D. J. Cohen (Eds.), *Developmental psychopathology* (vol. 2, pp. 332–368). New York: John Wiley & Sons.

Berndt, T. J. (1996). Transitions in friendship and friends' influence. In J. A. Graber, J. Brooks-Gunn, & A. C. Petersen (Eds.), *Transitions through adolescence: Interpersonal domains and context* (pp. 57–84). Mahwah, NJ: Lawrence Erlbaum & Associates.

Beyth-Marom, R., & Fischhoff, B. (1997). Adolescents' decisions about risks: A cognitive perspective. In J. Schulenberg, J. L. Maggs, & K. Hurrelmann (Eds.), *Health risks and developmental transitions during adolescence.* New York: Cambridge University Press.

Botvin, G. J., Schinke, S. P., Epstein, J. A., & Diaz, T. (1994). Effectiveness of culturally-focused and generic skills training approaches to alcohol and drug abuse prevention among minority youths. *Psychology of Addictive Behaviors, 8,* 116–127.

Botvin, G. J., Schinke, S. P., Epstein, J. A., Diaz, T., & Botvin, E. M. (1995). Effectiveness of culturally-focused and generic skills training approaches to alcohol and drug abuse prevention among minority youths: Two-year follow-up results. *Psychology of Addictive Behaviors, 9,* 183–194.

Brooks-Gunn, J., Burrow, C., & Warren, M. P. (1988). Attitudes toward eating and body weight in different groups of female adolescent athletes. *International Journal of Eating Disorders, 7,* 749–757.

Brooks-Gunn, J., & Graber, J. A. (1994). Puberty as a biological and social event: Implications for research on pharmacology. *Journal of Adolescent Health, 15,* 663–671.

Brooks-Gunn, J., & Warren, M. (1985). The effects of delayed menarche in different contexts: Dance and nondance students. *Journal of Youth and Adolescence, 14,* 285–300.

Brooks-Gunn, J., & Zahaykevich, M. (1989). Parent-daughter relationships in early adolescence: A developmental perspective. In K. Kreppner & R. M. Lerner (Eds.), *Family systems and life-span development* (pp. 223–246). Hillsdale, NJ: Erlbaum.

Byely, L., Archibald, A. B., Graber, J. A., & Brooks-Gunn, J. (in press). Familial and social influences on body image and dieting behavior in early-adolescent girls. International Journal of Eating Disorders.

Carlton-Ford, S., Paikoff, R., Oakley, J., & Brooks-Gunn, J. (1996). A longitudinal analysis of depressed mood, self-esteem and family processes during adolescence. *Sociological Focus, 29,* 135–154.

Cauffman, E., & Steinberg, L. (1996). Interactive effects of menarcheal status and dating on dieting and disordered eating among adolescent girls. *Developmental Psychology, 32,* 631–635.

Collins, W. A., & Russell, G. (1991). Mother-child and father-child relationships in middle childhood and adolescence: A developmental analysis. *Developmental Review, 11,* 99–136.

Compas, B. E. (1993). Promoting positive mental health during adolescence. In S. G. Millstein, A. C. Petersen, & E. O. Nightingale (Eds.), *Promoting the health of adolescents* (pp. 159–179). New York: Oxford University Press.

Contento, I. R., Manning, A. D., Shannon, B. (1992). Research perspective on school-based nutrition education. *Journal of Nutrition Education, 24,* 247–260.

Crawford, P. (1996, September). *Changing eating patterns in adolescent girls: Is there cause for alarm?* Paper presented at the APA conference "Psychosocial and behavioral factors in women's health," Washington, DC.

Eccles, J. S., Midgley, C., Wigfield, A., Buchanan, C. M., Reuman, D., Flanagan, C., & MacIver, D. (1993). Development during adolescence: The impact of stage-environment fit in young adolescents' experiences in schools and in families. *American Psychologist, 48,* 90–101.

Eron, L. D., Huesmann, L. R., & Zelli, A. (1991). The role of parental variables in the learning of aggression. In O. J. Pepler & K. H. Rubin (Eds.), The development and treatment of childhood aggression (pp. 169–198). Hillsdale, NJ: Lawrence Erlbaum & Associates.

Fairburn, C. G., & Beglin, S. J. (1990). Studies of the epidemiology of bulimia nervosa. *American Journal of Psychiatry, 147,* 401–408.

Fitzgibbon, M. L., Stolley, M. R., & Kirschenbaum, D. S. (1995). An obesity prevention pilot program for African-American mothers and daughters. *Journal of Nutrition Education, 27,* 93–99.

Gargiulo, J., Attie, I., Brooks-Gunn, J., & Warren, M. P. (1987). Girls' dating behavior as a function of social context and maturation. *Developmental Psychology, 23,* 730–737.

Garfinkel, P. E., & Garner, D. M. (1980). *Anorexia nervosa: A multidimensional perspective.* New York: Brunner/Mazel.

Garmezy, N., & Master, A. (1991). The protective role of competency indicators in children at risk. In E. M. Cummings, A. L. Green & K. H. Karraker (Eds.), Life-span developmental psychology: Perspectives on stress and coping (pp. 151–174). Hillsdale, NJ: Lawrence Erlbaum & Associates.

Graber, J. A., & Brooks-Gunn, J. (1998). *Depressive affect and eating problems: Comorbidity in adolescent girls.* Manuscript submitted for publication.

Graber, J. A., & Brooks-Gunn, J. (1999). "Sometimes I think that you don't like me:" How mothers and daughters negotiate the transition to adolescence. In M. Cox & J. Brooks-Gunn (Eds.), *Conflict and closeness in families: Consequences for children and youth development.* (pp. 207–242) Hillsdale, NJ: Lawrence Erlbaum & Associates.

Graber, J. A., Brooks-Gunn, J., Paikoff, R. L., & Warren, M. P. (1994). Prediction of eating problems: An eight year study of adolescent girls. *Developmental Psychology, 30,* 823–834.

Graber, J. A., Lewinsohn, P. M., Seeley, J. R., & Brooks-Gunn, J. (1997). Is psychopathology associated with the timing of pubertal development? *Journal of the American Academy of Child and Adolescent Psychiatry, 36,* 1768–1776.

Gralen, S. J., Levine, M. P., Smolak, L., & Murnen, S. K. (1990). Dieting and disordered eating during early and middle adolescence: Do the influences remain the same? *International Journal of Eating Disorders, 9,* 501–512.

Herzog, D. B., Keller, M. B., Sacks, N. R., Yeh, C. J., & Lavori, P. W. (1992). Psychiatric comorbidity in treatment-seeking anorexics and bulimics. *Journal of the American Academy of Child and Adolescent Psychiatry, 31,* 810–818.

Hoy, M. K., Contento, I., Brooks-Gunn, J., Graber, J. A., & Warren, M. P. (1996, July). *Eating patterns of adolescent girls who report dieting.* Paper presented at the annual meeting of the Society for Nutrition Education, St. Louis, MO.

Humphrey, L. L. (1989). Observed family interactions among subtypes of eating disorders using structural analysis of social behavior. *Journal of Consulting and Clinical Psychology, 57,* 206–214.

Kandel, D. B. (1985). *Advances in alcohol and substance abuse.* New York: Haworth Press.

Keating, D. P. (1990). Adolescent thinking. In S. Feldman & G. Elliott (Eds.), *At the threshold: The developing adolescent* (pp. 54–90). Cambridge, MA: Harvard University Press.

Killen, J. D., Taylor, C. B., Hammer, L. D., Litt, I., Wilson, D. M., Rich, T., Hayward, C., Simmonds, B., Kraemer, H., & Varady, A. (1993). An attempt to modify unhealthful eating attitudes and weight regulation practices of young adolescent girls. *International Journal of Eating Disorders, 13,* 369–384.

King, M. B. (1989). Eating disorders in a general practice population: Prevalence, characteristics and follow-up at 12 to 18 months. *Psychological Medicine* (Monograph suppl. 14), 1–34.

Levine, M. P. (1994). Beauty myth and the beast: What men can do and be to help prevent eating disorders. *Eating Disorders, 2,* 101–113.

Levine, M. P., & Smolak, L. (1992). Toward a model of the developmental psychopathology of eating disorders: The example of early adolescence. In J. H. Crowther, D. L. Tennenbaum, S. E. Hobfoll, & M. A. P. Stephens (Eds.), *The etiology of bulimia nervosa: The individual and familial context* (pp. 59–80). Washington, DC: Hemisphere Publishers.

Levine, M. P., Smolak, L., & Hayden, H. (1994). The relation of sociocultural factors to eating attitudes and behaviors among middle school girls. *Journal of Early Adolescence, 14,* 472–491.

Levine, M. P., Smolak, L., Moodey, A. F., Schuman, M. D., & Hessen, L. D. (1994). Normative developmental challenges and dieting and eating disturbances in middle school girls. *International Journal of Eating Disorders, 15,* 11–20.

Lewinsohn, P. M., Hops, H., Roberts, R. E., Seeley, J. R., & Andrews, J. A. (1993). Adolescent psychopathology: I. Prevalence and incidence of depression and other DSM-III-R disorders in high school students. *Journal of Abnormal Psychology, 102,* 133–144.

Marshall, W. A., & Tanner, J. M. (1969). Variations in the pattern of pubertal changes in girls. *Archives of Disease in Childhood, 44,* 291–303.

Matthews, K. A. (1992). Myths and realities of the menopause. *Psychosomatic Medicine, 54,* 1–9.

Millstein, S. G., Petersen, A. C., & Nightingale, E. O. (Eds.). (1993). *Promoting the health of adolescents.* New York: Oxford University Press.

Minuchin, S., Rosman, B. L., & Baker, L. (1978). *Psychosomatic families: Anorexia nervosa in context.* Cambridge, MA: Harvard University Press.

Montemayor, R., & Hanson, E. (1985). A naturalistic view of conflict between adolescents and their parents and siblings. *Journal of Early Adolescence, 5,* 23–30.

Nader, P. R., Sallis, J. F., Patterson, T. L., Abramson, I. S., & Rupp, J. W. (1989). A family approach to cardiovascular risk reduction: Results from the San Diego Family Heart Project. *Health Education Quarterly, 16,* 229–244.

Neumark-Sztainer, D., Butler, R., & Palti, H. (1995). Eating disturbance among adolescent girls: Evaluation of a school-based primary prevention program. *Journal of Nutrition Education, 27,* 24–31.

Offord, D. R., Kraemer, H. C., Kazdin, A. E., Jensen, P. S., & Harrington, R. (in press). Lowering the burden of suffering from child psychiatric disorder: Trade-offs among clinical, targeted and universal interventions.

Paikoff, R., & Brooks-Gunn, J. (1991). Do parent-child relationships change during puberty? *Psychological Bulletin, 110,* 47–66.

Paikoff, R. L., Brooks-Gunn, J., & Carlton-Ford, S. (1991). Effect of reproductive status changes upon family functioning and well-being of mothers and daughters. *Journal of Early Adolescence, 11,* 201–220.

Paikoff, R. L., Carlton-Ford, S., & Brooks-Gunn, J. (1994). Mother-daughter dyads view the family: Associations between divergent perceptions and daughter well-being. *Journal of Youth and Adolescence, 22,* 473–492.

Paxton, S. J., Wertheim, E. H., Gibbons, K., Szmukler, G. I., Hillier, L., & Petrovich, J. (1991). Body image satisfaction, dieting beliefs, and weight loss behaviors in adolescent girls and boys. *Journal of Youth and Adolescence, 20,* 361–379.

Perry, C. L. (1984). Health promotion at school: Expanding the potential for prevention. *School Psychology Review, 13,* 141–149.

Perry, C. L., Luepker, R. V., Murray, D. M., Hearn, M. D., Halper, A., Dudovitz, B., Maile, M. C., & Smyth, M. (1989). Parent involvement with children's health promotion: A one-year follow-up of the Minnesota Home Team. *Health Education Quarterly, 16,* 171–180

Petersen, A. C., Compas, B. E., Brooks-Gunn, J., Stemmler, M., Ey, S., & Grant, K. (1993). Depression in adolescence. *American Psychologist, 48,* 155–168.

Pike, K. M., & Rodin, J. (1991). Mothers, daughters, and disordered eating. *Journal of Abnormal Psychology, 100,* 198–204.

Resnick, M. D., Bearman, P. S., Blum, R. W., Bauman, K. E., Harris, K. M., & Jones, J. (1997). Protecting adolescents from harm: Findings from the national longitudinal study on adolescent health. *Journal of the American Medical Association, 278,* 823–832.

Rolls, B. J., Federoff, I. C., Guthrie, J. F. (1991). Gender differences in eating behaviors and body weight regulation. *Health Psychology, 10,* 133–142.

Rubin, C., Rubenstein, J. L., Stechler, G., Heere, Halton A., Housman, O., Kasten, L. (1992). Depressive affect in normal adolescents: relationship in life stress, family, and friends. *American Journal of Orthopsychiatry, 62,* 430–441.

Schuman, M., Contento, I., Graber, J. A., & Brooks-Gunn, J. (1994). *Eating disorder prevention in adolescent girls.* Paper presented at the Society for Nutrition Education Conference.

Smetana, J. G. (1988). Adolescents' and parents' conceptions of parental authority. *Child Development, 59,* 321–335.

Smith, S. (1995). *Two-generation programs for families in poverty: A new intervention strategy.* Norwood, NJ: Ablex Publishing Corporation.

Smolak, L., & Levine, M. P. (1994). Toward an empirical basis for primary prevention of eating problems with elementary school children. *Eating Disorders, 2,* 293–307.

Smolak, L., Levine, M. P., & Schermer, F. (1998). Lessons from lessons: An evaluation of an elementary school prevention program. In W. Vanderrycken & G. Noordenbos (Eds.) The prevention of eating disorders (pp. 137–172). London: Athlone.

Steinberg, L. (1990). Autonomy, conflict, and harmony in the family relationship. In S. Feldman & G. Elliott (Eds.), *At the threshold: The developing adolescent* (pp. 255–276). Cambridge, MA: Harvard University Press.

Story, M., Rosenwinkel, K., Himes, J. H., Resnick, M., Harris, L. J., & Blum, R. W. (1991). Demographic and risk factors associated with chronic dieting in adolescents. *American Journal of Diseases in Children, 145,* 994–998.

Striegel-Moore, R. H., & Kearney-Cooke, A. (1994). Exploring parents' attitudes and behaviors about their children's physical appearance. *International Journal of Eating Disorders, 15,* 377–385.

Striegel-Moore, R. H., & Smolak, L. (1996). The role of race in the development of eating disorders. In L. Smolak, M. P. Levine, & R. Striegel-Moore (Eds.), *The developmental psychopathology of eating disorders: Implications for research, prevention, and treatment* (pp. 259–284). Mahwah, NJ: Erlbaum & Associates.

Swarr, A. E., & Richards, M. H. (1996). Longitudinal effects of adolescent girls' pubertal development, perceptions of pubertal timing, and parental relations on eating problems. *Developmental Psychology, 32,* 636–646.

Tyrka, A. R., Graber, J. A., & Brooks-Gunn, J. (in press). A developmental perspective on disordered eating. In M. Lewis & A. J. Sameroff (Eds.), *Handbook of developmental psychopathology* (2nd ed.). New York: Plenum Press.

Vollrath, M., Koch, R., & Angst, J. (1992). Binge eating and weight concerns among young adults: Results from the Zurich cohort study. *British Journal of Psychiatry, 160,* 498–503.

Waller, G., Calam, R., & Slade, P. (1988). Family interaction and eating disorders: Do family members agree? *British Review of Bulimia and Anorexia Nervosa, 3,* 33–40.

Wonderlich, S. (1992). Relationship of family and personality factors in bulimia. In J. H. Crowther, D. L. Tennenbaum, S. E. Hobfoll, & M. A. P. Stephens (Eds.), *The etiology of bulimia nervosa: The individual and familial context* (pp. 103–126). Washington, DC: Hemisphere.

Wonderlich, S. A., & Swift, W. J. (1990). Perceptions of parental relationships in the eating disorders: The relevance of depressed mood. *Journal of Abnormal Psychology, 99,* 353–360.

CHAPTER

Lori M. Irving

A Bolder Model of Prevention: Science, Practice, and Activism

The "Boulder model" of clinical psychology was born in the late 1940s in Boulder, Colorado, at a conference of directors of clinical psychology training programs (American Psychological Association [APA], 1947). At this conference, the Boulder model was defined as an approach to training and professional activity in clinical psychology that places equal emphases on clinical skills *and* research skills. More specifically, according to the Boulder model:

> A clinical psychologist must be trained first and foremost as a *psychologist* in the sense that he (sic) can be expected to have a point of view and a core of knowledge and training in common with all psychologists. This would include an acquaintance with the primary body of psychological theory, research, and methods on which further training and interdisciplinary relationships can be built. (p. 543)

According to the Boulder model, then, clinical psychologists are *clinical scientists,* and should function in accordance with the principles of *any* science; for example, as scientists, clinical psychologists should be committed to efficiency (i.e., parsimony), objectivity, and methodological rigor in describing, explaining, predicting, and manipulating or changing human behavior.

The "Bolder Model" of psychology evolved between 1995 and 1997 at consecutive annual conferences of the organization Eating Disorders Awareness and Prevention (EDAP). The term "Bolder Model" was first used by Michael Levine, EDAP Board Member and President (and an editor of this book), to describe the

I am honored to be included alongside the other contributors to this book—pioneers in the field of eating disorders prevention. I gratefully acknowledge the students and colleagues who provided the instrumental, motivational, and emotional support that made the work described here possible: Arlene Anderson, Susan Berel, Kris Bluett, Zsaneil Bower, Sandy Brown, Linda Brownlee, Ronda Cannon, Cheryl Cody, Julie DuPen, Kristine Graff, Deanna Green, Amalia Icreverzi, Faye Jackson, Michael Levine, Michael Morgan, Niva Piran, and Monica Riddle. This work is supported in part by grants from the Southwest Washington Forward Trust (SWIFT), the Washington Institute for Mental Illness Research and Training (WIMIRT), and the Washington State University Department of Psychology and College of Liberal Arts (the Meyer Fund Faculty Project Award).

work of clinical psychologists simultaneously involved in clinical work, research, and activism. Michael has referred to my work as characteristic of the "Bolder Model"; however, he has not explained exactly why he considers my work "bold" or "bolder." In this chapter, I describe the work that I do and explain how and why it could be considered "bolder." I strive to accomplish this by explaining how my work differs from traditional approaches to clinical science; more specifically, I describe how my work differs from previous, more traditional approaches to eating-disorders prevention.

☐ The Context in Which I Work

A description of my work must begin with a description of the context in which I work. I live in Vancouver, Washington; I work at the Vancouver branch campus of Washington State University (WSU-V). WSU-V is located 180 miles south of Seattle, 10 miles north of Portland, Oregon, and 360 miles west of Pullman, a college town that is the home of the main campus of WSU. My work situation is somewhat unique. WSU-V is a small campus (1200 students) that offers upper-division undergraduate education (i.e., junior and senior level classes) and a handful of Master's programs (e.g., Master of Business Administration, Masters in Teaching, Master of Public Affairs). In addition to working with undergraduates at WSU-V, I am the major advisor for several students in the doctoral program in clinical psychology at WSU Pullman. Because of my distance from the Pullman campus, I communicate with my graduate students through e-mail, interactive television, and, if necessary, by telephone. Because I have no graduate-student assistants at my campus in Vancouver, I rely heavily on undergraduate research assistants (many of whom are "nontraditional," i.e., are older, have families, or have returned to school after an extended absence), high school student research assistants, and members of my local community. My WSU-V research group meets weekly; my WSU Pullman graduate student research group meets biweekly via interactive television. My contact with community members takes place monthly, at meetings of our regional "chapter"[1] of EDAP, Eating Disorders Awareness and Prevention of Southwest Washington (EDAP-SW).

Although those located in a more traditional academic setting (i.e., a department with graduate and four-year undergraduate programs on-site) might consider my situation undesirable or even unacceptable, I have come to view my situation as an asset. Involvement with undergraduate and high school students keeps me energized, motivated, and up-to-date on youth culture and issues that face families today; contact with graduate students keeps me intellectually stimulated and up-to-date on research literature; finally, involvement with the community prevents me from being sequestered in the ivory tower, and up-to-date about the needs of professionals and citizens in my region. I hope to make the advantages of my situation clearer in the following pages.

☐ Overview of the "Bolder" Model

The approach to prevention of eating disorders and weight and shape preoccupation that I have adopted interweaves research, clinical application, and social and political activism. This approach could be considered "Bolder" because it differs in a number of ways from the standard rules and guidelines that govern the science of clinical psychology. More specifically, this "Bolder" approach to clinical science in general, and eating disorders prevention specifically, does the following: (a) targets social and cultural norms and values (i.e., macro-level factors) in addition to characteristics of the individual (micro-level factors), the latter of which are most often targeted by clinical interventions; (b) is informed by the voices of community members (children, adolescents, parents, teachers, and policy makers) in addition to members of the academy; (c) emphasizes research methods that can be used in field settings (e.g., quasi-experiments, surveys, and qualitative data) and does not demand that field settings conform to traditional methodologies (e.g., the randomized clinical trial); (d) emphasizes human resiliency and empowerment rather than deficiency and treatments administered by experts; and (e) includes *in its mission* the growth and/or recovery of the individuals involved in research, practice, and activism.

This Bolder Model may be particularly appropriate for academic psychologists who adopt a feminist perspective, work at an institution with limited resources (e.g., no available research funds, graduate students), or at institutions that emphasize, value, and reward faculty for bridging the historical fissure between the university and the community. It is my hope, however, that this approach appeals to those whose theoretical perspective and work situation fall outside the boundaries of these descriptions.

In the remainder of this chapter, I elaborate upon the five tenets of the Bolder Model; describe research, clinically oriented activity, and activism that I, my students, and my colleagues have completed in accordance with this approach; and discuss briefly the advantages and disadvantages of a Bolder perspective.

Emphasis on Macro-level and Micro-level Change

Few would argue with the contention that eating disorders are multiply determined, the result of social and cultural influences (e.g., family, peers, and media) as well as individual difference factors (e.g., self esteem) (Stice, 1994). However, an emphasis on sociocultural influences is antithetical to traditional research and practice in clinical psychology. Most clinical psychologists are trained to understand behavior and administer "treatment" at the micro-level; that is, to impact problems that originate *within the individual* (e.g., psychopathology is the study of [-*ology*] suffering [*pathos*] of the mind [*psyche*], *not* the study of suffering created by social and cultural influences!). Most clinical psychologists are not trained to understand the impact that macro-level factors (e.g., social norms and values) have on the individual; not surprisingly, clinical scientists know little about how to intervene and assess outcomes at the macro-level. Experts in the field of eating disorders seem to agree that effective preventions must target social and cultural influences (Franko & Orosoan-Weine, 1998; Russell & Beumont, 1995); however, these same experts remain at a loss for how to intervene or measure outcomes at the sociocultural level.

How can we embolden ourselves to move beyond the micro-level focus of traditional clinical science? One strategy is to become familiar with the work of public health professionals and communications researchers who acknowledge and are knowledgeable about the importance and effectiveness of macro-level interventions (e.g., policy changes, public education programs) in altering health behaviors (Eisenberg, 1995). For example, much can be learned from public health campaigns that have been successful at preventing cigarette smoking (e.g., Flynn et al., 1994) and other negative health behaviors; similarly, much can be gained from media education campaigns developed by communications researchers to challenge how we think about advertisements (Austin & Johnson, 1997; Voojis & van der Voort, 1993).

Eating disorders *are* related to sociocultural as well as individual-level variables; therefore, psychologists must step outside of our comfort zone by becoming familiar with literature on how to design and implement interventions and outcome evaluations that include macro-level outcomes. Subsequently I describe work that my research group has done to implement and evaluate the impact of a media literacy program designed to have an impact on micro-level, individual-difference factors *and* macro-level factors that convey societal norms and values (Irving, DuPen, & Berel, 1998).

Listening to the Voices of the Community

Clinicians are encouraged to rely on techniques and corresponding theories of behavior change that have received empirical support (e.g., cognitive-behavioral therapy for bulimia nervosa); approaches that have not been investigated empirically are presumed to be ineffective.[2] This strategy is of little use in the field of eating disorders prevention, where interventions that are theory-based (Carter, Stewart, Dunn, & Fairburn, 1997) or methodologically rigorous (Killen et al., 1993) have met with limited success. Several pessimistic explanations have been given for these null findings, including: (a) we do not know what to prevent because there is insufficient evidence about specific risk factors for eating disorders (Grilo, Devlin, Cachelin, & Yanovski, 1997), (b) eating disorders cannot be prevented with large-scale interventions that have the goal of primary prevention (Killen et al., 1993), and (c) prevention programs inadvertently "do more harm than good" by teaching participants how to be successfully eating disordered (Carter et al., 1997; Grilo et al., 1997; Mann et al., 1997).

I would like to propose a competing explanation for the lack of success of eating-disorders prevention programs: *We have listened to the voice of the academy (i.e., empirically supported techniques and theory) and ignored the voices of the community.* We assume that, because the "best" preventive interventions conducted by the "best" investigators in the field have not been effective, no prevention program can be effective. We have failed to explore what is going on locally, through state and county agencies, in public schools, at university health centers and counseling programs, through interest groups and other grass roots organizations, and so on. In addition to ignoring the voices of our communities, few programs have been developed with the needs of a specific community culture or context in mind (for an exception, see Piran, 1996; see also Chapters 9 and 16).

One risk of ignoring the voices and needs of the community is a failure to fully understand, from the perspective of community members, the problem that we are trying to prevent. A wonderful example of this comes from Nichter and Vuckovic's (1994) work on body image among adolescent girls. Through ethnographic interviews with adolescent girls, Nichter and Vuckovic found out that, to girls, "fat talk" (i.e., discussing body weight) was a way of communicating how girls think and feel about themselves rather than a sign of "pathology." To provide another example, the clinical scientist may view bulimia nervosa as a form of psychopathology associated with affective instability and impulsivity; to the person engaged in binge eating and purging, these same behaviors may be seen as a strategy for dealing with incompatible cultural messages that encourage self-indulgence and, at the same time, demand self-control and restraint (Bordo, 1993). In both of these examples, interpretations of target behavior that reflect an awareness of the meaning of the behavior to community members (i.e., "fat talk" as ritual exchange; bulimia as a coping strategy) might lead to more effective, community-specific prevention or intervention strategies.

Piran's work (1996, in press; see also Chapter 16) at an elite ballet school illustrates the importance of listening to the voices of the community in the context of prevention of eating disorders and related problems. Prior to implementing her systemic intervention, Piran immersed herself in the culture of the elite ballet school in which her 10-year prevention effort took place (Piran, 1996). By the time that Piran began her intervention, she understood the culture; moreover, both students and staff knew that this university professor and "research psychologist" cared about the students as individuals. Consistent with the process in which her research was conducted, in writing about this project, Piran uses the voices of her students to describe and explain what she did, why she did it, and how and why it was successful (Piran, 1996).

Methodological Flexibility

The randomized clinical trial is the "gold standard" in clinical research. Indeed, the text for my graduate course in clinical research methods emphasized experimental methods and discouraged the use of less rigorous strategies and qualitative data (Kazdin, 1980). Despite the popularity of the randomized clinical trial, experimental methods often are not practical in the field, and, when used, may have little application to what typically happens in the "real world" (Seligman, 1995). In addition to being impractical and of limited external validity, controlled experimental methods are difficult to integrate with the Bolder Model goals of targeting macro-level factors and developing or modifying a program based on feedback from community members.

In order to achieve methodological soundness, target macro-level factors, and consider the voices of community members, eating disorders prevention researchers may need to consider more flexible methods—in some cases, methods borrowed from other disciplines. Ethnomethodology, often used by anthropologists, can offer a rich, authentic understanding of community norms and values (Nichter & Nichter, 1991; Nichter & Vuckovic, 1994). Quasi-experimental methods (Irving, DuPen, & Berel, 1998) and other creative methodologies (Piran, in press) can be used to avoid the ethical dilemmas and logistical problems created by random assignment to intervention and control groups. These methods are different than but not inferior to traditional research methods in psychology (i.e., the randomized clinical trial); on the contrary, alternative methods can provide more meaningful results than could be obtained by a controlled experiment.

To illustrate this point, contrast the rigorous methodology of Killen et al. (1993) to the nontraditional, feminist-informed approach used by Piran (1996, in press; see Chapter 16). Killen and colleagues' highly structured, 18-session program had no long-term effect on behavior. In contrast, Piran's less controlled, feminist-informed approach was associated with a linear decrease, over a 10-year period, in eating disordered behavior and the attitudes that underlie that behavior. This comparison demonstrates that methodological control does not always correspond to better outcomes; furthermore, this example demonstrates the power of the first two tenets of a Bolder approach: namely, that programs that intervene at the macro-level (in this case, at the level of the school "culture") and develop through the process of listening and responding to the voices of a specific community may be particularly effective.

Human Resiliency

Clinical training focuses on human vulnerability, or "illness" (as defined by the Diagnostic and Statistical Manual; American Psychiatric Association, 1994); clinical psychologists receive little instruction about resiliency, or wellness.[3] This focus on pathology can be seen in research on eating disorders prevention. According to a recent, small survey of college prevention programs ($n = 18$ programs; Mann et al., 1997), university-based programs often focus on information about clinical eating disorders rather than teaching skills to prevent the development of disturbed eating practices[4]; more specifically, most programs provide information about symptoms (89%), consequences (83%), and treatment (56%) of clinical eating disorders; a minority of programs teach skills such as how to cope with poor body image (33%), stress reduction (11%), or how to think critically about cultural messages (6%). Results of this survey indicate that, at many college campuses, prevention means teaching about eating disorder pathology. One can easily imagine the toxic consequences of a focus on pathology; a young person concerned about her weight may view compensatory behaviors (e.g., self-induced vomiting, laxative use) as a way to cope with pressures to be thin. Such prevention programs may indeed do more "harm than good" (Carter et al., 1997).

Rather than focus on teaching about signs and symptoms of eating disorders (i.e., pathology), greater emphasis must be placed on what many consider to be the most important ingredients in prevention: empowering individuals, encouraging them to value themselves, and teaching them to derive power and control from things other than weight and appearance.

Recovery and Growth

For me, a Bolder approach to preventing eating disorders includes *as part of its mission* the growth and recovery of those involved with the work. In other words, the process of doing the work *in and of itself* promotes recovery or growth in those who are involved in efforts to prevent eating disorders. The work may promote or help to sustain recovery for those who have experienced an eating disorder; among those who have not had an eating disorder, the work promotes increased awareness of how personal actions and beliefs support or contribute to a cultural context that encourages eating disorders.

My research, clinical work, and activism are motivated in part by my own experience with and recovery from an eating disorder.[5] In addition, a number of students and community members have gained support for their recovery through the process of working with me on research, clinical, and activism activities. Although I did not anticipate or hypothesize that recovery would be a consequence of participating in these activities, my experience with many girls and women has led me to include growth and recovery as important, overt goals of the work that I do. Reflecting on this, it seems fitting that those who are involved in developing and evaluating programs that empower others would themselves be empowered as a function of being part of such programs. In my case, then, a Bolder approach to the prevention of eating disorders and related problems has come to include taking an interest in the health, well-being, and, in some cases, the recovery of those who contribute to the work.

☐ The Bolder Model in Action: Washington State University—Vancouver

In the remainder of this chapter, I describe research, clinical, and activism activities undertaken in my capacity as a faculty member in the Department of Psychology at WSU-V and as the Coordinator of EDAP-SW. I encourage the reader to note the overlap in my roles as university professor and EDAP-SW coordinator; also of note is that my three "domains" of work (research, clinical, and activism activities) benefit and inform one another and, often, operate together.

Research

I maintain two research groups; one for graduate students, at the Pullman campus of WSU; and one for undergraduate and high school student research assistants, at WSU-V. Research group is a place where new responsibilities are assigned, progress on existing responsibilities and projects is discussed, and problems and barriers to goals are worked through and overcome. An equally important, complementary mission of these groups is to provide *support* for all members of the group. Research group is a place where spirits are lifted, motivation established or rekindled, and professional and personal accomplishments celebrated (e.g., papers accepted; theses defended; birthdays, pregnancy, and engagements celebrated). Because I am located on a campus with a small number of colleagues in my area, *and* because of my feminist foundation, my students are my collaborators as well as my advisees (Irving, Nelson, Hanke, & Gravel, 1996). I treat students with personal and professional respect; in addition, I have high expectations accompanied by an understanding of and willingness to work through insecurity and self doubt. It is in this context of high expectations, collaboration, and support that we conduct our work.

Each year, the research group is involved in three or four research projects. Some of these are theses or dissertations, others are projects developed and completed by the group. Here, I describe a "group" project, the development and evaluation of a peer-led media-literacy program to provide high school females with tools for resisting media pressures to conform to the current, thin standard of beauty (Irving, Dupen, & Berel, 1998). I present this work because it epitomizes the collaborative spirit of the research group and illustrates the tenets of the Bolder approach.

This project evolved out of my experience—in the classroom—with the power of media literacy. More specifically, the project was borne of my experience with Jean Kilbourne's (1987) powerful and provocative film, *Still Killing Us Softly*. This film graphically illustrates how advertisers portray women and communicate that in order to be valued, women should be young, thin, beautiful, white, child-like but sexually mature, virginal but sexually experienced; the film also points out how advertisers frequently use violence against women by men as a strategy for selling a product. I have shown this film many times; without exception, it elicits a strong, emotional response and increased interest in evaluating media critically. Students have borrowed the film to show it to a spouse, a partner, or their children. More impressive to me (as a clinical psychologist) is that, in some cases, the film has led to enduring behavior change. For example, after watching the film, one student in her 40s realized that she had begun to dye her hair because of her shame about looking "old." The film made her realize that this shame was founded in values conveyed through media and other cultural messengers. Stunned and angered by this realization, this student stopped dyeing her hair. To this day, her head is full of the silvery gray distinction that she has earned with age.

My experience with this film provided anecdotal evidence that, regardless of their age, people can be taught to think critically about the media, and that thinking critically about media can change behavior. In 1998, graduate student Susan Berel and I reviewed literature from the field of communications that supported this and suggested that consumers are not passive "casualties" of media, but active participants in the process of selecting and responding to the media that we view (Berel & Irving, 1998). This reading made us wonder what would happen if individuals were encouraged to think critically about appearance related media, to reject its unrealistic standards, and to become part of action to protest offensive and unrealistic images. Perhaps active, critical consumers of appearance-related media would be less inclined to internalize unrealistic beauty standards, become dissatisfied with their bodies, and, ultimately develop eating disorders. Perhaps, in successive generations, media literacy education could have a "ripple effect"; adolescents who resist or subvert media messages might become parents (or educators, coaches, or business people) who promote healthy eating practices in their own daughters (or students, athletes, or consumers) and encourage young people to value themselves for who they are and how they act rather than what they look like (Berel & Irving, 1998).

Media literacy originated in the field of communications and has been used successfully in changing children's attitudes about the importance of a variety of media. For example, media literacy programs have been successful at reducing children's approval of violence shown on television (Voojis & van der Voort, 1993) and decreasing children's intentions to drink alcohol (Austin & Johnson, 1997).

Although it was developed and studied primarily by communications researchers, media literacy's importance has been discussed by those interested in preventing body dissatisfaction and eating disorders (Kilbourne, 1994; Levine & Smolak, 1996; Shisslak & Crago, 1994; see also Chapter 6). Concern has been raised, however, that critical thinking about appearance-related media may not result in greater body satisfaction; that is, teaching individuals to be more critical of *external* images may not translate into greater acceptance of diverse body shapes and of one's own body, in particular. Because of this concern, it has been suggested that programs to promote critical thinking about appearance-related media would benefit from adopting a feminist approach, one that goes beyond raising consciousness about media by *empowering* participants to take action and reject cultural norms on a personal and political level (Berel & Irving, 1998; Steiner-Adair, 1994) and challenging participants to derive self-worth from accomplishments other than conformity to attractiveness norms (Srebnik & Saltzberg, 1994).

During the 1996–97 school year, my research group put these thoughts into action; we completed a peer-led media literacy program to teach high-school females to be more critical consumers of appearance-related media (Irving, DuPen & Berel, 1998). (During this same year, graduate student Susan Berel developed a similar program for use with college females at WSU in Pullman.) The program incorporated techniques from communications research (Austin & Johnson, 1997) and feminist therapy (Brown, 1994; Srebnik & Saltzberg, 1994).

The effectiveness of the program was determined by comparing the intervention group (media literacy) to a no-intervention control group on measures of critical thinking about media and satisfaction with appearance. Compared with those students in the control group, female students who participated in the media-literacy program were expected to demonstrate greater ability to think critically about media, as indicated by: (a) less internalization or acceptance of the thin standard of beauty; (b) less perceived realism of media images; (c) less reported desire to look like media images; and (d) fewer positive expectations of looking like a media image. We were dubious about the ability of the intervention to impact body dissatisfaction; however, measures were included to assess whether, compared with the control group, students who participated in the media literacy program would report more positive feelings about their body and less anxiety about their physical appearance.

Participants were 41 female high school students enrolled in sophomore English courses. Participants were 15 to 16 years of age ($M = 15.3$, $SD = .48$) and ethnically homogenous (80% White), body mass index (BMI) scores for the sample ranged from 16.8 to 31.4. Participants were not compensated for their time; all participants complied with informed consent procedures and were debriefed regarding the purpose of the study.

Dependent measures included: the body dissatisfaction scale of the Eating Disorders Inventory (Garner, 1991), worded as a state measure to assess dissatisfaction with one's body *"right now, at the present time"*; the weight subscale of the Physical Appearance State/Trait Anxiety Scale (state version; Reed, Thompson, Brannick, & Sacco, 1991), to assess current anxiety about physical appearance, particularly attributes associated with weight; the internalization subscale of the Social Attitudes Toward Appearance Scale (Heinberg, Thompson, & Stormer, 1995), to assess *internalization* of the thin ideal of beauty (e.g., "Photographs of thin women make me wish that I were thin"); and the Media Attitudes Questionnaire (Irving, Dupen & Berel, 1998), to assess *perceived realism* of media images (e.g., "Real women look like models in ads"), desirability of looking like individuals portrayed in media (e.g., "I would like to have a body like the models in ads"), and *positive expectancies* associated with being thin (e.g., "Being thin makes you happier").

The study took place at a high school in Vancouver, Washington. It was not feasible to administer a pretest or randomly assign students to groups; therefore, a quasi-experimental, post-test only design was used to evaluate the impact of the media literacy program on dependent measures. Two sophomore English classes participated in the study; one served as the experimental (media literacy) group, the other served as the control group. In the control group, female students ($n = 17$) were excused from their English class to complete the survey. The survey took approximately 20 minutes to complete and was administered in the school cafeteria.

Twenty-four female sophomores participated in the peer-led media-literacy program. The group was led by Julie DuPen, a junior at the high school who completed this project as part of requirements for her Honors' Biology and Psychology classes. Students in the experimental group were excused from English class and taken to another classroom where they sat in a circle. The group leader provided a brief introduction to the study, followed by a short discussion regarding the standard of beauty portrayed in the media. Following this, a 15-minute excerpt was shown from *Slim Hopes: Advertising and the obsession with thinness*, a film by Jean Kilbourne (1995). The 15-minute excerpt revealed tricks used by the media to make fashion models look flawless and slender, including how airbrushing is used to transform women's bodies to the waif look that is so popular today. After the video, participants discussed their reactions and participated in a loosely structured discussion regarding the realism of media images, how individuals think and behave in ways that reinforce media images, what individuals can do personally and politically to challenge unrealistic images, and the importance of basing self esteem on factors other than physical appearance. The guided discussion included specific tools for evaluating critically and "de-construct" media images of women. After completing this discussion, the experimental group completed the same survey that was completed by the control group.

After determining that the groups were comparable on age, ethnicity, and BMI, t-tests were used to compare the experimental and control groups on all dependent measures (see Table 1). Compared to the no-intervention control group, the group that participated in the media literacy intervention was more likely to report attitudes consistent with critical media viewing. More specifically, the media literacy group reported less internalization or acceptance of the thin standard of beauty and less perceived realism of media images. There were no group differences in awareness of the standard of beauty portrayed in media, desirability of looking like a media image, and positive expectations associated with being thin; likewise, there were no group differences in body dissatisfaction and anxiety about weight-related appearance.

Pearson correlations between dependent measures were computed; of particular interest were correlations between the two outcome measures that were influenced by the media literacy intervention (internalization and realism) and other dependent measures. Greater internalization of the thin beauty standard was significantly associated with a constellation of attitudes that are common in those who report disturbed eating practices (all $ps < .05$). More specifically, greater internalization of the thin standard of beauty was associated with greater body dissatisfaction ($r = .54$) and anxiety about weight-related appear-

TABLE 1. Differences on dependent measures for control and experimental groups

Dependent Measure	Control Group M (SD) n = 17	Experimental Group M (SD) n = 24	t-Value[a]	p
EDI-BD	31.24 (8.99)	29.76 (10.37)	< 1	.65
PASTAS-W	14.82 (8.37)	11.08 (8.85)	1.38	.18
PANAS-PA	26.20 (6.78)	23.00 (9.57)	1.17	.25
PANAS-NA	21.81 (10.40)	17.24 (8.66)	1.42	.17
SATAQ-Aware	21.94 (3.97)	21.46 (5.52)	< 1	.75
SATAQ-Internal	28.38 (8.02)	22.08 (10.01)	2.20	.03
MAQ-Realism	14.31 (4.22)	9.79 (3.82)	3.44	.001
MAQ-Desirability	25.29 (.94)	23.15 (10.62)	< 1	.53
MAQ-Expectations	12.71 (6.72)	12.71 (4.87)	< 1	.99

Note. EDI-BD = Eating Disorders Inventory, Body Dissatisfaction Subscale; PANAS-PA = Positive and Negative Affect Scale, Positive Affect; PANAS-NA = Positive and Negative Affect Scale, Negative Affect; SATAQ = Sociocultural Attitudes Toward Appearance Questionnaire; MAQ = Media Attitudes Questionnaire.
[a]Because of missing data, degrees of freedom range from 34 to 39.

ance ($r = .61$), greater awareness of the thinness standard ($r = .46$), greater desirability of looking like a media image ($r = .81$), and more positive expectancies associated with being thin ($r = .61$). Realism was associated with few other dependent measures; greater perceived realism was correlated with greater desirability of looking like a media image ($r = .40$). Internalization and perceived realism were not related ($r = .25$, *ns*).

The program appeared to affect those attitudes that, upon reflection, could be considered the most likely to change as a result of a brief intervention focused on media literacy. It is understandable that education and awareness regarding tricks used to create "flawless" female bodies (e.g., computer "morphing" of models' bodies) would lead to reductions in the perceived realism of such images. Similarly, critical discussion regarding media images may make students more conscious and critical of how they internalize and compare themselves with these unrealistic images (e.g., "I would like to look like the models in magazines," "I tend to compare my body to people in magazines and on TV"). Participants were encouraged to challenge media images by asking critical questions such as: "Is this real?" "Is this message right?" and "How does my own thinking and/or behavior reinforce the message portrayed in the media?" Participants' answers to these questions might reduce the perceived realism of media and lessen their tendency to use media images as a standard against which to compare themselves.

Why were group differences not found on desirability of looking like a model, positive expectations of thinness, and body dissatisfaction? The intervention taught participants that media images are unrealistic, even false, and that individuals evaluate their own worth in comparison to these false images. These important lessons do not change the reality that, in this culture at this time, individuals are evaluated and rewarded on the basis of these standards, regardless of whether they are honest or representative of the public. A longer-term, more extensive intervention, or an intervention that directly teaches participants how to act to challenge norms promulgated by media (e.g., letter-writing campaigns in response to offensive ads, participation in Eating Disorders Awareness Week activities), may be needed to make looking like a model less desirable.

We were skeptical about the program's ability to affect body satisfaction and anxiety about body weight; therefore, we were not surprised when group differences on these variables were not found. By the time that girls in this culture reach adolescence, they know that, for women, thinness is equated with attractiveness (i.e., the "thinness schema," Smolak & Levine, 1994). Therefore, adolescent females already are engaged in the process of evaluating and berating their own body in comparison to media images. It is doubtful that a brief intervention could change beliefs that have evolved as a result of years of messages provided by media, family, and peers.

Although we were pleased by certain results of this brief intervention, we were not able to evaluate the longer-term impact of the intervention on dependent measures; in addition, we did not include measures of eating practices (e.g., dietary restriction, symptoms of eating disorders), behaviors related to media (e.g., reading fashion magazines), and interest in engaging in media activism. We also were interested about the impact of the program if administered in a coeducational setting. To address these questions and limitations, we are replicating this study; more specifically, we have added the following to the design: (a) a pretest/post-test design with a long term follow-up; (b) pretest and follow-up measures of eating behaviors and media viewing practices; (c) a larger sample; (d) same-sex and coeducational groups; and (e) objective measures of participants' willingness to participate in media activism, and events to promote body esteem (i.e., yoga; meditation; poetry readings held during Everybody, Every Body Week, a week-long series of events developed for the purposes of this project by high school students Julie DuPen and Amalia Icreverzi).

Practice: Clinical Education and Training

I am a licensed clinical psychologist and an advisor for students in the doctoral program in clinical psychology at WSU-Pullman; however, I do not have a clinical practice, nor do I provide clinical supervision to graduate students in training to become psychologists. Although I am not actively engaged in work as a therapist, given my (privileged) position as a clinical research psychologist who studies eating disorders, I believe that I have a duty to assist those working in the field of eating disorders treatment to stay informed about innovations in treatment and prevention. I have a similar duty to see that individuals and families seeking help for an eating-related problem have access to accurate information about resources available in their own community. For all of these reasons, I have become heavily involved in providing education and information regarding eating disorders and their prevention to professionals and laypersons in my community. My entry into these activities was more accidental than planned; however, becoming involved in this work has opened doors that have made it easier for me to do my research; in addition, this work has made me aware of resources that have ignited my interest in, and efforts at activism.

I have worked at WSU-V since 1993. Upon taking the position, I often was sought out as a source of referrals for eating disorders treatment. Working in a university setting, I was fairly isolated and knew little about resources in my area. As I searched for resources in response to referral requests, I learned that there were few eating disorders resources available in my community. In 1995, out of my desire to locate or create resources for people needing help with an eating problem, I became a member of, and a Coordinator for EDAP in Southwest Washington (we now call ourselves EDAP-SW). A colleague and I established an organizing committee to develop educational and training opportunities and to create resources in our area. The organizing committee was multidisciplinary and diverse, and included a school nurse, a dietitian, a staff member from the Washington State health district, and college students—some of whom were in recovery from an eating disorder.

In that first year (1995–96), EDAP-SW established a free peer-support group (in cooperation with Anorexia Nervosa and Associated Disorders [ANAD]) and organized educational events in recognition of Eating Disorders Awareness Week (EDAW). EDAW events included a low cost, half-day workshop for professionals and a free evening presentation for community members. The EDAW half-day workshop, held in the midst of a torrential northwestern storm, drew 25 nurses, dietitians, and counselors; the community presentation drew 30 citizens. Unsure whether the low turnout was due to the weather or a lack of interest, we repeated our efforts the following year. In 1996–97, attendance at our EDAW events quadrupled; our 1997 all-day workshop drew over 100 nurses, dietitians, and counselors from Vancouver and Portland; and the community presentation drew over 100 people. During that year, we also compiled a list of professionals in the Southwest Washington area (including Portland, Oregon) trained to work with eating disorders and related problems. In only its second year, EDAP-SW had become a visible, respected resource in our region; in spring of 1997, the Vancouver newspaper, *The Columbian,* featured speakers from the 1997 EDAP-SW workshop in a four-part series on eating disorders and related problems (Allen, 1997a,b,c; Sisson, 1997). This four-part series led to the growth of our support group (we recently started a support group for parents), increased interaction with professionals in our community, and a greater number of requests for educational materials and referral information.

The EDAP-SW organizing committee now includes over 20 members, including school nurses, psychiatric nurses, school counselors, therapists, social workers, dietitians, a mental health administrator, a member of our local substance-abuse advisory board, a member of a local puppeteer troupe, and graduate, undergraduate, and high-school students. A number of these individuals are involved because they are in recovery or are close to someone in recovery from an eating disorder. The 1997–98 EDAW workshop attracted 155 professionals, and our community presentation drew 125 community members.

My involvement with EDAP has strengthened my commitment to a Bolder perspective to my work. Through EDAP, I have met academicians (e.g., Michael Levine, Niva Piran), clinicians, administrators, and laypersons locally and across the United States and Canada who are engaged in creative, impactful prevention interventions. Without EDAP, I might believe what others have said about eating disorders prevention being impossible, impractical, or doing "more harm than good" (Carter et al., 1997). Because of the annual EDAP conferences and network of Coordinators, I meet and dialogue with individuals who are engaged in prevention programs in their communities and in their schools. I am aware of scores of programs that are *not* represented by published studies. At the same time, because of my training as a research psychologist, I bring to EDAP my skills at designing outcome evaluations for some of the creative prevention programs being developed and implemented by others across the country (Irving, 1997).

Activism

My commitment to activism grew out of my interest in media literacy, and awareness of the importance of informing people of what they can do with the awareness, energy, and emotions (often anger) that media literacy can elicit. My commitment to activism also is born of a variety of personal and academic influences; I hold strong feminist beliefs and teach in the area of feminist psychology; in addition, for the past 7 years, I have studied the benefits of a "hopeful" dispositional style (Irving et al., in press; Irving, Snyder, & Crowson, 1998; Irving et al., 1997; Snyder, Irving, & Anderson, 1991) and am a strong advocate of goal-oriented thinking—teaching people to find and implement strategies for solving problems and overcome obstacles. Activism fits with my feminist perspective and respect for hopeful persistence in pursuit of goals. Activism also sustains my own process of recovery by redirecting my "self-critical" voice (my "eating disorder" voice) into anger about advertisements or social policies that promote self-criticism and inhibit wellness; activism reminds me of how far I have come and challenges me to be a role model for students, colleagues, and community members; finally, activism motivates me to help create a culture that promotes acceptance of oneself and diversity in general and prevents girls and women from feeling ashamed of who they are and what they look like. For all of these reasons, activism has become integral to my work in the area of eating disorders. Below I demonstrate how empowering activism can be by describing EDAP-SW's recent successful battle to stop a highly offensive national ad campaign demonstrate, how empowering activism can be.

Media Activism

Because WSU-V is a small campus, many faculty and staff members know that my research involves exploring social and cultural factors that contribute to preoccupation with body weight and shape. One morning in October of 1997, I was visited by Doug Baker, a professor in the Business department. Doug had in his hand a copy of *React for Teens: The News Magazine that Raises Voices,* a magazine that appears in each Tuesday's edition of *The Oregonian,* the Portland, Oregon, newspaper. Doug, father of young daughters, was extremely upset about an advertisement for Fetish cologne that had appeared in *React* on this particular day. In the advertisement, a thin, jaundiced-appearing adolescent woman wearing an orange bikini top and heavy, pink eye make-up has a vial of Fetish cologne clipped to the center of her bikini top. Text written across her chest reads, "Fetish #16: Apply generously to your neck so he can smell the scent as you shake your head 'no.'" The advertisement's promotion of a "heroin-chic" look and its false, dangerous message that girls and women mean "yes" when they say "no" were utterly appalling. Doug asked whether, given my area of research and my community involvement, there was something that I could or would do about this.

I agreed with Doug that the advertisement was offensive, but I was reticent to take the time to write a letter to the editor or advertiser. I was about to say, "I'm sorry but I can't, I'm extremely busy, I'm up for tenure next year" (tenure is an excuse honored by all academics), when I remembered that the EDAP-SW organizing committee was meeting that night. I told Doug that I would bring it up at the meeting. Speaking with other committee members confirmed my initial impression of the advertisement and fueled my motivation to do something. Consequently, we composed a letter, and 12 people (including Doug) signed it. We sent the letter to *The Oregonian* and to Dana Perfumes, the company that makes Fetish. There was no response; consequently we sent the letter again.

After the second letter, we received good news from the *The Oregonian*. The president of the newspaper called me personally to inform me that he had received my letters and forwarded them to the publishers of *React*. After our second letter, *React* decided to pull the advertisement entirely. In my e-mail note to all those who had signed the letter, I wrote, "I cannot tell you how good it felt to get this call. This makes all of our hard work worthwhile. A group of committed people truly CAN make a difference. What an awesome experience. Thanks to all of you for being a source of inspiration and collective action! P.S. Keep us posted about future sightings of the 'Fetish' ad!"

I felt triumphant. Victorious. We had fought Goliath, and we had won! Naturally, I thought that the entire episode was over. We had succeeded—achieved our goal; it was time to rest on our laurels—at least, that is what I thought. Two days later, I received an e-mail message from a student: "On Friday, right after I talked to you about the Fetish ad, I went to a pharmacy in Salmon Creek and guess what I saw? It was a Fetish perfume display in the cosmetic department. The advertisement looked exactly like the *The Oregonian* ad! What might I do to encourage the store manager to reconsider displaying the ad? Thought you might be interested!"

I was discouraged, but I remained energized by our previous success. In response to this Fetish sighting, we sent a letter to the owners of the pharmacy, and they immediately honored our request. Although I was grateful for their prompt response, this "sighting" of the advertisement left me discouraged: This was a *national* campaign that, despite our efforts locally, would continue across the country until it ran its course, unless, of course, Dana Perfumes would really listen to our letters. I was outwardly confident but inwardly doubtful that this was possible. After all, we were a local organization; how much legitimate power did we wield?

In November (remember, this began in early October), I received a call that communicated wonderful news. I described this call to other supporters in an e-mail message. In the message, I stated that I received

a call from the General Manager of Dana Perfumes, the producer of "Fetish" perfume and ads. The General Manager called me in response to a letter that we wrote to the General Manager of [name deleted] pharmacy after a student of mine spotted a "Fetish" display (complete with the infamous photo and text) in their store. The pharmacy forwarded my letter to the West Coast Division of Dana Perfumes. The West Coast Division forwarded it to the General Manager, who, in turn, called me tonight. Minutes after our conversation ended, the pharmacy called me to follow-up. All calls were cordial, both Dana Perfumes and the pharmacy wanted to do all they could to assure me that my concerns were taken seriously (Dana will send me a letter to this effect). Dana Perfumes has agreed to pull the ad. Entirely. Forever. Why? According to the General Manager, Dana is the #2 fragrance company in the country and they "cannot afford" this type of negative or bad publicity. Victory! I felt incredibly empowered and relieved. —Empoweredly yours, Lori

This victory was made sweeter by the calls and letters that I received congratulating us on our efforts to discontinue the "Fetish" campaign. One of my favorites was sent to me indirectly, through Michael Levine, whom I had been updating about our progress on a regular basis. (Michael, in turn, had been forwarding my letters to others around the country who are interested in media activism.)

Michael,
    Thanks for forwarding the correspondence from Lori Irving re: the Fetish ad. I am fascinated with this chain of events, and thrilled to see that consumer outcry has resulted in this ad being pulled. That in itself is an undeniable message to the Fetish company and its ad agency, in spite of the fact that they don't get "the big picture." Speaking of which, I did a program on campus this week on "Slim Hopes; Advertising and the Obsession with Thinness" using Jean Kilbourne's video. The audience was a group of about 25 women and 5 men. For the most part, most of these students didn't get it either, and discussion played out the feminist perspectives of the video with the men taking the position of "this is crap, and if the women do stupid things like diet and vomit then there is something wrong with them." (Has compassion become old fashioned I wondered?) While the women were basically unwilling to challenge the men and appear what?; bad, bitchy, smart, powerful, unfeminine? At any rate, I eventually projected a slide of the Fetish ad and told them the story of finding this in my 15 year old daughter's *Seventeen* magazine. The slide was such a powerful and clear example of the advertising industry's deliberate use of very dangerous messages and images that the students began to "get it." Perhaps I should thank the Fetish folks for such a helpful tool in prevention programming. Two steps forward in a journey of many, many steps!
    Thanks again Michael and Lori. Astoundedly Yours,—

Astounding, indeed! Excited about all that had happened, I called our local paper, *The Columbian*, to see if they would be interested in covering the story in the newspaper. Within the week, a reporter was out to interview me; he also interviewed Ronda Cannon, one of my research assistants and a co-signer of the letter, and the general manager of Dana Perfumes. I was surprised and delighted when this story made the front page of the newspaper (Vogt, 1997; Figure 1). I am more convinced than ever that activism works, and that consumers and citizens wield more power than they assume. I also am convinced that, had it not been for my involvement with EDAP-SW, I would not have had the motivation or courage to write the letter. In our work with high school and college students, we are trying to teach them not only how to be critical thinkers about media, but also how to organize their energies to conduct similar media activism campaigns on their campuses and in their day-to-day lives.

The Columbian

SERVING CLARK COUNTY, WASHINGTON ■ THURSDAY, DEC. 4, 1997

DAVE OLSON/The Columbian

Sweet smell of success: *Assistant psychology professor Lori Irving and Ronda Cannon are members of Eating Disorders Awareness and Prevention, which persuaded a perfume company to stop a national ad campaign.*

ON THE SCENT

Group that fights eating disorders takes aim at Fetish perfume ad

By TOM VOGT
Columbian staff writer

A local group has persuaded the country's second-largest perfume company to halt a national advertising campaign.

Lori Irving said the ads for "Fetish" fragrance sent a couple of wrong messages to girls.

Officials with the manufacturer, Dana Perfumes, said it does not believe the advertising campaign was in poor taste. However, the company with headquarters in Stamford, Conn. is not in the business of offending the public, Lynne Myers, general manager, said.

The advertisement featured a slender teen-age model with red-ringed eyes and a perfume flask clipped to her orange bikini top; the ad included this tip for using "Fetish:"

"Apply generously to your neck so he can smell the scent as you shake your head 'no.'"

Irving, assistant professor of psychology at Washington State University at Vancouver, led the protest. In addition to teaching several psychology courses, Irving does extensive research in the field of eating disorders and how girls develop attitudes toward their bodies.

Irving also is coordinator of Eating Disorders and Prevention of Southwest Washington.

Irving said the advertisement was not

unusual, as far as the standards of the industry go. However, "It was in a magazine targeting adolescents who are trying to figure out who they are," Irving said. "It's a very vulnerable time."

And that's not just something Irving learned by analyzing data. Irving said she suffered through a four-year battle with anorexia, starting when she was 15.

"It was hell. They were the worst years of my life," she said. "I see something like this, and it really upsets me."

Irving said she is not trying to foster a generation of pudgy teens.

"Overweight is a risk factor for a lot of problems. I don't deny that's a problem," Irving said.

But the "Fetish" concept goes too far the other way, she said.

"Ads like this promote the idea that she has power because she is attractive," Irving said. "I want to help girls find ways to feel powerful other than appearance."

Ronda Cannon, a senior at WSU Vancouver and member of the eating-disorder prevention group, was surprised at how early the focus on waistline starts.

"I have a son in elementary school and when I help out at school, I hear kids 5 and 6 — mostly girls — talk about how fat they are," Cannon said.

The "shake your head 'no'" message also bothered Irving. It implies that any girl who wants to look attractive — and smell

nice — should expect to fend off sexual advances. And if the girl wants to say "no," there are better ways than shaking her head, Irving said.

Dana Perfumes placed the ads in several national magazines geared toward teen-age girls. It came to Irving's attention through Doug Baker, professor of management systems at WSU Vancouver and father of two pre-teen girls. He saw the ad in a weekly magazine published by Parade Publications

"It was open on the table and I was stunned by it," Baker said. "I knew of Lori's work with eating disorders, and she picked it up and ran with it."

Ironically, the magazine's cover story was about an eating disorder, bulimia.

Irving said the model in the ad represented a style known as "heroin chic."

"That gaunt look is not unlike what heroin addicts look like when they are seriously into their addiction," Irving said.

FETISH/ *please see A7*

> **"I'd like people to know that they wield more power than they assume. ... The reason ads like this continue is that people don't speak out."**
> LORI IRVING

FIGURE 1. *The Columbian* story on the campaign against "Fetish."

At the time of writing this chapter, EDAP-SW is involved in writing letters in support of legislation recently introduced in the Washington State Senate that would mandate third-party payors to reimburse mental health care provided as part of eating disorders treatment. Currently, the Bill is in "sunrise," under study for approximately one year. I assure you that EDAP-SW will have something to say before that bill hits "sunset."

☐ Advantages and Disadvantages of a "Bolder" Approach

Merriam Webster's 1973 dictionary defines *bold* as (among other things) "adventurous; daring" (p. 124). Not surprisingly, there are dangers and rewards associated with adopting a bolder approach. For example, a Bolder approach may not be respected by those who rest comfortably with, and strive to be accepted by, "mainstream" psychological science. To those who believe in the sanctity of objectivity and the experimental method, the Bolder approach might seem reckless or undisciplined. A Bolder approach may be difficult to follow or poorly received in a traditional academic department. Perhaps this is why many faculty members do not do the research that they *really* want to do until they have tenure, or job security. Last but not least, a Bolder approach can involve a heavy commitment in time and energy—both intellectual and emotional.

All of this is true. For me, however, the advantages of a Bolder approach outweigh the disadvantages. Following my heart and mind to a Bolder approach has been highly rewarding, both personally and professionally. In the past several years, I have been able to weave together my personal and professional goals with my philosophical and political beliefs. It has been a coming home of sorts, a return to or movement toward "genuineness" (Rogers, 1961). Adopting a Bolder approach also has led me to ask more interesting questions and develop more appropriate methods for coming up with meaningful answers; finally, and importantly, the Bolder approach has allowed me to experience personally the implications of the work that I do. What could be more rewarding than that?

☐ References

Allen, A. (1997a, April 27). Cutting a deal with thinness: Ridgefield High teen finds path to recovery afterwar with anorexia nervosa. *The Columbian,* A1, A3.

Allen, A. (1997b, April 29). Conquering fears: Dietitians help people with eating disorders get their lives back. *The Columbian,* Food, 1, 2.

Allen, A. (1997c, May 6). A quest for understanding: Psychologist studies how perceptions of beauty and weight affect our eating habits. *The Columbian,* Food, 1, 2.

American Psychiatric Association (1994). *Diagnostic and statistical manual of mental disorders* (4th ed.). Washington, DC: Author.

American Psychological Association (1947). Recommended graduate training programs in clinical psychology. *American Psychologist, 2,* 539–558.

Austin, E. W., & Johnson, K. K. (1997). Effects of general and alcohol-specific media literacy training on children's decision making about alcohol. *Journal of Health Communication, 2,* 17–42.

Berel, S., & Irving, L. M. (1998). Media and disturbed eating: An analysis of media influence and implications for prevention. *Journal of Primary Prevention, 18,* 415–430.

Bordo, S. (1993). *Unbearable weight: Feminism, western culture, and the body.* Berkeley: University of California Press.

Brown, L. S. (1994). *Subversive dialogues: Theory in feminist therapy.* New York: Basic Books.

Carter, J. C., Stewart, D. A., Dunn, V. J., & Fairburn, C. G. (1997). Primary prevention of eating disorders: Might it do more harm than good? *International Journal of Eating Disorders, 22,* 167–172.

Eisenberg, L. (1995). Social policy and the reality of prevention. In B. Raphael & G. D. Burrows (Eds.), *Handbook of studies on preventive psychiatry* (pp. 31–50). New York: Elsevier Science.

Flynn, B. S., Worden, J. K., Secker-Walker, R. H., Pirie, P. L., Badger, G. L., Carpenter, J. H., & Geller, B. M. (1994). Mass media and school interventions for cigarette smoking: Effects 2 years after completion. *American Journal of Public Health, 84,* 1148–1150.

Franko, D. L., & Orososan-Weine, P. (1998). The prevention of eating disorders: Empirical, methodological, and conceptual considerations. *Clinical Psychology: Science and Practice.*

Garner, D. M. (1991). *Eating Disorder Inventory-2: Professional manual.* Odessa, FL: Psychological Assessment Resources.

Grilo, C. M., Devlin, M. J., Cachelin, F. M., & Yanovski, S. Z. (1997). Workshop Report: Report on the National Institutes of Health (NIH) workshop on the development of research priorities in eating disorders. *Psychopharmacology Bulletin, 33,* 321–333.

Heinberg, L. J., Thompson, J. K., & Stormer, S. (1995). Development and validation of the sociocultural attitudes towards appearance questionnaire. *International Journal of Eating Disorders, 17,* 81–89.

Irving, L. (1997, Winter). Research: A tool to prove that EDAP makes a difference. *EDAP Matters: Newsletter of Eating Disorders and Prevention, Inc., 1,* 4–5.

Irving, L. M., DuPen, J., & Berel, S. (1998). A media literacy program for high school females. *Eating Disorders: The Journal of Treatment and Prevention, 6,* 119–131.

Irving, L. M., Nelson, N., Hanke, J., & Gravel, L. (1996, March) *A cooperative research group for undergraduate women.* Paper presented at the annual meeting of the Association for Women in Psychology, Portland, OR.

Irving, L. M., Seidner, A. L., Burling, T. A., Pagliarini, R., & Robbins-Sisco, D. (1998). Hope and recovery from drug/alcohol dependence in homeless veterans. *Journal of Social and Clinical Psychology, 17,* 389–406.

Irving, L. M., Snyder, C. R., & Crowson, J. J. (1998). Hope and coping with cancer by college women. *Journal of Personality, 66,* 195–213.

Irving, L. M., Telfer, L., & Blake, D. (1997). Hope, coping, and social support in combat-related posttraumatic stress disorder. *Journal of Traumatic Stress, 10,* 463–477.

Kazdin, A. E. (1980). *Research Design in Clinical Psychology.* New York: Harper & Row.

Kilbourne, J. (1987). *Still Killing Us Softly: Images of Women in Advertising* [video]. Cambridge, MA: Cambridge Documentary Filming.

Kilbourne, J. (1995). *Slim hopes: Advertising and the obsession with thinness* [video]. Available from the Media Education Foundation, 28 Center St., Northampton, MA, 01060.

Kilbourne, J. (1994). Still killing us softly: Advertising and the obsession with thinness. In P. A. Fallon, M. A.. Katzman, & S. C. Wooley (Eds.), *Feminist perspectives on eating disorders* (pp. 395–418) New York: Guilford Press.

Killen, J. D., Taylor, C. B., Hammer, L. D., Litt, I., Wilson, D. M., Rich, T., Hayward, C., Simmonds, B., Kraemer, H., & Varady, A. (1993). An attempt to modify unhealthful eating attitudes and weight regulation practices of young adolescent girls. *International Journal of Eating Disorders, 13,* 369–384.

Levine, M. P., & Smolak, L. (1996). Media as a context for the development of disordered eating. In L. Smolak, M. P. Levine, & R. H. Striegel-Moore (Eds.), *The developmental psychopathology of eating disorders: Implications for research, prevention, and treatment* (pp. 235–237). Mahwah, NJ: Lawrence Erlbaum Associates.

Mann, T., Nolen-Hoeksema, S., Huang, K., Burgard, D., Wright, A., & Hanson, K. (1997). Are two interventions worse than none? Joint primary and secondary prevention of eating disorders in college females. *Health Psychology, 16,* 215–225.

Merriam-Webster, A. (1973). *Webster's New Collegiate Dictionary.* Springfield, MA: G. & C. Merriam Co.

Nichter, M., & Nichter, M. (1991). Hype and weight. *Medical Anthropology, 13,* 249–284.

Nichter, M., & Vuckovic, N. (1994). Fat talk: Body images among adolescent girls. In N. Sault (Ed.), *Many Mirrors: Body Image & Social Relations* (pp. 109–131). New Jersey: Rutgers University Press.

Piran, N. (1996). The reduction of preoccupation with body weight and shape in schools: A feminist approach. *Eating Disorders: The Journal of Treatment and Prevention, 4,* 323–333.

Piran, N. (in press). Eating disorders: A trial of prevention in a high risk school setting. *The Journal of Primary Prevention.*

Reed, D. L., Thompson, J. K., Brannick, M. T., & Sacco, W. P. (1991). Development and validation of the physical appearance state and trait anxiety scale (PASTAS). *Journal of Anxiety Disorders, 5,* 323–332.

Rogers, C. R. (1961). *On becoming a person.* Boston, MA: Houghton Mifflin.

Russell, J. D., & Beumont, P. J. V. (1995). Risk and prevention in eating disorders. In B. Raphael & G. D. Burrows (Eds.), *Handbook of studies on preventive psychiatry* (pp. 459–476). New York: Elsevier Science.

Seligman, M. E. P. (1990). *Learned optimism.* New York: Pocket Books.

Seligman, M. E. P. (1995). The effectiveness of psychotherapy: The Consumer Reports Study. *American Psychologist, 50,* 965–974.

Seligman, M. E. P. (1998, January). Building human strength: Psychology's forgotten mission. *APA Monitor, 2.*

Sher, B. (1989). A national directory of college and university mental health services for eating disorders. In L. C. Whitaker & W. N. Davis (Eds.), *The bulimic college student: Evaluation, treatment and prevention* (pp. 299–307). New York: Haworth Press.

Shisslak, C. M., & Crago, M. (1994). Toward a new model for the prevention of eating disorders. In P. Fallon, M. A. Katzman, & S. C. Wooley (Eds.), *Feminist perspectives on eating disorders* (pp. 419–437). New York: Guilford Press.

Sisson, B. (1997, May 13). Prescription for change: New diet pills can help the truly obese—but only as part of an overall weight-loss regimen. *The Columbian,* Food, 1, 2.

Smolak, L., & Levine, M. P. (1994). Critical issues in the developmental psychopathology of eating disorders. In L. Alexander & D. B. Lumsden (Eds.), *Understanding eating disorders* (pp. 37–60). Washington, DC: Taylor & Francis.

Snyder, C. R. (1994). *The psychology of hope: You can get there from here.* New York: Free Press.

Snyder, C. R., Irving, L. M., & Anderson, J. R. (1991). Hope and health: Measuring the will and the ways. In C. R. Snyder & Donelson Forsyth (Eds.), *The handbook of social and clinical psychology: The health perspective* (pp. 284–300). Elmsford, NY: Pergamon.

Srebnik, D. S., & Saltzberg, E. A. (1994). Feminist cognitive-behavioral therapy for negative body image. *Women and Therapy, 15,* 117–133.

Steiner-Adair, C. (1994). The politics of prevention. In P. Fallon, M. A. Katzman, & S. C. Wooley (Eds.), *Feminist perspectives on eating disorders* (pp. 381–394). New York: Guilford Press.

Stice, E. (1994). Review of the evidence for a sociocultural model of bulimia nervosa and an exploration of the mechanisms of action. *Clinical Psychology Review, 14,* 633–661.

Vogt, T. (1997, December 4). On the scent: Group that fights eating disorders takes aim at "Fetish" perfume ad. *The Columbian,* A1, A7.

Voojis, M. W., & van der Voort, T. H. A. (1993). Learning about television violence: The impact of a critical viewing curriculum on children's attitudinal judgments of crime series. *Journal of Research and Development in Education, 26,* 133–142.

☐ Notes

[1]Eating Disorders Awareness and Prevention (EDAP, Inc.) was established in 1987 by mental health professionals around the country in response to the growing number of individuals afflicted with eating disorders, including anorexia, bulimia, and compulsive overeating. With headquarters in Seattle, EDAP is a growing nonprofit organization with a national Board of Directors, distinguished Advisory Council, and Coordinators throughout the United States and Canada. EDAP does not have any formal "chapters" or "divisions." Therefore, the word "chapter" is used informally, in quotation marks; EDAP-SW comprises individuals in our region who are members of EDAP and strongly believe in its mission. The national office of EDAP may be contacted at (206) 382-3587, 603 Stewart St., Suite #803, Seattle, WA 98101.

[2]Seligman (1995) has called this reliance on empirically based approaches the "inertness assumption" and described this as the assumption that "if some form of treatment is not listed among the many which have been 'empirically validated,' the treatment must be inert, rather than just 'untested' . . . The inertness assumption is a challenge to practitioners, since long-term dynamic treatment, family therapy, and more generally, eclectic psychotherapy, are not on the list of treatments empirically validated by efficacy studies, and these modalities probably make up most of what

is actually practiced" (p. 966). Although Seligman was speaking of intervention (i.e., psychotherapy), not prevention, the "inertness assumption" could be applied to prevention. Little research attention has been given to nontraditional approaches to prevention, including art, music, media activism, and programs designed to promote "body pride." Much could be gained by pairing clinical scientists with professionals and community members who have developed creative approaches to the prevention of eating disorders.

[3]The tide may be turning. In January, 1998, APA president Martin Seligman stated, "Psychology is not just the study of weakness and damage, it is also the study of strength and virtue" (The APA *Monitor*, p. 2). Reflective of this shift from illness to wellness is a growing body of research on hope (Snyder, 1994; Seligman, 1990), which suggests that, even in dire circumstances, human beings believe in their ability to make good things happen in their lives (Irving, et al., 1997; Irving, Seidner, Burling, Pagliarini, & Robbins-Sisco, 1998).

[4]It should be noted that items on the survey used by Mann et al. (1997) emphasized clinical eating disorders (e.g., incidence, causes, and treatment of anorexia and bulimia), and provided few options for discussing alternative, "wellness-oriented" activities. Furthermore, survey respondents were selected from a resource list published 10 years ago (Sher, 1989). Consequently, this survey does not represent all that is being done currently on college campuses to prevent eating disorders.

[5]The idea of "research as 'me'-search" is understandable intuitively; however, disclosing personal motivations for one's work can be controversial, even stigmatizing if the investigator studies a behavior considered by the culture to be "deviant" (e.g., a mental disorder, homosexuality). I would argue that my passion for my subject matter is no different than the highly conscientious, analytic individual who is passionate about complex instrumentation and methodological control; or a scholar who has a "Type A" personality and studies anger management. Concerns about the "objectivity" of research motivated by personal experience are offset by examples of individuals whose research is personally motivated *and* professionally respected (Kay Redfield Jamison, whose research on bipolar disorder was motivated by her own manic depression; E. Fuller Torrey, whose research on schizophrenia was motivated by his sister's experience with schizophrenia).

II

PREVENTION PROGRAMS FOR ELEMENTARY AND MIDDLE SCHOOLS

Educational settings are important sites for prevention work. Schools have a role in promoting critical thinking in their students, encouraging the development of varied coping skills, and adopting institution-wide policies and norms that are conducive to healthy body- and self-esteem (European Network of Health-Promoting Schools Information Booklet, 1993). Programs also should be tailored to the developmental stages of the students (Shisslak, Crago, Estes, & Gray, 1996). Interventions at the elementary and middle school levels allow for primary prevention to occur prior to the establishment of unhealthy eating patterns. Constructive peer norms and relationships may help girls and boys navigate through the process of bodily and social changes at puberty in a healthy way. This section addresses developmental and relational challenges in the lives of children.

To date, very little prevention work has been conducted with elementary school students. In Chapter 5 Linda Smolak offers a developmental perspective to facilitate prevention efforts by teachers and other professionals who work with elementary school children. In Chapter 6 Catherine Steiner-Adair and Amy Purcell Vorenberg discuss the exploration of "weightism" and media literacy with young children. This work helps children develop a critical perspective and media literacy skills that have the potential to protect them against adverse influences.

Challenges involved with early adolescence, ages 10 to 14 years, are addressed in the next three chapters of the section. This phase in girls' lives has been found to be associated with a disruption in girls' senses of self and in their confidence in their knowledge and internally guided voices (Gilligan, 1993). This stage also has been found to be a period of risk for disordered eating (Killen et al., 1994; Smolak & Levine, 1996). In Chapter 7 Sandra Friedman describes her program for helping middle school girls to decode the influence of culture on themselves and to develop confidence in voicing their concerns and in deepening their relationships.

The theme of peer relations and peer norms is continued in the following two chapters. These two chapters describe approaches to prevention that apply to students all the way from middle school to high school. In chapter 8, Susan Paxton presents the implications for primary prevention of her research on friendship groups among middle and high school girls. In Chapter 9, Niva Piran describes key feminist concepts that can inform prevention work with middle and high school girls. This approach emphasizes knowledge anchored in life experiences, empowerment, relationships, and systemic interventions.

Despite documented body weight and shape preoccupation among girls as young as 9 years old (Maloney, McGuire, Daniels, & Specker, 1989), few programs are available for young children. The chapters in this section describe several possible approaches to working with children towards prevention. Further developments are needed to enrich prevention work at this important stage of life.

☐ References

European Network of Health-Promoting Schools Information Booklet. (1993). Denmark, Copenhagen, World Health Organization, Regional Office for Europe.

Gilligan, C. (1993). *In a different voice.* Cambridge, MA: Harvard University Press.

Killen, J. D., Taylor, D. B., Hayward, C., Wilson, D. M., Hammer, L. D., Robinson, T. N., Litt, I., Simmonds, B. A., Varady, A., & Kraemer, H. (1994). The pursuit of thinness and onset of eating disorder symptoms in a community sample of adolescent girls: A three year prospective analysis. *International Journal of Eating Disorders, 16,* 227–238.

Maloney, M., McGuire, J., Daniels, S., & Specker, B. (1989). Dieting behavior and eating attitudes in children. *Pediatrics, 84,* 482–489.

Shisslok, C., Crago, M., Estes, L., Gray (1996). Content and method of developmentally appropriate prevention programs. In L. Smolak, M. P. Levine & R. Striegel-Moore (Eds.), *The developmental psychopathology of eating disorders: Implications for research, prevention, and treatment* (pp. 341–364). Hillsdale, NJ: Erlbaum.

Smolak, L., & Levine, M. P. (1996). Adolescent transitions and the development of eating problems. In L. Smolak, M. P. Levine, & R. Striegel-Moore (Eds.), *The developmental psychopathology of eating disorders: Implications for research, prevention, and treatment* (pp. 207–233). Hillsdale, NJ: Lawrence Erlbaum Associates.

CHAPTER

5

Linda Smolak

Elementary School Curricula for the Primary Prevention of Eating Problems

There is a clear trend among those interested in the primary prevention of eating disorders and problems to call for programs aimed at elementary-school children (Franko & Orosan-Weine, in 1998; Shisslak, Crago, Estes, & Gray, 1996; Smolak & Levine, 1994). There are several reasons for this. First, although problematic eating attitudes and behaviors exist among elementary school-aged children (i.e., children 11 years old and under), these may be less consolidated than they are in adolescents or adults (Shisslak, Crago, McKnight et al., 1998; Smolak, Levine, & Schermer, 1998b). Ties among the components of the thinness schema underlying eating disorders—such as beliefs about attractiveness, self image, and weight control—seem to be weaker. This may make it easier to effectively intervene. Relatedly, educators may be interested in catching behaviors and attitudes such as dieting and weight concerns as they first appear, before they are entrenched habits that are difficult to change. Finally, the majority of elementary school children, even girls, are not dieting nor are they dissatisfied with their bodies. This, in combination with the relative weakness of the thinness schema, suggests that elementary-school programs may be aimed effectively at *preventing* such behaviors. By adolescence, programs must aim to change as well as prevent body dissatisfaction and eating problems.

Thus, elementary school primary prevention programs may represent an opportunity to actually decrease the incidence of eating problems. This chapter is intended to explore three issues in designing such programs. The first section discusses the target of the programs: Should they be aimed at preventing or at changing behavior? The second section considers the content of the programs, including discussions of general (e.g., disorder specific versus general health as a focus) as well as specific suggestions for what lessons might cover. The third section examines the incorporation of a developmental perspective, noting the constraints and opportunities presented by child developmental levels.

☐ Prevention or Change?

In general, programs aimed at preventing eating problems actually have tried to prevent some problems (typically clinically diagnosable eating disorders) and change others (such as calorie-restrictive dieting). Research from other prevention fields, ranging from alcohol to pregnancy prevention, suggests that it is extremely difficult to change existing behaviors within a school-based curriculum (e.g., Frost & Forrest, 1995; Hansen, 1993). Frost and Forrest (1995), for example, found that a program encouraging contraceptive use had its greatest effect among teenagers who had not initiated sexual intercourse at the time of the program. In other words, they had not yet had unprotected sex and so such a habit did not need to be changed. Instead, they adopted the use of contraceptives when they did become sexually active.

Curriculum designers must make conscious decisions as to whether they are trying to prevent or change behaviors and attitudes. Focusing on prevention holds several implications. First, it is important to intervene at a time when there is a low rate of the target behavior (e.g., dieting). Elementary school children are, then, an especially appropriate audience. Second, a preliminary evaluation of the sample is essential to assess whether the rates of dieting, body dissatisfaction, and other behaviors are sufficiently low to permit prevention of the behavior and attitudes in a substantial proportion of the children. Third, short-term follow-up is not adequate to assess the effectiveness of the curriculum. Such a design is not able to indicate whether a behavior has failed to emerge, which is the goal of prevention programs. Short-term outcome data from a prevention program may only be able to document change in knowledge, attitudes, or some behaviors. If knowledge or attitude change is seen as a first step in prevention, then such evaluation may be useful. Fourth, outcome evaluation of the curricula should be conducted at a point in time at which it is expected that the behavior would emerge. Thus, for example, evaluations of elementary school programs require evaluating the participants' weight concerns, dieting, and so forth in middle and possibly high school.

☐ Focus of Programs

Most primary and secondary prevention programs in the area of eating problems have focused on changing the *individual* girl or woman, particularly in terms of her attitudes and behaviors concerning body image and weight control. This emphasis on individual pathology and prevention is generally consistent with etiological models of eating disorders. Most etiological models adopt a medical model perspective, focusing on how the individual developed her illness because of, for example, family, personality, or trauma influences (e.g., Connors, 1996; Johnson & Connors, 1987; Shisslak, Crago, McKnight et al., 1998). However, sociocultural and feminist models of eating disorders point to the importance of broader societal change in prevention efforts (e.g., Piran, 1995, 1996). Any of these approaches might serve as a basis for elementary school prevention programs.

Programs Aimed at Individual Change

Specific Risk and Protective Factors

One approach to developing programs for the primary prevention of eating disorders is to identify a set of risk factors and intervene to reduce their impact. Risk factors are those influences that increase the likelihood that an eating disorder will occur (Kraemer et al., 1997). Some risk factors are more amenable to classroom intervention than are others (Neumark-Sztainer, 1996). For example, many theorists believe that dysfunctional family relationships play a role in the development of eating disorders (Strober & Humphrey, 1987). Enmeshment and family conflict are not likely candidates for a classroom presentation. However, teasing, which has been associated with eating problems (Heinberg, 1996), could be effectively considered in a lesson. Prevention programs also might include protective factors, i.e., influences that decrease the likelihood of developing eating problems. The most commonly considered protective factors are life and coping skills, such as the ability to withstand peer or media-based pressure (Levine, 1999).

A complete model would include both risk and protective factors. Table 1 exemplies this approach. For example, not only would a balanced program provide information about the relative ineffectiveness of dieting, it would teach children skills for responding to negative comments and images that encourage dieting. Such a program also would work to provide support from adults and peers as the children try to resist such messages. In general, risk factors have received more attention within prevention curricula than have protective factors.

Numerous programs for the primary prevention of eating disorders have been developed, several of which have been evaluated (e.g., Carter, Stewart, Dunn, & Fairburn, 1997; Killen, 1996; Mann et al., 1997; Moreno & Thelen, 1993; Moriarity, Shore, & Maxim, 1990; Neumark-Sztainer, Butler, & Palti, 1995; Paxton, 1993; Piran, 1997; Shisslak, Crago, & Neal, 1990 ; Smolak, Levine, & Schermer, 1998a, 1998b; Winzelberg et al., in press). Most of these have been aimed at adolescents in middle and high school. Although there are, of course, differences among the programs, there tends to be considerable overlap in their goals. These goals, which are listed in Table 2, indicate that prevention programs have been aimed specifically at eating problems as opposed to more general systemic (e.g., school policy) or pathology-related (e.g., self-esteem) issues.

One challenge posed by trying to develop prevention programs for elementary school children involves the selection of issues to be targeted and addressed by the program. Most middle-school and high school programs focus on precursors or symptoms of eating disorders, particularly of anorexia nervosa (AN) and bulimia nervosa (BN). This approach reflects the underlying assumption that there is a continuum of eating problems, ranging from preoccupation with weight and shape and occasional dieting to frank eating disorders (Shisslak, Crago, & Estes, 1995). The idea, then, is to prevent girls (and to a lesser extent boys) from moving along the continuum from experimenting with dieting and worrying about getting fat to eating disorders. Indeed, there are data indicating that early dieting plays a role in the development of binge eating (in both BN and binge-eating disorders; Polivy & Herman, 1993; Striegel-Moore, 1993) and AN (Tobin, Johnson, Steinberg, Staats, & Dennis, 1991). Furthermore, weight

TABLE 1. An example of a risk and protective factor model applied to a primary prevention program (From: Smolak, Levine, & Schermer, 1998b)

	Predispositions: Individual Personality	Predispositions: Systems	Precipitators/ Triggers	Developmental Tasks
Reducing Risk Factors	Provide information about effects and effectiveness of dieting Provide information about genetic effects on weight and shape	Discourage peer and family teasing and criticism Discourage negative parental modeling of weight concerns	Discourage sexual harassment Teach media literacy	Provide information about pubertal weight changes Discourage gender stereotyping
Enhancing Protective Factors	Provide role models of all sizes and shapes who are praised for accomplishments *and* appearance Encourage definitions of "beautiful" that focus on self-respect, assertiveness, and generosity of spirit Teach problem-oriented coping Teach assertiveness Focusing on health, functionality, and self-respect in developing positive body image	Provide support and information to parents concerning adolescents and resources; explore pathways to success not related to beauty/appearance Help provide support from adults Help organize peer support		

Note. From "Lessons from Lessons: An Evaluation of an Elementary School Prevention Program," by L. Smolak, M. P. Levine, and F. Schermer, in press, in. G. Noordenbos and W. Vandereycken (Eds.), *The Prevention of Family Disorders.* London: Athlone.

concerns, as reflected in fear of weight gain and attempts to control weight, predict the onset of eating problems (Killen et al., 1994). It is, nonetheless, still unclear whether dieting and weight concerns are really risk factors for eating disorders or whether they actually represent the early stages of the disorder, at least for some people (Franko & Orsan-Weine, 1998).

Almost all research on risk and protective factors has been conducted with children in late childhood (10–12 years old) or in adolescence. Although weight concerns in middle school predict the onset of eating problems in later adolescence (Killen et al., 1994), it is unclear whether or not weight concerns in elementary school predict eating disorders. The difference in correlations among components of the thinness schema in children versus adolescents (Smolak et al., 1998a) suggest that the relationships observed in adolescence may not be

TABLE 2. Topics commonly included in primary prevention eating problems curricula

1. Increase knowledge and promote acceptance of:
   a. Body fat and fat people
   b. Diversity and heritability of weight and shape
   c. Exercise for fun and fitness
   d. Pubertal changes
   e. The nature and dangers of eating disorders
2. Discourage calorie-restrictive dieting and promote healthy eating.
3. Reduce weight and shape related teasing.
4. Increase knowledge of, and promote resistance to, negative media, peer, and family influences on eating and body image.
5. Promote self acceptance and development of a positive body image.

Adapted from "Prevention of Eating Disorders, Eating Problems, and Negative Body Image," by M. P. Levine, 1999, in R. Lemberg (Ed.), Controlling Eating Disorders with Facts, Advice, and Resources (2nd ed., pp. 64–72) Phoenix: Oryx Press.

found among younger children. Because we have little research concerning childhood precursors of eating disorders, it is difficult to ascertain which risk factors might be amenable to intervention. There are even fewer data available on protective factors.

Developing programs without empirical information about risk and protective factors raises the possibility that the wrong topics will be emphasized in the curricula. This risk is particularly high in multicultural student groups, because research suggests that the symptoms and etiological factors associated with AN and BN show cultural differences (Striegel-Moore & Smolak, in press; see also Chapter 11). Selection of the wrong topics might lead to undesirable outcomes and to reduced effectiveness.[1] Perhaps, for example, young girls are dieting not simply because they believe it will make them thinner but also because they view dieting as a normative female behavior. If this is true, improving knowledge about the ineffectiveness of dieting is not likely to lower the current rate of dieting. Furthermore, it is not even likely to prevent dieting, at least in the near future.

A more disturbing outcome of selecting the wrong topics might be that a program actually increases eating disorders (Carter et al., 1997; Mann et al., 1997; Smolak, Levine, & Schermer, 1998b). For example, children and adolescents have a different understanding of future consequences than adults do. Their cognitive egocentrism may lead them to believe that they are less likely to suffer negative consequences than are other people. Elkind (1967) has called this a "personal fable." The personal fable may help us understand why teens are more likely to take risks, for example in terms of driving, birth control, and alcohol. If children and teenagers hear about a dangerous weight loss technique, they may well believe that they can use the technique without falling victim to it. This may explain why girls and young women and young male wrestlers can "learn" purging behaviors from a friend (Crandall, 1988). Programs that discuss symptoms of clinical eating disorders in great detail, then, may run the risk of introducing children and adolescents to these behaviors and initiating their use.

General "Problem" Behavior

Research generally indicates that children and adolescents who suffer from one problem often suffer from several (e.g., Cohen, Brook, Cohen, Velez, & Garcia, 1990; Robins & McEvoy, 1990). Indeed, eating problems themselves show substantial comorbidity with depression, anxiety disorders, personality disorders, and, in the case of BN, alcohol and other drug abuse (Zerbe, 1993). Research also indicates that adolescents who participate in one health risk behavior, such as failure to use contraception, also engage in others, such as not using seat belts or smoking. Such findings have led prevention experts in other fields to suggest that problem-specific approaches may not be effective because they tend to miss the real causes of the problems: stress and poor coping mechanisms. Instead, programs that emphasize self development and life skills seem more effective. For example, Allen, Philliber, Herrling, and Kuperminc (1997) found that the opportunity to participate in a volunteer program reduced a variety of academic and social problems among at-risk adolescents.

Approaches that address general challenges in the lives of children and adolescents are only beginning to be introduced in the field of eating disorders. Building on Harter's (1986) model of self development, Shisslak and associates (1998) recently suggested that mentoring programs might be used to build self-esteem in specific areas, such as physical or social competence, so that girls do not rely so heavily on attractiveness as an indicator of worth. These types of prevention programs may be especially appealing to those interested in easing several of the risks of the early adolescent transition for girls.

Girls and Early Adolescence

There is no longer doubt that early adolescence is an especially difficult developmental transition for girls (see, e.g., Smolak & Levine, 1996). Following, but not prior to, this stage, girls are found to be more depressed than boys (Hankin et al., 1998; Nolen-Hoeksema & Girgus, 1994). Unlike boys, girls never recover from the drop in self-esteem that occurs during early adolescence. Similarly, girls start to show less interest in school, especially in math and science, relative to boys (Eccles & Midgley, 1990). Declines in social support from teachers and parents, as well as increased peer pressure, seem to leave girls with no one to turn to with difficult questions concerning sexuality and sexual harassment (Brumberg, 1997). Indeed, girls seem to gradually lose their ability to express their own concerns, a loss sometimes so dramatic that the girls no longer seem to know what they would say if they could speak. They have lost touch with their selves (Brown & Gilligan, 1992; Taylor, Gilligan, & Sullivan, 1994).

In terms of eating problems, early adolescence marks a notable upswing in weight control behaviors (Smolak & Levine, 1996). This is especially noticeable as girls go through the pubertal process. Thus, early maturers start dieting sooner. There also seems to be a consolidation in eating attitudes and behaviors, such that combinations of these (as captured, for example, in Killen et al.'s [1994] Weight Concerns Scale) now predict later eating disorders. There also seems to be an increase in diagnosable eating disorders, especially AN, at this time (Smolak & Levine, 1996).

Elementary-school prevention programs may be aimed at preparing girls for this transition in hopes of *preventing* the onset of these problems. Again, the few extant elementary-school programs (e.g., Levine, Schermer, Smolak, & Etling, 1996) have focused on providing relevant cautionary information about, for example, dieting and pubertal weight gains in hopes that such knowledge will lead to an appreciation for an adult body and recognition of the dangers and futility of calorie restriction. Programs aimed at providing girls with coping mechanisms to deal with these transitions have been successful in preventing problems such as teen pregnancy, with older peers helping girls sort through the peer pressures concerning sexuality (Frost & Forrest, 1995).

The field of prevention of eating disorders has just started to incoporate components that address challenges girls face during and following the developmental stage of early adolescence. Piran (1996) has implemented a program with girls at an elite ballet school that emphasizes the shared generation in focus groups of knowledge and solutions relevant to their body and self esteem (see also Chapter 16). Friedman (1994) has created a prevention program for girls that operates outside of the school system. The program focuses on groups of girls finding ways to express their responses to a challenging environment other than the "language of fat."

Programs Aimed at Environmental and Societal Change

Targeting Peers

Peer groups are important in the development of eating problems in at least three ways: They provide information about and support for dieting and other weight control behaviors; they engage in "fat talk," thereby focusing girls on weight and shape (Nichter & Vuvkovic, 1994); and they tease children about weight and shape. Among adolescents, those girls whose female friends are invested in weight and shape or participate in dieting are at higher risk for disordered eating attitudes and behaviors (Levine, Smolak, & Hayden, 1994; Levine, Smolak, Moodey, Shuman, & Hessen, 1994). Adolescent girls who have elevated scores on measures of weight concern and weight control (e.g., the Eating Attitudes Test) report more teasing about weight and shape (Heinberg, 1996; Levine, Smolak, & Hayden, 1994). Limited data also suggest that such teasing is important in the *development* of eating problems (Cattarin & Thompson, 1994). There are no data tracing the development of weight related teasing from elementary school on.

Data concerning peer influences suggest that prevention of eating problems might be well served by changing attitudes of children and adolescents who themselves neither suffer from nor appear to be at risk for eating disorders. Programs might be aimed at preventing the development of a culture of dieting in which children freely (and negatively) comment on each others' bodies, weight, and eating patterns. For example, Paxton (1996) has noted that prevention programs should aim not only to inoculate girls against peer pressure but also to encourage friendship groups to adopt healthier, more positive attitudes about weight and shape (see also Chapter 8).

The limited success of primary prevention programs in middle school and high school has led some researchers to suggest that efforts focus on secondary prevention, which has been somewhat more successful (e.g., Killen, 1996; Powers & Johnson, 1996). However, secondary prevention programs miss the opportunity to alter the behavior, and hence the influence, of peers not at risk.

Targeting Parents

Smolak and Levine (1994) have pointed out that elementary school children have only limited input into what types of food they eat, when they eat, and how much they eat. These decisions are influenced, if not controlled, by parents. Parents also may simply be more influential in children's compared with adolescents' decision making (Graber & Brooks-Gunn, 1996; see also Chapter 3). Thus, the younger the children involved in a nutrition or eating disorders program, the more important it is to engage their parents.

In addition, parental comments to their children about weight and shape negatively impact children's eating attitudes and behaviors. This seems to be especially true for girls. These effects have been documented in children as young as fourth grade. Parental modeling also seems to be correlated with children's weight related attitudes and behaviors, although the relationship is weaker (Smolak, Levine, & Schermer, in press, Thelen & Cormier, 1995).

Clearly, then, parents are an important audience in preventing eating problems and should be included in elementary-school prevention efforts. This topic is addressed more fully in Chapter 3.

Institutional Change

AN and BN, as well as subclinical variants of eating disorders, are problems that affect many more females than males. Similarly, at all ages (at least elementary school through young adulthood), females are more likely to report body dissatisfaction, concern about being fat, and use of weight control techniques, even if they are of normal or below expected weight. The pervasiveness of the gender difference across the continuum of eating problems and disorders suggests that there are substantial gendered sociocultural factors at work (Murnen & Smolak, 1997).

These sociocultural factors include proximal influences, that is, behaviors and attitudes in the girls' immediate environment. The vast majority of adolescent girls report sexual harassment at school. This harassment is so severe that as many as one third of girls have thought about missing school in order to avoid it (Bryant, 1993). Yet, many schools do not have harassment policies. Indeed, girls report that they do not know what to do when they are harassed and that they do not expect to be taken seriously if they try to report harassment (Larkin, 1994; see also Chapter 13). Even worse, our society has sent girls mixed messages about harassment, sexuality, and body image such that girls may think they should feel flattered by the attention (Brumberg, 1997). This, too, prevents girls from coming forward and leads them to silence themselves publicly and personally, denying their own discomfort with and dislike of the comments, leers, and groping they routinely endure.

There are not data on sexual harassment in elementary school per se, but retrospective reports indicate that girls remember being harassed as early as the third grade (Bryant, 1993). Attempts by schools to design and enforce sexual-harassment policies, especially in elementary schools, often have met with media ridicule. Piran (1997, 1998) has suggested that sexual harassment is one of the key factors affecting adolescents' body image. As part of her prevention work with elite ballet students, she was able to engage the school's administration and teaching staff in responding to the girls' reports of sexual harassment in ways that improved the girls' reported confidence and body esteem (see Chapter 19).

Thus, helping schools design and institute effective sexual harassment policies, as well as finding ways to encourage girls to come forward, may be a valuable part of the long-term prevention of eating problems in multiple cohorts of girls. Similarly, school policies concerning teasing about weight and shape might be developed. Finally, in so much as gender role constraints (especially emphasizing beauty over other sources of achievement) might contribute to the development of eating problems (Murnen & Smolak, 1997; Worell & Todd, 1996), changes in the school environment, ranging from ensuring that women of achievement are included in classroom posters and the curriculum to valuing girls' sports participation, might reduce eating problems. Although such changes are difficult, they are not impossible, as indicated by the broad societal changes in racial attitudes or attitudes towards smoking or drunk driving. Furthermore, silence by educators on these issues may well be viewed by the girls as collusion between the eating disorder specialists and the school that accepts sexual harassment and gender discrimination (Piran, 1996).

☐ Developmental Constraints

Much of the theorizing concerning eating disorders has been based on the status of adolescent and adult clients. Similarly, much of the research has focused on adolescent and adult (especially college-aged) samples (Smolak et al., 1998a). Not surprisingly, then, many of the available evaluation instruments, such as the Eating Disorders Inventory (Garner, Olmstead, & Polivy, 1983) and the Eating Attitudes Test (Garfinkel & Garner, 1982), were developed using adult samples. Although some of these have been revised for children, simple wording changes often result in questionable measures (Smolak, 1996).

Prevention work has followed the same path, focusing on adolescents and adults. There is a real risk that programs designed for adolescents and adults will simply be revised so that their language is more accessible to young children. Such an approach may well miss the mark. Both generally and in terms of eating issues per se, young children may have self and cognitive structures that require an entirely different approach to primary prevention. The relative immaturity of the self and cognitive structures may provide unique opportunities as well as special challenges for prevention programs.

Self Structures

There are at least three important differences in self concept in elementary school children and that of adolescents and adults. First, self-esteem tends to be higher, and perhaps unrealistic, especially among early elementary school children. This higher self-esteem may be attributable partly to the limited influence of social comparison. Second, the elementary-school child shows less integration of the personality and concrete physical characteristics that make up his or her self schema. A similar statement might be made about self-esteem, which, over the course of childhood, becomes organized into an increasingly hierarchical structure (Harter, 1990). Finally, elementary school children emphasize different determinants of self than adolescents do (Ewell, Smith, Karmel, & Hart, 1996).

Self Esteem

By the second year of life, there is evidence of incipient self-esteem, for example, in mastery smiles or in calling parental attention to accomplishments (Kagan, 1982). In preschool and early elementary school, self-esteem tends to be quite global and unrealistically high. However, even young children can distinguish competence (how well they do something) from social acceptance (how well people like them). By age 7 or 8 years, self-esteem is differentiated into at least physical, academic, and social self-esteem. These areas become more refined and specific with age (Marsh, 1990), although even first graders can define their academic selves, for example, in terms of reading, arithmetic, and classroom behaviors (Entwisle, Alexander, Pallas, & Cadigan, 1987). Harter (1985) reported that by third grade there is a moderate correlation between each of the individual self-esteem domains (scholastic competence, social acceptance, athletic competence, physical appearance, and behavioral conduct) and global self-esteem.

Self-esteem becomes more realistic and differentiated partially because of increased social feedback as a child moves from a home or preschool environment to elementary school. Self ratings in first grade, for example, are not particularly related to teacher and peer ratings but self ratings in second grade are (Stipek, 1981). Eating disorders curricula aimed at very young elementary school children must reflect the fact that children are just learning to make social comparisons and use social feedback for self evaluations. This would seem to be a valuable age for helping children develop strategies for interpreting such feedback, keeping in mind that they probably cannot make multiple comparisons simultaneously. This seems to be a particularly valuable strategy given that social comparison is an important factor in problematic eating attitudes and behaviors among older girls and women (Paxton, 1996). This also may be a good age for helping children to see the effects of teasing. The children's ability to adopt the perspective of others is still developing (Selman, 1976), so it is probably important to give the children very direct experience in this realm through role plays and, perhaps more importantly, through adult interventions in situations in which they observe teasing about weight and shape. This is also a good time for schools and parents to use policy and rules to send children strong messages about the meaning and effects of teasing.

Self definition

It used to be widely held that young children relied exclusively on physical, concrete characteristics; whereas older children were thought to be more oriented toward general personality characteristics in defining their selves. Research now indicates that this description of self concept development is oversimplified (Ewell et al., 1996) and that even young elementary school children can refer to personality and psychological characteristics in describing themselves.

Younger children are less likely to view personality and psychological characteristics as being "trait-like," that is, consistent across situations, and less likely to believe that such characteristics predict future behavior (Ewell et al., 1996). Thus, one might argue that the self structures of young children are less consolidated and, perhaps, less schematic. Smolak and Levine have made a similar argument in terms of a "thinness schema," suggesting that young children have not effectively integrated beliefs about dieting and thinness with beliefs about attractiveness and self (Smolak & Levine, 1994; Smolak et al., 1998). If it is true that self and thinness schema are less consolidated in the early elementary school years, there is a real possibility of *preventing* the development of the self structures associated with eating problems. Elementary school prevention programs might focus, for example, on providing children with experiences that help them develop self definitions that do not have attractiveness and thinness at their core. This might mean using mentors to provide self enhancing experiences (Shisslak, Crago, Renger, & Clark-Wagner, 1998). Programs also might demonstrate that body shape does not predict success by providing children with images of people of all sizes who are successful in a variety of fields. This tactic may have contributed to the improvement in attitudes towards fat people found among fifth graders who participated in a prevention program (Smolak et al., 1998a).

Theory of Self

Children and adolescents have theories of self. In children, these theories focus on the self as a determinant. In other words, children think they are as they are because they want to be. By adolescence, peer and family context become more important as explanations for one's characteristics (Ewell et al., 1996). Girls seem particularly interested in considering their connections to others as they define themselves (Brown & Gilligan, 1992; Ewell et al., 1996; Taylor et al., 1994).

The developmental shift in the experience of the self again suggests that childhood may present special opportunities for the prevention of eating problems. Not only may young children be less susceptible to social and peer pressure, but they may believe themselves to be more in control of who they are and how they behave. For example, they may be more willing to be assertive with people who tease them or who urge them to lose weight. Indeed, Gilligan and her colleagues (Brown & Gilligan, 1992; Taylor et al., 1994) frequently report that girls lose their ability and willingness to be so assertive as they move into adolescence. This is partly because society fails to support such behavior in girls since the female gender role is defined as passive, compliant, and deferential to others (including not hurting others' feelings even at the expense of your own). The more assertive female gender role that is common in the African-American culture has been posited as one of reasons African-Americans have lower rates of AN and BN (Striegel-Moore & Smolak, 1996). Curricula that encourage this assertiveness *specifically in girls* and help girls to maintain this attitude as they move into adolescence may go a long ways toward preventing eating disorders.

Cognitive Structures

It seems obvious to say that children's cognitive functioning differs from that of adults. Yet, in both eating disorders assessment techniques and curricular design, there seems to be little recognition of these differences. It is not within the scope of this chapter to review all of the cognitive differences. Instead, three differences are highlighted: the concreteness of child thought, the limits of children's ability to use evidence to question their theories, and children's ability to integrate multiple components of a schema to analyze and predict behavior. It should be emphasized that all of these cognitive abilities develop during elementary school and so curricula designers need to become familiar with the skills specific to the age group they are targeting.

First, children tend to be much more tied to perceptual information than adults are, particularly if they are dealing with novel information (Siegler, 1991). Ludwig (1997) provides an interesting example of this. The Partnership for a Drug-Free America ran a public service announcement (PSA) showing a picture of a fried egg with the caption, "This is your brain on drugs." This was intended to provide a powerful image to accompany the colloquialism of "frying your brain." But children did not understand the image or the metaphor. Cotts (cited in Ludwig, 1997), reports that many children refused to eat eggs after seeing this PSA. Although no one interviewed children to understand this phenomenon, it is likely that they somehow equated eggs, drugs, and bad. They were tied to the concrete image of the egg coupled with the word *drugs*.

Second, children do not evaluate evidence the same way adolescents and adults do. Even young children form theories of how things happen or work. However, they are not able to analyze their belief systems as well as adolescents are. They tend to view these theories as accurate reflections of reality. This tendency leads young children (e.g., third graders) to discount evidence that contradicts their belief system (Kuhn, 1989, 1993). Children often ignore or even distort information in order to maintain their own theories. So, for example, in one project aimed at altering gender stereotypes, children were shown films of other children engaging in cross-gender play. The children who most strongly endorsed gender stereotypes (prior to viewing the movie) actually tended to misremember the play, reporting that children played in gender-consistent ways (Signorella, 1987). This is one more reason why preventing the development of an attitude or behavior is easier than changing it.

Third, young children tend to focus on one component or element of a concept or problem. This is most famously illustrated in Piaget's studies of conservation. Similarly, preschool children can list various components of gender roles (Martin, 1989). They know, for example, that women wear dresses, that boys play football, and that girls cry more than boys. But, it is not until at least six years of age that one aspect of the stereotype can be used effectively to predict the presence of another characteristic or behavior in an unfamiliar child. By age 11, they can consider an individual's unique characteristics as well as gender roles in predicting a child's behavior (Martin, 1989). Thus, younger children are less able to integrate various pieces of information as they try to understand or solve a problem.

These cognitive constraints have several implications for eating disorders primary prevention programs:

1. Materials, such as photos, videos, stories, and slogans, used successfully with adults or even adolescents are likely to be interpreted more literally by young children.
2. Complex material is likely to be distilled into one principle, probably one that fits a pre-existing belief. So, for example, a message that dietary fat is impor-

tant but should be limited is likely to be interpreted either as endorsing an "eat what you want" position or as indicating that you should eat no fat. Messages that there is no such thing as a "forbidden food" might be viewed as a license to eat however many cookies one would like.

3. Children who already hold beliefs about weight loss techniques, body fat, and so on are likely to be difficult to persuade by a simple presentation of evidence. Simply telling children or showing them that some fat people eat less than some thin people is not likely to convince them.

4. One should build on the children's strengths, including, ironically, the lack of integration of various schematic components. For example, although children as young as six years old indicate negative attitudes about fat people (Lerner & Jovanovic, 1990; Staffieri, 1967), children do befriend and play with fat children (Cohen, Klesges, Summerville, & Meyers, 1989; Phillips & Hill, in press). By encouraging continued interaction among children of all sizes and exposing children to successful role models of all sizes, one might prevent eventual behavioral discrimination (including teasing) against heavier people and, perhaps, gradually break down the negative attitudes.

5. One should provide repeated exposure to the messages. For example, instead of just discussing issues in health one should integrate them into math, science, and literature lessons. If body size, for example, is the issue, the children can actually observe small animals of different sizes (such as a few mice) and see if the bigger animals really eat more than the smaller ones. Then they might read a book about a successful big person and talk about how being heavier affected (or did not affect) the person's success. They might look at pictures of relatives (their own or famous families such as the British royals) and look for trends in physical characteristics of all sorts, including body shape, weight, and height. This exercise could be a history lesson, a science lesson, or an opportunity to write a story.

6. The previous examples also underscore the importance of active participation by the children. Piagetian theory has long established the importance of direct experience for the gradual evolution of children's cognitive functioning. Although more recent formulations have questioned the likelihood of Piaget's cognitive structures, there is no doubt that direct experience with material not only increases knowledge in that area but also raises the sophistication of thought (e.g., in terms of classification and abstraction abilities) about that material.

7. Themes and materials must be chosen carefully, and children's *understanding and interpretation* of the materials being used must be evaluated periodically.

☐ Conclusions

Primary prevention advocates have long noted the advantage of blocking the development of a behavior over altering an existing behavior (e.g., Albee, 1987). In the case of eating disorders, this means intervening before the weight concerns that may lead to eating disorders become entrenched. This, in turn, indicates that intervention with elementary school children may be a particularly fruitful approach in preventing eating problems.

The question, of course, is what such a program would look like. Should it focus specifically on risk factors for eating disorders? Although we do not know precisely which childhood attitudes and behaviors are risk factors for later eating disorders, it is probably not imperative to fully understand these links prior to instituting primary prevention (Albee, 1987). For example, dieting and body dissatisfaction probably do not fully explain the development of eating disorders, but they almost certainly are involved. Furthermore, preventing dieting and body dissatisfaction, in and of itself, is a valuable goal.

Prevention specialists have sometimes argued that these disorder-specific approaches are not likely to be successful (Albee, 1987). Certainly, self esteem, social support, coping styles, and other characteristics that are risk factors for, but not specific to, eating disorders might be considered as targets. Providing children with positive development in these areas might help in preventing eating disorders as well as drug, alcohol, pregnancy, and delinquency problems. Such an approach might be especially palatable to educators who find that they do not have time to institute all of the health-related prevention programs.

Another possibility is that prevention programs should not target children exclusively. Changes in parental and teacher attitudes are likely to have important long-term effects. Similarly, changes in institutional policies concerning harassment, public weighings, and teasing might have powerful effects.

Developmental levels, for example in terms of self and cognitive functioning, must be considered in designing prevention programs. Developmental phenomena raise challenges in terms of presenting information so that it will not be misinterpreted. Equally, however, these developmental differences provide opportunities because the children's concepts concerning weight and shape are also immature.

Perhaps the most important conclusion to be reached about elementary school prevention programs is the need for research. For those interested in problem-specific, individual-focused programs, research into risk and protective-factors is imperative. Similarly, more research on the impact of sociocultural influences, including sexual harassment, is essential. It is also important to further evaluate what children know and understand about eating problems; this needs to be done even as programs are ongoing. Finally, evaluation research, particularly of the sort that allows the examination of prevention rather than change, is crucial.

☐ **References**

Albee, G. (1987). The rationale and need for primary prevention. In S. Goldston (Ed.), *Concepts of primary prevention: A framework for program development* (pp. 7–20). Sacramento, CA: California Department of Mental Health.

Allen, J., Philliber, S., Herrling, S., & Kuperminc, G. (1997). Preventing teen pregnancy and academic failure: Experimental evaluation of a developmentally based approach. *Child Development, 64,* 729–742.

Brown, L., & Gilligan, C. (1992). *Meeting at the crossroads.* Cambridge, MA: Harvard University Press.

Brumberg, J. J. (1997). *The body project: An intimate history of American girls.* New York: Random House.

Bryant, A. (1993). Hostile hallways: The AAUW survey on sexual harassment in America's schools. *Journal of School Health, 63,* 355–357.

Carter, J., Stewart, D., Dunn, V., & Fairburn, C. (1997). Primary prevention of eating disorders: Might it do more harm than good? *International Journal of Eating Disorders, 22,* 167–172.

Cattarin, J., & Thompson, J. K. (1994). A three-year longitudinal study of body image, eating disturbance, and general psychological functioning adolescent females. *Eating Disorders: The Journal of Treatment & Prevention, 2,* 114–125.

Cohen, P., Brook, J., Cohen, J., Velez, C., & Garcia, M. (1990). In L. Robins & M. Rutter (Eds.) *Straight and devious pathways from childhood to adulthood* (pp. 242–258). New York: Cambridge University Press.

Cohen, R., Klesges, R., Summerville, M., & Meyers, A. (1989). A developmental analysis of the influence of body weight on the sociometry of children. *Addictive Behaviors, 14,* 463–476.

Connors, M. (1996). Developmental vulnerabilities for eating disorders. In L. Smolak, M. P. Levine, & R. Striegel-Moore (Eds.), *The developmental psychopathology of eating disorders: Implications for research, prevention, and treatment* (pp. 285–310). Hillsdale, NJ: Lawrence Erlbaum Associates.

Crandall, C. (1988). Social contagion of binge eating. *Journal of Personality and Social Psychology, 55,* 588–598.

Eccles, J., & Midgley, C. (1990). Changes in academic motivation and self-perception during early adolescence. In R. Montemayor, G. Adams, & T. Gullota (Eds.), *From childhood to adolescence: A transitional period?* (pp. 134–155). Newbury Park, CA: Sage.

Elkind, D. (1967). Egocentrism in adolescence. *Child Development, 38,* 1025–1034.

Entwisle, D., Alexander, K., Pallas, A., & Cadigan, D. (1987). The emergent academic self-image of first graders: Its response to social structure. *Child Development, 58,* 1190–1206.

Ewell, F., Smith, S., Karmel, M., & Hart, D. (1996). The sense of self and its development: A framework for understanding eating disorders. In L. Smolak, M. P. Levine, & R. Striegel-Moore (Eds.), *The developmental psychopathology of eating disorders: Implications for research, prevention, and treatment* (pp. 107–134). Mahwah, NJ: Lawrence Erlbaum Associates.

Franko, D., & Orosan-Weine, P. (1998). The prevention of eating disorders: Empirical, methodological and conceptual considerations. *Clinical Psychology: Science and Practice, 5,* 459–477.

Friedman, S. (1994). *Girls in the 90s facilitator's manual.* Vancouver, BC: Salal Books.

Frost, J., & Forrest, J. (1995). Understanding the impact of effective teenage pregnancy prevention programs. *Family Planning Perspectives, 27,* 188–195.

Garfinkel, P., & Garner, D. (1982). *Anorexia nervosa: A multidimensional approach.* New York: Brunner/Mazel.

Garner, D., Olmstead, M., & Polivy, J. (1983). The development and validation of a multidimensional eating disorder inventory for anorexia nervosa and bulimia. *International Journal of Eating Disorders, 2,* 15–34.

Graber, J., & Brooks-Gunn, J. (1996). Prevention of eating problems and disorders: Including parents. *Eating Disorders: The Journal of Treatment & Prevention, 4,* 348–363.

Hankin, B., Abramson, L., Moffitt, T., Silva, P., McGee, R., & Angell, K. (1998). Development of depression from preadolescence to young adulthood: Emerging gender differences in a 10-year longitudinal study. *Journal of Abnormal Psychology, 107,* 128–140.

Hansen, W. (1993). School-based alcohol prevention programs. *Alcohol Health & Research World, 7,* 54–60.

Harter, S. (1985). *Manual for the self-perception profile for children.* Unpublished manuscript, University of Denver, Colorado.

Harter, S. (1986). Processes underlying the construction, maintenance, and enhancement of self-concept in children. In S. Suhls & A. Greenwald (Eds.), *Psychological perspectives of the self* (pp. 136–182). Hillsdale, NJ: Lawrence Erlbaum Associates.

Harter, S. (1990). Issues in the assessment of the self-concept of children and adolescents. In A. La-Greca (Ed.), *Through the eyes of a child* (pp. 292–325). Boston: Allyn and Bacon.

Heinberg, L. (1996). Theories of body image disturbance: Perceptual, developmental, and sociocultural factors. In J. K. Thompson (Ed.), *Body image, eating disorders, and obesity: An integrative guide for assessment and treatment* (pp. 27–48). Washington, DC: American Psychological Association.

Johnson, C., & Connors, M. (1987). *The etiology and treatment of bulimia nervosa: A biopsychosocial perspective.* New York: Basic Books.

Kagan, J. (1982). The emergence of self. *Journal of Child Psychology and Psychiatry, 23,* 363–381.

Killen, J. (1996). Development and evaluation of a school-based eating disorder symptoms prevention program. In L. Smolak, M. P. Levine, & R. Striegel-Moore (Eds.), *The developmental psychopathology of eating disorders: Implications for research, prevention, and treatment* (pp. 313–340). Hillsdale, NJ: Lawrence Erlbaum Associates.

Killen, J., Taylor, C., Hayward, C., Wilson, D., Hammer, L., Robinson, T., Litt, I., Simmonds, B., Varady, A., & Kraemer, H. (1994). The pursuit of thinness and onset of eating disorder symptoms in a community sample of adolescent girls: A three year prospective analysis. *International Journal of Eating Disorders, 16,* 227–238.

Kraemer, H., Kazdin, A., Offord, D., Kessler, R., Jensen, P., & Kupfer, D. (1997). Coming to terms with the terms of risk. *Archives of General Psychiatry, 54,* 337–343.

Kuhn, D. (1989). Children and adults as intuitive scientists. *Psychological Review, 96*, 674–689.

Kuhn, D. (1993). Connecting scientific and informal reasoning. *Merrill-Palmer Quarterly, 39*, 74–103.

Larkin, J. (1994). *Sexual harassment: High school girls speak out.* Toronto: Second Story Press.

Lerner, R., & Jovanovic, J. (1990). The role of body image in psychosocial development across the life span: A developmental contextual perspective. In T. Cash & T. Pruzinsky (Eds.), *Body images: Development, deviance, and change* (pp. 110–127). New York: Guilford.

Levine, M .P. (1999). Prevention of eating disorders, eating problems, and negative body image. In R. Lemberg (Ed.), *Controlling eating disorders with facts, advice, and resources* (2nd ed., pp. 64–72). Phoenix: Oryx Press.

Levine, M. P., Schermer, F., Smolak, L., & Etling, C. (1996). *Eating smart, eating for me.* Columbus, OH: Ohio Dept of Education.

Levine, M. P., Smolak, L., & Hayden, H. (1994). The relation of sociocultural factors to eating attitudes and behaviors among middle school girls. *Journal of Early Adolescence, 14*, 471–490.

Levine, M. P., Smolak, L., Moodey, A., Shuman, M., & Hessen, L. (1994). Normative developmental challenges and dieting and eating disturbances in middle school girls. *International Journal of Eating Disorders, 15*, 11–20.

Ludwig, M. J. (1997). The cultural politics of prevention: Reading anti-drug PSA's. In K. T. Frith (Ed.), *Undressing the ad: Reading culture in advertising* (pp. 151–174). New York: Peter Lang.

Mann, T., Nolen-Hoeksema, S., Huang, K., Burgard, D., Wright, A., & Hanson, K. (1997). Are two interventions worse than none? Joint primary and secondary prevention of eating disorders in college females. *Health Psychology, 16*, 1–11.

Marsh, H. (1990). The structure of academic self-concept: The Marsh/Shavelson model. *Journal of Educational Psychology, 82*, 623–636.

Martin, C. (1989). Children's use of gender-related information in making social judgments. *Developmental Psychology, 25*, 80–88.

Moreno, A., & Thelen, M. (1993). A preliminary prevention program for eating disorders in a junior high school population. *Journal of Youth and Adolescence, 22*, 109–124.

Moriarty, D., Shore, R., & Maxim, N. (1990). Evaluation of an eating disorders curriculum. *Evaluation and Program Planning, 13*, 407–413.

Murnen, S., & Smolak, L. (1997). Femininity, masculinity, and disordered eating: A meta-analytic review. *International Journal of Eating Disorders, 22*, 231–242.

Neumark-Sztainer, D. (1996). School-based programs for preventing eating disturbances. *Journal of School Health, 66*, 64–71.

Neumark-Sztainer, D., Butler, R., & Palti, H. (1995). Eating disturbances among adolescent girls: Evaluation of a school-based primary prevention program. *Journal of Nutrition Education, 27*, 24–31.

Nichter, M., & Vukovic, N. (1994). Fat talk: Body image among adolescent girls. In N. Sault (Ed.), *Many mirrors: Body image and social relations* (pp. 109–131). New Brunswick, NJ: Rutgers University Press.

Nolen-Hoeksema, S., & Girgus, J. (1994). The emergence of gender differences in depression during adolescence. *Psychological Bulletin, 115*, 424–443.

Paxton, S., (1993). A prevention program for disturbed eating and body dissatisfaction in adolescent girls: A one year follow-up. *Health Education Research, 8*, 43–51.

Paxton, S. (1996). Prevention implications of peer influences on body image dissatisfaction and disturbed eating in adolescent girls. *Eating Disorders: The Journal of Treatment & Prevention, 4*, 334–348.

Piran, N. (1995). Prevention: Can early lessons lead to a delineation of an alternative model? A critical look at prevention with schoolchildren. *Eating Disorders: The Journal of Treatment & Prevention, 3*, 28–36.

Piran, N. (1996). The reduction of preoccupation with body weight and shape in schools: A feminist approach. *Eating Disorders: The Journal of Treatment & Prevention, 4*, 323–333.

Piran, N. (1997). Prevention of eating disorders: Directions for future research. *Psychopharmacology Bulletin, 33*, 419–423.

Piran, N. (1998). A participatory approach to the prevention of eating disorders in a school. In G. Noordenbos & W. Vandereycken (Eds.). *The prevention of eating disorders.* (pp. 173–186) London: Athlone.

Phillips, R., & Hill, A. (in press). Fat, plain, but not friendless: Self-esteem and peer acceptance of obese pre-adolescent girls. *International Journal of Obesity.*

Polivy, J., & Herman, C. P. (1993). Etiology of binge eating. In C. Fairburn & G. T. Wilson (Eds.), *Binge eating: Nature, assessment, and treatment* (pp. 173–205). New York: Guilford.

Powers, P., & Johnson, C. (1996). Small victories: Prevention of eating disorders among athletes. *Eating Disorders: The Journal of Treatment & Prevention, 4,* 364–377.

Robins, L., & McEvoy, L. (1990). Conduct problems as predictors of substance abuse. In L. Robins & M. Rutter (Eds.), *Straight and devious pathways from childhood to adulthood* (pp. 182–204). New York: Cambridge University Press.

Selman, R. (1976). Social-cognitive understanding: A guide to educational and clinical practice. In I. Lickona (Ed.), *Moral development and behavior: Theory, research, and social issues* (pp. 299–316). New York: Holt, Rinehart, & Winston.

Shisslak, C., Crago, M., & Estes, L. (1995). The spectrum of eating disorders. *International Journal of Eating Disorders, 18,* 209–219.

Shisslak, C., Crago, M., Estes, L., & Gray, N. (1996). Content and method of developmentally appropriate prevention programs. In L. Smolak, M. P. Levine, & R. Striegel-Moore (Eds.), *The developmental psychopathology of eating disorders: Implications for research, prevention, and treatment* (pp. 341–364). Mahwah, NJ: Lawrence Erlbaum Associates.

Shisslak, C., Crago, M., McKnight, K., Estes, L., Gray, N., & Parnaby, O. (1998). Potential risk factors associated with weight control behaviors in elementary and middle school girls. *Journal of Psychosomatic Research, 44,* 301–314.

Shisslak, C., Crago, M., & Neal, M. (1990). Prevention of eating disorders among adolescents. *American Journal of Health Promotion, 5,* 100–106.

Shisslak, C., Crago, M., Renger, R., & Clark-Wagner, A. (1998). Self-esteem and the prevention of eating disorders. *Eating Disorders: The Journal of Treatment & Prevention, 6,* 105–117.

Siegler, R. (1991). *Children's thinking.* Englewood Cliffs, NJ: Prentice-Hall.

Signorella, M. (1987). Gender schemata: Individual differences and context effects. In L. Liben & M. Signorella (Eds.), *Children's gender schemata* (pp. 23–38). San Francisco: Jossey-Bass.

Smolak, L. (1996). Methodological implications of a developmental psychopathology approach to the study of eating problems. In L. Smolak, M. P. Levine, & R. Striegel-Moore (Eds.), *The developmental psychopathology of eating disorders: Implications for research, prevention, and treatment* (pp. 31–56). Mahwah, NJ: Lawrence Erlbaum Associates.

Smolak, L., & Levine, M. P. (1994). Toward an empirical basis for primary prevention of eating problems with elementary school children. *Eating Disorders: The Journal of Treatment and Prevention, 2,* 293–307.

Smolak, L., & Levine, M. P. (1996). Adolescent transitions and the development of eating problems. In L. Smolak, M. P. Levine, & R. Striegel-Moore (Eds.), *The developmental psychopathology of eating disorders: Implications for research, prevention, and treatment* (pp. 207–233). Mahwah, NJ: Lawrence Erlbaum Associates.

Smolak, L., Levine, M. P., & Schermer, F. (1998). A controlled evaluation of an elementary school primary prevention program for eating problems. *Journal of Psychosomatic Research, 44,* 339–354.

Smolak, L., Levine, M.P., & Schermer, F. (1998b). Lessons from lessons: An evaluation of an elementary school prevention program. In G. Noordenbos & W. Vandereycken (Eds.). *The prevention of eating disorders.* (pp. 137–172). London: Athlone.

Smolak, L., Levine, M.P., & Schermer, F. (in press). Parental input and weight concerns among elementary school children. *International Journal of Eating Disorders.*

Staffieri, R. (1967). A study of social stereotype of body-image in children. *Journal of Personality and Social Psychology, 7,* 101–104.

Stipek, D. J. (1981). Children's perceptions of their own and classmate's ability. *Journal of Educational Psychology, 73,* 404–410.

Striegel-Moore, R. (1993). Etiology of binge eating: A developmental perspective. In C. Fairburn & G. T. Wilson (Eds.), *Binge eating: Nature, assessment, and treatment* (pp. 144–172). New York: Guilford.

Striegel-Moore, R., & Smolak, L. (1996). The role of race in the development of eating disorders. In L. Smolak, M. P. Levine, & R. Striegel-Moore (Eds.), *The developmental psychopathology of eating disorders: Implications for research, prevention, and treatment* (pp. 259–284). Mahwah, NJ: Lawrence Erlbaum Associates.

Streigel-Moore, R., & Smolak, L. (in press). The influence of ethnicity on eating disorders in women. In Eisler & Hersen (Eds.), *Handbook of gender, culture, and health.* Mahwah, NJ: Lawrence Erlbaum Associates.

Stipek, D. (1981). Children's perceptions of their own and their classmates' ability. *Journal of Educational Psychology, 73,* 404–410.

Strober, M., & Humphrey, L. (1987). Familial contributions to the etiology and course of anorexia nervosa. *Journal of Consulting and Clinical Psychology, 55,* 654–659.

Taylor, J., Gilligan, C., & Sullivan, M. (1994). *Between voice and silence.* Cambridge, MA: Harvard University Press.

Thelen, M., & Cormier, J. (1995). Desire to be thinner and weight control among children and their parents. *Behavior Therapy, 26,* 85–99.

Tobin, D., Johnson, C., Steinberg, S., Staats, M., & Dennis, A. (1991). Multifactorial assessment of bulimia nervosa. *Journal of Abnormal Psychology, 100,* 14–21.

Winzelberg, A., Taylor, C., Altman, T., Eldredge, K., Dev, P., & Constantinou, P. (in press). Evaluation of a computer-mediated eating disorder intervention program. *International Journal of Eating Disorders, 24,* 339–350.

Worell, J., & Todd, J. (1996). Development of the gendered self. In L. Smolak, M. P. Levine, & R. Striegel-Moore (Eds.), *The developmental psychopathology of eating disorders: Implications for research, prevention, and treatment* (pp. 135–156). Mahwah, NJ: Lawrence Erlbaum Associates.

Zerbe, K. (1993). *The body betrayed: Women, eating disorders, and treatment.* Washington, DC: American Psychiatric Press.

☐ Note

[1]It is possible that methodological problems have led to a misunderstanding of the effects of primary prevention. For example, without a control group it is difficult to interpret Carter et al.'s (1997) findings. See Franko & Orosan-Weine (1998) for a discussion of some of these issues.

CHAPTER

6

Catherine Steiner-Adair
Amy Purcell Vorenberg

Resisting Weightism: Media Literacy for Elementary-School Children

In order for eating disorders prevention to be effectively woven into the fabric of essential school-based preventative health education, the field needs to offer several paradigms and approaches that join with other prevention initiatives. This chapter offers both theoretical and practical suggestions that support the increasing recognition of the necessity for school-based eating-disorders prevention. Central to this paper are the following ideas: (1) Eating disorders per se are not "the problem" but, rather, behaviors that many girls and some boys turn to in order to deal with a wide range of experiences; (2) body intolerance, disordered eating, and eating disorders are a culturally informed and mediated problem; (3) therefore, students need knowledge and skills that enable them to challenge cultural messages and norms that lead to disordered eating behavior and body intolerance; (4) eating disorders need to be linked to weightism (Steiner-Adair, 1987, 1994) and reformed as a social justice issue; and (5) misperceptions about who is affected by disordered eating and eating disorders influence whether eating disorders prevention is acknowledged as a priority in health education.

☐ Understanding the Cultural Context

Numerous studies point to the importance of a feminist analysis in understanding, treating, and preventing eating disorders (e.g., Fallon, Katzman, & Wooley, 1994). It is generally believed that eating disorders are culturally mediated illnesses, in part because at least 90% of sufferers are females (Becker, 1996). In order to approach the process of effective eating disorders prevention, it is im-

The ideas reflected in this paper represent the authors' collaborative work in the areas of media literacy, the healthy development of children, and the prevention of eating disorders. In this paper, the pronoun "I" refers to Dr. Steiner-Adair in the first and third sections and to Ms. Vorenberg in the second.

portant to understand the cultural contexts in which girls develop and are at increased risk for developing eating disorders.

Findings from the Harvard Project on the Psychology of Girls and Women's Development provide substantial evidence (from a number of studies involving girls from different racial, cultural, and economic backgrounds) that as girls approach adolescence, their psychological strength and health is at risk (see, e.g., Brown & Gilligan, 1992). As they grow in to adolescence, many girls suffer a series of losses. They lose confidence in themselves as sources of authority; they lose their sense of efficacy and ambition; and, simultaneously, they adopt risky and dangerous behaviors and attitudes toward eating and their bodies, a concurrence that is not coincidental (Steiner-Adair, 1986). As girls approach adolescence, they begin to see that there are cultural norms about female adulthood, about what can be known and said, and about how one presents oneself to the world, and they discover the risks of authenticity, self knowledge, and self acceptance (Brown & Gilligan, 1992).

More specifically, Becker (1996) calls our attention to contemporary values in Westernized societies that teach females, in particular, the idea that the body is a commodity, something that can and should be personally changed, and that working on your body in order to perfect the narrow cultural ideal image of beauty is a form of identity development. Furthermore, girls, through the media and at school, are often exposed to harassing comments about female bodies. Thus, on the one hand, girls are told that their bodies are commodities they should strive to enhance. On the other hand, girls are told that their bodies are the appropriate recipients of sexual, physical, and verbal abuse. For example, it is not uncommon for girls to be teased about their "tits," to have their skirts pulled up on the playground, to be called "sluts," or to have their breasts grabbed walking down the hall in school. It is also not uncommon for girls to respond with silence and shame to the combined messages that their bodies need to be improved upon and the idea that their bodies are targets for harassment (see Chapters 9, 12 and 16). As girls learn to distrust their own voices, experiences, and knowledge, their bodies become the "selves" that speak—too often "telling tales" of self-loathing. For some girls, their growing preoccupation with weight, clothes, and bodies overrides other sources of confidence, identity, and self expression.

Clearly the cultural overvaluation of thinness and height and the vilification of bodies that fall into the wide range of "other" contribute to a cultural milieu that sets the stage for the high prevalence of body dissatisfaction and dieting, precursors to disordered eating and eating disorders. However, cross-cultural research suggests that the existence of a beauty ideal does not inevitably lead to the belief in the possibility or necessity of changing one's body in order to match the ideal image (Becker, 1995). In addition to the portrayal of thinness as a beauty ideal, there is also an underlying assumption in our culture that one's body is a central aspect of one's self or identify, and just as one can create a self, so too one can and should create a body; furthermore, in our achievement-oriented society, the extent to which one successfully creates an ideal body is an important index of achievement (Becker, 1996; Steiner-Adair, 1986). This joining of body image with character traits, moral virtue, and desirability contributes to the motivation to alter one's body in the name of self-development. The media portray to children the goal of the American ethos of self-cultivation.

When the cultural message of creating oneself through one's body is joined with an increasingly restrictive definition of the ideal body, a climate is created in which it is difficult to challenge cultural images and messages about adulthood, messages that, although normative, are unhealthy, unreal, and harmful. In other words, in order to successfully deconstruct the impact of the culture on the prevalence of eating disorders, we need to look not only at which images are presented, but at how they are rendered so compelling, and why females feel so motivated and capable of changing their bodies (Becker, 1996).

Girls and women are more likely than males to be affected by the cultural value and message that it is possible to recreate your body and use your "new and improved" body as a product for yourself (Becker, 1996). A thin body image as the essence of a positive self image sends girls the message that who they appear to be is more powerful and important than who they actually are. Consequently, girls learn at an early age to "work" on cultivating a body image that will link them with success. The ideal image of the thin, successful woman and all her ideally positive characteristics is easily identifiable by children and adults. The media reinforce this image by using thin models to enhance the marketability of products. Thus, the message is doubly reinforced: "Look this way and you'll be a success. This is what success looks like" (Becker, 1996). These messages are particularly harsh and destructive now because the images that are portrayed as ideal often are not even human bodies. In addition to whatever unhealthy eating and body sculpting behaviors models may use, the use of plastic surgery and computer graphics to perfect (or invent!) ideal body images has moved the current image of beauty beyond an image of natural beauty and has redefined "natural" and "healthy". In search of success, control, healthy, sexiness, and so forth, in the form of an unnatural image of beauty, girls internalize messages that lead to body disparagement, disordered eating, and dieting, and these attitudes and behaviors become normative among females (Kilbourne, 1994; Wolf, 1991).

However, negative body image, dieting, and disordered eating are not benign developmental rites of passage. They have serious negative physiological, psychological, and behavioral consequences, such as fatigue, depression, constipation, amenorrhea, mental sluggishness, lowered intake of calcium and iron, impaired physical growth, impaired school performance, and increased conflict within the family (Bull, 1988; MacDonald, Wearring, & Moase, 1983, Neumark-Sztainer, Butler, & Palti, 1995; Nylander, 1971). Eating disorders are the third most common chronic illness among females in the United States (Kreipe et al., 1995; Lucas, Beard, O'Fallon, & Kurland, 1991), constituting a major health concern. Research suggests that 1–2% of female adolescents develop anorexia nervosa, a slightly higher percentage develop bulimia nervosa, and the prevalence of eating disorders among preteens and younger adolescents is still on the rise (Goldman, 1996). Dieting for weight loss, a common precursor and frequent precipitant to the later development of eating disorders, is extremely common among teenage girls (Huon, 1994). Over 50% of adolescent girls think they are overweight and, consequently, diet (Fisher et al., 1995; Neumark-Sztainer et al., 1995). Research suggests that 13% of teenage girls, although not yet diagnosed with full-blown eating disorders, engage in anorectic and bulimic behaviors such as self-induced vomiting, laxative and diet pill abuse, skipping meals, and cycles of binge eating and dieting (Killen et al., 1986). In children ages 8–10, approximately half the girls were dissatisfied with their size and wanted to be thinner (Mellin, Scully, & Irwin, 1986). Fifty-two percent of 14-year-old girls report that they feel better about themselves if they are on a diet (Johnson, Tobin, & Lipkin, 1989). In practical terms, it is not unusual for a 14-year-old girl to think that she will be in better control of and happier with her life—as evidenced by more friends, closer ties with teachers, higher grades, and more celebrated accomplishments—if she skips lunch.

Although dieting is offered as a solution for many of life's dilemmas, as well as a means to a good life, dieting ultimately meets with extremely little success: 90–98% of dieters regain weight within 2–5 years (Burgard & Lyons, 1994). Moreover, as noted, dieting often leads to negative and immediate health and academic consequences. Dieting is also associated with nicotine addiction; young girls, especially teenage white girls, are the fastest growing population of smokers and are consciously using cigarettes to enhance their "image" and suppress their appetites.

Ironically, dieting is probably a contributing factor in the rising rates of obesity among American girls, because unhealthy dieting routinely results in unhealthy eating, particularly binge eating and consumption of high-fat junk foods (Gortmaker, Must, Perrin, Sobol, & Dietz, 1993). Along with numerous serious health consequences, obesity can influence girls' social and economic potential in a culture that values thinness in females and does not offer women of different body sizes equal access to a wide range of social and career achievement.

The common notion persists that only middle- and upper-middle-class white girls develop disordered eating and eating disorders. This is a misperception. Research indicates that girls from African American, Asian, Native American, Hispanic, and Latino families, as well as girls from every socioeconomic background, are affected by disordered eating (Crago, Shisslak, & Estes, 1996; Smith & Krejci, 1991; Thompson, 1994; Willard & Maresh, 1996). African American girls, who in early adolescence sometimes demonstrate higher levels of self esteem and a greater resilience to loss of voice and self knowledge than do white girls, (see Chapter 11) have been shown to develop disordered eating (as well as unwanted pregnancy and drug addiction) as signs of their profound disappointment in what society does—and does not—offer them (Thompson, 1994). It is not uncommon for low-income girls (White girls as well as girls of color) who aspire to be assimilated into mainstream White culture to either overeat or diet in attempts to deal with daily losses and frustrations (Thompson, 1994). Unfortunately, because of the persisting myth that eating disorders are an exclusive phenomenon of White culture, many girls of color are being underserved and, yet again, marginalized by prejudice.

Eighty percent of women in America, across race, class, and ethnic differences, report that the experience of being female means "feeling too fat" (Rodin, Silberstein, & Streigel-Moore, 1985). Given the prevalence of dieting and body preoccupation among women, it is hardly surprising that young girls who struggle with issues of voice, vision, and courage, resort to body obsession and disordered eating as attempts to manage life's challenges. Because body image dissatisfaction, expressed through mild-to-severe disordered eating, is a strong predictor of low self esteem, girls who get caught in the "body trap" risk stunting their psychological, emotional, and intellectual growth as well. Preoccupied with physically altering themselves, girls shrink from realizing their full range of competencies and from taking healthy risks in school, at home, and in relationships of all kinds.

Mainstream American culture offers girls (and women) two primary "skills" for coping with life's ups and downs: shopping and dieting or overeating. Following the loss of a boyfriend, an academic failure, or conflict with parents and friends, girls often turn to self- and body-injurious behavior: "I was so mad at myself for getting a C, I pigged out on ice cream. Then I made myself run an extra six laps even though my ankles were killing me." Unfortunately, new beginnings and noteworthy successes propel many girls to similar unhealthy behaviors: "You're going to try out for the play? That's so cool! Lose five pounds and you'll feel much more confident," or, "Let's go to the mall and get you a new outfit," rather than, "Go ask Amy what tryouts are like and I'll help you practice." Clearly, dieting, eating, and shopping are not adequate "skills" for coping with life's ups and down, yet in the cultural contest that values and promotes body improvement as an achievement and tool for self development, it is not surprising that girls turn to these self limiting behaviors in times of need.

Primary prevention of eating disorders must help girls identify the larger sociocultural values that direct girls toward dieting and shopping as coping mechanisms and, in so doing, contribute to maintaining various attitudes and contexts that set the stage for disordered eating, body disparagement, and eating disorders (Becker, 1996; Steiner-Adair, 1994). The field of media literacy (Silverblatt, 1995; Worsnop, 1994) offers a pedagogy for teaching children and adults how to deconstruct cultural messages in order to offer them real skills for healthy resistance and resilience. Media literacy offers students the ability to think critically about messages that glorify and normalize self-limiting and injurious behavior such as dieting, excessive shopping, and cigarette smoking (see Chapters 1 and 4).

Because the field of media literacy is perhaps unknown to many clinicians as well as some educators, the following section describes a unit on media literacy, developed by Amy Purcell Vorenberg, a third grade teacher at the Shady Hill School, Cambridge, Massachusetts. We believe that this unit is a good example of the kind of prevention education for young girls that should precede prevention aimed specifically at eating disorders. By offering girls the skills of media literacy prior to age 10 or so, when dieting becomes more of a perceived desirable behavior (Smolak & Levine, 1994), girls might be better able to resist the pressure of messages to participate in the culture of dieting, body intolerance, and shopping. Media literacy offers a feminist method for teaching girls to identify the cultural value placed on "working on your body" and in so doing offers students the possibility of empowering themselves to resist the false definitions of power associated with harmful images. If students have the opportunity to study and discuss and "experience" the process involved in image making, as well as the politics and ethics, they are better able to be skeptical consumers. In addition, media literacy should set the stage for further identifying and resisting forms of cultural prejudice and bias associated with thinness and body shape.

☐ Teaching Media Literacy to Third Graders

Media literacy is a relatively new, but fast-growing, academic discipline. Media literacy is defined as the ability of a citizen to access, analyze, and produce information for specific outcomes (Aufderheide, 1993). To be media literate means more than being able to watch television and read magazines. For me, as a third grade teacher, it means being prepared to teach students to think critically about different forms of media and media messages, and to understand that media are created through conscious and specific decision-making processes, processes that are primarily for-profit ventures. Teaching students to be media literate means that I am helping them to learn to decode, "read," and discuss visual images, just as I would teach them to read, write, listen, and speak effectively. I believe that teachers must support the development of media-literacy skills, because such skills are necessary to navigate the complicated waters of the mass media culture.

Today, children in the United States are growing up in homes in which the television is on seven hours daily (Huston, 1992). Children start watching television in infancy and continue on into adulthood. By the time an average viewer graduates from high school, the child has watched over 18,000 hours of television, compared with 11,000 hours spent in school (Huston, 1992). During that time, the child has been exposed to countless hours of commercials, literally thousands of acts of violence, and daily messages about beauty, dieting, and humor that are profoundly critical and disrespectful of bodies (Kilbourne, 1994). With this ongoing paradigm shift from a print-based culture to one in which some prominent media operate primarily on the basis of images and sounds (e.g., television), while others feature images, words, and sounds (e.g., the World Wide Web), children need to be equipped with the skills to better understand and interpret the messages, both implicit and explicit.

Media literacy is a "through line" in my classroom, a highly prioritized conceptual theme around which I frame lessons that will empower my students in new ways. It is a thread that is woven throughout my curriculum, on varying levels, all year. At times, I do direct teaching about the concepts of media literacy. Other times, media literacy discussions emerge from spontaneous conversations initiated by students. For example, I respond to student conversations about the latest movie they have seen by asking, "What was that movie all about? Did you like it?" These questions prompt conversations that reveal interesting perceptions that my students share, notions about what it means to be female or male in our culture or what a "perfect" body looks like. Our spontaneous media literacy conversations touch upon many types of media, from favorite television shows, to movies, to toys connected with mass marketing campaigns, to advertisement jingles. However, when I am teaching media literacy concepts, the class focus narrows to television. Using examples from television as a primary source, students develop skills to understand how media are created. With these skills, they are then able to look at other forms of media through new lenses, ready to understand magazines or movies, newspapers, or national advertising campaigns in new ways.

My primary goal is to help students to see that all media images are constructed (Worsnop, 1994) every media story, from the sitcoms we watch to the news stories featured at 6:00, is a construction of someone's point of view, someone's version of the truth. Someone, somewhere, is putting together the story we view at home. It is literally impossible to tell the "whole" story about anything, so decisions have to be made about what pieces of the whole will be presented, what perspectives will be shared.

On the news, for example, the construction of each story requires many decisions: which story to tell first; who is going to be interviewed; which pictures are going to be shown; in what order will they be shown; which words will go with the pictures to make the story complete. As we watch carefully constructed, smooth programming, it can be easy to assume that we are being told "The Truth," rather than a construction of the events to fit the format of the nightly news.

A second, related goal is to help students to understand that *seeing is not believing.* The old saying, "I've got to see it to believe it," doesn't apply in the image-based culture of today. We can "see" all sorts of things because images have been manipulated and transformed through the use of cinematographic tricks. Because special effects can make anything happen on screen, we, as audience, simply cannot trust our eyes anymore.

A third goal is for students to understand that, if all shows are constructed, the creations represent points of view. We forget this most of the time we watch, unless a dramatic technique is used, such as dropping the camera down to show another perspective, for example, a child's take on the world or a dog's point of view. In most television, the point of view is designed to make viewers feel as if they are in the same room as the characters on the screen. Viewers are meant to feel included and, therefore, part of the perceived truth on screen. This informs how we view, judge, and evaluate ourselves.

A fourth goal is to build specific skills as a media-literate consumer. Most television programming is financed primarily by advertisers. Therefore, viewers need to know that. Media-literate consumers understand how commercials convince and influence.

In some ways, children already are experts on the technologies they use regularly. They are comfortable with computers, video games, remote controls, and videocassette recorders and as young as age three, many can turn on the television, insert a video, and change the channels. But my third grade students (ages 8–9) have surprised me by their lack of knowledge about how images get "into" the television or how programs are made. They had been content to turn on the television and watch, assuming the shows were just "there" without effort. Their questions are fascinating: Where do the people go when you turn off the set? How do the pictures fly through the air? How do people get shrunk down to fit in the screen? I was shocked at their disjointed, illogical constructions, and their naive attempts to make sense of the magical box. Thus, in the beginning of our work to understand the media, we discussed the basis of what makes a television work. Using books for reference, such as *Eureka! It's Television* (Bendick & Bendick, 1993), I introduced students to simple concepts of electronics and began to develop their understanding of the complicated nature of television transmissions.

Because I believe that project-based learning offers multiple entry points for the widest range of learners, I designed a project for the class to participate in: *The Third Grade News.* The class assignment was to create a news program that would accurately cover the happenings in school during "Flex Week." Flex Week is special because all specialist classes are canceled and teachers are given free reign to develop innovative and fun curricula, without the limits of the school schedule. Our Flex Week project involved developing media literacy skills through the creation of the "IIIPurcell News Program." Empowering my students as authors of the program gave them direct experience with the many decisions that need to be made to create a show.

We secured the school video camera for recording stories, and students took on the roles of camera crew, anchorperson, weather reporter, and news reporters. They turned the classroom into a studio, designing an anchor desk and a weather reporting station. The students also made props and wrote a jingle for the program. They worked hard to create a logo, deciding on a whale fluke because our regular study focused on whales.

As they constructed their news program, decisions had to be made and compromises reached through intensive collaborative work. It was clear we could not cover every event happening at every moment on the campus. Students debated over which stories were most important to tell: Would it be the making of fairy houses around the school paths? The Greek dancers? Work that our partner class was doing? An artist-in-residence creating a play about a Japanese folk tale? What were the other third grade classes doing? Would it be important to include our best friends or our brothers and sisters at school? These conversations were powerful examples of the complicated negotiating that can go on as decisions about what we, as television viewers, see. The students, deciding how to construct their "news" story, began to think more critically about options and point of view.

To connect our work to media literacy concepts, we watched a local network news broadcast and applied critical thinking skills to our viewing. We wondered about the stories that the network chose tell us and discussed why news programs featured stories that students perceived as violent, dangerous, and scary. One student commented, "I wish we could see good news instead of scary news!"

Watching the broadcast news in class, one student was assigned to count the commercial messages. We were surprised that 19 commercials were aired during the 30-minute news show. This realization led us to conversations about advertising. Using two videos produced by Consumer Reports, *Buy Me That* and *Buy Me That, Too,* the students learned some of the special effects and editing techniques that are used to make commercials. Because many of the products were familiar to children, the conversations reflected the fact that many of them had been "tricked" by advertisements, had bought products that were disappointing, or were members of Kids' Clubs that were actually marketing schemes. The students were stunned, then outraged. Through dialogue, they were able to process their frustrations at being misled, and later they felt empowered to write letters to companies about disappointments they had experienced. As a class project, we wrote to a few companies, but no letter was ever acknowledged.

We also watched some children's cartoons. The themes throughout the cartoon programs were issues of violence and gender equity. Children saw helpless girls being rescued by male superheroes. In the random samples I videotaped one morning there were literally dozens of acts of violence. Interestingly, the girls noticed that when girls in cartoons had problems, they tried to solve them with kindness and love. That is, girl characters used love, hearts, rainbows, and butterflies to overwhelm their enemies. Boys, on the other hand, were clever and used trickery or problem-solving skills to resolve a situation. Boys were also far more likely to use violence.

Viewing these clips and then generating a list of powerful characters on television brought the group to one of the most powerful, troubling conversations I have led as a teacher. Girls in the classroom, eyes wide and arms waving as they begged to be called upon, shared story after story about the times they have seen girls portrayed unfairly in the media. They spoke about how girls on television were unrealistic and never allowed to do anything interesting. It was as though I had opened a flood gate: The girls were full of tales and could not get enough time to talk about their perceptions of, and feelings about, girls in the media. They shared their stories, with recurring themes of exclusion, helplessness, striving for boys' attention, stereotypic female roles, and vanity. It was already clear to these 8- and 9-year-old girls that watching these television shows creates an early developmental context in which girls are taught through the media that it is important to cultivate skills for changing their bodies and for developing roles in order to influence their future desirability. The girls were angry at the directions that the media were giving them about how to be successful as young females.

The boys, on the other hand, sat back and seemed puzzled by the girls' stories and their passion for the conversation. One boy, in particular, sat back listening for while, and then decided it was time for his voice to be heard. "You are lying," he accused the girls. He could not, simply could not, conceive of the stories the girls were telling. The girls rallied together and protested. They were furious, as was I, that they were having a chance to talk honestly and openly, only to have one of their classmates respond so negatively.

The girls demanded to be heard. They continued to dominate the conversation, with that one boy fighting back and arguing each point. He struggled to prove them wrong. They pointed out many painful places in which each girl had felt their gender as a barrier, as a limitation. One girl talked about loving to play ice hockey and trying out for a boys' team. She expressed her frustration at buying hockey cards and never getting a card with a woman hockey player. Another girl talked about stories she loved, stories that have male characters, and how she has pretended that the boy is a girl. She even said she switched the characters' names, for example, turning Joe into Joanna. Another student said she bought a game called Guess Who? by Milton Bradley. The object of the game is to guess the mystery person chosen by your opponent. The student explained that when she plays that game, she *never* picks a girl because there are only a few girls in the deck. As she explained, "If you pick a girl, you'll never win." The examples went on, with the male student desperately trying to find inconsistencies in the girls' stories and ideas. This boy was unopposed by all the other boys in the class and, thus, became the spokesperson for all the boys in the class. For me as a teacher, I could see that by the third grade these boys had become completely socialized in their expectations of whom the girls should be and their expectation that girls should be happy with these gender roles. In the conversation that followed, I could hear how the early feminist protest met with enormous resistance from the boys who were well positioned in a patriarchal culture.

This class conversation happened over three years ago, and I recently asked one of the girls in that class what she remembered about the week of media focus. Her words stay with me. "It was the greatest. I loved how we talked about stuff that teachers usually never let us talk about. We talked about real stuff. I loved it."

To complete our Flex Week study, we videotaped our IIIPurcell News show and reflected on the process. Our program was rough and unpolished, unlike the highly edited broadcast television news shows the class was familiar with.

This, too, was a lesson for us. Our "homemade" version was simple. We learned that with our basic equipment we were unable to produce slick, fancy productions like the television we see regularly. However, regardless of the production quality, the students were proud of their efforts and felt that they better understood what is involved in creating media news messages.

The following year, another media literacy project focused on print media, looking specifically at models in magazines. Using advertisements from many magazines, including *Glamour, Vogue,* and *Mademoiselle,* a wide variety of different and dramatic poses were chosen. In one picture, the model had red hair, flying wildly back from her face—basically going straight up in the air. When asked to state characteristics that they saw in the picture, third graders said, "weird hair, crazy, about to fly, tall and skinny, strong, trying to be beautiful, white." The next picture was a woman whose hair was dark brown, but her make-up made her look pale. Her pose accentuated her long neck. Children said, "ugly, naked, white/pale, make over, lips, staring." In another image, the class saw a woman sitting down with her legs crossed, her clothes conservative, her arm held up. They saw "normal, athletic, making a sign (with hand), casual, wants something." Many other images were shown, including a well-dressed woman getting out of a car. Comments included "independent, snobby, rich, mean, fancy, bossy, self-centered, showoff." This photo led the class to a rather hostile discussion of the model's motivation for being in the images. The kids were certain it was just for the money, and they spoke very negatively about the women posing in the pictures.

After the discussion subsided, I revealed the secret of the activity. *All* of the women in *all* of the pictures were the *same* model. With the help of a small army of photographers, make-up specialists, hairstylists, and computer graphic experts, the model—Kristen McMenamy—has the ability to transform herself to appear different in many images. The kids were shocked! They had seen such different messages and ideas in each of the photographs, and they were certain that each photograph was a different person. Kids saw the same woman as ugly, beautiful, normal, crazy, fancy, casual, and so forth. We generated a list of what the model had to have done to look so different in each photograph: change hairdos; change clothes; change backgrounds; new props and objects; change pose or body shape; change make-up; change expression. By changing all of these things, the students saw that the woman could look completely different. We asked, "Which one is the real Kristen McMenamy?" and the students agreed there was no way to tell.

After discovering the transformation in appearances that model Kristen Mc-Menamy and her associates are able to construct for different advertisers, we brainstormed a list of characteristics that an image can portray. Students suggested many: funny, snobby, mean, scared, impressive, nice, angry, rude, intense, far out, shy, horrified, sweet, innocent, active, gentle, and so on. From the list, each student decided on one word to transform themselves. Playing with props of scarves, eye glasses, and hats, students tried on different "images." For some, it was safest to choose an image that was comfortable and familiar. Others tried on images that were new and unfamiliar.

After some play with the props, the "photo shoot" was scheduled. With the help of parent volunteers, a photographer and make-up artist arrived in class. It was exciting—lights, cameras, backdrops. All students wore a black skirt or pants so only their props, hair, makeup, and facial expressions would build the image. They were thrilled by the idea of transforming themselves because it was fun and it was exciting, and it gave them permission to try on a new look, a new "them."

The photographer took Polaroids to test light and poses, and worked with each student to encourage her or him to try really hard to "be" the word chosen. For some, it was easy and natural. One student had braided her hair and worn dark sunglasses. She made sure her lipstick clearly defined her lips; she leaned into her pose and stared into the lens. She was most definitely "hip."

Another student had been experimenting with her power all year, sometimes challenging me, and often challenging her classmates about their opinions and ideas. She chose the word "powerful" and experimented with multiple poses in front of the mirror. She practiced with her hands folded across her chest and then with her hands on her hips. In front of the camera, she told the photographer, "I have to be above you—you have to look up at me." Her power is clear in her image. Later that month, after the project, she arrived at school with a crew cut. When the class gasped in shock as she entered the meeting area, she boldly said, "Just remember, it's only an image." She certainly drew power and powerfully from this work.

Other students found it harder to participate in the photo shoot, as they were nervous about being in front of the camera and less confident in how to transform themselves. As the photographer set up his equipment, one student started to cry and stated that she just could not be "cute," her original choice. We talked about other possibilities and she settled on "brave," perhaps to convince herself she could be brave enough to do it. She turned herself into an explorer and her image tells the viewer nothing of her nervousness! She truly was brave as she worked through her anxiety and posed for this picture.

All the children, posing and projecting images, saw and experienced their power and ability to create themselves in an image. They had fun transforming themselves and later discussed how much fun the work was. We returned to a conversation we had about a model's motivation. I asked, "Was it fun? Or do you think the models just do it for the money?" The entire class could see that it was both fun and work to change an image and to get a message across through an image. To understand the fun and challenge of a model's work allows students new ways of understanding the media. As they become more skilled at seeing the elements that help shape images, they are less likely to be tricked or seduced by what looks "perfect" in the media.

In regard to the nature and power of "images," we also looked at print and television advertisements to see what we could learn about the "language" that they speak to us. We talked about the images built around certain products and our desires to connect to certain images, perhaps more so than the products themselves. Then we designed imaginary soda pops, created product names, and worked on commercials to sell. The children considered colors that were appealing and developed ads to show how their "pop" was the best. In one video commercial the students created a full scene showing how the "pop" would change the quality of the drinker's life. Sitting around a table, without the soda, the group was sad and bored. Then someone brought a pack of "Purple Pop," the fun soda, and with one sip, joy and good times!

Watching this commercial evolve, it was frightening how many "adult" messages were unknowingly integrated into this piece. The soda was the ticket to fun, just as many alcohol commercials proclaim about their products. The messages are learned on many levels, and the class conversation about a drink's ability to change a group from bored to happy was interesting and telling. All of the class wanted to buy "Purple Pop" more than any of the others created by the class.

We also visited an advertising agency, where we were shown various components of advertising work. We saw dozens of pictures being considered for one Keds advertisement. Students also saw clips from advertisements directed at different target audiences and they learned that for the Union Bay print advertisements, over 15,000 pictures were taken in order to choose just six "perfect" images. The question was posed, "If you had 15,000 chances to look good in a picture, with the additional support of ideal lighting, hair and make-up stylists, wardrobe specialists, and the finest camera equipment, couldn't you look good in at least *one* of those pictures?" The answer to all was obvious: With all the techniques and manipulations that go on behind the scenes as media is produced, anything can look *great*. The children came to understand completely that the image created has very little to do with what's "real." Rather, it has everything to do with painstaking, masterful construction of the image.

In summary, teachers should consider the following educational concepts in thinking about teaching media literacy to students as part of health education and the prevention of disordered eating:

1. It is essential for students to be able to understand the process by which images are constructed and promoted.
2. Students need strategies to be resilient against images and cultural messages that may undermine their healthy development.
3. Media literacy needs to be taught throughout a student's academic career both in highly focused curricula and in spontaneous discussions as they occur in response to students' concerns, questions, and experiences.
4. Students need to be aware that everything they see in the media represents a point of view, a pocketbook, and a desire to prevail.
5. "Seeing is not believing" anymore, because of the impact of technology in inventing and representing reality.
6. We live in a culture of consumption in which it is very hard to know when you have and are enough.
7. Curricula for media literacy must involve current examples, hands-on materials, and experiential learning.
8. Teachers should be aware of the likelihood that gender biases in the culture will be reflected in the classroom and prepared to identify and address these dynamics as they emerge in the students' behavior and their own behavior.

In conclusion, developing students' abilities to critique and question the media was an explicit goal as each media literacy activity was introduced into the curriculum. Less explicit goals included my desire to empower my students, primarily girls, to question the messages that the media deliver about gender identity and body image. I wanted to help boys see how difficult it is to grow up in a female body in our culture, as well as how inequitably power is depicted in the media. I wanted all the students to understand that the media are seductive and present images that can be both appealing and appalling at the same time. It is my observation that if students are provided with tools for critical thinking about the media, they broaden their understanding and reject limiting, stereotypic attitudes and behaviors that mainstream media cultivate and reinforce.

Specifically, students learn to question media messages that glorify the power of men and the sexualized, thin bodies of women.

☐ Diversity Education and Weightism

In conjunction with the concept of media literacy, children as young as kindergarten and elementary school need to be taught, in a developmentally appropriate way, about "weightism" as a form of prejudice. One of the most insidious underlying factors propeling the surge of all of the aforementioned threats to girls' healthy development (i.e., body dissatisfaction, disordered eating, eating disorders, obesity) is a set of beliefs, attitudes, and behaviors that, in mainstream Western cultures, idealize thinness and vilify large bodies and weight gain (Steiner-Adair, 1987). This form of prejudice affects all girls and women and is powerfully reinforced by the ethos of "working on your body." Weightism is firmly established in most elementary schools as both boys and girls joke about, tease, and bully classmates whose body sizes do not fit the cultural norm. As noted, the media are also a major transmitter of the wide range of thinking and judgment that can be identified as weightist by children.

It is not unusual for children in kindergarten to tease each other and exclude one another based on body size (Ikeda & Naworski, 1994). Calling a child fat, saying "oink" in a cafeteria line, thumping the ground chanting "earthquake" as a child is about to sit on a chair, or saying, "You can't play, you're too fat," are all too frequent events in school. The most common disciplinary remark made, if any is made, is "that's not nice." We live in a culture in which fat jokes are so popular (for example, Garfield the cat) and so much the norm that their meanness often is ignored. However, if a child makes a racial comment about another child's skin color, most teachers use that moment to offer anti-bias training, teach about diversity and racism, and sternly discuss what kinds of personal comments will and will not be tolerated.

It is very easy to teach children in kindergarten that personal comments about body size and body color are equally unfair and harmful and not allowed. Weightist thinking can be found in the popular press in books expressly written for children. For example, in the children's book *A Baby For Max* (Lasky, 1987) about the arrival of a new baby, the mother says, "If our new baby is a boy, how about naming him Jacob?" The sibling says, "No, Mommy, Jacob is a chubby name."

As often happens with prejudice, the people who are being oppressed turn the prejudicial thinking against themselves and their peers. Weightism teaches girls to identify with the oppressive culture of body- and self-loathing; consequently, girls are vicious to themselves as well as each other. Unfortunately, girls often observe adult women critiquing their own bodies and calculating their own and other women's worth based on body weight—lower weight, higher worth. I have often heard girls cite the model Kate Moss (the Twiggy of the 1990s) as personifying the ideal definition of female beauty and quickly rattle off the common numbers of ideal beauty: a young woman standing 5'8" to 5'10" and weighing 110 to 120 pounds (body mass index = 16.8–17.4). Weightism and the "beauty bias" extend even further: Thin females are commonly (often mistakenly) assumed to possess other desirable traits simply as a result of their "ability to achieve" an ideal weight. In the author's experience working with school children, by the end of elementary school, girls commonly associate thinness and weight loss with high achievement, intelligence, and success and competence. In contrast to the ideal image based on models, it is helpful for girls and women to encounter poster images such as the Body Shoppe's (1997) "Ruby" (a large, voluptuous, and clearly pleased-with-herself nude woman), who reminds girls that "there are three billion women who don't look like supermodels and only 8 who do."

One intervention I use at schools to expose the prejudice of weightism is to ask students (preferably with boys and girls separately) the following question: "If a woman walks down the street and looks like she just stepped off the cover of *Vogue* or *Seventeen*, what are the assumptions and judgments you make about her life?" Students quickly describe this thin woman as extremely "successful, very well-educated (like at an ivy league college), she has a really high status professional job (like a doctor or lawyer), she is assertive, confident at work, in control, has great friends, a perfect relationship, perfect kids, a beautiful home, really rich, she is in control of herself, really happy with herself, and she is respected by everyone." And inevitably, the negative aspects come out in three common ways: "She's an air-head, she's anorectic, and [from the girls] we hate her!"

Then I ask students to imagine a woman walking down the street who looks the opposite of this ideal image (short, not tall, big round body, not thin) and tell me how they think people judge her and the quality of her life. In seconds the sadly predictable adjectives fly: "lazy, stupid, pathetic, depressed, a loser, working a menial job, lonely, unmarried, no friends, no self-control, she's depressed, she hates herself." In this discussion I introduce the idea of weightism to students (or parents or teachers) as a mean and irrational form of prejudice that erupted in our culture as a form of backlash against women's equality, against women equally throwing their weight around in the world. I make the analogy to racism and the parallel structure in which body color evokes irrational and cruel judgments. I teach students about the dynamics of prejudice and the concept of identifying with the aggressor, which helps girls understand why they are so mean and critical to themselves and to each other. I also teach students about how all forms of prejudice hold those who are being oppressed to a different standard of moral development. For example, lighter skin is seen as more worthy of respect than darker skin, or vice versa, in some forms of racism. Students easily make the analogy to weightism. Still working in the frame of the dynamics of prejudice, students also can see how moral character can be irrationally connected to a physical feature. And, finally, by joining weightism to other forms of prejudice and social injustice, I offer students a media-literacy analysis of the cultural context that mediates eating disorders. I have been impressed by how this approach to prevention strengthens their ability to choose not to participate in this form of prejudicial thinking, which predisposes girls to body- and self-loathing, disordered eating, and eating disorders. It also deepens students' awareness of the dynamics and politics of all forms of bias and prejudice by drawing parallels between weightism and sexism, racism, classism, homophobia, ableism, and other forms of bias.

In weightism there is also a "morality of orality," through which women and girls determine their self worth by what they eat (e.g., "Let's be good today, let's skip lunch," or, "Let's be bad today, let's eat dessert"). This skewed form of moral reasoning, adopted predominantly by females, takes root during the elementary years ("Mommy, am I too fat?" a six-year-old first grader asks, probably looking for reassurance that she is lovable, that she is worthy). As they grow toward womanhood, girls internalize the cultural message to (literally) weigh their self-esteem, as well as the implicit threat that females will suffer negative repercussions if they "throw their weight around."

Unfortunately, there is nothing new about fat children being viciously teased at school and at home, or virtue being associated with certain eating patterns. What is new is that teasing children for being fat and idealizing children for being thin is now occurring in a culture in which eating disorders are a serious health problem. By joining weightism to other forms of diversity education and consciousness raising, including media literacy, teachers can shift the conceptualization of eating disorders as just a physical or mental health issue to a social-justice issue; teachers can help children identify bias in our culture based on body shape and weight, by having children become ethnographers and social scientists; help children identify their own internalized weightist thinking, which may predispose them to risk for disordered eating or eating disorders; help children identify the ways in which children either bond together or reject each other through weightist thinking; In these ways teachers help children resist messages to judge their self-worth by assessing their body shape, while deepening children's understanding of the general dynamics of prejudice.

In order for eating disorders prevention to be successful, it is necessary to reveal the layers of cultural values, bias, and attitudes that create the contexts that encourage people to turn to disordered eating and eating disorders to deal with life's challenges (Levine, 1994; Steiner-Adair, 1992, 1994). With the skills of media literacy, students are better able to discern the high premium (at a high cost) placed on the following culturally mediated notions: One's identity can be defined by one's body; and one's body can be changed and self-made; one's self can be known and truly seen through one's image; one's worth, moral sensibility, and achievement can be determined via one's body. Although students are casually bombarded with unhealthy, mean-spirited, and unreal values and images in the media, they are quite capable of seeing with their hearts. If taught the concept of weightism and offered an understanding of eating disorders as a social justice issue, students have an opportunity to know deeply what they sometimes sense to be true—that the cultural focus on bodies and images and what people weigh is unfair and immoral and can lead to dangerously unhealthy disordered eating and eating disorders.

☐ References

Aufderheide, P. (1993). *National leadership conference on media literacy.* Washington, DC: Aspen Institute.

Becker, A. E. (1995). *Body, self, and society: The view from Fiji.* Philadelphia: University of Pennsylvania Press.

Becker, A. E. (1996). Culture, media, and eating disorders. *Harvard Review of Psychiatry, 1,* 163–167.

Bendick, J., & Bendick, R. (1993). *Eureka! It's television!* Brookfield, CT: Millbrook Press.

The Body Shoppe. (1997). *The full voice* [on-line]. (Available from http://www.the-body-shoppe.com/fullvoice/fullvoice1/index.html)

Brown, L., & Gilligan, C. (1992). *Meeting at the crossroads: Women's psychology and girls' development.* Cambridge, MA: Harvard University Press.

Bull, N. L. (1988). Studies of the dietary habits, food consumption and nutrient intakes of adolescents and young adults. *World Review of Nutritious Diets, 57,* 24–74.

Burgard, D., & Lyons, P. (1994). Alternatives in obesity treatment: Focusing on health for fat women. In P. Fallon, M. Katzman, & S. C. Wooley (Eds.), *Feminist perspectives on eating disorders* (pp. 212–230). New York: Guilford Press.

Crago, M., Shisslak, C. M., & Estes, L. S. (1996). Eating disturbances among African American minority groups: A review. *International Journal of Eating Disorders, 19,* 239–248.

Fallon, P., Katzman, M., & Wooley, S. C. (Eds.). (1994). *Feminist perspectives on eating disorders.* New York: Guilford Press.

Fisher, M., Golden, N. H., Katzman, D. K., Kreipe, R. E., Rees, J., Schebendach, J., Sigman, G., Ammerman, S., & Hoberman, H. M. (1995). Eating disorders in adolescents: A background paper. *Journal of Adolescent Health, 16,* 420–437.

Goldman, E. L. (1996). Eating disorders on the rise in preteens, adolescents. *Psychiatry News, 24* (2), 10.

Gortmaker, S. L., Must, A., Perrin, J. M., Sobol, A., & Dietz, W. H. (1993). Social and economic consequences of overweight in adolescence and young adulthood. *New England Journal of Medicine, 329,* 1008–1012.

Huon, G. F. (1994). Dieting, binge-eating, and some of their correlates among secondary school girls. *International Journal of Eating Disorders, 15,* 159–164.

Huston, A. (1992). *Big world, small screen: The role of television in American society.* Lincoln: University of Nebraska Press.

Ikeda, J., & Naworski, P. (1992). *Am I fat? Helping young children accept differences in body size.* Santa Cruz, CA: ETR Associates.

Johnson, J., Tobin, D., & Lipkin, J. (1989). Epidemiologic changes in bulimic behavior among female adolescents over a five-year period. *International Journal of Eating Disorders, 8,* 647–655.

Kilbourne, J. (1994). Still killing us softly: Advertising and the obsession with thinness. In P. Fallon, M. A. Katzman, & S. C. Wooley (Eds.), *Feminist perspectives on eating disorders* (pp. 395–418). New York: Guilford.

Killen, J. D., Taylor, C. B., Telch, M. J., Saylor, K. E., Maron, D. J., & Robinson, T. N. (1986). Self-induced vomiting and laxative and diuretic use among teenagers: Precursors of the binge-purge syndrome? *Journal of the American Medical Association, 255,* 1447–1449.

Kreipe, R. E., Golden, N. H., Katzman, D. K., Fisher, M., Rees, J., Tonkin, R. S., Sibler, T. J., Sigman, G., Schebendach, J., & Ammerman, S. D. (1995). Eating disorders in adolescents: A position paper of the Society for Adolescent Medicine. *Journal of Adolescent Health, 16,* 476–480.

Lasky, K. (1987). *A baby for Max.* New York: Alladdin Books.

Levine, M. P. (1994). Beauty myth and the beast: What men can do and be to help prevent eating disorders. *Eating Disorders: The Journal of Treatment & Prevention, 2*(2), 101–113.

Lucas, A. R., Beard, C. M., O'Fallon, W. M., & Kurland, L. T. (1991). 50-year trends in the incidence of anorexia nervosa in Rochester, Minnesota: A population-based study. *American Journal of Psychiatry, 148,* 917–922.

MacDonald, L. A, Wearring, G. A., & Moase, O. (1983). Factors affecting the dietary quality of adolescent girls. *Journal of American Dietetic Association, 82,* 26–263.

Mellin, L. M., Scully, S., & Irwin, C. S. (1986, October). *Disordered eating characteristics in preadolescent girls.* Paper presented at American Dietetic Association Meeting, Las Vegas.

Neumark-Sztainer, D., Butler, R., & Palt i, H. (1995). Eating disturbances among adolescent girls: Evaluation of a school-based primary prevention program. *Journal of Nutrition Education, 27,* 24–31.

Nylander, I. (1971). The feeling of being fat and dieting in a school population: An epidemiological investigation. *Acta Socialis Medicus Scandinavia, 1,* 17–26.

Rodin, J., Silberstein, L. R., & Streigel-Moore, R. H. (1985). Women and weight: A normative discontent. In T. B. Sonderegger (Ed.), *Psychology and gender: Nebraska symposium on motivation* (pp. 267–307). Lincoln: University of Nebraska Press.

Silverblatt, A. (1995). *Media literacy: Keys to interpreting media messages.* Westport, CT: Praeger.

Smith, J. E., & Krejci, J. (1991). Minorities join the majority: Eating disturbances among Hispanic and Native American youth. *International Journal of Eating Disorders, 10,* 179–186.

Smolak, L., & Levine, M. P. (1994). Toward an empirical basis for primary prevention of eating problems with elementary school children. *Eating Disorders: Journal of Treatment & Prevention, 4,* 293–307.

Steiner-Adair, C. (1986). The body politic: Normal female adolescent development and the development of eating disorders. *American Academy of Psychoanalysis, 14 ,* 95–114.

Steiner-Adair, C. (1987). Weightism: A new form of prejudice. *National Anorexic Aid Society Newsletter, 10,* 4.

Steiner-Adair, C. (1992). When the body speaks: Girls, eating disorders and psychotherapy. In C. Gilligan, A. Rogers, & D. Tolman (Eds.), *Women, girls, and psychotherapy: Reframing resistance* (pp. 253–267). Binghamton, NY: Haworth Press.

Steiner-Adair, C. (1994). The politics of prevention. In P. Fallon, M. Katzman, & S. C. Wooley (Eds.), *Feminist perspectives on eating disorders* (pp. 381–394). New York: Guilford Press.

Thompson, B. W. (1994). *A hunger so wide and so deep: American women speak out on eating problems.* Minneapolis: University of Minnesota Press.

Willard, S. G., & Maresh, R. D. (1996). Anorexia nervosa in an African-American female of a lower socioeconomic background. *European Eating Disorders Review, 4,* 95–99.

Wolf, N. (1991). *The beauty myth.* New York: William Morrow.

Worsnop, C. M. (1994). *Screening media: Ideas for media education.* London: The Falmer Press.

Sandra Susan Friedman

Discussion Groups for Girls: Decoding the Language of Fat

Just for Girls is an open discussion group for girls in grades five through nine. The program, which was developed in British Columbia in 1993, views eating disorders and the preoccupation with food and weight as coping strategies that evolve out of the adaptations girls make as they grow up female in a male world (Friedman, 1993). The program is grounded in girls' experiences and in the realities of their lives. It combines health promotion with contemporary theories of female development to help girls make a healthy transition through adolescence.

☐ Theoretical Background

Adolescence can be a difficult time for girls. Unlike boys, who develop their masculine identity through separation and individuation (Erikson, 1968), the central organizing feature of girls' development is an inner sense of connection with others (Gilligan, 1982, Gilligan & Brown, 1992; Surrey, 1991). Yet even though the desire for connection and mutually responsive and engaging relationships makes up an integral part of female identity, when girls approach adolescence they learn to silence themselves in their relationships rather than risk open conflict that may lead to rejection, isolation, and perhaps even violence against themselves (Gilligan and Brown, 1992). Girls are bombarded with messages from the culture that it is better to be kind and nice and not hurt anyone's feelings than to be honest and say what they really think and feel. The tyranny of kind and nice (Gilligan and Brown, 1992) causes girls to cover their strong feelings, hold back their opinions, and hide their own truths from themselves. As girls censor themselves they move from being the center of their own experiences to looking outward for definition and pleasing other people. They lose their authentic voice (Gilligan, 1992) and disconnect from each other and from themselves.

As girls enter puberty their hips get bigger and they accumulate the fat necessary for them to become sexual women in a culture that values thinness and has an extreme hatred of fat. As the discrepancy between the societal standard of beauty and their own biological (and often genetic) heritage begins to widen (Poulton, 1996), girls come to believe that the changes in their bodies are not normal and that their bodies are unacceptable or deformed (Jasper, 1993a). Because the inevitable weight gain and feeling of being out of control occurs at the same time that girls experience societal restrictions in their behaviors and activities, many girls learn to deal with the changes in their lives by focusing on the changes in their bodies. Their bodies become the context for their experiences, and the "language of fat" becomes their means of expression (Friedman, 1994).

When girls speak of "feeling fat" they usually are not referring to the fat on their bodies. Thin girls feel fat and fat girls feel fat. Nobody feels fat all the time. If at 2:00, for example, someone felt fine and at 2:30 she felt fat, the change that took place was not physical. It was emotional. Girls "feel fat" to displace feelings that they generally are encouraged to repress, and to describe experiences for which they often have little language or that make them feel unsafe. By encoding their feelings and experiences in the "language of fat," girls reinforce the alienation from themselves and from their bodies that occurs as they approach adolescence (Friedman, 1994). As they begin to engage with the language of fat and to diet instead of addressing the issues that lie underneath, they become vulnerable to eating disorders and to the other health risks that girls face such as smoking, alcohol and drug abuse, and sexually transmitted diseases.

The Just for Girls program addresses the silencing of girls' voices as they make the transition through adolescence. It helps girls decode the language of fat by teaching them about the *grungies*—the term coined to describe the negative self-deprecating voice that girls learn to use when they cannot be direct with their feelings and experiences. The program helps girls become aware of their grungies and encourages them to tell the stories that lie underneath. Through the use of group discussion, role play, art, and writing girls are able to express their feelings and articulate their experiences.

The Just for Girls program helps girls recognize and validate those aspects of the female culture that they are in danger of losing or negating as they try to fit into the dominant male culture. By reframing their stories in terms of female development, the program helps girls recognize their interdependence with one another and celebrate the importance of their friendships and the relational style and rituals of communication that they practice among themselves. Because girls tend to blame themselves in situations that make them feel badly and to view their reactions as abnormal or unique, the program also provides them with a societal context for their experiences. This allows them to recognize that they are not alone in how they feel and that they have a right to feel the way they do.

As girls approach adolescence they experience changes in the ways that they practice their relationships. When girls cannot be honest with one another and express their feelings directly, their friendships develop a dark side. Girls tell secrets, they talk behind one another's backs, they form cliques and they exclude one another (Bjorkvist, Osterman, & Koakianen, 1992). In the process of trying to please others, girls lose their boundaries or the sense of where they end and other people begin. Often, they negate their own needs and give to others at the expense of themselves. The Just for Girls program teaches girls conflict resolution and communication skills so that they can support one another and at the same time maintain their senses of themselves.

☐ Aims of the Program

The aims of the Just for Girls program are threefold: to help girls become aware of and decode the language of fat before it becomes an entrenched means of self-expression and an internalized way for them to deal with difficult situations in their lives; to help girls develop and maintain a positive sense of themselves by encouraging their self-expression, validating their experiences, and providing them with an understanding of their behavior, experiences, and feelings that is framed in the context of their female development and socialization; and to help girls build support systems for themselves by encouraging and facilitating the connections that they have with each other and with adult women.

☐ The Program

Content: The Issues that Girls Raise

Negative Self-talk: The Grungies

Just for Girls attempts to defuse any incipient (or already existing) preoccupation with food and weight before it can become entrenched by making girls aware of what they tell themselves when they are feeling down and providing them with an alternative means of expression. It does this by teaching girls about the grungies. Although the most common grungie is "feeling fat," the program helps girls identify other grungies such as feeling stupid, ugly, too tall, or anything else that makes individual girls feel different from their friends (Friedman, 1994).

Girls are asked during each session of the group to remember a time the previous week when they were "hit by a grungie." They pay attention to the time of day, the activity they were involved in, the thoughts they were thinking, and whatever feelings they had that they are aware of. The girls then are encouraged to talk about what was happening at that time. In doing so they shift their focus away from "fat" and tell the stories that lie underneath—stories that contain the feelings and experiences that are of real concern to them. The facilitator validates the girls' stories. She lets them know that they have a right to their feelings and that they are not alone in how they feel. She helps them understand why they feel the way that they do by reframing their stories in terms of female development and culture, and by providing them with an understanding of the societal pressures that they face. It is through the telling and validation of their stories that girls are able to retain or reclaim their voices and their selves.

Some sessions build upon the concerns raised when girls talk about the grungies. Others are centered around a specific topic. The flexibility of the program allows for activities that teach girls to become media-literate, for discussions about what happens when they diet, for providing girls with information relevant to their developmental stage and interests, and for addressing the issues that girls identify as important to them.

> *Example:* When 11-year-old Lindsay felt fat, the group was able to help her connect her grungie to her dance recital the previous weekend. Lindsay wore a two-piece costume and was in the front row. Telling herself that she *should* feel good that people were looking at her body, she encoded her real feelings of discomfort in the language of fat. The other girls validated Lindsay's feelings by talking about similar experiences in which they also felt uncomfortable at having their bodies on display (Friedman, 1997). This led to a discussion about how girls are objectified in the media and in turn are expected to objectify themselves, and the shame that they feel when their bodies do not match what society considers to be the ideal (Jasper, 1993b).

> *Example:* Twelve-year-old Eva felt fat when her best friend Angie was chosen for the part in the school play for which Eva also had auditioned. "I should be there for her and want to help her," she said when she talked about what was underneath her grungie, "but how can I do that when I feel angry and jealous that she got the part instead of me?" The girls in the group talked about the times when they too felt that they had to chose between their own realities and those of someone else. The group discussion helped the girls understand that they could have more than one feeling at a time and that they did not have to censor or repress themselves in order to maintain their friendships with others.

Communication Styles: Understanding the Gender Differences

Just for Girls helps girls recognize and validate the contextual, personal style of communication that they learn when they are very young and that is different from the goal-oriented, impersonal style that is practiced in the male world (Tannen, 1990). For example, unlike men who tend to solve problems on their own, girls *schmooze* with one another or engage in a communication ritual that is based on mutual sharing and validation. The girl with the problem describes it to her friends. As she articulates the problem it becomes concrete and real. This is important because girls tend to quickly negate and discount their realities. Her friend's first response is usually an empathic one that lets the girl know that she has the right to the way that she feels. The friend then shares a similar problem that she herself or someone that she know experienced. This lets the girl know that she is not alone in how she feels—something that is very common in girls. It is only after the schmoozing ritual has taken place that girls can address the practicalities involved in solving the problem.

> *Example:* When 13-year-old Janie talked about feeling criticized because her father told her how she should change her school project in order to get a better grade, her discomfort came because he had not schmoozed with her or validated her efforts and shared something of his own. As she told her story a chorus of voices chimed in with similar complaints. This prompted a discussion about different styles of communication and how they made girls feel. The girls described the goal-oriented way that Janie's father tried to "help" her as the same as the times when parents and teachers tried to "fix" things or began their feedback by pointing out mistakes. Instead of feeling encouraged when this happened, the girls felt criticized. They felt that what they were doing was not good enough. When asked how others could help them, they concluded that they would respond more positively

to feedback that took into account the process as well as the goal. For Janie, this meant that she could have seen her father's comments as helpful if he first acknowledged what she did well before he tried to help her make it even better (Friedman, 1997).

Negotiating Friendships: Dealing with Interpersonal Relationships

The girls speak of the importance of relationships and of the complexities inherent in them. They struggle between the need to express themselves and the fear of hurting others. Teaching girls about boundaries and providing them with communication and conflict resolution skills help them maintain the honesty in their friendships, support one another, and deal with the other people in their lives.

> *Example:* In one group 12-year-old Cara expressed her dilemma between needing to set her own boundaries and wanting to be there for her friend Becky, whose parents were going through a divorce. "Becky's my best friend," she said. "I want to be there for her, but I don't want her to live with me. She's so angry and upset all the time. But I'm afraid that if I say no to her I'm going to hurt her and make her feel worse" (Friedman, 1997).

The girls talk about being nice, about wanting to be liked. They speak of peer pressure to be like everyone else and of the pain of rejection and isolation that comes from being perceived as different. They talk about the dark side of female friendship—about secrecy and cliques and the pain of exclusion and about dealing with anger and hurt. In some groups the girls talk about the growing violence among girls and their fears of being beaten up. Through role playing girls are able to practice setting limits and making choices that feel right for them. They also can practice verbal self-defense that they can use individually or with the help of a friend for support. It is through standing up to the girls who tease them that they are able to stop being victimized and to start reclaiming their pride and dignity in who they are.

Living in a Changing Body

Girls going through puberty talk about their ambivalence about their changing bodies. They describe their anxiety around not knowing if they will be able to fit into their clothes. They worry about hormone swings and about changes that they do not understand and that therefore make them feel abnormal.

> *Example:* In one grade-seven group Jenny described her premenstrual syndrome saying, "Sometimes I feel like I'm in a bubble and I can't hear anything. It feels like there are hands pressing tighter and tighter against my head. I want to scream and scream and scream. I'm scared that I'm really crazy."

> *Example:* In a grade-six group Georgia asked in a very small voice, "Sometime my breasts hurt. Does this mean that I have cancer?" Amy wanted to know what the gunk in her pants was. Girls also express their fears about eating too much during their growth spurts and as a result getting fat, and their fear of not eating enough and becoming anorexic. Asked 10-year-old Rachel, "Can I go through puberty without gaining weight?"

Many girls feel self-conscious about their bodies. Thirteen-year-old Kate felt fat when she went swimming. It happened when she saw a group of her classmates looking at her and whispering among themselves. "I knew they were talking about me," she said. "I always wear a tee shirt when I go into the water because I don't want the other kids to make fun of my body," she told the group. This opened the door for a discussion about the immense pressure on girls to be thin and the pain that comes from the teasing that goes along with being large.

The older girls equate the unrelenting images of physical perfection with which they are bombarded by the media with pressure to be perfect—and thus never insecure—in their lives. The girls also struggle with their emerging sexuality. Younger girls talk about their changing perception of boys when friends or adversaries are suddenly under consideration as boyfriends. Older girls talk about wanting approval from boys and about their feelings about being pressured to have sex. Regardless of what her fears are about, each girl feels that she is the only one who feels the way that she does and is convinced that she is abnormal or sick.

Process: Helping Girls Express Themselves

The Talking Stick

The girls use the talking stick, a custom borrowed from the First Nations people (North American Indians). As the talking stick is passed around the circle, only the girl who is holding it may speak, and she may speak as long as she pleases without being interrupted. In the Just for Girls groups the custom has been modified so that the facilitator can respond in order to provide each girl with feedback, validate her experience, and complete the kind of responsive interaction that is needed to make the speaker feel safe. The use of the talking stick allows girls to plan what they will say, to elaborate on the details of their stories, and to share their feelings and perceptions. It validates not only what girls have to say but also how they say it. The talking stick teaches girls that they have a right to be listened to and that what they have to say is important. It helps each girl retain her voice at a time at which she is most in danger of losing it. In the telling of their stories girls validate themselves and one another and increase their self-esteem.

Role Playing

Although a good part of the Just for Girls program is centered around discussion, the program also includes activities to encourage self-expression so that girls can remain the center of their own experiences. Girls use role playing to act out their grungies. The girls are divided into smaller groups. Each group has a turn to perform for the other groups who are the audience. The girl whose turn it is assigns parts to the other girls in her group so that they can act out the story underneath. Often the grungies are about the times when girls censored themselves rather than hurt someone else. Girls are encouraged to try to change the endings of their stories so that they can express what they really felt at the time. Role playing gives them the opportunity to deal with their feelings in a direct and constructive way and in the process help them feel more positive about themselves.

Encouraging Different Means of Expression

The Just for Girls program also makes use of movement, art, and writing as additional means of self-expression. Movement and body drawings foster body awareness and help girls regain the kinesthetic experience of their bodies, which they are in danger of losing (or have already lost). They also allow girls to experience and relate to their bodies in a manner other than through how they look. Artwork and writing allow girls to express their feelings and share their ideas. In one group the girls created an ongoing advice column as a way of articulating and dealing with some of the issues that were important to them. In each group girls are given a journal and are encouraged to write the stories underneath their grungies as well as the other things that are of concern to them. The girls decorate their journals, put pictures in them, and draw in them. One girl wrote poetry. Another used her journal to write a book. Each week she read a new chapter to the group. Although the girls encourage each other to share their journals, it is important for them to recognize that their journals are private and that they can choose to say no.

Giving Positive Feedback

The girls are encouraged to say something positive about themselves at the close of each session and to identify something about themselves that makes them interesting. They are also encouraged to give each other verbal bouquets that describe the qualities and characteristics that draw them to the other person. This gives girls a broader framework in which to see and experience themselves (besides how they look) and an opportunity to receive concrete, specific feedback from others. It counteracts the tendency that girls have to define themselves and each other mainly in terms of "pretty" and "nice."

☐ Program Set-up

The Just for Girls program is held over a 10- to 12-week period of time. The group format of the program is built upon mutual support and commonality of experience. It provides girls with a safe environment in which to talk about their concerns, learn new skills, and try out new behaviors. Girls are invited to try out a group program that centers around "girl talk" and the issues of concern to them. They are told that the open format means that they can talk about anything that they want. Although the concept of feeling fat is included in the invitation, the words *eating disorders, body image,* and *self-esteem* never appear. These are "adult words" and have little to do with the realities of girls' lives and their concerns.

Each session is 1.5 hours. If the group is too short it is hard to develop good group dynamics and to ensure that each girl has a chance to speak and feel heard. If the group is too long, it runs the risk of losing the girls' attention, especially with girls in the younger grades.

Ideally the group is self-selected and runs on a drop-in basis so that girls can test the program without making a commitment and can feel free to miss sessions because of other demands on their time. However, it also can be adapted to fixed attendance and to professionally selected participants in accordance with the needs of the facilitators or the sponsoring school or organization.

The Just for Girls groups described in this chapter were drawn from two grade-six, two grade-seven, and two grade-eight drop-in groups and one grade-six group in which the mothers registered their daughters for the full program ahead of time. Once the groups began about two to four girls in each of the drop-in groups failed to return after the first two sessions. The remaining 8 to 10 girls in each group formed a core group that attended regularly, with an additional four to six girls who dropped in whenever they could. In the group with fixed attendance all of the eight participants attended for the duration of the program.

The steady attendance seems to be based upon the degree of safety that girls feel in the group. Because of the relational way in which girls develop, they feel safest in small groups. Although 8 to 10 seems to be an ideal number, some groups can accommodate up to 12 girls. However, once the group gets too big the dynamics change. Girls clam up and stop speaking or they form smaller subsets of girls within the larger group. They stop listening to each other and tend to speak all at once.

☐ The Facilitators

It is important that the facilitators of the group be women. Women model the kind of healthy, female-oriented relationships that are based on reciprocity and equality. Girls respond if they feel an emotional bond with women who are honest about their feelings and opinions. Through sharing their similar experiences with girls, women validate those of the girls and form a connection with them that facilitates their growth.

Facilitating a Just for Girls group requires that women bring their personal selves into their professional lives. This can be difficult at first for women who have been trained to view their professionalism as based on hierarchy and on distance. Remembering their own adolescence can be painful for some women because it brings up memories that they consider best left forgotten. Often women are unwilling to talk about their own experiences in the mistaken belief that if they do not "burden" girls with their own pain, they can spare the girls from experiencing it. Instead of talking with girls, they talk at them. This creates a void for girls because it robs them of a context and of feedback at a time when they need it the most. It sends them into uncharted territory without a guide, and it threatens the connections that women have tried so hard to build up.

It is important, also, that facilitators be able to recognize weight prejudice in themselves and be able to monitor their language and actions for signs of it. Women who work with girls are a product of the same culture in which girls mature and are influenced by the same pressures. Despite their best intentions, they pass their attitudes on to girls. In one Just for Girls group one of the participants talked about a well-meaning teacher who brought cookies in for the students. Realizing that there were not enough cookies to go around, the teacher said, "Only the thin kids will get cookies. The fat kids don't need them."

Facilitators also must be able to accept a range of body types and sizes. This means that they do not fall prey to the myth that equates being fat with being unhealthy, or that everyone wants to be thin—and can be if they try hard enough. Facilitators who see fat as bad tend to feel sorry for fat girls. In their misguided attempts to "protect" them, they tend to talk around their size rather than acknowledge it. Instead of helping girls to be fat with dignity, they discount and negate them. Women who are dieting or are overly concerned with losing weight or counting grams of fat or being in shape may run the risk of reinforcing the very beliefs that they are trying to counteract.

☐ Potential Pitfalls

Parents

Although most parents support the Just for Girls program, some parents do not. If the groups require preregistration, parents can prevent their daughters from attending. In drop-in groups for which no consent form is required or if the group is integrated into the school curriculum, girls often attend even though their parents may not know or may be against it. When one participant in a grade eight group cried during a session, she became concerned that her eyes were red. "My parents don't want me to come to the group," she said. "They think it's a waste of time. I tell them that on Tuesdays I play volleyball."

Even if parents consent to their daughters' participation they sometimes do not realize that addressing girls' issues and concerns often involves changes in girls' behavior. In one group a father complained because his daughter was speaking her mind more. "She used to be such a good girl," he said, "She would do everything that I told her to. Now she disagrees with me and it's all because of that group."

Girls who attend the group despite their parents' wishes have to deal with the conflict between the values taught at home and the skills and philosophy taught in the group. This is especially true of girls who come from cultures in which women are seen as inferior to men and their voices are not supposed to be heard. If girls continue to attend the group even with opposition at home, the group can encourage them to practice their communication skills and to use their voices in situations that are less threatening to them than outright confrontation with their parents. It can also validate girls' feelings of being caught between needing to be themselves and being pressured to conform to their families' ideal.

Schools

Some schools are reluctant to offer the Just for Girls program because it excludes the boys. Teachers want to include boys in the group because they think that boys need to learn about and from girls. When the question "But what about the boys?" arises, it is important to differentiate between the different kinds of learning in which children participate. Although all children would benefit from learning about gender differences and from communication skills, the purpose of the Just for Girls program is for girls to learn about themselves in the context of their female culture. Once even one boy is introduced to the group, the dynamics change as the girls begin to silence themselves. One solution for including the boys is to run parallel programs. In Saskatchewan, Canada, a pilot project called Kids in the 90s is underway in the elementary schools. While the female teachers facilitate groups for girls, the male teachers work with the boys to address the issues common to them.

Because the Just for Girls program encourages girls to talk about their concerns, one of the issues that can arise is sexual harassment—either by boys or by male teachers. Some schools may be reluctant to deal with harassment, especially if a teacher is involved. They may deny it, trivialize it, and even bar the program or the facilitators from the school. It is important, therefore, that before programs are offered or girls recruited from a specific school that a policy be set in place by the facilitators, school administration and teachers to ensure that the school will address harassment and to develop a procedure that can be followed should this issue arise.

Group Dynamics

Although most girls are eager to participate in the Just for Girls Program, the composition of the group sometimes makes it difficult for them to do so. The girls in one grade-six group all came from the same school and were engaged in a bullying dynamic that they brought with them into the group. Each week one girl was picked on. The next week she became one of the victimizers and picked on someone else. The facilitators talked about bullying and exclusion. They worked with interpersonal communication skills. Despite their efforts, the dynamic that existed among the girls was too entrenched for them to have much of an impact. Regardless of what happened in the group the girls knew that they had to deal with the school situation the next day. Because the school was unwilling to address the issue of bullying, it was impossible to establish the trust necessary to proceed. In the end the group was terminated before it had run its full course. The experience with this group drove home the lesson that despite the facilitators' skill and best efforts some groups just do not work because of the composition of the group.

☐ Evaluation

In the last session of each program, girls are asked to fill out an evaluation form asking them to describe what they liked and did not like about the group, the activities that were the most useful and least useful, and the changes that they see in themselves. They also are asked to rank the degree to which knowing about the grungies has helped them feel better about themselves. Filling out the feedback form is important for both the facilitators and the participants. The facilitators need to know about the program from the girls' perspective so that they can continue to adapt future groups to suit the needs of the girls. Asking the girls to fill out the feedback form gives them an opportunity to assess their experiences and to examine what works for them and what does not. It allows them to see the changes that they perceive in themselves and in others and lets them know that the facilitators value their ideas and opinions.

Girls write about being less shy and less embarrassed and more assertive at the end of the group. They are more able to speak their minds. They see knowing about the grungies as helpful because this means that they do not have to feel badly about themselves. Although girls describe activities that they have enjoyed, the most important part of the group is the opportunity to talk about their concerns and know that other girls feel the same way.

The girls report changes in their own and each other's behavior. Most of them feel that they have become more assertive and less shy and less afraid to speak to boys, or to talk to teachers when they feel unfairly treated or need help in class. For some of the girls, these changes in their behavior are supported by their parents. Others find that their parents are not happy if they become more assertive.

It has not been possible to conduct a long term evaluation of the Just for Girls program because of a lack of funding. This is unfortunate, because there is no way of knowing how long girls can sustain the positive changes made during the group and whether the skills that they learned are still of use to them as they make the transition through adolescence into adulthood.

☐ Conclusion

The Just for Girls program addresses what happens to girls in the process of growing up female that makes them lose their self-esteem and define themselves in terms of how they look. It teaches girls to recognize and decode the language of fat (and self-deprecation) before it becomes integrated into the ways in which they interpret and respond to situations in their lives, and before it becomes a major substitution for their feelings. It provides girls with skills that are set within the framework and context of their own lives. It introduces girls to the concept and value of a support system and encourages the mutually responsive relationships that are part of the female culture and are necessary in order for girls to develop and maintain their self-esteem. In doing so, the program validates both the girls who participate and the women who facilitate the group.

As steady attendance in the program has indicated, the optimum time to run a Just for Girls program as an after-school program is when girls are in grades five, six, seven, and eight. Even though some girls feel fat before then, this is the time when developmentally girls can benefit most from the group. However, although the short-term evaluation shows positive change after the girls have participated in the group, care must be taken to provide these girls with ongoing support as they make the transition to high school and through adolescence into adulthood. No matter how positive girls feel in the early stages of puberty, they need support if they are to deal successfully with the societal messages and the pressures on them to conform that they continue to receive.

The Just for Girls program was designed to be facilitated by women of different professional orientations and with varied skills and interests. It can be adapted for use with different age groups and can be integrated into existing programs using existing resources and personnel. Regardless of how the program is used, it is important to continuously find a balance between the process that is at the heart of the program and the structure that allows for the development of skills. If there is too much emphasis on the process, the program cannot teach the girls skills or provide them with an opportunity to try out new behavior. However, too much emphasis on structure leaves the group at risk of sacrificing the girls' voices and experiences to activities that center on problem solving.

Although the program originally was intended as a group program, its skills and philosophy can be adapted for use in individual counseling. In teaching girls about the grungies and encouraging their self-expression, care must be taken to respect and practice the female-oriented reciprocal style of communication. Girls learn through their connection with others. If adults assume their authoritative voices, girls close down, act out, or succumb to the "tyranny of kind and nice."

The Just for Girls program can be used not only for eating-disorder prevention, but also to address such issues as smoking, contraception, teen pregnancy, sexually transmitted diseases, and abusive versus healthy relationships in a framework of female culture and development and in the context of girls' lives and experiences. Its flexibility and generic nature make it a prototype for programs that involve girls and ensure its longevity in a time of shrinking resources and decreased funding.

Regardless of how the Just for Girls program is used, its underlying philosophy and skills development offer girls an image of women that is different from the prevailing one reinforced by our society. It encourages activity instead of passivity, self-expression instead of repression and self-control, and teaches girls to focus on their lives instead of on their looks. In providing girls with an alternative way of seeing themselves and being in the world, the Just for Girls program puts them at risk of being different from other girls and of meeting disapproval and reaction from parents, teachers, and other girls. It is important, therefore, that adults who teach girls new behaviors and encourage a different way of being in the world be there to support girls as they try out these behaviors, learn the skills to support one another, and take their places in the world.

☐ References

Bjorkvist, K., Osterman, K., & Kaukianen, A. (1992). The Development of direct and indirect aggressive strategies in males and females. In K. Njorkqvist, & P. Niemela (Eds.), *Of mice and women: Aspects of female aggression*. New York: Academic Press.

Erikson, E. (1968). *Identity, youth and crisis*. New York: W.W. Norton.

Friedman, S. (1993). Decoding the language of fat: Placing eating disorder groups in a feminist framework. In C. Brown, & K. Jasper, (Eds.), *Consuming passions: Feminist approaches to weight preoccupation and eating disorders*. Toronto: Second Story Press.

Friedman, S. (1994). *Girls in the 90s facilitator's manual*. Vancouver, BC: Salal Books.

Friedman, S. (1997). *When girls feel fat: Helping girls through adolescence*. Toronto: HarperCollins Publishers.

Gilligan, C. (1982). *In a different voice*. Cambridge, MA: Harvard University Press.

Gilligan, C., & Brown, L. M. (1992). *Meeting at the crossroads: Women's psychology and girls' development*. Cambridge, MA: Harvard University Press.

Jasper, K. (1993a). Monitoring and responding to media messages. *Eating Disorders: The Journal of Treatment and Prevention*. 109–114.

Jasper, K. (1993b). Out from under body image disparagement. In C. Brown, & K. Jasper (Eds.), *Consuming passions: Feminist approaches to weight preoccupation and eating disorders*. Toronto: Second Story Press.

Poulton, T. (1996). *No fat chicks: How women are brainwashed to hate their bodies and spend their money*. Toronto: Key Porter Books.

Surrey, J. L. (1991). The self-in-relation: A theory of women's development. In J. Jordan, J.B., Miller, I.P. Stiver, & J.L. Surrey (Eds.), *Women's growth in connection*. New York: Guilford Press.

Tannen, D. (1990). *You just don't understand: Women and men in conversation*. New York: Ballantine Books.

CHAPTER

8

Susan J. Paxton

Peer Relations, Body Image, and Disordered Eating in Adolescent Girls: Implications for Prevention

An expanding body of research has confirmed the high incidence of body-image dissatisfaction and unhealthy dieting behaviors in adolescent girls (e.g., French, Perry, Leon, & Fulkerson, 1995; Grigg, Bowman, & Redman, 1996; Patton et al., 1997; Paxton et al., 1991; Rosen & Gross, 1987). These are associated with low self-esteem and depression (Rosen, Gross, & Vara, 1987; Wertheim et al., 1992), potential health risks (e.g., Gibbons, Wertheim, Paxton, Petrovich, & Szmukler, 1995; Lifshitz & Moses, 1988; NIH Panel, 1992), and the later development of disordered eating (Attie & Brooks-Gunn, 1989; Killen, et al., 1994; Patton, Johnson-Sabine, Wood, Mann, & Wakeling, 1990). In addition, the incidence of severe eating disorder in adolescents remains unacceptably high (e.g., Ben-Tovim, Subbiah, Scheutz, & Morton, 1989; Rooney, McClelland, Crisp, & Sedgwick, 1995).

Although the causes of poor body image, weight loss behaviors that pose health risks, and eating disorders are not well understood, individual and sociocultural factors that may contribute to the development of such difficulties have been identified. Individual risk factors most reliably demonstrated are high body mass index (BMI) and previous weight concerns (French, Perry, Leon, & Fullerton et al., 1995; Killen et al., 1994; Patton et al., 1990; Shisslak et al., 1998; Thompson, Coovert, Richards, Johnson, & Cattarin, 1995). Proposed sociocultural factors contributing to an environment conducive to the development of unhealthy weight-control behaviors include media, family and parental, and friendship pressures (e.g., Levine, Smolak, & Hayden, 1994; Pike, 1995; Stice, 1994; Stice, Nemeroff, & Shaw, 1996; Strong & Huon, 1998). Theorists agree that, during adolescence, peer influences and friendships typically assume greater significance in the world of teenaged girls (Heaven , 1994), and the first section of this chapter reviews the emerging research reflecting on the relationships among peer factors, body dissatisfaction, and disturbed eating. The second section considers implications of these findings for the structure and content of prevention interventions designed to redress body image dissatisfaction and dieting disorders.

Peer Influences and Friendship Relations, Body Image, and Eating Behaviors

There is growing empirical evidence that a girl's immediate friendship environment provides a subculture that may enhance or diminish the importance of thinness and engaging in weight-loss behaviors and establish norms in these areas. Regular discussion of weight and dieting may assist in establishing and emphasizing the social value of thinness and rejection of fatness, placing particular pressure on those of higher BMI. Weight and weight control have been observed to be frequent topics of conversation for adolescent girls. Levine, Smolak, & Hayden (1994) found that 41.5% of middle school girls reported talking with their friends at least sometimes about weight, shape, and dieting. Nichter and Vuckovic (1994) identified a number of functions that "fat talk" (talk about weight) could serve in peer-group interactions, including as a means for soliciting encouragement from friends and promoting group affiliation. Although serving these roles, "fat talk" is likely to simultaneously reinforce the understanding within a friendship group that the importance of thinness and the rejection of fatness are shared values. Talk about dieting also serves as a means of giving and receiving weight control information, as indicated by the finding of Desmond, Price, Gray, and O'Connell (1986) that 50% of ninth-grade girls reported receiving information about weight control from their friends. Among friends there is little direct encouragement to diet (Paxton et al., 1991; Wertheim, Paxton, Schutz, & Muir, 1997) or comment on another's weight gain (Nichter & Vuckovic, 1994). If it does occur, however, it may be especially powerful, as retrospective accounts of patients with eating disorders frequently cite encouragement from a friend to lose weight as a trigger for disordered eating (Mitchell, Hatsukami, Pyle, & Eckert, 1986; Pyle, Mitchell, & Eckert, 1981).

Talking about dieting is likely to be one indicator of a broader construct of peer investment in thinness and dieting. Observable dieting behaviors are likely to be another indicator. Levine and colleagues (Levine, Smolak, & Hayden, 1994; Levine, Smolak, Moodey, Shuman, & Hessen, 1994) have found perceived peer investment in dieting (assessed using a scale gauging how often friends talk about weight and weight loss, how many friends would like to be thinner, and how many friends are on a diet) made small but significant contributions to the prediction of individual investment in thinness, eating disturbance, and use of weight-management strategies. A girl's perceptions of the number of weight-loss techniques used by her friends predicted the extent of her own recent weight-management attempts (Levine, Smolak, Moodey et al., 1994).

Not only do perceptions of friends' investment in thinness and dieting predict a girl's own behavior, but also friends' actual body-image attitudes and dieting behaviors have been found to be related. In best-friend dyads, significant correlations between self-reported dietary restraint, crash dieting, fasting, and drive for thinness have been observed (Paxton, Williams, & Wertheim, 1998). In friendship groups, Crandall (1988) and Pike (1995) have reported a positive relationship between a girl's binge-eating symptoms and those of her friends. Paxton, Schutz, Wertheim, and Muir (in press) found within–friendship group similarity in body image concerns, dietary restraint, and use of extreme weight-loss behaviors. Further, mean friendship-group scores on measures of these variables were positively correlated with mean group scores on measures of the importance of thinness, the extent to which friends were a source of dieting information and influence, the extent of friends' concerns regarding thinness and dieting, the frequency of talk within groups about dieting and weight, the frequency of comparison of one's body with that of others, and teasing from peers. These data suggest that in groups in which there is frequent dieting, there is a constellation of accompanying weight and shape concerns. Friends' concerns regarding weight and shape, talk among friends about dieting, and the extent to which friends were a source of information and influence in dieting matters significantly predicted an individual girl's body-image satisfaction and dieting over and above the contribution of BMI and psychological and familial factors. Wertheim et al. (1997) suggested that one of the motivations recognized by girls who employ similar extreme weight-control strategies was the provision of mutual support in weight-loss efforts.

Particular vulnerability to body dissatisfaction and dieting may be conveyed to girls who inhabit multiple subcultural environments that each strongly endorse thinness as an ideal. Consistent with this hypothesis are data from Levine, Smolak, & Hayden (1994) indicating that girls who perceived both high peer and high family investment in thinness were at greater risk of poor body image and involvement in weight control. The cumulative effect of multiple pressures also is suggested by data indicating that synchronous early puberty and dating also have been shown to confer increased vulnerability to the development of eating concerns (Levine, Smolak, Moodey et al., 1994; Smolak, Levine, & Gralen, 1993)

Teasing may be viewed as another, less subtle, way in which peers reinforce the thin body-image ideal. In an interview study of grade-10 girls, it was observed that teasing about weight was directed at both heavier and normal-weight girls and that although sometimes taunts were recognized as inaccurate, more frequently they were taken literally (Wertheim et al., 1997). In addition, a number of studies have reported that frequency of teasing and comment on weight status predicts body dissatisfaction (Cash, 1995; Fabian & Thompson, 1989; Levine, Smolak, & Hayden, 1994; Paxton et al., in press) and dietary restraint (Grigg et al., 1996; Paxton et al., in press) independent of BMI. Thompson and colleagues (1995) have used a combination of covariance structure modeling and longitudinal (3-year follow-up) designs to examine the relationship among BMI, teasing, and body dissatisfaction. Their cross-sectional research revealed that actual level of obesity had no unique impact on body image: Rather, its effect was mediated by teasing history. In the longitudinal component, time 1 levels of obesity and teasing predicted time 2 levels of weight and appearance satisfaction.

Nichter and Nichter (1991) highlight that girls "are involved in a highly comparative world where little goes unnoticed" (p.261). The frequency of body comparison (comparison of one's body with those of others), however, does vary across individuals. Research in college-aged women has shown that social comparison in the body shape domain is an important predictor of body dissatisfaction (Heinberg & Thompson, 1992a,b; Stormer & Thompson, 1996), feeling fat (Striegel-Moore, Silberstein, & Rodin, 1986), and bulimia and drive for thinness scores (Stormer & Thompson, 1996). Similar findings have been reported in teenaged girls. In an interview study, frequent comparison of one's body with that of others and comparison with others on diets were reported as sources of distress and motivators to diet (Wertheim et al., 1997). Body comparison also has been found to contribute uniquely to the prediction of body image satisfaction and dieting (Paxton et al., in press) with the main targets for body comparison in teenaged girls being immediate peers (friends, other girls at school, popular girls) and fashion models in magazines (Schutz, Paxton, & Wertheim, 1997). A potentially related construct, competition with friends on weight, shape, and appearance issues, also has been observed to be a strong predictor of dieting initiation (Huon et al., in press).

The relationships between popularity, quality of friendships, thinness, body dissatisfaction, and weight-control behaviors have been examined from a range of perspectives. In a study of 9- to 11-year-old children, Oliver and Thelen (1996) observed that the belief that peer likeability would be improved by being thin was the strongest predictor of eating and body concerns, an effect mediated by BMI. However, the substantial majority of adolescents in one study (Nichter & Vuckovic, 1994) reported that thinness was not considered a prerequisite for friendships with other girls, a view supported by the finding that few girls believed they would have more friends if they were thinner (Paxton et al., 1991). It was suggested, however, that thinness was an important factor for membership in the popular groups (Nichter & Vuckovic, 1994). These relationships appear complex, as popularity, measured by the frequency with which a girl was nominated as a friend, has not been found to be related to BMI or dieting behaviors in a further sample of teenage girls (Paxton et al., in press). The extent to which deficient social relationships play a part in the development of disordered eating is at present poorly understood. French, Story, Downes, Resnick, and Blum (1995) have reported dieting frequency to be associated with lower connectedness to others. Further, Killen Taylor, Hammer, Litt (et al., 1993) have observed self-rated unpopularity and aggressiveness to be greater in girls who later developed eating disorder symptomatology compared with asymptomatic girls. The literature supporting insecurity in social relationships, low levels of perceived social support from friends, and low levels of social competence in those diagnosed with an eating disorder is much stronger (e.g., Grissett & Norvell, 1992; Mallick, Whipple, & Huerta, 1987; Steinhausen & Vollrath, 1993; Wilfley et al., 1993).

Heterosexual peer influences have received some research attention. Recent onset of dating has been shown to account for a small but significant amount of variance in weight-management scores (Levine, Schutz et al., 1994) but this effect diminishes across adolescence (Gralen, Levine, Smolak, & Murnen, 1990). About a quarter of one female adolescent sample believed that being thinner would improve their number of dates (Paxton et al., 1991), and body shape is believed to be an important component in attractiveness of girls to boys (Damhorst, Littrell, & Littrell, 1988; Nichter & Vuckovic, 1994). Recent data from an Australian study (Norris, 1995) indicate that girls' concerns are not entirely unjustified. Although the ideal female figure selected by grade 10 boys was larger than that selected by girls, it was smaller than girls' self-reported current figure size. Further, in response to the question, "Generally, how important do your friends think a slim figure is in determining a girl's attractiveness?" 27% of boys replied "very important" and 61% replied "fairly important." Such responses suggest that boys, not surprisingly, have internalized sociocultural beliefs regarding the relationship among thinness, attractiveness, and success. Indeed, it is probable that boys themselves are under increasing pressure to have the perfect body size and shape.

With attention focused on negative peer influences on body image and weight loss behaviors of adolescent girls, the potentially positive influences of friends have been ignored somewhat. It might be argued that, although some friendship networks may have intense investment in weight and shape and provide a dangerous environment for a girl vulnerable to an eating disorder on other grounds (e.g., higher BMI, low self-esteem), other networks are less invested in these areas and may provide a protective environment for a girl who is otherwise vulnerable. Wertheim et al. (1997) found that a number of girls reported that other girls had stopped vomiting after friends dissuaded them from such a weight-loss strategy. Consistent with this finding are reports of the value of friends in the recovery from bulimia. Rorty, Yager, and Rossotto (1993) found that friends very often were regarded as helpful in providing emotional support, and seldom were regarded as actively harmful in the recovery process from bulimia. When those suffering from eating disorders were asked to give advice to others suffering from an eating disorder, the advice most frequently given was to reach out to others such as a friend or other bulimic women for support. Thus, it is likely that the friendship environment has the potential to offer protection against the development of eating concerns and to provide a healing environment for those who already have these problems.

☐ Intervention Implications

In response to high incidences of body image dissatisfaction and disordered eating in adolescent girls, prevention interventions increasingly are being implemented and evaluated. Although tertiary prevention strategies in the eating-disorder domain are relatively well established, primary and secondary prevention programs are still in developmental phases. The few primary prevention programs to date that have been assessed using quantitative methods have used school-based educational programs that have combined didactic presentations and small group activities. The content of these programs typically has informed students about healthy eating patterns, negative consequences of extreme weight-control strategies, normal female body composition, and awareness of media and social pressures to be thin (Killen et al., 1993; Paxton, 1993; Smolak, Levine, & Schermer, 1998). Carter, Stewart, Dunn, and Fairburn (1997) have included skills training in challenging problematic thoughts about shape and weight, while Mann et al. (1997) provided information about eating disorders to college students.

These educational primary interventions have been successful in moderating attitudes towards fat people (Smolak et al., 1998), intentions to diet (Moreno & Thelen, 1993), and knowledge about healthy eating and eating disorders (Carter et al., 1997; Killen et al., 1993; Shisslak, Crago, Neal, & Swain 1987; Smolak et al., 1998). But those programs that have assessed the critical indicator of self-reported weight loss behaviors have provided no encouragement for such educational approaches (Carter et al., 1997; Killen et al., 1993; Mann et al., 1997; Paxton, 1993; Smolak et al., 1998). These initially disappointing results raise the question of how the structure and content of prevention interventions might be made more effective. In light of the review presented here, it appears that a crucial aspect of adolescent girls' experience in relation to body image and dieting, that of peer group interactions and norms, has been neglected in the conceptualization of these programs. Thus, the following section considers how peer relations may be harnessed in the service of prevention of body dissatisfaction and disordered eating.

Primary Prevention

All primary prevention programs described in the literature to this point have used school-based approaches, and these are clearly the most practical to deliver and the most efficient in terms of reaching the target group. The friendship issues described in the previous section suggest that this is an appropriate structural base. Although all members of a friendship group will not necessarily be contained within a school setting, friendship groups are very often school-based, and it is likely that a school group will contain many relevant peers. The research suggests, however, that the friendship group is an important subcultural unit to be considered in intervention. It is likely that the more activities that could be conducted at the level of the friendship group and the greater the extent to which members of friendship groups could work together to explore healthy approaches to eating and their bodies, the more powerful a program would be in bringing about both individual and subcultural change.

This view is supported by Piran's (1996) observations of a prevention program at a ballet school in which she facilitated small group discussions around body image and eating issues using a feminist framework. This program allowed for the safe exploration of the sensitive issues of shame over body shape and function, powerlessness in the face of criticism of their bodies, and the negative impact of comments from peers. These intensely personal experiences were crucial to the young women, and although they could be discussed in a small peer group they were unlikely to be explored in a larger classroom environment.

In addition to structural modifications, the content of primary prevention programs also may be modified in light of current conceptualizations of the role of peer relations in body-image dissatisfaction and disordered eating. Friendship-group similarity in body dissatisfaction and dieting has a number of applied implications, although these are somewhat dependent on the unknown cause of these similarities. Two dominant possibilities exist, with different, although not incompatible, implications. Girls may adopt the behaviors and attitudes of their friends (peer influence) or, alternatively, girls may choose friends like themselves (peer selection).

The peer influence explanation of friendship similarity indicates the value of program content addressing pressures to conform within the friendship environment. Students could be taught skills to identify the source and triggers of body image concern and inclination to diet, such as discussion of weight, shape, and dieting or eating behaviors of friends, and then to reframe these as reflections of concern on the friends' part or as "fat talk," without personal implications for themselves. Understanding the social role of "fat talk" may diminish its power to invoke anxiety. Further, cognitive skills for managing teasing and direct weight-related comments are likely to be effective. These approaches have elements in common with successful prevention programs for smoking, which have incorporated cigarette refusal skills training (Dent et al., 1995; Murray, Richards, Luepker, & Johnson, 1987). It is also notable that most girls are unaware of the pressure that they inadvertently exert on others when they engage in "fat talk," or the potentially damaging consequences of teasing (especially as it relates to larger girls). In the small group context, Piran (1996) found that identification of the destructive effects of ongoing mutual peer evaluation enabled group members to resolve to stop such evaluation, potentially enhancing self perceptions but also strengthening friendship relations.

The peer-influence model also recognizes that peer influence may work in a positive direction (Aloise-Young, Graham, & Hansen, 1994), potentially improving body image and decreasing disordered eating. This model supports the use of peer leaders, shown to be effective in smoking-prevention programs (Dent et al., 1995) and in modifying intentions to diet (Moreno & Thelen, 1993). Capitalizing on the positive supportive nature of adolescent friendship relations, girls may be encouraged to replace joint dieting with mutually supportive attempts to improve eating, body image, and self-esteem. This approach is also supported by Piran's (1996) observations, within the ballet school environment, of a number of situations in which peers provided support for individuals in challenging deprecating comments, and in which peer groups felt more empowered than a single individual to act against particular sources of damage to body image satisfaction and self-respect.

The peer selection model, which proposes that girls select into groups with similar attitudes and behaviors as their own, is not necessarily a negative one for primary prevention interventions (Ennett, Bauman, & Koch, 1994). It suggests that programs could highlight the benefits of friendship relations with non-dieting girls and of friendship environments supportive of positive body image and eating behavior. Further, this model suggests that, in addition to inoculating the individual against peer pressures for thinness, prevention should aim to alter the whole friendship group's eating and body image norms, encouraging friendship groups to actively adopt positive body attitudes and healthful eating practices.

The content of intervention programs also could address the consequences of body comparison and competition between friends. Although the causal direction is unclear, more frequent body comparison is associated with greater body dissatisfaction and weight loss behaviors. Within the experiential ballet school group intervention, recognition of the competitive environment has been shown to have a powerful impact (Piran, 1996). Prevention programs also could contain a cognitive coping skills component teaching the recognition of body-comparative thoughts (e.g., "My thighs are larger than hers"; "If she is on a diet, I ought to be on a diet"), the emotional and behavioral consequences of such thoughts (e.g., negative mood and commitment to go on a crash diet), and alternative, more adaptive thoughts (e.g., "I am a healthy weight for my body"; "Regular eating and exercise patterns are the best ways to maintain a healthy weight"; "Losing weight is not the answer to all problems").

Although there is strong evidence that those with eating disorders often have disturbed social relationships, the extent to which this is causative is unresolved. However, this finding suggests that primary prevention programs could redress systematically the notion that losing weight will improve relationships and be the solution to loneliness or social isolation. It also implies the importance of teaching social skills, the identification of other emotional difficulties, and appropriate help-seeking behaviors. Similarly, as has previously been suggested (Shisslak et al., 1987), raising awareness of the connection between food and emotion is a potentially useful program component. In this area, it would seem important to be able to offer other resources or referrals for girls who wanted to resolve interpersonal problems in another forum.

Recognition of the potential power of the friendship subculture to support or negate prevention programs opens up creative opportunities in the development of primary prevention programs. Girls typically treasure their friendship relations and could themselves be challenged to consider how members of their friendship groups could support each other in the development of positive self-image.

Secondary Prevention

Given the difficulties in changing sociocultural influences, some authors have recommended focus on secondary prevention (Vandereycken & Meerman, 1984). Friendship relations could be harnessed as a valuable resource in early detection. Friends are very often the first to notice a substantial weight loss, but most girls are unsure what they should do if they suspect a friend has an eating problem and they do not feel empowered to act. Do they ignore it, discuss it with the girls, or talk to a teacher? Although circumstances vary, rather than being asked to inform on friends, girls could be encouraged to raise their concerns with their friend and offer support in seeking help. Information on relevant resources should be readily available to adolescent girls for such circumstances.

Research described previously suggests that some friendship environments are particularly focused on weight and shape issues and involved in the use of extreme weight loss behaviors. It would be valuable if teachers and others involved in the welfare of adolescents were aware of these groups and, if possible, could make more intensive intervention programs and resources available to such at-risk groups. Similarly, interventions could be provided especially for peer groups in identified high-risk environments such as ballet schools (e.g., Piran, 1996), gymnastics and diving schools, and those involved in the fashion and modeling industries.

Tertiary Prevention

Although many treatment programs for adolescent anorexia and bulimia nervosa patients recognize, in their use of family therapy as a therapeutic approach, the power of environmental influences in maintaining eating disorders (Russell, Szmukler, Dare, & Eisler, 1987), few have specifically considered drawing on the friendship environment. Consideration of friendship issues could be valuable in the cognitive therapy component of treatment. Cognitive therapy approaches could be used to challenge irrational beliefs regarding the importance of thinness to friendship relations and acceptance by friends, and to reduce negative comparisons being made between one's body and the bodies of peers. Further, therapy could focus on resolving issues related to unsatisfactory or deficient peer relations, an approach consistent with the success of interpersonal psychotherapy in adult binge eaters (Wilfley et al., 1993).

The patient's friendship subculture itself also could be targeted. For those whose friendships are still intact, a friend could be involved in some sessions of therapy, in which the patient's and the friend's concerns could be explored about return to school, expectations of particular difficulties for each, and ways in which support from the friendship network could be enhanced. Very often friends are keen to help but are unclear about the best ways to do this. Depending on the wishes of patient and friends, a clinician could talk to friends about the nature of eating disorders and the positive roles a friendship network can play in a patient's recovery. For patients who have withdrawn from their friends, active measures to reestablish supportive friendships could be implemented.

☐ Challenges to a Peer-focused Approach

It has been established that peer similarity in weight-loss behaviors is more than the perception of teenaged girls, but research into the mechanisms accounting for peer similarity is still in its early phases. As described previously two hypotheses proposed to account for peer similarity are peer influence and peer selection. Crandall's (1988) finding that college-aged women become more like their friends in binge eating over time suggests the operation of peer influence. However, studies of smoking similarity between young adolescent friends suggest that selection plays a greater part than influence (Ennett & Bauman, 1994; Fisher & Bauman, 1988), and this also could be the case in body image and eating behaviors. Because of the popular notion of "peer pressure" it often is assumed that peer influence is the dominant mechanism, but it is important to recognize in the development of intervention programs that girls may be selecting a weight-conscious group to which to belong because it reflects attitudes compatible with her own. Teaching peer-resistance techniques is unlikely to be helpful in such a situation. On the other hand, it is difficult to see how it would do any harm. Until demonstrated otherwise, for the purpose of developing intervention programs, it is probably most appropriate to assume both processes operate.

While small group discussions have been shown to alter negative food- and body-related attitudes in young women (Huon, 1994), authors have warned against the possible iatrogenic effects of prevention programs (Carter et al., 1997; Garner, 1985; Russell & Beumont, 1995; Mann et al., 1997). A similar caution is warranted in a consideration of the use of friendship groups as a unit of intervention. In small-group interactions, there is substantial evidence for "group polarization" effects, that is, for groups to produce more extreme attitudes and decisions than those produced by their individual members acting alone (Eagly & Chaiken, 1993). If friendship groups are given opportunities to discuss body-image ideals and so forth, and prevailing views of members reject current stereotypes, group views may shift toward attitudes firmly rejecting unrealistic pressures on females to obtain a certain body shape. In this manner, an individual girl may receive peer support in rejecting unrealistically thin goals.

On the other hand, if group sentiments are initially favorable to the current thin ideal, group discussion could reinforce the perceived value of this body shape, and in fact its value may be enhanced to the group members. Thus, the resulting attitudes may be even more damaging to personal self-image. Counterproductive attitudes that may be reinforced in this way, as they are widely held in the community, include the views that being very thin will bring success and happiness, that a girl's value rests in her appearance, and that boys only like very thin girls. Thoughtful facilitation of group activities may be required to ensure that group dynamics work in favor of, not against, prevention goals.

Body-image and eating issues in adolescent girls and boys are substantially different (e.g., Paxton et al., 1991). Consequently, it is difficult to design a combined curriculum that is equally relevant to both sexes. However, research reviewed previously indicates how important it is that boys be aware of the pressures girls are under to be very thin, and the ways in which the boys can exacerbate or reduce this pressure. Although information presented to boys that is in any way blaming is likely to be counterproductive, it would be valuable in changing the wider social pressures on girls if boys were aware that they are responding to and reflecting the social influences supporting the very thin female ideal. Clearly, if the girls at a school make gains in their own body-image satisfaction, these are more likely to be sustained if boys also reject the unhealthy ideal.

Indeed, recognizing the importance to girls of the heterosexual environment is part of a recognition that it is insufficient to attempt intervention at the immediate subcultural level only. Much wider social and systemic changes are required. Within school environments it is important that teachers and curricula provide consistent messages regarding the importance and attractiveness of a health body weight. More generally, if powerful institutions and the dominant culture support an unhealthy thin female beauty ideal, peer subcultures will do so, too, despite efforts to support them in taking an alternative view.

Although more creative ways of addressing prevention in body image and disordered eating are required, so too is evaluation of these ideas. It is essential to examine the practicality of smaller group formats for intervention, which necessarily are more resource-intensive than larger classrooms, and to assess the impact of new approaches to the content of intervention programs. We increasingly are being warned to ensure that our well meant attempts at prevention are not counterproductive, and only carefully controlled studies will indicate this.

☐ Conclusion

This chapter explores ways in which peer relations may be harnessed to reduce body-image dissatisfaction and disordered eating in adolescent girls. The peer environment of adolescent girls is intensely salient and provides a dominant set of subcultural norms in many attitudes and behaviors, including those related to the importance of weight and shape and the acceptability of dieting and disordered eating. Peer groups may vary in their investment in thinness and dieting as indicated by their talk about these issues and their actual behaviors. Although it is unclear at present whether girls select peer environments consistent with their own beliefs and behaviors or become more like their peers, there is growing evidence that a girl's dieting behaviors are predicted by both her perceptions of her friends' dieting and her friends' actual dieting behaviors. These findings indicate the salience of the peer environment in relation to body image and eating behaviors. Teasing from peers, a means of reinforcing group norms, predicts later body-image concerns and disordered eating. Girls also may perceive pressure from boys to be very thin and to diet though the extent to which this is perceived or actual is still unclear. Further, a girl's interactions with her peers in terms of her comparison of her body with those of peers and possibly the quality of her friendship relations may contribute to poor body image and unhealthy dieting. Although friend relations may intensify weight and shape concerns, there is also evidence that they may act in a protective, supportive, reassuring manner.

Despite the relevance of the peer environment in the lives of adolescent girls, intervention programs quantitatively evaluated to this point have failed to address any of the peer interactions that may contribute to poor body image and unhealthy weight loss strategies or capitalize on their potential to effect favorable change. The positive observations from one descriptive study of peer group exploration of body-image issues among those at a ballet school (Piran, 1996) and the peer and body image literature do suggest this may be effective. In relation to primary prevention it is likely that interventions at the peer group level may be powerful. The content of primary prevention programs could include identification of peer pressures to diet and skills to counteract them. The impact of "fat talk," teasing, and body comparison and competition could be explored, and beliefs regarding the importance of thinness to friendships and social success might be challenged. Although body-image concerns largely effect females, boys should not be ignored in primary prevention, as they are part of the peer environment of girls. In relation to secondary and tertiary prevention, friends may be a valuable source of support in help seeking and in reassurance of personal value independent of weight and shape. At all levels of prevention, peer groups could be encouraged to be supportive of healthy body image and eating rather than of body concern and dieting.

☐ References

Aloise-Young, P. A., Graham, J. W., & Hansen, W. B. (1994). Peer influence on smoking initiation during adolescence: A comparison of group members and group outsiders. *Journal of Applied Psychology, 79,* 281–287.

Attie, I., & Brooks-Gunn, J. (1989). Development of eating problems in adolescent girls: A longitudinal study. *Developmental Psychology, 25,* 70–79.

Ben-Tovim, D. I., Subbiah, N., Scheutz, E., & Morton, J. (1989). Bulimia: Symptoms and syndromes in an urban population. *Australian and New Zealand Journal of Psychiatry, 23,* 73–80.

Carter, J. C., Stewart, D. A., Dunn, V. J., & Fairburn, C. G. (1997). Primary prevention of eating disorders: Might it do more harm than good? *International Journal of Eating Disorders, 22,* 167–172.

Cash, T. F. (1995). Developmental teasing about physical appearance: Retrospective descriptions and relationships with body image. *Social Behavior and Personality, 23,* 123–130.

Crandall, C. S. (1988). Social contagion of binge eating. *Journal of Personality and Social Psychology, 55,* 588–598.

Damhorst, M., Littrell, J., & Littrell, M. (1988). Age differences in adolescent body dissatisfaction. *Journal of Psychology, 121,* 553–562.

Dent, C. W., Sussman, S., Stacy, A.W., Craig, S., Burton, D. & Flay, B. R. (1995). Two-year outcomes of Project Towards No Tobacco Use. *Journal of Consulting and Clinical Psychology, 63,* 676–677.

Desmond, S. M., Price, J. H., Gray, N., & O'Connell, J. K. (1986). The etiology of adolescents' perceptions of their weight. *Journal of Youth and Adolescence, 15,* 461–472.

Eagly, A. H., & Chaiken, S. (1993). *The psychology of attitudes.* Fort Worth, TX: Harcourt Brace Jovanovich College Publishers.

Ennett, S. T., & Bauman, K. E. (1994). The contribution of influence and selection to adolescent peer group homogeneity: The case of adolescent cigarette smoking. *Journal of Personality and Social Psychology, 67,* 653–663.

Ennett, S. T., Bauman, K. E., & Koch, G. G. (1994). Variability in cigarette smoking within and between adolescent friendship cliques. *Addictive Behaviors, 19,* 295–305.

Fabian, L. J., & Thompson, J. K. (1989). Body image and eating disturbance in young females. *International Journal of Eating Disorders, 8,* 63–74.

Fisher, L. A., & Bauman, K. E. (1988). Influence and selection in the friend-adolescent relationship: Findings from studies of adolescent smoking and drinking. *Journal of Applied Social Psychology, 18,* 289–314.

French, S. A., Perry, C. L., Leon, G. R, & Fulkerson, J. A. (1995). Dieting behaviors and weight change history in female adolescents. *Health Psychology, 14,* 548–555.

French, S. A., Story, M., Downes, B., Resnick, M. D., & Blum, R. W. (1995). Frequent dieting among adolescents: Psychosocial and health behavior correlates. *American Journal of Public Health, 85,* 695–701.

Garner, D. M. (1985). Iatrogenesis in anorexia nervosa and bulimia nervosa. *International Journal of Eating Disorders, 4,* 701–726.

Gibbons, K. L., Wertheim, E. H., Paxton, S. J., Petrovich, J., & Szmukler, G. I. (1995). Nutrient intake of adolescents and its relationship to desire for thinness, weight loss behaviours, and bulimic tendencies. *Australian Journal of Nutrition and Dietetics, 52,* 69–74.

Gralen, S. J., Levine, M. P. Smolak, L., & Murnen, S. K. (1990). Dieting and disordered eating during early and middle adolescence: Do the influences remain the same? *International Journal of Eating Disorders, 9,* 501–512.

Grigg, M., Bowman, J., & Redman, S. (1996). Disordered eating and unhealthy weight reduction practices among adolescent females. *Preventive Medicine, 25,* 748–756.

Grissett, N. I., & Norvell, N. K. (1992). Perceived social support, social skills, and quality of relationships in bulimic women. *Journal of Consulting and Clinical Psychology, 60,* 293–299.

Heaven, P. C. L. (1994). *Contemporary adolescence: A social psychological approach.* Melbourne: Macmillan.

Heinberg, L. J., & Thompson, J. K. (1992a). The effects of figure size feedback (positive vs. negative) and target comparison group (particularistic vs. universalistic) on body image disturbance. *International Journal of Eating Disorders, 12,* 441–448.

Heinberg, L. J., & Thompson, J. K. (1992b). Social comparison: Gender, target importance ratings and relation to body image disturbance. *Journal of Social Behaviour and Personality, 7,* 335–344.

Huon, G. (1994). Towards the prevention of dieting-induced disorders: Modifying negative food- and body-related attitudes. *International Journal of Eating Disorders, 16,* 395–399.

Huon, G., Hayne, A., Gunewardene, A., Strong, K. G., Lunn, N., Piira, T, & Lim, J. (in press). Accounting for differences in dieting status: Steps in the refinement of a model. *International Journal of Eating Disorders.*

Killen, J. D., Taylor, C. B., Hammer, L. D., & Litt, I. Wilson, D. M., Rich, T., Hayward, C., Simmonds, B., Kraemer, H., & Varady, A. (1993). An attempt to modify unhealthy eating attitudes and weight regulation practices of young adolescent girls. *International Journal of Eating Disorders, 13,* 369–384.

Killen, J. D., Taylor, C. B., Hayward, C., Wilson D. A. M., Haydel K. F., Hammer, L. D., Simmonds, B., Robinson, T. N., Litt, I., Varady, A., & Kraemer, H. (1994). Pursuit of thinness and onset of eating disorder symptoms in a community sample of adolescent girls: A three-year prospective analysis. *International Journal of Eating Disorders, 16,* 227–238.

Levine, M. P., Smolak, L. & Hayden, H. (1994). The relation of sociocultural factors to eating attitudes and behaviours among middle school girls. *Journal of Early Adolescence, 14,* 471–490.

Levine, M. P., Smolak, L., Moodey, A. F., Shuman, M. D., & Hessen, L. D. (1994). Normative developmental challenges and dieting and eating disturbance in middle school girls. *International Journal of Eating Disorders, 15,* 11–20.

Lifshitz, F., & Moses, N. (1988). Nutritional dwarfing: Growth, dieting and fear of obesity. *Journal of the American College of Nutrition, 7,* 367–376.

Mallick, M. L., Whipple, T. H., & Huerta, E. (1987). Behavioral and psychological traits of weight conscious teenagers: A comparison of eating-disordered patients of high- and low-risk groups. *Adolescence, 22,* 157–168.

Mann, T., Nolen-Hoeksema, S., Huang, K., Burgard, D., Wright, A., & Hanson, K. (1997). Are two interventions worse than none? Joint primary and secondary prevention of eating disorders in college females. *Health Psychology, 16,* 215–225.

Mitchell, J. E., Hatsukami, D., Pyle, R. L., Eckert, E. D. (1986). The bulimia syndrome: Course of the illness and associated problems. *Comprehensive Psychiatry, 27,* 165–179.

Moreno , A., & Thelan, M. (1993). A preliminary prevention program for eating disorders in a junior high school population. *Journal of Youth and Adolescence, 22,* 109–124.

Murray, D. M., Richards, P. S., Luepker, R. V., & Johnson, C. A. (1987). The prevention of cigarette smoking in children: Two- and three-year follow-up comparisons of four prevention strategies. *Journal of Behavioral Medicine, 10,* 595–611.

Nichter, M., & Nichter, M. (1991). Hype and weight. *Medical Anthropology, 13,* 249–284.

Nichter, M., & Vuckovic, N. (1994). Fat talk: Body image among adolescent girls. In N. Sault (Ed.), *Many mirrors: Body image and social relations* (pp. 109–131). New Brunswick, NJ: Rutgers University Press.

NIH Panel. (1992). Methods of voluntary weight loss and control: Technology Assessment Conference statement. *Annals of Internal Medicine, 116,* 942–949.

Norris, M. (1995). *Body image, weight loss behaviours and "dating" in adolescent girls.* Unpublished honours thesis, University of Melbourne.

Oliver, K. K., & Thelen, M. H. (1996). Children's perceptions of peer influence on eating concerns. *Behavior Therapy, 27,* 25–39.

Patton, G. C., Carlin, J. B., Shao, M. E., Hibbert, M. E., Rosier, M., Selzer, R., & Bowes, G. (1997). Adolescent dieting: Appropriate weight control or borderline eating disorder*? Journal of Child Psychology and Psychiatry, 38,* 299–306.

Patton, G. C., Johnson-Sabine, E., Wood, K., Mann, A. H., & Wakeling, A. (1990). Abnormal eating attitudes in London schoolgirls: A prospective study: Outcome at twelve month follow-up. *Psychological Medicine, 20,* 383–394.

Paxton, S. J. (1993) A prevention program for disturbed eating in adolescent girls: A one year follow-up. *Health Education Research: Theory and Practice, 8,* 43–51.

Paxton, S. J., Schutz, H. K., Wertheim, E. H., & Muir, S. L. (in press). *Friendship clique and peer influences on body image attitudes, dietary restraint, extreme weight loss behaviors and binge eating in adolescent girls.* Journal of Abnormal Psychology.

Paxton, S. J., Wertheim, E. H., Gibbons, K. Szmukler, G. I., Hillier, L., & Petrovich, J. C. (1991). Body image satisfaction, dieting beliefs and weight loss behaviors in adolescent girls and boys. *Journal of Youth and Adolescence, 20,* 361–379.

Paxton, S. J., Williams, M., & Wertheim, E. H. (1998, April). *Peer environment factors and extreme weight loss behaviors in adolescent girls.* Paper presented at the Eighth New York International Conference on Eating Disorders, New York.

Pike, K. M. (1995). Bulimic symptomatology in high school girls: Towards a model of cumulative risk. *Psychology of Women Quarterly, 19,* 373–396.

Piran, N. (1996). The reduction of preoccupation with body weight and shape in schools: A feminist approach. *Eating Disorder: The Journal of Treatment and Prevention, 4,* 323–333.

Pyle, R. L. Mitchell, J. E., & Eckert, E. D. (1981). Bulimia: A report of 34 cases. *Journal of Clinical Psychiatry, 42,* 60–64.

Rooney, B., McClelland, L., Crisp, A. H., & Sedgwick, P. (1995). The incidence and prevalence of anorexia nervosa in three suburban health districts in south west London, UK. *International Journal of Eating Disorders, 18,* 299–307.

Rorty, M., Yager, J., & Rossotto, E. (1993). Why and how do women recover from bulimia nervosa? The subjective appraisals of forty women recovered for a year or more. *International Journal of Eating Disorders, 14,* 249–260.

Rosen, J. C., & Gross, J. (1987). Prevalence of weight reducing and weight gaining in adolescent girls and boys. *Health Psychology, 6,* 131–147.

Rosen, J. C., Gross, J. C., & Vara, L. (1987). Psychological adjustment of adolescents attempting to lose or gain weight. *Journal of Consulting and Clinical Psychology, 55,* 742–747.

Russell, J. D., & Beumont, P. J. V. (1995). Risk and prevention in eating disorders. In B. Raphael & G. D. Burrows (Eds.), *Handbook of studies of preventive psychiatry* (pp. 459–476). Amsterdam: Elsevier.

Schutz, H., Paxton, S. J., & Wertheim, E. (April, 1997). *Precursors to eating disorders? Body comparisons and "fat talk" among adolescent females.* Paper presented to the Third London International Conference on Eating Disorders, London.

Shisslak, C. M., Crago, M., McKnight, K. M., Estes, L. S. Gray, N., & Parnaby, O. G. (1998). Potential risk factors associated with weight control behaviors in elementary and middle school girls. *Journal of Psychosomatic Research, 44,* 301–313.

Shisslak, C. M., Crago, M., Neal, M. E., & Swain, B. (1987). Primary prevention of eating disorders. *Journal of Consulting and Clinical Psychology, 55,* 660–667.

Smolak, L., Levine, M. P., & Gralen, S. (1993). The impact of puberty and dating on eating problems among middle school girls. *Journal of Youth and Adolescence, 22,* 355–368.

Smolak, L., Levine, M. P., & Schermer, K. (1998). A controlled evaluation of an elementary school primary prevention program for eating problems. *Journal of Psychosomatic Research, 44,* 344–354.

Steinhausen, H., & Vollrath, M. (1993). The self-image of adolescent patients with eating disorders. *International Journal of Eating Disorders, 13,* 221–227.

Stice, E. (1994). Review of the evidence for a sociocultural model of bulimia nervosa and an exploration of the mechanisms of action. *Clinical Psychology Review, 14,* 633-661.

Stice, E., Nemeroff, C., & Shaw, H. E. (1996). Test of the dual pathway model of bulimia nervosa: Evidence for dietary restraint and affect regulation mechanisms. *Journal of Social and Clinical Psychology, 15,* 340–363.

Stormer, S. M., & Thompson, J. K. (1996). Explanations of body image disturbance: A test of maturational status, negative verbal commentary, social comparison and sociocultural hypotheses. *International Journal of Eating Disorders, 19,* 193–202.

Striegel-Moore, R. H., Silberstein, L. R., & Rodin J. (1986). Towards an understanding of risk factors for bulimia. *American Psychologist, 41,* 246–263.

Strong, K. G., & Huon, G. F. (1998). An evaluation of a structural model for studies of the initiation of dieting among adolescent girls. *Journal of Psychosomatic Research, 44,* 315–326.

Thompson, J., Coovert, M., Richards, K. J., Johnson, S., & Cattarin, J. (1995). Development of body image, eating disturbance, and general psychological functioning in female adolescents: Covariance structure modelling and longitudinal investigation. *International Journal of Eating Disorders, 18,* 221–236.

Vandereycken, W., & Meerman, R. (1984). Anorexia nervosa: Is prevention possible? *International Journal of Psychiatry in Medicine, 14,* 191–205.

Wertheim, E. H., Paxton, S. J., Maude, D., Szmukler, G. I., Gibbons, K., & Hillier, L. (1992). Psychosocial predictors of extreme weight loss behaviours and binge eating in adolescent girls and boys. *International Journal of Eating Disorders. 12,* 151–160.

Wertheim, E. H., Paxton, S. J., Schutz, H. & Muir, S. L. (1997). Why do adolescent girls watch their weight? An interview study examining sociocultural pressures to be thin. *Journal of Psychosomatic Research, 42,* 345–355.

Wilfley, D., Agras, W. S., Telch, C. F., Rossiter, E. M., Schneider, J. A., Cole, A. G., Sifford, L. & Raeburn, S. D. (1993). Group cognitive behavioral therapy and group interpersonal therapy for the non purging bulimic. A controlled comparison: *Journal of Consulting and Clinical Psychology, 61,* 296–305.

CHAPTER

Niva Piran

The Reduction of Preoccupation with Body Weight and Shape in Schools: A Feminist Approach

In this chapter I discuss elements that I have come to regard as key aspects of a feminist approach to the prevention of body-weight and shape preoccupation (BWSP) among young women in schools. The impetus to propose a feminist framework for intervention emerges from three sets of experiences. First, interest in prevention has grown dramatically in the past 10 years because of the documented high prevalence of BWSP even in prepubescent girls (Maloney, McGuire, Daniels, & Specker, 1989). BWSP has been associated with social and medical morbidity (Fisher, 1992; Killen et al., 1987). Second, a review of existing programs for the prevention of BWSP (Piran, 1995) showed aspects of intervention that contradicted feminist principles of counseling. Third, similar issues challenge preventative interventions with youth in other domains, such as substance abuse and smoking (Gerstein and Green, 1993). The preventative paradigm developed in this chapter is presented as a rudimentary basis for dialogue and discussion rather than as a fixed model, with the hope that other practicing therapists will add to and revise these ideas. The central themes of this approach include the following key topics: Expertise and transformation originate in life experiences, discovered in the process of dialogue; systemic interventions facilitate the transformation of knowledge into power; change occurs within a matrix of relationships; and intervention guided by feminist principles counters dominant prejudices, mores, and sociopolitical structures that may contribute to the development of body weight and shape preoccupation.

For the past 12 years I have been involved in the prevention BSWP in different settings. The decision to become involved in prevention work followed my experience as a feminist psychologist and clinical director of a hospital center for the treatment of eating disorders. This center was inundated by referrals of young women with severe eating disorders, some with stunted growth and osteoporosis and some on the verge of death.

My most intensive and long-term involvement in prevention has been in a residential dance school in Toronto. Here, my understanding of the need to extend ideas about feminist counseling to health promotion was deepened. The prevention program implemented in that school followed the health-promoting school model developed by the World Health Organization (European Network of Health-Promoting Schools, 1993). This model describes a collaborative process of intensive dialogues with all members of the school community towards the creation of a changed school environment that addresses target areas of concern. The program at the dance school aimed to reduce body weight and shape preoccupation and the incidence of full-blown eating disorders. The program and its outcome have been described in greater detail elsewhere (Piran, 1998, in press) and therefore are outlined only briefly in this paragraph. The program involved ongoing interventions with school administration and staff. Meetings with staff included the exploration and identification of factors within the school system that impacted favorably or adversely on students' body- and self-image, adopting strategies for change, as well as educational sessions. Educational sessions covered information requested by staff, such as developmental challenges for girls in puberty, set-point theory, and social theories of body weight and shape preoccupation. These meetings occurred 10 to 20 times annually. In addition, a focus group was conducted two to six times annually in small gender- and grade-cohesive groups of students, throughout the 8 years the students stayed at the school. In these groups, students were invited to explore what affected their experience of their body at the school and to devise strategies to address desired changes in the school system. Educational material requested by the students was provided as well. This chapter shares new information learned through implementing the program at the school. To anchor the ideas presented, examples are used from records of group meetings with girls between the ages of 10 and 15 years. All identifying information has been omitted or disguised. The first concept, the most crucial one, involves the location of authority and expertise.

☐ Expertise and Transformation Originate in Life Experiences Discovered in the Process of Dialogue

Adolescent women in the dance school at which I counseled had the knowledge and expertise both to describe and contextualize their BWSP and to devise wise solutions responsive to the circumstances of their lives.

Example: I asked the young women in one group how they felt about their bodies at the school. They also were questioned about what may affect them to feel dissatisfied with their bodies and weight.

They talked about the shame associated with having a woman's body. They described conflicting pressures about the shape and size of their breasts, their buttocks, and their thighs. Their bodies were never quite right. They described a television star who lost a lot of weight and "looked anorexic." They had seen a program on TV that showed how this anorexic star had to wear a special girdle that forced her flesh up towards the neckline to appear as if she still had breasts even though she was emaciated. That way she could be "both anorexic and sexy." The use of the girdle led to a discussion of how rough and devaluing the producers were towards this woman's body. They felt that using a girdle still was better than cosmetic surgery "even though it looked as if nobody could breathe in this girdle."

The girls commented that a similar manipulation of women's bodies occurred often in the dance world, in which different companies had specific conflicting physical requirements for female dancers. For example, some dance companies wanted longer legs and shorter backs; others preferred different body proportions. The many ideals for body shape not only were impossible to achieve but often conflicted. The girls in the group were angry at how conflicting norms were prohibiting talented women from dancing professionally. The discussion seemed to relieve pressures caused by internalizing these conflicting sets of socially constructed expectations and to mitigate experiences of shame and self-doubt.

The girls continued by describing the way a particular teacher blamed half of them for being too thin and the other half for being too fat even though they all looked the same. The following day, the classification might arbitrarily and capriciously change. It felt to them as if the teacher was toying with them and with their feelings through their body. Collectively, they became angry as they began to realize the teacher was abusing his power by freely deprecating their bodies. They also commented that they noticed a worsening in this teacher's attitude. As a group, they realized that the teacher's behavior might reflect his own difficulties regarding his aging rather than problems with their body shape. The anger and discussion helped the students locate the problem with the teacher rather than with themselves. They decided to approach the administration about this teacher. The teacher was given relevant feedback by the administration and another teacher was assigned to work with him in some classes.

Another student was disturbed when one of her male classmates blamed her angry outburst on her menstrual cycle rather than on his refusal to follow her request of wanting to be alone. His claim that she was "bitchy" because she was having a period discounted the real reason for her anger. The girls in the group described how shamed they felt about their menstrual periods and how vulnerable they felt if anybody mentioned their periods or even saw them buying menstrual pads. They said that boys used information about their periods to make embarrassing comments. As an outcome of the discussion a group of five girls decided to call this boy to educate him about their menstrual processes. They needed, as they put it, "to be in power" while educating him about menstruation and about separating body experiences from social issues. They said they felt safer in a group with a five-to-one ratio. In order to give him a sense of their experience they asked him to describe his experiences of wet dreams. Whether he developed new insight was not revealed, but the girls emerged with more power to address their concerns about harassing comments.

These are examples of how, through group discussion, knowledge emerges and is voiced about the meaning of the social experience of owning a young woman's body. From a discussion of body shape, bodily functions, and expectations of one's appearance, the dialogue is transformed into a discussion about power and voice. Through the articulation of the problems within the safety of the group, wise solutions emerge.

What gradually became apparent to me as a facilitator was the lack of correspondence between this "lived" experience and professional models of interventions employed in BSWP programs. Although the young women discussed and attempted to address a myriad of social issues, such as power, harassment, violence, and racism, existing prevention programs typically stressed healthy eating and weight management or media-conveyed pressures for thinness (Piran, 1995). Moreover, the didactic format of these expert-driven packages seemed to limit the emergence of valued lived knowledge and left little room for the expression of diversity in social and personal experiences. Professionally contrived programs were observed to restrict successful solutions that might emerge through dialogue and inquiry (Piran, 1995).

A feminist-guided prevention program honors the transformative power of lived knowledge (MacKinnon, 1989; Nielsen, 1990; Sullivan, 1990) and relies on *inquiry and dialogue* to derive and give a voice to this knowledge. Instead of the traditional authoritative model in which the expert interprets the meaning and motivation that underlie behavior, participants explain their behavior and assign personal meaning to it (Sullivan, 1990). Similarly, participants offer their own solutions. Although the location of expertise within the client is a core principle of feminist counseling, it has not been extended consistently to prevention interventions with youth in schools. The offering of relevant information in the context of inquiry may aid in the process of transformation (Oakley, 1992). In that context, feminist research conducted with and for women is informative to both facilitators and participants.

☐ Systemic Interventions Facilitate the Transformation of Knowledge into Power

New knowledge, which emerges in focus groups with students, has the potential to guide school-wide systemic transformations, making the school a safer and more equitable environment for adolescent women. It is recommended that, prior to direct interventions with students, school staff receive special training that emphasizes the impact of staff on students' body image as well as how to listen undefensively to students. Within this context, students' feedback is more likely to be heard and incorporated (Piran, 1995). A cycle then ensues whereby group discovery leads to successful action that, in turn, leads to further discoveries and further action. Discussion about issues of appearance and weight, for example, might be followed by intensive work related to sexual harassment or to the exploration of disclosures of sexual abuse. The process of change is enhanced and made credible by the extent to which the school system is capable of addressing issues raised. Conversely, if the school system stifles understanding and action, knowledge that emerges in the group may only exacerbate experiences of vulnerability and helplessness.

> *Example:* A group of girls began a session by joking about their body shapes. Their dialogue seemed scattered and they could not listen to each other. Gradually the girls became more focused. Different girls hesitantly mentioned that they were not sure if adult staff were "really listening" to them. I needed to reassure them that I would do my best to listen. A girl then started to tearfully describe how a staff member told her she looked like a whore in her outfit because it was tight around her developing breasts. Similar complaints emerged about this staff person. When I took the information seriously and suggested that this should be discussed with administration, they tearfully related difficulties with an additional staff member whom they saw as constantly leering at their developing bodies and encroaching on their privacy. As their voices grew more confident in the group, they requested to see the director about these experiences. The director saw them promptly and appropriately responded through personnel changes.

Changing the system includes more than shifting the attitudes of staff and administration. Revisions in peer relations among students are an equally important objective. Peers can be encouraged to form support groups to combat the expression of prejudices and inequities. The program established consensual norms about many aspects of the school milieu, including ways teachers and peers (girls to girls, boys to girls, girls to boys, and boys to boys) could and could not talk to each other. Specific norms were established around comments about the body. Therefore, if norms were violated students felt empowered to voice their experience directly and with authority to staff and peers.

> *Example:* A group of girls victoriously described how they dealt with a negative comment from their dance teacher. The teacher told a girl in the group that she was getting "chunky," actually violating rules about teachers' behaviors that were agreed upon in staff meetings as part of the prevention program. The particular rules that this teacher violated were that teachers were not allowed to make any comments about their students' body shapes, and that they were not allowed to treat students' bodies disrespectfully. Indignantly, the girl responded by telling the teacher that she was in a growth spurt and that restricting her nutritional intake at this time could threaten both her health and her growth. Failing to get the message, her teacher continued to insist that she should do something about her weight. Risking altercation with the teacher, her peers formed a strong and united supportive network around her and insisted that the teacher retract this dangerous perspective. Following the class they approached another staff person requesting that the incident in the class be explored. With administrative support, the system was able to effect a change in attitude. The teacher has not repeated these comments.

These examples demonstrate how crucial the reinforcing reaction of staff and peers is in transforming group knowledge into power. Moreover, they demonstrate that the students can guide ongoing interventions with staff. Intervention within a particular school may facilitate the creation of a healthier system, a subculture, that can buffer adverse effects of the larger culture (Paxton, 1993). In contrast with this systemic approach, a review of school-based prevention programs for BWSP revealed that most programs have focused on inducing change within individual students without a parallel effort at inducing changes in their social environment (e.g., school staff, coaches, parents, or peers) (Piran, 1995). For example, programs tried to help individual students combat cultural pressures for thinness by providing them with information about natural weights and set-point theory without at the same time addressing teasing by their peers or parental pressures for weight loss. Directing students to change without concurrently guiding changes in their social environment may put undue stress on students and render interventions inefficient (Piran, 1993; Stermac, Piran, and Sheridan, 1993).

From a feminist perspective, BWSP may be seen as the expression by women of the prejudicial, unequal, and harsh treatment of themselves and their bodies in their social context and an attempt to cope with these challenges. A feminist prevention program critically examines the many varied contextual factors that affect women's experience of themselves, their bodies, and their eating. It then targets aspects of the social and political environment for direct intervention. The changed context reinforces the process of transforming bodily expressions of oppression into authoritative voices, which, in turn, guide further systemic changes.

☐ Change Occurs Within a Matrix of Relationships

The knowledge that emerged at the dance school about BWSP and the changes that followed occurred within the context of intense reciprocal relationships. The opening of relational dialogues occurred among students (within and across genders), between students and myself as program facilitator, and between students and different staff members. Regarding peer relations, one consistent observation was that peers in small groups, by their own initiative, examined and worked to improve their interrelationships before targeting changes outside of the group.

> *Example:* The group discussed the way in which a particular teacher was putting students down through commenting on their appearance. They then realized that they also were commenting on each other's appearance. They discovered that this ongoing mutual peer evaluation was introducing power disparity among friends, and this corrupted their relationships: "If you evaluate me you have power over me this is not good friendship." They therefore decided to stop evaluating one another. Only after they were satisfied that they had addressed this peer issue fully did they decide to approach the teacher requesting a change in her behavior.

Although members of this group felt strongly connected to one another and engaged in an ongoing relational dialogue during and between group meetings, members of other groups sometimes reacted to adverse social pressures and experiences by withdrawing from connections and competing in a way that kept them feeling alienated from one another. Nonetheless, members of all groups were seeking connections and felt relieved and excited to rediscover them in the groups. Similar to the pattern of connected groups, members of alienated groups sought to repair and establish their own connections before dealing with external pressures.

> *Example:* A competitive and alienated group found it initially hard to talk to one another about different mundane events that had occurred during the past week. They soon realized that they had been competing so hard in ballet and in every one of their academic subjects that they all secretly felt on the verge of physical and psychological collapse. Revealing these experiences in the group provided immediate relief expressed through both laughing and crying. Group members decided to hold hands in a circle for a while in order to help one another relax. Before the group session ended, members made a decision to help one another deal with their demanding ballet teacher by using a particular hand movement during class to convey the following message to one another: "You are doing fine, the teacher is in a bad mood today." They left the group more unified and less intimidated by the teacher.

Relationships between myself as the group facilitator and the young women involved long-term commitments and been mutually transformative. In order to voice silenced knowledge and channel the knowledge into action, the young women needed to feel that I cared for them and their experiences and that I trusted and cherished their voices, respected their need for safety, and honored their authority. The young women's openness, courage, insights, relational understanding, and creative solutions consistently awed me. My experiences during childhood and adolescence and as an adult woman and mother resonated with aspects of their experiences. I shared personal reactions and experiences, which I thought would be validating and constructive to the young women. As well, I explicitly described my values and attitudes regarding pertinent issues such as harassment, violence, or norms of thinness, while recognizing different views. Although we were located in different places in terms of age and power in the school, the young women's and my life intersected in many ways. I found facing the adversity of so-called normative conditions in young women's lives, outside of the counseling office, to be both revealing and devastating. At times, I needed to talk about different reactions to this work with colleagues. This happened, for example, if a new teacher or guests exposed girls to harsh treatment, or if the girls rehearsed elsewhere. At the early phases of the work at the school, before many positive changes took place in the school and in students' self- and body-image, I found myself reacting to the degree to which the girls had internalized the harsh external treatment of their bodies. In those situations I had to face and go beyond my own experiences of discouragement before I could fully validate and support the women in their experiences of despair and betrayal.

> *Example:* Having gone through puberty, a group of girls in midadolescence were assessing their developed bodies. A pretty, thin, and only slightly developed girl said: "Me and my mom are going to have breast reduction surgery together, isn't it cool?" Most girls felt that this news were indeed exciting and "cool." The reasons that were related to me for the surgery mainly suggested that the mother was feeling vulnerable, and that there was considerable misinformation about the benefits (exaggerated and unfounded) and risks (minimized) of the operation. Most girls in the group talked about their hatred of their body *shape*, their breasts and their menstrual cycles. They followed these themes by chanting the most demeaning rhymes I have ever heard about women and their bodies, how women nag, their stomachs droop like bags, and their breasts sag. These expressions of internalized aggression and deprecation made me feel hopeless about changing the school and about women's status in general. At that time, I was feeling drained and betrayed by the lack of gender equity at my workplace. I had to be aware of my own experience before I could emotionally connect with the girls and say, "Yes, sometimes it is hard to be a woman and to have a woman's body." That comment started many discussions about the context within which we live that may make us, women, so hard on our bodies and ourselves.

Often, we would emerge from these experiences more committed to networking and to social and political changes. Older girls in the school would become advocates of younger girls, wanting to protect them from adverse experiences. The overall process was that of mutual growth and transformation for all involved.

Commitment to one another and to the process of change was an additional aspect of the relational matrix in the program. The young women's commitment to one another's welfare and the care of older students for younger students in a true spirit of sisterhood was often moving. In the difficult process of initiating change, the young women needed to know that I was committed to advocate for them in the school and that I had the power to effect changes in the school system. They needed to know that different staff members in leading positions at the school were behind them. For example, I noticed that they often would assess accurately, through changes at the school, whether I had followed a particular advocacy task they requested of me during a group meeting. They also needed to see that in my advocacy role I did not go beyond their guidance and left for them the work they wanted to do. Most often we worked in a coordinated and parallel way to effect changes.

In light of the key role of the relational context of the intervention in the school, it is striking to note that programs for the prevention of BWSP have paid little attention to relational issues (Piran, 1995). This resembles a tendency within different streams of psychotherapy to concentrate on particular techniques or contents of intervention irrespective of their meaning within a relational context (Butler and Strupp, 1986).

A feminist prevention program honors change and growth that occur within a matrix of relationships typified by mutual respect, empathy, and responsibility. If oppression has alienated young women from one another, a prevention program for BWSP aims to help young women reclaim the quality of their relationships and thus develop resistance. Such a program facilitates the opening of relational dialogues across generations, positions of power, gender, race, and other social barriers. Similar to models of feminist counseling, a feminist prevention program aims to minimize the power differential between facilitator and participants.

The three elements that have been described so far—reliance on knowledge anchored in diverse life experiences, the targeting of systemic factors for change, and the emphasis on the relational context of change—are components of the next broader principle.

Intervention Guided by Feminist Principles Counters Dominant Prejudices, Mores, and Sociopolitical Structures that May Contribute to the Development of Body Weight and Shape Preoccupation

In emphasizing lived diverse knowledge, the program counters social and professional power structures (Nielsen, 1990; Sullivan, 1990), honors knowledge derived from life experiences and in relationships (Belenky, Clinchy, Goldberger, & Tarule, 1986), respects diversity and the enrichment in understanding derived from diversity (Nielsen, 1990; Thompson, 1994), and focuses on the process of unsilencing knowledge of oppressed groups as a depathologizing, healing, and empowering process (Herman, 1992; MacKinnon, 1989; Wooley, 1993). By targeting the system as a focus of change, and especially guiding systemic interventions by students' voices, the program empowers the students, assures greater likelihood of success and safety (Orenstein, 1994), and hightlights the responsibility of adults for the welfare of children and adolescents, a responsibility often unrecognized in prevention programs with schoolchildren (Stermac et al., 1993). In emphasizing the importance of relationships in the life of women, the program aims to mitigate the relational crisis women experience in early adolescence (Gilligan, Rodgers, & Tolman, 1991). Based on her understanding of BWSP and her social experiences and values, a program facilitator may elect to focus on countering different aspects of adverse societal prejudices and mores. The choices should be outlined explicitly and examined continuously. My own social and professional experience has led me to value the relevance of issues of voice, relationships, power, and equality in BWSP.

The challenge to create an intervention space that does not collude with adverse societal structures, prejudices, or mores is elusive and maybe impossible. Societal prejudices and mores are so insidious and pervasive that their inclusion may be unavoidable. A suggestion made in one of the first documents published about the prevention of eating disorders (Crisp, 1988) may serve to illustrate the risk of collusion with adverse prejudices. Among other ideas, the author suggested putting pregnant women on a diet in order to prevent overweight off-spring, which is a risk factor for the development of eating disorders. Not only does such a suggestion put the mother at risk for developing an eating disorder, but it colludes with myths that a woman's body and appetites, especially during this powerful event of pregnancy, should be externally controlled and managed (Bordo, 1993). Varied programs have been differentially successful in combating negative prejudices and mores. A review of different prevention programs for BWSP revealed occurrences of sexist or weightist attitudes (Piran, 1995). Pro-grams also failed to include material that has been silenced by the larger culture. Although all prevention programs address pressures for thinness, they do not address other social factors such as harassment and violence, sexism and equity, or membership in minority groups (Piran, 1995). These omissions perpetuate the social silencing of issues of trauma and social power (Wooley, 1993).

The decision whether to address particular issues in prevention programs of BWSP may at times be controversial among feminist activists and depend on a facilitator's values and biases. One example of a controversial issue is the inclu-sion of healthy weight-management training in prevention programs for BWSP. Such training has been a staple of most prevention programs for BWSP. The ra-tionale for this training has been that knowledge of healthy weight manage-ment will prevent young women from resorting to unhealthy eating patterns. Although I support the importance of healthy lifestyle training that includes principles of healthy eating and healthy exercise, I tend to separate such train-ing from prevention programs for BWSP. In my view, one of the significant goals of a prevention program for BWSP is to dispel cultural myths that maintain that a woman's body is inherently deficient and in need of external management and control (Bordo, 1993). The inclusion of a weight management program may contradict this goal. Similarly, although I support a stronger emphasis for girls and women on involvement in different sport activities, I have tended, un-like other feminist women who work with youth, to focus on the benefit of sport activities for improved fitness and vitality, rather than for weight manage-ment. Inevitably, assumptions, attitudes, and values in our work need to be ex-plicitly discussed and explored through ongoing dialogues so we can arrive at more diverse ways of understanding.

Even if the different issues covered by a prevention program in a school do not collude with adverse societal mores, the process of administration nonethe-less may reveal the pervasive impact of adverse societal factors. For example, a common prevention activity for BWSP in schools involves a slide presentation of emaciated models to a group of adolescent women and men. Although the presentation aims to convey the potential destructiveness of media pressures for thinness, it is very common for young men in the crowd to whistle and express other admiring reactions to the women in the slides. I have seen repeatedly how these presentations make adolescent women feel inadequate in their bodies and how the men's response to the slides degrades the women and makes them feel vulnerable and unsafe, similar to experiences of sexual harassment. The typi-cally vocal reactions of young men to discussions that follow these presentations and the relative silence by the young women in the audience is a further indica-tion that a certain trauma has been recreated by the presentation.

Feminist-informed programs for BWSP put a strong emphasis on assuring that the content or process of the interventions does not replicate adverse societal conditions. This goal requires ongoing review and critical assessment.

Potential Challenges in Implementing a Feminist-Informed Participatory Program

In planning to implement a feminist-informed participatory program that targets the school system as a whole for change, it is valuable to consider several challenges. One challenge relates to the important goal of engaging all possible parties of the school community: administrators, teachers, other staff, parents, and students. This engagement allows both for the active and collaborative scrutiny of protective and adverse systemic factors that affect body- and self-image and for the implementation of school-wide changes as agreed upon by all sides. Support by the school administration empowers the facilitator to initiate and bring forth changes suggested by students and other staff and empowers students to voice their perceptions and solutions directly to administration. The response of administration to such initiatives is essential to the success of the program. A process enlisting the support and participation of members of the school community may take some time, possibly a few months to a year, but the program cannot be effective without it. Even if rapport has been established, challenges may surface as the program progresses. The program may reveal that personnel changes are indicated, that new policies (for example, regarding sexual abuse or compromising the athletic regimen of a particular team) need to be implemented, or that external agencies need to be involved (for example, if sexual or physical abuse is revealed). These situations, at times, pose challenges to the ongoing rapport and to the support for the program. Restating the shared goals of the program and assessing its success usually lead to renewed commitment.

Following the successful engagement of staff and students, different members of the school community and the program facilitators work towards the shared goal of creating a school culture that promotes positive body and self images among its students. Because different personnel address different aspects of the program, it is important to schedule meeting times when all involved have the opportunity to communicate and coordinate their efforts. It is also important to create a network of support for personnel, parents, and students who take the lead in changing aspects of the school. Unlike a time-limited preplanned prevention program, a participatory program requires more ongoing monitoring. At the same time, if the program is successful, the systemic changes allow for the maintenance of gains.

Another challenge in implementing such a program model relates to the selection of program facilitators. Facilitators of such programs have to be comfortable with the emerging and relatively unstructured nature of the programs, because the programs develop through multiple dialogues, often in focus groups with staff and students. Facilitators have to be familiar and comfortable with the facilitation of groups. The program relies both on the understanding and experienced knowledge of members of the community, especially students, and on the empowerment of these members. For that purpose, facilitators need to feel comfortable in a facilitative, rather than an expert, role. Because facilitators have to explicitly counter adverse societal prejudices, they need to be informed about developmental challenges in the lives of girls and hold feminist values. They also should be comfortable discussing their values openly with students and other members of the school community. Because the program relies on activism within the school system, it would be fitting for the facilitator to model activism outside of the school system as well. Understanding of the political implications of the program and the challenge they may pose in working with the school administration and others is also an asset. Most importantly, the facilitator needs to feel committed to the program, the students, and the school as a whole. The program therefore poses greater demands on facilitators compared with time-limited didactic programs, and facilitators should assess how realistic such an engagement is for them at a particular point in time. This way of work, on the other hand, is enriching, engaging, and rewarding.

The participatory method of health promotion poses special challenges in terms of outcome evaluation. Although the principles of a program generally can be outlined, the program may take on very different forms in its process of implementation in two different schools. Outcome comparisons therefore are challenging. In addition to the relatively easier task of assessing favorable individual changes among students of participating schools, the program evaluation needs to address systemic changes. Changes in the school system are a stated goal of the program. Yet the field of health promotion as a whole is still facing challenges in trying to assess systemic change (McKinlay, 1997; Piran, 1997). In addition, a participatory program involves multiple qualitative changes, but qualitative changes often are not incorporated into outcome-evaluation studies.

☐ Conclusion

Through describing a prevention approach that follows the participatory and dialogic principles of the health-promoting schools model of the World Health Organization, this chapter explores key aspects of a feminist-informed approach to the prevention of BWSP in schools and extends principles of feminist counseling to prevention programs. A feminist program acknowledges the importance of voice, power, lived experience, and relationships. The program works towards creating a safe and equitable school system in which the voices of diverse women are heard and women's bodies are no longer a site of societal oppression. Although the program requires both time and emotional commitment on the part of its facilitators, it has been found to be an effective way of combating BWSP in a school. In addition, its systemic nature allows for gains to be maintained over time.

☐ References

Belenky, M. F., Clinchy, B. M., Goldberger, N. R., & Tarule, J. M. (1986). *Women's way of knowing: The development of self, voice, and mind.* New York: Basic Books.

Bordo, S. (1993). *Unbearable weight: Feminism, western culture, and the body.* Berkeley: University of California Press.

Butler, S.F., & Strupp, H.H. (1986). Specific and nonspecific factors in psychotherapy: A problematic paradigm for psychotherapy research. *Psychotherapy, 23,* 30–40.

Crisp, A.H. (1988). Some possible approaches to prevention of eating and body weight/shape disorders, with particular reference to anorexia nervosa. *International Journal of Eating Disorders,* 7(1), 1–17.

European Network of Health-Promoting Schools. (1993). *World Health Organization Regional Office for Europe.* Copenhagen, Denmark.

Fisher, M. (1992). Medical complications of anorexia and bulimia nervosa. *Adolescent Medicine: State of the Art Reviews, 3,* 481–502.

Gerstein, D. R., & Green, L.W. (1993). *Preventing drug abuse: What do we know?* Washington, DC: National Academy Press.

Gilligan, C., Rodgers, A., & Tolman, D. (1991). *Women, girls and psychotherapy: reframing resistance.* New York: Harrington Park Press.

Herman, J.L. (1992). *Trauma and recovery.* New York: Basic Books.

Killen, J.D., Taylor, C.B., Telch, M.J., Robinson, T.N., Maron, D.J., & Saylor, K.E. (1987). Depressive symptoms and substance use among adolescent binge eaters and purgers: A defined population study. *American Journal of Public Health, 77,* 1539–1541.

MacKinnon, C. (1989). *Towards a feminist theory of the state.* Cambridge, MA: Harvard University Press.

Maloney, M. J., McGuire, J., Daniels, S.R., & Specker, B. (1989). Dieting behavior and eating attitudes in children. *Pediatrics, 84,* 482–489.

McKinlay, J. B. (1997, April). *Appropriate levels of intervention and analysis for community health interventions.* Presented at the One Hundred and Fifth Annual Convention of the American Psychological Association, Chicago.

Nielsen, J. M. (1990). Introduction. In J.M. Nielsen (Ed.), *Feminist research methods* (pp. 1–37). Boulder, CO: Westview Press.

Oakley, A. (1992). Interviewing women: A contradiction in terms. In H. Roberts (Ed.), *Doing feminist research* (pp. 30–61). New York: Routledge Press.

Orenstein, P. (1994). *School girls.* New York: Bantam Doubleday Dell Publishing Group.

Paxton, S. J. (1993). A prevention program for disturbed eating and body dissatisfaction in adolescent girls: A 1-year follow-up. *Health Education Research, 8,* 43–51.

Piran, N. (1993). Let's put treatment and prevention of eating disorders on an equal footing: The effect of prejudices, social structure, and social mores. *Eating Disorders. The Journal of Treatment and Prevention, 1,* 105–108.

Piran, N. (1995). Prevention: Can early lessons lead to a delineation of an alternative model? A critical look at prevention with schoolchildren. *Eating Disorders: The Journal of Treatment and Prevention, 3*(1), 28–36.

Piran, N. (1997). Prevention of eating disorders: Directions for future research. *Psychopharmacology Bulletin, 33,* 419–423.

Piran, N. (1998). A participatory approach to the prevention of eating disorders in a school. In W. Vandereycken & G. Noordenbos (Eds.), *The Prevention of eating disorders.* (pp. 173–186). London: Athlone Press.

Piran, N. (in press). Eating disorders: A trial of prevention in a high risk school setting. *Journal of Primary Prevention.*

Stermac, L., Piran, N., & Sheridan, P. M. (1993). Sexual abuse, eating disorders, and prevention: Political and social realities. *Eating Disorders: The Journal of Treatment and Prevention, 1,* 250–258.

Sullivan, E. (1990). *Critical psychology and pedagogy: Interpretation of the personal world.* Toronto: OISE Press.

Thompson, B. (1994). Food, bodies, and growing up female: Childhood lessons about culture race and class. In P. Fallon, M. A. Katzman, & S. Wooley (Eds.): *Feminist perspective on eating disorders* (pp. 355–380). New York: Guilford Press.

Wooley, S. (1993). Recognition of sexual abuse: Progress and backlash. *Eating Disorders: The Journal of Treatment and Prevention, 1,*(3 & 4), 298–314.

II

PREVENTION PROGRAMS FOR HIGH SCHOOLS AND COLLEGES

Adolescent students in high school who have completed their process of puberty and young adult students in college are at the stage at which they go through an intensive process of negotiating issues of identity, social roles, and expectations, all within the context of dominant societal institutions, mores and prejudices. This age range is the most common age of onset of eating disorders (Striegel-Moore, 1993). The common onset of eating disorders among high school and young adult women warrants an examination of prevention programs designed for high school and university students.

Themes related to peer groups and challenges faced in the school system—relevant to both middle and high school—are mentioned in the last two chapters of Part II. Part III continues the examination of the experience of girls in high school and describes programs that aim at enhancing critical awareness and empowerment. This section also includes two chapters that describe prevention programs on campus in general, and in sororities in particular.

In Chapter 10, LeAdelle Phelps, Monica Dempsey, Jennifer Sapia, and Linda Nelson apply knowledge derived from research on resiliency and girls' development to the development of a prevention program for high school students which is evaluated using a variety of outcome measures. Mimi Nichter, Nancy Vuckovic, and Sheila Parker, in Chapter 11, integrate knowledge derived from their multimethod studies of African American, Hispanic, and White high school students in Arizona. The multifaceted impact of sexual harassment on high school girls rarely has been included in the examination of poor body image. In Chapter 12, June Larkin, Carla Rice, and Vanessa Russell describe the common occurrence of sexual harassment in the lives of high-school students, the impact of this harassment on body image, and ways to help adolescent women and schools combat this adverse social phenomenon.

The transition from high school to the college environment involves pressures that increase the risk for eating disorders (Smolak & Levine, 1996; Striegel-Moore, Silberstein, Frensch, & Rodin, 1989; Whittaker & Davis, 1989). In Chapter 13, Kathy Hotelling describes the introduction of an integrated program on campus that includes a variety of services and strategies for the prevention and treatment of eating disorders. In Chapter 14, Brenda Alpert Sigall describes her efforts to work with sororities to create healthier norms regarding body shape and eating. The program emphasizes peer support and peer and professional collaboration.

☐ References

Smolak, L., & Levine, M.P. (1996). Adolescent transitions and the development of eating problems. In L. Smolak, M.P. Levine, & R. Striegel-Moore (Eds.), *The developmental psychopathology of eating disorders: Implications for research, prevention, and treatment* (pp. 207–233). Mahwah, NJ: Lawrence Erlbaum Associates.

Striegel-Moore (1993). Etiology of binge eating: A developmental perspective. In C. Fairburn & G.T. Wilson (Eds.), *Binge eating: Nature, assessment, and treatment* (pp. 144–172). New York: Guilford Press.

Striegel-Moore, R.H., Silberstein, L.R., Frensch, P., & Rodin, J. (1989). A prospective study of disordered eating among college students. *International Journal of Eating Disorders, 8,* 499–509.

Whittaker, L.C., & Davis, W.N. (Eds.). (1989). The bulimic college student: Evaluation, treatment, and prevention [special issue]. *Journal of College Student Psychotherapy, 3*(2/3/4).

LeAdelle Phelps
Monica Dempsey
Jennifer Sapia
Linda Nelson

The Efficacy of a School-based Eating Disorder Prevention Program: Building Physical Self-Esteem and Personal Competencies

☐ Development of a Prevention Model

Effective psychosocial prevention programming is dependent upon the identification of specific risk and protective factors that significantly influence the onset of a particular disorder. Always preceding the onset of the illness, risk and protective factors encompass both environmental ingredients and intrapsychic or personal variables. Risk catalysts are associated with higher probability of onset, greater severity, and longer duration of the disorder, whereas protective variables are affiliated with improved resistance and resilience. After successful identification of such factors, highly specific strategies then can be developed with the prevailing intent to reduce risk factors and enhance protective factors. It should be noted that the goals of decreasing risk and increasing protection are not mutually exclusive and, in fact, may be highly similar (Mrazek & Haggerty, 1994). Thus, the broad aims of a risk/protective model of prevention research are deterrence of a specific disorder, reduction of risk status, and mental-health promotion (Reiss & Price, 1996).

Modifiable factors such as coping skills and self-efficacy, which can be taught and increased effectively, are of particular interest (NIMH Committee on Prevention Research, 1995). Past research has indicated that elevating self-esteem and enhancing social competence strengthen resistance to stress (Albee, 1996). Nowhere may this be more true than in the prevention of eating disorders among adolescent females. Beginning in preschool and peaking during adolescence and early adulthood, a large proportion of a female's self-esteem is linked to her perception of her physical appearance (Akan & Grilo, 1995; Grilo, Wilfley, Jones, Brownell, & Rodin, 1994; Wertheim et al., 1992). It is now generally accepted that sociocultural mores and mass media portrayals promoting an unrealistic thin ideal play major roles in the development of eating disorders among females (Levine, Smolak, & Hayden, 1994; Stice, Schupak-Neuberg, Shaw, & Stein, 1994; Tiggemann & Pickering, 1996; Wiseman, Gray, Mosimann, & Ahrens, 1992). In fact, Levine et al. concluded that some girls live in a "subculture of dieting," surrounded by many weight-control messages emanating from the media, peers, and family. These youngsters have high levels of body dissatisfaction, engage in frequent weight-control activities, and evidence elevated disturbed eating behaviors.

Social pressure from peers and family members as well as the media depiction of the perfect body type are not the only antecedents of weight dissatisfaction and disordered eating. Although the cultural mores and media models of thinness are ubiquitous, the majority of teenagers do not develop long-term dysfunctional weight-related eating or behavioral patterns. A factor-analytic study of adolescent girls suggested, instead, that compliance with the model skeletal look generally first required psychological distress, such as feelings of insecurity and social self-doubt (Phelps & Wilczenski, 1993). Stice (1994) concurred with this conclusion and outlined an etiological model for eating disorders wherein low self-esteem and identity confusion increased the internalization of sociocultural and media pressures. Other studies have validated the relationship between eating-disordered behaviors and feelings of personal and physical inadequacy in adolescents (Adams, Katz, Beauchamp, & Zavis, 1993; Bennett, Spoth, & Borgen, 1991).

In order to prevent eating disorders, we must not only identify such risk and protective factors as mentioned previously but also distinguish which precursors are the strongest predictors and how such variables interact. Prospective data analyses using adolescent samples have substantiated that *body dissatisfaction* is the single strongest predictor of eating-disorder symptomatology (Button, 1990; Leon, Fulkerson, Perry, & Cudeck, 1993). According to the sociocultural model, body dissatisfaction occurs if an individual internalizes a culturally determined body ideal and then, upon self-comparison, determines her or his body to be discrepant from that ideal. Body dissatisfaction can vary from generalized displeasure, such as dislike of the entire body shape or size, to vexation with a specific part. It is important to note that large epidemiological studies have shown the majority of adolescent females to be dissatisfied with their bodies yet few are overweight (Bunnell, Cooper, Hertz, & Shenker, 1992). Thus, body dissatisfaction is intimately tied to *subjective opinions* of weight, and this subjective view is more predictive of dieting behaviors than actual weight (Button, 1990; Bunnell et al., 1992).

The identification of variables predictive of body dissatisfaction would aid significantly in the development of early prevention programs designed to intervene *before* a youngster is evidencing risk status. Recall that there are three subcategories within the realm of prevention programming: universal preclusion activities designed for general populations with no identified risk status; selective programming targeted to meet the needs of individuals or subgroups who, because of biological, psychological, or social considerations, are at significantly higher risk than the general population; and specific procedures intended for high-risk persons who have minimal but nonetheless detectable symptoms of the disorder (Mrazek & Haggerty, 1994). Thus, identification of variables *predictive of body dissatisfaction* would facilitate the development of a broad-based prevention program designed for adolescents with no discernable risk status.

In order to develop such a prevention model, Phelps, Johnston, and Augusty-niak (in press) surveyed 830 adolescent females attending a middle school (grades 6–8) or high school (grades 9–12) in a suburban school district in western New York. Using hierarchical multiple regression analyses and subsequent path analyses, Phelps et al. explored the relationships and interactions of numerous variables related to body dissatisfaction. Four areas of self-concept were of particular interest: physical (i.e., evaluation of one's physical appearance and ability), social (i.e., appraisal of one's peer relationships and social success), competence (i.e., judgment of personal efficacy and goal attainment), and academic (i.e., assessment of one's success in scholarly pursuits). These variables were measured using the Multidimensional Self Concept Scale (MSCS), a recently published self-report inventory having excellent reliability and validity (Bracken, 1992). Results of the final path-analysis model indicated that assisting adolescent females in the recognition of positive attributes of their physical appearance (i.e., physical self-concept) coupled with increasing their sense of personal efficacy or power (i.e., competence) significantly reduced the internalization or acceptance of current sociocultural mores (as measured by the drive-for-thinness subscale of the Eating Disorders Inventory-2 [EDI-2]; Garner, 1991). Subsequently, less endorsement of the thin ideal resulted in notably lower scores on the body-dissatisfaction subscale of the EDI-2. This, in turn, significantly reduced participation in disordered eating behaviors (e.g., use of laxatives, diuretics, or diet pills; participation in excessive exercise in order to control weight; and episodic bingeing and purging). Thus a risk/protective prevention program based on this model would include activities designed to increase physical self-esteem and feelings of personal competence, reduce individual acceptance and adherence to the current ideal of extreme thinness, and diminish the body dissatisfaction so ubiquitous among adolescent and young adult females.

☐ A Six-Session Eating Disorder Prevention Program

Two significant limitations of previously published intervention efforts are the reliance upon didactic presentations of factual information and the exclusive focus on risk factors. For example, past research on prevention models for AIDS, unprotected sex, drug use, and drinking/driving programs have proven that increasing an adolescent's *knowledge* about the risk associated with certain behaviors is simply not enough to significantly change future *actions* (Dielman, 1994). As the old adage goes: "Insight seldom changes behavior." Instead, the goals of this program were to facilitate a critical evaluation of current sociocultural mores, encourage personal values clarification, and enhance individual resilience via interactive lessons which included group discussions, problem-solving, and cooperative exercises. Thus, this prevention program was unusual in that it utilized active individual participation and collaborative learning (as opposed to a passive lecture format), and highlighted strengthening specific personal attributes that attenuate the sociocultural pressures promoting disordered eating behaviors (e.g., physical self-esteem and personal competence). If programs address only negative risk factors (e.g., chronic dieting, peer pressure, body dissatisfaction) or utilize a prescriptive informational format, participants are not likely to develop the necessary adaptive coping skills shown to mitigate future eating disorder symptomatology.

The final nuance of this prevention program was the inclusion of male participants. Although the vast majority of individuals suffering from eating disorders are female, the role of males in the development and maintenance of symptoms should not be overlooked. It appears appropriate for adolescent males to be included in prevention programming so that they can be challenged to examine their own beliefs regarding beauty and become aware of the pressures they may be placing on their female peers to engage in unhealthy eating practices.

The resulting eating-disorder prevention program was integrated within existing school curricula and utilized active participation by classroom teachers. It consisted of six sessions, with the objectives described here.

Session One

Session one was intended to reduce the internalization of sociocultural pressures by:

1. Discussion of the impact of sociocultural mores for thinness. During this session, the group leaders depicted how the definition of beauty and acceptable weight limitations had altered over the past 50 years. Photos of Betty Gable, Marilyn Monroe, and Twiggy were used as examples. The group participants were then asked to share their own perceptions of current mores.
2. Illustration of the roles of media, peers, and family modeling in disseminating weight-control messages. Numerous examples from magazine ads that were age-appropriate for each particular group were displayed (e.g., *Seventeen, Young and Modern, Vogue, In Style,* and *Cosmopolitan*). Typical comments from peers (particularly boyfriends) and parents regarding food consumption, weight distribution, and weight gain were delineated. The participants were then encouraged to share their own experiences regarding media, peer, and family pressures.

Session Two

Session two was devised to increase physical self-esteem by:

1. Provision of feedback on personal positive physical attributes. Most of the participants had never focused on positive aspects of their physical status. Group facilitators first provided examples of constructive feedback regarding such qualities as attractive hairstyle, eye color, physical endurance, and athleticism. Then each attendee had to complete the open-ended statement, "What I like about my physical appearance is . . ." Finally, group members were encouraged to provide positive feedback to one another.
2. Encouragement for improvement of personal physical fitness and strength. Alternatives to dieting and fasting were provided. Group leaders discussed how one's percentage body fat was a more accurate measure of physical fitness than weight (e.g., muscle weighs more than fat). Tables illustrating caloric burn for various activities such as walking, jogging, aerobics, and weight lifting were distributed. Finally, specific information regarding local fitness centers and evening exercise classes offered at the school was disseminated.

Session Three

Session three was designed to build personal competence by:

1. Facilitation of the development of internal locus of control. Group leaders guided a lengthy group discussion highlighting the importance of self-determination as opposed to responding to external influences. Participants were encouraged to share situations in which they chose to act in accordance to their personal values rather than be swayed by group pressure.
2. Cultivating better and more effective adaptive coping skills. The discussion then focused on constructive ways to respond to external pressures. Group facilitators provided examples of assertive responses and ignoring or not responding to negative comments.

Session Four

Session four was directed toward reducing body dissatisfaction by:

1. Illustration of the natural weight and fat gain during puberty. The group first was provided information about the biological aspects of puberty. Participants then shared their feelings about personal height and weight gains.
2. Depiction of visual normative reference points for body shape and size. Participants studied numerous photos of normal-weight teenagers that were age-appropriate for each particular group. These were compared with the photos presented in session one that depicted extreme models of thinness. The session was summarized by the statement that most models were 15% below their expected body weight, one of the criteria for a diagnosis of anorexia.

Session Five

Session five sought to explore appropriate methods of weight control by:

1. Elucidation of the negative consequences of restrictive dieting and other weight-reduction and weight-maintenance techniques. Information about the ill effects of "yo-yo" weight variation, starvation, and a deficiency in necessary nutrients was provided. Group leaders outlined the scientific data supporting the notion of a robust biogenetic disposition to maintain weight within a certain range (i.e., set-point theory) and the ineffectiveness of most diets.
2. Provision of information regarding appropriate methods of weight modification and maintenance. The participants then were asked to generate a list of more suitable techniques for maintaining a healthy, physically fit physique. Group leaders guided participants to consider such issues as frequency, length, and duration of physical exercise as well as proper eating habits (e.g., three meals a day, regular intake of vegetables and fruits, and limited consumption of fats and sugars). A food pyramid developed by the US Department of Health was distributed at the end of the session.

Session Six

Session six consisted of a presentation and question and answer session featuring a young adult woman who had recovered from an eating disorder. Hearing a personal story added significantly to the program and provided excellent closure.

☐ Was the Program Effective?

Middle-School Experience

The program was completed with 1066 middle-school students (grades 6–8, ages 11–15 years) utilizing a pre-post experimental-control design. Assimilated into the home and careers curriculum, the sessions incorporated both genders (530 females, 536 males) in coeducational groupings (i.e., each discussion group had approximately equal numbers of females and males). The control group consisted of students enrolled in a music-education class that ran concurrently with home and careers. After completion of the prevention program with the experimental group, the adolescents in the control group rotated into the program. Thus, by the completion of the academic year, nearly every student in the middle school had participated in the prevention program.

To evaluate program efficacy, the senior researcher developed a scale assessing future behavioral intentions. That is, students were asked to indicate whether they planned in the future to participate in fasting, excessive exercise, or purging, or intended to use diet pills, water pills, or laxatives to control their weight. The scale utilized a four-point Likert-type rating system (i.e., daily, weekly, monthly, rarely, or never). Likewise, students were assessed both pre- and postintervention regarding their *current* use of such activities or pharmaceutical aids, and levels of body dissatisfaction (EDI-2), drive for thinness (EDI-2), physical self-concept (MSCS), and competence (MSCS).

Pre- and posttest comparisons with the females in the experimental and control groups indicated that the program was successful in lowering the current incidence of as well as the future intent to use fasting, excessive exercise, purging, diet aids, water pills, and laxatives as methods of weight control. Likewise, reported levels of body dissatisfaction and drive for thinness decreased, whereas levels of physical self-concept and competence increased for program participants. None of these changes, however, reached statistical significance.

After examining the statistical results as well as reviewing the qualitative feedback solicited from the student participants and the classroom teachers, the research team reached two conclusions. First, at this young age (range, 11–15 years) very few of the female students were engaging in weight-control activities or evidencing elevated disturbed eating behaviors. Therefore, it was virtually impossible to achieve statistically significant decreases in either current dysfunctional actions or future intentional behaviors. A better measure of treatment efficacy likely would be tracking the females through their high-school years to determine the *long-term* effects of program participation. Twice-yearly "booster sessions" would be appropriate with such a research design.

The second conclusion focused on male participation. The maturational level of middle-school males is notably lower than their female counterparts. As a result, there were striking gender differences in the ability to actively and appropriately participate in this prevention program. In short, many of the males at this age were unable to critically examine their beliefs about feminine beauty or scrutinize current sociocultural mores. As a result, the research team concluded that coeducational sessions were not efficacious. Although incorporation of males in the global prevention model still was viewed as essential, we decided that the six-session program would best be devoted solely to female partici-pants, and a separate procedure shortened to two sessions would better meet the needs of male students.

High-School Experience

The six-session program then was completed with 9th-, 10th-, and 11th-grade (ages 13–16 years) girls. The sessions were incorporated within the physical ed-ucation curriculum utilizing an experimental-control research design (control group $N = 159$, experimental group $N = 153$). Because girls were assigned ran-domly to the experimental or control group, a pretest measure was not deemed necessary. In addition to assessing current methods of weight control (i.e., caloric-intake restriction, excessive exercise, purging, and use of diet aids or water pills), the senior researcher developed a new treatment efficacy scale con-sisting of 10 questions to better assess adolescent beliefs about feminine beauty and weight control as well as evaluate future behavioral intentions (Table 1).

In comparison with the middle-school program, the high-school sessions were not as structured, with less group-facilitator involvement and more time devoted to group discussion, personal disclosure, and directed feedback. This modification worked very well, as the older girls were far more open to sharing (most likely because of the lack of male presence as well as their increased ma-turity). Likewise, the high-school group interacted in a more socially appropri-ate manner with the young woman who had experienced an eating disorder (session six). Their questions were sensitive and directed more toward the social aspects of, emotional functioning during, and fight for recovery from an eating disorder as compared to the middle-school youngsters who sought grisly de-scriptions of purging (we instructed the presenter to quietly sidestep these ques-tions) or physical outcomes (e.g., "Did vomiting hurt?" "Weren't you hungry?" "Did your teeth rot out?"). Finally, as previously indicated, pictorial illustrations of excessively slender models compared with normal-weight teenagers utilized in sessions one and four were selected to be age-appropriate.

The posttest experimental-control group comparison resulted in a significant total raw-score difference in the treatment efficacy scale (t-test $= -2.01$, $p \leq .05$). Thus, the six-session program did have a notable effect on changing participants' attitudes and beliefs about sociocultural mores, unwillingness to engage in dysfunctional disordered eating behaviors, and future intentions re-garding weight control. Likewise, the qualitative feedback from the students and the classroom teachers was positive. Finally, it was clearly evident to the re-search team that the choice to present the program to single-gender groups was appropriate. The breadth and depth of interest, active participation, and self-dis-closure showed marked improvement over the middle school coeducational program.

Although the high-school program did lower *current* uses of fasting, excessive exercise, purging, diet aids, water pills, and laxatives as methods of weight con-

TABLE 1. Treatment efficacy scale

1. I believe the media and ads encourage adolescent females to feel that their bodies are too fat.
   (a) strongly agree, (b) agree, (c) disagree, (d) strongly disagree
2. Looking at female models in magazines and on tv makes me want to be thin.
   (a) strongly agree, (b) agree, (c) disagree, (d) strongly disagree
3. By exercising, dieting, or fasting, I can make my body look anyway I want it to.
   (a) strongly agree, (b) agree, (c) disagree, (d) strongly disagree
4. Our height and weight is determined primarily by genetics.
   (a) strongly agree, (b) agree, (c) disagree, (d) strongly disagree
5. Physical attractiveness has far too many important social rewards.
   (a) strongly agree, (b) agree, (c) disagree, (d) strongly disagree
6. In order to get positive attention from my peers, I would diet, fast, or use other methods to be thinner.
   (a) strongly agree, (b) agree, (c) disagree, (d) strongly disagree
7. The best methods of weight control are moderate exercise coupled with eating three meals a day that include fruits and vegetables.
   (a) strongly agree, (b) agree, (c) disagree, (d) strongly disagree
8. Too much emphasis is placed on physical appearance today.
   (a) strongly agree, (b) agree, (c) disagree, (d) strongly disagree
9. In the future, I plan to exercise moderately to control my weight.
   (a) strongly agree, (b) agree, (c) disagree, (d) strongly disagree
10. In the future, I plan to eat three healthy and moderate meals a day in order to control my weight.
    (a) strongly agree, (b) agree, (c) disagree, (d) strongly disagree

Notes on scoring. Items 1, 4, 5, 7, 8, 9, and 10 are scored in the positive direction (i.e., a = 3, b = 2, c = 0, d = 0). Items 2, 3, and 6 are scored in the negative direction (i.e., a = 0, b = 0, c = 2, d = 3). Higher scores indicate better treatment efficacy.

trol in the experimental group, the data did not reach statistical significance. As with the middle-school sample, these randomly selected high-school females were not participating in these activities to the extent as to allow for a statistically significant drop.

College Sample

Given the notable success with the high-school sample, the research team decided to expand their efforts to college-aged females via evening programming at the students' place of residence. Two comparable sororities were identified: one as an experimental group that participated in the entire program and the other as a control group with nonparticipation. Although group assignment was, therefore, obviously not random, we wished to avoid treatment contamination that may occur when participants discuss the prevention activities openly with cohorts in the control group. This is likely to happen if the two groups of females (i.e., participants versus nonparticipants) live together in close proximity. Thus, the research team chose to implement the control-experimental group design with two separate analogous sororities that were separated by some geographical distance.

Forty-five females (ages 18–25 years) living together in one sorority participated in the eating-disorder prevention program, which was reformatted to four

1.5-hour sessions (i.e., session one incorporated the curriculum from the original session one; session two was a compilation of the prototype sessions two and three; session three combined the original sessions four and five; session four consisted of the presentation and question and answer interaction with a recovered client). This change was necessary to better accommodate the busy schedules of university undergraduate students.

Information provided by the group facilitators and pictorial illustrations shown during the program were altered to be age-appropriate. As with the high-school group, the sessions were less structured, with considerable participant discussion and self-disclosure. In fact, most of the sessions went longer than expected because of the fervor of the group interchanges. Finally, 18 females residing in a sorority closely matched to the experimental group on the variables of perceived university social status, socioeconomic status, and student majors served as the control group.

Experimental-control posttest comparisons indicated that the program was successful in significantly lowering *current* utilization (t-test = -2.23, $p \leq .05$) as well as *future* intentional use (t-test = -2.33, $p \leq .05$) of fasting, excessive exercise, purging, diet aids, water pills, or laxatives as methods of weight control. Likewise, pre- to posttest comparisons with the experimental group verified the program's efficacy in significantly increasing physical self-esteem (as measured by the physical subscale of the Tennessee Self-Concept Scale: 2nd Edition [TSCS:2]; Fitts & Warren, 1996; t-test = -4.19, $p \leq .0001$); notably increasing personal efficacy or competence (as measured by the personal subscale of the TSCS:2; t-test = -8.03, $p \leq .0001$); and, significantly decreasing body dissatisfaction (as assessed by the body-dissatisfaction subscale of the EDI-2; t-test = 2.35, $p \leq .05$). Qualitative comments from the participants were very positive, focusing primarily on the opportunity to discuss openly the impact of peer and boyfriend pressures, as well as the constant inundation of media images portraying impossibly thin role models.

Although these results are very promising, it should be noted that the experimental-control groups were not randomly assigned, and there was no pretest measure given to the control group to ascertain if the two groups were comparable before treatment. This research design has been advocated by some investigators who believe that having members of the control group answer questions on a pretest sensitizes, and possibly alters, their posttest answers. Yet, if the experimental-control groups are not truly randomized, it is difficult to assert that they were similar on the variables being assessed prior to treatment. Thus, although we carefully selected two sororities that by all outward appearances were analogous, we cannot guarantee that such was the case.

☐ Potential Pitfalls

As with any prevention or intervention program utilized with a wide variety of clientele, there are inevitably procedures and strategies that work and others that do not. From our experience, we would offer professionals implementing this program the following suggestions:

1. Although it seems logical to provide prevention activities as early as possible, this program is not suitable for elementary school–aged children. The activi-

ties require personal evaluation, abstract reasoning, empathy, and sensitivity for others. These characteristics are only marginally present with middle-school children. Therefore, other programs would be more appropriate with younger children.

2. Do not utilize coeducational groupings. Notwithstanding the appeal of such an approach (i.e., facilitating a critical analysis by males of the role they play in the promotion of eating disorders among their female counterparts), the presence of males consistently decreased the amount and depth of group discussion and self-disclosure. There were numerous instances during the middle-school programming wherein a male initiated a hurtful interchange (e.g., "Well your boyfriend is right; you do have a fat stomach"), responded inappropriately to group discussions (e.g., "You're wrong. I think this picture is real bad [*attractive* in today's lingo]"), or abruptly cut off personal concerns or self-disclosure (e.g., "Why are you talking about that? It is so stupid."). After completion of all the program sessions, the researchers asked the high-school and college participants about their recommendations regarding coeducational participation in future groups. Most responded negatively, indicating that males would hamper honesty and open discussion.

3. It is imperative that the discussion groups be limited in number (i.e., 6–8) to facilitate active participation and encourage quality interchanges. When implementing this program, be certain to have enough trained group facilitators available to divide classes into these smaller groupings.

4. Finally, although we utilized teachers throughout the curriculum, they need to be trained in the methods of active listening, the process of offering nonjudgmental feedback, and provision of information without falling into a "lecture" format. Teachers are so accustomed to the role of "instructing" that they sometimes have difficulty engaging in a more experiential, discovery-learning process or open-ended discussion format. There are clearly terminal goals to this program (i.e., decreasing internalization of sociocultural mores and body dissatisfaction, and increasing physical self-esteem, personal competence, and participation in appropriate activities for physical fitness and weight control). But these goals are better achieved if participants actively explore their own thoughts and feelings and reach such objectives as a result of personal exploration and evaluation.

☐ Conclusions

Eating disorders have become more prevalent in recent decades, resulting in 5% of the population, primarily adolescent females, meeting restrictive criteria (American Psychiatric Association, (1994) for anorexia or bulimia. Likewise, over one third of the adolescent female population reports participation in such aggressive methods of weight control and reduction as chronic dieting, excessive exercise, self-induced vomiting, and abuse of laxatives, diet medications, and water pills (Phelps, Andrea, & Rizzo, 1994). Research supports an etiological model that links sociocultural pressures to the acceptance of a thin, yet unrealistic, ideal. The internalization of this ideal leads to body dissatisfaction, which in turn provides motivation for one to adopt the use of stringent weight-control methods. The use of various weight-management techniques, particularly restrictive dieting, provides significant risk for the establishment of an eating disorder. However, protective factors have been identified (i.e., physical self-esteem and personal competence) that serve as buffers to the development of disordered symptomatology (Phelps et al., 1998).

Utilizing this etiological model, prevention programming was directed toward female adolescents (ages 11–16 years) and young adults (ages 18–25 years) with an orientation toward increasing the factors that attenuate risk status while reducing elements that place these young women in jeopardy. The program was very successful in facilitating an acknowledgement of the ubiquitous pressures for attainment of the model skeletal look; changing attitudes about standards of beauty; altering the participants' current and future intentional use of pharmaceutical aids or disordered eating behaviors (e.g., fasting, strenuous dieting, purging, excessive exercise) as methods of weight control; building physical self-esteem and personal competence; and, reducing body dissatisfaction. Thus, by stringent statistical criteria, this six-session program attained the rigorous goals of a risk/protective prevention model (i.e., deterrence of eating-disorder symptomatology, reduction of risk status, and mental-health promotion).

The perceived strengths of this program are its distinct theoretical foundation (i.e., sociocultural etiological model); implementation of data-driven procedures (i.e., attention to specific risk and protective factors; the integration of factual information coupled with in-depth group discussions and personal evaluations; positive qualitative responses from the participants and classroom teachers; and its proven treatment efficacy (i.e., significant *t*-test differences between both experimental pre-post measures as well as experimental-control posttest evaluations). Perceived weaknesses of the program include age limitations for participants and the need for development, implementation, and quantitative and qualitative assessment of a separate curriculum for male students.

It is recommended that future research efforts focus on testing the long-term efficacy of this program. That is, we must now seek to determine if participation in this or a similar prevention program significantly reduces eating-disorder symptomatology over time. It is likely that "booster sessions" will be necessary to maintain the positive effects evidenced thus far. Comparisons of a multiplicity of follow-up procedures that vary in length and frequency would be most beneficial.

☐ References

Adams, P. J., Katz, R. C., Beauchamp, K., & Zavis, D. (1993). Body dissatisfaction, eating disorders, and depression: A developmental perspective. *Journal of Child and Family Studies, 2,* 37–46.

Akan, G. E., & Grilo, C. M. (1995). Sociocultural influences on eating attitudes and behaviors, body image, and psychological functioning: A comparison of African-American, Asian-American, and Caucasian college women. *International Journal of Eating Disorders, 18,* 181–187.

Albee, G. W. (1996). Revolutions and counterrevolutions in prevention. *American Psychologist, 51,* 1130–1133.

American Psychiatric Association. (1994). *Diagnostic and statistical manual of mental disorders* (4th ed.). Washington, DC.

Bennett, N. M., Spoth, R. L., & Borgen, F. H. (1991). Bulimic symptoms in high school females: Prevalence and relationship with multiple measures of psychological health. *Journal of Community Psychology, 19,* 13–28.

Bracken, B. A. (1992). *Multidimensional self concept scale.* Austin, TX: Pro-Ed.

Bunnell, D. W., Cooper, P. J., Hertz, S., & Shenker, I. R. (1992). Body image concerns among adolescents. *International Journal of Eating Disorders, 11,* 79–83.

Button, E. (1990). Self-esteem in girls aged 11–12: Baseline findings from a planned prospective study of vulnerability to eating disorders. *Journal of Adolescence, 13,* 407–413.

Dielman, T. E. (1994). School-based research on the prevention of adolescent alcohol use and misuse: Methodological issues and advances. *Journal of Research on Adolescence, 4,* 271–293.

Fitts, W. H., & Warren, W. L. (1996). *Tennessee self-concept scale* (2d ed.). Los Angeles: Western Psychological Services.

Garner, D. M. (1991). *Eating disorder inventory-2.* Odessa, FL: Psychological Assessment Resources.

Grilo, C. M., Wilfley, D. E., Jones, A., Brownell, K., & Rodin, J. (1994). The social self, body dissatisfaction, and binge eating in obese females. *Obesity Research, 2,* 24–27.

Leon, G. R., Fulkerson, J. A., Perry, C. L., & Cudeck, R. (1993). Personality and behavioral vulnerabilities associated with risk status for eating disorders in adolescent girls. *Journal of Abnormal Psychology, 102,* 438–444.

Levine, M. P., Smolak, L., & Hayden, H. (1994). The relation of sociocultural factors to eating attitudes and behaviors among middle school girls. *International Journal of Eating Disorders, 15,* 11–20.

Mrazek, P. J., & Haggerty, R. J. (Eds.). (1994). *Reducing risk of mental disorders: Frontiers for preventive intervention research.* Washington, DC: National Academy Press.

NIMH Committee on Prevention Research. (1995, May 15). *A plan for prevention research for the National Institute of Mental Health (A report to the National Advisory Mental Health Council).* Washington DC.

Phelps, L., Andrea, R. K., & Rizzo, F. G. (1994). Weight control techniques among female adolescents: A comparative study. *Journal of School Psychology, 32,* 283–292.

Phelps, L., Johnston, L. S., & Augustyniak, K. (in press). Prevention of eating disorders: Identification of predictor variables. *Eating Disorders: The Journal of Treatment and Prevention.*

Phelps, L., & Wilczenski, F. (1993). Eating disorders inventory-2: Cognitive-behavioral dimensions with nonclinical adolescents. *Journal of Clinical Psychology, 49,* 508–515.

Reiss, D., & Price, R. H. (1996). National research agenda for prevention research: The National Institute of Mental Health report. *American Psychologist, 51,* 1109–1115.

Stice, E. (1994). Review of the evidence for a sociocultural model of bulimia nervosa and exploration of the mechanisms of action. *Clinical Psychology Review, 14,* 633–661.

Stice, E., Schupak-Neuberg, E., Shaw, H. E., & Stein, R. I. (1994). Relation of media exposure to eating disorder symptomatology: An examination of mediating mechanisms. *Journal of Abnormal Psychology, 103,* 836–840.

Tiggemann, M., & Pickering, A. S. (1996). Role of television in adolescent women's body dissatisfaction and drive for thinness. *International Journal of Eating Disorders, 20,* 199–203.

Wertheim, E. H., Paxton, S. J., Maude, D., Szmukler, G., Gibbons, K., & Hiller, L. (1992). Psychosocial predictors of weight loss behaviors and binge eating in adolescent girls and boys. *International Journal of Eating Disorders, 12,* 151–160.

Wiseman, C. V., Gray, J. J., Mosimann, J. E., & Ahrens, A. H. (1992). Cultural expectations of thinness in women: An update. *International Journal of Eating Disorders, 11,* 85–89.

11

CHAPTER

Mimi Nichter
Nancy Vuckovic
Sheila Parker

The Looking Good, Feeling Good Program: A Multi-Ethnic Intervention for Healthy Body Image, Nutrition, and Physical Activity

Research has generally concluded that there is an "epidemic" of dieting among girls, with estimates that as many as 60–80% of White adolescent girls are dieting at any given time (Berg, 1992; CDC, 1996; Rosen & Gross, 1987). Concern has been expressed that the use of extreme methods is escalating and that such dieting behaviors may lead to a higher incidence of eating disorders (Berg, 1992). Although research on body image and dieting behaviors among minority populations is limited compared with that on White women, data suggest that African American women are less likely to diet and are more satisfied with their body shape than their White counterparts. This chapter begins with an overview of the literature on ethnic differences in body image and dieting practices among adolescent girls, with a specific focus on the findings of a largely ethnographic research project carried out in Tucson, Arizona. The chapter then moves to a discussion of how cultural differences informed the development of an intervention focused on media awareness, nutrition, and physical activity for adolescent girls.

☐ Ethnic Differences in Body Image and Weight Concerns

Compared with White and Hispanic girls, African American adolescents are less likely to perceive themselves as overweight (Morbidity and Morality Weekly Report ["body weight perceptions"], 1991). In an item-by-item comparison, African American adolescents had fewer thoughts about dieting, were less fearful of weight gain, and had a less negative valuation of overeating (Casper & Offer, 1990). Rosen and Gross (1987) concluded that African American girls were more likely to be engaged in weight gain than weight loss efforts compared with their White and Hispanic counterparts.

175

Differences in cultural standards for acceptable weights have been reported both among adult women as well as adolescent females. Allen (1989), in a study of weight management activities among African American women, reported that although most of her informants had been overweight for years by biomedical standards, they did not perceive themselves to be overweight. Awareness of being overweight came from outside the immediate family. As Allen (1989) notes, these women had not evaluated their body size "in relation to the White ideal in the media but in comparison to other African American women who on the average are heavier than white women" (p. 17). Moreover, most informants did not define overweight as unhealthy. These findings are corroborated by a National Health Interview Survey that demonstrated that fewer African American women than White women considered themselves overweight, even if they were overweight, measured by actual weight (Dawson, 1988).

Drawing on a sample of African American adult women, Kumanyika, Wilson, and Guilford-Davenport (1993) found that about 40% of women in the overweight categories (based on Body Mass Index) considered their figures attractive or very attractive. Almost all of these women recognized that they were overweight by biomedical standards. Further, only half of the women who were moderately or severely overweight reported that their husbands or boyfriends were supportive of their dieting efforts. Almost unanimously, overweight women reported that their body size had not been the source of difficulties in their personal or family relationships.

Nationwide survey results indicate that, in contrast to African American females, White and Hispanic girls perceive themselves to be overweight even if their weight for height falls within "normal" parameters as established by the National Center for Health Statistics ("Body weight perceptions", 1991). Robinson and colleagues (1996) found that Hispanic middle school girls reported significantly greater body dissatisfaction than White girls. Of the three ethnic groups studied (White, Hispanic, and Asian adolescents), no significant differences were found in desired body shape (Cohn et al., 1987; Robinson et al., 1996). With respect to body image and self-image, several studies have suggested that Hispanic girls are at elevated risk for mental health problems such as depression. Between the ages of 9 and 15 years, Hispanic girls show the most precipitous decline in the likelihood of endorsing the statement "I am happy the way I am" (American Association of University Women, 1992). White girls also express increasing dissatisfaction with themselves as they grow older (Simmons & Blyth, 1987). By contrast, African American girls report a relatively stable and positive sense of self worth. Orenstein (1994) has noted that Hispanics are an "at risk" population because they lack both the high self-esteem characteristic of African American girls and the academic opportunities available to some (but certainly not all) White girls.

Anorexia nervosa and bulimia nervosa are estimated to affect 1% to 3% of the White population (Fairburn & Beglin, 1990; Lucas, Beard, O'Fallon, & Kurland, 1991). With regard to the prevalence of eating disturbances, studies indicate that their frequency among Hispanic girls and women is similar to that among White females (Pumariega, 1986; Smith & Krejci, 1991). In fact, recently researchers have begun to question whether eating disorders and unhealthy eating attitudes are actually much more prevalent among Hispanic and Asian girls and women than previously recognized (Robinson et al., 1996). It has been suggested that the overrepresentation of middle-class and upper-class Whites as those who have eating disorders may be both an artifact of the samples studied and a result of referral bias (Dolan, 1991; Robinson et al., 1996).

To date, few cases of anorexia nervosa and bulimia nervosa among African American females have been reported in the literature. A comparative study of bulimia nervosa among African American and White college women found that fewer African American women experienced a sense of fear and discouragement concerning food and weight control than did their White counterparts (Gray, Ford, & Kelley, 1987). There has been some concern, however, that increased affluence and acculturation of African Americans into White culture may result in a higher incidence of eating disorders as African Americans seek to emulate White middle class ideals (Hsu, 1987). In a study of African American female college students, higher levels of assimilation to White racial identity were associated with greater food restriction, fear of fat, and drive for thinness (Abrams, Allen, & Gray, 1993). Researchers who have studied eating disorder symptoms among obese populations have found significant rates of disordered eating in overweight Black women (Yanovski, 1993). Silber (1986) has suggested that professionals misdiagnose eating disorders among African Americans because of stereotypical ideas that such problems are restricted to White women.

Striegel-Moore and Smolak (1996) note that if African American girls or women experience weight-related social pressures, they are likely to want to be thinner, to attempt to lose weight, or both. These authors warn that "the dominant 'White model of eating disorders' limits researchers' understanding of the etiology of eating disorders" (p. 260). It is of particular concern to these researchers that the present understanding of eating disorders is based almost exclusively on data obtained from clinical samples.

Drawing on in-depth interviews with African American and Latina women, Thompson (1994) highlights the risk of generalizing about class and thinness among women of color. The diversity of experiences among her informants makes it clear that African American and Latina women are equally or perhaps more vulnerable to the emphasis on thinness. She notes that "media permeation of even the most remote areas of the country makes it unlikely that any ethnic or racial group is unaware of the premium placed on dieting and thinness" (p. 361).

Research findings reported on ethnic differences in dieting, body weight, and eating disorders have drawn largely on the findings of survey research, although Thompson's (1994) work is a notable exception. When ethnic differences are reported, explanations typically revolve around the statement that "cultural factors" somehow are implicated. Indeed, little emphasis has been placed on exploring what type of self-presentation is valued culturally by diverse ethnic groups, in what context, and for what reasons. In the next section, we draw on in-depth interviews and focus group data from the Teen Lifestyle Project to discuss cultural factors that have an impact on weight perception, body image, beauty, and style, with particular emphasis on differences between African American and White adolescent girls.

☐ Body Image and Dieting: Findings of the Teen Lifestyle Project

The Teen Lifestyle Project was a three-year longitudinal study (1989–1992) of body image, dieting, and smoking among adolescent girls in Tucson, Arizona, funded by the National Institute of Child Health and Human Development. Two hundred and fifty participants from a range of socioeconomic and ethnic back-grounds, including White, Hispanic, and African American girls, were followed from junior high school through high school. Data collected annually from each participant included an ethnographic interview, two telephone interviews, food records, and a survey on dieting and smoking attitudes and behaviors. In addi-tion, many girls participated in focus group interviews across the three years of the study. At the end of the third year of the project, another study was initiated with 46 African American girls who participated in a one year cross-sectional study. These girls completed surveys and participated in individual and focus group interviews.

During ethnographic interviews, we learned that White and Hispanic girls had similar beauty ideals and shared a uniform vision of what constituted the "perfect" girl (Nichter & Vuckovic, 1994). These findings, and the literature pre-viously discussed, led us to combine Hispanic girls and White girls into a single group for analysis. Typically, their ideal girl was described as being 5 ft., 7 in. tall and between 100 and 110 pounds (45.35 to 49.89 kg). She was usually a blonde, and her hair was long and flowing. Descriptions mirrored those of fash-ion models: "I think of her as tall with long legs, naturally pretty, like a model's face with high cheekbones." Among White and Hispanic girls, results of a sur-vey question about satisfaction with body shape revealed that almost 90% of these informants expressed some degree of negative concern about their body shape (Parker, Nichter, Nichter, Vuckovic, Sims, & Ritenbaugh, 1995).

African American perceptions of beauty were markedly different than White perceptions despite frequent media images of African American models and dancers who depict White beauty ideals. In response to the question, "How sat-isfied are you with your weight?" 70% of the African American girls responded that they were satisfied or very satisfied with their current weight. Although 82% of these girls were at or below the normal weight for height range for African American girls of their age, 18% were significantly overweight (above the 85th percentile). Only 12% of girls who were of normal weight expressed dissatisfaction with their present weight.

In focus groups, African American girls were asked to describe their sense of an ideal girl. Commonly, girls responded with a request for clarification: Were we asking about an African American ideal girl or a White one? This response signaled to us that the girls were keenly aware of differences in ideals of beauty between the African American and the dominant White culture. This was con-firmed in a survey that we developed for only African American girls, in which they were asked whether there was a difference between their ideal of beauty and that of White girls. Over 60% of these African American girls agreed that there was, while the remainder reported that there was little difference. In re-sponse to the open-ended question, "If yes, what is the difference?" African American girls wrote comments such as, "White girls have to look like Barbie dolls and Cindy Crawford to be beautiful," and, "White girls want to be perfect." African American girls noted that "their attitudes and the way they wear their clothes is different" and that White girls "want to be tall, be thin, and have long hair."

When we asked African American girls for their description of an ideal African American girl, their response often began with a list of personality traits rather than physical attributes. The ideal African American girl was smart, friendly, not conceited, easy to talk to, and fun to be with and had a good sense of humor. Many girls noted that their ideal girl did not have to be "pretty," just "well-kept" (i.e., well-groomed).

What was particularly striking in African American girls' descriptions, compared with those of White adolescents, was their deemphasis on external beauty as a prerequisite for popularity. Beauty was not described in relation to a particular size or set of body statistics. It was important to be beautiful on the inside as well as on the outside, and to be beautiful a girl had to "know her culture." Having a positive attitude and "not worrying about your looks too much" were important components of a beautiful woman. Attitude eclipsed body parts as a measure of value (Parker, Nichter, Nichter, Vuckovic, Sims, & Ritenbaugh, 1995).

Standards for body image and beauty among African American adolescents were described by these girls as "looking good." "Looking good" or "got it goin' on" entails "making what you've got" work for you, by creating and presenting a sense of style. "Looking good" had to do with projecting self-image and confidence—having "'tude" (i.e., attitude) and "flavor." "Throwing your attitude" involves establishing a presence, creating a "certain air about yourself," being in control of your image and "things around you," being able to improvise effectively, and maintaining poise under pressure.

African American girls in the study reported routinely receiving compliments from other African Americans of both genders for "looking good" and having it "goin' on." Girls reported receiving far more positive feedback for creating their own style around their given attributes than White girls, who received support for altering their looks to fit established beauty ideals. Support for dieting was commonly articulated by White girls but rarely mentioned by African American girls.

☐ Moving from Research to Intervention

During the Teen Lifestyle Project, we observed that girls valued talking about issues related to body image, eating, and dieting behaviors. At the end of the study, more than 75% of the girls who had participated in the longitudinal component said they would be willing to continue in the project. A follow-up study of these girls is presently being conducted with funding from the Robert Wood Johnson Foundation. When asked if they would like to receive information about nutrition and physical activity, girls enthusiastically responded that they would. The research team was eager to develop and implement an effective intervention for healthy body image, nutrition, and physical activity for adolescent girls. We believed that there was much that girls could learn by listening to each other talk about how they felt about themselves and by sharing their experiences. Our goal was to reinforce positive health-related attitudes and behaviors and to address negative attitudes and potentially harmful behaviors identified among this population (Nichter, Ritenbaugh, Nichter, Vuckovic, & Aickin, 1995).

Public health practitioners increasingly have noted that the prevalence of overweight and obesity among youth has reached alarming proportions (Troiano, Flegal, Kuczmarkski, Campbell, & Johnson, 1995). Indeed, one in five adolescents aged 12–19 years is classified as obese, and there is concern that this number will increase (Troiano et al., 1995). Sedentary lifestyles and the consumption of fast foods are becoming increasingly commonplace among youth. However, we did not conceptualize the program as specifically aimed at the prevention of obesity or eating disorders, although it was informed by a recognition of these problems. Rather, our goal was the development of a curriculum that would command the attention of adolescent girls and provide them with tools to make more healthful decisions to better navigate in the worlds in which they lived. Our program was targeted at girls who might experience varying degrees of concern with their weight and appearance during adolescence and beyond. Our intention was to introduce nutrition and exercise training that would set the stage for healthy eating and physical activity habits throughout adolescence and adulthood. Given the growing public health concern about obesity, we reasoned that all girls could benefit from training in nutrition and exercise.

The causes of obesity, like the causes of eating disorders, are multifactorial and include the influences of cultural pressures and low self-esteem. Positioning education about nutrition and exercise within the framework of body image and self-esteem is also important from the perspective of obesity prevention. Although anorexia nervosa and bulimia nervosa affect 1–3% of girls, obesity is far more prevalent (21% for Whites; 30% for African Americans) (Troiano et al., 1995). The prevalence of obesity in adolescent girls has increased in the past 30 years, with rates of obesity climbing faster for African American girls than for White girls (Troiano et al., 1995). Moreover, because obesity during youth and adolescence predisposes one to adult obesity (Serdula et al., 1993), establishing good nutrition and exercise patterns in young people is critically important.

Having spent several years in middle and high schools, we were struck with how little information girls received about how to achieve positive health goals, particularly in regard to healthy eating and exercise. In the high schools in which we worked, health education was required as a one-semester course. As a result, over the course of the four years of high school, the average student was exposed to a maximum of five class periods of nutrition education. There was considerable latitude as to what was included in these classes, and some health education teachers chose to include only one or two lessons on nutrition. Considering the paucity of education for making healthy food choices, coupled with the overaccessibility of high fat foods in the schools, was it realistic to expect teens to eat differently than they did? Although we recognized that much of the socialization into eating and taste preferences occurred in the context of the family, it seemed clear that youth also learned about eating from their peers in and out of school settings. It was also apparent that mass media, particularly food advertisements and nutritional "advice" given in fashion magazines, were influencing girls' ideas about eating. Our discussions with girls in the Teen Lifestyle Project revealed that there was a lot of confusion about terms such as *lite, low-fat, fat-free, cholesterol,* and so forth, as well as a great deal of interest about what constituted appropriate food choices.

Our previous research had concluded that although talk about body dissatisfaction and the belief that one needed to diet were pervasive among White adolescent females, this did not always result in sustained dieting behaviors (Nichter & Vuckovic, 1994; Nichter et al., 1995). Many girls talked about "watching what they ate" as a strategy to maintain their weight and to be healthy. As opposed to dieting, "watching" was a positive behavior that entailed eating less junk and eating more vegetables and fruits. Although this was often difficult to maintain in a world saturated with junk food, girls did have a knowledge base about what foods they believed were good for health. In our intervention, we wanted to build on what girls already knew, particularly positive attitudes and behaviors such as watching, and directly address the concerns they had voiced in interviews. What healthy choices could they make when they went to fast food restaurants? What did nutritional labels mean and how could that help them better understand what they were eating? What was the difference between a food labeled "low fat" and one labeled "low calorie?" For those girls who wanted or needed to lose weight, was there a way that they could "do it right?" Rather than adopt a top-down expert approach we wanted to acknowledge girls' lived experience and build upon their existing knowledge base. We felt that teenaged girls, regardless of their ethnicity, could benefit from such discussions.

Was it enough to teach about nutrition without putting food and eating in the context of girls' lives? We thought not. For many teenage girls, health work—including the "work" of eating—is closely aligned with beauty work. Girls' beauty ideals have direct implications for their food intake. It seemed clear that a program that has as one of its goals to promote better nutrition must raise girls' awareness of unrealistic body images promoted through the media and discuss the possibilities for more realistic body shapes. Having heard so much of the anguish that girls (particularly White and Hispanic girls) experienced from being teased for their body shapes, we recognized the importance of teaching tolerance of others and acceptance of self.

Differences between African American and White adolescent girls with regard to body image and dieting practices were particularly intriguing, so we hoped that bringing girls of different ethnic backgrounds together to articulate cultural differences would help them understand and reflect upon the cultural underpinnings of how girls and women felt about their bodies. Changing the focus of the discussion from the individual level to the cultural could provide girls with a much-needed perspective on their own attitudes and behaviors. We felt that White and Hispanic girls could benefit from learning about African American perceptions of beauty and their greater acceptance of self regardless of their weight. At first glance it might seem that African American girls, who certainly were aware of the dominant culture's ideals of beauty even if they did not espouse them, might not receive equal benefit from these discussions. However, the multi-ethnic intervention team believed that as a result of these discussions, there would be a positive reinforcement of cultural values for African American girls, as well as an opportunity for them to learn from other girls whose embodied experiences might be quite different from their own.

Our guiding philosophy was that there was much girls could learn from one another and from the process of exploring their own experiences. We had learned in the course of our research that discussion and dialogue can serve as an intervention that empowers participants and allows them to take ownership of the knowledge that they gain (see Chapters 7, 9, and 16). Therefore, our educational program incorporated few didactic elements and relied heavily on group discussion and experiential activities.

The opportunity to pilot an intervention for adolescent girls came in the form of funding from Canyon Ranch, a health spa located in Tucson, Arizona. The multidisciplinary intervention team was comprised of a public health nutritionist, a medical anthropologist, an adolescent specialist, and a physical activity expert. Over a 9-month period, our intervention was implemented with 70 girls at three field sites, allowing us to test the applicability and effectiveness of the project among girls of different ages and ethnic groups in both community and after school settings. There were no control groups. The three sites were a community setting (a Boys and Girls Club), a largely African American church-related afterschool program, and a high school. The discussion in this chapter focuses largely on the highschool setting; for a complete review of the three interventions see work by Parker, Nichter, Vuckovic, Sims, and Teufel (1995).

The content of the intervention at all sites focused on meeting specific program objectives utilizing the following strategies:

Objective 1

To provide girls with practical understanding and skills for making healthy food and exercise choices within the demands and limitations of their everyday lives
Strategies:

A. Provide nutrition education that is relevant and practical for teen life styles.

B. Discuss and evaluate existing weight-management and dieting strategies and suggest healthy alternatives

C. Involve girls in assessing patterns of teen eating behavior inside and outside the home

D. Discuss and evaluate current exercise behavior

Objective 2

To heighten awareness of media influences on the perception of self.
The strategy was to:

A. Expose girls to media images and advertisements that influence body image and allow them to reflect on and critically evaluate the problematic meaning behind the messages.

Objective 3

To help girls become aware of and understand cross-cultural differences with regard to body image and weight control.
The strategy was to:

A. Facilitate discussion by girls of various ethnic groups of issues relating to body image, self-esteem, eating behavior, exercise patterns, and weight control.

☐ The High School Site

Our third intervention site was a public high school and involved 22 girls from the 9th through the 12th grade. The high school group was approximately one-third White, one third Hispanic, and one third African American. The program

TABLE 1. Components of the high school–based intervention

Session 1 (Saturday)	Pretest
	Food recalls
	African Dance/creative movement
	Funk aerobics
	Media awareness
Session 2 (after school)	Review of food recalls
	Healthy food choices
	Food labels
Session 3 (after school)	Cooking demonstration
	Question-and-answer session
Session 4 (after school)	Weight training I
Session 5 (Saturday)	Goal setting for healthy lifestyles
	Weight training II
	Putting your best foot forward
	Post-test

was held during two 6-hour Saturday workshops and three 90-minute after school sessions, rather than during class time. Table 1 lists the components of the five sessions.

There were three reasons why we chose to pilot the project outside of regular school hours. First, we wanted to develop a program exclusively for girls in order to facilitate dialogue and engender rapport among participants, particularly around sensitive topics such as body image. In public schools, where coeducation is mandated, there is little opportunity for a single-gender classroom experience. Second, the extracurricular program provided a setting for younger students to interact with older students. High school juniors and seniors in the Teen Lifestyle Project had expressed an interest in talking with younger girls about the difficulties of being a first-year student and the pressures they felt to fit in with their peers. This format gave older girls that opportunity. Third, conducting the sessions outside of class also gave us time flexibility not possible during the school day. After school and Saturday sessions allowed us to schedule longer time periods during which members of the group could explore personal topics in depth and interact in a variety of ways.

☐ The Media Awareness Program

A 20-minute multiple-projector slide show developed specifically for the intervention by the first two authors was shown to participants on the first day of the program. The show used images from magazine advertisements of White, African American, and Hispanic women to illustrate the pervasiveness of the dominant culture's influence on beauty ideals. It was shown how women of color are often depicted in the media (e.g., in magazines such as *Seventeen* and *Glamour*) as looking extremely similar to White women. The diversity of shape and color that exists in real life is not pictured.

The script for the show included phrases taken verbatim from Teen Lifestyle Project interviews and was performed by girls from a drama class at a local high school. The lines they spoke portrayed how girls felt about themselves when they saw advertisements of women in the media or real girls who were beautiful: "I'd kill for her body"; "Oh, she's so perfect, I hate her"; "When I go to the mall and I see all these beautiful girls, I just wonder why I was born". The purpose of the presentation was to provide girls with an opportunity to critically evaluate media messages and to begin to reflect on how these messages made them feel about themselves and other girls (see Chapter 1). One of the themes highlighted in the narrative was how notions of beauty negatively influenced social relations between girls by creating jealousy. Images and dialogue in the show also highlighted themes such as "having it all" (by eating diet foods and cheating just a little) and media representations of women as body parts rather than as whole people. The dialogue and the discussion that followed guided girls to view the images and cultural ideals behind them as unrealistic and problematic, rather than something to aspire towards (see Chapters 1 and 4).

After viewing the slide presentation, girls were encouraged to discuss concepts of beauty, body image, and weight control. Referring to pictures of African American, White, and Hispanic women incorporated in the slide show, the two members of the project team who had designed the media component facilitated the discussion to address cross-cultural perceptions of beauty. The participants noted cultural differences in ideal body type, and they listened intently when girls of differing cultural backgrounds talked about male expectations of women and the media's influence and portrayal of beauty. The discussion made it obvious to all participants that media images were marketing discontent, and even girls who appeared to match the dominant cultural ideal (i.e., white, blonde, and thin) were driven to be dissatisfied with their appearance.

The African American, Hispanic, and White girls learned much through their honest communication and interactions. African American girls talked about body acceptance and the importance of "makin' what you got work for you" rather than striving for an ideal image portrayed in magazines. White and Hispanic girls became more aware of the cultural dimensions of beauty and body image and discovered that what was desirable in White culture was not generally the ideal among African Americans. All of the girls learned that how they felt about themselves was culturally as well as individually mediated, providing girls with insights into their own behaviors and attitudes. It also provided opportunities to expand their notions of what was beautiful. For African American girls, these discussions and the reactions of the White and Hispanic girls reinforced the positive nature of their cultural models of beauty. When African American girls heard White girls talk about their ideals of being "perfect," they also gained a greater understanding of the problems caused by rigid and unrealistic beauty ideals.

In keeping with the theme of "makin' what you got work for you," a presentation entitled "Putting Your Best Foot Forward" was held during the last session, to allow girls to explore their own styles through color, line, and clothing style. The lesson was designed to introduce the participants to factors other than body shape and size that influence body image, the appearance that a person presents to others, and how good she feels about herself. Discussion during this segment focused on how it is important to feel good about ourselves, and how we need to recognize our assets and limitations.

☐ Nutrition

The nutrition component of the intervention was provided at both Saturday sessions, as well as during two of the afterschool sessions. Topics included dietary assessment, information on nutritious eating, and a cooking demonstration. The first Saturday session began with participants completing "food recalls" of what they had eaten on the previous day. The recalls were analyzed and used for discussion about nutrient intake that took place during the next session. In the afterschool session, girls were introduced to the role of nutrients in health and how to interpret information on food labels. The group also discussed how to make the best food choice given the demands and limitations of their everyday lives. This discussion allowed girls to share their knowledge about nutrition and gave the instructor an opportunity to correct some misconceptions about nutrition and weight control. Questions that arose included, "Why can some people eat and eat and eat and never gain weight and other people just look at food and get fat?" "Why do we need fat anyway?" "Is there a way that we can turn fat into muscle?" "What does the word 'metabolism' really mean? Is it fixed over your life or can you change it?" "What can I do if I've really pigged out?"

The next afterschool session featured a cooking demonstration of nutritious and easy to prepare foods. Girls observed and participated in the food preparations and tasted the final product. A nutritionist led a discussion about making nutritious food choices in a variety of social contexts and facilitated a second question-and-answer session, allowing the participants to further explore nutrition topics that were of interest to them.

The objective of the nutrition component was to deemphasize weight control and to teach and encourage nutritious eating that would promote good health now and in the future. We recognized that it is important to establish good eating habits in adolescence in order to minimize future disease risks associated with obesity, high fat intake, and low calcium consumption.

☐ Exercise

The physical activity components of the intervention were meant to introduce participants to exercise options. In the first of these components, a creative-movement specialist and artist in African dance engaged the girls in discussion about body movement and self-esteem and led the group in body movement routines. Her presentation, which emphasized moving gracefully with confidence, embodied African American notions of presence and sense of style. She followed the dance activity with a discussion of how movement and grace come from within and how we as individuals are much more than how we look on the outside. This session was followed by a funk aerobics class led by an instructor from Canyon Ranch. The instructor used popular music and current dance steps to make the exercise fun as well as vigorous.

In an afterschool session, a member of our team and an exercise specialist from Canyon Ranch demonstrated strength training exercises. The emphasis was on weight training that could be done at home using conventional 5- and 8-pound barbells or milk jugs filled with water or sand. The exercise specialist talked to the girls about strength basics and proper alignment for each exercise. Girls had the opportunity to practice a variety of low-tech exercises that they could replicate in their homes. At the request of participants, a follow-up session on strength training was scheduled for the final Saturday session of the program. At this session girls worked one-on-one with a fitness trainer from Canyon Ranch who answered their questions, corrected their form, and gave them handouts to use for future reference. Girls were able to purchase barbells used during the sessions, which we had bought at a used sporting goods store, for $5 a set. All sets were sold, suggesting that many girls had decided to begin a home exercise program.

☐ Project Evaluation

Evaluation data were generated through group discussion with the participants conducted by an independent evaluator; pre- and post-tests of knowledge, attitudes, and behavior; and a telephone interview conducted eight months after participants had completed the project. The group discussion yielded important information about the format and content of the project. We learned that girls valued the participatory nature of the curriculum because it provided an opportunity for open discussion and critical thinking among the participants. The participants were eager to talk and ask questions during the program, and, because they felt it was a nonjudgmental environment, they were willing to openly discuss sensitive issues about appearance and their feelings about their bodies. Although we knew girls frequently talked about their appearance and body image with friends, discussing the same topics with a more diverse group (in terms of age, social group, and ethnicity) during the program sessions was eye-opening. Several girls acknowledged that through these discussions they realized that others shared similar concerns. Through a recognition that issues about the body were not simply individual problems, girls became less critical of themselves and more critical of media representations of beauty.

As anticipated, the all-girl composition of the group facilitated dialogue and engendered rapport among the participants. Many girls commented how different the experience seemed "without boys being there," and how they felt more free to talk about issues that were important to them without worrying about being judged or teased by their male peers. This was substantiated in another school setting in which the first author showed the synchronized slide show on representations of women in the media to a coeducational middle school audience. As boys watched the onslaught of scantily dressed women, the catcalls became louder. The ensuing discussion between girls and boys was hostile, with girls stating that boys had no right to comment on girls' bodies in the ways that they typically did. Whereas the all-girls group discussion in the intervention setting had moved to a discussion of strategies to deal with the comments of males toward girls' bodies, the coeducational group discussion did not. Rather than teaching girls to critically evaluate the media, the coeducational middle school experience brought up issues of boys critically evaluating girls. In the high school intervention site, because no boys were present, girls felt more comfortable discussing subjects such as boys' preference for girls' body shapes. Cross-cultural comparisons of "what a boy is looking for" made for lively discussion and again underscored the variability in standards of attractiveness across ethnic groups.

Although some of the topics discussed in the intervention had been introduced previously in the regular school curriculum (e.g., cooking, nutrition), girls felt that they enjoyed the learning experience of the intervention more, because they were not under pressure to take an examination about what they had learned. In addition, because they were not being evaluated academically, the girls felt more at ease asking what might otherwise have been perceived as "stupid" questions.

Another advantage of the extracurricular format was the inclusion of multiple presenters who were experts in particular fields of exercise, nutrition, self image, and so forth. Girls felt that there was status attached to having people from the "outside" come in to talk to them. The enthusiasm and expertise of the Canyon Ranch staff were particularly appreciated and enjoyed by the participants. There were many requests for them to return and teach more "hands-on classes." It is important to note that although Canyon Ranch is known as an exclusive health spa, the activities that these experts presented in the intervention did not emphasize the use of expensive facilities or supplies. Rather, they used inexpensive equipment (including homemade hand weights) and common foods (e.g., tortillas, potatoes).

Participants expressed a keen interest in developing an ongoing project similar to the one they had just completed. Although we recognized that our pilot project needed much refinement, we took these comments as an indication of girls' need and desire to have opportunities to discuss issues of body image, nutrition, and physical activity in a nonthreatening environment. It was clear to us that this was not available to students at this high school prior to our intervention.

Girls were asked how a project like this could be structured in the school setting. After some discussion, participants suggested that a club would be a suitable format for a continued program. Girls mentioned that they would like to bring in "experts" to talk to club members about specific topics of concern such as how to eat more nutritiously and how to work out. Their enthusiasm about the funk aerobics class led them to request an afterschool aerobics class at their school, for which they were willing to pay a small fee. This idea was equally endorsed by girls in the intervention across ethnicity. This signaled to us that some girls wanted to be more physically active than they currently were but did not have opportunities to do so. It also may have indicated that exercising in a supportive environment with other girls was valued.

When asked if the curriculum should be expanded to include discussion of risky health behaviors such as smoking cigarettes and the use of alcohol and other drugs, participants said they already received considerable information on these topics within their regular school curriculum. They thought that it would be "boring" to discuss these issues again. The girls did request more information on the following: preparing nutritious meals, how to make healthy food choices in their everyday environment, food labeling and deceptive advertising, and how to work out with weights. Although these topics already were included in the curriculum, the participants believed that more sessions on dealing with these issues would help them to expand their knowledge and establish behaviors in these topic areas.

☐ Impact Evaluation

Participants completed a 25-item survey at the start and end of the program. Although it is beyond the scope of this chapter to review all the results of the pre- and post-tests, several points can be highlighted (see Parker, Nichter, Vuckovic, Sims, & Teufel, 1995, for a fuller presentation of the results). Three questions were used to evaluate participants' attitudes and behaviors with regard to their weight: Are you trying to change your weight now? What do you think about your present weight? How often do you worry about your weight? There were no differences between girls' responses to these questions at time 1 and time 2. These findings are not surprising, however, given the short duration of the program. Importantly, almost two-thirds of the girls who participated in the program indicated that they were satisfied with their weight at time 1.

Several questions were asked to assess the participants' knowledge of a variety of nutrition issues, including appropriate food choices, calories, carbohydrates, fiber, fat, and protein. At time 2, over two-thirds of our participants were able to identify what constituted a healthy choice from a fast-food restaurant, compared with one-third of girls at time 1. They learned that foods that initially seemed to be a healthful choice might actually have hidden fats and calories. At time 2, girls had a better understanding of nutritionists' recommendations for a healthy diet for adolescents and demonstrated a better understanding of the meaning of terms such as *fiber, protein,* and *calories.* These concepts were unfamiliar to many of the girls at time 1. For more complex topics such as food labeling (e.g., the meaning of the term *lite*), no gain in knowledge was found. Most probably, to improve comprehension of a topic as complex as this, there must be more than one presentation during the course of the intervention.

The exercise component was difficult to evaluate with a quantitative instrument because the teaching about this subject had utilized an experiential rather than a didactic learning approach. As was noted in the discussion of the process evaluation, participants seemed extremely enthusiastic about the practical demonstrations with weights and aerobics.

☐ Outcome Evaluation

Eight months after the intervention was completed, participants were called to determine the effect of the intervention on their present health behavior. The response rate was 60%. Of those girls, 69% were exercising regularly, compared with 31% who had made no change in their exercise behavior. With regard to ethnicity, 60% of the African American and Hispanic girls made changes in their exercise behavior, as compared with 85% of White girls who had done so. Girls who were exercising reported a range of activities including dancing, running, physical education classes, and sit-ups. When asked if they had made changes in their eating habits, 69% responded "yes" and 31% responded "no." Changes in eating behaviors were similar across all ethnic groups and included eating more fruits and vegetables, eating a more balanced diet, avoiding excess fat, reading food labels, and "watching" what they ate. Almost half of the girls reported making changes in both their exercise and eating habits. All of the participants reported that the project had made a positive difference in how they presently

felt about themselves and had provided them with a more positive personal out-
look and greater self acceptance.

How Ethnographic Research Contributed to the Success of the Intervention

The research team's experience with the Teen Lifestyle Project enabled us to create
an intervention that matched the needs and interests of adolescent girls (Nichter &
Vuckovic, 1994; Nichter, Ritenbaugh, Nichter, Vuckovic, & Aikin., 1995; Parker,
Nichter, Nichter, Vuckovic, Sims, & Ritenbaugh, 1995). For example, in our interviews with teenage girls, we learned that girls often danced in their rooms at
night. Even though this could be a vigorous aerobic activity, few girls recognized
that this "qualified" as a physical activity. Their perception was that only organized
sports or activities done at a gym constituted "exercise." The funk aerobics class
was extremely popular because it demonstrated that a favorite activity (dancing)
was a fun and effective way of exercising. Providing inexpensive options for exercise equipment (hand weights and milk jugs) also helped to dispel notions that exercise could only be done in a gym on expensive equipment. We had learned in
our research that some girls were hesitant to participate in physical activity because they thought if they breathed hard or sweated it was an indication that they
were out of shape. Because of this awareness, we directly addressed this issue in
our intervention. After learning that sweating and breathing hard were expected
outcomes of exercising, girls were more willing to be physically active.

Our ethnographic research also helped us to design nutrition components
that were consistent with girls' concerns and lifestyles. The sessions devoted to
nutrition addressed common misconceptions about nutrients, and provided
strategies for healthy eating in places in which teens eat—the school cafeteria
and fast-food restaurants. Cooking demonstrations offered healthier ways to
prepare popular teen food items, including taco salad and French fries.

Most importantly, our research pointed out that education about nutrition
and exercise—that is, a healthy lifestyle—cannot be separated from girls' concerns about body image, including concerns about weight and body shape. We
recognized that many White and Hispanic girls routinely compared themselves
with other girls and women whom they considered "perfect." These practices
undermined self-esteem and placed girls at risk for unhealthy eating when they
set unrealistic standards for weight and body shape. Carried into the future,
these disordered patterns of eating could lead to nutrient deficiencies and might
result in obesity if metabolic set points become altered through repeated cycles
of dieting and weight gain. Although African American girls' more flexible standards of acceptable weight were adaptive during adolescence, they may put girls
at risk for obesity as they transition into adulthood (Serdula et al., 1993).

Challenges to Implementation

Although we obtained encouraging results from our intervention, we recognize
that the program did have limitations. The project was short-term and offered to a
only small number of girls. The number of participants, although appropriate for
the funding level and pilot nature of the program, nevertheless limited the types

of analyses we could conduct and the power of our findings. Still, the process measures and qualitative evaluation, together with the pre- and post-tests and follow-up survey results, lead us to believe that we had a positive influence on participants and that a larger-project of this kind could work in our community.

The program we developed was based on several years of ethnographic research in Tucson and was tailored to the local population. It would be difficult to predict how such a program would fare in other communities. The African American population in Tucson is small and dispersed, and African American girls are in the minority at their schools and in many other social situations. There are, however, places in which African Americans cluster, such as churches and community centers, and there is a strong sense of community and common values at these sites. Despite their small number, there was little evidence from our Tucson project that African American girls were more at risk for approximating the White beauty ideals or adapting the White girls' patterns of restricted eating. The intervention team, which is itself multi-ethnic, believed that bringing girls of diverse ethnic and cultural backgrounds together could be beneficial for all participants involved. We felt that it was important to acknowledge and celebrate the positive cultural models of body image found in African American culture, just as it was important to build on the positive health-oriented behaviors that had been identified among White and Hispanic girls.

With regard to the location in which a program is implemented, it is important to note several issues related to placement within a community site. The community sites at which we worked were not viewed generally as places of learning by youth, but rather as places where teens come to socialize and participate in sports activities. Because there was a constant turnover in membership, it was difficult to predict the number and ages of participants available at these sites at any given time. The continuity of the learning process in the intervention therefore was compromised. Such issues should be considered in the placement of future prevention programs at community sites. In comparison with a community site, a high school setting is an established learning site that can provide a structured environment for an intervention and a large established population from which to recruit participants. School-based settings also provide greater options for facilities, such as demonstration kitchens and exercise or dance rooms. The fact that our program targeted only girls made it difficult for us to enter a public school setting, in which coeducational programs are mandated. Although it would be important to mainstream prevention efforts so as to reach a larger audience, consideration would have to be given to how this could be done within the existing school culture.

Before planning any intervention, it is critically important to assess local conditions, including the needs of participants and resources available in the community. Our project had the valuable resource of years of ethnographic fieldwork, but more rapid methods of environmental assessment (e.g., rapid appraisal methods; see Harris, Jerome, & Fawcett, 1997) can also yield crucial information that can make or break a program.

☐ Conclusion

The success of the intervention is most readily apparent in the enthusiasm of the participants at the conclusion of the project. Girls indicated that they would be willing to pay a small fee for the opportunity to have an afterschool fitness program that continued beyond our no-cost intervention. Their willingness highlights the limited opportunity for high school girls to participate in regular physical activity if they are not part of athletic teams. The interest expressed by the participants in creating a regular workout program for high school students and their desire to gain more nutritional knowledge reflects their desire to be physically healthy and fit.

It is also important to note that the participants were interested in having presenters who were "experts" in their respective fields. The project team initially had thought that participants in each phase of the project would be more accepting of health information if it came from trained peer facilitators rather than adults. In fact, in the community intervention sites we had trained and utilized older adolescent girls as facilitators. In the high school intervention site, the older ages of the presenters as compared with the adolescent participants were not barriers but were interpreted as an indication of the presenters' expert status. The mixed group of older and younger teens in the high school site did allow for some of the benefits of peer interactions and leadership.

An important issue of concern to those involved in the prevention of eating disorders has been at what age programs should be introduced for maximum benefit (see Chapter 5). Some researchers have suggested that programs geared toward middle and high school students come too late in girls' development and that programs are best introduced in elementary school, followed by booster sessions in middle school and high school (Franko & Orosan-Weine, 1998; Shisslak, Crago, Estes, & Gray, 1996). Our intervention identified differences in what was appropriate for high school–aged girls as compared with girls ages 10–13. In the community sites, some of the participants had not yet gone through puberty, and so weight and other body changes were not issues for them. In the high school site, participants noted that the program was particularly relevant for girls their age because of their level of physical and social maturity. As one girl commented, "A couple of years ago, I wouldn't have learned anything." These girls felt that at their present age they were capable of implementing the food choices and other behavioral changes that were discussed in the sessions. In addition, older girls were able to identify with the images and themes introduced in the media awareness slide show and thus were able to engage in a more insightful discussion of how such images effected them. Future interventions need to pay close attention to the changing developmental concerns of girls across adolescence (Shisslak et al., 1996).

We found that an important influence on the success of our program was the opportunity to bring together girls of various ethnic and racial backgrounds. Their discussions during the program helped the girls to realize the cultural underpinnings of beauty ideals, and to expand their own ideas of what "looking good" is all about.

☐ References

Abrams, K. K., Allen, L. R., & Gray, J. J. (1993). Disordered eating attitudes and behaviors, psychological adjustment, and ethnic identity: A comparison of black and white female college students. *International Journal of Eating Disorders, 14,* 49–57.

American Association of University Women (1992). *The AAUW Report: How schools shortchange girls.* Washington, DC: The AAUW Educational Foundation and National Educational Association.

Allen, J. D. (1989, November). *Weight management activities among Black women*. Paper presented at the Annual Meeting of the American Anthropological Association, Washington, DC.

Berg, F. (1992, July/August). Harmful weight loss practices are widespread among adolescents. *Obesity & Health*, 69–72.

Casper, R., & Offer, D. (1990). Weight and dieting concerns of adolescents: Fashion or symptom? *Pediatrics, 86*, 384–390.

Centers for Disease Control and Prevention (CDC). (1996). *MMWR CDC surveillance summaries. 45* (SS-4).

Cohn, L., Adler, N., Irwin, C., Millstein, S., Kegeles, S., & Stone, G. (1987). Body-figure preferences in males and female adolescents. *Journal of Abnormal Psychology. 96*, 276–279.

Dawson, D. (1988). Ethnic differences in female overweight: Data from the 1985 National Health Interview Survey. *American Journal of Public Health, 78*, 1326–1329.

Dolan, B. (1991). Cross cultural aspects of anorexia nervosa and bulimia: A review. *International Journal of Eating Disorders, 10*, 67–78.

Fairburn, C. G., & Beglin, S. J. (1990). Studies of the epidemiology of bulimia nervosa. *American Journal of Psychiatry, 147*, 401–408.

Franko, D. L., & Orosan-Weine, P. (1998). The prevention of eating disorders: Empirical, methodological, and conceptual considerations. *Clinical Psychology: Science and Practice, 5*, 459–477.

Gray, J. J., Ford, K., & Kelly, L. M. (1987). The prevalence of bulimia in a black college population. *International Journal of Eating Disorders, 6*, 733–740.

Harris, K. J., Jerome, N., & Fawcett, S. B. (1997). Rapid assessment procedures: A review and critique. *Human Organization, 56*, 375–378.

Hsu, L. K. G. (1987). Are eating disorders becoming more common among Blacks? *International Journal of Eating Disorders, 6*, 113–124.

Kumanyika, S., Wilson, J., & Guilford-Davenport, M. (1993). Weight-related attitudes and behaviors of Black women. *Journal of the American Dietetic Association, 93*, 416–422.

Lucas, A. R., Beard, M., O'Fallon, W. M., & Kurland, L. T. (1991). 50-year trends in the incidence of anorexia nervosa in Rochester, Minn: A population-based study. *American Journal of Psychiatry, 148*, 917–922.

Morbidity and Mortality Weekly Report (MMWR). (1991). Body weight perceptions and selected weight management goals and practices of high school students—United States, 1990. *Morbidity and Mortality Weekly Reports, 40*, 741–750.

Nichter, M., Ritenbaugh, C., Nichter, M., Vuckovic, N., & Aickin, M. (1995). Dieting and watching among adolescent females: Report of a multimethod study. *Journal of Adolescent Health, 17*, 153–162.

Nichter, M., & Vuckovic, N. (1994). Fat talk: Body image among adolescent females. In N. Sault (Ed.), *Mirror, mirror: Body image and social relations.* (pp. 109–131). New Brunswick, NJ: Rutgers University Press.

Orenstein, P. (1994). *Schoolgirls: Young women, self-esteem, and the confidence gap.* New York: Doubleday.

Parker, S., Nichter, M., Nichter, M., Vuckovic, N., Sims, C., & Ritenbaugh, C. (1995). Body image and weight concerns among African American and White adolescent females: Differences that make a difference. *Human Organization, 54*, 103–114.

Parker, S., Nichter, M., Nichter, M., Vuckovic, N., Sims, C., & Teufel, N. (1995). *The final report of the Looking Good, Feeling Good Health Promotion Project.* Unpublished manuscript, University of Arizona, Department of Anthropology and Department of Family and Community Medicine.

Pumariega, A. J. (1986). Acculturation and eating attitudes in adolescent girls: A comparative and cultural study. *Journal of the American Academy of Child and Adolescent Psychiatry, 31*, 802–809.

Robinson, T., Killen, J., Litt, I., Hammer L., Wilson D., Haydel, K., Hayward, C., & Taylor, C. B. (1996). Ethnicity and body dissatisfaction: Are Hispanic and Asian girls at increased risk for eating disorders? *Journal of Adolescent Health, 19*, 384–393.

Rosen, J., & Gross, J. (1987). Prevalence of weight reducing and weight gaining in adolescent girls and boys. *Health Psychology, 6*, 131–147.

Serdula, M. K., Ivery, D., Coates, R. J., Freedman, D., Williamson, D., & Byers, T. (1993). Do obese children become obese adults? A review of the literature. *Preventive Medicine, 22*, 167–177.

Shisslak, C. M., Crago, M., Estes, L. S., & Gray, N. (1996). Content and method of developmentally appropriate prevention programs. In L. Smolak, M. P. Levine, & R. Striegel-Moore (Eds.), *The developmental psychopathology of eating disorders* (pp. 341–364). Mahwah, NJ: Lawrence Erlbaum Associates.

Silber, T. (1986). Anorexia nervosa in Blacks and Hispanics. *International Journal of Eating Disorders, 5*, 121–128.

Simmons, R., & Blyth, D. (1987). *Moving into adolescence: The impact of pubertal change and school context.* Hawthorne, NJ: Aldine.

Smith, J. E., & Krejci, J. (1991). Minorities join the majority: Eating disturbances among Hispanic and Native American youth. *International Journal of Eating Disorders, 9*, 179–186.

Striegel-Moore, R., & Smolak, L. (1996). The role of race in the development of eating disorders. In L. Smolak, M. P. Levine, & R. Striegel-Moore (Eds.), *The developmental psychopathology of eating disorders* (pp. 259–284). Mahwah, NJ: Lawrence Erlbaum Associates.

Thompson, B. (1994). Food, bodies, and growing up female: Childhood lessons about culture, race, and class. In P. Fallon, M. A. Katzman, & S. C. Wooley (Eds.), *Feminist perspectives on eating disorders* (pp. 355–378). New York: Guildford Press.

Troiano, R. P., Flegal, K. M., Kuczmarkski, R., Campbell, S., & Johnson, C. (1995). Overweight prevalence and trends for children and adolescents. *Archives of Pediatric and Adolescent Medicine, 149*, 1085–1091.

Yanovski, S. (1993). Binge eating disorder: Current knowledge and future directions. *Obesity Research, 1*, 306–318.

12
CHAPTER

June Larkin
Carla Rice
Vanessa Russell

Sexual Harassment and the Prevention of Eating Disorders: Educating Young Women

Women's preoccupation with their body weight, size, and physical appearance starts early and gets played out in ways that range from periodic monitoring of food intake and regulation of body presentation to perpetual dieting to full-blown anorexia and bulimia. For many young girls, dieting has become a standard practice. One Canadian study found that 80% of young women "worried a lot" about appearance (Canadian Teachers Federation, 1990). In addition, researchers have found that as many as 80% of 10-year-old girls report having been on a diet (Mellin, Scully, & Irwin, 1992), half of young women between the ages of 14 and 18 years believe they are too fat, and almost 45% are trying to lose weight (Day, 1990). Researchers investigating the gender dimensions of such struggles find that the level of body-image disturbance in adolescent females far exceeds the body dissatisfaction of young men (Paxton et al., 1991; Richards, Petersen, Boxer, & Albrecht, 1990; Rodriquez-Tome et al., 1993; Offer, Ostrov, & Howard, 1981). The diagnosis of eating disorders is particularly prevalent among young women and girls (Malson, 1998).

There is a growing body of literature on the possible relationship between women's troubled relationships with their bodies and a past history of sexual trauma and physical abuse (Rice, 1995; Rice & Langdon, 1991; Root & Fallon, 1988; Thompson, 1994; Vanderlinden, Vandereycken, Van Dyck, & Vertommen, 1993; Waller, Hamilton, Rose, Sumra & Baldwin, 1993; Wooley, 1994). However, researchers have yet to seriously consider the links among sexual harassment, body-image issues, and eating problems as they explore the cultural factors that account for young women's loathing of their own bodies. Although a few researchers have suggested that "childhood teasing" is implicated in the development of depression, low self-esteem, body-image dissatisfaction and eating disorders, none have investigated the gendered and racialized nature of this "teasing" (Cattarin & Thompson, 1994; Fabian & Thompson, 1989).

194

Sexual harassment is so pervasive that it often is perceived as normal. As one women put it: "Sexual harassment happens so much it's almost a background of what going out the door seems to mean" (Kelly, 1987, p. 53). In this chapter, we examine the nature and impact of sexual harassment on adolescent girls. We explore how experiences of harassment can contribute to young women's un-easiness about their developing bodies, which can lead to intense body monitoring and disordered patterns of eating. We conclude by offering suggestions for doing educational work on harassment and body image with preadolescent and adolescent girls.

☐ Sexual Harassment: Its Nature and Impact

Although the term *sexual harassment* was coined only recently, sexually harass-ing behavior is not a new phenomenon. As early as 1911, the National Women's Trade Union League complained about the abusive and insulting language that female workers endured from men in their jobs, but there was no label for this behavior (Bulzarik, 1978).

It is Farley (1978) who is credited with creating the term *sexual harassment,* but there is wide disagreement about what constitutes sexually harassing be-havior (Debruin, 1998). Although the need for legal sanctions against cases of quid pro quid harassment (trading sex for favors) generally is accepted, the more common forms of harassment are often dismissed as ordinary and natural heterosexual interaction. Roiphe (1993), for example, is critical of the inclusion of "leering and ogling, whistling, sexual innuendo, and other suggestive or of-fensive or derogatory comments, humor and jokes about sex" (p. 100) in sexual harassment policies and claims that women should be able to handle such trivial and mundane behavior without appealing to policy or legislation. It is, however, the more common and mundane forms of sexual hassling that are key to the regulation and subordination of women. This is because mundane harassment can have a cumulative impact:

> It's crucially important to name the "dripping tap" behaviours, events, and situa-tions as *sexual harassment*: by doing so we recognise that they're important and common, rather than trite and confined to "just me" and "my peculiarities," and we see them as limiting, oppressive and wrong *political* behaviours because they at-tempt to disempower us. Out of this we come to see that "politics" is about power, influence and control and can be located in the most humdrum and supposedly "insignificant" of things. (Wise and Stanley, 1987, p. 114)

Over the past 20 years, there has been a wide range of surveys documenting the nature and prevalence of sexual harassment in the lives of adult women. In a survey conducted by *Redbook* magazine in 1976, 88% of the 9000 respondents reported that they had received unwanted sexual attention at work (Sanford, 1979). The US Merit Systems Protection Board conducted the first national sur-vey of sexual harassment with 20,000 people in 1981 and found that 42% of fe-male and 15% of male respondents reported experiencing "unwanted sexual attention" in the workplace over the previous 2 years (Merit Systems Protection Board, 1981). In the same year, the Canadian Human Rights Commission con-ducted a survey and found that 49% of women and 33% of men who responded had experienced "unwanted sexual attention" (CHRC, 1983). The statistics on the prevalence of workplace sexual harassment for men and women internationally is comparable with reports of workplace harassment in Canada and the United States (International Labor Organization, 1992).

Notably absent from these earlier studies was an inquiry into the sexual harassment experiences of girls and younger women. As the symptoms of physical and emotional distress affecting adult women became well documented (see, e.g., Backhouse & Cohen, 1978; Bannerji, 1995; Fredrickson & Roberts, 1997; Larkin, 1994/1997, 1997), researchers began to consider the problem of harassment in relation to younger females. In a study conducted with 2000 female students in the United States, 89% of the girls reported having experienced inappropriate sexual comments, gestures and looks; 83% had been touched, pinched, or grabbed; and 40% said that these incidents occurred daily at school (Stein, Marshall, & Tropp, 1993). In an Ontario study, 83% of female high-school students reported having been sexually harassed in the school setting (Ontario Secondary School Teachers' Federation, 1994).

The alarmingly high incidence of sexual harassment reported by girls in survey-based studies can provide a basis for making broad claims: If 89% of 2000 girls responding to a questionnaire report that they have experienced inappropriate sexual comments, gestures, and looks at school, then one can reasonably make the case that sexual harassment is a problem in the educational setting. What may get missed in surveys are questions that may be relevant to the phenomenon of sexual harassment but have yet to be identified by the researcher. This was the case for Larkin, who had not made the connection between harassment and body image until she conducted a qualitative study in which she explored the phenomenon of sexual harassment in the lives of a group of high-school girls.

Larkin's study involved students from schools in urban, rural, and small-town school settings and represented a variety of racial, cultural and economic backgrounds. Such a diverse sample was necessary to understand the various ways sexual harassment gets played out in young women's lives. Traditionally, sexual harassment has been understood in the context of an "undifferentiated notion" (Bannerji, 1995, p. 126) of woman. Bannerji argues that the "woman" who is referred to in typical sexual harassment complaints is a White woman, who must be identified as such if we are to conceive of sexual harassment policy and law that is expanded to serve women of color:

> The "woman" in question, serving as the base type for sexual harassment complaints, is a *white* woman. She demands *this* specific adjective, if we are to stretch the law beyond her to other women. Otherwise, though we can deal with her case, we cannot even begin to address the wrongs of her sister, the *black* woman . . . whose difference enters into the peculiar type of sexual harassment meted out to her. And yet, *normally*, daily, why is this category "woman" non-adjectivized for a white woman, while all others have their differences "raced" or "coloured?" (p. 126, italics in the original)

Factoring in race, class and other oppressive factors is crucial to expanding the concept of sexual harassment beyond the limited notion of a problematic heterosexual dynamic (Bannerji, 1995).

As part of the research project, Larkin ran focus groups in which female students were invited to share incidents of sexual harassment that they had recorded in their personal journals. Considering the backlash experienced by adult women who have dared to label certain forms of males' behaviour as sexual harassment (see, e.g., McIntyre, 1986; Ramazanoglu, 1987), Larkin believed that a journal might be a safe place for young women to express and reflect upon what they were choosing to record as sexual harassment. She also believed that the process of keeping a journal, coupled with reflection on the comments made in group discussions, would prepare the students for their individual interviews.

Students' misconceptions and confusions about what behavior constituted sexual harassment made it difficult for Larkin to get a valid picture of the extent to which they were dealing with harassment. Most young women were familiar with the term *sexual harassment* but had a limited notion of the scope of sexually harassing behavior; many assumed it meant rape or sexual assault. One student believed that sexual harassment had to involve "molesting." In her words, "I never thought of it as being vocal" (Larkin, 1994/1997, p. 66). The young women had come to accept as natural those forms of harassment they experienced on a daily basis. For some students, this behavior was part of the backdrop of their daily school life:

> You don't think about it really . . . because it happens all the time, it happens so often it's just part of life. How can I explain it? It's like you are walking down the street and someone whistles at you . . . It's like whistles all the time, honks all the time—you don't even pay attention to it. It's part of life.

There was much behavior students did not identify as sexual harassment because "it was just what happened every day at school."

In Larkin's study, the harassment leveled against the female students ranged from routine experiences of insults and objectifying comments to periodic threats of rape and murder. If harassment was laced with racial slurs and stereotypes, the experience was qualitatively different. For example, although being rated by male students in school corridors was a common experience for girls, the lowest scores were reserved for Black students.

> The guys would play this game. They would all have . . . a number and [they would score] girls who passed by them in the hallway. If it was a pretty girl they'd say, "Ten, right on, you've got *her*!" If a Black girl walked by they'd go, "Oh my God, she's got such a big ass. . . ." They'd give her a low score. (Larkin, 1994/1997, p. 92)

Being labeled a "2" by a group of young men as other students milled about the halls was a form of public diminishing that shook many young women's precarious sense of self. Such diminishment was more common for Black girls, who tended to receive lower scores than their White peers. It is no coincidence that young Black women were attacked and devalued because of their buttocks, a part of African Canadian and American women's anatomy that historically has been both denigrated and eroticized by Europeans (Mama, 1995).

Sexual harassment must be understood in the context of women's situated histories. The process of objectification that is the essence of sexual harassment "takes on a particular virulence with the overlay of race upon gender stereotypes" (Cho, 1997, p. 205). For example, Davis (1997) points out that sexual harassment "forces African American women to realize that the ideologies of slavery still exist" (p. 195). Comments such as, "I hear Black girls like White guys' dicks," leveled against girls in Larkin's study, resonated with the common pornographic image of Black women as willing slaves to their White masters and are steeped in a history of colonial relations (Mayall & Russell, 1993).

Wise and Stanley (1987) point out that most sexual harassment does not involve extreme or "sledgehammer" (p. 114) behavior but consists of smaller, cumulative intrusions that are limiting, demeaning, and disempowering. The more infrequent but threatening sledgehammer behavior, however, renders every incident of harassment a violent threat. This was the case for many students in Larkin's study. The young women never knew when a seemingly minor incident of harassment could escalate to a more extreme form of abuse. As one young woman explained, "You know these little incidents can lead to big incidents" (Larkin, 1994/1997, p. 101).

Unfortunately, such concerns often were validated. One young woman told Larkin she was "terrified" when she learned that a male student who had been following her around the school was part of a group of young men who had harassed and then sexually assaulted another female student. Another young woman dropped out of school after being sexually assaulted by a group of male students who had been hassling her because she had refused to date one of their friends. When Larkin began to work in elementary schools she was contacted about a seventh-grade girl who had attempted suicide in a desperate attempt to avoid facing her male classmates who had stepped up their gendered insults to threats of sexually assaulting her.

The hostile environment created through sexual harassment prevented many girls from participating fully and comfortably in school life. Compared with the results of the survey studies conducted by the American Association of University Women (1993) and the Ontario Secondary School Teachers' Federation (1994), the responses of students in Larkin's study were similar. These included not wanting to go to class, finding it hard to pay attention in school, staying home from school or cutting a class, making a lower grade in school, not speaking up in class, dropping courses, and leaving school. Of course, the regulatory effect of harassment is not limited to girls' experience in schools. What has to be considered, also, is the impact of the pervasive harassment girls face on the streets and in other public places (Larkin, 1997). One young woman summarized it this way:

> There is always a sense of watching where you step, watching where you go, watching who you meet . . . You have to be careful, watch out, there are idiots out there, there are creeps, there are weirdos, watch out. (Larkin, 1997, p. 128)

In addition to regulating women's movement and behavior, sexual harassment has been found to affect girls' and women's mental well-being (Carmen, Russo, & Miller, 1990; Larkin, 1994/1997). Backhouse and Cohen (1978) have described a variety of distress-related consequences such as depression, headaches, nausea, hypertension and insomnia. Missing from this cluster of symptoms that Backhouse and Cohen label as the "sexual harassment syndrome" are the body-image and eating problems that are additional results of the pervasive harassment inflicted on girls.

Larkin's study and the Embodying Equity Project conducted by Rice and Russell (1995) revealed the strong link between sexual harassment and body-image problems. The Embodying Equity Project, a joint program between the Toronto Board's Equity Studies Centre and the Women and Body Image Project of the

Regional Women's Health Centre, involved support groups for female students in over fourteen schools. The groups created a context for girls and young women to begin to talk about a range of concerns about their bodies and their lives. In comparing the results of our two studies, we found similar stories about body-based harassment. For example, girls complained that being constantly compared to the pin-up girls boys stashed away in their desks or lockers or having to fend off comments about being "as flat as the walls" created a growing uneasiness about their developing bodies. As one student put it: "I felt bad about my body and I wished that I was a boy" (Larkin, 1994/1997, p. 110).

In the next section we describe the ways sexual harassment contributes to a young woman's disdain about her developing body and, subsequently, to her vulnerability to disordered eating.

☐ Getting Cut Down to Size: The Effects of Harassment on Body Image

Body image and self-esteem are developed through interactions with people and the social world. The association between a history of being "teased" about physical appearance and the occurrence of both body-image and eating disturbances has been well documented (Berscheid, Walster, & Bohrnstedt, 1973; Fabian & Thompson, 1989; Rice, 1993; Striegel-Moore & Kearney-Cooke, 1994; Thompson, 1994; Thompson & Psaltis, 1988). However, the gendered nature of this "negative verbal commentary" (Cattarin & Thompson, 1994, p. 123) has yet to be acknowledged and named as sexual harassment. Moreover, the effect of harassment on the developing body images and identities of young women has yet to be explored.

Harassment is a tool of oppression that can alienate women from their bodies and embed them with a precarious sense of self. Harassing words thrown at a girl slowly are absorbed into the child's identity and developing sense of self, becoming an essential part of who she sees herself to be. This is especially true if the slurs are reinforced by systemic forces in her environment that brand her as less worthy, inferior, and defective. For example, a harassing comment targeted at her body may interact with a stigmatized assessment of her body as deviating from the ideal shape to create poor body- and self-esteem (Rice and Russell, 1995).

The messages we receive about our bodies shape our sense of body consciousness; that is, our ability to reside comfortably within our own bodies (Thompson, 1994). In the different focus groups conducted by Rice and Russell (1995) and by Larkin (1994/1997), the facilitators heard countless accounts of body-based harassment: The girl who was afraid to walk home from school each day because she was forced to walk past a gang of adolescent boys who routinely called her a "fat bitch" and pelted her with stones; the girls who avoided a certain hallway in their high school because they were afraid of being publicly rated on a scale of 1 through 10 and coming out on the low end; the girls who were subjected to barking, grunting, and mooing calls and labels of "dog, "cow," or "pig" when they passed by groups of male students; the girls who were teased about not measuring up to the buxom, bikini-clad girls that drape the pages of various newspapers; and the girls who were grabbed, pinched, groped, and fondled as they tried to make their way through the school corridors. There was a double sting for girls who were members of marginalized groups: the young black woman who was nicknamed "chia pet" because of her kinky hair; the Chinese girl who was asked about her "slanted cunt"; and the girls with disabilities who were branded with names such as "hunchback."

Experiences of harassment can engender a sense of shame. Kaschak (1992) writes that a "sense of shame leads to a desire to disappear, to hide the body, to become invisible" (p. 202). Shame occurs if people evaluate themselves relative to a cultural ideal and determine they do not measure up (Fredrickson & Roberts, 1997). The Western standard of beauty is the basis of body shame for many young women, particularly those who do not fit the thin, white, able-bodied ideal. Although some women of color have created oppositional standards of beauty and others have inherited subcultural ideals that are different from dominant standards, few women who are socialized in mainstream Western institutions escape pressure to conform to its notions of beauty (Mama, 1995; Russell, Wilson, & Hall, 1992). Fredrickson & Roberts (1997) argue that the fear of social exposure of one's deficiencies is a powerful component of shame. Much of the harassment directed at young women invokes shame because it is a public judgment of their bodies as flawed and imperfect. Shame can generate "an intense desire to hide, to escape the painful gaze of others, or to disappear, alongside feelings of worthlessness and powerlessness" (Fredrickson & Roberts, 1997, p. 181). Shame reinforces the splitting of the bodies from minds, while it compels young women to engage in relentless body criticism and improvement in an effort to bolster their shattered self-esteem. Rice (1995) has suggested

> For someone faced with unrelenting discrimination in the form of blatant public hostility and disgust, demeaning and dehumanizing jokes, unwanted advice and comments and systemic economic oppression, losing weight becomes an attractive means of attempting to retrieve lost self-esteem as well as gaining and achieving success. (p. 22)

The experience of conducting focus groups in schools (Larkin, 1994/1997; Rice & Russell, 1995) has alerted us to a disturbing process whereby girls' excitement about their developing bodies is being crushed by the harassing comments that accompanied their physical maturation. In her article "Growing up in a Sexual Jungle," Fraser (1991) writes that:

> At some point in their physical development, all female children lose the protection of baby fat and barrettes and become prey in a game in which there are rules only if the laws are broken. It is pretty much open season on their self-confidence and aspirations and propriety. (p. 21)

Our awareness of the impact of sexual harassment on body image and self-esteem has expanded our work to include the prevention of sexual harassment as an important strategy in curbing the development of eating disorders and intensive body monitoring in girls.

☐ Facing Sexual Harassment: Toward the Goal of Prevention

Our educational work in the area of harassment and body image has been informed by the knowledge we have acquired through the interviews as well as the focus and support groups we have conducted in our respective projects with adolescent girls. Providing a supportive space in which girls can feel comfortable to articulate, test, revise, or conform their perceptions of events is crucial. This is best accomplished in all-female settings with ample time to share stories, process information, and build relationships.

Opportunities to do education can be offered in varying degrees in single, multiple, and extended same-gender sessions and should be included as part of a regular educational program. To this end, we have worked to develop educational materials focused on harassment as well as materials addressing body image and related issues. We also have worked to address sexual harassment and body-image problems at systemic levels, helping teachers and administrators in educational systems understand and respond to harassment in all its manifestations.

Individual and Group Interventions

Feminist theorizing on consciousness raising has been particularly influential in shaping our work with adolescent girls. Consciousness raising is an approach to theorizing women's experiences in society from within the social context and the first person (MacKinnon, 1983, 1989). Traditionally, it has been through the process of consciousness raising

> that women's understandings of our lives are transformed so that we see, understand and feel them in a new and quite different way at the same time as we see them in the "old way." This "new way" of seeing the same reality . . . involves a situation in which women come to understand the seemingly endless contradictions within our life. (Stanley & Wise, p. 54)

The notion of consciousness raising may seem old hat to some, but for the young women we worked with, coming together in a safe and supportive environment was a novel experience. Having the opportunity to share similar stories was liberating, as the young women realized that they were dealing with common experiences that had little to do with their personal inadequacies. Historically, this is the way through which women have come to see their personal incidents of harassment and abuse as part of the larger problem of women's inequality, and this is also the way through which women have come to form strong connections with each other. Some feminists have expressed concern about the move away from consciousness raising as an important component of feminist research and activism. For example, Heilburn (1988) stresses the need to

> return to strengths of the earlier stages of this wave of feminism which, at least in the case of . . . [working to] combat sexual harassment and coercion, we may have left behind too soon. In particular, we need to return to consciousness raising as a form of mutual support and as a way to reach clarity of understanding of the tactics used to keep us down. We must begin to tell the truth, in groups, to one another. Modern feminism began that way, and we have lost, through shame or fear of ridicule, that important collective phenomenon. (p. 45)

According to Raymond (1986) the development of strong bonds between women provides them with "a common reference point so they do not lose their grounding in the larger world" (p. 8). Our focus groups provided this reference point. The groups also provided a context in which young women could develop new norms and values concerning their responses to standards of beauty and reinterpret negative feedback from their environment regarding their bodies and selves.

Consciousness raising evolved as a practice to transform the "muted condition of women" (Spender, 1980, p. 130) by providing a forum in which women could "hear each other into speech" (Morton, cited in Frye, 1990, p. 179). Initially, when Larkin met with high-school girls in focus groups and asked them to share their experience of harassment, there was silence. Eventually, a young woman would cautiously relay an incident she thought might be sexual harassment. Her story would often provoke a symphony of voices: "That happened to me, too." And then the stories flowed. Many young women explained they had been afraid to open up because they did not know "how much it happened to everyone else." They had been ashamed to speak up because they believed they were deserving of such defilement or they had provoked it. The increased facility in labeling harassment acquired in the groups seemed to increase the likelihood that recall of incidents would occur. The interpretation of distressing incidents shifted as well with the ability to label events as incidents of harassment.

In their body image groups, Rice and Russell (Larkin, Rice, & Russell, 1996) found that young woman made the links between sexual and racial harassment and body image. Although some young women have been more concerned about pressures to conform to thin ideals within their families and peer groups, others have talked about light-skin color bias within the dominant culture and among some members of their own communities. Connections between sexual and racial harassment and body image have been raised and discussed by young women in virtually every body image group, regardless of the range of ages, classes, or races of the participants. Themes related to harassment have tended to emerge in the 6th and 7th weeks of an 8-week group process, after the young women have made personal connections and a sense of trust has been established.

The diversity of our groups offered the young women the opportunity to understand that they were "living in a world organized to differently benefit race, class, gender, and sexuality interests (Chauhan, 1994, p. 36). Despite their differences, however, alliances among the young women began to flourish as the groups met over a period of time. Amid the heterogenity among women, Fredrickson and Roberts (1997) propose that having a maturing female body may create a shared set of experiences. A student in Larkin's study explained it this way:

> You got to put yourself in somebody else's position. . . . I can understand that person a lot better now because they've gone through the same thing that I have. . . . I can associate with them now, maybe not on every level, but on one—*as a woman*. (Larkin, 1994/1997, p. 141)

Moving the problem from personal experience to political understanding gave the young women a way of interpreting the larger picture. There was a sense of outrage when the young women connected issues about their bodies to experiences of violence and harassment. This was an important moment. Anger is the flip side of shame. Shame is the internalization of oppression that marks an individual. Anger moves the problem beyond the self. This crucial transition provides the momentum for resistance. In recalling her history of harassment one young woman declared, "Before I used to put up with it. Not anymore. It makes me so mad. How dare they!" In Larkin's study, the students became a force to pressure the administration to deal with the sexual harassment that was prevalent in their schools. In collaboration with supportive teachers, they developed an educational workshop for students, articles for the school newspaper, and a series of classroom resources on the issue of sexual harassment.

Systemic Interventions

For many young women, a sense of collective empowerment often follows when they understand that there is systemic protection from their school board against harassment and violence. We have been active at systemic levels, developing and implementing sexual-, racial-, and homophobic-harassment policies and supporting students who have been forced to make complaints. We also have worked to help educators and school administrators understand the connections between verbal taunting and the development of eating and body image problems.

As a student-program worker, Russell has been involved with developing and administering harassment policies, ensuring that students and teachers in her system understand what constitutes harassment, what support is available for victims, and how the board of education is mandated to respond to complaints. In her capacity as a counselor working closely with various systems, Rice has supported both adolescent and adult women in identifying sexually and racially harassing behavior and, if necessary, in making formal sexual and racial harassment complaints.

We realize, however, that the implementation of a policy will not resolve the problem of harassment. Although a policy is a statement of institutional support and can offer redress to those who are the targets of harassing behavior, it takes a punitive approach to dealing with harassment. The ultimate goal is to change the attitudes that perpetuate sexually harassing behaviour. As one student put it, "Education is the key to prevention" (Larkin, 1994/1997, p. 135).

Over the past 10 years in her capacity as a consultant and a researcher, Larkin has conducted workshops with educators, students, and parents across Canada on the problem of school-based harassment. A crucial component of Larkin's educational work is raising awareness about the ways harassment can damage body image and self-esteem. Standard insults, such as, "You're so flat the walls are jealous," and, "You're a carpenter's dream, flat as a board and never been nailed," are well known to many adults and students, but few have made the connection to girls' preoccupation and struggles with issues around food and body image.

As a general strategy, we encourage educators to move beyond the "quick-fix" approach of dealing with isolated incidents of harassment and to consider, instead, the systemic nature of the problem: the ways in which the very structure of our educational system creates a climate that fosters harassment and other forms of abuse against females and other marginalized groups. We suggest that educators begin by examining their curriculum content and classroom practices for gender and race bias. Who takes up most verbal space in the classroom? What groups of people are highlighted in the curriculum?

There is strong evidence that boys get the bulk of the teacher's attention and that the experiences of White men are highlighted in educational texts (Morgan, 1996; Sadker & Sadker, 1994). What does this mean for girls? Without a knowledge of the history and traditions of women, girls are less likely to develop a sense of themselves as significant and constructive members of society. This has serious implications for girls' self-esteem. A male-centered education confers upon boys "a lived sense of valued integrity" (Morgan, 1996, p. 117); girls get the message that they are second-rate. In considering the reasons for women's silence in response to sexual harassment, Cairns (1997) argues that

> the absence from public discourse of any positive mention of women's contributions to the creation of our cultures and institutions [prevents girls] from seeing the effects of their foremothers' contributions and from establishing role models for agency. (p.102)

This is not to suggest that girls are passive victims of harassment, but to point out that the messages relayed in harassing incidents often reflect the general devaluing of women that girls perceive as part of the cultural backdrop. Many girls have come to accept the negative perceptions of women, having no knowledge basis with which to reject them.

Parents, educators, and counselors can work to eliminate harassment by ensuring that young women and young men are well versed in the important contributions women have made to the social, artistic, scientific and domestic domains. Armed with a pride and knowledge of their own history, girls may be more resistant to the sting of harassment and both girls and boys may be less likely to engage in harassing behavior.

Interpersonal and Systemic Struggles and Challenges

In raising issues related to sexual harassment and society's negative images of women, there is a danger that we might increase young women's sense of fear and vulnerability. We find it helpful to end each session, workshop, or focus group with positive stories of resistance. Young women are delighted to realize the extent to which they have, and use, their personal power. The challenge here is to work against the stereotype of the helpless female victim without avoiding the tough issues and dilemmas girls are facing in their everyday lives.

As a way of encouraging girls to develop a positive connection with their bodies, we stress the importance of fitness and physical activity. Our focus is not competitive sports (although that may be the choice of some girls) but the value of experiencing one's body as an important part of the larger world. This notion can be liberating for girls who are constantly bombarded with messages about the need to regulate their movement as a personal-safety strategy.

Bringing parents and educators on side can be a serious challenge. Our work in schools often is limited to those settings that have educators who are concerned about harassment and the related issues of body image and self-esteem. Offering to provide workshops for educators on professional-development days and speaking to members of parent-school councils has been an effective way of targeting large groups of adults who are responsible for the education and well-being of girls. The most effective approach to raising the issues is to relay the stories of the young women who have participated in our research. The wrenching accounts of sexual and racial hassling have a familiar ring for most adults. Many have added their personal accounts to the litany of incidents we have documented in our work with girls in schools.

In working with young women, it is important that we do not replace the oppressive rules of dominant society with a different, yet equally oppressive, set of rules and values. We do not seriously expect everyone to stop wearing make-up, give up shaving their legs, throw out their television sets, or vow never to go to another Hollywood film. We do believe, however, that we can offer young women some tools to buffer the harmful messages that can wear them down. These tools include giving them alternative images that celebrate women's nonconformity to the ideal, providing and sharing stories of resistance and empowerment, instilling a sense of pride in their bodies and themselves, facilitating an understanding that connections between women are important, and encouraging greater investment in body and self acceptance (Rice and Russell, 1995). These are important antidotes to the pervasive harassment that can contribute to disruptive eating patterns and distorted body image in girls.

☐ Conclusion

Certainly, sexual harassment is only one of a myriad of factors that contribute to the conflicts that young women may develop around eating and body image, but it is one of the more pervasive ways in which they are reminded of the hazards of living within a woman's body. The documented evidence of the high prevalence of harassment and disordered eating patterns in girls, the data collected in our respective body-image and harassment projects, and the links we have made between these two issues are strong evidence of the need to do preventive work with girls. It is our hope that parents, educators, and counselors will recognize these important links and will work to end the harassment that interfers with young women's ability to develop healthy relationships with their own bodies.

☐ References

American Association of University Women. (1993). *Hostile hallways: The AAUW survey on sexual harassment in America's schools*. Washington, DC: Louis Harris and Associates.

Backhouse, C., & Cohen, L. (1978). *The secret oppression*. Toronto: MacMillan.

Bannerji, H. (1995). *Thinking through: Essays on feminism, marxism, and anti-racism*. Toronto: Women's Press.

Berscheid, E., Walster, E., & Bohrnstedt, G. (1973, November). The happy American body: A survey report. *Psychology Today, 11*, 119–131.

Bulzarik, M. (1978). Sexual harassment in the workplace: Historical notes. *Radical America, 12*, 25–43.

Cairns, K. (1997). "Femininity" and women's silence in response to sexual harassment and coercion. In A. Thomas & C. Kitzinger (Eds.), *Sexual harassment: Contemporary feminist perspectives* (pp. 91–130). Buckingham, England: Open University Press.

Canadian Human Rights Commission (CHRC). (1983). *Unwanted sexual attention and sexual harassment: Results of a survey of canadians*. Ottawa: CHRC/Research and Special Studies Branch.

Canadian Teachers' Federation. (November, 1990). *A capella: A report on the realities, concerns, expectations and barriers experienced by adolescent women in Canada*. Ottawa: Author.

Carmen, E.H., Russo, N.F., & Miller, J.B. (1981). Inequality and women's mental health: An overview. *American Journal of Psychiatry, 138*, 1319–1330.

Cattarin, J.A., & Thompson, J.K. (1994). A three-year longitudinal study of body image, eating disturbance, and general psychological functioning in adolescent females. *Eating Disorders, 2*(2), 114–125.

Cho, S. (1997). Converging stereotypes in racialized sexual harassment: Where the model minority meets Suzie Wong. In A. K. Wing (Ed.) *Critical race feminism: A reader* (pp. 203–220). New York: New York University Press.

Chauhan, J. (1994). Racism and gender. *Canadian Woman Studies/les cahiers de la femme, 14*(2), 34–37.

Day, D. (1990). *Young Women in Nova Scotia: A Study of Attitudes Behaviour and Aspirations*. Halifax: Nova Scotia Advisory Council on the Status of Women.

Davis, D. (1997). The harm that has no name: Street harassment, embodiment, and African American women. In A. K. Wing (Ed.) *Critical Race Feminism: A Reader* (pp. 192–202). New York: New York University Press.

Debruin, D. (1998). Identifying sexual harassment: The reasonable woman standard. In S. French, W. Teays, & Pury L. M. (Eds.), *Violence against women: Philosophical perspectives* (pp. 107–122). Ithaca, NY: Cornell University Press.

Fabian L.J., & Thompson, J.K. (1989). Body image and eating disturbance in young females. *International Journal of Eating Disorders, 8*, 63–74.

Farley, L. (1978). *Sexual Shakedown: The Sexual Harassment of Women on the Job*. New York: Warner Books.

Fraser, M.B. (1991). Growing up in a sexual jungle. *Canadian Woman Studies/les cahiers de la femme, 11*(4), 20–21.

Fredrickson, B., & Roberts, T. A. (1997). Objectification theory: Towards understanding women's lived experiences and mental health. *Psychology of Women Quarterly, 21*, 173–206.

Frye, M. (1990). The possibility of feminist theory. In D. Rhode (Ed.), *Theoretical perspectives on sexual difference* (pp. 174–184). New Haven, CT: Yale University Press.

Heilburn, C. (1988). *Writing a woman's life*. New York: W.W. Norton & Co.

Kaschak, E. (1992). *Engendered lives: A new psychology of women's experience*. New York: Harper Collins.

Kelly, L. (1987). The continuum of sexual violence. In J. Hanmer & M. Maynard (Eds.), *Women, violence and social control* (pp. 114–132). Beverly Hills, CA: Sage.

Larkin, J. (1994/1997). *Sexual harassment: High school girls speak out*. Toronto: Second Story Press.

Larkin, J. (1997). Sexual terrorism on the street: The moulding of young women into subordination. In A. Thomas and C. Kitzinger (Eds.), *Sexual harassment: Contemporary feminist perspectives* (pp. 115–130). Buckingham, England: Open University Press.

Larkin, J., Rice, C. & Russell, V. (1996). Slipping through the cracks: Sexual harassment, eating problems and the problem of embodiment. *Eating Disorders: The Journal of Treatment and Prevention, 4*(1), 5–26.

MacKinnon, C. (1983). Feminism, marxism, method and the state: An agenda for theory. In E. Abel & E. Abel (Eds.) *The signs reader: Women, gender and scholarship* (pp. 227–256). Chicago: University of Chicago Press.

MacKinnon, C. (1989). *Toward a feminist theory of the state*. Cambridge, MA: Harvard University Press.

MacKinnon, C. (1993). *Only words*. Cambridge, MA: Harvard University Press.

Malson, H. (1998). *The thin woman: Feminism, post-structuralism, and the social psychology of anorexia nervosa*. London: Routledge.

Mama, A. (1995). *Beyond the masks: Race, gender and subjectivity*. New York: Routledge.

Mayall, A., & Russell, D. (1993). Racism in pornography. *Feminism & Psychology, 3*(2), 275–281.

McIntyre, S. (1986). *Gender bias within the law school: Memo to faculty*. Kingston: Queen's University, Canada.

Mellin, L., Scully, S. & Irwin, C. (1992). Prevalence of disordered eating in girls: A survey of middle-class children. *Journal of the American Diet Association, 92*, 851–853.

Merit Systems Protection Board. (1981). *Sexual harassment in the Federal workplace: Is it a problem?* Washington, DC: US Government Printing Office.

Morgan, K. (1996). Describing the Emperor's new clothes: Three myths of educational (in-)equity. In A. Diller, B. Houston, K. Morgan & M. Ayim (Eds.) *The gender question in education: Theory, pedagogy & politics* (pp. 50–63). Boulder, Colorado: Westview Press.

Offer, D., Ostrov, E., & Howard, K. (1981). *The adolescent: A psychological self-portrait*. New York: Basic Books.

Ontario Secondary School Teachers' Federation (1994). *Student to student sexual harassment*. Toronto.

Paxton, S., Wertheim, E., Gibbons, K., Szmukler, G. Hillier, L., & Petrovich, J. (1991). Body image satisfaction, dieting beliefs and weight loss behaviours in adolescent girls and boys. *Journal of Youth and Adolescence, 20,* 361–379.

Ramazanoglu, C. (1987). Sex and violence in academic life or you can keep a good woman down. In J. Hanmer & M. Maynard (Eds.), *Women, violence and social control* (pp. 61–74). London: Macmillan.

Raymond, J. (1986). *A passion for friends.* Boston: Beacon Press.

Rice, C. (1993). Freeing future generations: Raising our children without food and weight problems. *Nutrition Quarterly, 17*(3), 55–71.

Rice, C. (1994). Out from under occupation. *Canadian Woman Studies/les cahiers de la femme, 14*(3), 44–50.

Rice, C. (1995). *Trauma, eating problems and the problem of embodiment: A comprehensive annotated bibliography.* Unpublished Manuscript.

Rice, C., & Langdon, L. (1991). Women's struggles with food and weight as survival strategies. *Canadian Woman Studies/les cahiers de la femme, 12*(1), 30–33.

Rice, C., & Russell, V. (1995). Embodying equity: Putting body and soul back into equity education. *Our Schools. Ourselves, 7,* 42–54.

Richards, M., Petersen, A., Boxer, A., & Albrecht, R. (1990). Relation of weight to body image in pubertal girls and boys from two communities. *Developmental Psychology, 26,* 313–321.

Rodriquez-Tome, H., Bariaud, F., Cohen Zardi, M. F., Delmas, C., Jeanvoine, B., & Szylagyi, P. (1993). The effects of pubertal changes on body image and relations with peers of the opposite sex in adolescence. *Journal of Adolescence, 16,* 421–438.

Roiphe, K. (1993). *The morning after: Sex, fear and feminism.* London: Hamish Hamilton.

Root, M., & Fallon, P. (1988). The incidence of victimization experiences in a bulimic sample. *Journal of Interpersonal Violence, 3*(2), 161–173.

Russell, K., Wilson, M., & Hall, R. (1992). *The color complex: The politics of skin color among African Americans.* New York: Anchor Books.

Sadker, M., & Sadker, D. (1994). *Failing at fairness: How America's schools cheat girls.* New York: Charles Scribner's Sons.

Sanford, W. (1979). *Fighting sexual harassment: An advocacy handbook.* Boston: Alyson Publications.

Spender, D. (1980). *Man-made language.* London: Routledge & Kegan Paul.

Stanko, E. (1986). *Intimate intrusions.* London: Routledge & Kegan Paul.

Stanley, L. & Wise, S. (1985). *Breaking out: Feminist consciousness and feminist research.* New York: Routledge and Kegan Paul.

Stein, N., Marshall, N., & Tropp, L. (1993). *Secrets in public: Sexual harassment in our schools.* Wellesley, MA: Center for Research on Women at Wellesley and the NOW Legal Defense and Education Fund.

Striegel-Moore, R., & Kearney-Cooke, A. (1994). Exploring parents' attitudes and behaviours about their children's physical appearance. *International Journal of Eating Disorders, 15*(4), 377–385.

Thompson, B. (1994). "A Way Outa No Way:" Eating problems among African American, Latina and White women. *Gender & Society, 6,* 546–561.

Thompson, J.K., & Psaltis, K. (1988). Multiple aspects and correlates of body figure ratings: A replication and extension of Fallon and Roxin (1985). *International Journal of Eating Disorders, 7,* 813–817.

Vanderlinden, J., Vandereychen, W., Van Dyck, R., & Vertommen, H. (1993). Dissociative experiences and trauma on eating disorders. *International Journal of Eating Disorders, 13,* 187–193.

Waller, G., Hamilton, K., Rose, N., Sumra, J., & Baldwin, G. (1993). Sexual abuse and body image distortion in the eating disorders. *British Journal of Clinical Psychology, 32,* 350–352.

Wise, S., & Stanley, L. (1987). *Georgie Porgie: Sexual harassment in everyday life.* London: Pandora Press.

Wooley, S. (1994). Sexual abuse and eating disorders: The concealed debate. In P. Fallon, M. Katzman, & S. Wooley (Eds.), *Feminist perspectives on eating disorders.* New York: The Guilford Press.

Kathy Hotelling

An Integrated Prevention/Intervention Program for the University Setting

Until 1989, when *The Bulimic College Student: Evaluation, Treatment, and Prevention* (Whitaker & Davis, 1989) addressed the problem of bulimia nervosa among college students, scant literature existed regarding the prevention and treatment of eating disorders on college campuses. In that volume, Clark, Levine, and Kinney (1989) and Hotelling (1989) proposed models of prevention and treatment of eating disorders for higher education, and Sesan (1989b) described a campus-based program utilizing peer educators. In that same year, in another publication, Sesan (1989a) focused on female student athletes. Subsequently, some articles (Mann, et al. 1997; Martz, Graves, & Sturgis, 1997) and an unpublished dissertation (Babb, 1996) have featured college-based programs, but they, too, have been limited in number. Undoubtedly a major arena that specifically addresses and encourages campus programs for the prevention and treatment of eating disorders is not a single publication, but rather an annual conference that began in 1995 at Penn State: Eating Disorders on Campus: The Institutional Response. Each year this conference features keynote speakers and workshops that address educational and treatment programs at universities across the United States.

This chapter describes the multifaceted and integrated eating disorder program at Northern Illinois University (NIU). This program has evolved over the past 12 years through the commitment of many professionals and professionals-in-training who have comprised the University's Eating Disorder Task Force. Each year the efforts of the group have taken a slightly different emphasis, which has resulted in a broad-based program that is continually developing to take into account member interests and to meet the changing needs of the student body.

☐ Multidisciplinary Nature of the Eating Disorder Task Force

Prior to 1991, a handful of professional staff who treated students with eating disorders in the Counseling and Student Development Center and in the University

Health Service cooperated in treatment by obtaining releases of information from those students and communicating on the phone or through memos. It should be noted that these two departments are separate entities with different administrative structures, budgets, and campus locations. A few workshops on topics such as the signs and symptoms of eating disorders or helping a friend with an eating disorder were held annually in residence halls and sororities. There was, however, a growing sense among those involved in these efforts that a broad-based, coordinated effort was needed on campus to address the educational and treatment issues related to this problem. Eating disorders were widespread among the student population and certainly one or two staff members could not begin to address the educational needs of the campus community, to say nothing of providing treatment for those who would be identified with eating disorders as a result of such efforts. In 1991, the Eating Disorders Task Force was established and represented the commencement of a program based on a multidisciplinary approach to the problem of eating disorders. Over time the membership of the group has included (in addition to the original psychologist and family practice physician who worked together informally) various professionals who have an interest eating disorders: nutritionists, a psychiatrist, athletic trainers, an exercise physiologist, physical and health educators, an advisor to sororities and fraternities, recreation center staff, housing and food service staff, and counselors of student athletes. Student involvement has included athletes, nutrition majors, officers of the Panhellenic Council and the Student Dietetic Association, and graduate students associated with the professionals who attend. The changing nature of the group over the past seven years, the increased knowledg base of the members, and the changing needs of students have prompted the development of new ideas and a breadth to the program that otherwise would not be possible.

☐ Goals of the Eating-Disorder Task Force

The purpose of the Task Force is to address both the educational and treatment issues related to eating disorders on our campus. Specific goals include to: (1) educate key staff on campus (such as physicians, coaches, residence-hall staff, faculty in departments that have had a significant number of affected students) about eating disorders; (2) serve as a networking mechanism for campus staff and faculty interested in eating disorders; (3) establish a variety of services for prevention and treatment; (4) increase educational efforts for the university community, including planning and implementing Eating Disorder Awareness Week; (5) troubleshoot difficult situations with students suspected of having an eating disorder; (6) develop and implement protocols for the identification, referral, and treatment of those with eating disorders; (7) precipitate early identification and referral of those with eating disorders; and (8) coordinate care of individual students with eating disorders through formal meetings, called *eating disorder staffings* (see section on treatment).

☐ Philosophy of the Eating Disorder Task Force

This program is guided by the conviction of the professionals involved that individuals acting in isolation cannot affect the prevention of eating disorders or successfully resolve the behavioral and physical symptoms of eating disorders, to say nothing of the underlying issues. Consequently, each professional involved in the program, whether she or he provides educational programs or treatment, is an important team member working to reduce the incidence, prevalence, and effect of eating disorders on our campus. Whether it is the fitness expert educating students about the benefits of exercise and the risks of over-exercise, the dietitian speaking to students about the differences between disordered eating and eating disorders, or the psychologist lecturing about fostering positive body image, each contributes to the mission of the Task Force through dissemination of information germane to her or his discipline and role on campus.

There is also a strong commitment to coordinated and multidisciplinary treatment as vital to our efforts on behalf of students. Obviously eating disorders are psychiatric disorders that can have potentially severe, even fatal physical complications. Because of this, our philosophy is that it is unethical for mental health professionals to treat students with eating disorders if they are not under the care of a physician who knows about the existence of an eating disorder and is knowledgeable about the medical treatment of eating disorders. Waiting for the associated medical problems to become discernible to the eye is inappropriate; the physician needs to be involved from the beginning of treatment. Service at the Counseling Center can be, and on one occasion has been, denied to students with eating disorders who refuse to comply with physician assessment and treatment recommendations. Although this is a difficult stance to take, we are unwilling to collude with the denial that we believe such refusal signifies and with the physical damage, even death, that potentially could occur. Also, severe physical complications can compromise talk therapy because of the cognitive effects, for example, of starvation. Conversely, because eating disorders are psychiatric disorders, therapy must be part of the treatment; nutritional counseling or medical treatment alone or in combination with each other is not sufficient. Students who refuse therapy, however, cannot be and are not denied physician and nutrition services at the University Health Service. If a student refuses to follow recommendations for medical treatment, the health service physician attempts to manage potential medical complications and to connect the student to other resources within the community or his or her hometown to assist in that management.

Furthermore, the team approach encompasses the belief that nutritional education is best provided by a dietitian. Often physicians or mental health professionals assume that they can address the nutritional issues. The reality is that this information is not within those respective disciplines' competencies and, therefore, the information will not be addressed in the sustained and concentrated manner needed no matter what the knowledge level of the individual practitioners. Another important factor of the team approach is that each student with an eating disorder receives a similar message from each member of the team. This assists in breaking down the denial that is part of the eating disorder symptomology and thus advances the effects of psychotherapy. Also, it aids in the prevention of the "splitting" of caregivers that can occur when there is more than one professional treating an individual client.

Feminism also underlies the work of the Eating Disorder Task Force. Although there is a chair of the Task Force to set meeting schedules, send out mailings, and so forth, all members take responsibility for the work of the group by contributing ideas for initiatives, making decisions, and carrying out the details of the activities planned. An understanding of the role of societal expectations based on gender is infused throughout the work of the Task Force. For example, primary and secondary prevention efforts address the strong sociocultural underpinnings of eating disorders (sex-role conflict, media images of women, the beauty myth, lack of assertiveness, and so forth). These programs seek to empower women through information and skills that provide a basis for challenging cultural norms that contribute to the development of eating disorders. Psychological treatment also empowers women with eating disorders in similar ways and provides an environment wherein they can challenge those societal messages and develop ways of being in the world that are conducive to their relationships with others and to growth and health.

☐ Accomplishments of the Eating Disorder Task Force

The accomplishments of this group of committed individuals are impressive. A general knowledge and understanding of eating disorders exists among the Task Force members who represent different departments on campus, such as the Campus Recreation Center, Athletics, Housing and Dining Services, Family Consumer and Nutrition Sciences Department, University Programming and Activities, Health Service, the Counseling and Student Development Center, and so forth. This has produced a "ripple effect," that is, other staff and faculty associated with Task-Force members know about their involvement with the group, which has led to an increased awareness across campus and to improvements in the identification and referral of students with eating disorders. Consultation regarding students with eating disorders occurs much more frequently now than in the past and involves a wide range of professionals. Other accomplishments include expanded programming and services, the development of guidelines for evaluation and treatment, and the identification of students interested in learning about eating disorders for use in their future careers. Task-Force members have also been actively involved in sharing their experiences and knowledge with others through, for example, conference presentations, dissertation committees, and the distribution of over 400 copies of protocols for the identification and treatment of students with eating disorders (Hotelling & Liston, 1998) to interested professionals.

The specifics of the program encompass the three traditional levels of prevention: primary, secondary, and tertiary. Before proceeding with a description of the different aspects of our program, however, I must assert a word of caution. Several years ago I was a strong advocate of primary prevention on university campuses (Hotelling, 1989). Although we continue to provide primary prevention activities, the intervening years have tempered my belief in the potential impact of such efforts. Increasing numbers of students entering colleges have diagnosable eating disorders and may already have been treated and even hospitalized for these behaviors. The age of onset of eating disorders for many of these students was between 10 and 12 years. This observation is reinforced by the increasingly frequent calls I receive from nurses, counselors, and parents of elementary school and middle school children struggling with dieting, laxative abuse, vomiting, and other eating disorder–related symptomology. This has led me to believe that the primary prevention of eating disorders, in order to be most effective, must occur in elementary and middle schools, *not* on university campuses. It is at these ages that children are effected by many of the precipitating factors, such as cultural norms, that contribute to the development of eating disorders (see, e.g., Chapter 6). It is also true that eating disorders still can and do develop during students' college careers, partially in response to the developmental challenges of this period of life (Dickstein, 1989), and primary prevention should not be ignored in this arena. Hopefully, programmatic efforts such as those described here do avert the development of eating disorders for some individuals. Such efforts, however, need to be viewed realistically in terms of their effectiveness in averting the development of eating disorders in most traditional college-aged individuals.

☐ Primary Prevention on Campus

In primary prevention, the focus of intervention is targeting groups of "currently unaffected people for purposes of helping them to continue functioning in healthy ways, free from disturbance" (Coyne, 1987, p. 6). Of course, we must realize that "affected" students also attend primary prevention programs, partly in recognition of their need for the information being presented. Thus, an unanticipated result of primary prevention efforts is that these students often seek assistance for their problems.

Primary prevention efforts of the Task Force have addressed existing policies or practices that may inadvertently undermine health by focusing on weight loss and appearance. For example, through education of and consultation with staff responsible for athletics, weekly weigh-ins by all coaches of women athletes and weigh-ins of a dance performance squad have been eliminated. Also, an athletics policy now states: "A student-athlete's criteria for participation is based on overall physical health, not the absence of an eating disorder. Athletes with a suspected or identified eating disorder should be assured that such concern or identification will not be used as punishment to deny them athletic participation" (Hein, Michalski, Hotelling, & Liston, 1998, p. 47). Departments such as theater, dance, and athletics have requested educational sessions to help staff and faculty be supportive of and appropriate in their interactions with students who are identified as having an eating disorder. Although such consultation is sought for the purpose of learning how to deal with students with eating disorders (and thus could be seen as tertiary prevention), inevitably a discussion ensues about current departmental or individual practices (including advice, teasing, or other comments) that may contribute to the development of negative body image, unhealthy eating and exercising, and eating disorders. This, in turn, has resulted in changes that benefit all students—for example, weight reduction or gain not being commented upon if it is not germane to performance.

The Task Force works with various offices of the university to help them offer presentations that focus on mental, physical, and nutritional health and thereby encourage students to develop individual and social strengths. For example, staff at the Counseling and Student Development Center periodically offer one-time presentations and structured groups on self esteem, stress reduction, assertiveness, handling anger, body image, and similar topics with the primary goal of teaching students life skills that will increase their overall resilience.

These workshops are offered in residence halls, Greek houses, and classes, and to student organizations.

Programming during our annual Eating Disorder Awareness Week has been expanded to include topics that may benefit all students as well as help students who are at particular risk for the development of eating disorders. For example, daily seminars at noon and each evening have included the media's portrayal of women, body image, mothers and daughters, disordered eating or eating disorder, exercise, and factors in the development of eating disorders. Each year the Task Force sponsors one event that all women athletes and sorority members must attend. These offerings have included videotapes followed by a panel of team members and recovering students, a one-woman show, and a social-issue theater. Periodically programs for men have explored the attitudes and values they have toward women and relationships with women.

The Counseling and Student Development Center's homepage has a section devoted to eating disorders which also provides links to other sites about eating disorders. This website plays a role in both primary and secondary prevention. Another form of visual media that we began to use this year in primary prevention is "Barbie." An artist was commissioned to produce a life-sized Barbie on canvas that is displayed in different locations on campus and at various events; wherever displayed, we have observed that this depiction serves as an important consciousness-raising function.

The Campus Recreation Center has been very successful in integrating nutrition into their overall fitness programming. For example, nutrition options include a class designed for those interested in a healthy weight-loss program that combines both nutrition and fitness information to deal with the many factors involved in sensible and safe weight control. All personal training clients receive a nutrition consultation. Diet analysis, body composition analysis, and fitness assessments are offered alone or in combination with each other. "Hot topic" presentations focus on a variety of popular topics of interest to many: ergogenic aids, dairy products and enhancing physical fitness, dietary fat, protein in the diet, holiday dieting, creatine supplements, "bulking up," and exercise and fluid replacement. Graduate interns in nutrition present all topics, so not only is a service provided to the campus community, but also the graduate students receive training, supervision, and experience in primary prevention. Nutrition education is incorporated into the overall fitness program through other means also: in-service training for aerobics instructors, fitness weeks, question and answer bulletin boards, newsletters, and staff available for drop-in questions and information.

Another form of primary prevention is our involvement in the education of future dietitians, elementary school teachers, school administrators, counselors, health educators, and so forth. In classes and seminars, material is presented to challenge the current culture that glorifies slenderness and vilifies fat with the hope that information presented now will affect their interactions in the field with at risk students, clients, and other consumers.

☐ Secondary Prevention on Campus

The focus of secondary prevention is early identification and treatment of health problems (Caplan, 1964) and, indeed, prevention efforts of all kinds at universities serve as awareness campaigns that may lead to identifying those with clinical or subclinical eating disorders and encouraging them to seek prompt treatment. Task Force efforts in this regard have been varied. For example, we have used a variety of media to enhance awareness of eating disorders: electronic bulletin boards, public service announcements on cable television and in newspapers, television and radio interviews, displays across campus, and tables set up in high traffic areas in campus buildings. Utilizing the broadcast background of a counseling graduate student, the Task Force produced an 8-minute videotape that featured theater students portraying students with eating disorders and an affected boyfriend; this tape has been shown at wellness fairs and has provided the basis for class discussions. There is wide dissemination on campus of two brochures, one targeted toward participation in a support group for those with eating disorders [ANAD], (using the model of the National Association of Anorexia Nervosa and Associated Disorders Box 7, Highland Park, IL, 60035, 847-831-3438) and another for allies of those with eating disorders; both provide basic information about eating disorders and a bibliography. We target classes in majors that we know may attract students with eating disorders, such as the health-related fields, and also those in fields that prepare students who are likely to have contact with individuals at risk for developing eating disorders, such as education, nursing, dance, and so forth.

As noted previously, there has been a "ripple effect" from the Task Force members to others on campus, as evidenced by the frequency with which we serve as consultants (either by phone or in person) to coaches, faculty, peers, professional staff and secretaries in various offices, and significant others of those with eating disorders. These same individuals may be the ones who invite us to their departments, teams, or classes to speak. Questions often include how to confront a friend with an eating disorder, how to refer the person for treatment, and how to act around food when the affected person is present. A specific example of the circumstances that may bring about a consultation is a health-education professor reading the journal of a student who appears to have severe body image distortion and disordered eating. Another situation that has resulted in consultation is when the cleaning staff finds vomit on a regular basis in the bathroom of a residence hall floor.

In the near future, we will be consulting with the organizers and participants of an annual body-building contest; this was initiated because a student was hospitalized for medical complications caused by the diet used in preparation for competition. Providing a seminar regarding eating disorders to aerobics instructors at the Campus Recreation Center increases the likelihood that they will be able to identify participants who use exercise inappropriately or who have an eating disorder. Campus Recreation Center staff in general now notice when students "overuse" the facilities and have made interventions with the purpose of referring them for at least a medical examination, if not an eating disorders assessment. In another instance, a laboratory supervisor in an academic department referred to the Health Center a student who passed out while conducting an experiment. Suspecting that she had an eating disorder, he also asked the Counseling and Student Development Center for information about eating disorders. In this regard, Health Service clinical staff are educated as to the various symptomologies and physical findings suggesting an eating disorder, and now they routinely refer or consult with in-house physicians or nutritionists or the Counseling and Student Development Center as appropriate.

In 1996 we participated in the first National Eating Disorder Screening Project. At that time we utilized the suggested format of setting up several sessions that consisted of an educational presentation and videotape about eating disorders, followed by having participants complete a screening instrument (which was scored immediately so that feedback could be given to the individuals involved). Because of the limited draw to these sessions, since that time we have disseminated screening tools, instructions for scoring the questionnaire, and a list of referral sources to all attending the Eating Disorder Awareness Week events. This both encourages students to look at their own eating patterns and attitudes (but allows them not to do so if they do not wish to) and assists us in identifying and referring students with problems ranging from disordered eating to eating disorders. Through this method we reach over 600 students during this week alone, which is substantially more than the 25 students who attended the advertised "screenings" in 1996.

I have had the opportunity for several semesters to speak to a class for future middle school administrators on the development of networks and resources regarding student problems, especially in rural areas where it is very likely that a local "expert" is not available. The illustration that I use is how, when coming to Northern Illinois University, I established a network of resources in regard to eating disorders. Thus, in fulfilling the outcome desired by the professor of this class, I am also educating these future principals about eating disorders, a problem they will encounter during their tenure in middle school.

☐ Tertiary Prevention on Campus (Treatment)

The focus of tertiary prevention is treating a health problem once it has developed (Caplan, 1964) so as to eliminate the problem or prevent the problem from worsening. The existence of the Task Force has both contributed to the expansion of treatment components and to the coordination of the actual care of students with eating disorders. Through the addition of types and modalities of services over time, the development of protocols, and an eating disorder staff meeting (the staffing), a comprehensive, intensive, outpatient treatment program has been developed.

With the advent of the Task Force in 1991, an ANAD support group led by a counseling graduate student and a nutrition graduate assistant in the Health Service was added. A full-time psychiatrist also was hired in the Counseling and Student Development Center and Health Service that year in order to provide students with psychotropic medication when appropriate. In 1993 we began offering a 7-week structured psychoeducational group for women with bulimia; this group utilizes *The Road to Recovery,* a manual developed by the Toronto Hospital (Davis et al., 1989; it should be noted that their program has been revised and now includes videotapes and new materials. We continue to use the original format because of financial constraints.). Various time-limited, structured groups, such as Body Love, Binge Eating, Assertiveness Training, and Increasing Self Esteem, have been utilized as adjuncts to individual counseling. The availability of these groups has been dependent on the interests and skills of trainees and on the participation of other Counseling and Student Development Center staff members not on the eating disorder team.

The Counseling and Student Development Center primarily provides time-limited therapy, although each staff member treats a few students in a long-term modality. Thus, if chronicity and severity are extreme or if all eating disorder specialists have a full caseload, students with eating disorders are referred to off-campus practitioners, assuming that the student has insurance to pay for these services. Being referred off-campus does not preclude involvement in the structured groups and workshops, therapy groups, or the ANAD support group, all of which are offered by the Counseling and Student Development Center, nor does it preclude the services of physicians and nutritionists at the Health Service.

In general, the basic treatment for those with eating disorders includes therapy, physician monitoring, the ANAD group, and nutritional counseling. Other treatment options are added as appropriate. The existence of different treatment components and caregivers provides the student with several touchstones each week. This is especially important in that Counseling and Student Development Center policy, again based on budgetary considerations, prohibits more than one individual therapy session per week, unless there is an emergency. Also, students cannot participate in both individual and group therapy at the same time at the Counseling Center, but they can have individual counseling and attend structured groups concurrently. We have had some success in first treating a student in individual treatment and then moving her to a therapy group (such as Hope and Healing for abuse survivors, or a women's therapy group) after the eating disorder symptomology has been eliminated. This allows the student to deal in an intense manner with underlying issues such as abuse or relationships, in a peer group, which is a very appropriate arena in which to address those concerns. Sequencing therapy in this way also allows for optimal use of limited individual services. If the student has a relapse after referral to group, she then reenters individual therapy for a brief period to get control over the symptoms. This is similar to what we might do if a group member has a suicidal crisis and needs additional support for the duration of the crisis.

Part of the power of the availability of many treatment options is that the treatment program can be customized in terms of intensity for each student. For example, the nutritionist would offer the nutrition major who has an eating disorder information that she may already have; this same client, however, could benefit from the psychoeducational group that is co-led by a nutritionist and counselor, because the focus and context of the information presented is different in the group than in individual consultations. In reality, of course, treatment options in the outpatient setting also are determined by the students' class schedule (and, to a lesser degree, their work schedules) and, to some extent, their willingness to participate in certain modalities. Nonetheless, we attempt to provide as intensive an outpatient program as appropriate and as possible.

In 1993 the treatment providers on the Task Force organized monthly eating disorders staffings (meetings where the care of students with eating disorders is coordinated); within a year the frequency of the staffings was increased to occur biweekly to accommodate adequately the students whom we are collaboratively caring for. The multidisciplinary team includes myself (a licensed psychologist who is the director of the Counseling and Student Development Center), a family practice physician who has expertise in eating disorders, a psychiatrist, a registered dietician, and trainees in nutrition and psychology who directly provide services to students with eating disorders. Other individuals can include treating therapists, the athletic trainer, coaches, and residence hall personnel, any of whom might attend the staffing if a student with whom they are involved is discussed. Each student is asked to sign a release of information for the staffing and, therefore, is fully aware of who is in attendance at the staffing. The purpose of the staffing is to discuss the progress, compliance, and treatment dilemmas of those being treated. For a particular student, the caregivers may only "touch base" by sharing information, while for other students the team may actually devise or refine treatment approaches or strategies. Setting this regular time to coordinate treatment allows excellent, ongoing communication that is precluded if less formal communication is relied upon. We have found that students may share information about their symptoms and sometimes history differentially with their caregivers, especially in the early phase of treatment. This may be because of differing levels of comfort that the student has with individual caregivers, members of different disciplines emphasizing certain parts of histories more than others, or certain individuals pursuing information more aggressively or concretely than others. Thus, the staffing leads to a more comprehensive understanding of dynamics than would be possible otherwise, which provides the basis for joint treatment plnning and makes "splitting" of caregivers much more difficult than it was when only periodic contact occurred between practitioners. We are aware of how other team members work and easily can seek clarification if recommendations attributed to another on the team seem unlikely. The staffing also provides an important model of multidisciplinary cooperation for the trainees and provides a continuing education arena for all involved; participants, for example, may share relevant information that they recently read or experiences they had that increased their understanding of the conceptualization and treatment of eating disorders. In order for the staffing to be effective, attention to the following factors is important: A special release must be signed; there must be regular meetings with regular attendance; a systematic review of individuals needs to occur, with additional attention during crisis periods; and discussions need to be documented. A notebook is kept that has a staffing report for each student. Depending on the information shared at the staffing, the physician may add a note to the student's clinical chart at the Health Service.

A special note about student athletes with eating disorders is vital. To discuss the treatment and progress of affected student athletes, staffings include the athletic trainer, and, at times and with student permission, coaches. Communication between the physician and the trainer or coach occurs on a regular basis because the importance of thorough monitoring of the physical health of the affected student. If physical health is or might be compromised because of low weight or other medical complications attributable to the eating disorder, the physician, athletic trainer, student, and perhaps the coach draw up a contract to clearly state the limitations to be placed on practice or competition. The physician on the Task Force is also the head team physician for athletics, which has facilitated communication between Athletics Department and the Task Force.

On some occasions members of the treatment team have met with a student's parents to discuss the student's progress, to educate parents about eating disorders so as to encourage beneficial interaction around the topic, to answer questions, and to communicate the need for continued care. This approach has been a comfort to parents in that they know that a team of professionals is looking out for their daughter or son. It also has facilitated hospitalization if this has been necessary. In the beginning of our work together, the issue of informing parents of the medical complications of their child's eating disorder, without the permission of the student, arose in the team. Because of legal statutes and ethical standards regarding confidentiality and, practically speaking, because of the effect of such action on the treatment team's relationships with the student, this is not appropriate. Another issue that has been discussed is the removal from the university of students who do not comply with treatment recommendations. Because we are a state institution that complies with the Americans with Disabilities Act, such mandatory withdrawal from the university is illegal.

One of the early outcomes of the Task Force was the development of protocols that serve as a basis for understanding how each team member thinks about and treats the shared clients (Hotelling & Liston, 1998). These have been updated as necessary, and new sections have been added as other staff members develop guidelines, as in the recent addition of a Campus Recreation Center protocol. This set of guidelines was established to handle students whose health may be compromised by exercise or students suspected of overusing exercise as part of an eating disorder.

Professional Training About Eating Disorders on Campus

The Eating Disorder Task Force has utilized the predoctoral internship and practicum in psychology and the graduate program in nutrition both to train new professionals and to broaden service delivery. This established specialization in the predoctoral training program allows these psychology students the opportunity to develop an advanced knowledge of eating disorder prevention and treatment. Since 1991 we have had five interns who have chosen eating disorders as a specialty. Each entered the internship with a strong interest in the area of eating disorders, but the knowledge and experience of this group has varied considerably from year to year. This diversity in backgrounds has produced individual variations in the kind of primary and secondary interventions that the interns have implemented for our student body and for students in local school districts; for example, some interns have been especially interested in binge eating, whereas others have been interested in body image. Another important variation is seen in the methodology favored by the interns: For example, one intern used popular songs to demonstrate societal expectations of thinness and beauty and of societal acceptance of disordered eating. Thus, not only has the specialization program in eating disorders increased intern knowledge about eating disorders and intern experience in the types of intervention possible, but also the student body has profited from the specific interests and services that the interns provided during their year on campus.

Although the opportunity for a psychology or social work practicum student to specialize in eating disorders is much more limited and less structured than the intern specialization, the student who is in the early stages of training and experience does receive valuable exposure to this clinical area. The extent of each student's participation has been dependent on hours available on campus, the flexibility of schedules, and the requirements of individual academic programs. Nevertheless, opportunities have included training and experience in facilitating various groups, counseling individuals with eating disorders, participating in the Eating Disorder Task Force and in the staffing, consulting with concerned others, and presenting workshops for public-school children and college students.

Selected nutrition graduate students can receive practical experience in Task Force activities through participation in several arenas: the Campus Recreation Center, the Health Service, Housing and Dining Services, or the Counseling and Student Development Center. Responsibilities may include assisting in the organization, publicity, and activities of Eating Disorder Awareness Week, making "hot topic" presentations at the Campus Recreation Center, providing individual nutritional services to students who present with a variety of concerns at the Health Service, co-leading the psychoeducational group at the Counseling and Student Development Center, or writing articles for the student newspaper. Students who provide direct service at the Health Service come to the staffing. This past year I began offering a one-credit workshop in eating disorders through the dietetics department. This course is primarily for graduate students in nutrition, although I encourage students in other disciplines, such as psychology and counseling, to participate, which adds to the cross-disciplinary nature of the course. This course was requested by the dietetics department as a supplement to their course offerings to raise awareness and interest in eating disorders as an area of specialization for training, through the assistantships in the Health Service and internships in the Campus Recreation Center, and future practice. In this course, as well as a counseling graduate course regarding eating disorders that has been offered twice, Eating Disorder Task Force members share their knowledge and expertise with the graduate students.

☐ Questions and Directions

There is no question that the Task Force has raised awareness of eating disorders on our campus and has created options both for those students who are at risk and for those who are seeking treatment. A troubling question remains: How effective is our work? Like many practitioner-based programs, it seems impossible to find the time to evaluate the impact of our program in a scientific manner, although a physician at the Health Service recently started working with medical records and quality assurance personnel to design some outcome studies there. Our impressions about the effectiveness of our work are based on the observations of Task Force members and the feedback that we receive from students, parents, teachers, coaches, and others who have participated in some aspect of our efforts. Participants report that the programming of the Task Force elicits thought and introspection about beliefs about food and weight inherited in part from their families, differential societal expectations based on gender, the role of the media in promulgating fatism and weight-loss obsessions, and so forth. They state that their awareness, for example, of the bias and influence of the media has been heightened, and this affects whether they just accept information at face value; they now view television advertisements and read magazines with a discerning eye.

Programming results in calls from individuals wanting to help others and in students seeking help. Clients in treatment report that the awareness that they have so many individuals looking out for their welfare is encouraging and supportive. Many clients change their eating disordered behaviors. So the feedback we receive from different constituency groups is very positive and appreciative of our efforts to raise awareness and to change attitudes that are harmful and may predispose, precipitate, or perpetuate an eating disorder.

On the other hand, resources do not allow us to present as many primary and secondary prevention efforts as are needed. Nor do we have the resources to always provide treatment in a timely manner or to the degree that we know is needed (given that we must refer many students out after assessment for therapy). For example, more of an emphasis on body image in both prevention and treatment is needed. We do not sufficiently challenge the weightism of our society (Steiner-Adair, 1994; see also Chapter 6). We could offer other kinds of groups or offer others on a regular basis. As we do more outreach, a presence is acknowledged, which leads to more demand for services, which becomes increasingly difficult to meet.

☐ Conclusion

An important component of the Eating Disorder Task Force is that scarce resources from one department or from one "eating-disorder person" are not unduly drained. Numerous individuals, representing many offices and professional disciplines have worked diligently for more than a decade to make a difference in this particular area of concern. This type of program represents a significant commitment on the part of the participating university departments and the individuals involved, but it is a shared responsibility and is a worthwhile and rewarding endeavor. Our efforts benefit both professional staff and the primary recipients of our services, students. Prevention is being approached from many different angles. Organizing a campus-wide series of events during Eating Disorder Awareness Week receives its impetus and attention to detail from a group of individuals, the Task Force members, and not an individual. Caregivers also work as part of a group and are less likely to feel isolated and demoralized, because of joint decision making and support from other professionals. These interconnections that are central to the way the work of the Eating Disorder Task Force has been accomplished also are focal to the feminist issues that underlie eating disorders and the prevention and treatment of those disorders. As Steiner-Adair (1994) and others have repeatedly reminded us, to work in the area of eating disorders necessitates challenging the values of our society and thus is political work. Women value their connections with each other, in fact rely on them. I hope that the model of cooperation and feminism that the Task Force work embodies sends several messages to the students on whose behalf we are working. They have a support network in the team. They can create that type of support in other parts of their lives. We all are working to provide the groundwork for the development of their potential for academic and interpersonal success by challenging societal standards and values.

☐ References

Babb, E. J. (1996). *A qualitative investigation of eating disorder programs on selected college campuses.* Unpublished doctoral dissertation, University of Virginia, Charlottesville.

Caplan, G. (1964). *Principles of preventive psychiatry.* New York: Basic Books.

Clark, L. V., Levine, M. P., & Kinney, N. E. (1989). A multifaceted and integrated approach to the prevention, identification, and treatment of bulimia on college campuses. In L. C. Whitaker & W. N. Davis (Eds.), *The bulimic college student: Evaluation, treatment, and prevention* (pp. 257–298). New York: Haworth Press.

Coyne, R. K. (1987). *Primary preventive counseling.* Muncie, IN: Accelerated Development.

Davis, R., Dearing, S., Faulkner, J., Jasper, K., Olmsted, M., Rice, C., & Rockert, W. (1989). *The road to recovery.* Toronto, Ontario: The Toronto Hospital.

Dickstein, L. J. (1989). Current college environments: Do these communities facilitate and foster bulimia in vulnerable students? In L. C. Whitaker & W. N. Davis (Eds.), *The bulimic college student: Evaluation, treatment, and prevention* (pp. 107–133). New York: Haworth Press.

Hein, A. A., Michalski, S., Hotelling, K., & Liston, L. K. (1998). Athletic guidelines. In K. Hotelling & L. K. Liston (Eds.), *Guidelines for the outpatient management of individuals with eating disorders in the university setting* (pp. 47–50). DeKalb, IL: Counseling and Student Development Center.

Hotelling, K. (1989). A model for addressing the problem of bulimia on college campuses. In L. C. Whitaker & W. N. Davis (Eds.), *The bulimic college student: Evaluation, treatment, and prevention* (pp. 241–255). New York: Haworth Press.

Hotelling, K., & Liston, L. K. (Eds.). (1998). *Guidelines for the outpatient management of individuals with eating disorders in the university setting.* DeKalb, IL: Counseling and Student Development Center.

Mann, T., Nolen-Hoeksema, S., Huang, K. Burgard, D., Wright, A., & Hanson, K. (1996). Are two interventions worse than none? Joint primary and secondary prevention of eating disorders in college females. *Health Psychology, 16,* 1–11.

Martz, D. M., Graves, K. D., & Sturgis, E. T. (1997). A pilot peer-leader eating disorders prevention program for sororities. *Eating Disorders: The Journal of Treatment and Prevention, 5,* 294–308.

Sesan, R. (1989a). Eating disorders and female athletes: A three-level intervention program. *Journal of College Student Development, 30,* 568–570.

Sesan, R. (1989b). Peer education: A creative resource for the eating disordered college student. In L. C. Whitaker & W. N. Davis (Eds.), *The bulimic college student: Evaluation, treatment and prevention* (pp. 221–240). New York: Haworth Press.

Steiner-Adair, C. (1994). The politics of prevention. In P. Fallon, M. A. Katzman, & S. C. Wooley (Eds.), *Feminist perspectives in eating disorders* (pp. 381–394). New York: Guilford Press.

Whitaker, L. C., & Davis, W. N. (Eds.). (1989). *The bulimic college student: Evaluation, treatment, and prevention.* New York: Haworth Press.

CHAPTER 14

Brenda Alpert Sigall

The Panhellenic Task Force on Eating Disorders: A Program of Primary and Secondary Prevention for Sororities

Body image, weight and shape concerns amongst girls and women occur so widely that they have been termed a "normative discontent" (Rodin, Silberstein, and Streigel-Moore, 1985). Multiple studies have confirmed the high prevalence of body-weight and body-shape preoccupation as well as eating disorders (Feingold & Mazzella, 1998; Rosen, 1990). There is considerable evidence of their frequency and seriousness on college campuses (Harris, 1995; Klemchuck, Hutchinson, & Frank, 1990; Mintz & Betz, 1988; Shisslak, Crago, & Estes, 1995). In a prospective study, Streigel-Moore, Silberstein, Frensch, & Rodin (1989) documented an increase in disordered eating symptoms among students during their first year of college. The growing awareness of the scope of the problem has resulted in the development and recommendation of multifaceted models for treatment and prevention (Clark, Levine, & Kinney, 1989; Hotelling, 1989). The conference entitled Eating Disorders on Campus: The Institutional Response has been held annually since 1995, exemplifying the proliferation of interest and efforts on campuses across the country.

Several studies (Crandall, 1988; Kurtzman, Yager, Landsverk, Wiesmeier, & Bodurka 1989; Meilman, von Hippel, & Gaylor, 1991; Schulken, Pinciaro, Sawyer, Jensen, & Hoban, 1997) have identified sororities as a high risk population within the campus. Crandall (1988) described both the social contagion factor in bulimic behaviors and the power of conformity to group norms in sororities in the maintenance of disordered eating patterns. Schulken et al. (1997), in a study of 627 sorority women, reported that they exhibited greater fear of fat, body dissatisfaction, weight preoccupation, and concern with dieting than nonsorority college women included in other studies.

The Panhellenic Task Force on Eating Disorders, its creation, development, and management has in every way been a joint effort of the author and Patricia Preston. For giving life to our design with their energy and commitment, I would like to thank the members of the task force.

Prevention efforts have met with limited success. In their extensive study with middle-school girls, Killen et al. (1993) found that curriculum intervention aimed at healthy weight management resulted in increased knowledge about eating disorders but no differences in eating attitudes or behaviors, a finding echoed by other researchers. Levine, Smolak, and Schermer (1996), evaluating the effects of a media literacy curriculum administered to fourth and fifth graders, found a moderate increase in knowledge and some shift in attitudes, but no changes in behavior. Studies conducted on university campuses similarly yielded negative or inconsistent results. Franko (1998), in a small pilot study of college women, introduced a curriculum intervention and found improvements in attitude but no changes in disturbed eating behaviors. Possible explanations for the failure to achieve desired changes included the pervasiveness of weight concerns and disordered eating behaviors and the time-limited exposure (one or a few presentations) to the intervention.

A number of other prevention models have emerged that are of particular interest here. Piran (1995, 1996), Shisslak and Crago (1994), and Steiner-Adair and Purcell (1996) have pointed to the importance of involving students themselves in the process of education, consciousness raising, and change. Piran's (1998) successful work in the Toronto Ballet School rests on certain critical features. Students' knowledge that is anchored in their life experiences, and which is discovered and shared through discussion with each other, is used in those students' interventions to improve school policies and atmosphere.

The impact of peers on attitudes and behaviors also has been a subject of study in the field of eating disorders. Levine, Smolak, and Hayden (1994) and Nichter and Vuckovic (1994) found that the high frequency of diet- and weight-related talk among friends seemed to reinforce the thinness ideal and eating disturbances. Levine, Smolak, Moodey, Shuman, and Hessen (1994) also have reported that girls' weight-management techniques are predictable from their perceptions of their friends' weight-management techniques. There is evidence that in college women social comparison is related to body dissatisfaction (Stormer & Thompson, 1996), feeling fat (Streigel-Moore, McAvay, & Rodin, 1986), bulimia and drive for thinness (Stormer & Thompson, 1996). Paxton, Schutz, Wertheimer, and Muir (1996) observed that adolescents exhibited behaviors regarding dieting, weight loss, and body dissatisfaction that resembled their friends and reflected group attitudes and norms.

Paxton (1996) posited that given the power of the group, as revealed by all of these studies, friendships may have the potential for exerting a positive influence if the group was educated toward healthier attitudes and behaviors and if the value of selecting and associating with peers with healthier views were promoted. In this vein, Huon (1994) had used small-group peer discussions, which did produce positive change in dieting attitudes among college women. Sesan (1989) recommended using peers as educators to provide workshops on eating disorders to a campus community. Martz, Graves, & Sturgis (1997) trained peers as leaders of a primary and secondary prevention program in sororities. This was a pilot study of 1 month's duration that did not yield predicted outcomes, but the limited time and the small sample may have restricted the probability of finding the desired effects.

This chapter describes a model that relies on peer-based interventions and developed as an outreach to sororities on a large college campus. Beginning in 1993, the author and a colleague, Patricia Preston, both experienced mental-health providers on campus, felt the need to intervene more intensively with the Greek community. Despite multiple educational presentations to sorority houses and consultations with the Panhellenic Association, sorority presidents' association, and individual sorority-house boards, the incidence of disordered eating and weight and shape preoccupation did not seem to change. Although the reactions to presentations were favorable, the unchanged incidence indicated a lack of carry-over effects and no preventative benefit. Rather than continue our time-limited presentations and crisis response mode, a radically different approach was envisioned. In this model, interventions would be ongoing and systematic, thus maximizing the opportunities for successful outcome. During the preliminary stage of our planning, the author became aware of a similarly constructed program, Sorority Education for Lifetime Fitness (SELF) on another campus (Ousley, 1993, personal communication), which helped guide the development of our format.[1]

☐ The Panhellenic Task Force on Eating Disorders

The model involved the creation of a permanent task force, made up of representatives from each sorority, who carried out within their sororities a program for the prevention of body image problems, unhealthy dieting and eating disorders. The peer-centered prevention program addressed the following issues:

- Body image: cultural myths and messages that impact women's feelings about their bodies; media portrayal of women; acceptance of individual differences in size and shape; ways to enhance body acceptance and improve body image
- Healthy eating and weight: dangers of dieting and deprivation; contributions of heredity in weight and shape determination; proper nutrition and normal eating and their importance to well-being; moderate, nonexcessive exercise as a component of good health
- Eating and emotions: the relationship of food and feelings; ways in which food is used to deal with emotions
- Self-esteem: Valuing nonappearance and non–weight-related aspects of self; assessing and appreciating personal strengths; developing interests and skills
- Eating disorders: signs, symptoms, risks and consequences; suggestions for helping oneself and helping a friend; treatment resources and recovery process.

The guiding principles for the Panhellenic Task Force on Eating Disorders (PTFED) were to involve students, provide ongoing programming, work towards changing the norms of the community, and create a permanent and collaborative prevention structure.

☐ Student Involvement

The sororities themselves would become involved in acknowledging, understanding, and solving the problems. It appeared that most of the sorority leaders knew that body image and eating disorders existed in their houses. Not surprisingly, however, these problems were shrouded in secrecy and shame. By involving every sorority in the task force, it was hoped that as a community they could take the issues out of the shadows, talk openly about their common existence, and work together to address them. Owning the problem was the first step. Taking responsibility for dealing with it would be the next. It was hoped that this method of active participation would result in a more dynamic process than seemed to flow from the standard authority/speaker to passive recipient/listener modality. This approach is similar in concept to the participatory model discussed by Piran (1998), which requires involving students in the collective acquisition of knowledge through dialogue and empowering them to bring about change through systemic interventions.

☐ Continuous Programming

Given the disappointing results of the previously mentioned one-shot interventions, we sought to introduce an education and awareness paradigm that would be woven into the fabric of sorority life. Although speakers, workshops, films, and so forth would continue to be offered, they would be but a part of a permanent structure. Representatives who were educated about the issues would provide a presence in the sororities that reflected knowledge, healthy attitudes, and positive behaviors. Information would be integrated into the sorority houses through resource centers, announcements, bulletin boards, commentary at routine sorority meetings, spontaneous or planned group discussions, awareness of relevant on- or off-campus activities, with the opportunity to participate in or to become activists through local or national programs to which representatives draw attention.

☐ System Change

In addition to changing individuals' knowledge, attitudes, and behavior, a primary goal of the program was to affect the norms of the community. Piran (1996) points to systemic interventions as a critical part of her prevention work in the residential dance school. Affecting the norms of a community is a daunting task, but one that seems imperative in dealing with problems that flow in part from cultural attitudes, mores, and biases (Gordon, 1990). Without consciousness raising about sociocultural messages, sororities like most institutions reinforce the prescribed value, whether it be thinness, dieting, or binge eating (Crandall, 1988). Our objective was to introduce information, stimulate dialogue, and encourage involvement with the relevant issues. By educating sororities about the risks and consequences of disordered eating and weight preoccupation, and facilitating critical thinking about media messages and images, we hoped to begin to shift the norms in the sororities regarding what was acceptable and desirable. A long-term goal was that the sororities would become agents for prevention rather than reinforcers of negative cultural messages.

☐ Permanent Prevention Structure

Our goal was to create a permanent structure within the university that was dedicated to the prevention of body image problems and eating disorders and, specifically, to do so in collaboration with campus administrators. In this process we were naming and describing the problem, and officials in the administration were being educated about its existence. By supporting the formation of the task force as an institutional structure, the university acknowledges and owns the problem, much as the sororities do through their representative participation.

The first step in developing PTFED was to meet with the campus Greek life administrators to propose the program and seek institutional approval and sponsorship. Included in these discussions were relevant information about body image and eating disturbances and observations of problems occurring in the sororities. The task force model was described, including its key concepts of student involvement, ongoing programming, and systemic change, and an overview of why these principles might result in a more successful intervention. The administrators were receptive and granted their support. They then directed us to student leaders who would be crucial liaisons to the Greek community. We met, assessed needs, planned, and set goals. The Panhellenic Association adopted the task force as a part of its formal programming.

The mission of the task force, as set forth in its official description is:

1. To prevent the development of body-image problems and eating disorders by increasing understanding and awareness of unhealthy culturally prescribed standards of size and shape for women, harmful dieting practices, and the damaging emphasis on appearance as a measure of self-worth.
2. To enhance awareness in sororities of eating disorders and to provide representatives with appropriate guidelines for offering information, support, and evaluation/treatment referrals for house members who are struggling with these problems.

This bimodal mission reflects the intention of the task force to be a program of primary and secondary prevention.

Membership of the task force is constituted by two elected or appointed representatives from each sorority house. Members are asked to serve for a minimum of 1 full academic year, with the invitation to serve longer, as some have. It is recommended that each team have one older and one younger student. This has a two-fold advantage. First, representatives relate to two age cohorts in their houses. Second, it increases the probability of continuity on the task force: If a senior graduates, the younger representative continues and is able to guide and help integrate the replacement representative on her team.

Leadership for the task force is provided by three of the representative and the two founding clinicians. Forming an executive board, this group oversees the functioning of the task force and assumes responsibility for its operation. Input, however, is sought continually from the whole membership for direction, programming, and focus. The task force seeks to make the needs of the houses, as reflected through their representatives, central to its agenda. Also, we recognize that it is the students, not the professionals, who have the capacity to integrate the task force into the sororities and make it vital and credible.

An early benefit of the participatory model occurred in our 2nd year of operation. At the initiative of several students, the PTFED was given a seat on the Panhellenic Cabinet, the governing body that oversees and coordinates sorority functioning. This gave us increased visibility and power in the Greek community. In keeping with our philosophy of ownership and responsibility, this cabinet post is held by one of the task force student leaders, giving us a direct liaison with the Panhellenic leadership.

Recruitment and selection of the representatives is an important and evolving process for the task force. Our current procedure is described here:

☐ Recruitment

Sororities

At a full house meeting, current representatives review the task force mission, workings, and responsibilities of representatives. A recruitment flyer (Appendix A) is distributed that fully articulates this information, including a clause that addresses attitudes and behaviors required for participation:

> This is *not* an eating disorders support group. If you have experienced these problems, it is expected that you are at a level of recovery where you are not actively struggling with eating disordered behaviors, and you are making a conscious attempt to accept yourself and others on the basis of qualities not connected to weight and size.

In addition to the recruitment flyer, an application form (Appendix B) is distributed. This form asks for identifying information, a brief explanation of interest in the position, and a signed statement that the person is prepared to make a 1 year commitment and handle sensitive information in a trusted manner.

Panhellenic Association

The Panhellenic Cabinet member solicits the assistance of the organization in communicating the importance of the position and appropriate reasons for participation. Also, a PTFED student leader attends the annual sorority presidents retreat held at the start of the academic year. She speaks to the group about the task force, its purpose, its functioning, and the need for house representatives.

☐ Selection

The planned next phase in the process is for the executive board to review the applications, set up brief in-person interviews, and select our full complement of house representatives. Often, however, the sororities present us with representatives before the interviews have actually taken place. In the beginning, we were met with a number of recurring problems. First, representatives were sometimes women with anorexia or bulimia, who thought the task force would be a support group for eating disorders. Second, representatives sometimes idealized thinness, restraint, and exercise and expected and wanted the task force to support the cultural emphasis on fitness and fat avoidance. Third, some representatives were fulfilling a sorority activity requirement and had no real interest in the task force mission.

Over the years, we have refined our recruitment and selection process, and these problems have decreased. We hypothesize that this has been a function of increased visibility of the PTFED and concomitant understanding of what it is and what it is not. We continue to work to improve our functioning in this area.

As with any participatory model, our work can only be as good as our student members, thus our desire to attract women who will be committed, passionate, and energetic.

☐ Training

Part of the responsibility for the effectiveness of our representatives lies with the professional leadership and their ability to provide good training. Formal training sessions are held at the beginning of each academic year and encompass the following:

1. History and organization of the task force is presented, including goals, responsibilities and activities.
2. Ground rules, including confidentiality, attendance and acceptance of responsibility, are discussed. Given the sensitive nature of the problems that representatives encounter in their houses, we ask that no names be used in group discussion. Inevitably, however, descriptions of situations sometimes suggest identification to some members in the room. We, therefore, operate with the same rules of confidentiality that one would use in a therapy group.
3. Information about eating disorders, weight, dieting, and body dissatisfaction is given, including their cultural context. The particular manifestations of these problems on college campuses are addressed. A film segment is used to stimulate small-group discussion and dialogue.
4. Guidance for approaching a friend with a problem is given with the aid of written case studies and role playing. Representatives are trained to offer help with care and concern and take care of themselves in the process.
5. A manual describing the task force and containing articles, handouts, resources for referral, the task force membership directory, and evaluation forms is distributed at the training sessions. These manuals serve as the representatives' handbook for functioning in their positions.
6. An initial group project is worked on that reflects the learning and dialogue that has occurred in the sessions. For example, representatives construct posters illustrating relevant issues that they take with them to put up in their houses. These posters are the start-up for the creation of in-house resource centers (described here subsequently). This activity has the value of engaging the new representatives in a hands-on way, promoting personal involvement as well as group interaction.
7. The first task of representatives who conclude training is to introduce themselves and the task force to their houses at their next regular sorority meeting.

This formal training is supplemented informally through additional handouts and discussion of pertinent issues as they arise in the course of the year. Professional leaders are vital to the integrity of the task force as they serve as educators and as links to the treatment and prevention communities.

☐ Roles and Responsibilities

The heart of the program is in the roles and responsibilities of the representatives. With some overlap, items 1 through 3 and 4 and 5 below constitute, respectively, the primary and secondary prevention components of the program. It is expected that each rep will:

1. Be a role model in her sorority, promoting healthy attitudes about self and body image. Assuming principles of social learning theory (Bandura, 1977), it is anticipated that the posture of the representatives vís a vís attitudes and behaviors associated with weight and shape can facilitate the promotion of healthier, less stereotypic house mores.

2. Provide information and resources. Representatives are encouraged to reproduce and share all knowledge and materials acquired through the task force with their houses and to supplement them with items of interest that they seek and find independently. Each representative is required to set up a resource center in her house with information, flyers, announcements of events, and resources for consultation and treatment. The nature of the center is left up to the discretion and creativity of the individual representative and her assessment of her sorority's needs.

3. Plan and present educational programs. In addition to the ongoing funneling of knowledge and integration of countercultural messages into their houses, each representative has two formal programming requirements. The first is to plan one structured event per year, one per semester if possible. Events might be lectures, films, panel discussions, peer presentations, joint sorority or sorority-fraternity discussions, body-image activities, and so forth. Houses are encouraged to participate in national programs, such as the Eating Disorders Awareness and Prevention Media Advocacy Campaign (a structured program of assessing and giving feedback to media advertisers). The second requirement is for the representative to coordinate her house's participation in Eating Disorders Awareness Week (EDAW). Since PTFED's inception, EDAW has been a focal point of Spring-semester activities. The person power of the task force, in fact, has been critical to the success of EDAW on the campus. Task force members create events and help in the production and distribution of flyers, posters, and educational materials across the campus. They have held information fairs, conducted an awareness ribbon campaign, and assisted in the organization of feature events, such as nationally known speakers, dramatists, film showings, panels, and so forth, to which they have facilitated record campus audience turnouts of as many as 600 students. The task force also has helped organize the National Eating Disorders Screening Project on campus. Publicizing our work during EDAW serves as another teaching tool for the students as they think through and articulate the issues being addressed. By giving accurate and corrective information to newspaper reporters and television and radio programmers, the representatives are operationalizing one of our primary objectives, that is, to counter unhealthy media messages with more positive ones.

4. Offer support to members of her sorority. A major function of our representatives is to be identified as people who understand body image and disordered eating problems and who can be a resource for support and assistance. During regular task force meetings, representatives are invited to share feelings about situations of concern in their houses. The group helps formulate a plan for responding to these problems and gives support to the representative.

5. Act as a liaison to campus mental health professionals. Representatives do consult with clinicians and work with them to make appropriate referrals or

accompany a sorority sister to the clinician's office, if she desires. Often, clients come for treatment without the representative's knowledge but as a result of a task force function that informed the client about eating disorders or about available campus resources.

As a result of some problems encountered, we learned that we needed to articulate what was *not* a representative's role or responsibility:

1. Representatives do not try to diagnose eating disorders or body image problems.
2. Representatives do not provide counseling. Anyone needing or seeking help should be referred to campus mental health providers.
3. Representatives should not administer questionnaires or surveys designed to detect eating disorders or body-image problems. Such instruments are very sensitive, can cause distress, and are designed to be administered and interpreted by trained professionals, in keeping with professional ethical guidelines and university regulations.

☐ Challenges in Implementation

As with any theory, this one is easier to write than apply. The parameters of the real work of the college campus do not fit neatly into a preconceived model. Working in an institutional structure over which we have no control presents unexpected obstacles. Some of the major problems encountered, not heretofore mentioned, are described, in this section. Wherever possible, the solution found, attempted, or envisioned is indicated.

Continuity

One serious problem that arose early on was that of shifting membership. In a program that relies on training and acquired knowledge, it is difficult to be faced routinely with new members. Our model involves a minimum 1-year tenure for representatives, beginning in the Fall semester. The sorority calendar does not fit with the two-semesters-equal-a-year formula. Sororities may hold elections midyear, in April, or so forth. At these times, positions change. Our efforts to obtain a year-long commitment have met with mixed results. A new solution being tested involves having the Greek life administrators work with the Panhellenic Association to have PTFED representatives exempted from the normal calendar cycle. The task force representative would be defined as in a different category of office from other sorority positions.

Black Sororities' Noninvolvement

Although we have ethnic diversity among our representatives, the Black sororities, who operate under a separate umbrella organization, have opted not to participate on the task force. They do not see eating disorders and body image problems as priorities, although, as clinicians, we see increasing numbers of African American clients presenting with these problems. We will continue our outreach to these groups, but thus far we have been unsuccessful in our attempts to gain their interest.

Fraternities' Noninvolvement

Although the original concept for the task force included fraternity participation, these organizations were not interested in the program. Ultimately, we believe we must increase understanding and awareness among men to successfully bring about change for individual women and within the system. On a very limited scale, our efforts have included outreach to the fraternities. In the coming year, for the first time, we have plans to work programmatically with them. The campus fraternity advisor has expressed interest in our work and will join with us to reach the fraternity community.

Membership Problems

Recruiting and selecting representatives who were appropriate to our mission was a challenge and is addressed in a previous section.

Attendance

Attendance at meetings has been a recurring problem. In addition to the normal demands of student life, such as academic pressures, social commitments, and so forth we must compete with the very considerable requirements of sorority participation. The sorority calendar is a busy one, necessitating members' presence at many routine and special functions. As a result, meeting attendance sometimes suffers. If one member of a team is present, the problem is manageable, although certainly not ideal. When a house is totally unrepresented, we must follow up individually with them to bring them on board with whatever they missed. A solution to this problem is enforcement of mandatory attendance. As a cabinet-level Panhellenic function, attendance is required, with nonattendance resulting in the imposition of fines to houses. We have not employed this policy but intend to in the future.

Another attendance problem has been representatives sending substitutes in their place, when they cannot make a meeting. This is the normal operating procedure with all other sorority positions. Clearly, this is not acceptable for our work, given the necessity for training, knowledge, group cohesiveness, and confidentiality adherence. This problem has significantly diminished over the years, but we do have to revisit our policy in this regard periodically.

Greek Life Administration Support

Greater involvement from the institutional authorities is needed to support our mission and operational procedures. As noted in the section on continuity, there is movement in that direction.

Financial Resources

PTFED is given a budget of approximately $200 by the Panhellenic Association. Small contributions come from the counseling center and from the health center, with some additional support for EDAW activities from the Maryland Association for Anorexia Nervosa and Bulimia and other campus departments. The need for more funding is currently under discussion with Panhellenic and the Greek-life administration. One proposal, which fits with our philosophy of sorority involvement, ownership, and responsibility, is for each sorority to give financial support to PTFED. With 16 sororities, even a nominal amount per house could amount to a substantial contribution to our operating budget.

☐ Outcome and Evaluation

We have not conducted a formal evaluation of the outcome of the task force as a prevention intervention. Our information about its effectiveness comes from evaluations filled out by our representatives at the end of each year since 1993 and evaluations of house events collected in 1997 and 1998.

Representative Evaluations

All evaluations are anonymous. Questions are asked about training, the experience of being a representative, and perceived impact of their office on their sorority. Suggestions for additions or changes in the task force are solicited. Based on this feedback, our impressions are that

1. Representativess had very positive feelings about being on the task force. They indicated that they were challenged and had learned a lot and felt that they were part of something useful and important.
2. Media awareness, educational handouts, and information about approaching a friend were highly valued training components.
3. All representatives reported feeling that they had a positive impact on their sororities as resources for support, information, and referral for individuals with disordered-eating problems, and as facilitators of positive change in group norms. Reps felt that they raised awareness about unhealthy dieting and damaging cultural messages. They reported some behavioral changes in diet and fat talk and dieting practices. For example, prior to the existence of the task force, whole houses were known to go on commercial diets, such as NutriSystem or Weight Watchers. Cooks were ordering prepared packaged foods from these companies in huge lots. The task force, working with the Panhellenic Association, was successful in discouraging these practices. Representatives are encouraged to work with cooks to plan healthy, satisfying meals that are not diet-centered. Several houses have initiated policies that are aimed at diminishing fat and calorie commentary during meals. "Don't Yuk My Yum" is the slogan banner decorating one sorority house's dining room wall.

4. Changes suggested include a monthly newsletter to all sororities, more funds for programming, more group interaction, and more task force visibility on campus. More help with in-house programming frequently is requested. Of interest, long-term representatives (more than 1 year of service) indicated that their effectiveness increased over time. They reported having more confidence commensurate with accumulated knowledge, skills, and experience. With more confidence, they were able to be more assertive in introducing system interventions and talking with peers with problems. This feedback is certainly not surprising, but it is important data for us as it comes directly out of the students' experiences. It should be helpful to us in enlisting the support of campus leadership in pushing for our need for continuity.

House Event Evaluations

Unfortunately, few events were evaluated. Those that were generally were well received and recipients indicated benefiting from them. In particular, students who participated in the Eating Disorders Prevention and Awareness Media Advocacy Campaign reported that it was a good learning experience and they were excited to be a part of a national effort. It is our intention to firm up the evaluation system so that we have more feedback in the future.

Representatives' Personal Change

There has been an additional and unexpected outcome of PTFED, a two-tiered effect. Our goal was to impact the sorority community. Our method was to use sorority members as representatives of that community who would connect us with the houses. What we did not anticipate was that the task force representatives themselves have become a group of young women with heightened feminist sensibilities and awareness of body image and disordered eating issues. We have been gratified by this development. A number of the representatives have gone on to graduate school with the intention of working in the field of treatment or prevention of eating disorders.

☐ Conclusion

The Panhellenic Task Force on Eating Disorders is a work in progress. As noted in this chapter, policies have evolved as we have responded to unforeseen obstacles and new ideas leading us in unplanned directions.

Our commitment to sorority ownership remains strong as we observe the experiences reported by our representatives. They are excited about their involvement and are able to reach their house members in ways that outside presenters never could. Paxton's (1996) comments certainly fit with our experience that there is indeed potential for friends to be positive influences.

Our experience also has reinforced the importance of the educative role of the professionals. For example, relying solely on their collective experience, college women could rightly conclude that indeed men prefer slimmer women and society values thin bodies more than fuller ones. Without educational intervention, this conclusion predictably could lead to attitudes and behaviors that conform to these social pressures. Thus it is critical to provide the knowledge that can inform women's understanding of these values and to be able to help students deal with the very real struggle posed by the conflict between fact and social fiction. By inviting open discussion about the information, we believe that we maximize the potential for understanding, acceptance and integration of new ideas. On the basis of our experience with the task force, we believe that that our ability to do this effectively is a function of the fact that we have an established and ongoing relationship with the group.

It has been encouraging to observe some systemic changes in sorority houses. We do not expect to transform this subculture, but we do see that the possibility for change and movement does exist. With more institutional support and inclusion of not-yet-reached populations, we hope to increase the efficacy of our future efforts.

☐ References

Bandura, A. (1977). *Social learning theory.* Englewood Cliffs, NJ: Prentice Hall.

Clark, L. V., Levine, M. P., & Kinney, N. E. (1989). A multifaceted and integrated approach to prevention, identification, and treatment of bulimia on college campuses. *Journal of College Student Psychotherapy, 3,* 57–73.

Crandall, C. S. (1988). Social contagion of binge eating. *Journal of Personality and Social Psychology, 55,* 588–598.

Feingold, A., & Mazzella, R. (1998). Gender differences in body image are increasing. *Psychological Science, 9,* 190–195.

Franko, D. L. (1998). Secondary prevention of eating disorders in college women at risk. *Eating Disorders: The Journal of Treatment and Prevention, 6,* 29–40.

Gordon, R. A. (1990). *Anorexia and bulimia: Anatomy of a social epidemic.* Cambridge, MA: Basil Blackwell.

Harris, S. M. (1995). Body image attitudes and the psychosocial development of college women. *Journal of Psychology, 129,* 315–329.

Hotelling, K. (1989). A model for addressing the problem of bulimia on college campuses. *Journal of College StudentPsychotherapy, 3,* 241–255.

Huon, G. F. (1994). Towards the prevention of dieting-induced disorders: Modifying negative food- and body-related attitudes. *International Journal of Eating Disorders, 16,* 395–399.

Killen, J. D., Taylor, C. B., Hammer, L. D., Litt, I., Wilson, D. M.,Rich, T., Hayward, C., Simmonds, B., Kraemer, H., & Varady, A. (1993). An attempt to modify unhealthful eating attitudes and weight regulation practices of young adolescent girls. *International Journal of Eating Disorders, 13,* 369–384.

Klemchuck, H. P., Hutchinson, C. B., & Frank, R. I. (1990). Body dissatisfaction and eating -related problems on the college campus: Usefulness of the Eating Disorder Inventory with a nonclinical population. *Journal of Counseling Psychology, 37,* 297–305.

Kurtzman, F. D., Yager, J., Landsverk, J., Wiesmeier, E., & Bodurka, D. C. (1989), Eating disorders among selected student populations at UCLA. *Journal of the American Dietetic Association, 89,* 45–53.

Levine, M. P., Smolak, L., & Hayden, H. (1994). The relation of sociocultural factors to eating attitudes and behaviors among middle school girls. *Journal of Early Adolescence, 14,* 471–490.

Levine, M. P., Smolak, L., Moodey, A. F., Shuman, M. D., & Hessen, L. D. (1994). Normative developmental challenges and dieting and eating disturbances in middle school girls. *International Journal of Eating Disorders, 15,* 11–20.

Levine. M. P, Smolak, L., & Schermer, F. (1996). Media analysis and resistance by elementary school children in the primary prevention of eating problems. *Eating Disorders: The Journal of Treatment and Prevention, 4,* 310–322.

Martz, D. M., Graves, K. D., & Sturgis,, E. T. (1997). A pilot peer-leader eating disorders program for sororities. *Eating Disorders: The Journal of Treatment and Prevention, 5,* 294–308.

Meilman, P. W., von Hippel, P. A., & Gaylor, M. S. (1991). Self-induced vomiting in college women: Its relation to eating, alcohol use, and Greek life. *Journal of American College Health, 40,* 39–41.

Mintz, L., & Betz, N. (1988). Prevalance and correlates of eating disordered behaviors among undergraduate women. *Journal of Counseling Psychology, 35,* 463–471.

Nichter, M., & Vuckovic, N. (1994). Fat talk: Body image among adolescent girls. In N. Sault (Ed.), *Many mirrors: Body image and social relations* (pp. 109–131). New Brunswick, NJ: Rutgers University Press.

Paxton, S. J. (1996). Prevention implications of peer influences on body image dissatisfaction and disturbed eating in adolescent girls. *Eating Disorders: The Journal of Treatment and Prevention, 4,* 334–347.

Paxton, S. J., Schutz, H. K., Wertheim, E. H., & Muir, S. L. (1996). Friendship clique and peer influences on body image attitudes, dietary restraint, extreme weight loss behaviors and binge eating in adolescent girls. Unpublished manuscript.

Piran, N. (1995). Prevention: Can early lessons lead to a delineation of an alternative model? A critical look at prevention with school children. *Eating Disorders: The Journal of Treatment and Prevention, 3,* 28–36,

Piran, N. (1996). The reduction of preoccupation with body weight and shape in schools. A feminist approach. *Eating Disorders: The Journal of Treatment and Prevention, 4,* 323–334.

Piran, N. (in press). Eating disorders: A trial of prevention in a high risk school settting. *Journal of Primary Prevention*

Rodin, J., Silberstein, L. R., & Striegel-Moore, R. H. (1985). Women and weight: A normative discontent. In T.B. Sondregger (Ed.), *Nebraska Symposium on Motivation: Vol 32. Psychology and Gender* (pp. 267–307). Lincoln: University of Nebraska Press.

Rosen,, J. C. (1990). Body-image disturbances in eating disorders. In T. F. Cash & T. Pruzinsky (Eds.), *Body Images, Development, Deviance, and Change* (pp. 190–214). New York: Guilford Press.

Schulken, E. D., Pinciaro, P. J., Sawyer, R. G., Jensen, J. G., & Hoban., M.T. (1997). Sorority women's body size perceptions and their weight-related attitudes and behaviors. *Journal of American College Health, 46,* 69–74.

Sesan, R. (1989). Peer educators: A creative resource for the eating disordered college student. *Journal of College Student Psychotherapy, 3,* 221–240.

Shisslak, C. M., & Crago, M. (1994). Toward a new model for the prevention of eating disorders. In P. Fallon, M. A. Katzman, & S. C. Wooley (Eds.), *Feminist perspectives on eating disorders* (pp. 419–437). New York: Guilford Press.

Shisslak, C. M., Crago, M., & Estes, L. S. (1995). The spectrum of eating disturbances. *International Journal of Eating Disorders, 18,* 209–219.

Steiner-Adair, C., & Purcell, A. (1996). Approaches to mainstreaming eating disorders prevention. *Eating Disorders, 4,* 294–309.

Stormer, S. M., & Thompson, J. K. (1996). Explanations of body image disturbance: A test of maturational status, negative verbal commentary, social comparison, sociocultural hypotheses. *International Journal of eating Disorders, 19,* 193–202.

Striegel-Moore, R., McAvay, G., & Rodin, J. (1986). Psychological and behavioral correlates of feeling fat in women. *International Journal of Eating Disorders, 5,* 935–947.

Striegel-Moore, R., Silberstein, L., Frensch, P., Rodin, J. (1989). A prospective study of disordered eating among college students. *International Journal of Eating Disorders, 8,* 499–509.

☐ Note

[1]I want to thank Dr. Ousley for generously sharing her ideas and materials.

☐ **Appendix A**

WANTED:

TWO DEDICATED AND CARING WOMEN TO REPRESENT YOUR HOUSE AS MEMBERS OF THE PANHELLENIC TASK FORCE ON EATING DISORDERS

WHAT IS THE PANHELLENIC TASK FORCE ON EATING DISORDERS?

The PTFED is a group founded in 1992 by Brenda Alpert Sigall, Ph.D., from the Counseling Center, and Patricia Preston, L.C.S.W., from the Health Center. This group meets monthly with sorority women to discuss eating disorder and body image issues in the houses, and to work together in education and prevention efforts.

WHAT IS ITS MISSION?

The PTFED is dedicated to:

1. Educating sorority women on the prevention and treatment of eating disorders
2. Increasing awareness of the recovery resources available on campus
3. Promoting health attitudes about self and body image
4. Increasing understanding of unhealthy, culturally prescribed standards of size and shape for women, and their detrimental effects on women's sense of self-worth

WHAT WOULD MY RESPONSIBILITIES AS A PTFED MEMBER BE?

1. To be a role model in your sorority, promoting healthy attitudes about self and body image
2. To provide educational information at chapter meetings and through the Resource Center you create in your house
3. To plan and present educational programs in you house
4. To be available to house members to offer support
5. To act as a liaison to campus mental health professionals
6. To attend one meeting a month and take an active part in Eating Disorders Awareness Week

PLEASE NOTE

*You are *not* expected to diagnose eating disorders or body image problems, or provide counseling; this role is for the trained professionals only.

*This is *not* an eating disorders support group. If you have struggled with these issues, it is expected that you are at a level or recovery where you are not actively struggling with eating disordered behaviors, and you are making a conscious attempt to accept yourself and others for qualities not connected to weight and size.

*You must be a committed member; due to the close-knit nature of the group, sending a substitute is not an option. At least one representative is required for attendance at meetings.

☐ **Appendix B**

PANHELLENIC TASK FORCE ON EATING DISORDERS
APPLICATION FOR REPRESENTATIVE

Tell us about you. . . .

Name _____

  Sorority _____

Address _____

Telephone number _____

Year in School _____

  Major _____

Other Activities and Interests _____

_____

_____

_____

_____

Please explain briefly why you are interested in applying for this position

_____

_____

_____

_____

  Yes, I will be able to be a committed representative for at least one academic year, and I can be trusted to handle the confidential, sensitive nature of this responsibility.

Signed _____

  Date _____

If you have further questions, please call Brenda Sigall:
Pat Preston:
Or the Task Force Rep. to Panhel:

Please send the completed application to
Pat Preston, University Health Center,
College Park, MD 20742

V

SPECIAL CHALLENGES: HIGH-RISK POPULATIONS AND SECONDARY PREVENTION

Special challenges in the domains of both primary and secondary prevention are posed by specific populations that are at a higher risk of developing eating disorders, such as elite athletes, ballet dancers, and youth with diabetes. Special challenges regarding primary and secondary prevention are also faced by medical professionals whose work involves conveying norms regarding eating, body shape, and growth to children, adolescents, and their parents. As such, these professionals make up an important group that guides all members of the family, and society in general, in dealing with issues of physical development and mental health, especially during times of transition, such as puberty and pregnancy. This section contains work that describes strategies for both primary and secondary prevention in these different fields. An important issue that is addressed in this section is the challenge of integrating secondary and primary prevention, an issue that has raised considerable controversy (Mann et al., 1997). Prevention work in these domains has received limited professional and research attention.

The first three chapters in this section cover issues related to primary and secondary prevention in populations found to have a higher prevalence of eating disorders. In Chapter 15, Pauline Powers and Craig Johnson describe risk factors for the development of eating disorders among elite athletes, as well as ways in which the identification of disordered eating among athletes has led to changes in policy and training in influential athletic organizations. In Chapter 16, Niva Piran describes the multiphasic introduction of an integrated prevention program in an elite ballet school. The active participation of all stakeholders in the school community has been a central component in this prevention program, which has included components of tertiary, secondary, and primary prevention. In Chapter 17, Patricia Colton, Gary Rodin, Marion Olmsted, and Denis Daneman describe an approach which uses psychoeducational principles in the prevention of eating disorders among adolescents with insulin-dependent diabetes mellitus.

The last two chapters in this section describe the roles general practitioners may play in the primary and secondary prevention of eating disorders. In Chapter 18, Roslyn Weiner discusses ways in which she, as a clinical psychologist and director of an eating-disorder clinic, works with primary-care physicians to improve their care of adolescent patients. Her work strengthens the effectiveness of physicians in identifying and in treating children and adolescents who display early eating symptomatology, and in so doing she enhances the role of physicians in preventing preoccupation with body weight and shape. In Chapter 19, Debra Katzman, a pediatrician, describes ways in which physicians can detect eating difficulties early and avoid medical complications, especially during the time of maturation and growth.

☐ Reference

Mann, T., Nolen-Hoeksema, S., Huang, K., Burgard, D., Wright, A., & Hanson, K. (1997). Are two interventions worse than none? Joint primary and secondary prevention of eating disorders in college females. *Health Psychology, 16*(3), 1–11.

15
CHAPTER

Pauline S. Powers
Craig L. Johnson

Small Victories: Prevention of Eating Disorders Among Elite Athletes

During the past decade, multiple studies have demonstrated an increase in the prevalence of eating disorders and disordered eating among athletes of all skill levels (Clark, Nelson, & Evans, 1988; Rosen & Hough, 1988; Rucinski, 1988; Thompson & Sherman, 1993). Female athletes are especially at risk in sports that emphasize a thin body or appearance such as gymnastics, figure skating, swimming, and distance running. Sports in which anaerobic activities predominate (e.g., gymnastics) appear to increase risk compared with sports in which aerobic activities predominate. Males in sports such as body building and wrestling are also at greater risk for disordered eating than males in general (Dick, 1991; Pope, Katz, & Hudson, 1993).

The possible role of exercise in the etiology of eating disorders, especially anorexia nervosa, has been the focus of recent studies. Terms such as *obligatory exercise, exercise dependence,* and *anorexia athletica* all point to a dawning awareness of the importance of exercise in a comprehensive understanding of eating disorders. Epling and Pierce (1992) have developed an animal model in which overexercise can precipitate a set of behaviors very similar to those seen in anorexia nervosa patients. At the same time, we have witnessed a positive interest among women in sports and exercise that may presage a model of femininity that incorporates strength, power, and vitality.

In this chapter we describe some of the dilemmas that complicate prevention of eating disorders among athletes. It is hoped that prevention efforts in this high-risk group may offer hope for effective prevention strategies in the general population.

☐ Dilemmas in Prevention Among Athletes

Our efforts to prevent eating disorders always have been plagued by the dilemma that we are attempting to affect a set of beliefs and behaviors that is highly reinforced within our Westernized culture medically, socially, and financially. Several investigators (Garner, 1997; Orbach, 1986) have argued convincingly that the increase in the prevalence of eating disorders is directly correlated, and perhaps caused by, a shift toward glamorizing or idealizing thinness among women beginning in the mid- to late 1960s. Twiggy's phenomenal emergence during this era as one of the most successful and celebrated fashion models of all times often is seen as the beginning of the glamorization of the anorexic look for women. Garner, Garfinkel, and Olmstead (1983) demonstrated that from the early 1960s to the late 1970s there was a consistent downward trend in the height/weight ratios of fashion models, Miss America pageant contestants, and *Playboy* centerfolds. Paralleling this idealization of thinness, the culture increasingly devalued and discriminated against individuals who were fat, and a multibillion dollar weight-loss industry was developed to try and protect people from falling prey to this fate (Wooley & Garner, 1991).

Another dilemma for female athletes is the paradox related to early sports participation by girls. On the one hand, research suggests that early participation in sports may improve girls' self-esteem (Sands, Tricker, Sherman, Armatas, & Maschette, 1996) and increase the likelihood of healthy physical activity in adulthood. On the other hand, as girls become more proficient at sports they paradoxically may be increasing their vulnerability to eating disorders in the highly competitive elite athletic culture.

This Western cultural idealization of thinness for women has affected significantly the women's athletic community, which has seen a dramatic rise in the incidence of eating disorders over the past 10 to 15 years. The primary risk factors for eating disorders among women athletes emanate from two slightly different belief systems. The first relates to what we have termed *appearance thinness*. The idealization of thinness seen in the general culture over the past several decades appears particularly to have affected women's sports such as gymnastics and figure skating. Judges progressively have rewarded thinner athletes. Predictably, the incidence of eating disorders among athletes is highest among the sports that have the most emphasis on appearance thinness. In some sports, youth is also a factor. For example, certain feats performed by skaters, dancers, and gymnasts are best performed with a prepubescent body. Breast development and growth in height may interfere with capacity to perform some of these activities and shorten the athlete's career.

The second risk factor that is unique to the athletic community is the emphasis on what we have termed *performance* thinness. Essentially, over the same time period, a belief system has developed that lower body fat content enhances performance, particularly in the endurance sports such as track, cross country, and swimming. Although this is a passionately held belief among many coaches, trainers, and athletes, the databases that support this belief are less than compelling, particularly for female athletes.

Consequently, the dilemma for prevention of eating disorders among athletes is slightly more complicated than for even other high-risk occupations such as the entertainment or fashion industry. In addition to the idealization of appearance thinness, we have a belief widely propagated by coaches and trainers that achieving a low percentage of body fat will give athletes a competitive advantage.

Many elite athletes are perfectionistic and able to focus attention exclusively on a competitive goal. Often coaches of elite athletes are similarly highly competitive. This joint capacity of the athlete and coach to focus on a competitive goal often leads to success in the sport. Unfortunately, for some athletes and coaches, an inappropriate focus on a competitive goal, coupled with inaccurate information about fat content and performance, may lead to an eating disorder. The ability to lose perspective may be necessary to become an elite athlete in this day and age. If there is a hint that achieving thinness from either an appearance or performance perspective will give the athlete a competitive edge, the threat of an eating disorder or other medical complications from these training practices probably will fall on deaf ears. Similarly, coaches who are under tremendous stress to succeed (and whose jobs actually may depend on success of the athletes) also may lose perspective and fail to recognize the hazards of dangerous training practices. The enormous social and financial rewards for being successful (both for the athlete and the coach) dwarf the medical and psychological risks in this belief system.

☐ Primary Prevention

Criteria for Effective Prevention Programs

Primary prevention efforts aim to prevent the emergence of an illness or disorder, usually by influencing risk factors that contribute to the development of the condition. For example, in the 1970s, massive public-education efforts were undertaken to modify risk factors identified as contributing to coronary artery disease among sedentary middle-aged, mostly White, middle-class men (Kannel, 1976).

Public education messages urged the public to lower consumption of cholesterol-containing foods (because elevated cholesterol levels had been shown to be associated with an increased risk of myocardial infarction), to exercise regularly, and to combat obesity in order to prevent heart attacks. These educational messages were aimed at (and received by) a broad spectrum of the public, some of whom were not apparently at risk (for example, normal weight women). One positive effect of this campaign has been a reduction in the incidence of myocardial infarction, at least in the group of middle-aged men initially identified at risk (Gillum, 1994). However, there have been unexpected, often dangerous, consequences of this campaign. The increased prevalence of eating disorders may be caused partly by this prevention effort, which influenced the population in general. Many of the public-service messages encouraged the entire population to consume less fat, eat fewer cholesterol-containing foods, lose weight, and exercise more. Although this advice is appropriate for individuals who are overweight, who do not exercise, or who have elevated cholesterol levels, weight loss is not appropriate for normal-weight individuals, and more exercise is not necessarily helpful to those who already exercise moderately. Furthermore, since this educational prevention campaign began, more specific risk factors for myocardial infarction have been identified. For example, waist/hip ratios above certain levels may be a more accurate means of identifying coronary risk than body mass index or fat content (Flynn, Codd, Gibney, Keelan, & Sugrue, 1993). Hence, excessive focus on fat content and weight may be inappropriate.

The three main lessons to be learned from this effort to prevent coronary artery disease are as follows. First, prevention efforts are best directed to "at risk" groups, because unexpected side effects may be more likely if efforts are directed to the population in general. Second, risk factors need to be accurately identified so that prevention efforts can be narrowly and specifically focused. Third, it is important to anticipate that unintended consequences *will* occur, so that efforts can be made to alter the prevention program to obviate these negative effects. Garner (1985) noted that education efforts actually may have increased the likelihood of certain behaviors that lead to eating disorders by suggesting dangerous weight-loss strategies to previously naive adolescents.

These observations do not mean that primary prevention efforts should be forsaken but do imply that we should be cautious when we design large prevention programs aimed at groups that are not necessarily at risk. It is important to assess the results of a prevention program not only in reducing the disorder in question but also in terms of whether or not other unanticipated problems have been created.

Competitive Female Athletes: An At-risk Group

Competitive female athletes in sports that emphasize appearance thinness or performance thinness are an at-risk group for the development of subclinical and full syndromal eating disorders. They are also more likely to develop disturbed attitudes toward body shape, weight, and eating than their nonathletic peers. Thus, this group fulfills the first criterion for selecting a group that may be an effective target for a primary prevention program.

Risk Factors in Athletes

Multiple studies have attempted to identify the factors that mediate the development of eating disorders among adolescent females in general. Several studies have found that body dissatisfaction is predictive of eating disorder symptoms among nonclinical samples of nonathletic adolescent girls and young women (Attie & Brooks-Gunn, 1989; Killen et al., 1994; Rosen, 1992). However, in order to develop effective primary prevention programs it is necessary to identify factors that antedate the development of body dissatisfaction. Williamson and colleagues (1995) recently have proposed a new model for the development of eating disorders in female athletes that may permit identification of factors that occur prior to the development of body dissatisfaction in the female athlete.

The model is as shown in Figure 1.

Three factors may influence and antedate the development of concern about body size and shape (that is, the attitudinal aspect of body image or body dissatisfaction). These three factors are social influence, performance anxiety, and athlete self-appraisal. The researchers used three tests to assess these three antecedent variables. The tests were a newly designed five-item social influence scale; the Sports Competition Anxiety Test (Martens, 1977); and a five-item

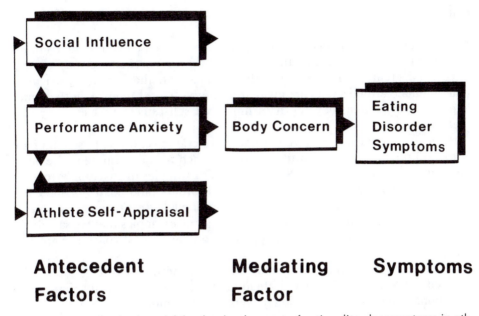

FIGURE 1. Hypothesized model for the development of eating-disorder symptoms in athletes. Adapted, with permission, from Williamson et al. (1995, p. 389).

scale for the athlete to rate her own athletic performance. The proposed mediating variable, body dissatisfaction, was measured with the Body Shape Questionnaire (Cooper, Taylor, Cooper, & Fairburn, 1987). The researchers studied 94 female college athletes and used structural modeling analysis to assess the importance of the three proposed antecedent factors in the development of body dissatisfaction. They found that social pressure from coaches and peers for thinness combined with anxiety about athletic performance and negative self-appraisal of athletic achievement was associated with body dissatisfaction. High scores on individual antecedent variables did not predict that body concern would develop, but high scores on all three variables did. Without the presence of body concern, eating-disorder symptoms did not develop. Anxiety about athletic performance may relate to some of the irrational beliefs about performance thinness.

The advantage of the model is that it suggests ways of identifying factors among competitive athletes that antedate the development of body dissatisfaction. Athletes dissatisfied with their performance or who have significant performance anxiety may be more likely to believe that thinness per se improves performance. Because genetic endowment, muscle mass, and motivation are the key factors associated with enhanced athletic performance (Birrer & Levine, 1987; Orlick, 1990), an educated coaching staff may be able to counter some of the false beliefs about performance thinness. Weight loss results in loss of both lean body mass and fat content, and initially loss of lean body mass predominates (Brownell, Steen, & Wilmore, 1987). Hence, exclusive focus on weight loss or fat grams consumed may be counterproductive in enhancing performance in competitive female athletes.

Role of the Coach

The coach is usually a very powerful figure in the life of a competitive athlete. The coach may be with the athlete more than the parents and may come to have even greater influence over the athlete than the parents, particularly young female athletes who are away from home. This influence on the athlete is often positive and may result in improved self-esteem that endures for a lifetime.

However, some coaches have very negative effects on the self-esteem of athletes, and the behavior and attitudes of the coach may contribute to the development of an eating disorder. Some infamous examples of coaching errors that have facilitated the development of eating disorders (and deaths of some elite female athletes) are detailed in the book entitled *Little Girls in Pretty Boxes* by Ryan (1995). Although these examples, and some examples that we saw during the 1996 Summer Olympics, are appalling, probably most coaches want their athletes to win *and* be healthy.

In an interesting study by Smoll, Smith, Barnett, & Everett (1993), they showed that coaches who were trained to increase their supportiveness and instructional effectiveness had team players who had more fun and worked better together than players of untrained coaches. Two key factors are important. First, a supportive, noncritical relationship with the athlete is likely to increase the athlete's self-esteem. Second, knowledge about nutrition, body composition, and its relationship to performance allows the coach to properly instruct female athletes. For example, pubescent girls have an increased need for both calories and calcium. Also, body fat content probably needs to be over 17% for females to have initial onset of menses (Frisch, 1988). Finally, there is very little evidence that reduction of fat content below that needed for normal menstruation improves performance.

Role of Judges

The judge is key in both developing appropriate coaching methods and encouraging normal nutrition and weight in athletes. Judges who reward emaciated short childlike gymnasts who have stress fractures with first-place honors contribute to the increased prevalence of eating disorders. Although rarely considered, it might come within the judge's purview to prohibit competition by an athlete who has developed physical symptoms. It is not only the athlete who notices that judges have been rewarding progressively thinner and younger athletes; the coaches have taken note as well.

☐ Small Victories for Primary Prevention Efforts

International Olympics Committee

Primary prevention efforts within the athletic community have increased dramatically over the past 5 years. In the fall of 1995, representatives from 11 national and international sports organizations met to review current and proposed models for prevention of eating disorders among athletes. As a consequence of the proposal emanating from this meeting, the International Olympic Committee has appointed a task force to study eating disorders among female athletes.

National Collegiate Athletic Association

The National Collegiate Athletic Association, led by its sports science division, has identified eating disorders as one of its chief concerns among women athletes. Their prevention efforts include two excellent videos that detail the range of eating disorders and have several athletes discussing their personal struggles with the disorders. They also have supported a large-scale research project investigating the nature and extent of eating disorders among student athletes (Dick, 1991). They also provide extensive written information to coaches, trainers, and athletes about the risk factors for eating disorders.

USA Gymnastics Prevention Efforts

USA Gymnastics, which is the national governing board for gymnastics in the United States, called a task force in 1994 to make recommendations about how to prevent eating disorders within their sport. In many ways, the gymnastic organization, which has been highly criticized for the prevalence of eating disorders among their athletes, has accomplished the most in terms of prevention.

The prevention efforts that have been created include the following:

- The artistic and rhythmic national teams both have contracted team sports psychology consultants and nutritionists to work with the athletes, parents, and coaches.
- The International Gymnastics Federation has increased the age limit for participation in artistic gymnastics in the 2000 Olympics to 16 years old.
- The United States coaches have developed methods of training older athletes that have resulted in improved performance and an increased length of competitive careers. The top 10 gymnasts of the 1996 National Team included three members of the 1992 Olympic Team and four athletes who were 18 years old or older. These athletes are projecting a more mature image for gymnasts, which can only aid in combating the preoccupation with body image and weight, because adolescent gymnasts strive to become like their idols.
- Information and training, available to coaches through the Talent Opportunity Program (TOP), national-team meetings, and other coaching certification programs, have assisted in training coaches about ways that they can contribute to the overall physical and mental health of their athletes.
- Initial efforts at parent education have included parent sessions at national-team meetings and at TOP camps.
- Nutritional information is available to athlete members through the USA Gymnastics magazine. Additionally, an athlete's cookbook has been printed, and numerous educational videos on nutrition and eating disorders are available through USA Gymnastics educational-product sales.

- Recognition and awareness of the problems of the female athlete triad (disturbed eating behavior, amenorrhea, and osteoporosis) is reflected in the emphasis on educational sessions at the state, regional, and national congresses of USA Gymnastics.
- Educational programs for athletes are conducted at training camps, national-team meetings, and at the TOP training camps by the team nutritionist and sports psychology consultants.

World Tennis Council

In an effort to avoid the female athlete triad as well as other psychological problems that affect young female tennis players, the World Tennis Council encouraged the World Tennis Association to increase its age eligibility to 18 for players to be able to compete on its tour on an unrestricted basis. This group noted that there was a myth that the full potential of a tennis player should be reached by age 11 years, and that the prepubescent shape contributed to better performance in tennis. They found no evidence for either of these ideas. They concluded that the young age of the tennis competitors contributed to impaired social and emotional development, was likely to shorten their career, and might increase to the likelihood of developing an eating disorder. In addition to changing the age requirement, this group also has recommended yearly medical examinations, limitation of evening play (after 9:00 PM) for players under age 16 years, availability of counseling and mentoring programs for players, and ongoing research into the medical and psychological aspects of women's tennis.

Injunction Against Steroid Use in Athletes

Steroid abuse is high among athletes, particularly among male body builders, weight lifters (Perry, Andersen, & Yates, 1990), wrestlers, and football players (Wang, Downey, Perko, & Yesalis, 1993). Up to 20% to 30% of body builders may use steroids on an intermittent but chronic basis (Kleiner, Bazzarre, & Litchford, 1990). The most commonly used ergogenic drugs are anabolic-androgenic steroids (AASs) (Smith & Perry, 1992). *Anabolic* refers to the "growth-promoting" effect and *androgenic* refers to the "masculinizing" effect. The AASs are believed to improve performance, endurance, and appearance. In a metaanalysis of studies of the possible positive effects of the AASs, Elashoff, Jacknow, Shain, and Braunstein (1991) found that among previously trained athletes there was slightly greater improvement in strength in the AAS-treated group than in the placebo group, with a median difference of 5% across the nine studies that could be evaluated. However, in the larger studies the differences in performances were smaller, and all studies used relatively small doses of the AASs, probably significantly less than frequently used by the athletes.

The evidence for significant side effects from the AASs is strong. Although it may be correct that athletes who use AASs for one cycle may be at a relatively small physiological risk, it is likely that use will become chronic, and there are probably long-term physiological complications (DePiccoli, Giada, Benettin, Sartori, & Piccolo, 1991). On the other hand, there is strong evidence that even transient use of steroids can be associated with behavioral changes and mood changes (especially irritability and possibly violence) (Choi & Pope, 1994).

The scandals of the 1988 Olympic Games in Seoul, Korea, resulted in a ban against steroid use, and sophisticated detection methods were developed. Most sports organizations now ban the use of steroids. Because athletes may serve as role models, one intriguing question has been whether or not the ban against steroid use among professional and elite athletes has resulted in a decline in steroid use in the general population. There is some evidence that this has been the case. In one meta-analysis of the studies of prevalence of steroid abuse among high school students prior to the Olympic ban (Smith & Perry, 1992), 5% to 10% of high-school students used steroids, and in a recent study (Drewnowski, Kurth, & Krahn, 1995) 0.6% of male high-school students acknowledged using steroids.

Recent efforts undertaken to prevent steroid abuse among high-school and college students have produced interesting results. One group (Perko, Cowdery, Wang, & Yesalis, 1995) found that students with lower grade-point averages were less likely to believe steroids are a threat to health and more likely to believe that anabolic steroids enhance performance than students with higher averages. Goldberg, Bents, Bosworth, Tevisan, and Elliot (1991) evaluated the effect of education about steroids. They found that a balanced view of steroids (there are some ergogenic benefits but there are also multiple complications) was more effective in altering attitudes toward steroids than an approach emphasizing only the negative consequences.

Although there is some indication that steroid abuse may have decreased in the general male adolescent population, the findings among athletes, particularly body builders, is not as hopeful. In a recent dissertation (Bassett, 1996) in which detailed interviews with body builders were undertaken, widespread abuse of AASs, obtained through illicit means, was found. Furthermore, the body builders used larger doses of the steroids than have been scientifically studied in terms of ergogenic effects, and all had experienced increased muscle size and strength and weight gain, which routinely was experienced as positive. Most of the body builders wanted to "be bigger." The fact that the bodybuilders obtained drugs illegally and the fact that the desired effect was achieved with steroids suggests that this is a group of athletes who may require specialized prevention techniques.

The Female Athlete Triad

In the past decade, disturbed eating behavior, amenorrhea, and osteoporosis have been identified as a common triad of findings in female athletes (Nattiv, Agostini, Drinkwater, & Yeager, 1994). Other similar syndromes such as anorexia athletica and athletic amenorrhea have been identified. Initially, athletic amenorrhea was thought to be benign, but further studies have demonstrated that amenorrhea in athletes may be associated with loss of bone mineral mass. Anorexia athletica and the female athlete triad are very similar and probably are best conceptualized as subclinical eating disorders (Beals & Manore, 1994).

The terms *anorexia athletica, athletic amenorrhea,* and *female athlete triad* have served to heighten awareness of some of the problems faced by female athletes.

However, these terms may be misleading, in that they may be used to avoid the stigma of a mental disorder and thus may delay appropriate early intervention. There may be differences between classic anorexia nervosa and anorexia athletica (or individuals with the female athlete triad) but, so far, the similarities are more apparent. For example, weight loss, amenorrhea, lower than normal fat content, osteopenia, elevated cortisol levels, and decreased levels of sex hormones are common to both groups (Huberland, Seddick, Marcus, & Backrach, 1995; Lindholm, Hirschbert, Carlstrom, & von Schoultz, 1995).

The "Pursuit of Strength"

There are encouraging signs that a cultural shift toward valuing strength and fitness in women, as compared to simply thinness, may be occurring. Although the most popular female United States Olympians in 1996 were the childlike gymnasts, very powerful women also emerged as admirable and effective. The female synchronized swimming team and baseball team are two examples. Bonnie Blair and Jackie Joyner-Kersee are individual stars that model strength and agility.

In another example, in her plenary address at the 1996 International Conference on Eating Disorders, Joan Brumberg showed pictures of her female students modeling their biceps. The heroine of *Beauty and the Beast* is thin but is also sufficiently strong to lift the Beast onto a horse when he is injured.

Although the heroines in films and in the Olympics are normal to thin, many now are also strong. The pursuit of strength, as opposed to the pursuit of thinness, may be associated with better health consequences. However, as shown by the body-builder studies, the relentless pursuit of strength also can be associated with hazards.

☐ Secondary Prevention: Early Detection

Psychological and Physiological Screening Methods

Various psychological and physiological screening methods have been proposed to detect eating disorders among athletes. The best-known psychological screening questionnaires are the Eating Attitudes Test (Garner & Garfinkel, 1979) and the Eating Disorders Inventory-2 (Garner, 1991). Although these questionnaires do not substitute for a clinical assessment and may produce false negative results, they are useful in detecting disturbed attitudes toward eating, weight, and appearance that may progress to an eating disorder.

Because amenorrhea is a key feature of anorexia nervosa, certain physiological measures might be useful in the early detection of eating disorders. For example, assessment of body fat content might be used to determine if the female athlete was likely to have menses (Frisch, 1988). This is controversial for a number of reasons, some of which are legitimate and some of which are related to the set of beliefs regarding performance thinness and the erroneous conclusion that lower fat content is *necessarily* associated with better performance.

Team Physician

Team physicians and other healthcare providers often can detect eating disorders early and facilitate entry into appropriate treatment. Van DeLoo and Johnson (1995) have devised a screening questionnaire for the female athlete for use in the physician's office (see Appendix 1). Completion of the questionnaire by the athlete usually takes fewer than 5 minutes and can alert the physician to inquire further if symptoms of an eating disorder are present. Working with the athlete who acknowledges symptoms requires skill and understanding of the usually fervent desire of the athlete to continue in his or her sport. For some sports, such as gymnastics, specific weight guidelines have been proposed for gradually increasing participation in various levels of activities with appropriate weight gain.

Coaches and Trainers

The coach or trainer may be the first to notice than an athlete is developing an eating disorder. Encouragement from the coach is often a powerful inducement to the athlete to seek appropriate medical and psychological treatment. Kratina (1996) has prepared a list of 10 things that coaches can do to help prevent eating disorders in their athletes (see Appendix 2). These very straightforward guidelines usually can guide coaches toward appropriate intervention early in the development of eating disorders among their athletes.

☐ Conclusions

The increased rate of eating disorders among different groups of elite athletes suggests the importance of prevention efforts in this area. Exposure to both widespread societal pressures and special demands that operate in the field of athletics put elite athletes at an increased risk for eating disorders. Prevention work should occur at all levels. Governing bodies should provide as much relevant information as possible to parents, coaches, trainers, and athletes about risks involved with attempts to lower athletes' weight and percentage of body fat, as well as delay female athletes' puberty. Similarly, information should be widely distributed about the signs, symptoms, and perils of eating disorders. Judges should be informed about the risks involved with overvaluing thinness in their judging process. Research may have a role in countering the widely held belief that a lower percentage of body fat increases performance among female athletes. The practice of requiring female athletes in certain sports to perform feats that cannot be performed after puberty inappropriately limits athletes' careers and may result in attempts by athletes to maintain a prepubescent body shape and in associated eating disorders and stunted growth.

Increased screening efforts need to be instituted to identify athletes at risk prior to developing eating related symptoms. Because early detection remains one of the best prognostic indicators of recovery, screening strategies utilizing instruments such as the Eating Attitude Test, the Eating Disorders Inventory, or the Health History Questionnaire for the Female Athlete can be used to identify athletes who have developed eating-disordered symptoms. Systematic assessment of prevention efforts could guide further developments in this field.

☐ References

Attie, I., & Brooks-Gunn J. (1989). Development of eating problems in adolescent girls: A longitudinal study. *Developmental Psychology, 25,* 70–79.

Bassett, J. D. (1996). Psychological correlates in induced hypomasculine and hypermasculine physiques: Male anorexics and body builders. Unpublished doctoral dissertation, Smith College School for Social Work, Northampton.

Beals, K. A., Manore, M. M. (1994). The prevalence and consequences of subclinical eating disorders in female athletes. *International Journal of Sport Nutrition, 4,* 175–195.

Birrer, R. B., & Levine, R. (1987). Performance parameters in children and adolescent athletes. *Sports Medicine, 4,* 211–227.

Brownell, K. D., Steen, S. N., & Wilmore, J. H. (1987). Weight regulation practices in athletes: Analysis of metabolic and health effects. *Medicine and Science in Sports and Exercise, 19,* 546–556.

Choi, P. Y., & Pope, H. G., Jr. (1994). Violence toward women and illicit androgenic-anabolic steroid use. *Annals of Clinical Psychiatry, 6,* 21–25.

Clark, N., Nelson, M., & Evans, W. (1988). Nutrition education for elite female runners. *Physician and Sports medicine, 16,* 124, 128, 130, 133–134.

Cooper, P. J., Taylor, M. J., Cooper, Z., & Fairburn, C. G. (1987). Development and validation of the Body Shape Questionnaire. *International Journal of Eating Disorders, 6,* 485–494.

DePiccoli, B., Giada, F., Benettin, A., Sartori, F., & Piccolo, E. (1991). Anabolic steroid use in body builders: An echocardiographic study of left ventricle morphology and function. *International Journal of Sports Medicine, 12,* 408–412.

Dick, R. W. (1991). Eating disorders in NCAA athletic programs. *Athletic Training, 26,* 136.

Drewnowski, A., Kurth, C. L., & Krahn, D. D. (1995). Effects of body image on dieting, exercise and anabolic steroid use in adolescent males. *International Journal of Eating Disorders, 17,* 381–386.

Elashoff, J. D., Jacknow, A. D., Shain, S. G., & Braunstein, G. D. (1991). Effects of anabolic-androgenic steroids on muscular strength. *Annals of Internal Medicine, 115,* 387–393.

Epling, W. F., & Pierce, W. D. (1992). *Solving the anorexic puzzle: A scientific approach.* Toronto: Hogrefe & Huber.

Flynn, M. A., Codd, M. B., Gibney, M. J., Keelan, E. T., & Sugrue, D. D. (1993). Indices of obesity and body fat distribution in arteriographically defined coronary artery disease in men. *Irish Journal of Medicine Science, 162,* 503–509.

Frisch, R. (1988). Fatness and fertility. *Scientific American, 258,* 88–95.

Garner, D. M. (1985). Iatrogenesis in anorexia nervosa and bulimia nervosa. *International Journal of Eating Disorders, 4,* 701–726.

Garner, D. M. (1991). *The Eating Disorder Inventory-2 professional manual.* Odessa, FL: Psychological Assessment Resources.

Garner, D. M. (1997). Psychoeducation principles in treatment. In D. M. Garner & P. E. Garfinkel, *Handbook of Treatment for Eating Disorders* (2d ed. pp 145–177). New York, The Guilford Press.

Garner, D. M., & Garfinkel, P. E. (1979). The eating attitudes test: An index of the symptoms of anorexia nervosa. *Psychological Medicine, 9,* 273–279.

Garner, D. M., Garfinkel, P. E., & Olmstead, M. P. (1983). An overview of the sociocultural factors in the development of anorexia nervosa. In P. L. Darby, P. E. Garfinkel, D. M. Garner, & D. V. Coscina (Eds.), *Anorexia nervosa: Recent developments* (pp. 65–82). New York: Alan R. Liss.

Gillum, R. F. (1994). Trends in acute myocardial infarction and coronary heart disease death in the United States. *Journal of the American College of Cardiology, 23,* 1273–1277.

Goldberg, L., Bents, R., Bosworth, E., Tevisan, L., & Elliot, D. L. (1991). Anabolic steroid education and adolescents: Do scare tactics work? *Pediatrics, 87,* 283–286.

Huberland, C. A., Seddick, D., Marcus, R., & Backrach, J. K. (1995). A physician survey of therapy for exercise-associated amenorrhea: A brief report. *Clinical Journal of Sports Medicine, 5,* 246–250.

Kannel, W. B. (1976). Coronary risk factors: II. Prospects for the prevention of atheroscleorsis in the young. *Australian and New Zealand Journal of Medicine, 6,* 410–419.

Killen, J. D., Taylor, C. B., Hayward, C., Wilson, D. M., Haydel, K. F., Hammer, L. D., Simmonds, B., Robinson, T. N., Litt, I., Varady A., & Kraemer, H. (1994). Pursuit of thinness and onset of eating disorder symptoms in a community sample of adolescent girls: A three-year prospective analysis. *International Journal of Eating Disorders, 16,* 227–238.

Kleiner, S. M., Bazzarre, T. L., & Litchford, M. D. (1990). Metabolic profiles, diet, and health practices of championship male and female body builders. *Journal of the American Dietetic Association, 90,* 962–967.

Kratina, K. (1996, Spring). Ten things coaches can do to help prevent eating disorders in their athletes. *National Eating Disorders Organization (NEDO) Newsletters,* 6.

Lindholm, C., Hirschberg, A. L., Carlstrom, K., & von Schoultz, B. (1995). Altered adrenal steroid metabolism underlying hypercorticolism in female endurance athletes. *Fertility and Sterility, 63,* 1190–1194.

Martens, R. (1977). *Sports competition anxiety test.* Champaign, IL: Human Kinetics.

Nattiv, A., Agostini, R., Drinkwater, B., & Yeager, K. K. (1994). The female athlete triad: The interrelatedness of disordered eating, amenorrhea, and osteoporosis. *Clinics in Sportsmedicine, 13,* 405–418.

Orbach, S. (1986). *Hunger strike: The anorectic's struggle as a metaphor for our age.* New York: W. W. Norton.

Orlick, T. (1990). *In pursuit of excellence* (2 ed.). Champaign, IL: Leisure Press.

Perko, M. A., Cowdery, J., Wang, M. Q., & Yesalis, C. S. (1995). Associations between academic performance of division 1 college athletes and their perceptions of the effects of anabolic steroids. *Perceptual and Motor Skills, 80,* 284–286.

Perry, P. J., Anderson, K. H., & Yates, W. R. (1990). Illicit anabolic steroid use in athletes: A case series analysis. *American Journal of Sports Medicine, 18,* 422–428.

Pope, H. G., Jr., Katz, D. L., & Hudson, J. I. (1993). Anorexia nervosa and "reverse anorexia" among 108 body builders. *Comprehensive Psychiatry, 34,* 406–409.

Rosen, J. C. (1992). Body image disorder: Definition, development, and contribution to eating disorders. In J. Crowther, D. Tennebaum, S. Hubfoil, & M. Stephens (Eds.), *The etiology of bulimia nervosa: The individual and family context* (pp. 157–177). Washington, DC: Hemisphere.

Rosen, L. W., & Hough, D. O. (1988). Pathogenic weight-control behaviors of female college gymnasts. *Physicians and Sportsmedicine, 16,* 141–146.

Rucinski, A. (1989). Relationship of body image and dietary intake of competitive ice skaters. *Journal of the American Dietetic Association, 89,* 98–100.

Ryan, J. (1995). *Little girls in pretty boxes: The making and breaking of elite gymnasts and figure skaters.* New York: Doubleday.

Sands, R., Tricker, J., Sherman, C., Armantas, C. & Maschette, W. (1996). Disordered eating patterns, body image, self-esteem, and physical activity in preadolescent school children. *International Journal of Eating Disorders, 21,* 159–166.

Smith, D. A., & Perry, P. J. (1992). The efficacy of ergogenic agents in athletic competition: Part 1: Androgenic-anabolic steroids. *Annals of Pharmacotherapy, 26,* 520–528.

Smoll, F. L., Smith, R. E., Barnett, N. P., & Everett, J. J. (1993). Enhancement of children's self-esteem through social support training for youth sports coaches. *Journal of Applied Psychology 78,* 602–610.

Thompson, R. A., & Sherman, R. T. (1993). *Helping athletes with eating disorders.* Champaign, IL: Human Kinetics.

Van DeLoo, D. A., & Johnson, M. D. (1995). The young female athlete. *Clinics in Sports Medicine, 14,* 687–707.

Wang, M. Q., Downey, G. S., Perko, M. A., & Yesalis, C. E. (1993). Changes in body size of elite high school football players: 1963–1989. *Perceptual and Motor Skills, 76,* 379–383.

Williamson, D. A., Netemeyer, R. G., Jackman, L. P., Anderson, D. A., Funsch, C. L., & Rabalais, J. Y. (1995). Structural equation modeling for risk factors for the development of eating disorder symptoms in female athletes. *International Journal of Eating Disorders, 17,* 387–393.

Wooley, S. C., & Garner, D. M. (1991). Obesity treatment: The high cost of false hope. *Journal of the American Dietetic Association, 91,* 8–11.

254 Preventing Eating Disorders

☐ Appendix 1: Supplemental Health History Questionnaire for the Female Athlete (From Van DeLoo & Johnson, 1995)

1. How old were you when you had your first menstrual period? _____

2. How many periods have you had in the last 12 months? _____

3. Have you ever gone for more than 2 months without having a menstrual period? _____ Yes _____ No

4. How long do your periods last? _____

5. When was your last menstrual period? _____

6. Do you take birth control pills or hormones? _____ Yes _____ No

7. Have you ever been treated for anemia? _____ Yes _____ No

8. What have you eaten in the last 24 hours? _____

_____

9. Are there certain food groups you refuse to eat (i.e., meats, breads)?

_____

10. Are you happy with your present weight? _____ Yes _____ No

11. If not, what would you like to weigh? _____

12. Have you ever tried to control your weight with:

_____ fasting? _____ vomiting? _____ using laxatives?

_____ diuretics? _____ diet pills?

13. Do you have questions about healthy ways to control weight?

_____

☐ Appendix 2: 10 Things Coaches Can Do to Help Prevent Eating Disorders in Their Athletes (From Kratina, 1996)

1. Instruct coaches and trainers to recognize the signs and symptoms of eating disorders and understand their role in helping to prevent them. Those with eating problems often hide their symptoms to avoid calling attention to them. They are often aware the behavior is abnormal.

2. Provide athletes with accurate information regarding weight, weight loss, body composition, nutrition and sports performance in order to reduce misinformation and to challenge practices that are unhealthy and even counterproductive. Be aware of local professionals who will help educate the athletes.

3. Emphasize the health risks of low weight, especially for female athletes with menstrual irregularities or amenorrhea. The athlete should be referred for medical assessment in these cases.

4. Refer to a sports psychologist or other therapist skilled at treating disorders if an athlete is chronically dieting and/or exhibits mildly abnormal eating. Early detection increases the likelihood of successful treatment—left untreated, the problem may progress to an eating disorder.

5. De-emphasize weight by not weighing athletes and by minimizing (eliminating) comments about weight. Instead, focus on other areas in which athletes have more control in order to improve performance, i.e., focus on strength and physical conditioning, as well as the mental and emotional components of performance. (There is no risk in improving mental and emotional capacities!)

6. Do not assume that reducing body fat or weight will enhance performance. While weight loss or a reduction in body fat can lead to improved performance, studies show this does not apply to all athletes. Additionally, many individuals respond to weight loss attempts with eating disorder symptoms. Improved performance should not be at the expense of the athlete's health.

7. Understand why weight is such a sensitive and personal issue for many women. Since weight is emotionally charged for many, eliminate derogatory comments or behaviors, no matter how slight, about weight. If there is concern about an athlete's weight, the athlete should be referred for an assessment to a Registered Dietitian and Sports Psychologist skilled in treating eating disorders.

8. Do not automatically curtail athletic participation if an athlete is found to have eating problems, unless warranted by a medical condition. Consider the athlete's health, physical and emotional safety and self-image when making decisions regarding an athlete's level of participation in his/her sport.

9. Sport personnel should explore their own values and attitudes regarding weight, dieting and body image, and how these values and attitudes may inadvertently affect their athletes. They should understand their role in promoting a positive self-image and self-esteem in their athletes.

10. Take warning signs seriously. Take eating disorder behaviors seriously. There is a 10–15% mortality and 25% suicide rate for those with eating disorders.

Niva Piran

On the Move from Tertiary to Secondary and Primary Prevention: Working with an Elite Dance School

It has been suggested repeatedly that training for professions that involve appearance-related criteria, thinness in particular, such as ballet dancing or modeling, may result in an increased risk for eating disorders (Garfinkel & Garner, 1982). Increased risk for eating disorders also has been found among athletes training in sports that involve an emphasis on appearance and on a thin body shape (see Chapter 15). Although reports of a higher incidence of eating disorders and related medical complications among dancers and in specific sports have raised concerns among professionals (Brooks-Gunn, Burrow, & Warren, 1998; Evers, 1987; Garner, Garfinkel, Rockert, & Olmsted, 1987; Nattive, Agostini, Drinkwater, & Yeager, 1994; Weeda-Mannak & Drop, 1985) and the public (Carreiro & Verhaeghe, 1992; Terry, 1997) alike, there is very limited information about tertiary, secondary, and primary prevention work with these groups. Similarly, to date, only an overwhelming minority of training settings have recognized the importance of including mental-health professionals who specialize in the area of eating disorders and body image among their multidisciplinary staff. Within the field of dance, professionals in the area of body image rarely have been included in training schools or companies (Staines, personal communication, April 10, 1998). At times, dancers in training have approached the media to request the involvement of such personnel in their setting (Carreiro & Verhaeghe, 1992; Hench, cited in Terry, 1997). Within the field of athletics, the gymnastic association has taken initial steps to incorporate such expertise into settings of training (see Chapter 15).

For the past 13 years I have been involved in intensive prevention work in a world-class competitive residential ballet school for female and male students ages 10 to 18 years. In addition, I have seen a considerable number of dancers, at different stages of their training and careers, for consultation and counseling. I also have served as a consultant to different high schools that had competitive athletic programs. This chapter describes several key observations and findings derived from this work for the purpose of facilitating and encouraging the involvement of health and mental health professionals in this area of work. The chapter first addresses factors within the training setting that may affect a dancer to develop an eating disorder. The observed ambivalence to the involvement of personnel who specialize in body-weight and shape preoccupation is discussed in the following section. The chapter then continues with the discussion of the move from tertiary to secondary and primary prevention. A discussion of potential pitfalls in such work leads to the conclusion of the chapter.

☐ Beyond Thinness: Expanding the Understanding of Pressures in the Body Domain

Similar to theories regarding eating disorders in the general population, the single most widely sanctioned risk factor implicated in the increased incidence of eating disorders among ballet dancers has been the pressure to achieve a thin body shape. Indeed, in the ballet world, pressures for an ethereally thin body shape are accentuated. The pressures are particularly severe among top companies of classical ballet as compared with top companies of modern dance (Staines, personal communication, April 10, 1998). Among companies that do not compete at the world-class level, pressures for thinness vary according to the demands of the artistic director of each company. Different dancers and directors in the ballet world have suggested to the author that to be a member of top classical ballet companies in the world, a female dancer may need to be in the range of 75% to 80% of average body weight. Variations among ballet companies do exist, as several companies have taken the stance of supporting a healthier and stronger image of the female dancer (Walker, 1998) while others seem always to have accepted a fuller image of the female dancer (Staines, personal communication, 1998). Nonetheless, the most pervasive norms of thinness in the ballet world are the extreme ones, and they are conveyed through ethereally thin idealized role models, artistic directors and teachers who strongly hold to these ideals, and judges in international and national competitions. Young adult ballet dancers typically have dedicated their childhood to dance, and their wish to be gainfully employed as a dancer and their love for this form of art may drive them to subject their bodies to harsh nutritional regimens in the pursuit of thinness. Indeed, changing the norms of thinness within the ballet world is an essential aspect of successful prevention in this field (Piran, in press).

Although pressures for thinness are important in the field of ballet, preventative work in ballet and related fields should be guided by a comprehensive understanding of factors that may relate to eating disorders in these fields. In a 10-year qualitative study that examined in focus groups with dancers in training their perceptions of what may affect them to lose weight (Piran, 1996a), as well as in my 15 years of work with top professional dancers, a broader array of adverse factors have surfaced (Piran, 1995; 1997). Dancers describe the current lack of acceptance of a fully developed woman's figure in the classical ballet world as an additional appearance-related factor that may pressure them to lose weight. Even within a very thin figure dancers feel that breasts, rounded hips, or thighs are a liability to a career in dance. Slight bloating before menstruation similarly is experienced as a barrier to ideal shape and performance. Acquiring a full woman's figure therefore is experienced as a negative experience among aspiring dancers. I have found that even young adolescents who dance in non-competitive or nonprofessional schools strive for the "ballerina look", meaning an early pubescent figure. Related to the power of this ideal, I have seen professional dancers who, even upon their retirement in their late 30s, sought counseling to address struggles regarding body shape. Often, in struggling to feel more positive about owning a full woman's figure, they recalled the way their body shape was challenged and criticized by their dance teachers once they experienced puberty. They therefore were barred from connecting with their bodies more positively until their retirement.

Other pressures dancers in training describe that may affect them to lose weight are challenges related to their experience of ownership of their bodies. The body of the dancer continually is examined and scrutinized from the outside: shape and lines, movements, eating patterns, training and resting periods. In addition, in the process of training, the dancer often is expected to deny her own pain related to varied injuries or ignore her safety when asked to perform movements that repeatedly injure her or lifts that put her at the risk of falling or being dropped. In the process of training, some teachers feel the liberty to be physically rough. Some dancers experience the sexualization of the relationship with teaching staff or directors. These factors lead to struggles around body ownership, boundaries, and control and may result in the experience of alienation from one's body. I have heard dancers describe this experience as living in the body from the "outside in" rather than from the "inside out." Within the context of alienation from the body, it is harder for the dancer to care for the body in a compassionate way, including to experience eating as a form of self-care and regulating it from the inside.

Other factors that dancers describe as challenging to their body image and eating patterns relate to prejudices they feel as women in ballet. Female dancers describe feeling disadvantaged compared with male dancers because their sheer larger number forces them into harsher competition with one another, competition that may get diverted into the body shape arena. Ethnic or racial origin can cause an additional prejudice that may drive some dancers towards a greater pursuit of thinness in order to combat racism.

Varied expectations from female classical ballet dancers on and off the stage have been cited by ballet dancers in training as another type of adverse pressure leading them to feel uncomfortable with their physical self. They often have related in small groups that they feel uncomfortable with their strength and power. In different roles in classical ballet they have to portray a certain ethereal ascetic quality. Although their experience has taught them that their strength is essential to successful *pas-de-deux* parts, they still are expected stereotypically to be small and thin enough to be lifted. Unlike their male partners, they have felt the expectations off stage as well to be ascetic, amenable, good, polite, and quiet, images that are concordant with a smaller body and presence.

Overall, the pressures in the classical ballet world and in varied training settings may expose female dancers to complex accentuated factors that can affect their experiences of their bodies, their body image, and the experience of eating. A fuller understanding of the complex factors that may affect body shape and eating increases the likelihood of a successful outcome of preventative interventions (Piran, 1995, 1996b). It is important to recognize that every training school and dance company may have a somewhat different constellation of adverse factors, as well as strengths. It is therefore important to get familiar with the unique qualities and culture of each setting before and during the implementation of prevention interventions. The process of gaining entry as a professional in the area of body image to a dance company or school is in itself revealing about the setting.

Understanding Ambivalence: Shifting from Initial Ambivalence to Professional Rapport

Many professionals in the area of eating disorders have asked me over the years what has allowed me to implement a prevention program at the ballet school, because they faced strong ambivalence to such interventions from companies or schools they tried to approach. As mentioned earlier in the chapter, despite widespread concerns and difficulties with eating disorders, entry of professionals to dance companies or schools has been limited. In attempting to gain access to such settings it is important to understand the ambivalence towards the interventions of professionals who work in the area of body image and eating disorders.

There are different sources of ambivalence from administrators and directors of dance companies and schools. Elite companies and training schools are not favorable to programs that they perceive as potentially adversely affecting their training practices or appearance norms and, ultimately, their hard-won success. In addition, a prevention program may be seen as potentially contradicting key norms and policies advocated by training staff and administration. As such, a prevention program may be seen as challenging the authority of staff. Outsiders possibly may be seen as not understanding of or compassionate towards the challenges faced by training staff and students. In addition, artistic freedom often is seen as involving freedom from external monitoring. A preventative program inherently implies a stance of responsibility on the part of the school and company for the well-being of dancers, a domain seen by many training settings as outside their mandate. Moreover, preventative programs inherently involve the long-term well-being of the individual; most training settings focus on short-term gains.

Specifically in the area of eating disorders, dance companies and schools are worried about being associated with eating disorders. Having a professional who specializes in the area of eating disorders work at the setting is seen by staff as confirming common negative beliefs about the association between dance and eating disorders, a belief they wish to dispel. Moreover, the direct experience of administration and training staff with eating disorders is often negative. Because most companies will not address a dancer's eating disorder until it is quite severe, most staff members have experienced eating disorders as a devastating and irreversible affliction leading to the loss of talented dancers. Addressing the issue of eating disorders therefore is seen as a venture involving anticipated losses and few gains.

In light of the many sources of ambivalence in a dance company or school, it is especially important for a professional seeking entry into a setting to connect with and emphasize any positive motivations voiced by the administration of the setting. For example, administration or staff may mention the problem of losing talented dancers to eating disorders or of being worried about the well-being of some students, or they may be bothered by particular symptoms some students display (e.g., compulsive exercise that may result in injuries, or signs of vomit in the washroom). They may be affected by bad publicity about the setting related to problems with eating disorders. Although dance personnel who had successful careers themselves tend to idealize their own, sometimes harsh, past training, at times they are open to examine domains that were not adequately addressed in their schools. For example, if they struggled with an eating disorder for which they sought counseling, they may be particularly open to inviting help for their students. However, if they were left on their own to struggle with an eating disorder, they may refuse to examine the long-term impact of such oversight and to invite a professional to help the students. It is essential that the dance company or school feel that it benefits from the implementation of the program at the school. Such support and sanctioning by administration and staff is crucial to a successful implementation of the program.

Often, one finds administration and teaching staff who are quite open to the program and motivated to help in its success, and staff who are more resistant to the program. Enlisting the active collaboration of motivated staff gradually leads to making connections and rapport with other staff. Outside professionals need to have some power in the system in order to be successful.

Within the context of growing rapport, a multicomponent program can be developed. I believe that every competitive program in the area of dance or athletics, especially in domains in which appearance is related to success, requires the implementation of tertiary, secondary, and primary components.

☐ Tertiary Prevention

It is most common for a dance company or school to become involved in addressing the phenomenon of eating disorders if a crisis situation with a dancer occurs. Although a crisis may have occurred with one student, it is likely that other dancers display clinical or subclinical symptomatology. The availability of a trusted consultant to the school or company in the area of eating disorders inherently facilitates the process of prompt referral. It gives the administration, all other staff members, and students an ongoing resource to turn to with any concern in the area of eating disorders. The more available and present the consultant is, the more likely it is that people in the setting will contact her or him with questions and concerns. The consultant then can be involved in the initial consultation and, based on her or his assessment, facilitate the provision of proper treatment for the dancer. It is most helpful for the consultant to develop a network of local professionals in the area of psychotherapy, nutrition, and medicine who have acquired an interest and specialized knowledge in the area of athletics or dance and who can work together in a collaborative way.

In addition to the availability of a professional as a resource person in the area of eating disorders, the eating disorder consultant has to provide education to all staff about the nature of eating disorders, their manifestations, their complications, and warning signs. In a dance school or company, weight loss and excessive exercise easily can be interpreted as signaling devotion, high motivation, dedication, and ambition. Without adequate education about eating disorders, some teachers may idealize students who intensively engage in these behaviors until severe medical crises occur. At times, teachers may deny the connection between a severe exercise regimen and disordered eating. Teachers often are not informed about the multiple medical, social, psychological, and vocational complications of eating disorders. I have found teachers to be very interested in this information and relieved to have the consultant as a resource if difficulties arise. Although it is made explicit that staff members' role is not to diagnose eating disorders or treat them, it is expected that they will contact both the dancer and the consultant if any concerns exist. I have found that, following the educational sessions in the ballet school, accurate referrals came from teachers, administrators, physiotherapists, and residence staff.

The 10 students referred to me during the first 2 years of my work at the school had all fulfilled criteria for anorexia nervosa or bulimia nervosa (American Psychiatric Association, 1987) and had displayed significant eating symptomatology for an average duration of over 2 years. Two of these students had developed anorexia at the ages of 10 and 11 years, five and four years prior to joining the school. At the time of referral to me they were of extremely short stature (under 5 feet, 150 cm.) and of average weight for their height. They displayed symptoms of bulimia nervosa. Medical assessment suggested that their growth likely had been stunted, probably because of their early untreated anorexia. Students were advised to stop training until their eating disorders were under control and/or they regained average weight. In considering this decision, medical status as well as psychological factors are important. If medical status is compromised in any way and the particular psychological challenges involved in continued performance may compromise the process of recovery, it is important to temporarily stop all involvement in dance performances and training. Medical considerations are crucially important in dealing with students in early adolescence whose eating disorders may affect their processes of growth and physical maturation (see Chapter 19). Once significant healing has occurred, most can return to their dance careers. Others, however, may find that past experiences (such as physical or sexual abuse) may make them too vulnerable to the demands of a career in dance, or that their process of recovery may be too lengthy to pursue a career in dance. Others may find that they do not wish to pursue a career that emphasizes body shape. These are important decisions that individual dancers or students should be supported in making.

The decision to temporarily prohibit participation in the dance or training program until significant healing occurs is important not only for the dancer or student, but also for the other dancers or students. These decisions reflect the stance of the school towards eating disorders. It reflects the ultimate importance the school or company puts on the medical safety of its dancers or students. It also reflects the importance the school puts on the psychological well-being of students. I have seen students and company members examine the attitude of their schools or companies about eating disorders as demonstrated through the actual practice of prohibiting talented dancers from performing while suffering from eating disorders, rather than through the publicly stated policy of the school. Keeping talented dancers who develop clinical eating disorders in school shows or performances signifies support for eating disorders even if the public policy says otherwise. It is interesting to mention in this regard a well-established company whose visibly emaciated key female dancer had described publicly severe difficulties with eating. Students at the school attached to this company have discussed publicly the impact of having an ethereally thin role model who has eating difficulties, and their challenges with body image and eating patterns.

Short-term evaluation of outcome revealed that all but one student were treated with at least some success on an outpatient basis. The 10th student improved following a stay in an inpatient unit and continued to dance in the school upon complete recovery. Although no systematic long-term evaluation of students with clinical eating disorders has been possible, it is not unusual for past students at the school to keep in touch with me either through short notes or, less often, through further professional contacts. Three of the original 10 students developed a second bout of an eating disorder 5 to 10 years into their careers in dance, following personal or ballet-related crises. Although all three recovered from these bouts, two decided on their own to withdraw from dance. Two others chose to withdraw from dance despite a successful career to avoid continued pressures in the body domain. The two students with stunted growth could not pursue successful dance careers, because their bodies did not fulfil the aesthetic requirements of company directors. Overall, this clinical picture suggests that the development of a full-blown eating disorder, in addition to taking a serious personal toll, challenges a career in dance and requires long-term treatment and follow-up. Further, this evaluation reinforces the value of secondary and primary prevention.

When I reflect about my 2 years of exclusive involvement in tertiary prevention, I do view such involvement positively in that it has assisted students who, previous to such involvement, were struggling without appropriate professional help. However, I view these 2 years as especially important in that they gave me the opportunity to introduce a more comprehensive program at the school. During these 2 years, in addition to seeing students who displayed eating symptomatology at the school, I spent time talking with key personnel at the school about body image and eating disorders. When I suggested implementing a primary and secondary prevention at the school, the school embraced this suggestion. A few processes that occurred during these 2 years seemed to relate to this positive response on the part of the school as well as to the success of the prevention program. First, the school developed trust in my professional services, and a solid rapport was formed between key personnel at the school and myself as a professional at the community. Second, I became familiar with the school culture and its strengths and weaknesses, as well as with key personnel at the school. Third, through dialogue with me as a service provider and through observing the processes of growth among girls who were healing from their difficulties, the attitudes of key personnel shifted from viewing eating disorders as irreversible aberrations affecting the weaker few to seeing eating disorders as understandable and mostly treatable reactions to pressures in the body domain. In an interesting way, this resulted in a greater openness to identify the spectrum of eating difficulties at the school. Fourth, the more hopeful view of recovery from eating disorders made key personnel hopeful about the possibility that the school would be helped as a whole. Fifth, key personnel assumed a stance of responsibility for examining and changing body-related pressures and the occurrence of eating disorders at the school. Sixth, key personnel had the opportunity to voice and discuss their motivations for actively involving the school in curtailing eating disorders. Seventh, despite possible ambivalence towards my explicitly stated values regarding healthy weights and related issues, key personnel felt that I could work with their school in a way that would take into consideration the goals and challenges of the school and allot the system as a whole the time it needed to change. This period of initial rapport had a powerful impact throughout the process of successful implementation of the other components of the program.

☐ Secondary Prevention

The addition of a secondary prevention component to the tertiary component at the school was a natural expansion of the latter. Similar to tertiary prevention, the secondary component involved the subcomponents of identification, consultation, and intervention. Because the goal of secondary prevention is the identification of and intervention with individuals at increased risk for the development of clinical eating disorders, the process involves the identification of individuals displaying lower levels of symptomatology on the continuum of body weight and shape preoccupation.

Special presentations were prepared for the purpose of early identification of students at high risk at the school. These presentations were made every 2 or so years to the different staff groups. Presentations also were made annually to all students in the school in grade- and gender-cohesive groups, albeit in a briefer "booster" format in repeat years. Although the presentations to staff and students were similar, presentations to students were more cautious about describing any eating symptomatology in order to minimize the effect of contagion (Crandall, 1988; Mann et al., 1997). In addition, although these presentations included didactic information, the format was always that of exploration and discussion, letting students and staff pursue relevant aspects of knowledge in their own terms. In introducing the different components of the presentations, I describe them as they were structured when conducted with students.

Presentations aimed at secondary prevention included several aspects. One was exploration of the pressures that exist at and outside of the school that may make students susceptible to becoming preoccupied with body weight and shape. The goal of this aspect was to make disordered eating an understandable occurrence and to take away the personal stigma involved in developing difficulties. It was emphasized repeatedly that a person at times may become preoccupied with his or her weight if different pressures accumulate and make it difficult for him or her to cope. These could include feeling challenged at dance classes or not feeling accepted by friends, feeling sad about a crisis in the family, or feeling bad about the way that somebody treated the person or his or her body. The body then can become a "scapegoat," an avenue to express and deal with other feelings and experiences. It further was suggested that students take notice if this was happening to them at any time. The goal was not to develop a comprehensive theoretical understanding, but to accustom students to questioning what different issues may be operating in their or their friends' lives that may make them preoccupied with their body and to suggest that students who become preoccupied with body weight and shape seek a counseling arrangement that would give them the opportunity to examine the challenges they were facing in their life at the time.

The second component included a discussion of complications of a considerable preoccupation with body weight and shape. This discussion included descriptions of possible medical complications of poor nutrition (weakening of the body, cardiac complications, disrupted growth processes, lowered metabolic rate, and so forth), possible psychological complications (preoccupation with eating, lowered concentration, low mood, sleep disturbance, and so forth), social complications (withdrawal, shame), and vocational and academic complications (especially the impact on the ability to dance).

The third component included a discussion of signs of strong preoccupation with body weight and shape. In these presentations, a strong emphasis was put on the heightened discomfort with body weight and shape rather than on eating symptomatology. A strong preoccupation with body weight and shape was described as a degree of preoccupation that affects one's mood, ability to dance comfortably, and feelings about oneself. It also was mentioned that a student who is uncomfortable with her or his body weight and shape, at times, might try to change her or his body shape in different means, such as changing calorie consumption or exercising relentlessly. Because the format of these presentations always has been interactive, I tended to listen to the existing knowledge in the class about ways of undoing the act of eating. In some classes, usually older classes, students mentioned the behaviors of vomiting or laxatives. When these behaviors were mentioned I always explored with the students their knowledge of specific risks involved in these behaviors, as well as describing why these measures do not work in the short and long run. Similarly, the futility and short- and long-term risks involved in all measures of trying to alter one's natural body shape, especially during the process of growth, were described. The importance of a healthy lifestyle involving healthy nutrition and a balanced exercise routine and its advantage in supporting a natural body shape and in enhancing a career in dance always were highlighted.

Because the presentation emphasized the importance of confronting issues that underlie preoccupation with body weight and shape rather than alter one's own body, the last component included a concrete action plan for students to follow if they detected a strong degree of body-shape preoccupation in themselves. Students were to approach people they knew and felt comfortable with who were assigned by the school to respond to these issues—the school counselor, a key teaching staff member who had special knowledge and sensitivity in the area, an administrative secretary who was responsible for making appointments with outside consultants—or they could contact me directly. These people had to make themselves easily accessible to students' inquiries and refer them to me for consultation if students displayed ongoing preoccupation with body weight and shape. In order to prepare them for this role, I spent time with each of these people training them about ways to respond to the students if they were approached with preoccupation with body weight and shape. This system of on-site support and referral was checked on an ongoing basis.

Consultations included an assessment of level and duration of symptomatology and degree of preoccupation with body weight and shape, and assessments of mood states and of the experience of oneself. Precipitating factors and individual, familial, and social histories were included. History of physical or sexual abuse or other body-related trauma was explored. Coping strategies, strengths and weaknesses, and available supports were assessed. Physical and mental symptomatology associated with different means of starvation and purging was explored. The report of any significant symptomatology indicated a referral for a medical consultation. Because the secondary prevention brought students with much lower levels of symptomatology and preoccupation for consultations, generally these students showed a larger variety of adaptive coping strategies, ego strengths, healthy social connections, active psychological exploration, and openness to explore affecting factors. In addition, the onset of weight preoccupation and eating symptomatology was recent and not entrenched in the students' life. It was therefore much easier to reverse adverse processes.

In terms of intervention, consultations with students revealed that students who developed preoccupation with body weight and shape or low-level symptomatology required varied outpatient services. A few discovered that the onset of weight preoccupation masked significant experiences and challenges that required longer-term counseling. The prompt identification, however, allowed them to proceed with counseling work that focused on the challenges at hand rather than on overcoming an entrenched eating disorder. Others required being seen just few times to get beyond the weight preoccupation, identify their underlying concerns, and develop strategies to deal with these challenges. Some needed to be seen just one time for a quick and focused intervention. For example, a student whose family recently immigrated from the Far East to Canada found herself at the beginning of the year getting preoccupied with her body size and eating. An exploration revealed that her Caucasian roommate who had just joined the school was masking a full-blown eating disorder and continuously measured the two of them with a tape measure and taught the Asian girl about food restriction and "bad" foods. During the session, we found that the immigrant student had a positive body image and had a healthy connection to food, especially her familial foods, as a source of sustenance and health. She also had strong and positive familial ties. The student needed to discuss the impact of her roommate on her and locate the problem with her roommate rather than with her own body. I encouraged her to take a few days vacation with her family to connect more healthily with her body and eating, while the school changed the sleeping arrangements. In a follow-up session, she was problem-free. The roommate was angry to find out that the school required her to address her eating problem if she wanted to be involved with the ballet program; in her previous school they had "left her alone," and she returned to her previous school. She and her family rejected all offers of help.

The idea of conducting groups, rather than individual interventions, with students preoccupied with body weight and shape seems plausible. However, within the context of the ballet school, students were not interested in such a program. On two occasions when this possibility was explored, students expressed a strong preference to meet with the consultant individually to discuss their own challenges in dealing with body-related pressures. It seems to me that students were seeking individual consultations because they get ample opportunity for group support and discussion as part of the primary prevention component.

Evaluation of the secondary prevention component yielded a revealing positive pattern (Piran, 1998a). For the purpose of this evaluation, all referrals for consultation during the 2 years prior to the implementation of the secondary component and the referrals during the 10 years following the implementation of the program were compared. First, students referred for consultation after the implementation of the secondary prevention component consistently displayed lower levels of symptomatology. Second, duration since onset of eating symptomatology was reduced from over 2 years to an average of 8 weeks. Third, after the introduction of the secondary prevention component about 50% of the students referred themselves for consultation, before staff detected any difficulty, while none of the students during the tertiary prevention stage referred themselves for treatment. Similar to the tertiary component, no systematic long-term evaluations were conducted, but following students throughout their years at school and a significant portion through their dance careers, I have not seen a relapse into a full-blown eating disorder by any of these students.

☐ Primary Prevention

Prior to describing my approach to the primary prevention of eating disorders in the ballet school it may be of value to address two issues that could be raised in relation the implementation of a combined secondary and primary prevention program in a particular setting. Based on a study of prevention on campus, Mann and her colleagues in Stanford University (Mann et al., 1997) have suggested that components of primary and secondary prevention may work at cross-purposes. They suggested that the dissemination of information about eating disorders for the purpose of early identification inadvertently may encourage some people to adopt such symptomatology and, hence, could result in increased incidence. My experience has been quite divergent from this conclusion, in that I have found a natural continuity and amplification of effectiveness in including both components in the same setting. In both components, students and staff were invited to explore factors that could cause themselves or others to develop preoccupation with body weight and shape. In both components they also were invited to take on initiatives aimed at dealing with these underlying factors directly rather than resorting to a diverted, often futile (in the long-term) and dangerous struggle with their body. In the secondary component students were invited to explore and address underlying adverse factors in counseling if they detected a high preoccupation with body weight and shape. In the primary component they were encouraged to examine their environment and their own experiences and guide changes in their school setting, and other domains of their lives, that would result in a positive experience of their body and their self esteem. In addition to overlapping explorations and initiatives, the secondary component implemented in the ballet school was most parsimonious in describing varied eating symptomatology and did not include information that could have glamorized or idealized eating disorders as a way of coping. The experience was, therefore, that the primary and secondary components were not working at cross-purposes.

The second issue that could be raised in relation to a multicomponent program is the overlap between these two components. For example, the inclusion of information about the complications of severe preoccupation with body weight and shape and disordered eating patterns may be relevant both to primary and secondary prevention. In this chapter, I have included this material in the secondary prevention section for two reasons. First, extensive research in the area of primary prevention has shown repeatedly that this information does not lead to reduced incidence of disordered eating (see Chapters 1 and 8). Secondly, I have viewed primary prevention as requiring varied components such as empowerment, equity, and safety (Piran, 1996a, 1997, in press), elements not present in semididactic sessions on risks involved with eating-disorder symptomatology.

The primary prevention program, aimed at lowering the incidence of body weight and shape preoccupation, followed participatory processes of development similar to the European Network of Health Promoting Schools model developed by the World Health Organization (European Network of Health-Promoting Schools information booklet, 1993). The program has been described elsewhere (Piran, 1996b, 1998b; see also Chapter 9). The program started with a process of dialogue in focus groups with all stakeholders in the school setting, including students, administration, and teaching and residence staff, about the presence and causes of body-weight and shape preoccupation at the school. All groups expressed a high level of concern in that domain. The initial exploratory phase started a process of ongoing scrutiny of systemic factors at the school that could exert adverse effects on body image, self-esteem, and the experience of eating as a source of sustenance and as a social ritual (Piran, in press). Ways of addressing and changing adverse factors and amplifying positive factors were explored and their implementation planned. The process of dialogue, communication, collaboration, and systemic change has continued throughout the operation of the program and is a key component in this model of prevention. The model relies heavily on feminist (Piran, 1996) and participatory (Piran, in press) principles of change and on systemic approaches to prevention (McKinlay, 1997). The process of implementing the primary prevention component has been revealing both theoretically (Piran, 1996a) and in terms of guiding the practice of prevention (Piran, 1995; 1996b), in that students' expert communications about their experiences provided the basis of for systemic change.

A retrospective look at the systemic outcome of implementing the primary prevention program at the school reveals that the program worked to create a social subsystem (the school system) that counteracted adverse influences on students' experiences of their bodies and themselves. More specifically, it created a school system in which a healthy lifestyle is emphasized and practiced, natural growth processes are respected, and the role of food in sustenance and in social rituals is incorporated; students develop a critical perspective towards adverse social influences on body image and use this critical perspective to transform their environment; the body is not a site of maltreatment, prejudice, or constraining social roles; students can express problematic experiences in the body domain and have the power to change them; and students can unite in working on challenges they face in the body domain.

Creating an experientially healthier environment for students as well as facilitating an intellectually critical perspective in students are hallmarks of systemic interventions in schools (European Network of Health Promoting Schools information booklet, 1997). In the process of creating a healthier system for the students, based on students knowledge and agency, the ballet school had to examine and revise many norms, systems of prejudice, rules of operation, hierarchical structures, and structures of communications (Piran, in press). The writings of Foucault (1979) and critical social theorists, including feminists such as Rich (1986), are highly relevant in that they stress the role of the body as a medium through which rules about social power and social worth are both inscribed and learned. Scrutiny around students' experience of their body inherently led to scrutiny of the school system as a whole. The great value put on students' experiences and their empowerment in guiding changes in the school system are in line with participatory and feminist paradigms of intervention.

A retrospective examination of changes conducted at the school over the past 10 years suggests that these changes can be roughly divided into three temporal stages, somewhat different in focus although not mutually exclusive. During the first 3 to 4 years at the school, systemic changes focused on revising aesthetic, ideological, and behavioral norms around weight, shape, and eating. These included the acceptance of diverse body shapes, natural processes of growth and maturation, lifestyle education, and emphasis on stamina rather than appearance. The second stage, from the 3rd through the 8th year, included mainly issues related to harassment, equity, safety, power, and communication. During the third stage, from the 8th year and on, the school became involved in leading and advocacy roles in reforming ballet training and weight norms in the ballet world worldwide. For example, key personnel have started to work towards the acceptance of fuller figures for women in dance and to emphasize the importance of long-term health, and positive body and self-image of dancers (Staines, personal communication, April 10, 1998; Walker, 1997).

The outcome of the program has been described elsewhere (Piran, in press). The program has been associated with significant decreases in the incidence of new cases, in the incidence of subclinical difficulties, and in body-image disturbance.

☐ Challenges in the Implementation of a Multiple-Component Systemic Intervention in a Ballet School

The program relies on ongoing active monitoring and scrutiny of the system. Although systemic changes are known to be easier to sustain than individual changes, it is important to monitor the nature of systemic changes. Unfavorable changes may occur unexpectedly because of staffing change, a new student body, or an influential visitor from the dance community. Such changes need ongoing monitoring and interventions. The program relies on rapport with all stakeholders in the school setting. Keeping ongoing rapport with administration, teaching and residence staff, and students presents a challenge that requires ongoing monitoring as well.

At times, the primary prevention component may force the school to tackle hard issues, such as staff replacement. In addition, new administrators may oppose the changes introduced prior to their involvement.

I have found it useful to be involved in all three components of prevention in a particular school. It gives one the opportunity to get to know the culture "inside out" and intervene in the most efficient way. However, such intensive involvement is not always possible for the consultant.

☐ Conclusion

The program at the ballet school included tertiary, secondary, and primary components. These seemed to amplify one another and to follow similar principles, those of exploring the phenomena of eating disorders and actively pursuing solutions based on critical examination and understanding of students' and staff's life experiences. The program has worked successfully, most likely because of its emphasis on systemic change and students' empowerment.

☐ References

American Psychiatric Association. (1987). *Diagnostic and statistical manual of mental disorders* (3rd ed., revised). Washington, DC: Author.

Brooks-Gunn, J., Burrow, C., & Warren, M.P. (1988). Attitudes toward eating and body weight in different groups of female adolescent athletes. *International Journal of Eating Disorders, 7,* 749–757.

Carreiro, D., & Verhaeghe, M. (1992, April 5). Dancing on the ceiling: Dangerous role model, *The Winnipeg Sun.*

Crandall, C. S. (1988). Social contagion of binge eating. *Journal of Personality and Social Psychology,* 55, 588–598.

European Network of Health-Promoting Schools Information Booklet. (1993). *World Health Organization. Regional office for Europe, Denmark.*

European Network of Health-Promoting Schools Information Booklet. (1997). *World Health Organization, Regional Office for Europe, Denmark.*

Evers, C. L. (1987). Dietary intake and symptoms of anorexia nervosa in female University dancers. *Journal of the American Dietetic Association, 87,* 66–68.

Foucault, M. (1979). *Discipline and punish.* New York: Vintage Books.

Garfinkel, P. E., & Garner, D. M. (1982). *Anorexia nervosa: A multidimensional perspective.* New York: Brunner/Mazel.

Garner, D., Garfinkel, P., Rockert, W., & Olmsted, M. (1987). A prospective study of eating disturbances in the ballet. *Psychotherapy and Psychosomatics, 48,* 170–175.

Mann, T., Nolen-Hoekksema, S., Huang, K., Burgard, D., Wright, A., & Hanson, K. (1997). Are two interventions worse than none? Joint primary and secondary prevention of eating disorders in college females. *Health Psychology, 16,* 215–225.

McKinlay, J.B. (1997). Appropriate levels of intervention and analysis for community health interventions. Paper presented at the One Hundred and Fifth Annual Convention of the American Psychological Association, Chicago.

Nattive, A., Agostini. R., Drinkwater, B., & Yeager, K.K. (1994). The female athlete Triad: The interrelatedness of disordered eating, amenorrhea, and osteoporosis. *Clinics in Sports Medicine, 13,* 405–418.

Piran, N. (1995). Prevention: Can early lessons lead to a delineation of an alternative model? *Eating Disorders: The Journal of Treatment and Prevention, 4,* 323–347.

Piran, N. (1996a). Eating disorders: Culture, research paradigms and the transformation of knowledge. Paper presented at the One Hundred and Fourth Annual Convention of the American Psychological Association, Toronto.

Piran, N. (1996b). The reduction of preoccupation with body weight and shape in schools: A feminist approach. *Eating Disorders: The Journal of Treatment andPrevention, 4,* 323–330.

Piran, N. (1997). Prevention of eating disorders: Directions for future research. *Psychopharmacology Bulletin.* 33, 419–423.

Piran, N. (1998a). Outcome evaluation of a secondary prevention program in an elite ballet school. Unpublished manuscript.

Piran, N. (1998b). A participatory approach to the prevention of eating disorders in a school. In W. Vandereycken & G. Noordenbos (Eds.), The preventing of eating disorders (pp. 173–186). London: Athlone.

Piran, N. (in press). Eating disorders: A trial of prevention in a high risk school setting. *Journal of Primary Prevention.*

Rich, A. (1986). *Of woman born.* New York: W. W. Norton.

Terry, S. (1997, July 11). A ballet dancer, so very thin, dies, and the questions begin. *New York Times.*

Walker, S. (1997, November 22). Ballet shows its muscles. *The Toronto Star.* pp. 5–6.

Weeda-Mannak, W. L., & Drop, M. J. (1985). The discriminative value of psychological characteristics in anorexia nervosa: Clinical and psychometric comparison between anorexia nervosa patients, ballet dancers and controls. *Journal of Psychiatric Research, 19,* 285–290.

Patricia A. Colton
Gary M. Rodin
Marion P. Olmsted
Denis Daneman

CHAPTER

Preventing Eating Disorders in Young Women with Diabetes

It is now well established that disturbed eating attitudes and behavior are common in adolescent girls and young women, including those with type I diabetes mellitus (DM) (Powers, Malone, Coovert, & Schulman, 1990; Rydall, Rodin, Olmsted, Devenyi, & Daneman, 1997). It has been proposed that specific aspects of diabetes management, including strict dietary restraint, weight gain caused by insulin therapy, and the availability of insulin manipulation as a weight-control strategy, may predispose vulnerable individuals with DM to the spectrum of disordered eating, including bulimia nervosa (Figure 1) (Fairburn, Peveler, Davies, Mann, & Mayou, 1991; Rodin & Daneman, 1992; see Figure 1). The question of whether clinical eating disorders are more common in the diabetic population remains unresolved, although there is mounting evidence that even mild eating disturbances in this population are associated with poor blood sugar control and with increased risk of early diabetes-related medical complications. This chapter reviews the clinical presentation, detection, and potential consequences of eating disorders in young women with DM and considers several possibilities for primary and secondary prevention of eating disturbances in this high-risk group.

☐ Type I Diabetes Mellitus

Type I diabetes mellitus, previously known as "juvenile diabetes" and "insulin-dependent diabetes mellitus," is a common chronic medical condition that most often has its onset during childhood and adolescence. It affects 0.2–0.3% of individuals by the age of 20, with an equal gender distribution (Drash, 1987). One postulated cause of the disorder is autoimmune destruction of the body's insulin-producing cells in the pancreas (Atkinson & Maclaren, 1994), which leads to decreasing levels of insulin in the blood. Insulin is required for entry of blood sugar into the body's cells. In its absence, blood sugar levels rise dramatically, and sugar then is lost in the urine. If this happens, large quantities of water are lost with

From Diabetes
to Disturbed Eating Behavior

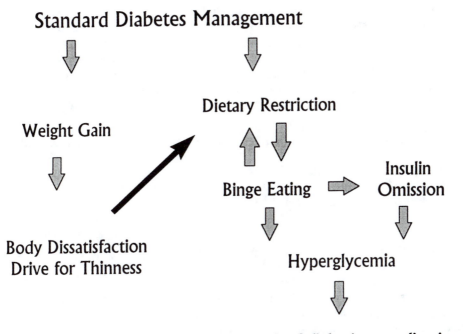

FIGURE 1. Pathways from diabetes to disturbed eating behavior.

the sugar, resulting in thirst, weight loss, excessive urination, and dehydration, all of which signal the onset of DM. Once DM is present, daily insulin injections are required to utilize nutrients, to maintain body weight, and to sustain life.

The diagnosis of DM initiates profound changes in lifestyle for the child and his or her family (for more information, see Jacobson et al., 1986). The main goal of diabetes management is to maintain blood sugar levels consistently within a narrow range. The usual management plan includes careful planning of meals and snacks, blood sugar measurements and insulin injections several times daily, and regular medical follow-up. Families learn about the symptoms and management of episodes of hypoglycemia (low blood sugar) and hyperglycemia (high blood sugar), both of which can be serious and life-threatening. After an initial period of medical stabilization and intensive family-based education about diabetes management, the majority of children with DM are healthy and active. However, in addition to the daily effort of managing their diabetes, individuals with DM face increased lifetime risk of a number of medical complications. These complications include heart disease, stroke, peripheral vascular disease, and damage to the kidneys, eyes, and peripheral nerves.

The Diabetes Control and Complications Trial (DCCT) demonstrated conclusively that maintaining blood sugar levels close to normal values decreases the risk of onset and progression of long-term diabetes-related complications affecting kidney, retina, and peripheral nerves (DCCT Research Group, 1993). The finding that better management of DM can improve the chance of remaining healthy over the lifespan has been very encouraging, both to individuals with DM and to the health care professionals who work with them. On the other hand, individuals with DM and their families often feel enormous pressure to maintain "perfect" blood sugar control and may experience feelings of guilt or failure if they are unable to do so. Blood sugar control is assessed both by patterns of daily blood sugar measurements and by measurement of hemoglobin A1c, an index of blood sugar control over the past two to three months.

☐ Psychological Adjustment to Type 1 Diabetes Mellitus

Following the diagnosis of DM, sadness, social withdrawal, anger, and increased dependence on parents are initially common in children and adolescents (Kovacs, Brent, Steinberg, Paulaskas, & Reid, 1986). A significant proportion of children and adolescents with DM is also at risk for subsequent psychological, social, and family difficulties (Rubin & Peyrot, 1992). Longitudinal studies of psychosocial functioning have documented high rates of depression and anxiety in children and adolescents with DM, with a cumulative risk for a major psychiatric disorder through adolescence of 48% (Jacobson et al., 1994; Kovacs, Goldston, Obrosky, & Bonar, 1997). The challenges of living with a medical illness also may interfere with consolidating a stable and positive self-concept and body image; as a group, adolescents with chronic medical conditions have poorer self-esteem and body image than their medically well peers (Wolman, Resnick, Harris, & Blum, 1994).

☐ Epidemiology of Eating Disturbances and Type 1 DM

The relationship between DM and eating disorders has been the focus of increasing interest and research since Bruch (1973) reported a case of anorexia nervosa in a young woman with DM. Following initial case reports of the coincidence of DM with anorexia nervosa and bulimia nervosa, numerous studies have examined the prevalence of eating disorders in individuals with diabetes, the nature of the relationship between eating disturbances and diabetes, and the health consequences of these disturbances.

Marcus and Wing (1990) provided an excellent review of the 57 cases of eating disorders in individuals with DM reported to that time. These cases demonstrated features that have been confirmed in subsequent systematic research. Ninety-five percent were women, mirroring sex ratios of eating disorders in the general population, and in 90% of cases the diagnosis of diabetes was made prior to the onset of an eating disorder. Steel, Lloyd, Young, and MacIntyre (1990) documented deterioration in body image over the first year following diagnosis of DM. This observation is compatible with the hypothesis that living with diabetes may lower the threshold for the expression of an eating disorder, in which body image disturbance is central.

The rate of clinical eating disorders reported in studies of individuals with DM varies widely, based on the age range and gender ratio of the study population, the method of evaluation, and the diagnostic criteria that are employed. The most recent DSM-IV criteria (American Psychiatric Association, 1994) tend to yield higher rates than earlier criteria in diabetic populations, because insulin manipulation qualifies as a "compensatory behavior." Although the prevalence of clinical eating disorders has ranged from none in preadolescent and adolescent girls (Striegel-Moore, Nicholson, & Tamborlane, 1992) to 16% in women with DM (Affenito et al., 1997), most surveys have found eating disorders in 5–10% of the samples studied (e.g., Fairburn et al., 1991; Mannucci et al., 1995). Bulimia nervosa and eating disorders not otherwise specified are more common than anorexia nervosa in young women with diabetes (Rydall et al., 1997), as in the general population. Some of these studies included a non-diabetic control group, but none have had sufficient statistical power to detect significant differences that may exist.

Although the data regarding clinical eating disorders are inconclusive, adolescent girls and young women with DM are more uniformly found to be at increased risk over their non-diabetic peers for milder, subclinical eating disturbances. These disturbances are not of sufficient severity to justify a psychiatric diagnosis but nevertheless can heighten the risk of poor blood sugar control and early diabetes-related medical complications (Colas, Mathieu, & Tchobroutsky, 1991; Rydall et al., 1997). In this regard, 12–58% of young women with DM admit to binge eating (Fairburn et al., 1991; La Greca, Schwarz, & Satin, 1987; Stancin, Link, & Reuter, 1989), and up to 40% manipulate insulin dosage or omit insulin injections in order to control or lose weight (e.g., Rydall et al., 1997; Stancin, 1989). Use of intense exercise to control weight is also common, although other purging behavior, such as self-induced vomiting and laxative or diuretic abuse, is much less common than either insulin manipulation or exercise for weight control (Fairburn et al., 1991; Powers et al., 1990; Stancin et al., 1989).

The Link Between Type 1 Diabetes Mellitus and Eating Disturbances

We have suggested (De Groot & Rodin, 1994) that eating disorders are associated with a disturbance in the psychological sense of self, and in the processing and awareness of affective states, hunger and satiety cues, and other aspects of subjective experience. Individuals with this relative inability to identify, trust, or modulate inner experience are likely to be more sensitive to environmental cues and pressures, including pressure to diet and be thin. This tendency to rely on environmental rather than inner cues may lead to states of dysregulation, including anorexia nervosa and bulimia nervosa. In individuals with DM, states of dysregulation may be triggered by the pressure to ignore inner hunger cues and to eat according to a prescribed meal plan.

Blood sugar control often worsens significantly during the adolescent years (Jacobson et al., 1987); adolescent girls have particular difficulty following the strict diabetic regimen that is designed to minimize their risk of developing diabetic complications (Gordon & Mansfield, 1996). This failure to adhere to the management plan may be explained partially by the disturbed eating behavior that is common among adolescent girls and young women. This behavior is rooted in the body dissatisfaction, preoccupation with weight and shape, and drive for thinness that are endemic among young women in Western countries. Specific aspects of diabetes and its management, particularly strict dietary control and restraint, weight gain associated with insulin therapy, and manipulation of insulin use to control weight, may put vulnerable individuals with DM at heightened risk for disturbed eating behavior.

Dietary Restraint

Rigorous planning of food intake is the cornerstone of diabetes management. A traditional diabetic meal plan is well balanced and contains adequate calories for healthy growth and development. It is, however, similar to many weight-loss diets in its prohibition or strict limitation of the intake of certain foods, particularly simple carbohydrates, and its encouragement of individuals to follow an imposed eating plan rather than respond to their own hunger and satiety cues.

Prospective studies of non-diabetic adolescent and young women have confirmed that dieting is a significant predictor of the onset of more disturbed eating behavior over the next several years (e.g., Attie & Brooks-Gunn, 1989). The dietary restraint that is dictated externally by a diabetic diet may lead, as does the restraint arising from the drive for thinness, to dysregulation of normal eating patterns (Polivy & Herman, 1985), with binge eating and compensatory purging behavior, including insulin-dosage manipulation. This dangerous cycle of dietary restraint, binge eating, and compensatory behavior may be self-perpetuating. Unfortunately, these girls may be reluctant to tell their families and physicians about their body image and eating problems and so may not have access to the support and treatment that they need.

Weight Gain

Weight and shape concerns tend to be heightened in young women during periods of rapid weight gain, in those who are heavier than their peers, and during the physical changes and significant weight gain associated with puberty. Several prospective general population studies have identified childhood obesity and an increased percentage of body fat in the early adolescent period as predictors of later disturbed eating (e.g., Attie & Brooks-Gunn, 1989; Killen et al., 1994). Obese girls with DM are significantly more likely than nonobese girls with DM to have a clinical eating disorder, and to suffer from a range of other psychiatric problems (Vila et al., 1995).

When diabetes treatment is first begun, patients rapidly gain back the weight that may have been lost prior to diagnosis. Intensive insulin therapy, to achieve the tight blood sugar control recommended by the Diabetes Control and Complications Trial, (DCCT), may require as many as four insulin injections daily and is associated with weight gain (Wing, Klein, & Moss, 1990). Females with DM have higher body mass index values than their non-diabetic peers (Diabetes Research Group, 1988). We have found that the combination of rapid initial weight gain and higher stable weight can be very distressing for girls who already are struggling with body shape and weight concerns, particularly in a culture that highly values a thin, prepubertal body ideal. Such young women may experience intense conflict between the desire to adhere to a management plan that lowers their risk of diabetic complications but causes weight gain, and the strong personal and social pressures to be slim. Negotiating a healthy compromise between the fear of weight gain and the desire for adequate diabetic management and prevention of medical complications is often a challenging therapeutic task.

Insulin Manipulation

Weight-control behaviors such as dieting, self-induced vomiting, the abuse of laxatives, diuretics, and diet pills, and compulsive exercise are associated with clinical and subclinical eating disorders. Individuals with DM have an additional weight-control method available to them. If they take less than the prescribed dosage of insulin, or omit an insulin injection entirely, blood sugar levels rise, and a large number of calories, in the form of sugar, is lost in the urine. The prevalence of insulin manipulation for weight control is shockingly high among adolescent girls and young women with DM, ranging from 13% (Mannucci et al., 1995) to 36% (Biggs, Basco, Patterson, & Raskin, 1994). In fact, this is the most common purging behavior in weight-preoccupied diabetics (Rydall et al., 1997). The simplicity and ready availability of this weight-control strategy may explain the low prevalence of other behaviors such as vomiting and laxative and diuretic use in diabetic women with eating disturbances. Insulin manipulation for weight loss does occur, although rarely, among men with DM (e.g., Powers et al., 1990).

Insulin dosage manipulation may occur in young women with diabetes for a variety of reasons. Although weight control is the most common reason for taking less than the prescribed dosage, other factors may contribute to difficulty adhering to this part of the management plan. These include fear of severe low blood sugar reactions, a wish to deny or "take a holiday" from diabetes, needle phobia, secondary gain, and, occasionally, suicidal intent (e.g., Polonsky et al., 1994). Insulin dosage manipulation is associated with more psychological distress, high rates of other clinically significant eating disturbances, poorer blood sugar control, more frequent hospitalizations, and higher rates of retinopathy, neuropathy, and other medical complications (Biggs et al., 1994; Polonsky et al., 1994). Some of the issues involved in insulin dosage manipulation are illustrated in the following case.

Laura, who was diagnosed with DM at age 12, began dieting and exercising intensely at age 22, hoping to attain a "flat stomach." She had just completed college, and was away from home for the first time, working as a counselor at a summer camp for children with diabetes. After restricting her diet and losing nearly 20 pounds, she began binge eating nightly. She also learned from a peer with diabetes that by taking less than her prescribed dosage of insulin, she could rapidly lose weight and compensate for her binges. At a psychiatric assessment several months later, Laura reported intense fears of gaining weight and of losing control of her eating. She often felt overwhelmed by strong emotions, although she frequently could not distinguish the nature of these feelings or their precipitants. Inducing high blood sugar levels through insulin omission allowed her to feel "numb" and "removed" from her intense distress. She was acutely aware and fearful that her poor blood sugar control could contribute to early medical complications. She felt physically flawed by her diabetes, "even though other people can't see it," and deprived and punished by the limitations of her diabetes management plan. Laura felt that the diabetic dietary restrictions imposed on her as a young girl made it difficult for her to enjoy food, or to eat without significant anxiety and guilt.

Consequences of Eating Disturbances in Individuals with Diabetes

In the general population, eating disorders are associated with significant morbidity and mortality (Jacobs Institute of Women's Health, 1996). In individuals with DM, even mild eating disturbances can have additional medical consequences; disordered eating is associated with poor blood sugar control and more frequent hospitalizations (La Greca et al., 1987; Stancin et al., 1989). Disordered eating also is associated with increased risk of diabetes-related medical complications (e.g., Colas et al., 1991; Rydall et al., 1997; Steel, Young, Lloyd, & MacIntyre, 1989). Colas et al. (1991) compared a series of 29 women with DM and eating disorders with age-matched diabetic women without eating disorders. Retinal damage was detected in 62% of the women with eating disorders, but in only 20% of the women without eating disorders ($p < .001$). In a longitudinal study of 91 adolescent girls and young women with DM, we (Rydall et al., 1997) demonstrated that girls with eating disturbances at baseline had a threefold increase in the prevalence of retinal damage four years later, compared with girls without eating disturbances (86% versus 24%). Trends for increased diabetic kidney damage (Rydall et al., 1997) and nerve damage (Colas et al., 1991; Steel et al., 1989) also have been noted.

Family Factors

The quality of family environments is an important factor in determining the adjustment of children and adolescents to DM, including the success of their diabetes management (e.g., Hauser et al., 1990). Poor compliance with diabetes management and resultant poor blood sugar control among adolescents with DM have been associated with disturbed family functioning (Maharaj, Rodin, Olmsted, & Daneman, 1998). Some of these disturbances are reminiscent of those documented in the families of girls with eating disorders (Dare & Eisler, 1997). They include rigidity, difficulty with conflict resolution, less open expression and discussion of feelings, and high levels of conflict (Hauser et al., 1990; Jacobson et al., 1994).

Our research (Maharaj et al., 1998) revealed a striking association of eating disturbances in adolescent girls with DM with poor blood sugar control, and family dysfunction. The girls with disturbed eating were significantly more likely to report poor communication with parents, and to perceive their families as having high levels of conflict and being inadequate in support. Specific family-based interventions may facilitate healthy eating attitudes and behavior and may prove to be powerful tools in the prevention or management of eating disturbances in this population.

☐ Screening for Eating Disturbances in Diabetes

Screening for disturbed eating attitudes and behavior should be a part of routine clinical care, because these disturbances are so common in girls and young women with DM, and because they can have serious medical consequences. In our clinic we ask young women with DM directly, in a respectful and nonjudgmental way, about body dissatisfaction, discrepancy between current and ideal weight, dietary restriction, overeating and binge eating, and insulin manipulation and other purging behavior. Particularly with the older girls, we try to ask these questions without their parents present. Screening tests such as the Eating Disorder Inventory (Garner, Olmsted, & Polivy, 1983) may increase the rate of detection of eating disorders in the diabetic population (Cantwell & Steel, 1996), although some items on such self-report measures need to be adjusted for patients with diabetes. Because problems evolve over time, and because individuals initially may be reluctant to admit to disordered eating behavior, questions about body image, eating, and purging behavior should be a part of ongoing regular clinic care. Several warning signs that may indicate undetected eating disturbances are outlined in the following subsections.

Poor Blood Sugar Control

Persistently poor blood sugar control, or a deterioration in the level of blood sugar control, may be the result of chaotic eating and purging behavior. Girls and women with eating disturbances are consistently much more likely to have poor blood sugar control than are their diabetic peers without symptoms of disordered eating (e.g., Rydall et al., 1997). Because ingesting as few as 500 calories without increasing insulin dosage can adversely affect blood sugar levels, it is understandable that even mild eating disturbances can have a dramatic negative effect on blood sugar control.

Recurrent Hospitalizations and Diabetic Ketoacidosis

Diabetic individuals with bulimic symptoms often have high blood sugar levels (hyperglycemia) because of binge eating and insulin dosage manipulation. If insulin administration is delayed for too long, or if other physiological stressors such as illness or vomiting are involved, diabetic ketoacidosis can result. Diabetic ketoacidosis is a state of severe insulin deficiency marked by acid-base and electrolyte abnormalities, severe dehydration, and symptoms such as nausea, vomiting, and abdominal pain. It usually requires hospitalization and can be life-threatening.

The most common precipitant of ketoacidosis is omission of insulin (Golden, Herold, & Orr, 1985), which may account for the increased rate of hospitalization in young women with diabetes compared with young diabetic men (Cohn, Cirillo, Wingard, Austin, & Roffers, 1997). Indeed, recurrent episodes of diabetic ketoacidosis and more frequent hospitalizations are more common in individuals with clinical and subclinical eating disorders (e.g. Stancin et al., 1989) and should be taken as serious warning signs of disturbed eating behavior and irregular insulin use.

Recurrent Hypoglycemia and Growth Failure

Anorexia nervosa is much less common in individuals with DM than are bulimia-type syndromes of restricting, binge eating, and purging behavior. Anorexia nervosa may be associated coincidentally with diabetes, although it has been suggested that deliberate food restriction, which dramatically reduces insulin requirements, may be an attempt to deny the reality of living with diabetes (Schechter, 1985). Recurrent episodes of severe low blood sugar (hypoglycemia), sometimes with loss of consciousness, can result from food intake that is not sufficient to maintain normal blood sugar levels. We also have noticed that low blood sugar reactions may trigger an eating binge, particularly in individuals who are already having trouble controlling their eating patterns, and so we regularly inquire about the management of low blood sugar reactions. Inadequate growth or delayed puberty also may result from excessive food restriction (Rodin, Daneman, Johnson, Kenshole, & Garfinkel, 1985).

Dietary Manipulation

We have found that teenaged and young adult women with DM who seek dietary advice frequently or who want to lower caloric intake, change to a vegetarian diet, or severely restrict fat or sugar intake may be showing early evidence of disturbed eating attitudes and behavior.

☐ Prevention and Management of Eating Disturbances in Individuals with Type I Diabetes Mellitus

In teens with poor blood sugar control, efforts usually are aimed at tightening up the diabetes management plan, with more attention to insulin regimens, blood glucose testing, and dietary compliance. If these efforts are not helpful, or if they actually worsen blood sugar control, we consider whether an eating disorder or milder eating disturbance is present. For these individuals, we have modified our treatment approach to encourage our patients and their families to be more flexible in making decisions about when and what to eat, and more responsive to the individual's hunger and fullness cues.

There is a wide range of responses to the diagnosis of diabetes, and this adjustment to diabetes is an ongoing, dynamic process. Healthcare providers should be sensitive to the stress associated with the diagnosis and management of DM. Individuals and their families can be helped to address their concerns, anger, and fears in a supportive context, particularly following initial diagnosis. Disturbances in family functioning are commonly related to eating disturbances in adolescent girls with diabetes and can contribute to the onset and the maintenance of these problems (Maharaj et al., 1998). Family involvement, education, and support is therefore an important part of both preventive and treatment efforts related to eating disturbances. Family therapy can be suggested for families in significant distress.

☐ A Psychoeducation Program for Adolescents with Type 1 DM

The increased risk of medical complications associated with eating disturbances and the evidence that these disturbances tend to persist in girls and young women with DM (Rydall et al., 1997) suggest that prevention and early intervention measures should be a high priority. However, there is no reported research regarding the benefit of primary or secondary prevention programs in this population. With the goal of preventing eating disturbances or intervening early in their course, we have developed and implemented a six-session group psychoeducation program for adolescent girls with DM (Olmsted, Rodin, Rydall, Lawson, & Daneman, 1997).

Brief group psychoeducation is an economical and highly structured treatment approach designed to promote changes in eating attitudes and behavior through education about the nature, precipitants, and consequences of eating disturbances, and about strategies for change (Davis et al., 1992). Psychoeducation has been shown to be an effective treatment modality for bulimia nervosa in non-diabetic individuals, particularly among those with less severe eating disturbances (Olmsted et al., 1991). Disturbed eating is common among adolescent girls with DM, is most often at the milder end of the spectrum of eating disturbances, and can have serious medical consequences. A psychoeducation intervention therefore seems appropriate for this high-risk group.

Our psychoeducation program is adapted from the one that has been used for several years in our outpatient eating disorder program. We believe that shame, embarrassment, and denial may interfere with seeking help or information regarding eating disturbances. The presentation of information in a group setting in which participants are not expected to provide personal information makes it easier for girls to acknowledge that there is a problem, and also demonstrates that other people have similar concerns and problems. The program is intended to change the perception of external expectations regarding weight and shape, to increase the young women's awareness of their own internal cues, and to draw attention to aspects of self worth unrelated to appearance. We have attempted to create a different external influence to counterbalance current cultural pressures that tie self-esteem to bodily appearance and weight, by encouraging girls to value other aspects of themselves, particularly their physical health and emotional well-being.

The intervention consists of six sessions of slide presentations and lectures co-led by an eating disorder specialist and a diabetes specialist in the setting of a diabetes clinic. An outline of the sessions is presented in Table 1. All group participants receive a detailed manual before the program commences. This is not group therapy; the girls are not required to disclose personal information but are encouraged to comment or ask questions. There are simultaneous sessions conducted for the girls' parents, with the same manual and presentation. The separate sessions allow participants to ask questions most relevant to their concerns. We think that involving the parents may enhance the program, by

TABLE 1. Outline of psychoeducation program sessions

	Discussion topics
First session	Why do people diet?
	Signs and symptoms of eating problems
	Diabetes-related signs of disturbed eating
	Health consequences of disturbed eating, especially in diabetes mellitus
Second session	Predisposing, precipitating, and perpetuating factors of eating problems
	Contribution of diabetes mellitus to body image and eating problems
	Sociocultural, personal, and family influences on eating and body image
Third session	Set-point theory of weight regulation
	Physical and psychological effects of dieting
	The connection between dieting and binge eating
	Dieting and diabetes
Fourth session	Developing a healthy relationship with food
	Strategies for healthy eating behavior
	Developing a nondieting meal plan
	Strategies for controlling overeating, binge eating, and purging
Fifth session	Feelings about your body
	Body image and diabetes
	Improving body image
	Family communication
	Parents and diabetes management
Sixth session	Cognitive distortions that maintain body-image and eating problems
	Strategies for maintaining changes in body image and eating behavior

ensuring that the girls and their parents have similar knowledge, and by facilitating a dialogue about some of the issues raised in the sessions.

We currently are completing an initial evaluation of this psychoeducation program as a prevention tool for teenage girls with DM with evidence of at least a mild eating disturbance, drive for thinness, or weight and shape preoccupation on self-report screening. Based on our criteria, just over half of the girls screened were eligible for the psychoeducation program. Seventy-seven young women aged 12–19 years attending the Diabetes Clinic at The Hospital for Sick Children in Toronto, Ontario, who met criteria were randomly assigned either to a psychoeducation group or to a conventional diabetes management condition. Assessment of body image and eating attitudes and behavior were carried out before the psychoeducation program, four weeks after completion of the program, and six months after the program. Participation in the psychoeducation group was associated with a significant reduction ($p < .05$) in binge eating episodes, and in eating restraint score on the Eating Disorder Examination (Cooper & Fairburn, 1987) at six-month follow-up. Differences in hemoglobin A1c levels between the two groups were not statistically significant ($p = .09$) at follow-up. One and two-year follow-up assessments are planned, and if the promising group differences seen at six months continue at one year, the psychoeducation program also will be offered to the girls who were randomized to the conventional diabetes management group. The psychoeducation program that we have implemented has been acceptable to both the girls and their parents in its current format. However, consideration is being given to developing briefer and modified versions for subsequent booster interventions. We also are considering offering preventive interventions to a younger group. The content, format, and language will need to be revised to be appropriate for the younger developmental level. In view of the strength of our findings regarding the association of disturbances in family functioning and disordered eating, we also are considering incorporating more information about this area into future psychoeducational interventions.

Management of Eating Disturbances

In the case of milder eating disturbances, several clinic-based strategies may be helpful. We believe that the dietary restraint and weight gain associated with insulin therapy are possible triggers of eating disturbances. The traditional approach to individuals with poor blood sugar control has been to promote a stricter and more controlled diabetes management plan. We have found that this approach may have an effect opposite to what is intended in those individuals in whom poor blood-sugar control is caused by disturbed eating attitudes and behavior. The increased pressure to control blood sugars and restrict the diet may lead to binge eating, worsening blood sugar control and increasing feelings of anxiety and guilt. Therefore, we reduce the emphasis on "perfect" blood sugar control and strict dietary control, and we encourage a more flexible approach to healthy eating, based on hunger and satiety cues rather than only on the requirements of a diabetic meal plan.

In the presence of clinically significant disturbed eating, improvements in diabetes management are unlikely to occur until the body image and eating disturbances are addressed directly. Prompt referral to an eating disorder treatment program or to a mental health professional experienced in working with individuals with eating disorders is therefore usually necessary. In our setting, a day hospital treatment program for eating disorders (Kaplan & Olmsted, 1997) has been effective in decreasing eating disturbances in several young women with coexisting DM and an eating disorder. Peveler and Fairburn (1992), who have noted that eating disorders may be particularly difficult to manage in the presence of diabetes, have suggested some modifications to a cognitive-behavioral treatment program to facilitate use with individuals with DM. Adjunctive pharmacological treatment with fluoxetine or another serotonin reuptake inhibitor may be helpful in reducing bulimic behavior. Because selective serotonin reuptake inhibitors can decrease insulin requirements, vigilance for hypoglycemic episodes is important if these medications are used. A common difficulty for parents who have a child with DM is in finding the optimal balance between providing support that is needed and permitting age-appropriate autonomy. Family therapy may be helpful, particularly if patterns of family functioning appear to be directly contributing to the maintenance of eating disturbances and problems with diabetes management.

☐ Summary and Future Directions

Disturbances in body image and eating behavior, including clinical eating disorders, are common in adolescent girls and young women with DM. Disturbed eating behavior can worsen blood sugar control and increase the risk of diabetes-related medical complications. For these reasons, efforts at prevention and management of eating disturbances are particularly important in this population. We have developed a clinic-based approach to these problems, with a psychoeducation program targeting body image and eating disturbances in adolescent girls with DM, and a parallel set of sessions for parents. Evaluation is needed to determine whether a more relaxed approach to diabetes management also has an independent effect in preventing eating disorders. Although the benefits of preventive interventions in general population groups of young women have not been striking, we believe that the increased health risks and the greater motivation of these young women and their families may contribute to more positive outcomes from prevention interventions in the diabetic population.

We have found that relatively mild eating disturbances may carry profound health risks in young women with diabetes. Although these disturbances often have not been taken into account in diabetes clinics, we have shown that they can be identified easily and are amenable to relatively brief group psychoeducational interventions. Longitudinal research is needed to confirm whether such improvement is sustained and whether structured interventions in a younger population have preventive value. Research also is needed to determine whether assistance with family interactions can be provided in a group psychoeducation format, or whether it must be tailored to individual families and provided in a family-based format.

☐ References

Affenito, S. G., Backstrand, J. R., Welch, G. W., Lammi-Keefe, C. J., Rodriguez, N. R., & Adams, C. H. (1997). Subclinical and clinical eating disorders in IDDM negatively affect metabolic control. *Diabetes Care, 20,* 182–184.

American Psychiatric Association. (1994). *Diagnostic and statistical manual of mental disorders* (4th ed.). Washington, DC: Author.

Atkinson, M. A., & Maclaren, N. K. (1994). The pathogenesis of insulin-dependent diabetes mellitus. *New England Journal of Medicine, 331,* 1428–1436.

Attie, I., & Brooks-Gunn, J. (1989). Development of eating problems in adolescent girls: A longitudinal study. *Developmental Psychology, 25,* 70–79.

Biggs, M. M., Basco, M. R., Patterson, G., & Raskin, P. (1994). Insulin withholding for weight control in women with diabetes. *Diabetes Care, 17,* 1186–1189.

Bruch, H. (1973). *Eating disorders: obesity, anorexia and the person within.* New York: Basic Books.

Cantwell, R., & Steel, J. M. (1996). Screening for eating disorders in diabetes mellitus. *Journal of Psychosomatic Research, 40,* 15–20.

Cohn, B. A., Cirillo, P. M., Wingard, D. L., Austin, D. F., & Roffers, S. D. (1997). Gender differences in hospitalizations for IDDM among adolescents in California, 1991. *Diabetes Care, 20,* 1677–1682.

Colas, C., Mathieu, P., & Tchobroutsky, G. (1991). Eating disorders and retinal lesions in type 1 (insulin-dependent) diabetic women. *Diabetologia, 34,* 288.

Cooper, Z., & Fairburn, C. (1987). The Eating Disorder Examination: A semi-structured interview for the assessment of the specific psychopathology of eating disorders. *International Journal of Eating Disorders, 6,* 1–8.

Dare, C., & Eisler, I. (1997). Family therapy for anorexia nervosa. In D. M. Garner & P. E. Garfinkel (Eds.), *Handbook of treatment for eating disorders.* (2nd ed., pp. 307–326). New York: Guilford at press.

Davis, R., Dearing, S., Faulkner, J., Jasper, K., Olmsted, M. P., Rice, C., & Rockert, W. (1992). The Road to Recovery: A manual for participants in the psychoeducation group for bulimia nervosa. In H. Harper-Giuffre & K. R. MacKenzie (Eds.), *Group psychotherapy for eating disorders* (pp. 281–341). Washington, DC: American Psychiatric Press.

De Groot, J. M., & Rodin, G. (1994). Eating disorders, female psychology, and the self. *Journal of the American Academy of Psychoanalysis, 22,* 299–317.

Diabetes Control and Complications Trial Research Group. (1988). Weight gain associated with intensive therapy in the Diabetes Control and Complications Trial. *Diabetes Care, 11,* 567–573.

Diabetes Control and Complications Trial Research Group. (1993). Effect of intensive diabetes treatment on the development and progression of long-term complications in adolescents with insulin-dependent diabetes mellitus in the Diabetes Control and Complications Trial. *Journal of Pediatrics, 125,* 177–188.

Drash, A. L. (1987). The epidemiology of insulin-dependent diabetes mellitus. *Clinical and Investigative Medicine, 10,* 432–436.

Fairburn, C. G., Peveler, R. C., Davies, B., Mann, J. I., & Mayou, R. A. (1991). Eating disorders in young adults with insulin dependent diabetes mellitus: A controlled study. *British Medical Journal, 303,* 17–20.

Garner, D. M., Olmsted, M. P., & Polivy, J. (1983). The Eating Disorder Inventory: A measure of cognitive-behavioral dimensions of anorexia nervosa and bulimia. In P. Darby, P. E. Garfinkel, D. M. Garner, & D. V. Coscina (Eds.), *Anorexia nervosa: Recent developments in research* (pp. 173–184). New York: Alan R. Liss.

Golden, M., Herold, A., & Orr, D. (1985). An approach to prevention of recurrent diabetic ketoacidosis in the pediatric population. *Journal of Pediatrics, 107,* 195–200.

Gordon, C. M., & Mansfield, M. J. (1996). Changing needs of the patient with diabetes mellitus during the teenage years. *Current Opinions in Pediatrics, 8,* 319–327.

Hauser, S., Jacobson, A., Lavori, P., Wolfsdorf, J., Herskowitz, R., Milley, J., Bliss, R., Wertlieb, D., & Stein, J. (1990). Adherence among children and adolescents with insulin-dependent diabetes mellitus over a four year longitudinal follow-up: II. Immediate and long-term linkages with family milieu. *Journal of Pediatric Psychology, 15,* 527–542.

Jacobs Institute of Women's Health. (1996). *Women's health data book* (2nd ed.). Washington, DC: Elsevier.

Jacobson, A. M., Hauser, S. T., Lavori, P., Willett, J. B., Cole, C. F., Wolfsdorf, J. I., Dumont, R. H., & Wertlieb, D. (1994). Family environment and glycemic control: A four-year prospective study of children and adolescents with insulin-dependent diabetes mellitus. *Psychosomatic Medicine, 56,* 401–409.

Jacobson, A. M., Hauser, S. T., Wertlieb, D., Wolfsdorf, J. I., Orleans, J., & Vieyra, M. (1986). Psychological adjustment of children with recently diagnosed diabetes mellitus. *Diabetes Care, 9,* 323–329.

Jacobson, A. M., Hauser, S. T., Wolfsdorf, J. I., Houlihan, J., Milley, J. E., Herskowitz, R. D., Wertlieb, D., & Watt, E. (1987). Psychologic predictors of compliance in children with recent onset of diabetes mellitus. *Journal of Pediatrics, 110,* 805–811.

Kaplan, A. S., & Olmsted, M. P. (1997). Partial hospitalization. In D. M. Garner & P. E. Garfinkel (Eds.), *Handbook of treatment for eating disorders* (2nd ed., pp. 354–360). New York: Guilford Press.

Killen, J. D., Hayward, C., Wilson, D. M., Taylor, C. B., Hammer, L. D., Litt, I., Simmonds, B., & Haydel, F. (1994). Factors associated with eating disorder symptoms in a community sample of 6th and 7th grade girls. *International Journal of Eating Disorders, 15,* 357–367.

Kovacs, M., Brent, D., Steinberg, T. F., Paulaskas, S., & Reid, J. (1986). Children's self-reports of psychologic adjustment and coping strategies during first year of insulin-dependent diabetes mellitus. *Diabetes Care, 9,* 472–479.

Kovacs, M., Goldston, D., Obrosky, D. S., & Bonar, L. K. (1997). Psychiatric disorders in youths with IDDM: Rates and risk factors. *Diabetes Care, 20,* 36–44.

La Greca, A. M., Schwarz, L. T., & Satin, W. (1987). Eating patterns in young women with IDDM: Another look. *Diabetes Care, 10,* 659–660.

Maharaj, S. I., Rodin, G., Olmsted, M. P., & Daneman, D. (1998). Eating disturbances, diabetes and the family: An empirical study. *Journal of Psychosomatic Research, 44,* 479–490.

Mannucci, E., Ricca, V., Mezzani, B., Di Bernardo, M., Piani, F., Vannini, R., Cabras, P. L., & Rotella, C. M. (1995). Eating attitude and behavior in IDDM patients: A case-controlled study. *Diabetes Care, 18,* 1503–1504.

Marcus, M. D., & Wing, R. R. (1990). Eating disorders and diabetes. In C. S. Holmes (Ed.), *Neuropsychological and behavioural aspects of diabetes* (pp. 102–121). New York: Springer-Verlag.

Olmsted, M. P., Davis, R., Rockert, W., Irvine, M. J., Eagle, M., & Garner, D. M. (1991). Efficacy of a brief group psychoeducational intervention for bulimia nervosa. *Behavior Research and Therapy, 29,* 71–83.

Olmsted, M. P., Rodin, G., Rydall, A., Lawson, M., & Daneman, D. (November 1997). The effect of psychoeducation on disordered eating attitudes and behaviours in young women with IDDM [abstract]. Eating Disorder Research Society Meeting.

Peveler, R. C., & Fairburn, C. G. (1992). The treatment of bulimia nervosa in patients with diabetes mellitus. *International Journal of Eating Disorders, 11*, 45–53.

Polivy, J., & Herman, C. P. (1985). Dieting and bingeing: A causal analysis. *American Psychologist, 40*, 193–201.

Polonsky, W. H., Anderson, B. J., Lohrer, P. A., Aponte, J. E., Jacobson, A. M., & Cole, C. F. (1994). Insulin omission in women with IDDM. *Diabetes Care, 17*, 1178–1185.

Powers, P. S., Malone, J. I., Coovert, D. L., & Schulman, R. G. (1990). Insulin-dependent diabetes mellitus and eating disorders: A prevalence study. *Comprehensive Psychiatry, 31*, 205–210.

Rodin, G., & Daneman, D. (1992). Eating disorders and IDDM: A problematic association. *Diabetes Care, 15*, 1402–1412.

Rodin, G. M., Daneman, D., Johnson, L. E., Kenshole, A., & Garfinkel, P. (1985). Anorexia nervosa and bulimia in female adolescents with insulin dependent diabetes mellitus: A systematic study. *Journal of Psychiatric Research, 19*, 381–384.

Rubin, R. R., & Peyrot, M. (1992). Psychosocial problems and interventions in diabetes: A review of the literature. *Diabetes Care, 15*, 1640–1657.

Rydall, A. C., Rodin, G. M., Olmsted, M. P., Devenyi, R. G., & Daneman, D. (1997). Disordered eating behavior and microvascular complications in young women with insulin-dependent diabetes mellitus. *New England Journal of Medicine, 336*, 1849–1854.

Schechter, N. L. (1985). Self-starvation in a diabetic adolescent. *Journal of Adolescent Health Care, 6*, 43–45.

Stancin, T., Link, D. L., & Reuter, J. M. (1989). Binge eating and purging in young women with IDDM. *Diabetes Care, 12*, 601–603.

Steel, J. M., Lloyd, G. G., Young, R. J., & MacIntyre, C. C. A. (1990). Changes in eating attitudes during the first year of treatment for diabetes. *Journal of Psychosomatic Research, 34*, 313–318.

Steel, J. M., Young, R. J., Lloyd, G. G., & MacIntyre, C. C. A. (1989). Abnormal eating attitudes in young insulin-dependent diabetics. *British Journal of Psychiatry, 155*, 515–521.

Striegel-Moore, R. H., Nicholson, T. J., & Tamborlane, W. V. (1992). Prevalence of eating disorder symptoms in preadolescent and adolescent girls with IDDM. *Diabetes Care, 15*, 1361–1368.

Vila, G., Robert, J. J., Nollet-Clemencon, C., Vera, L., Crosnier, H., Rault, G., Jos, J., & Mouren-Simeoni, M. C. (1995). Eating and emotional disorders in adolescent obese girls with insulin-dependent diabetes mellitus. *European Child and Adolescent Psychiatry, 4*, 270–279.

Wing, R. R., Klein, R., & Moss, S. E. (1990). Weight gain associated with improved glycemic control in population-based sample of subjects with type I diabetes. *Diabetes Care, 13*, 1106–1109.

Wolman, C., Resnick, M. D., Harris, L. J., & Blum, R. W. (1994). Emotional well-being among adolescents with and without chronic conditions. *Journal of Adolescent Health, 15*, 199–204.

CHAPTER

Roslyn G. Weiner

Working with Physicians Toward the Goal of Primary and Secondary Prevention

I am a psychologist and I direct a child and adolescent outpatient eating disorders clinic located in a tertiary care hospital that is also a primary teaching hospital for a university medical school. For the past 10 years I have worked collaboratively with physicians to assist children and adolescents who have become compromised in their ability to care for their bodies. For the most part, my physician colleagues are pediatricians in private practice; however, some staff hospital outpatient pediatric clinics, while others provide care in neighborhood health centers. All of the physicians desire to detect these problems as soon as possible after onset to minimize risk to the child and to facilitate sustained remission. But, as collaborators, we question ourselves repeatedly as to how the problems could be detected even sooner and, more importantly, we ask how eating disorders could be prevented from occurring. This chapter describes my efforts in developing collaborative efforts with physicians in regard to secondary and tertiary prevention and offers some suggestions congruent with the long-term goal of primary prevention. Multidisciplinary prevention and treatment of eating disorders or any other illness requires that we engage each other with open minds and a clear understanding that each of us has something of value to contribute to patient care.

☐ Prevention

Importance of the Physician in Eating-Disorders Work

Although physicians often are consulted if illness or disease is present or suspected, medical specialists also serve an important role in the preservation and enhancement of good health. Prevention of illness contributes to the preservation of health and the development of resilience. Over time, physicians develop rapport and a relationship with those who choose to consult with them. They accumulate records and impressions to which they can refer, especially if the patient presents with new complaints or a puzzling change in demeanor or body appearance or functioning. The physician uses the relationship and appropriate medical tests and physical examinations to evaluate this instability of body functioning and to search for underlying causes of change. If either physical precipitants are ruled out or interaction among feelings, behavior, and symptoms is suspected, the physician is particularly qualified to educate the patient as to the need for consideration of mental and emotional factors that may be operative.

A physician must be unambivalent about referring a patient for a consultation with an eating disorder specialist. Understandably, few patients and their families greet such a recommendation with enthusiasm. The patient may fear that the doctor is abandoning her and must be reassured that the recommended referral is for a consultation to assist both the physician and the patient in determining what kind of problems exist and how they might work more effectively together. The approach requires that physicians be nondefensive in acknowledging that they do not have all the answers. This strategy permits the patient to hold an open mind, too. Additionally, the patient may imagine that her doctor thinks she is crazy or has some other mental disorder. This apprehension may not be verbalized, but it should be anticipated and acknowledged through a frank description of the interplay between mind and body that the physician has observed previously. Education as to the nature of a psychological evaluation also might be useful, including the need to obtain a family history, to consider what circumstances may have precipitated the eating disorder symptoms, and to explore whether there are any indications that other emotional problems or interpersonal conflicts may be finding expression through compromised eating behavior.

When a physician refers to me for the first time, we must attend to the creation of *our* relationship, not just to the relationship between me and the patient. There is a difference between being asked to share in the care of the patient and being asked to take on a patient in treatment. The latter often occurs if the physician is inexperienced in the relationship dimension of eating disorders treatment and expects that I will label the symptom state, prescribe the course of treatment, and attend to implementation of that prescription. Respectfully, I share the grim details of acting out, medical compromise, family distress, resistance, and denial that often precede and accompany restoration and repair. If the physician responds with interest or curiosity, I outline several models of collaboration as regards the nature of our communication and the kinds of oversight we each will provide, and then I inquire as to which might fit the practice or personal style of the physician. In the few cases in which physicians elect not to speak with me regularly, I have learned to politely refuse to accept the referral.

Defining Prevention as It Applies to the Physician's Role

Most mental health clinicians learn about eating disorders at the "tertiary" level of prevention. We expend considerable energy to prevent our patients from dying of the disorder, and then we do what we can to strengthen them so that the disease does not possess them in a chronic state. Pausing between crises, we wonder how we might detect symptoms and vulnerability earlier. Thus, we become motivated to explore secondary prevention, that is, whether there are early warning signs. However, strategies concerning primary prevention arise only out of the reflections that occur after many, many patients have struggled with us to effect their own recoveries. At that time, we challenge ourselves to consider whether the child might have been conditioned to resist temptations to harm her body and whether the messages transmitted by home, school, and culture need to be intercepted and radically changed.

Using this framework, we can infer that the physician, even without awareness, is always involved in primary prevention. The tradition of well-baby check-ups extended through adolescence permits physician, patient, and family to work collaboratively to build within the patient a positive body image and security about body use and function. The physician is also able to observe the degree of patient self-esteem and provide guidelines for food consumption and patterns of physical activity modified by age and stage. At the boundary between primary and secondary work, the physician can monitor changes in growth patterns or functioning and act expediently if irregular or unexpected finding are noted. Once problems are identified, the physician relies on the quality of the preexisting relationship, which reasonably must include trust and good will, to keep the family focused on getting help. If referrals to specialty clinicians are made, the physician monitors the treatment process, because without that monitoring the likelihood of crisis-free recovery is diminished.

In the current healthcare environment, physicians are increasingly the individuals who interact with third party payers to determine whether patients will receive specialty care. The importance of this responsibility is intensified in any discussion of prevention work. The acknowledgment that an eating disorder reflects dysfunction both of mind and body should cause the physician to advocate strenuously for immediate provision by the payer of psychological and nutritional counseling as soon as the requisite syndrome of symptoms is presented even in minimal form.

How Physicians Help Parents Raise Healthy Children

Pediatricians, adolescent medicine specialists, and family-care practitioners all are concerned about facilitating the growth and functioning of young people who are their patients. The physician's access to the child is mediated by the parents, who decide when and under what circumstances to contact the physician. Therefore, the physician strives to build a relationship with the parents by becoming acquainted with them as persons who are requesting the physician's assistance as they labor to raise their child. During this process, physician and parents trade information about goals and ideas concerning childrearing, enabling the physician to assess the level of parenting readiness and to determine what intellectual and emotional resources the parents possess as individuals and as a parental unit. Simultaneously, parents determine whether the physician's orientation, philosophy, and style of practice management are sufficiently compatible with their approach.

If disease prevention is the goal, the physician's role should not be limited to that of intermediary when physical symptoms are noted. Building upon the initial joint motivation for collaboration, the physician should seek to train the parents to serve as careful observers and candid reporters of a wide variety of data. Most important, parents need to be given a proactive communication orientation. Parent training is initiated by the kind of questions asked by the physician in both well-child and sick-child office visits and is reinforced by the empathic, attentive listening of the questioner to the respondent. Additionally, the parents need to experience the physician making constructive use of the data offered.

Collaborative physicians ask the parents how comfortable they feel about the process of communication both in the office and on the telephone. They inquire directly about what parents are observing and they take parent and child concerns seriously. For example, they never say to parents with overweight school-aged children, "Don't worry, she'll [or he'll] outgrow it" (depending on the degree of overweight, the child may not and the parent's expression of concern may mask or conceal the possibility that the child is not feeling accepted by the parent "as is"). How accessible the physician is to the parents also may determine the efficacy of the exchange of information between them. If the parents must struggle to reach the physician or if physician access is more likely to occur in response to physical symptoms than at other times, parents will be less motivated to offer social, psychological, and other observations, and children may be unconsciously provoked to provide physical symptoms in order to cue the physician that emotional and other kinds of issues have surfaced.

Because there is a developmental regularity to parent-child-physician interaction, the physician serves as a health educator for parents in a very natural way. As children mature, the physician also may elect to include them in physician-parent discussions. Parents of young children might be startled if the physician were to initiate a dialogue concerning the prevention of eating disorders. Nevertheless, there are several topics that fall easily under that heading. For example, physicians, in consultation with knowledgeable dietitians, could teach families about age-appropriate nutrition, emphasizing the importance of parental planning, supervision, and monitoring of food choices and amounts even if the child is not eating at home. Establishing patterns of physical activity is also important but is potentially a more complicated topic, because some families believe that children's participation in physical activities depends on their interest level and is less required than, for example, brushing teeth.

Physicians extend their educator function when they sensitize parents concerning the impact of societal and peer pressures on a child's body image and self-esteem (Heinberg, 1996). In addition, parents particularly appreciate being advised about the early warning signs of both physical and emotional difficulties that they might confront with their child. This requires that the physician offer the parents relevant information about normal development. The physician who is attuned to eating disorder prevention encourages parents to stress body competency skills over shape and appearance and provides data in regard to normal genetic and developmental variations in body growth and social and emotional behavior. Finally, the physician as educator anticipates for the parents key individual and family transition times at which children and adolescents may act out their ambivalence or emotional distress in the ways they choose to take care of (or fail to care for) their bodies. This is especially relevant at the onset and end-point of puberty and whenever children and their families face separations, even those fully expected by the family's culture, such as summer camp, a new school or home, or departure from home for college or work.

Physician as Role Models of Social Change

Magazines, newspapers, television, movies, fitness centers, and clothing manufacturers all have been targeted as promulgating views and standards about the acceptable and preferred body shape, type, and weight (see chapter 1). Few of us are immune to the impact of visual images and others' comments as we construct our beliefs and feelings about the adequacy or acceptability of our own body's size and shape. Some persons are particularly sensitive to their perceptions of external standards, and we suspect that this sensitivity plays a role in the formation of an eating disorder.

The concerned physician is in a position to promote primary prevention on at least three dimensions. First, as noted, physicians can help patients appreciate and emphasize body function over body shape and appearance. This requires a conscious, prophylactic effort on the physician's part, which is undertaken through conversation, sharing of written material, reinforcement of the patient's self-accepting communication about her own attitudes and experiences regarding her body, and through immediate intervention if negative self-referencing is observed. Second, physicians can guide patients to address their weight and shape concerns in healthy ways through education in the areas of nutrition and physical activity or through referrals for counseling if there is evidence that the patient has begun to doubt herself, especially on body terms. The physician should be particularly aware of the choices patients make regarding physical activity. There are a range of concerns here, from that of the patient who does nothing to the patient who is unrealistic about the demands she places on her body in order to be accepted in a peer group or on a team. Third, the physician committed to prevention can be visible in private practice, in hospitals, and in the general community as an advocate who publicly challenges harmful cultural standards for appearance, as well as sports and other activities that encourage alteration of body shape or limitations of growth as a condition of participation.

Physicians can encourage patients to boycott stores that offer a limited range of size and style choices and to write leaders in the entertainment, clothing, and cosmetic industries expressing displeasure with the emphasis on thinness that permeates contemporary advertising strategies (see Chapter 1). Further, the physician can help teach adolescent patients to be more selective in their purchasing of print media that glorify models whose bodies reflect a look that healthy eating and exercising could not produce. Through their own professional networks, physicians also should take leadership positions in challenging these same industries to be more responsible in their role as image makers. In this light it is important that the physician provide an office environment sensitive to the needs of adolescent girls, including procedures for safeguarding personal modesty in examining rooms, waiting room reading material that is teen-centered and reinforcing of attitudes emphasizing a healthy body and the total person, and general office procedures that communicate a sense of respect to these young persons who are learning how to respect themselves.

Schools are particularly likely to welcome the presence of physicians as educators of students, parents, and faculty concerning both prevention and treatment of eating disorders in young persons. By working collaboratively with the
schools, physicians also may be able to build alliances with coaches and athletic
trainers who, consciously or not, have tremendous power in determining how
young persons care for their bodies. As noted, the physician is in a key position
to act publicly as a political activist on behalf of eating-disorders prevention.
From a treatment perspective, third party payers need firm encouragement
and education to authorize services that respect the close alliance among medical, nutritional, and psychological services during the recovery process. The
availability of funds for both nutritional and psychological treatment still lags
woefully behind that for medical treatment. Legislative and other legal interventions may be necessary to compel service provision, and the physician's
raised voice in this effort would appear to be critical. In addition, there are numerous opportunities for physician involvement in national and statewide efforts to raise community consciousness and conscientiousness in regard to the
prevention, identification, and treatment of eating disorders.

The Role of the Annual Check-up

The focus of the annual check-up is to determine the status of the child's or adolescent's journey from one developmental stage to the next on dimensions both
biological and psychosocial in nature. Physician, patient, and parents collaborate in determining if anticipated physical and emotional growth has occurred
in the preceding year and if body parts and organs are of sufficient strength and
capacity for the tasks that they are next to accomplish. A positive report reassures everyone and often is perceived as a validation of family competency.
However, the visit is also an opportunity for the physician to detect deviations
from anticipated growth curves, tensions in the parent-child relationship, and
questions troubling the young patient or their parents about physical, emotional, or interpersonal well-being. The annual check-up is also an opportunity
for the physician to emphasize health, strength, and stamina (instead of slenderness), and to emphasize the importance of such simple things as fruits and
vegetables, as well as the special nutritional needs of, for example, girls going
through puberty.

How the annual appointment is structured varies depending on the age of the
child, the personalities of the child and her parents, and the press of the physician's responsibilities. The following discussion is presented as a flexible model
that might support prevention efforts. It is acknowledged that the prevailing
healthcare environment has seriously challenged even the most well-motivated
physicians to have enough time to do all that they wish to do with and for
patients.

The check-up blends physician supervision of the child's medical status with a
recognition and appreciation of the child's uniqueness, including style of expression and self-esteem. Similar to adult patient-physician interaction, as soon
as the child is sufficiently verbal, there should be opportunities for the physician
and the child to converse directly with each other. At least beginning at junior-
high age, the child might welcome some opportunities for dialogue without

parents present. In order to sanction such dialogue, some parents may require reassurance that they will be consulted if information is revealed indicating that the child is at either emotional or physical risk.

In the course of the examination and discussion, physicians extend their interest in many dimensions beyond the child's medical status. For example, questions about friends are very important in determining the child's social affiliation or isolation. Does the child have a best friend? Does she spend regular time with friends outside of the school environment? What are the friends teaching each other? How does the child, particularly if she is an adolescent, feel she compares to others, not just friends but also her siblings and her mother? The physician notes the child's manner of dress and self decoration and inquires about eating habits, academic interests and performance, and the quality of interactions with family and other adults in the community. Physicians makes it clear to their patients that they are interested in them as whole persons. Does she have summer plans, an afterschool job, a social life, ideas about her future? As she matures, the physician inquires about her opinion as to her family's adjustment to her increasing autonomy. The physician might even inquire about what magazines and television shows or movies she enjoys, as well as what sports or physical activities she prefers.

As the appointment proceeds, the physician also is participating in his or her own mental dialogue: Given what I know already about my patient and her current age and developmental stage, what did I expect to see today? What do I see? Are the observed physical and emotional differences within a normal range? Do I observe a progression in the skills of independence and self-care of my patient, and is that growth coupled with an appropriate diminution in the degree of parental oversight and direction? Does my patient reveal a sense of body competency, or does she appear preoccupied with her body, dissatisfied, and overly self-critical or ashamed? Is my patient's body shape significantly different from that of her mother's? Does that difference, if it exists, appear to affect the mother-daughter relationship?

The physician's skill at blending a well-informed internal dialogue with an authoritative but comfortable interaction with the patient contributes to eating disorder prevention efforts. Specifically, the physician who is able to clearly and thoroughly communicate observations to the patient and her parents motivates them to be forthcoming too. If the physician offers a description of a variety of adolescent eating styles, including skipping family meals, relying on junk food, and eliminating some food groups from the daily diet, and suggests that many adolescents experiment with their eating patterns, the adolescent may reveal her eating and dieting behaviors, and the parents can be encouraged to share their reactions to these behaviors. Parents and adolescents can be helped to establish some safety parameters, such as how much weight loss or gain is healthy, what information adolescents and parents should exchange about the adolescent's approach to nutrition, or what behaviors around food consumption should be brought to the attention of the physician. Parents could be encouraged to provide information about how eating and body concerns were managed when they were growing up, which alerts the physician to familial history of struggles around eating behavior and body image. For the purpose of educating parents and adolescents as to the pressures the adolescent may be experiencing within the family system, the present role and attitudes of other family members, especially grandparents, in reference to the child's body (shape and functioning) and eating and activity patterns also should be identified.

Other questions follow easily (however, not always with parents present): What specific things do you do to take care of your body, such as regular exercise and sufficient sleep? How do you decide when and what to eat? What do you know about your body's specific nutritional needs? How do you integrate your nutrition needs with your athletic and other physical activities? If the annual check-up coincides with a physical examination for a sport, there are additional eating disorder prevention opportunities. The thoughtful physician inquires about the patient's feelings in regard to the coach's behavior towards her, team relationships and competition pressures, and any demands the patient presently is facing to alter her body to meet sport requirements, such as weight standards. In addition, sport physicals could stimulate questions about the approach of the patient's coaches or trainers to fitness, training, and general body care.

At the conclusion of the visit, the physician integrates medical findings with the information obtained through discussion with the patient and other family members. The physician may request that additional tests or laboratory studies be performed. The physician might assure patient and parents that there were no findings that should evoke alarm, or he or she might validate some concerns that were shared at the outset of the meeting and then instruct the patient about particular care she should provide to herself. If the physician suspects that some symptoms of an eating disorder were revealed, he or she should speak candidly with the patient and parents and refer the patient for further evaluation. But it is also critical that the physician arrange for the patient to return for several brief office visits over the subsequent weeks to ensure that although the evaluation is undertaken, close medical oversight regarding the patient's dietary patterns and medical stability occurs.

☐ Identification and Treatment of Disordered Eating

The Physician's Role in the Diagnostic Process

Both early recognition of the symptoms or precursors that may signal an eating disorder and prompt referral for in-depth evaluation are crucial for facilitating symptom remission and for limiting chronic long-term impairment. The diagnostic process begins as soon as the physician suspects that there is not a physiological explanation for the alteration in growth, the changes in body function, or the reported shifts in the patient's social, intellectual, or emotional adjustment. The physician conducts an office examination and may order some basic laboratory studies, checking for cardiac, electrolytic, and gastrointestinal stability. But what is most critical is the discussion among physician, patient, and parents. The physician expresses his or her concerns and points out the specific changes in the patient's appearance and function that are alarming. Reported patient behaviors then are linked to the specified medical concerns. At the same time, the physician begins to prepare the patient and parents to commit to the recommended in-depth evaluation process. This process includes explaining how the consultants have been selected, defining the role and interests of each specialist, and describing as exactly as possible the purposes and structure of the evaluation process. Ultimately, the adequacy of referral preparation rests on the collaborative nature of the physician-specialist relationship. It is most effective if there is a group of mental health and nutritional colleagues with whom the physician consults regularly.

The emotional climate surrounding the referral is usually intense and pressured. The family is often anxious, frustrated by the failure of their various efforts to assist their family member. The physician is often alarmed by what has been observed in the office, such as conflict between parents and patients, intense emotionality, or denial of the seriousness of the problem. Depending on his or her own experience caring for persons with eating disorders, the physician may be hesitant to permit initial outpatient care. Both patient and parents may be apprehensive about talking to a stranger about personal or family matters. However, the fact that the physician and specialists are known to each other and have a format for working constructively together provides a context for helping the family make the transition from one office to another. The diagnostic process occurs on an outpatient basis only if despite medical findings (e.g., weight loss), the patient remains medically stable (e.g., laboratory studies are all within normal limits, vital signs are stable), and there is no reported cardiac dysfunction.

The physician seeks two kinds of consultation on behalf of the patient: confirmation of the diagnosis and development of a treatment plan. In a sense the physician must create and direct a unique diagnostic team for any patient suspected of having an eating disorder (see Chapter 13). Our standard eating disorder diagnostic protocol includes, first, a meeting with a mental-health clinician and the patient and her parents. Next there is a meeting attended only by the patient and the mental health clinician, followed by a nutrition consultation, part of which the parents should attend. Additionally, the physician might request further medical evaluation from a gastroenterologist, a gynecologist, a dentist, an endocrinologist, or from other medical subspecialties. If comorbid psychiatric diagnoses are suspected, an appointment with a psychopharmacologist should be scheduled.

The physician fulfills an important role as the diagnostic process unfolds, joining collaboratively with psychologist and nutritionist to frame questions, integrate medical, psychological, and nutritional findings, and monitor the patient's receptivity to learning about herself and to making changes in thoughts, attitudes, and behaviors. If the patient is a child, the physician serves also as mentor to the parents, anticipating confusion and concern as multiple appointments with specialists are arranged. It is useful if the physician contracts very precisely with the parents for the appointments that will be completed as part of the evaluation. The process may feel overwhelming, and the physician cannot assume that just because he or she refers the family to specialists, their recommendations actually will be followed.

An exchange of information among consultants and physician must occur promptly and in detail. It is important not only that there be agreement about the meaning of the observable symptoms, but also that the severity of the impairment and the patient's and family's openness to recovery work be assessed. The efficacy of the diagnostic process rests on the quality of communication among team members and the respect each holds for the expertise of the other. A physician who is uninformed or unsympathetic as to the power of distorted thinking secondary to malnourishment or low self-esteem cannot effectively support the treatment recommendations of either the nutritionist or the mental-health clinician.

Recognizing Negative Body Image and Disordered Eating

When is eating "disordered"? With busy families, multiple kinds of family structures, working parents, the proliferation of fast food opportunities, and the decline of incidence of family dinner time, what constitutes the early warning signs of a problem and when does a family need advice? Referring physicians usually call me if their patient presents with one or more of the following concerns: low weight for height and age, a fall-off in growth, a worried parent's suspicion of purging behavior or report of alteration in the child's eating habits or activity routines, or some collection of physical symptoms not explained or corrected by physically focused tests or interventions. These symptoms include hair loss, alteration in weight patterns, temperature deregulation, gastrointestinal complaints, and amenorrhea.

The *Diagnostic and Statistical Manual of Mental Disorders, Fourth Edition* (DSM-IV; American Psychiatric Association, 1994) provides very clear diagnostic criteria for guiding physicians to make the *tentative* diagnosis of an eating disorder and to communicate with the patient and her parents about a course of more detailed evaluation. The challenge faced by those engaged in "secondary" prevention efforts is to become aware of behaviors and attitude changes that precede the more serious symptoms. Appendix 1 presents the guidelines that I have found useful in my collaborative work with physicians. For example, adolescents reveal distortions in body image by refusing to wear bathing suits, choosing only very oversized clothing, spending inordinate time in front of a mirror, offering numerous and "harsh" personal body appraisals, and checking the bathroom scale several times each day. Children reveal eating concerns through dietary restriction, especially in regard to products containing (or perceived to contain) fat, report of loss of appetite (which subsequently is acknowledged as untrue), withdrawal from the family dinner table, assumption of the role of family cook without eating what has been prepared, and refusal to consume regular meals while leaving evidence of eating binges followed by efforts to rid their bodies of the consumed food. Shifts in exercise patterns, for example, very rigid, compensatory exercise after eating, also may signal eating or body concerns.

Eating-disorder symptoms such as binge eating, purging, and dietary restrictions may be "silent partners" in the creation of medical instability. Studies of adolescents who have insulin-dependent diabetes mellitus and a history of poor metabolic control despite close medical monitoring revealed that these patients were manipulating their insulin regimes to produce weight loss (Rydall et al., 1997; see also Chapter 17). In addition, chronic illnesses of early childhood, such as gastric reflux, failure to thrive, or irritable bowel syndrome, which require extensive medical intervention or close parental and physician oversight, may contribute to an adolescent's poor regard for her body or to a heightened need to reject parental efforts to supervise both eating and activity patterns.

In order to minimize disease impact and to enhance prevention opportunities, physicians must recognize eating disorder precursors and encourage their patients to accept referrals for diagnostic evaluations, even if the presenting symptoms meet only the DSM-IV diagnostic category of Eating Disorder Not Otherwise Specified. The younger the patient, the more prudent this strategy, because the preadolescent child is at risk for growth as well as function failure. Prompt referral to a multidisciplinary team protects the child and prepares her parents to recognize that the child may need psychiatric and nutritional as well as medical assistance.

Early Identification

An eating disorder is a mind and body problem with the potential to cause death if unrecognized or insufficiently treated. The value of early identification of an eating disorder is four-fold: healthy habits can be reestablished more quickly, family disruption is minimized, growth patterns are maintained, and mental and physical functioning remains relatively unimpaired. Early identification happens if physicians know what to look for *and* patients feel empowered to make observations about their own bodies because they believe that they will be listened to carefully and not judged critically if they reveal honestly how they are presently experiencing and treating their own bodies. This requires that a collaborative relationship exists between patient and physician in which both examine how the patient's thoughts, attitudes, and feelings about herself influence her behaviors concerning various aspects of body care, including nutrition, physical activity and rest, and use of alcohol and other drugs.

The following is the orientation I bring to my work with physicians. First, eating is both a biological necessity and often a social experience. As a regularly repeated activity, eating has as its intended outcome continued healthy functioning of the body, and in the case of children and adolescents, defined parameters of growth. From the start of life and at least through late adolescence, it is mediated through a relationship between a caregiver and the recipient of that care. By contrast, an eating disorder is a mind (cognition and emotion) and body problem, usually embedded in a familial (interpersonal) context, which disrupts normal growth and functioning because energy input and energy expenditure consistently are deregulated. Second, if a child or adolescent demonstrates symptoms of an eating disorder, a team of clinicians representing multiple disciplines must cooperate to evaluate the severity and meaning of the symptoms and to both prescribe and provide care (see Chapter 13). The referring or primary care physician is a key player on that team. Third, it follows that a strong, positive relationship between the physician and the key mental health specialist is a crucial element in providing a stable environment in which repair and recovery occurs. For the most part I have found physicians to be eager collaborators around the care of persons with eating disorders. This is particularly true if both the physician and I are candid with each other about our own perceptions of successful collaboration, and if we take the time to compromise or negotiate around variance in our points of view.

Physicians who choose to consult with a psychologist or other mental health clinician about care for their patients are usually persons who appreciate that physical illnesses may have emotional precipitants or consequences. Through interactions with their patients, they observe how the capacity for both accurate self-appraisal and adequate self-care can become compromised despite careful physician advice and instruction. Although an eating disorder is a serious illness with life-threatening consequences, it should *not* be experienced, at least by the clinicians, as a crisis. The human body is a marvelous instrument with amazing resilience. Consequently, although prompt and thorough intervention is required, frantic and dramatic interventions only trigger control battles with patients and agitate what is usually already a fragile family system. Unless an emergency intervention is warranted, I make a very conscious effort to engage with child, family, and physician in a calm, focused, empathic, curious, and informed manner. I do not assume there is a problem. I invite family and physician to join me in a detection effort; hence the emphasis on curiosity.

It has been my experience that physicians welcome well-informed colleagues who can assist them in the care of their eating-disordered pediatric patients. The presence of a starving or vomiting child in the office, usually accompanied by one or more very worried or agitated parents, evokes concern, worry, and often frustration as the physician explores medical precipitants while observing and absorbing the emotional excesses that frequently accompany office-based interactions between parent and child. Certainly, the physician first must ascertain the degree of physiological compromise of the body. Those physicians inexperienced in treating persons with eating disorders initially order a large number of medical tests, searching diligently for impaired body processes before questioning their patient's active role in the decompensation of body functioning. However, if multiple tests return with negative or equivocal findings, most physicians are amenable to exploring psychosocial explanations and are eager to share responsibility for altering the patient's biological, mental, and interpersonal state. Then a decision is made concerning the necessity for the evaluation to occur on an inpatient or outpatient basis. I advocate that such decisions be made through a process of consultation among the physician, a nutritionist, and a mental-health clinician. Together, these multidisciplinary colleagues determine a path for treatment and establish a mechanism for responsible oversight. That is the way in which established pathways of team collaboration become useful both to the ill child and to her concerned parents and physician.

As a society, we have not yet agreed upon all of the precipitants of eating disorders, nor have we taken sufficient responsibility for correcting those factors within society that may be perpetuating compromised body image and poor self-care. No physician has ever informed me that training opportunities in treatment or prevention of eating disorders were offered during medical school or specialty training. It is only recently that standards for care of persons with eating disorders have been disseminated by professional organizations (Academy for Eating Disorders, 1997; American Psychiatric Association, 1994; Society for Adolescent Medicine, 1995; Yager et al., 1993). Consequently, I provide on-the-job training to physicians, because the first time we treat a child together, I believe I am teaching the doctor as much as I am collaborating in the care of the child. The majority of physicians are consciously aware of this and express appreciation for the investment of time and effort I make outside of the treatment setting. The few physicians who are dismissive of my efforts usually do not refer to me again, and, although I regret the failure to achieve a real collaboration, I recognize that not everyone views the world the way I do and I accept that my approach is labor-intensive and may not fit the practice patterns of every physician.

What is my approach to effective and collaborative work with my medical colleagues? First, I see myself as having been invited to join the physician in the care of his or her patient. Therefore, I emphasize to the physician by telephone at the time of the referral that the primary responsibility for the well-being of the patient still resides with the physician, although at times the coordination component of treatment might be delegated to me. Second, I make explicit that successful resolution of a mind-body problem depends on satisfactory integration of medical and mental health efforts, with the priority of either of those efforts shifting depending on circumstances at any specific time. Third, I explicitly articulate to the physician the expertise that I can add to the treatment efforts and in so doing begin to build a framework for mutual understanding of the underlying nature of the eating problem. Concrete guidelines for monitoring the safety and recovery of the patient are determined collaboratively between the physician and me, and a system is designed to ensure regular but not overly intrusive communication. Finally, I introduce the idea of adding other professionals, such as a family therapist, nutritionist, psychopharmacologist, gynecologist, endocrinologist, dentist, gastroenterologist, orthopedist, or school administrators or guidance personnel, to the working team, always emphasizing how multidisciplinary teamwork enhances the likelihood of the patient's crisis-free recovery and balances the workload for any one of us (see Chapter 13).

The Physician's Role During Treatment

The evaluation of a child or adolescent is completed when all clinicians who have been involved in the evaluation from the perspective of multiple disciplines share their findings with the child or adolescent and her family. Usually that feedback is presented in integrated form to the family by the eating disorders specialist (the mental health clinician) who first has previewed the findings and treatment recommendations with the referring physician. The physician's understanding and approval of the treatment recommendations is positively linked to the family's likelihood of accepting and implementing them.

It is my practice to invite the referring physician to serve on the treatment team. Parents, patient, and physician in consultation with the mental health clinician then agree on a schedule of appointments with the physician during which time the patient will be weighed (in a hospital gown and sometimes backwards to prevent being upset by the number), a urine sample will be collected (to protect the patient who might be tempted to water-load), laboratory studies will be obtained as needed, and the physician and patient will have a brief chat concerning the patient's feelings about both the status of her recovery and the ongoing treatment process. This contact is critical for many reasons. Parents receive reassurance that their child is medically safe or are offered an immediate intervention if their child becomes medically unstable. The physician is attuned to the family's degree of comfort with the therapeutic process and is able to help the family stay in treatment despite the wearisome nature of the disease process and the treatment demands. The physician is experienced as appropriately protective by patient, family, and mental-health clinician. Moreover, by his or her consistent behavior around insisting on limits on physical activity if there are signs of noncompliance with recommended dietary plans, the important connection between quality of body care and degree of independence to regulate one's own physical behavior is established.

The physician also helps to buffer the relationship between the adolescent who is reaching for independence and the parent who wants to facilitate that release but is terrified because of the seriousness of the eating disorder symptoms. The physician clarifies for the patient, with whom his or her relationship is usually longstanding, that as long as the eating disorder is powerful within her, she may not be able to take care of herself with full effectiveness, but she will be expected to do what she can while the treatment team safeguards her until she recovers.

The close collaboration of physician and mental health clinician helps create a space in the psychotherapy office for the patient to talk safely about herself on any and all levels with the reassurance that her therapist will be able to listen compassionately without the therapist being overwhelmed with anxiety about the patient's current physical state. At a practical level, this collaboration works only if physician and mental health clinician (and other team members) have attended to the steps previously presented concerning the formation of their relationship. Also, it is very important that team members agree to make no changes in the treatment plan, even in regard to their own discipline, without consultation with all other team members. This usually can be managed through prompt use of the telephone and is often helpful in avoiding crises and forestalling "splitting"—efforts (perhaps unconscious) by some part of a system to cause other parts not to work collaboratively. As the patient and her family engage actively in a recovery effort, it is usually appropriate that changes be made in the treatment plan. Again, consultation among team members is advised.

The Physician's Role in Identifying and Managing a Crisis

For the purpose of this discussion I am defining *crisis* both as a condition of dangerous instability and as the point in the course of a serious disease at which a decisive change occurs, leading either to recovery or to death. Referring to the former definition, the first encounter in the physician's office represents a crisis: A child is perceived to be unstable in her attitudes about and her approach to caring for her body. When the physician acts assertively to correct this instability by referring the patient for specialty care, the patient is protected from experiencing more permanent physical damage. Over the course of eating disorder treatment, close medical monitoring serves to limit medical instability and to enable the physician to intervene with additional medical treatment, such as hospitalization, intravenous feedings, and restriction of physical activity, before a medical crisis occurs.

The decision to hospitalize a person with an eating disorder is appropriate if the assessment or treatment team determines that the patient cannot be kept safe in an outpatient setting. If communication between patient and team is open and complete, this decision should not provoke a crisis within the patient–care provider system. But, sometimes, as eating disorder symptoms recede in intensity, underlying psychiatric illnesses emerge, such as depression or anxiety disorder, and the patient may become unable to maintain her own safety. Alternatively, the eating disorder symptoms may worsen or operate in an intransigent manner, and the patient may require either carefully supervised refeeding or a trial of medication under close supervision because of the patient's fragile physical state.

Persons struggling with eating disorders are also at risk for psychosocial crises. At times they may present in the physician's office looking very emotionally fragile. The physician and his or her staff may become alarmed and question the efficacy of the outpatient plan or the competency of the collaborating mental health clinician. Again, the quality of the collegial relationship will determine the outcome of the physician's crisis of confidence in both plans and colleagues. If the physician and clinician are working well together, they will appreciate together that the patient's crisis may be signaling any or all of the following circumstances: the impact of prolonged malnourishment, the patient's alarm over weight gain, the emergence of a psychiatric comorbidity, the expression of underlying tension in the parent-patient relationship, and the parents' or patient's resistance to some aspect of the overall treatment plan.

The physician's calm demeanor and firm encouragement that patient and parents explore directly the issues underlying the current emotional crisis usually resolves the immediate instability. This process involves a rapid but thorough review by all involved of the possible precipitants to the current state and of the changes in plan that might be necessary, as well as an affirmation of those successful aspects of the ongoing work that must be continued. Additionally, markers such as blood pressure alteration, family tension, weight loss or gain, and alteration in pattern of binge eating and purging are identified that will be used to chart ongoing progress or to signal the necessity of subsequent changes in the treatment plan. Psychological and system crises are a natural part of the work of recovery from an eating disorder; only medical crises are preventable. Medical crises usually highlight some aspect of the child's emotional development that has become stuck. The risk of medical crises is that their presence may cause all participants to lose focus. In other words, psychological, systemic, and medical crises should be anticipated. Their successful resolution is often key in the accomplishment of secondary prevention, for example minimizing the impact of the eating disorder on healthy development and sustaining symptom remission.

The Mental-Health Clinician as Educator of, and Collaborator with, the Physician

Every patient-linked encounter between physician and mental health clinician is an opportunity for each to learn from the other. However, learning occurs only if there is mutual agreement that each has expertise of a particular sort and that the expertise of both (and others) is required by the patient suffering from an eating disorder. Although the eating disorder specialist possesses important knowledge and tools, the physician carries the unique responsibility for providing oversight of the patient's medical stability. In my experience, patient care will not be delivered effectively unless multidisciplinary collaborators have agreed upon answers to the following questions:

1. When and by what means will we communicate?
2. What kind of information will we exchange and who else will share information with us?
3. What are our goals and what are our strategies to accomplish them?
4. What are some signs that our collaboration is working, and what warns us that things are not working well?

There are few absolutely right answers to these questions. It is by listening, negotiating, and compromising that colleagues learn enough about each other to feel capable of weaving a safety net around their mutual patient while providing her with the tools to grow. In the process, the providers may grow, too. As soon as an eating disordered patient is referred to me, I open a prevention dialogue with the referring physician. I offer to come to the physician's office and talk with him or her, and with partners, nurses, and support staff, about my understanding of how eating disorders develop and how they can be identified before medical compromise has occurred. If asked, I teach the physicians dialogues about body care that they can use with their patients, and I encourage the practice to arrange for speakers to address groups of patients and their families concerning disease prevention and creation of good health. I invite the physician to join me when I speak in the community at the behest of managed care companies who, more and more, are engaging in preventive work.

All of these efforts take time, and not every effort is successful. Nevertheless, over time I have become convinced that I have a responsibility to alert physicians to behaviors that may obscure or compromise their desire to work constructively to treat or prevent eating disorders. First, physicians should avoid dismissing or minimizing potential worries brought to them by either the patient or family members. Examples include, "I feel fat," "I think there is something wrong with my child's eating," and "Do you think my wife [sister/daughter] could be vomiting?" Second, almost by contrast, physicians should be careful not to emphasize medical or physical explanations for problems in ways that neglect or obscure investigations of emotional or psychosocial dimensions of these problems. In this regard, it is important not to assume that psychological therapies are failing if the patient complains about the therapist; in fact, just the opposite may be true. Physicians treating eating disorders must be well informed about psychological resistance and denial. Finally, it is crucial that the physician not assume that the patient is well just because there is visible resolution of physical symptoms. In fact, it is not until malnourishment has been replaced by nutrient energy or binge-purge cycles have abated that the patient will have sufficient energy to attempt exploration of the issues underlying, precipitating, or perpetuating the symptom state.

I want to be clear that the physician is never the only learner. I have been the grateful student many, many times. Collaborative efforts always have provided me with support and enriched my work. Specifically, physicians provide in-struction about the effects of eating disorders on the body at a level of detail that enables me to appreciate better what the patient is experiencing physically. Consequently, I can respond more empathetically to my patients as we sort out what is going on inside of them emotionally from what is the result of physical impairment. When I trust my physician colleague to safeguard our patient's physical state, I can offer my services to patients whom formerly I would not have treated in an outpatient setting. When natural resistance occurs within the therapeutic alliance, I can depend on my physician colleague to help the patient stay with the struggle by providing a temporary ventilation opportunity and then redirection back to my office. Even if the patient becomes so resistant that she chooses to withdraw from our therapy, she can turn to the physician to help her stay stable while she considers other recovery options; this helps assuage my sense of treatment failure and reassures me that my patient has a chance to re-main safe. Respectful collaboration with my physician colleagues also has of-fered me a place to ventilate the fears and frustrations that cannot help but arise in the context of this difficult therapeutic endeavor. I hope I have remembered to say thank you.

☐ Conclusion

Recently, I presented much of what is written here at a meeting attended by hard-working, dedicated, community-based physicians. They listened atten-tively, but I knew by their questions that most of them had not yet worked as collaboratively as my model requires. They were doubtful, but not rejecting. They encouraged me to "boil it down" to some guidelines and then send like-minded mental health clinicians into their neighborhood. I saw and felt their point. I will redouble my efforts to persuade my mental health colleagues to ini-tiate more outreach to physicians and to be forthcoming in providing communi-cation about the nature of their work with mutual patients. And after some reflection, I offer the following as the "boiled down" model.

Physicians

Recognize (see) the disease.
Move on it more assertively, more quickly, and always collaboratively.
Work with your patient (and others) until the disease is over.
Then acknowledge your hard work and that of the team.
Acknowledge the patient and the family who work hard, too.
Tell your colleagues about this work you are doing and how and why you are doing it.
Advocate that they do it, too.

Mental health clinicians and community-based physicians may have different training and different skills, but our goal is the same: to engage with our pa-tients on behalf of their continued or renewed capacity to provide for their own good health and productive living. This shared intent requires us to work to-gether for our own and our patients' benefit.

☐ Appendix 1: Behavior of Parents and Children that Might Be Associated with Onset of Eating Disorders or Impaired Eating Attitudes and Behaviors: Guideline for Healthcare Providers

1. Parents express degree of worry about child's shape, appearance, or weight that is not supported by the primary care physician's clinical findings or observations.
2. Child expresses dissatisfaction with body shape and weight to parents or pediatrician.
3. Child imposes food restrictions in variety or quantity that
   a. compromises nutritional status
   b. stimulates family conflict
   c. suggests child is concerned about body shape, or weight or is engaged in a control battle with parents
4. In response to questions about the child/parent interaction around eating, parents or child reveal information that suggests that
   a. parent is uncomfortable with child having food preferences or feeding himself or herself.
   b. child is reluctant to experiment with food of variable textures, smells, consistency, taste.
   c. there is no structure to meal time and few family interactions around food consumption, or there is heightened tension in family when there are eating opportunities.
   d. parent's anxiety about child's eating behavior intrudes upon interactions with child around food purchase, preparation, presentation, and consumption.
   e. there is an intense emphasis in family, particularly by parents, on physical fitness and low-fat eating patterns, which may promote an overly restricted pediatric diet and a child who feels compelled to work out beyond child's interest and body capacity.
5. Child sneaks food.
6. Child chooses not to or resists parent's efforts to involve him or her in physical activities, or parents believe children should engage in physical activity only if it interests them.
7. Parents express discomfort about establishing expectations and consequences for children about eating behavior; compare this to parent's capacity to instruct regarding toilet training, sleep behavior, and brushing of teeth.
8. There is a history of eating disorders or impaired eating behavior in the family, including parent, grandparent, or member of child's generation.

©Roslyn G. Weiner, Ph.D.

☐ References

Academy for Eating Disorders. (1997). *Position statement on equity in insurance coverage for eating disorders* [on-line]. Available: http://www.acadeatdis.org.
American Psychiatric Association. (1994). *Diagnostic and statistical manual of mental disorders* (4th ed.). Washington, DC: Author.

Carney, C. P., & Anderson A. E. (1996). Eating disorders: Guide to medical evaluation and complications. In J. Yager (Ed.), *The psychiatric clinics of North America: Eating disorders* (Vol. 6, no. 4, pp. 657–679). Philadelphia: W.B. Saunders.

Heinberg, L. J. 91996). Theories of body image disturbance: Perceptual, developmental, and sociocultural factors. In J. K. Thompson (Ed.), *Body image, eating disorders, and obesity: An integrative guide for assessment and treatment* (pp. 27–47). Washington, DC: American Psychological Association.

Kreipe, R. E., Golden, N. H., Katzman, D. K., Fisher, M., Rees, J., Tonkin, R. S., Silber, T. J., Sigman, G., Schebendach, J., & Ammerman, S. D. (1995). Eating disorders in adolescents: A position paper of the Society for Adolescent Medicine. *Journal of Adolescent Health, 16,* 476–480.

Rydall, A. C., Rodin, G. M., Olmsted, M. P., Devenyi, R. G., & Daneman, D. (1997). Disordered eating behavior and microvascular complications in young women with Insulin-Dependent Diabetes Mellitus. *The New England Journal of Medicine, 336* (June 26), 1849–1854.

Stiegel-Moore, R. H., Silberstein, L. R., & Rodin, J. (1993). The social self in bulimia nervosa: Public self-consciousness, social anxiety, and perceived fraudulence. *Journal of Abnormal Psychology, 102,* 297–303.

Yager, J., Andersen, A., Devlin, M., Mitchell, J., Powers, P., & Yates, A. (1993). American Psychiatric Association practice guidelines for eating disorders. *American Journal of Psychiatry, 150,* 207–228.

CHAPTER

Debra K. Katzman

Prevention of Medical Complications in Children and Adolescents with Eating Disorders

Eating problems of children and adolescents occur along a continuum ranging from mild to severe. The most common are anorexia nervosa and bulimia nervosa. The period of greatest risk for development of an eating disorder is during adolescence, the age of onset ranging from 12 to 25 years (Garfinkel et al., 1995; Mitchell, Pyle, Eckert, Hatsukami, & Soll, 1990; Rastam & Gillberg, 1991; Rastam, Gillberg, & Garton, 1989; Woodside & Garfinkel, 1992). Because of the high prevalence among young people and the significant incidence of morbidity and death, prevention and early identification of these disorders are critical. Their physical impact on the growing and developing child and adolescent can be profound: Serious growth retardation, pubertal delay or interruption, peak bone-mass reduction, and abnormalities in brain structure can occur early in the course of the illness. The role of the physician is to identify and minimize these serious physical consequences.

This chapter provides healthcare professionals with an overview of the role of the primary-care physician in the prevention of the medical complications that can develop in children and adolescents. (Because most patients with eating disorders are female, we use the feminine pronouns *she* and *her* throughout the chapter.)

☐ Early Identification

Early identification of young people at risk for an eating disorder allows for prompt intervention, one of the few predictors of a positive outcome (Fisher et al., 1995). The few reports available on the early detection and diagnosis of eating disorders in the primary-care setting present a discouraging picture. According to one study (Bryant-Waugh, Lask, Shafran, & Fosson, 1992), diagnosis of early-onset eating disorders often is delayed or overlooked because physicians are unaware that younger patients can be affected. The study, which evaluated two case reports of young children with anorexia nervosa, found that only one third of pediatricians and 2% of family practitioners included an eating disorder in their differential diagnosis. Similarly, a study (Zinkand, Cadoret, & Widmer, 1984) of the obstacles to diagnosing bulimia nervosa found that primary-care physicians had difficulty diagnosing the disorder in patients as young as 14 years old because of patient secrecy and obesity.

The difficulty in identifying an eating disorder in a child or younger adolescent is caused by several factors. First, some of the clinical characteristics found in children and adolescents differ from those commonly seen in older adolescents and adults. Second, the definition of eating disorders as they apply to pre-pubertal and pubertal adolescents in the current classification schemes may be incomplete. Debate continues about the clinical features necessary for the diagnosis of an eating disorder in this population. Finally, community-based studies and case registers have shown that about half of those ill with an eating disorder do not receive help from their doctors (Pagsberg & Wang, 1994). Many young people are reluctant to seek help and typically conceal their disorder from family and friends. Most patients seek medical management with their illness well underway, and the physician's work begins by preventing further medical complications.

☐ Diagnosis

The division of opinion on the clinical features necessary for the diagnosis of eating disorders in children and younger adolescents is clear from a consideration of anorexia nervosa. The central features of this disorder, as outlined in the *Diagnostic and Statistical Manual of Mental Disorders, Fourth Edition* (American Psychiatric Association, 1994), are problematic when applied to younger patients. The first criterion states that patients with anorexia refuse to maintain their body weight over a minimally normal value for age and height or fail to make the expected weight gain during a period of growth, leading to a body weight 15% below that expected. However, children and younger adolescents may stop gaining weight early on in the illness even before there is any weight loss. In addition, some children and younger adolescents develop an eating disorder when they are overweight. When they come to medical attention, they may meet all the criteria except that their weight is relatively normal.

The criterion that suggests that postmenarchal girls should have missed at least three consecutive menstrual cycles poses additional problems. Because menarche may be delayed if anorexia nervosa develops before or early in puberty (Meyer, von Holtzapfel, Deffner, Engel, & Klick, 1986), this criterion cannot be applied to girls who have not begun to menstruate. After menarche, it is normal for healthy adolescents to experience amenorrhea for 3 months or more any time in the first 1 to 2 years (Emans & Goldstein, 1990). In addition, many adolescents are on medications that can alter menstrual function, particularly oral contraceptives. The utility of amenorrhea as a diagnostic criterion even has been questioned in the adult eating-disorder field (Garfinkel et al., 1996). In a large epidemiological survey using several relevant variables, amenorrhea did not appear to discriminate between women with anorexia nervosa and women with all its features except amenorrhea.

The diagnosis of an eating disorder should be considered in any child or young adolescent who has weight loss of unexplained cause and who avoids food. It is imperative to exclude underlying systemic disorders that could cause weight loss, such as a malignancy, brain tumors, seizure disorders, inflammatory bowel disease, endocrine and metabolic disease, and infection. Weight loss alone is not a common sign of a malignancy. Young people with a malignancy may develop pallor, lymphadenopathy, petechiae, hepatomegaly, splenomegaly, or abdominal mass. The most common malignancies in adolescents are leukemia, lymphomas, and brain tumors (Neinstein, 1996). Children and adolescents with inflammatory bowel disease not only lose weight but also experience abdominal pain, loose stools associated with mucus or blood, and anemia, and have a high erythrocyte-sedimentation rate. Adolescents with hyperthyroidism become hungrier and eat more but do not gain weight. They also may have tachycardia, sweating, tremors, and frequent bowel movements. With other causes of weight loss, body image is rarely distorted, and the adolescents themselves often become alarmed at the continued loss.

Eating disorders also have been reported in patients with diabetes mellitus, cystic fibrosis, and inflammatory bowel disease. Significant comorbidity exists between eating disorders and many other psychiatric illnesses, especially affective and substance-use disorders (Woodside, 1993). Adolescents using chemical agents that cause loss of appetite and weight, such as amphetamines and cocaine, also exhibit a rise in blood pressure, dilated pupils, tachycardia, dry mouth, and dry mucous membranes.

Other causes of weight loss in children and adolescents (< 14 years old) include food-avoidance emotional disorder, food refusal, pervasive refusal, selective eating, and appetite loss secondary to depression. The common theme underlying all of these eating disturbances is food refusal (Bryant-Waugh & Kaminiski, 1993). A thorough history and physical examination along with specific laboratory studies can help distinguish an eating disorder from these other diagnostic possibilities.

☐ Warning Signs of an Eating Disorder

Dissatisfaction with body image and dieting are major concerns of adolescent girls. A prospective study (Killen et al., 1996) that followed a community sample of adolescent girls of high-school age over 4 years found that weight concerns strongly predicted an eating disorder. Many adolescents believe that they are overweight and want to weigh less (Rodin, 1993). One study (Eisele, Hertsgaard, & Light, 1986) demonstrated that although 81% of young adolescent girls were within or below the range for ideal weight, 78% preferred to weigh less; only 14% were satisfied with their current weight. Dieting is widespread among children and adolescents, especially girls. By the age of 13 years, 80% of girls and 10% of boys have been on a diet (Melin, Irwin, & Scully, 1992). It is rare to find a girl by the age of 18 years who has not dieted (Davies & Furnham, 1986).

Dieting among adolescent girls has become an important issue because of its association with eating disorders (Killen et al., 1996). Five warning signs of an eating disorder in the child or adolescent have been described: dieting associated with decreasing weight goals, increasing criticism of the body, increasing social isolation, amenorrhea, and evidence of purging (Woodside, 1993).

Young girls at risk of an eating disorder never feel they are thin enough. They often describe some part of their body as too "big" or "fat." These girls resist gaining weight. As a girl continues to diet and her body gets thinner, she still remains critical of her shape and weight. In one series of 48 anorexic children under 14 years old, 56% expressed a dread of fatness (Fosson, Knibbs, Bryant-Waugh, & Lask, 1987). Assessing the patient's satisfaction with her body and her perceptions of body shape and size is therefore important. The physician might begin by exploring whether there is anything about the patient's body (size, shape, weight) that she wishes she could change? What does she see when she looks in the mirror? A response indicating body dissatisfaction ("I really dislike my body") or disturbances in the way she experiences her body (e.g., "My stomach and thighs are huge!") warrants further exploration. The physician might probe into the relative importance of the young person's body shape, weight, and size in the overall way she feels about herself. Does the patient believe that her life will change as a result of weight loss? Does she spend a lot of time thinking about her body? We ask all our patients what they think is their "ideal" body weight. If a young person reports that she is dissatisfied with her body then it is important to explore how she copes with these feelings. "How do you deal with the feelings?" "Have you tried to adjust your weight?" "How have you tried to lose weight?"

Amenorrhea in adolescents should be investigated for possible disordered eating, regardless of their weight. In one study, 40% of amenorrheic adolescents reported fasting or purging in the previous month (Selzer, Caust, Hibbert, Bowes, & Patton, 1996). Amenorrhea should be considered a marker for weight-control practices related to eating disorders. Under such circumstances, the primary-care physician should review the patient's eating attitudes and behavior and elicit a menstrual history.

Purging in an effort to lose weight also should alert the primary-care physician to a possible problem. An alarming number of young adolescents employ unhealthy weight-regulation strategies: one study (Killen et al., 1986) found that 11% of 15-year-old girls vomited, 8% used diet pills, and 7% abused laxatives. Another study reported that vomiting was a chief means of weight control in a sample of patients with anorexia nervosa who were 14 years old or less, while excessive exercise and laxative abuse also were important compensatory behaviors used by children and young adolescents (Fosson et al., 1987). Therefore, it is important to ask questions about purging behavior: vomiting, the use of laxatives, diuretics, ipecac, and diet pills, and exercise. "Have you ever had the feeling that you needed to vomit after meals?" "Have you ever vomited after you have eaten?" If the patient acknowledges using vomiting as a weight-control method then the physician should determine the method by which vomiting is self-induced. Patients often use a finger or foreign body (toothbrush or spoon) to elicit the gag reflux to induce vomiting. Vomiting gradually becomes easier and sometimes is induced by use of Valsalva's maneuver. Determining the frequency, age of onset, severity during the worst period, and periods of abstinence is important. It is also important to determine whether the patient is misusing laxatives, diuretics, diet pills, or syrup of ipecac. The type of medication used for prevention of weight gain and the quantity and frequency of use should be determined. Finding out how young people are purchasing these medications is also important, as they do not have the same opportunity to buy them as older adolescents and adults. Some patients ingest syrup of ipecac, an over-the-counter product used as first aid in cases of accidental poisoning. The physician should also characterize the type, amount, and frequency of exercise. Often, affected young people with anorexia nervosa participate in solitary forms of exercise, such as excessive calisthenics, walking, jogging, or riding an exercise bicycle. Patients should be asked what they do if they cannot exercise and how they feel about decreasing or modifying their regimen.

Primary health care providers are in a good position to recognize dieting that goes beyond that undertaken by many teenagers. If a young person exhibits hazardous eating behaviors, remedial strategies should be introduced before they become entrenched.

☐ Medical Complications of Children and Adolescents with Eating Disorders

Serious medical complications develop in children and younger adolescents with eating disorders early in the course of the illness (Fisher et al., 1995; Palla & Litt, 1988). Malnutrition caused by weight-control habits may result in permanent interference with growth in stature, prolonged delay in puberty, interruption of attainment of peak bone mass, and changes in brain structure. Healthcare providers need to be aware of these early complications so that prompt evaluation and intervention can prevent the long-term effects of these often irreversible conditions. The medical complications associated with eating disorders in adolescents have been extensively reviewed (Fisher et al., 1995) (Table 1). The following sections discuss the medical complications specific to children and adolescents with eating disorders and recommend ways to prevent the long-term effects of these conditions.

Growth Retardation

Eating disorders occurring before or during puberty may have devastating effects on the patient's development, particularly on growth in stature. Growth retardation and short stature have been reported in patients with anorexia, especially if it develops before the pubertal growth spurt or during active growth (Golden et al., 1994; Nussbaum, Baird, Sonnenblick, Cowan, & Shenker, 1985; Nussbaum et al., 1990; Root & Powers, 1983). The velocity of physical growth in adolescence requires an increase in energy and nutrients. The reported energy intake of adolescents with anorexia nervosa, however, is significantly lower than the recommended dietary allowance for energy in all adolescent age groups (Beaumont, Chambers, Rouse, & Abraham, 1981). Patients with bulimia nervosa also have significant energy and other nutritional deficits after binge eating, vomiting, and purging.

Studies of anorexic adolescents (Golden et al., 1994; Nussbaum et al., 1990) have shown that hypothalamic dysfunction and malnutrition contribute to the delay in growth. Basal growth-hormone levels have been reported to be elevated in about half of adults with anorexia but normal or low in adolescents

TABLE 1. Physical findings in adolescents with an eating disorder

Type	Anorexia Nervosa	Bulimia nervosa
General		
	Hyperactivity or lethargy	Weakness
	Cold intolerance	Irritable mood
Vital signs		
	Weight loss	Weight fluctuations
	Growth delay	Arrythmias
	Arrythmias (bradycardia)	
	Hypotension	
	Hypothermia	
Head and neck		
		Parotid hypertrophy
		Dental caries
Breast		
	Failure to develop or loss of secondary sexual characteristics	
Cardiac		
	Arrythmias (bradycardia)	Arrythmias
	Peripheral edema	Peripheral edema
	Congestive heart failure	
	Poor peripheral perfusion	
Abdomen		
	Masses (stool vs. abdominal mass)	Epigastric tenderness
	Abdominal tenderness	
	Constipation	
Genitalia		
	Failure to develop or loss of secondary sexual characteristics	
	Amenorrhea	Amenorrhea
		Oligomenorraga
		Menstrual dysfunction
Musculoskeletal		
	Muscle weakness	Muscle weakness
	Scoliosis	
Central nervous system		
	Seizures	Seizures
	Peripheral neuropathy	
	Myopathy	
Skin		
	Dry skin	Russell's sign
	Hair loss	
	Lanugo	
	Acrocyanosis	
	Yellow skin (hypercarotenemia)	
	Brittle hair and nails	

(Nussbaum et al., 1990). Somatomedin-c production also was found to be lower in adolescents with anorexia nervosa (Golden et al., 1994; Nussbaum et al., 1990). Altered growth-hormone secretion and action, which occur during the years of active growth, are reversible with refeeding (Golden et al., 1994). The nutritional deficiencies of an eating disorder may result in lifelong consequences for the growing adolescent (Schebendach & Nussbaum, 1992).

The physician should follow the young person's growth in height, weight, and sexual development carefully. To determine the patient's expected body weight, the primary-care provider needs to take into account a combination of previous height and weight percentiles, anticipated growth, heights and weights of family members, and the average weights of healthy adolescents of the same sex, height, and sexual-maturity rating.

In clinical practice, growth can be measured by height and weight. The most commonly used method is that of the smoothed growth curves on which clinicians traditionally plot height for age and weight for age throughout childhood (Hamill et al., 1979; Tanner, Whitehouse, & Takaishi, 1966a, 1966b). Growth curves are most useful if longitudinal data are available, as extrapolating from cross-sectional data collected at one point in time can be misleading. One needs to bear in mind that these charts are limited by a lack of adjustment for sexual-maturity rating and ethnicity as well as for individual variations in the onset of the pubertal growth spurt and development.

Quetelet's body-mass index (BMI) (Beumont, Al-Alami, & Touyz, 1988) is a weight-to-height relationship expressed as weight in kilograms divided by height in meters squared. Many clinicians assess body size by comparing the BMI with reference data. Percentile tables of BMI for age and sex based on the National Center for Health Statistics data have been developed for children and adolescents (Hammer, Kraemer, Wilson, Ritter, & Dornbusch, 1991).

Knowledge of the body composition in terms of fat and fat-free mass is used in pediatrics to estimate an adolescent's nutritional status. The combination of triceps (an index of peripheral subcutaneous fat) and subscapular skinfold (an index of central subcutaneous fat) measurements is one of the most useful ways to assess body fat in adolescents of all ages (Mahan & Rosebrough, 1984). In addition, the sum of four skinfold-thickness measurements can be used to estimate the percentage of total body fat from subcutaneous stores in older adolescents (Durnin & Rahaman, 1967)). Midarm muscle area provides an additional estimate of body-tissue composition if compared with reference data (Frisancho, 1990). These anthropometric techniques are easy and valuable to use in daily pediatric practice.

In the absence of a gold standard for establishing ideal body weight in adolescents, the methods described should be applied in combination to assess the adolescent's nutritional state.

If an adolescent is found to have an arrest in growth and development, hospitalization may be necessary and nutritional rehabilitation should be implemented immediately. Early identification and treatment of eating disorders is therefore crucial to ensuring a return to an optimum weight and normal growth patterns.

Pubertal Delay and Interruption

Malnutrition also may result in delayed sexual maturation. In premenarchal and pubertal girls with anorexia nervosa, normal pubertal development is disturbed and sexual maturation often is delayed. Manifestations include delay of breast and testicular development, depletion of auxiliary and pubic hair, and loss of growth of pelvic contours in girls (Russell, 1985). One report suggested that if the illness persists for many years, including the time of puberty, breast development simply may fail to occur (Russell, 1985).

Menstrual dysfunction is common with eating disorders. Weight loss interferes with the onset of menarche and causes secondary amenorrhea in the postmenarchal girl. From 20% to 50% of patients with anorexia nervosa lose their menstrual periods even before they lose a significant amount of weight (Golden & Shenker, 1992). Basal levels of both luteinizing and follicle-stimulating hormones are low or low to normal. Patients with anorexia have been shown to have a circadian luteinizing hormone secretory pattern, consistent with the immature patterns found in prepubertal children (Katz & Boyar, 1978). Pelvic ultrasound studies, which make it possible to observe the effects of past nutrition on ovaries and uterus, have confirmed the immaturity of the hypothalamic-pituitary-ovarian axis. In patients who are seriously ill, the reproductive organs appear infantile and show considerable regression of the ovarian and uterine size, shape, and morphology (Lai, Debruyn, Lask, Bryant-Waugh, & Hankins, 1994). Treasure, Wheeler, King, Gordon, and Russell (1988) have used pelvic ultrasound to establish target weights in adult patients with anorexia nervosa. At low weights, ovarian volumes were found to be similar to those of 8 to 12-year-olds, and changes in ovarian morphology resembled those of normal pubertal development but on a more rapid timescale. Their findings suggest that pelvic ultrasound is a good indicator of the weight required for full endocrine recovery. A recent study in adolescents with secondary amenorrhea revealed that ovarian volume in adolescents with good outcomes was significantly higher than in the poor-outcome group (Sobanski, Hiltmann, Blanz, Klein, & Schmidt, 1997). Those patients who had a BMI of 18 had an increased probability of recovered ovaries, suggesting that pelvic ultrasound may offer a method for monitoring ovarian growth and maturation in order to determine the target weight for adequate ovarian size and function in adolescents with secondary amenorrhea.

Other work has shown that menstruation is unlikely to resume in adolescents with anorexia nervosa if body weight is less than 90% of the median weight for height and age. In one study (Golden et al., 1997), 86% of patients who achieved this goal weight resumed menses within 6 months. In this same study a serum estradiol level of more than 110 pmol/L (30 pg/mL) was associated with the return of menstrual function at follow-up.

Patients with bulimia nervosa may experience oligomenorrhea, amenorrhea, and anovulatory cycles (Cantopher, Evans, Lacey, & Pearce, 1988). Factors thought to contribute to menstrual dysfunction include loss of body fat, excessive exercising, chaotic eating behaviors, emotional disturbances, and alterations in the regulation of the hypothalamic-pituitary function (Golden & Shenker, 1992).

Osteopenia

Osteopenia is one of the most serious and early consequences of anorexia nervosa in adolescents. Its causes include estrogen deficiency, elevated glucocorticoid levels, generalized malnutrition, calcium-intake deficiency, and reduced body mass. Because 45% to 60% of peak bone mineral normally is acquired during adolescence (Rubin et al., 1993), the impact of this disorder on bone-mineral accretion is significant. Complications may include increased risk of premature fractures and inability to reach height potential. Osteopenia that develops during adolescence as a result of anorexia nervosa may not be completely reversible (Bachrach, Guido, Katzman, Litt, & Marcus, 1990; Bachrach, Katzman, Litt, Guido, & Marcus, 1991). In order to monitor the bone-mineral status in adolescents with anorexia nervosa, a study of bone density should be considered (Bachrach, Guido, et al., 1990; Bachrach, Kateman, et al., 1991). A few treatments have been suggested in the prevention and treatment of low bone-mineral density in anorexia nervosa. Weight rehabilitation has been shown to be effective in increasing bone-mineral density, even before the return of menses (Bachrach, Guido, et al., 1990; Bachrach, Kateman, et al., 1991; Charig & Fletcher, 1987). If an eating disorder occurs in childhood or young adolescence, calcium intake may be significantly compromised at a critical time for bone mineralization. It has been recommended that young people take 1200 to 1500 mg per day of calcium.

In other studies, positive outcomes have been confined to adults. For example, exercise has been shown to protect against osteopenia in adults with anorexia nervosa (Rigotti, Neer, Skates, Herzog, & Nussbaum, 1991), but this effect has not been confirmed in adolescents (Bachrach et al., 1990; Biller et al., 1989). Nor has the effect of estrogen administration on bone-mineral density in adolescents with anorexia nervosa been evaluated. One randomized trial (Klibanski & Greenspan, 1986) on the effects of estrogen replacement in women with anorexia showed that bone-density improvement was greatest in those at the lowest percentage of ideal body weight. To date, no controlled trials of the effect of estrogen on bone mass in adolescents with anorexia nervosa have been reported. This awaits further study.

Structural Abnormalities of the Brain

Structural abnormalities of the brain have been reported in adolescents with anorexia nervosa (Katzman et al., 1996; Golden et al., 1996). In one study using magnetic resonance imaging, adolescents with anorexia nervosa of brief duration (3–24 months) showed marked brain changes (Katzman et al., 1996). Volumes of both gray and white matter were diminished, and cerebrospinal fluid volumes were increased. Gray-matter volumes were correlated positively with lowest body mass index and negatively correlated with 24-hour urine cortisol levels. These findings suggest that the brain changes found early in the illness may result from the degree of starvation. This study and others have reported significant correlations between magnitude of brain abnormalities and degree of starvation (Golden et al., 1996; Katzman et al., 1996; Kingston, Szmukler, Andrewes, Tress, & Desmond, 1996; Krieg, Pirke, Lauer, & Backmund, 1988).

Brain changes in adolescents with anorexia nervosa seem to have reversible and irreversible components. Return of cerebrospinal fluid volumes and white-matter volumes to normal range occurs with weight restoration, supporting the importance of prompt and early weight rehabilitation. Although grey-matter volumes also increase with weight restoration, current evidence suggests that deficits in the volume of this tissue persist (Katzman, Zipursky, Lambe, & Mikulis, 1997; Lambe, Katzman, Mikulis, & Zipursky, 1997). To date, we do not know the factors that predict whether brain abnormalities persist. There is evidence, however, that weight restoration reverses some of the brain changes observed.

Cognitive deficits have been described in patients with anorexia nervosa, specifically in the focusing and execution, verbal, memory, and visuospatial domains (Kingston et al., 1996; Pendleton-Jones, Duncan, Brouwers, & Mirsky, 1991). Some studies have documented improvement in cognitive function in patients with anorexia nervosa following weight gain. However, in view of inconsistencies in study findings, further investigation is needed of structural brain abnormalities in patients with anorexia nervosa and their associations with impaired cognitive functioning.

☐ The Role of the Primary-Care Physician

The primary-care physician plays many roles in the prevention of medical complications in children and adolescents with eating disorder. The most important role consists of the early identification of eating problems. A review of the outcome literature (Herzog, Nussbaum, & Marmor, 1996) over the past decade concludes that the outcome is good in approximately 50% of patients with anorexia nervosa, medium in 30%, and poor in 20%. Prognostic factors for a favorable outcome are early age at onset, good patient-parent relationship, and a low number of hospitalizations. The recovery rates for bulimia nervosa range from 17% to 71% (Herzog et al., 1996). With this disorder, early age at onset and friendships have been associated with a good outcome. These predictors strongly underline the importance of identifying young people at risk as soon as possible. For both anorexia nervosa and bulimia nervosa, the consistent predictor of a favorable outcome is early age of intervention: the earlier a child or adolescent is identified, the better the outcome.

Very little is known about the long-term prognostic value of medical comorbidity in anorexia nervosa. The literature suggests that the course of an eating disorder may be negatively influenced by the development of a comorbid physical disease (Herzog, Dieter, Fiehn, & Petzold, 1997). Long-term follow-up studies of osteopenia and structural brain abnormalities show that these medical complications, which develop early in the course of the illness, may not be completely reversible (Bachrach et al., 1991; Katzman et al., 1997; Lambe, et al., 1997). The implications of comorbidity of severe medical illnesses on the outcome of adolescents with eating disorders needs further evaluation. Again, early recognition and weight rehabilitation are important in modifying the outcome of the illness and any associated medical comorbidity (Bachrach et al., 1991; Katzman et al., 1997; Lambe et al., 1997).

The goals of treatment are two-fold: to help the adolescent achieve both physical and emotional health. Each aspect of treatment should be developmentally appropriate for the patient. The first objective is to achieve medical and nutritional stabilization as a prerequisite to psychological treatment. For an adolescent with anorexia nervosa, once a healthy weight range is determined, treatment should facilitate refeeding and the integration of normal eating patterns and behaviors that will result in attaining the target weight gain. Adolescents with bulimia nervosa need to learn how to sustain a normal nutritional intake without unduly restricting food intake, and to avoid binge eating and purging.

Outpatient management includes regular monitoring of weight, height, vital signs (especially pulse and body temperature), orthostatic changes, fluid and caloric intake and output, electrolyte balance, and urine specific gravity. The long-term medical complications that require follow-up include growth failure, pubertal delay, menstrual irregularities, and decreased bone-mineral density.

The physician needs to decide when and if hospitalization is necessary, as it can provide an opportunity to reverse potentially serious and life-threatening medical complications. Young people may require hospitalization for many reasons, depending on the severity and chronicity of the disorder's medical and behavioral components. Recommended criteria for hospitalization of adolescents with eating disorders are listed in Table 2. Adolescents require hospitalization if weight loss has been so prolonged or so rapid that life-threatening complications must be averted, or if weight loss continues despite outpatient treatment. The young adolescent who has lost a higher percentage of body weight sooner and whose growth and pubertal development may be compromised should be admitted earlier. Application of these criteria may prevent multiple hospitalizations, prevent irreversible medical complications, and increase the chances of a more complete recovery. Furthermore, discharge from hospital at a normal weight has been shown to reduce rates of rehospitalization significantly (Baran, Weltzin, & Kaye, 1995).

Healthcare providers are in a good position to provide basic information and developmentally appropriate health education on the topics of general adolescent growth and development, energy metabolism, and nutrition. This information should be reinforced throughout eating-disorder treatment in anticipation of a healthy adult lifestyle.

The primary physician alone is unable to provide the comprehensive treatment required by adolescents with eating disorders and should be able to assemble a team of professionals who are experienced and understand these problems. Depending on the availability and strength of staff members as well as the flexibility in the composition and roles of the team, a variety of professionals including pediatricians or family physicians, psychiatrists, nurses, occupational therapists, social workers, nutritionists, and psychologists can offer their specific expertise. A multidisciplinary team ensures a comprehensive approach to management because it involves focusing on the physical, social, and psychological factors. Young people should be encouraged to meet with a mental-health provider for evaluation and treatment of the symptoms distressing them. Adolescents with eating disorders can face numerous stressful issues related to autonomy, social skills, family interaction, substance use, and sexual behavior. Controlled studies (Crisp et al., 1991; Russell, Szmukler, Dare, & Elsleh, 1987) suggest that family therapy should be an essential part of treatment in the child and adolescent. Because these disorders have varied causes, a multimodal approach may offer the best chance for success (Garfinkel & Garner, 1982). Further work currently is being done to look at other effective treatment modalities.

Another important role of the primary-care physician is coordinating the team of professionals involved in the treatment of patient and family. Coordination of care requires regular communication with team members to avoid the manipulation, splitting, and confusion so commonly experienced by those who work with eating-disordered patients. A trusting and supportive relationship between the adolescent and her family and the treatment team is paramount. This

TABLE 2. Indications for hospitalization in an adolescent with an eating disorder

1. Severe malnutrition (weight < 75% ideal body weight)
2. Dehydration
3. Electrolyte disturbances
4. Cardiac arrythmia
5. Physiological instability (severe bradycardia, hypotension, hypothermia, orthostatic changes)
6. Arrested growth and development
7. Failure of outpatient treatment
8. Acute food refusal
9. Uncontrollable binge eating and purging
10. Acute medical complication of malnutrition (e.g., syncope, seizures, cardiac failure, pancreatitis)
11. Acute psychiatric emergencies (e.g., suicidal ideation, acute psychosis)
12. Comorbid diagnosis that interferes with the treatment of the eating disorder (e.g., severe depression, obsessive compulsive disorder, severe family dysfunction)
13. Diagnostic assessment

Adapted by permission of Elsevier Science from Eating Disorder in Adolescents: A Background Paper by Fisher, M., Golden, N. H., Katzman, D. K., Kreipe, R. E., Rees, J., Schebendach, J., Sigman, G., Ammerman, S., & Hoberman, H. M. Journal of Adolescent Health, 16(6), 420–37, Copyright 1995 by The Society for Adolescent Medicine.

is cultivated by a team that has a clear understanding of adolescent eating disorders, exhibits a caring attitude and a genuine concern for the patient and family, acknowledges the patients' feelings about her illness, and is truthful about the details of the treatment approach.

In summary, the primary healthcare provider should be familiar with the warning signs and serious medical sequelae that occur as a result of abnormal eating behaviors and eating disorders. They then will be able to play an integral role in the early of recognition of and intervention with young people at risk.

☐ References

American Psychiatric Association. (1994). *Diagnostic and statistical manual of mental disorders* (4th ed.). Washington, DC: Author.

Bachrach, L. K., Guido, D., Katzman, D. K., Litt, I. F., & Marcus, R. (1990). Decreased bone density in adolescent girls with anorexia nervosa. *Pediatrics, 86,* 440–447.

Bachrach, L., Katzman, D., Litt, I., Guido, D., & Marcus, R. (1991). Recovery from osteopenia in adolescent girls with anorexia nervosa. *Journal of Clinical Endocrinology and Metabolism, 72,* 602–606.

Baran, S. A., Weltzin, T. E., & Kaye, W. H. (1995). Low discharge weight and outcome in anorexia nervosa. *American Journal of Psychiatry, 152,* 1070–1072.

Beumont, P., Al-Alami, M., & Touyz, A. (1988). Relevance of a standard measurement of undernutrition to the diagnosis of anorexia nervosa: Use of Quetelet's Body Mass Index (BMI). *International Journal of Eating Disorders, 7,* 399–405.

Beaumont, P. J., Chambers, T. L., Rouse, L., & Abraham, S. F. (1981). The diet composition and nutritional knowledge of patients with anorexia nervosa. *Journal of Human Nutrition, 35,* 265.

Biller, B. M. K., Saxe, V., Herzog, D. B., Rosenthal, D. I., Holzman, S., & Klibanski, A. (1989). Mechanisms of osteoporosis in adult and adolescent women with anorexia nervosa. *Journal of Clinical Endocrinology and Metabolism, 68,* 548–554.

Bryant-Waugh, R., & Kaminiski, Z. (1993). Eating disorder in children: An overview. In B. Lask & R. Bryant-Waugh (Eds.), *Childhood onset anorexia nervosa and related eating disorders* (pp. 17–29). East Sussex, England: Lawrence Erlbaum Associates.

Bryant-Waugh, R. J., Lask, B. D., Shafran, R. L., & Fosson, A. R. (1992). Do doctors recognize eating disorders in children? *Archives of Disease in Childhood, 67*(1), 103–105.

Cantopher, T., Evans, C., Lacey, J. H., & Pearce, J. M. (1988). Menstrual and ovulatory disturbance in bulimia. *British Medical Journal, 297,* 836–837.

Charig, M., & Fletcher, E. (1987). Reversible bone loss in anorexia nervosa. *British Medical Journal, 295,* 474–475.

Crisp, A. H., Norton, K., Gowers, S., Halek, C., Bowyer, C., Yeldham, D., Levett, G., & Bha, T. A. (1991). A controlled study of the effect of therapies aimed at adolescent and family psychopathology in anorexia nervosa. *British Journal of Psychiatry, 159,* 325–333.

Davies, E., & Furnham, A. (1986). Body satisfaction in adolescent girls. *British Journal of Medical Psychology, 59,* 279–287.

Durnin, J. V. G. A., & Rahaman, M. M. (1967). The assessment of the amount of fat in the human body from measurements of skinfold thickness. *British Journal of Nutrition, 21,* 681.

Eisele, J., Hertsgaard, D., & Light, H. K. (1986). Factors related to eating disorders in young adolescent girls. *Adolescence, 21,* 283–290.

Emans, S. J., & Goldstein, D. P. (1990). *Pediatric and adolescent gynecology* (3rd ed.). Boston/Toronto/London: Little, Brown and Company.

Fisher, M., Golden, N. H., Katzman, D. K., Kreipe, R. E., Rees, J., Schebendach, J., Sigman, G., Ammerman, S., & Hoberman, H. M. (1995). Eating disorder in adolescents: A background paper. *Journal of Adolescent Health, 16,* 420–437.

Fosson, A., Knibbs, J., Bryant-Waugh, R., & Lask, B. (1987). Early onset anorexia nervosa. *Archives of Disease in Childhood, 62,* 114–118.

Frisancho, A. R. (1990). *Anthropometric standards for the assessment of growth and nutritional status.* Ann Arbor: University of Michigan Press.

Garfinkel, P. E., & Garner, D. M. (1982). *Anorexia nervosa: A multidimensional perspective.* New York: Brunner/Mazel.

Garfinkel, P. E., Lin, E., Goering, P., Spegg, C., Goldbloom, D., Kennedy, S., Kaplan, A. S., & Woodside, D. B. (1996). Should amenorrhea be necessary for the diagnosis of anorexia nervosa? Evidence from a Canadian community sample. *British Journal of Psychiatry, 168,* 500–506.

Garfinkel, P. E., Lin, E., Goering, P., Spegg, C., Goldbloom, D. S., Kennedy, S., Kaplan, A. S., & Woodside, D. B. (1995). Bulimia nervosa in a Canadian community sample: Prevalence and comparison of subgroups. *American Journal of Psychiatry, 152,* 1052–1058.

Golden, N. H., Ashtari, M., Kohn, M. R., Patel, M., Jacobson, J. S., Fletcher, A., & Shenker, I. R. (1996). Reversiblity of cerebral ventricular enlargement in anorexia nervosa, demonstrated by quantitative magnetic resonance imaging. *Journal of Pediatrics, 128,* 296–301.

Golden, N. H., Jacobson, M. S., Schebendach, J., Solanto, M. V., Hertz, S. M., & Shenker, R. (1997). Resumption of menses in anorexia nervosa. *Archives of Pediatric and Adolescent Medicine, 151,* 16–21.

Golden, N. H., Kreitzer, P., Jacobson, M. S., Chasalow, F. I., Schebendach, J., Freedman, S. M., & Shenker, I. R. (1994). Disturbances in growth hormone secretion and action in adolescents with anorexia nervosa. *Journal of Pediatrics, 125,* 655–660.

Golden, N. H., & Shenker, I. R. (1992). Amenorrhea in anorexia nervosa: Etiology and implications. In M. P. Nussbaum & J. T. Dwyer (Eds.), *Adolescent medicine state of the art reviews. Adolescent nutrition and eating disorders* (Vol. 3, pp. 503–517). Philadelphia: Hanley and Belfus.

Hamill, P. V. V., Drizid, T. A., Johnson, C., Reed, R. B., Roche, A. F., & Moore, W. M. (1979). Physical growth: National Center for Health Statistics percentiles. *American Journal of Clinical Nutrition, 32,* 607–626.

Hammer, L. D., Kraemer, H. C., Wilson, D. M., Ritter, P. L., & Dornbusch, S. M. (1991). Standardized percentile curves of body-mass index for children and adolescents. *American Journal of Diseases of Children, 145,* 259–263.

Herzog, W., Deter, H.-C., Fiehn, W., & Petzold, E. (1997). Medical findings and predictors of long-term physical outcome in anorexia nervosa: a prospective 12-year follow-up study. *Psychological Medicine, 27,* 269–279.

Herzog, D. B., Nussbaum, K. N., & Marmor, A. K. (1996). Comorbidity and outcome in eating disorders. *The Psychiatric Clinics of North America, 19,* 843–859.

Kaplan, A. S., & Garfinkel, P. E. (1993). *Medical issues and the eating disorders: The interface.* New York: Brunner/Mazel.

Katz, J. L., & Boyar, R. (1978). Weight and circadian luteinizing hormone secretory pattern in anorexia nervosa. *Psychosomatic Medicine, 40*, 549–567.

Katzman, D. K., Lambe, E. K., Mikulis, D. J., Ridgley, J. N., Goldbloom, D. S., & Zipursky, R. B. (1996). Cerebral gray matter and white matter volume deficits in adolescent females with Anorexia Nervosa. *Journal of Pediatrics, 129*, 794–803.

Katzman, D. K., Zipursky, R. B., Lambe, E. K., & Mikulis, D. J. (1997). Longitudinal MRI study of brain changes in adolescents with anorexia nervosa. *Archives of Pediatrics and Adolescent Medicine, 151*, 793–797.

Killen, J. D., Taylor, C. B., Hayward, C., Haydel, K. F., Wilson, D. M., Hammer, L., Kraemer, H., Blair-Greiner, A., & Strachowski, D. (1996). Weight concerns influence the development of eating disorders: A 4-year prospective study. *Journal of Consulting & Clinical Psychology, 64*, 936–940.

Killen, J. D., Taylor, C. B., Telch, M. J., Saylor, K. E., Maron, D. J., & Robinson, T. N. (1986). Self-induced vomiting and laxative and diuretic use among teenagers: Precursors of the binge-purge syndrome? *Journal of the American Medical Association, 255*, 1447–1449.

Kingston, K., Szmukler, G., Andrewes, D., Tress, B., & Desmond, P. (1996). Neuropsychological and structural brain changes in anorexia nervosa before and after refeeding. *Psychological Medicine, 26*, 15–28.

Klibanski, A., & Greenspan, S. (1986). Increase in bone mass after treatment of hyperprolactinemic amenorrhea. *New England Journal of Medicine, 315*, 542–546.

Krieg, J., Pirke, K., Lauer, C., & Backmund, H. (1988). Endocrine, metabolic, and cranial computed tomographic findings in anorexia nervosa. *Biological Psychiatry, 23*, 377–387.

Lai, K. Y. C., Debruyn, R., Lask, B., Bryant-Waugh, R., & Hankins, M. (1994). Use of pelvic ultrasound to monitor ovarian and uterine maturity in childhood onset anorexia nervosa. *Archives of Disease in Childhood, 71*, 228–231.

Lambe, E. K., Katzman, D. K., Mikulis, D. J., & Zipursky, R. B. (1997). Cerebral gray matter volume deficits after weight recovery from anorexia nervosa. *Archives of General Psychiatry, 54*, 537–542.

Mahan, L. K., & Rosebrough, R. H. (Eds.). (1984). *Nutritional requirements and nutritional status assessment in adolescence.* St. Louis: Times Mirror/Mosby.

Melin, L. M., Irwin, C. E., & Scully, S. (1992). Prevalence of disordered eating in girls: A survey of middle-class children. *Journal of the American Dietetic Association, 92*, 851–853.

Meyer, A. E., von Holtzapfel, B., Deffner, G., Engel, K., & Klick, M. (1986). Amenorrhea and predictors for remenorrhea in anorexia nervosa: A psychoendocrinological study in inpatients. *Psychotherapy and Psychosomatics, 45*, 149–160.

Mitchell, J. E., Pyle, R. L., Eckert, E. D., Hatsukami, D., & Soll, E. S. (1990). Bulimia nervosa in overweight individuals. *Journal of Nervous and Mental Disorders, 178*, 324–327.

Neinstein, L. S. (1996). Vital statistics. In L. S. Neinstein (Ed.), *Adolescent heatlh care: A practical guide* (3d ed., p. 1253). Baltimore: Williams & Wilkins.

Nussbaum, M., Baird, D., Sonnenblick, M., Cowan, K., & Shenker, I. R. (1985). Short stature in anorexia nervosa patients. *Journal of Adolescent Health Care, 6*, 453–455.

Nussbaum, M. P., Blethen, S. L., Chasalow, F. I., Jacobson, M. S., Shenker, I. R., & Feldman, J. (1990). Blunted growth hormone responses to clonidine in adolescent girls with early anorexia nervosa: Evidence of an early hypothalamic defect. *Journal of Adolescent Health, 11*, 145–148.

Pagsberg, A. K., & Wang, A. R. (1994). Epidemiology of anorexia nervosa and bulimia nervosa in Bornholm County, Denmark, 1970–1989. *Acta Psychiatrica Scandinavica, 90*, 259–265.

Palla, B., & Litt, I. F. (1988). Medical complications of eating disorders in adolescents. *Pediatrics, 81*, 613–623.

Pendleton-Jones, B., Duncan, C. C., Brouwers, P., & Mirsky, A. F. (1991). Cognition in eating disorders. *Journal of Clinical and Experimental Neuropsychology, 13*, 711–728.

Rastam, M., & Gillberg, C. (1991). The family background in anorexia nervosa: A population-based study. *Journal of the American Academy of Child and Adolescent Psychiatry, 30*, 283–289.

Rastam, M., Gillberg, C., & Garton, M. (1989). Anorexia nervosa in a Swedish urban region: A population-based study. *British Journal of Psychiatry, 155*, 642–646.

Rigotti, N. A., Neer, R. M., Skates, S. J., Herzog, D. B., & Nussbaum, S. R. (1991). The clinical course of osteoporosis in anorexia nervosa. A longitudinal study of cortical bone mass. *Journal of the American Medical Association, 265*, 1133–1138.

Rodin, J. (1993). Cultural and psychosocial determinants of weight concerns. *Annals Of Internal Medicine, 119*, 643–645.

Root, A. W., & Powers, P. S. (1983). Anorexia nervosa presenting as growth retardation in adolescents. *Journal of Adolescent Health Care, 4*, 25–30.

Rubin, K., Schirduan, V., Gendreau, P., Sarfarazi, M., Mendola, R., & Dalsky, G. (1993). Predictors of axial and peripheral bone mineral density in healthy children and adolescents, with special attention to the role of puberty. *Journal of Pediatrics, 123*, 863–870.

Russell, G. F. M. (1985). Premenarchal anorexia nervosa and its sequelae. *Journal of Psychiatric Research, 19*, 363–369.

Russell, G. F. M., Szmukler, G. I., Dare, C., & Elsleh, I. (1987). An evaluation of family therapy in anorexia nervosa and bulimia nervosa. *Archives of General Psychiatry, 44*, 1047.

Schebendach, J., & Nussbaum, M. P. (1992). Nutrition management in adolescents with eating disorder. *Adolescent Medicine: State of the Art Reviews, 3*, 541–548.

Selzer, R., Caust, J., Hibbert, M., Bowes, G., & Patton, G. (1996). The association between secondary amenorrhea and common eating disordered weight control practices in an adolescent population. *Journal of Adolescent Health, 19*, 56–91.

Sobanski, E., Hiltmann, W.-D., Blanz, B., Klein, M., & Schmidt, M. H. (1997). Pelvic ultrasound scanning of the ovaries in adolescent anorectic patients at low weight and after weight recovery. *European Child and Adolescent Psychiatry, 6*, 207–211.

Tanner, J. M., Whitehouse, R. H., & Takaishi, M. (1966a). Standards from birth to maturity for height, weight, height velocity and weight velocity: British children 1965. *Archives of Disease in Childhood, 41*, 454–471.

Tanner, J. M., Whitehouse, R. H., & Takaishi, M. (1966b). Standards from birth to maturity for height, weight, height velocity, and weight velocity: British children, 1965: II. *Archives of Disease in Childhood, 41*, 613–635.

Treasure, J. L., Wheeler, M., King, E. A., Gordon, P. A. L., & Russell, G. F. M. (1988). Weight gain and reproductive function: Ultrasonographic and endocrine features in anorexia nervsoa. *Clinical Endocrinology, 29*, 607–616.

Woodside, D. B. (1993). Anorexia nervosa and bulimia nervosa in children and adolescents. *Current Opinion in Pediatrics, 5*, 415–418.

Woodside, D. B., & Garfinkel, P. E. (1992). Age of onset of eating disorders. *International Journal of Eating Disorders, 12*, 31–36.

Zinkand, H., Cadoret, R. J., & Widmer, R. B. (1984). Incidence and detection of bulimia in a family practice population. *Journal of Family Practice, 18*, 555–560.

20

CHAPTER

Michael P. Levine
Niva Piran

Reflections, Conclusions and Future Directions

The contributors to this book leave little doubt that prevention of the continuum of eating problems is an immense task: immensely complicated and challenging, but also immensely interesting, exciting, important, and even transformative for those engaged in the collaborative process. Those who join in the process and take the time to look will find that various types and levels of prevention work have strong theoretical bases and impressive records of effectiveness (see, e.g., Albee, 1987; Albee & Gullotta, 1997; Bloom, 1996).

During the 1990s there has been a long overdue upsurge in professional interest in theory and research concerning the prevention of eating disorders (Franko & Orosan-Weine, 1998; Shisslak, Crago, Estes, & Gray, 1996; Levine & Piran, 1998; Piran & Levine, 1996; Vandereycken & Noordenbos, 1998). This has been accompanied by new or renewed prevention efforts in public schools (see Chapters 6 and 9), in the United States Federal government, and in influential organizations such as the International Olympic Committee and USA Gymnastics (see Chapter 15). The commercial successes of *The Beauty Myth* (Wolf, 1991) and *Reviving Ophelia* (Pipher, 1994) during this period also highlight the importance of the issue to many adolescents and adults in the general population in North America.

Such growth often produces "growing pains," and the development of the "field" of prevention of eating disorders is no exception. There is no shortage of criticism and controversy about research methodology (see Chapter 5), empirical findings (Carter, Stewart, Dunn, & Fairburn, 1997), competing models (Piran, 1995), and the funding of prevention work "versus" treatment or risk factor studies. Nevertheless, our recent review of more than 30 published and unpublished prevention studies (Levine & Piran, 1998) confirms Smolak's statement that "although no one yet has demonstrated definitively that the prevention of eating disorders works, the research collectively indicates that it very well *might* work" (personal communication, October 19, 1998). In this regard, Piran's (1996, in press; see also Chapter 16) successful application of the Feminist-Empowerment-Relational (FER) model to the prevention of eating problems in an elite ballet company is particularly encouraging. It was not that long ago that many people would have thought that an elite ballet company was an intractable breeding ground for disordered eating.

It is impossible to weave the different contributions to this volume into a consensual, unified guide for future developments in theory, research, programming, and activism. The contributors, like experts and groups of people everywhere, inevitably disagree over the best way to conceptualize the issues and proceed from there. Consequently, in concluding, we offer no "resolution" or "correct view," preferring to apply a feminist perspective that acknowledges diversity, recognizes the constructive potential in conflict and self-reflective critiques, and honors dialogue. In the early stages of building constructive relationships (in this case between scholars) and generating new ideas (in this case for prevention), such dialogue is often multifaceted, contradictory, open-ended, and ambiguous.

This state of affairs does not mean, however, that there are no useful principles or themes to be extracted from the chapters considered as a tapestry. In educating professionals and organizing his own work in prevention, Levine has found it helpful to develop a set of principles for prevention work (see, e.g., Clark, Levine, & Kinney, 1989; Levine & Hill, 1991). The following principles are definitely linked but, for purposes of illustration, are considered individually. These principles are offered as well-informed points for reflection and dialogue in the process of program development and evaluation. They are definitely not intended to be top-down, "expert" pronouncements as to how further work "must" proceed if progress is to be made (cf. Piran, 1995).

☐ Emerging Principles

Acknowledge and Welcome Complexity and Collaboration

The breadth and depth of contributions to this volume indicate that understanding and preventing eating disorders is very complex. Important topics include:

- The developmental biology of adolescence (see Chapter 14) and psychosomatic illness (see Chapter 17)
- The social psychology of peers (see Chapter 8) and television viewing (see Chapter 6)
- Path analysis (see Chapters 10 and 15)
- The impact of modernization on women's lives (see Chapter 2)
- Postmodern theories of epistemology and social change (see Chapters 9 and 16).

Collaboration is thus a nearly constant theme in this book. "Bold," determined individuals such as Irving, Friedman, Weiner, and Sigall can make a tremendous difference in the lives of girls and young women. Nevertheless, no one person alone can organize and synthesize the knowledge and skills required. As Hotelling (see Chapter 13) notes, no one person alone can navigate the multiple systems that must be affected to create and integrate the systemic and personal changes necessary for prevention. Moreover, if one is to adopt a "Bolder Model" of the prevention specialist (see Chapters 1 and 4), there is need for social support in monitoring the possibility of inadvertent iatrogenic effects (see Chapter 5) and in dealing with the inevitability of frustration and failure.

The corollary of embracing complexity is a healthy suspicion about simplicity. The contributors to this volume leave little doubt that we have lot to learn about the messages we give to elementary school children (see Chapter 5), about the undeniable *potential* for our messages to have a negative effect (see Chapter 5; see also Levine & Piran, 1998). We have a lot to learn about the adverse and protective influences of media (see Chapters 1 and 6), parents (see Chapter 3), peers (see Chapter 8), and "cultural factors," including ethnicity (see Chapters 2 and 11). It is also clear that one subtle form of the simplicity trap is the belief that "the more recent is the more creative and more effective." Nasser and Katzman (see Chapter 2), Larkin, Rice, and Russell (see Chapter 12), and Piran (see Chapters 9 and 16) demonstrate convincingly that important lessons about the causes and prevention of eating problems may be found, for example, in the writings of 19th-century physicians such as Lesegue, or the feminist literature of the 1970s concerning consciousness raising.

Eating Problems are "Existential" Problems

One aspect of the complexity that challenges (haunts) prevention specialists is the question: What exactly are we trying to prevent? The answer, we believe, must be framed with an acknowledgment that eating disorders are very "real" and very serious medical conditions created by problems with eating and weight management. These disorders need to be recognized early and treated effectively via collaboration between professionals (see Chapters 13, 17, 18, and 19). Yet, even this "fact" is quickly destabilized by Weiner's and Colton et al.'s insistence that we conceptualize the nature of the disorder and the nature of identification, referral, treatment, and prevention within the context of relationships and the social psychology of families, referral systems, medical communities, and so forth.

Eating disorders are relatively rare, in comparison with affective disorders or anxiety disorders (Levine, 1997). However, all the contributors agree that the "subthreshold" components—for example, negative body image, fear of fat, feeling powerless and insecure in regard to one's needs—are prevalent enough among girls and women in many countries to be considered "normative" and "epidemic." This horrible state of affairs, coupled with the astounding gender difference in eating disorders and the risk periods in early and late adolescence, points to the need to think about what "eating problems" mean in the context of the lives of girls and women (see, e.g., Chapters 5, 6, 7, 9, 12, and 16). This striking point is seen in the lengthy list of "ordinary" factors that have been found to be associated with risk for disordered eating: puberty, heterosexual dating, teasing, sexual harassment and others forms of sexual violence, certain forms of athletic participation, certain peer groups such as sororities, body-related monitoring and criticism by parents, and so forth (see, e.g., Chapters 3, 5, 8, 9, 12, and 16).

Prevention specialists (including Levine & Hill, 1991) have all too often avoided these issues because they are hard to address with a "5-Day Lesson Plan" and because they tend to make school boards, parents, teachers, and students uneasy (Piran, 1995; see also Chapter 9). Many of the programs described in this volume agree with Piran that although it may be "hard" and "controversial," it is crucial not to collude with silence; and it is indeed possible to create effective programs (e.g., Piran, in press) that work from within the "lived experience" of girls and women (see Chapters 6, 7, 9, 11, 12, and 16). Several of the contributors also agree that a full understanding of that "experience" requires that prevention specialists pay closer attention to developmental psychopathology (see Chapters 3, 5, and 8).

Prevention of Eating Disorders Requires Intensive, Multidimensional Efforts to Change Social Systems

With the exception of Piran's program, all the published prevention programs whose outcomes have been evaluated focus on changing the individual via relatively short-term classroom-like programs (see review by Levine & Piran, 1998; Piran, in press; see also Chapters 9 and 16). Her research strongly suggests that more long-term and intensive prevention programs, involving multiple dialogues and actions with multiple people operating at multiple levels within an organization, are much more effective. Many contributors to the present volume (Graber et al.; Hotelling; Larkin et al.; Levine et al.; Sigall; Smolak) agree with Piran that increases in individual "resistance" to negative influences must be supported and facilitated by active changes in the systems that define the lives of girls and women in general (see also Neumark-Sztainer, 1996). Media literacy needs to foment and be supported by media activism and advocacy (see Chapters 1 and 6). Programs for individual athletes and dancers need to change the people—including adults (e.g., coaches) and peers (e.g., captains)—and the social systems that influence and regulate the lives of those individuals (see Chapters 15 and 16). Curricular "lessons" and empowerment for constructive change need to be extended, not only to students but to administrators, teachers, and parents (see Chapters 3, 5, 9, 12, and 16).

Entering systems, understanding systems, changing systems, and evaluating systems are all very complicated prospects (see the first principle). They require attention to subtle and not so subtle forms of power and control, as well as to the "shameful," "silent" experience of those who are being dis-empowered and dis-connected (see Chapters 2, 9, 12, and 16). According to the FER model, the principle of systemic change is a reminder of one meaning of the phrase: "The personal [change] is the political."

Prevention Involves Empowerment Through Dialogue, Relationships, and Activism

Another meaning of that powerful cliche, and one found across very different approaches within this volume (cf. Levine et al.'s approach versus Friedman's approach versus Nichter et al.'s program), is that prevention is facilitated by converting awkward, unclear, and even shameful personal concerns (e.g., "My body is fat and disgusting") into an understanding of sociopolitical factors that support the underlying feelings ("I feel out of control") and the expression via "fat talk."

This process of constructing a "voice" for understanding and change is one of the pillars of the FER model (Piran, 1995, 1996, 1997, in press; see also Levine &

Piran, 1998; see Chapters 9 and 16). This paradigm is deserving of further application and development for at least four reasons. First, there is empirical evidence to suggest that it prevents disordered eating (Piran, in press). Second, it is the only paradigm that incorporates the strengths of other models with the principles articulated in this conclusion (e.g., complexity, collaboration, systemic emphasis). Third, the principles of dialogue, critical inquiry, activism, and advocacy that are at the heart of the FER paradigm are consistent with other promising developments in emancipatory education, such as media literacy (Hobbs, 1997), Freirian consciousness raising (Wallerstein, Sanchez-Merki, & Dow, 1997), and the development of critical consumers (Murray & Ozanne, 1991).

Finally, the FER model emphasizes that the body can be a powerful (empowering) site of knowledge-within-connection, and a source for experiencing and realizing the desire for action and transformation (Piran, 1996). The FER model encourages girls and women to work individually and collaboratively to change what *they* as a group have identified as unhealthy and unfair influences in their immediate lives. This intensely "personal" transformation of the body from site of shame into source of power, mastery, and connection holds a great deal of promise for addressing the disconnection, disempowerment, and disrespect identified by Nasser and Mervat as being a key "political" and "cultural" factor in the creation of disordered eating (see also Steiner-Adair, 1994).

Prevention Work Requires a Bolder Model of Professional and Personal Development

One of many ironies encountered in prevention work (Levine, 1994, 1995) is that participatory models of prevention and female development require enhanced attention to the role of adults in creating safe, respectful, nurturant, encouraging environments for children, adolescents, and adults themselves (Piran, 1995, 1996; see also Chapters 9, 12, and 16). Girls (and boys) need "spaces" to construct, tell, make sense of, and act on "their stories" of harassment and honor, anxiety and achievement—and conformity and resistance. In the process, young people and significant others (e.g., teachers, parents, coaches) can benefit tremendously from authoritative (versus authoritarian) professionals who know about group processes, who know about set-point theory and the clash between biology and culture, and who know how and when to infuse their own stories into that process (see Chapters 1, 6, 9, and 16). A poignant theme found throughout this book is that the creation of safe, respectful spaces for girls and women often requires personal courage as a bold political act of insisting on civil rights while negotiating with men and women (e.g., principals, school boards, athletic directors) in power. As seen in the work of Stoddard (see Chapter 1) Piran, Irving, Larkin et al., Powers, Johnson, Sigall, and other contributors, the prevention specialist as a bold model of assertion (and collaboration) is one way of creating the spaces needed for people, including youth, to tell their stories as they construct new, healthier possibilities.

As editors, we invited Lori Irving to tell her (evolving) "story" of "bolder" prevention work that integrates the personal (e.g., her values and her recovery from an eating disorder), the professional (e.g., her work as a psychologist), and the political (e.g., her organization of local professionals, her protest of the Fetish campaign). However, in keeping with the principle of complexity and multiple systems, it is important to note that Lori's work is situated squarely in traditional academic roles of teacher, mentor, supervisor of graduate students, researcher, specialist in statistics. In fact, this is true of a number of the contributors to this volume, such as Piran, Larkin, Levine, Powers, Rice, and Smolak. Irving's intentionally unorthodox chapter—and the work of many professionals committed to the prevention of eating disorders—is yet another facet of the statement, "The personal is (the professional, is) the political" (Levine, 1994, 1995).

Graduate Training and Opportunities Are Important Prevention Work

As highlighted in previous principles, there is a lot to be learned in order to do the work of prevention. There is also a lot to be taught. The work of several contributors to this volume demonstrates how the design, conduct, and evaluation of prevention programs provide an outstanding opportunity for the training— and, one would hope, personal development—of colleagues, be they other professionals, graduate students, undergraduates, and even high-school students (see Chapters 4, 5, 10, 13, 14, 17, and 18). That is, the participants (we dislike the word "targets") in our prevention work are not only patients or the recipients of classroom lessons or the audience at presentations during Eating Disorders Awareness Week; they are various types of "students" and "collaborators" who are learning about prevention or who could be learning about prevention.

For those working at a college or university, the scope of people whose education could contribute to prevention is breathtaking (Clark et al., 1989; see also Chapters 13 and 14). A short list includes students in the following areas: clinical or counseling psychology (see Chapter 10), obstetrics and gynecology or sports medicine (Levine, in press; see also Chapter 15), dietetics, cultural anthropology (see Chapter 11), public health, elementary education (see Chapter 6), communications and mass media (see Chapter 1), administration in higher education (see Chapter 14), art history and studio art, dramatic art, computer science (see Chapter 1), research methods in psychology (see Chapters 5 and 10), and women and gender studies (see Chapters 9, 12, and 16).

The opportunities for research, for art (e.g., in the creation of eye-catching visual messages; see Chapter 13) and for the furthering of graduate education are similarly staggering. A great deal is known about eating problems and about primary prevention (Levine & Piran, 1998; Shisslak et al., 1996). Nevertheless, the contributors to this volume make it crystal clear that much basic research and theory development needs to be done. Fertile topics for further work are, for example, the developmental psychology of eating problems in late childhood (see Chapter 5), the role of parents in risk and resilience (see Chapters 3 and 5), the role of personal vulnerability and social comparison processes in the effects of mass media (see Chapter 1), the operation of consciousness-raising groups (see Chapters 7, 9, 12, and 16), and the implications of ethnicity and multiculturalism for risk and resilience (see Chapter 2). Thus, in keeping with the FER model and as Irving (see Chapter 4) and Smolak (see Chapter 5) continue to illustrate in their work and their lives, mentoring of various types of students (including colleagues like Levine) can promote prevention through an expanding web of constructed and imparted knowledge.

In considering prevention through teaching and mentoring, one does well to recall a point made by Sigall (see Chapter 14) and by Piran (see Chapters 9 and 16). After reading scores of articles and books on eating disorders, and after giving scores of presentations to various audiences, one can all too quickly forget that negative body image, binge eating, purging, and eating disorders remain "shrouded in shame" and silence. This important observation reinforces the value of collaboration (the first principle) as a means of combating the sense prevention professionals sometimes have that they have "heard it all" and "said it all" so many times before.

Technology Will Play an Increasingly Important Role in Prevention

It is a truism that television, computer technology, and the World Wide Web have transformed the worlds of a vast number of people. Millions of people routinely seek and easily locate health information, social support, and intellectual excitement on television and "on line"—and very soon these will be one and the same thing. Extrapolating from the contributions to this book, prevention specialists will need to understand and work with at least four aspects of this revolutionary transformation. First, "sociocultural" as a factor in the creation and prevention of eating problems will continue to take on new, unstable meanings within the "cross-culture" of cyberspace (see Chapter 2). Second, it follows that key processes for prevention—"support" and "mentoring" and "consciousness raising" and "transformative consumer and political action" and "social marketing"—will need to be conducted in part "within" this new cultural "space" (see Chapters 1 and 2). As seen in EDAP, Inc.'s web-site based media advocacy campaign, for example, this effort is now underway (see Chapter 1).

Third, ideals of beauty and success, created especially for the young and the restless, likely will become more artificial (e.g., "virtually" constructed from images of "real" people and then modified to look "fantastically real") and more disdainful of biodiversity. In a culture that glorifies technology, this development and the ensuing dissatisfaction and disconnection with the body will likely intensify the allure of exercise machines, "plastic" surgery, and special pills and diets. This makes the fourth implication all the more pressing: the development of on-line resources for health promotion and preventive education (see Chapter 1). The success to date of the Stanford group's inchoate efforts to create such resources for at-risk college students is an encouraging development (Winzelberg et al., 1998a). This is also an area with a lot of possibility for prevention through teaching and research with graduate students (the first and sixth principles).

☐ Breaking More Silences

The FER model emphasizes the need to listen for, listen to, and honor what is being said by various contributors to a dialogue. It also acknowledges the importance of what is not being said and who is not being heard (Brown & Jasper, 1993; Piran, 1995).

The Contested Ground of Obesity

Irrational myths and fear about fat, coupled with prejudice against fat people in general and fat women in particular, contributes to the widespread development of eating problems (Garner & Wooley, 1991; see also Chapter 6). However, many people in our society, including a large number of physicians, health educators such as Nichter et al. and Phelps et al. (see Chapters 10 and 11), school teachers, and parents, are extremely concerned about the health risks of at least some forms of overweight or obesity (Dietz, 1998; Neumark-Sztainer, 1998).

The definitions of "overweight" and "obesity," the nature of the health risks (and benefits), the role of prejudice, and the implications of these phenomena for prevention and health promotion are, to say the least, the subject of controversy among eating-disorder specialists and health educators (e.g., Battle & Brownell, 1996; Brownell & Rodin, 1994; Garner & Wooley, 1991; Neumark-Sztainer, 1998). Is there an inevitable and unproductive conflict between prevention of eating disorders and prevention of obesity? Drawing from several lines of work (e.g., Burgard & Lyons, 1994; Ikeda & Naworski, 1992; Piran, 1996; Story & Neumark-Sztainer, 1996) we have argued elsewhere that this debate should be reframed as a dialogue concerning health promotion (Levine & Piran, 1998). Rather than "waging war" on either obesity or eating disorders, we advocate a de-emphasis on calories and weight and a (re)emphasis on (1) the nutritional needs of girls and women during transitions such as puberty and pregnancy; (2) the value of healthy nutrition, irrespective of weight and weight changes, such as eating more fruits and vegetables and less salt and saturated fats; (3) increasing self-acceptance and appreciation of the power and pleasures emerging from one's body; (4) enhancing tolerance of diversity in weight, shape, and ethnic food choices; (5) creating opportunities to exercise for fun, friendship and stamina; and (6) building respectful environments, supportive relationships, and effective coping skills so that stressors will be reduced as will the risk of coping with distress through bingeing or starving. These recommendations, however, are unlikely to be understood or well received by physicians, teachers, parents, and children unless those committed to the prevention of eating disorders develop a fuller understanding of "obesity" and work to create mutually instructive dialogues with those who want to prevent obesity. Evidence for the possibility of this rapprochement already can be found in the medical literature (Kassirer & Angell, 1998).

Where the Boys Are

The voices of boys and men are noticeably absent from the descriptions of prevention programs in this book, except as loud echoes of physical intimidation and verbal harassment (see Chapters 5, 6, 7, and 12), disruptive leers and catcalls in class (see Chapters 9, 10, and 11), weight-related teasing and criticism by fathers (see Chapter 3), and expressions of disinterest in prevention evidenced by the nonparticipation of fraternities (see Chapter 14). Powers and Johnson discussion of steroid use (see Chapter 15), does acknowledge that male athletes (and boys in general) have body-image and eating problems that are embedded in cultural definitions of a muscular, "hard" masculinity and of rapid self-transformation through technology (e.g., machines and drugs). Boys, men, their power, their fears, their dreams, and their capacity to care for themselves and others need somehow to be addressed in multidimensional programs for systemic and personal change (Levine, 1994; Maine, 1991).

Acknowledging and Respecting Diversity

Elementary school children, graduate students, athletes, and eating-disorder professionals are an increasingly diverse group of people in regard to ethnicity and culture. If prevention specialists are to understand the complexities of risk and resilience (see the first principle), then further investigation of—and connection to—such diversity is very important (see Chapters 9, 11, and 16). We have often heard the statement, "We can learn a lot from African American girls and women because they are at less risk for eating disorders than other women." This claim turns out to be true in some important respects and simplistic in other important respects (Striegel-Moore & Smolak, 1996; Thompson, 1994; see also Chapter 11). There are important qualifications pertaining to identity, acculturation to the dominant White value system, ethnicity (e.g., Hispanic versus African American), and experiences with prejudice. Moreover, although some African American girls apparently are quite willing to share their healthier perspective and style with non–African American girls (see Chapter 11), Sigall (see Chapter 14) reported that the African American sororities at the University of Maryland were not interested in participating in her prevention program.

We believe that people committed to the prevention of eating disorders must continue to struggle with the monstrosities of prejudice and the nuances of multicultural collaboration (Brown & Jasper, 1993; see also Chapter 11). Race, class, gender, and sexual orientations may sound to some like a clichés, but they remain important spaces of silence in the field of prevention as it is currently being constructed. As another example, work by Smolak and Levine (1996) and by others (see Chapters 3 and 8) highlights the role of "dating concerns" in risk for disordered eating during early adolescence. This is an important finding, but it clearly refers to heterosexual interests and activities. What if the young girls' emerging sexuality is lesbian in nature? Is there risk for disordered eating? If so, how is it to be construed and addressed (Siever, 1994)?

The theories, research, and various forms of knowledge provided in this book support the validity of trying to prevent eating disorders by joining girls and women in their struggles to develop all of the following: physical competencies and stamina, a critical and action-oriented sensibility, pride in self and culture, and strong connections to other women and to empowering traditions and ceremonies. But we also feel that it important to raise these issues of ethnicity and sexual orientation as a reminder to all (including ourselves) that it is important to keep asking: Who is defining "health" and "health promotion?" How is it being defined? For whom are the messages and programs and changes intended? Who determines the methods of evaluation and the use of the "data?" The Feminist-Empowerment-Relational model, which we believe should be a part of prevention in the next century, is clear in arguing that the process of thinking about and asking aloud this type of question is an important foundation for designing effective, far-reaching prevention programs (Piran, 1996, 1997, in press).

☐ References

Albee, G. W. (1987). The rationale and need for primary prevention. In S. E. Goldston (Ed.), *Concepts of primary prevention: A framework for program development* (pp. 7–20). Sacramento: California Office of Mental Health (Office of Prevention).

Albee, G. W., & Gullotta, T. P. (1997). Primary prevention's evolution. In G. W. Albee & T. P. Gullotta (Eds.), *Primary prevention works* (pp. 3–22). Thousand Oaks, CA: Sage.

Battle, E. K., & Brownell, K. D. (1996). Confronting a rising tide of eating disorders and obesity: Treatment vs. prevention and policy. *Addictive Behaviors, 21*, 755–765.

Bloom, M. (1996). *Primary prevention practices.* Thousand Oaks, CA: Sage.

Brown, C., & Jasper, K. (Eds.). (1993). *Consuming passions: Feminist approaches to weight preoccupation and eating disorder.* Toronto: Second Story Press.

Brownell, K. D., & Rodin, J. (1994). The dieting maelstrom: Is it possible and advisable to lose weight. *American Psychologist, 49*, 781–791.

Burgard, D., & Lyons, P. (1994). Alternatives in obesity treatment focusing on health for fat women. In P. Fallon, M. Katzman & S. C. Wooley (Eds.) *Feminist perspectives on eating disorders,* 17 (pp. 212–230). New York: Guilford press.

Carter, J., Stewart, D., Dunn, V., & Fairburn, C. (1997). Primary prevention of eating disorders: Might it do more harm than good? *International Journal of Eating Disorders, 22*, 167–173.

Clark, L. V., Levine, M. P., & Kinney, N. E. (1989). A multifaceted and integrated approach to the prevention, identification, and treatment of bulimia on campus. *Journal of College Student Psychotherapy, 3*, 257–298.

Dietz, W. H. (1998). Health consequences of obesity in youth: Childhood predictors of adult disease. *Pediatrics* 1998;101:518–525.

Franko, D. L., & Orosan-Weine, P. (1998). The prevention of eating disorders: Empirical, methodological and conceptual considerations. *Clinical Psychology: Science and Practice, 5*, 459–477.

Garner, D. M., & Wooley, S. C. (1991). Confronting the failure of behavioral and dietary treatments for obesity. *Clinical Psychology Review, 11*, 729–780.

Hobbs, R. (1997). Literacy for the information age. In J. Flood, S. B. Heath & D. Lapp (Eds.), *Handbook of research on teaching literacy through the communicative and visual arts* (pp. 7–14). New York: Simon & Schuster.

Ikeda, J., & Naworski, P. (1992). *Am I fat? Helping young children accept differences in body size.* Santa Cruz: ETR Associates.

Kassirer, J. P., & Angell, M. (1998). Losing weight: An ill-fated New Year's resolution [editorial]. *Journal of the American Medical Association, 338*, 52–54.

Levine, M. P. (1994). Beauty myth and the beast: What men can do and be to help prevent eating disorders. *Eating Disorders: The Journal of Treatment & Prevention, 2*, 101–113.

Levine, M. P. (1995, Summer). The satchel. *The Renfrew Perspective, 1*(2), 1–3.

Levine, M. P. (1997, April). *The developmental psychopathology of depression and disordered eating: Implications for treatment and prevention.* Paper presented at the Conference on Co-Occurrence of Eating Disorders and Clinical Depression sponsored by the NIMH's D/ART–Ohio Program, Columbus, OH.

Levine, M. P. (in press). Bulimia nervosa. In E. J. Quilligan & F. P. Zuspan (Eds.), *Current therapy in obstetrics and gynecology* (5th ed). Philadelphia: W. B. Saunders.

Levine, M. P., & Hill, L. (1991). *A 5 day lesson plan book on eating disorders: Grades 7–12.* Tulsa, OK: The National Eating Disorder Organization.

Levine, M. P., & Piran, N. (1998). *Approaches to health promotion in the prevention of eating disorders.* Manuscript submitted for publication.

Maine, M. (1991). *Father hunger: Fathers, daughters and food.* Carlsbad, CA: Gurze Books.

Murray, J. B., & Ozanne, J. L. (1991). The critical imagination: Emancipatory interests in consumer research. *Journal of Consumer Research, 18*, 129–144.

Neumark-Sztainer, D. (1996). School-based programs for preventing eating disturbances. *Journal of School Health, 66*(2), 64–71.

Neumark-Sztainer, D. (1998). *The weight dilemma: A perspective on the controversy. International Journal of Obesity.*.

Pipher, M. (1994). *Reviving Ophelia: Saving the selves of adolescent girls.* New York: Ballantine Books.

Piran, N. (1995). Prevention: Can early lessons lead to a delineation of an alternative model? A critical look at prevention with schoolchildren. *Eating Disorders: The Journal of Treatment & Prevention, 3*, 28–36.

Piran, N. (1996). The reduction of preoccupation with body weight and shape in schools: A feminist approach. *Eating Disorders: The Journal of Treatment & Prevention, 4,* 323–330.

Piran, N. (1997). Prevention of eating disorders: Directions for future research. *Psychopharmacology Bulletin, 33,* 419–423.

Piran, N. (in press). Eating disorders: A trial of prevention in a high risk school setting. *Journal of Primary Prevention.*

Piran, N., & Levine, M. P. (Eds.). (1996). [Special Prevention Issue]. *Eating Disorders: The Journal of Treatment & Prevention, 4*(4).

Shisslak, C. M., Crago, M., Estes, L., & Gray, N. (1996). Content and method of developmentally appropriate prevention programs. In L. Smolak, M. P. Levine, & R. Striegel-Moore (Eds.), *The developmental psychopathology of eating disorders: Implications for research, prevention, and treatment* (pp. 341–363). Mahwah, NJ: Lawrence Erlbaum Associates.

Siever, M. D. (1994). Sexual orientation and gender as factors in socioculturally acquired vulnerability to body dissatisfaction and eating disorders. *Journal of Consulting & Clinical Psychology, 62,* 252–260.

Smolak, L., & Levine, M. P. (1996). Adolescent transitions and the development of eating problems. In L. Smolak, M. P. Levine, & R. Striegel-Moore (Eds.), *The developmental psychopathology of eating disorders: Implications for research, prevention, and treatment* (pp. 207–233). Mahwah, NJ: Lawrence Erlbaum Associates.

Steiner-Adair, C. (1994). The politics of prevention. In P. Fallon, M. Katzman, & S. Wooley (Eds.), *Feminist perspectives on eating disorders* (pp. 381–394). New York: Guilford.

Story, M., & Neumark-Sztainer, D. (1996). School-based nutrition education programs and services for adolescents. *Adolescent Medicine: State of the Art Reviews, 7,* 287–302.

Striegel-Moore, R., & Smolak, L. (1996). The role of race in the development of disordered eating. In L. Smolak, M. P. Levine, & R. Striegel-Moore (Eds.), *The developmental psychopathology of eating disorders: Implications for research, prevention, and treatment* (pp. 259–284). Mahwah, NJ: Lawrence Erlbaum Associates.

Thompson, B. (1994). *A hunger so wide and so deep.* Minneapolis: University of Minnesota Press.

Vandereycken, W., & Noordenbos, G. (Eds.). (1998). *The prevention of eating disorders.* London: Athlone Press.

Wallerstein, N., Sanchez-Merki, V., & Dow, L. (1997). Freirian praxis in health education and community organizing: A case study of an adolescent prevention program. In M. Hinkler (Ed.), *Community organizing and community building for health* (pp. 195–211). New Brunswick, NJ: Rutgers University Press.

Winzelberg, A. J., Eldredge, K. L., Wilfley, D., Eppstein, D., Dasmahapatra, R., Dev, P., & Taylor, C. B. (1998a). *Effectiveness of an internet-based program for reducing risk factors for eating disorders.* Manuscript submitted for publication.

Winzelberg, A. J., Taylor, C. B., Sharpe, T., Eldredge, K. L., Dev, P., & Constantinou, P. S. (1998b). Evaluation of a computer-mediated eating disorder intervention. *International Journal of Eating Disorders, 24,* 339–350.

Wolf, N. (1991). *The beauty myth: How images of beauty are used against women.* New York: William Morrow.

AUTHOR INDEX

SUBJECT INDEX

Acculturation, 30
Achievement, 95
Adolescent girls. *See also* African American
    females; Hispanic females; White females
  consciousness raising with, 201–203
  development of eating problems in, 47–49
  issues facing, 121–124
  mass media and, 4, 5, 9 (*See also* Mass
    media)
  prevention programs for young, 92–93
  problems related to early, 47–48, 51, 92–93
Advertisements, 10–13
African American females
  beauty ideals of, 178–179, 181, 189
  binge-eating disorder in, 59
  eating disorders and, 30, 177
  media awareness program and, 183–184
  sexual harassment and, 197–198
  in sororities, 230–232
  Teen Lifestyle Project and, 177–179
  weight concerns and, 175–177
Alcohol abuse, 92
Amenorrhea, 304, 307
American Association of University Women,
  198
Anabolic-androgenic steroids, 248–249
Anorexia nervosa. *See also* Eating disorders
  African Americans and, 177
  comorbidity and, 92, 306, 313
  ethnic groups and, 176
  families of adolescents with, 50
  growth retardation and, 308–309
  historical background of, 27–28
  occurrence of, xv, 107
  osteopenia and, 311–312
  pubertal delay and interruption and,
    310–311
Anorexia Nervosa and Associated Disorders
  (ANAD), 10, 11
Anxiety disorders, 92
Appearance, 54–55
Arabs, 30–31
Argentina, 31
Art, 128
Asian Americans, 30, 31, 176
Athletes
  coaches and trainers of, 124, 251
  competitive female, 244

conclusions regarding, 251–252
eating problems and disorders among, 241,
  256
effective prevention programs for, 243–244
female athlete triad and, 249–250
International Olympics Committee and,
  246–247
judges of, 246
National Collegiate Athletic Association
  and, 247
prevention problems of, 241–242
psychological and physiological screening
  methods for, 250
pursuit of strength in, 250
risk factors in, 244–245
steroid use by, 247–249
team physicians and, 251
USA Gymnastics prevention efforts and,
  247–248
World Tennis Council and, 248
Avia, 12

A Baby for Max (Lasky), 117
The Beauty Myth (Wolf), 319
Behind Closed Doors, 15, 25n
Blood sugar control, 277, 278, 281–282
Bodies
  as commodities, 106
  dealing with changing, 126–127
Body image. *See also* Body weight and shape
    preoccupation (BWSP); Thinness
  EDAP campaign and, 11–13
  effects of negative, 107–108
  ethnic differences in, 178–179, 181, 189
  family cohesion and, 51–53
  friendship relationships and, 135–136
  GO GIRLS and, 13–22
  media activism and, 10–11
  media advocacy and, 11
  media audience and, 5
  media content and, 4–5
  media ideal and, 6–7
  media influence and, 5–6
  media literacy and, 9–10
  racial harassment and, 202
  role of physician in recognizing negative,
    294–295
  sexual harassment and, 199–200